Computer Graphics for Design

From Algorithms to AutoCAD®

Daniel B. Olfe

University of California, San Diego

PRENTICE HALL
ENGLEWOOD CLIFFS, NEW JERSEY 07632

Library of Congress Cataloging-in-Publication Data

Olfe, Daniel B.
    Computer graphics for design : from algorithms to AutoCAD / Daniel
B. Olfe.
      p.   cm.
    Includes bibliographical references and index.
    ISBN 0-13-159583-0
    1. Computer graphics. 2. Computer-aided design. I. Title.
    T385.0343 1995
    620´.0042´028566—dc20   94-28190
                            CIP

Acquisitions editor: Linda Ratts
Project manager: Irwin Zucker
Buyer: Lori Bulwin
Cover designer: DeLuca Design
Editorial assistant: Naomi Goldman

©1995 by Daniel B. Olfe
Prentice-Hall, Inc.
A Simon & Schuster Company
Englewood Cliffs, New Jersey 07632

Printed in the United States of America

10 9 8 7 6 5 4 3 2 1

ISBN 0-13-159583-0

Prentice-Hall International (UK) Limited, *London*
Prentice-Hall of Australia Pty. Limited, *Sydney*
Prentice-Hall Canada Inc., *Toronto*
Prentice-Hall Hispanoamericana. S.A., *Mexico*
Prentice-Hall of India Private Limited, *New Delhi*
Prentice-Hall of Japan, Inc., *Tokyo*
Simon & Schuster Asia Pte. Ltd., *Singapore*
Editora Prentice-Hall do Brasil, Ltda., *Rio de Janeiro*

Contents

Contents   v

Contents

Preface

This book is for designers: engineers, architects, industrial designers, and anyone else who designs with computers. Unlike most computer graphics books, this book provides examples of graphics implementation on a CAD (computer-aided design) system. Although this book was developed for students in CAD courses, it should also be of interest to practicing designers who wish to know more about the fundamental graphics behind their CAD software.

Topics are presented in three stages: first, the graphics algorithm is presented; second, a programming implementation of the algorithm is given; and third, the use of the algorithm in a CAD system is examined. For example, B-spline curves are introduced with a presentation of the equations and a discussion of their solution; then program subroutines are presented to draw these curves for a given set of data; finally, examples are given for using B-splines in AutoCAD.

By providing the theoretical basis and programming examples for CAD graphics, this book helps CAD users to understand more fully how their software works. Such an understanding will lead to an improved use of the software and help users diagnose and solve problems associated with modeling designs.

In order to go beyond generalities, a specific programming language (the C language) and a particular CAD package (AutoCAD) are used for examples. But because it emphasizes the fundamental computer graphics, the book should also be useful to people who use other programming languages and other CAD systems.

The programming procedures for C are similar to those for other languages; thus, the simple C programs in this book can be read and converted quite easily to other languages. Only the simplest C programming procedures are used; for example, arrays are used instead of C structures (structs) because arrays can be used in any of the common programming languages.

AutoCAD was selected for examples because it is the most widely used CAD software. Most other CAD systems used by designers have features similar to those of Auto-

CAD, so examples used in this book can be readily converted to other systems. After someone has learned to use one CAD program, it is much easier to learn another. In fact, we encourage our students to learn to use more than one CAD system (and more than one programming language).

Although many specific AutoCAD commands are discussed in this book, this is not a tutorial for AutoCAD, nor is it a tutorial for C programming. New CAD users and new programmers should refer to their software manuals or tutorial books for additional help.

Because this book is for CAD users, it is assumed that the reader has had some college-level mathematics. Specifically, familiarity with algebra, geometry, vectors, and matrices is assumed (although a review of matrix operations is given in appendix C).

The material in this book was developed in a course for upper-level undergraduates. The students' majors included mechanical engineering, aerospace engineering, structural engineering, and bioengineering. Most of the weekly assignments include both programming and the use of AutoCAD.

Some of the topics—2-D graphics and solid modeling—have also been presented in a beginning engineering graphics course (along with the more traditional engineering graphics topics). This lower-level course covers topics in chapters 1–5, 8, and 13.

The upper-level course briefly reviews the early chapters but concentrates on the material in chapters 6–14, with particular emphasis on spline curves, surface modeling, and solid modeling. Because these two one-quarter courses provide a rather limited amount of time to thoroughly cover all of the material in this book, some topics are treated more completely than others in our courses.

This is not only a hands-on book for users, but it has been a hands-on book for its author. All of the program lines were written by the author. Also, except where other sources are acknowledged (primarily student drawings), all of the figures were drawn by the author on either an IBM PC clone or a Macintosh computer. The use of ordinary microcomputers, rather than an advanced workstation, means that the features described in this book can be duplicated by most readers. Many of the figures use simple examples from engineering and architecture; the more complex figures are mostly from student projects.

The chapters in this book are divided into those that treat either 2-D graphics or 3-D graphics. Most of the topics include both programming and AutoCAD examples.

Chapter 1 presents an overview of computer graphics and CAD. Specific hardware and software are described for completeness, even at the risk of becoming dated.

In chapter 2, the development of computer graphics begins with the display of pixels (picture elements) on a computer screen. Presented next are the algorithms that arrange the illuminated pixels into a line at a prescribed angle on the screen. The line segments are used in chapter 3 to represent curves and polygons. Also, different line types and polygon fill patterns are described.

A relatively brief presentation of technical (engineering) drawings and graphs is given in chapter 4. Along with business graphics topics (bar graphs and pie charts), some examples are given from engineering and science.

In another short chapter (5), arrays of graphical elements are used to provide practice for programming loops and using AutoCAD commands. Examples have been chosen from art, architecture, and engineering.

The discussion of color theory in chapter 6 provides the background for the use of color in scientific visualization and in rendering. The extension of the palette of shades by ordered dithering is also discussed.

Chapter 7 on splines and other curves is one of the more mathematical chapters. The following interpolation curves are discussed: circular-arc fit (biarc curve), parabolic blend, and natural cubic spline. Also, the following approximation curves are developed: uniform B-splines, nonuniform B-splines (nonrational and rational), and Bézier curves.

Chapter 8 begins with a brief discussion of how lines and surfaces are represented in programs. Then AutoCAD DXF and script files are described. This chapter emphasizes the DXF file because it provides an easy interface for programming data into and out of CAD drawings.

Chapter 9 on interactive features presents program subroutines for simulating 2-D CAD programs. These features may be used for other interactive programs, such as the color pickers discussed in chapter 6.

A formal presentation of 2-D transformations is given in chapter 10, in preparation for introducing the 3-D transformations in chapter 11. Programming examples for the 2-D transformations include the addition of pan and zoom operations to a CAD program, the drawing of rotated and scaled letters, and an animation of a rotary engine. The 3-D transformations include viewing and perspective projections. An architectural walkthrough of a wireframe house is given as an interactive example of perspective transformation.

Chapter 12 on surface modeling is the longest chapter in the book. Surface types include individual polyfaces (pfaces or 3Dfaces), extruded surfaces, tabulated surfaces, surface of revolution, ruled surface, Coons patch, and rectangular meshes smoothed to form uniform and nonuniform B-spline surfaces. These surfaces are constructed with AutoCAD and with program subroutines. Example surface applications include gears, furniture, boat hulls, buildings, and fractal mountains.

Chapter 13 briefly reviews the different types of solid models, with emphasis on constructive solid geometry (CSG) and boundary representation (B-rep). Applications are provided with AutoCAD AME (Advanced Modeling Extension). Programming examples in computational geometry include the calculation of intersection curves and the evaluation of mass properties.

The final chapter (14) discusses rendering, from a simple illumination model to the ray tracing and texture mapping techniques used to produce photorealistic images. Animation is also considered.

In summary, this book provides a wide variety of topics for study by students and design professionals. Much of my pleasure in writing this book came from developing simple program subroutines for illustrating graphics algorithms and from creating CAD drawings. Readers will be able to expand and improve the programs and drawings. When I have used this material in courses, it has been a pleasure to observe the energy that students—even those who have not otherwise excelled in course work—have put into developing imaginative projects.

ACKNOWLEDGMENTS

The material for this book was developed with help from many people. I have benefitted greatly from discussions with colleagues who have taught computer graphics and design at UCSD, in particular, Mike Bailey, Geza Nagy, and Dick Seymour. Also, I appreciate the helpful comments and guidance provided by outside reviewers, particularly Josann Duane and Robert Wilke of The Ohio State University.

The success of a computer graphics/CAD course depends largely on the operations of the computer laboratory. Our laboratory sessions are very ably run by student teaching assistants. Among those who have helped in the past several years, I particularly recall the contributions of Mike Kilby, Jamie Anderson, Pierre Larochelle, Alan Payne, Chien Hsiung, Rachel Lau, Jeff Brown, Steve Sargent, Jim McCullough, Don O'Neil, and Jorge Aldana. Their help has been invaluable for this book as well as in the laboratory.

A book is completed only with considerable help from publishing professionals. I would like to thank former Prentice Hall Executive Editor Doug Humphrey for having the faith in my book concept to sign me up. Thanks are also due to Acquisitions Editor Linda Ratts and Editor-in-Chief Marcia Horton for their continued support and help. Production Editor Irwin Zucker should be singled out for his patience and care in producing an attractive book. The completion of this book was also greatly aided by the professional editing assistance I received from my wife, Julie T. Olfe.

Daniel B. Olfe

1

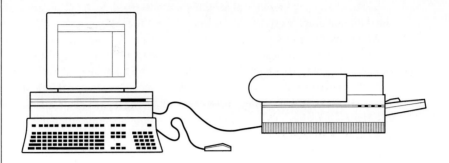

Introduction to Computer Graphics and CAD

Advancements in computer graphics are rapidly changing the technical design and analysis processes carried out by engineers, scientists, architects, and other professionals. Only a decade ago computer-aided design (CAD) was a luxury enjoyed only by design professionals who had access to mainframe computers equipped with graphics terminals and plotters. The use of expensive mainframe systems was justified only for large projects such as the design of aircraft or buildings. Nowadays, workstations have taken over the high end of the graphics market, and the personal computer has become a sufficient platform for running professional CAD software. To run CAD software, an IBM-PC compatible computer normally requires a 386, 486, Pentium, or PowerPC processor, and a Macintosh should be a Mac II (pictured above), a Quadra, or a PowerMac.

Powerful CAD software has been developed for personal computers, and many of the mainframe/workstation CAD packages have migrated down to personal computers. This book presents basic computer graphics algorithms, provides programming examples, and shows how the algorithms are implemented in a commercial software package, AutoCAD.® Although several software packages offer comparable CAD features on personal computers, AutoCAD was selected primarily because it is the most widely used package. Although examples are given for AutoCAD, the material presented in this book should be useful to those who have access to almost any CAD package.

The computer graphics algorithms are presented in the C programming language, with common graphics statements selected from the Macintosh QuickDraw library or from the Microsoft C/QuickC® library (equivalent graphics statements for some other systems are shown in table 1.1 in section 1.3). To aid readers familiar with BASIC and FORTRAN, the initial program in chapter 2 is presented in those languages as well as in C.

This chapter begins with a short history and overview of the computer-aided design process. In section 1.2 hardware is discussed, including input and output devices. Section 1.3, on software, includes discussion of graphics statements in programming languages. Illustrations are presented in section 1.4 to show how objects are graphically represented in two and three dimensions. Finally, to show how a CAD system is used, the chapter closes with a discussion of AutoCAD menus, including the setup and execution of a simple drawing.

1.1 DEVELOPMENTS IN COMPUTER-AIDED DESIGN

The first system that permitted a designer to graphically interact with a computer was SKETCHPAD, developed by Ivan Sutherland at MIT in 1962–63. Graphical interaction was achieved by the use of a light pen to directly touch items on the screen. During the 1970s CAD systems were developed so that mainframe computers could be used for designing large projects such as aircraft or buildings. During the 1980s professional CAD software was developed for personal computers, so that now computer-aided design is available in a wide range of levels and prices. Designers can choose from a variety of software for different stages of the design cycle.

Figure 1.1 illustrates the four main stages in the design of a product. The connecting structure for the design software is a graphics program—such as AutoCAD for personal computers or CADAM for mainframes and workstations—that provides the drafting and database framework for representing objects in two and three dimensions. Specialized software for various design functions should integrate with the main CAD software.

The specifications for the design and the analysis of need can be developed with standard database management software such as dBASE. To access the nongraphic data in external databases, AutoCAD uses the AutoCAD SQL Extension™ (ASE).

Specialized software for the initial or conceptual design phase has been developed in recent years. For engineering design, this type of software uses *parametric modeling,* so

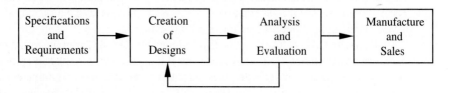

Figure 1.1   Stages of a design cycle.

that you can draw an item in a particular configuration, and then change sizes and orientations of the components to analyze the effect of the overall design parameters. Parametric modeling is similar to the work that a designer would do by hand when sketching various configuration arrangements and checking their effectiveness with calculations. When a product's appearance is most important, software featuring quick computer modeling and visualization can be used for conceptual design.

In figure 1.1, the arrow going back from the evaluation/analysis box to the creation box illustrates that the design process is an iterative procedure. Thus, an initial design can be repeatedly modified as a result of analysis. Although the acronym CAD means *computer-aided design*, it is often used for software that offers just computer-aided drafting. To emphasize the design component, the acronym CADD, *computer-aided design and drafting,* is sometimes used. Software that includes engineering analysis of designs is often described by the more general title CAE, *computer-aided engineering.* To differentiate software for mechanical engineering applications from electrical engineering applications such as printed circuit design, the following abbreviations are often used: MCAD, *mechanical computer-aided design,* and MCAE, *mechanical computer-aided engineering.* One of the most useful types of engineering analysis software packages involves FEA, *finite-element analysis*, which uses FEM, the *finite-element method* for structural analysis, or for calculating heat transfer and fluid flow. At least one software vendor uses the acronym FEM to signify *finite-element module.*

The last box in figure 1.1 shows that the design process continues through the manufacturing and sales phase. The designs developed in the earlier phases are used to make production drawings and help set up the production line. Software used in this final phase is often described by the acronym CAM, *computer-aided manufacturing.* The computer control of machines during manufacturing is termed CNC, *computer numerical control,* or NC, *numerical control,* as in NC lathes and NC mills. As an aid in producing manuals for products, the drawings from earlier design phases can be put in a form for use with DTP (*desktop publishing*) software. Also, realistic drawings called *renderings* can be developed for use in sales. In some areas, such as architecture, renderings may be produced at an earlier phase to lead to a visually pleasing design.

The term CAD/CAM is popular for describing the use of computers throughout the design and manufacturing phases. Another all-encompassing acronym is CIM, *computer-integrated manufacturing.* Although the term CIM may raise visions of computers and robots in a completely automated factory, it is commonly used to describe the integration of software (under a common database) in the design and manufacturing phases. Recently, *concurrent engineering,* or CE, has become a popular term to describe the computer integration of the overall design process. As you can see from the above discussion, the marketing directors of software firms have been busy coining acronyms, and their interpretation is often inexact.

Computer graphics has produced many technical terms. In section 1.4 we illustrate how computer graphics can represent 3-D (three-dimensional) objects with a *wireframe* model. A more complete representation of an object is done by *solid modeling,* of which CSG, *constructive solid geometry,* is a popular method. A common means of mathematically representing surfaces of complex objects is to build them out of *spline* curves and *spline* surfaces or patches. As mentioned above, realistic pictures of an object are called renderings, and the process of producing such pictures with illumination and shading is termed *rendering*.

The graphics image on the computer screen is broken down to its smallest constituents, called picture elements or *pixels.* The process of finding which pixels a graphic entity (line, polygon, etc.) covers is termed *rasterization* or *scan conversion.* The fineness of the pixels on your computer screen depends on the graphics card or graphics adapter in your computer; the original IBM PC had a CGA, or *computer graphics adapter,* giving 320 × 200 pixels in the horizontal and vertical directions, respectively. The screen resolution of personal computers was first increased by the EGA, or *enhanced graphics adapter,* to 640 × 350 pixels, and then by the VGA, or *video graphics adapter,* to 640 × 480 pixels. SuperVGA graphics adapters can extend the PC screen resolution to the workstation standard (1280 × 1024 pixels) and beyond.

1.2 HARDWARE

Hardware for computer graphics consists of a computer plus peripherals, including input and output devices. Besides the standard keyboard, input devices for graphics include the mouse, graphics tablet, trackball, joystick, scanner, knobs on a view control box, and exotic tools for 3-D, such as the spaceball and data glove. Although your graphics output will usually be plotted on your monitor, for design purposes you will often need hard copy from one of the following output devices: dot-matrix printer, laser printer, pen plotter, thermal printer, ink-jet printer, electrostatic plotter, or film recorder. Although computer hardware changes rapidly, approximate prices for equipment and even brand names are sometimes included in the discussion below to better present the current (1994) situation. Prices quoted are usually for devices to be used with personal computers or individual workstations; higher-priced versions often exist for use in large-volume commercial applications.

Personal Computers

The figure at the beginning of the chapter shows a simple CAD configuration consisting of a personal computer including monitor and keyboard, a mouse pointing device, and a printer. All of the figures in this book were produced on this type of system, namely an Apple Macintosh II series microcomputer with an Apple LaserWriter printer, or on 386- and 486-based IBM PC compatibles with a Hewlett-Packard LaserJet printer. Most figures were drawn with AutoCAD, although some were drawn with the illustration program Canvas, and others plotted directly from C programs. The C programs used were THINK C on the Macintosh and Microsoft C/QuickC on the PC.

The main unit of a personal computer contains the items illustrated in figure 1.2. This diagram represents the layout for a Macintosh II computer (the IBM PC has equivalent components arranged in a similar manner). These items include hard and floppy disk drives for magnetic storage, an electric power supply with a cooling fan, and an exposed part of the

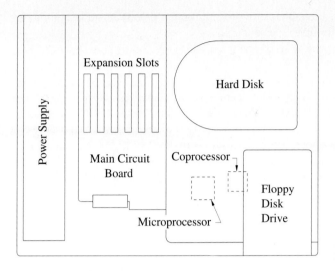

Figure 1.2 Diagram of components in the main unit of a personal computer.

main circuit board (motherboard) with expansion slots for insertion of cards (such as the video or graphics card). Hard disks for personal computers hold from 80M bytes to 1G bytes of memory, where M stands for *mega* (million), and G stands for *giga* (U.S. billion). CAD software requires a system with a hard disk because of memory requirements; also, information accessing and storage is much faster on a hard disk drive than on a floppy system.

If computers are not networked, floppy disks are useful for transferring programs and CAD drawings between computers. Many current PC systems are augmented with optical CD ROM (read-only memory) drives, so that the large amount of memory on a compact disk (CD) can be read. A compact disk holds approximately 600M bytes of information compared with floppy disks, which hold from 400K to 1.4M bytes (where K stands for *kilo*, or thousand).

Figure 1.2 includes the main microprocessor for the Macintosh, a Motorola series 68000 series chip (68000, 68020, 68030, or 68040), which is shown as a dashed square because it is located on the main circuit board under a metal sheet that holds the disk drives. On an IBM PC or compatible the microprocessor is an Intel series 8000 chip (8086, 8088, 80286, 80386, 80486, or Pentium). Although past versions of CAD software (such as Auto-CAD) have run on IBM compatible computers with the 80286 chip, new versions of CAD software often require the 386 or 486 chips because more memory capability is needed than the 640K RAM (random-access memory) limit accessible by the 286 chip. For a computer to run CAD software efficiently, or run complex programs fast, a math coprocessor chip is required (the coprocessor is integral with the 486 and Pentium chips). The coprocessor chip carries out floating-point operations much faster than the main microprocessor. Not shown in figure 1.2 are two types of memory chips located on the main circuit board under the region of the hard disk. These are the RAM and ROM chips.

One expansion slot on the main circuit board is used for a standard video (graphics) card or for special cards that accelerate graphics operations and increase screen resolution and color capabilities. The other slots may hold cards for a variety of purposes; for example, cards for input devices such as a tablet, a joystick, or (on the IBM PC) a mouse; for a modem; for extra memory; or for other special purposes.

Workstations

Workstations are optimized for high-speed operation in engineering, science, and design. Major producers of workstations include Silicon Graphics, Sun, Hewlett Packard, IBM, and DEC (Digital Equipment Corporation). High-speed workstations for graphics typically cost from $10,000 to $100,000 or more, compared with approximately $2,000 to $10,000 for a personal computer system capable of running relatively advanced CAD software. As personal computers have become more advanced, and as workstation prices have fallen, considerable overlap has developed in the performance and prices of personal computers and workstations. However, the most advanced workstations produce extremely high-speed graphics output; that is, graphic entities such as lines and shaded polygons can be drawn on a graphics workstation in a small fraction of the time required on a personal computer. This speed is mainly achieved by transferring graphics operations from software to hardware and firmware. Graphics operations like line drawing, polygon filling, and even transformations (translation, scaling, and rotation) can be incorporated into special graphics chips. Current (1994) high-end graphics workstations can plot over 100 million pixels per second and over 1 million 3-D vectors or polygons per second. These numbers sound large, but they are needed for plotting complex screen images at approximately 60 frames per second, as required for real-time animation.

Besides higher performance, the workstation environment more often provides a networked system of computers with access to database management software. A linked CAD management system can provide access to drawing changes and data at all stages of the design process, yielding considerable savings in time and money over the design cycle.

Figure 1.3 illustrates some of the special features of a high-speed graphics workstation. The mouse and keyboard are connected directly to the computer CPU (central processing unit). In the dashed rectangle on the right of the bus (common line of conductors) there are a number of special items for processing high-speed graphics. The display list stores graphics information for quick retrieval and display of scenes. The transform pipeline uses hardware (chips) to carry out graphics transformations such as translation, rotation, scaling, clipping, perspective views, etc. (see chapters 10 and 11 for transformation algorithms). The rasterizer uses hardware to change lines and polygons into pixels (see the algorithms given in chapters 2 and 3). The Z-buffer stores the depth of the closest object for each pixel so that a scene can be displayed with hidden surfaces removed. The frame buffer (discussed in chapter 2) stores pixel information such as color. The frame buffer is shown double to illustrate double-buffering, in which the back buffer is being written into while the front buffer is being drawn on the monitor. An updated scene can be quickly transferred to the monitor by switching buffers. The box labeled VTC represents video timing and control, which refreshes the monitor with the contents of the frame buffer. The monitor is refreshed at a rate of 60 times per second to prevent flickering of the screen image. The CLT box is the color lookup table, which sets the specific colors to be displayed on the monitor (see chapter 2).

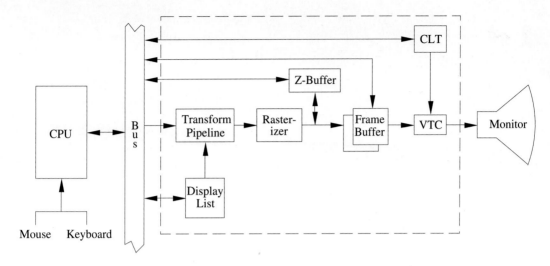

Figure 1.3   Generic workstation architecture (from a diagram supplied by Michael Bailey, San Diego Supercomputer Center).

Input Devices

Every computer has at least one input device, the keyboard. Although graphics programs and CAD software can be run exclusively with a keyboard, it is extremely useful to have a mouse, tablet, or other device for handling menu items and for selecting points or graphic entities on the screen.

The mouse is a standard input device with the Macintosh computer and with advanced graphics workstations. The mouse senses position as it is moved on a desktop (or on a mouse pad). A mechanical mouse detects position through the rolling ball beneath it. An optical mouse detects movement by means of a light beam reflected from the roughened desk surface (or from a ruled mouse pad). In each case the moving mouse positions a cursor on the screen so that menus or graphic entities can be selected by clicking a button on the mouse. The Macintosh mouse has only one button, but others often have two or three buttons that can be programmed for separate functions; see figure 1.4.

A device similar to the mechanical mouse is the trackball, which consists of a ball facing upward in a holder. The user rotates the ball in its holder, rather than moving it around a desk. The trackball is particularly useful with laptop personal computers because there may be no desktop available for using a conventional mouse.

A graphics tablet has a mouse-like device called a puck (figure 1.4) that moves over a tablet surface to which the user can attach a template for a CAD menu. A schematic representation of the AutoCAD menu template is illustrated in figure 1.17 in section 1.5. A graphics tablet is an efficient input device because it contains practically all of the commands on a single surface, instead of in nested menus like those that appear on the screen. A blank area on the tablet represents the computer screen, so that the puck can be used like a mouse to select points or menus from the screen. Both the tablet and mouse can be used

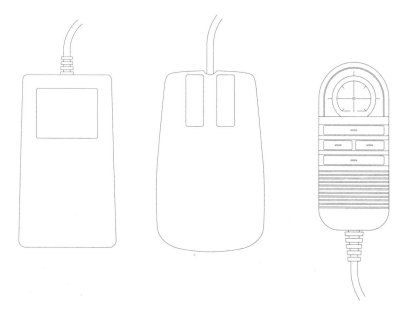

Figure 1.4 Input devices, including (from left) the Apple Macintosh one-button mouse, the Microsoft two-button mouse, and the puck from a Hewlett-Packard graphics tablet.

for simple digitizing, that is, for tracing over drawings to put them into the software database. Graphics tablets replace the puck with a pen to improve the accuracy of selecting points for digitizing. Less popular nowadays are light pens for selecting menus from a light-sensitive computer screen, although "touch-screen" monitors sensitive to fingers are still useful for general public applications such as selecting an option from a list of choices (for example, an object to purchase, or a location on a map).

The joystick is an input device often used for computer games, but it has limited use for CAD applications because its input is limited to the small number of directions and signals appropriate for games.

For advanced workstations that have the hardware features illustrated in figure 1.3, a simple box with control dials is convenient for rapidly translating, rotating, and scaling the screen image.

Another useful input device is the optical scanner. Scanners transfer drawings or pictures from images on paper to a computerized record. This record is a raster file that provides a photographic representation of the image as gray-scale dots, typically 300-dpi (dots per inch) resolution, which is also the standard laser printer resolution. Although desktop publishing software can directly use scanned images, converting paper drawings to CAD drawings requires two steps, of which scanning is just the first. The second step is to use the raster file created by the scanner to produce a CAD drawing, either with specialized software for directly converting the raster file to the CAD drawing file or by using the scanned image as a reference to create a new CAD drawing. This latter approach is similar to digitizing from a tablet except that the image appears on the screen to provide better access for overlaying a new CAD drawing.

Advanced input devices include three-dimensional digitizers, the spaceball, and a wired glove. For 3-D digitizing, either a stylus or a laser beam is used to input the x-, y-, and z-coordinates on the surface of a 3-D object. The spaceball is similar to the trackball except that the spaceball remains stationary; it is exposed so that it can sense normal and tangential forces from the user's hand and interpret them as translations and torques along all three axes.

The wired glove, marketed as DataGlove by VPL Research, Inc., carries sensors that monitor flection and extension of the fingers, as well as the position and orientation of the hand. The glove, which fits on the user's right hand, can be used to grasp objects on the screen in a manner similar to the way objects are handled in the real world. The programming interface for the DataGlove enables gestures to be interpreted as commands for convenient maneuvering and selection in the "screen world." The wired glove is an example of an input device that creates a *virtual reality.* The user may be put into an artificial world or virtual reality by coupling the wired glove with a head-mounted display (helmet-mounted display with sensors that move the displayed images as the head is moved). Another type of input for creating a virtual reality is a treadmill with steerable handlebars, coupled to a head-mounted display, to permit the user to "walk through" buildings. The oldest type of virtual reality is the flight simulator used for training airplane pilots. The input devices for the flight simulator are the actual aircraft controls, which are programmed to move the high-resolution displays in the simulator windows in response to the controls. Additional reality is provided by the active cockpit control panel, and by mounting the cockpit on gimbals to provide accelerations and vibrations appropriate to the simulation of flight.

Output Devices

The first hard copy from computers was produced by impact printers for text and by pen plotters for line drawings. Nowadays there is a wide range of hard-copy output devices, each with its own price-performance niche in the graphics market. Below we discuss dot-matrix impact printers, laser printers, ink-jet printers, thermal printers, pen plotters, electrostatic plotters, and film recorders. Performance ranges from a simple low-resolution *screen dump* (black-and-white copy of screen image at screen pixel resolution) on A size paper (8.5 × 11 in.) from a $200 dot-matrix printer, to a high-resolution plot including color area fill on E size paper (32 × 44 in.) from a $50,000 electrostatic plotter. Figure 1.5 shows the relative size of American standard plotting paper; European sizes A4–A0 correspond

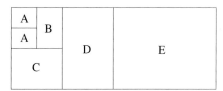

Figure 1.5   Standard U.S. engineering plotting paper sizes A–E: 8.5 × 11, 11 × 17, 17 × 22, 22 × 34, and 34 × 44 in. Architectural plotting paper is slightly larger: 24 × 36 for size D and 36 × 48 for size E.

approximately to American sizes A–E, but starting with a size of 21 × 29.7 cm (approximately 8.3 × 11.7 in.) rather than 8.5 × 11 in.

The particular printer or plotter to use depends not only on your pocketbook but also on the graphic requirements of your application. The quality of the graphic output will depend on software as well as hardware. CAD software often has drivers for a large number of printers and plotters; for example, many of the preliminary figures for this book were made by using the AutoCAD PLOT command to produce drawings on a laser printer. Still higher resolution was achieved for final printing by producing a file in PostScript (page description language) for printing directly on Linotronics or Compugraphic printers used in the publishing industry, which achieve resolutions up to 2540 dpi.

Dot-matrix printers are the least expensive output devices. Following common usage, here dot-matrix printer refers to the dot-matrix *impact* printer, even though essentially all other printers and plotters except pen plotters are dot-matrix (raster) devices. Although used mainly for text, the dot-matrix printer can produce graphics either in a simple screen dump mode or as higher-quality output if an appropriate driver is available on a higher-resolution printer. High-speed line printers can have a print bar that extends across the entire page; however, most dot-matrix impact printers have one or two lines of pins (also called wires, needles, or hammers) that are carried across the paper by the motion of the printhead; see figure 1.6. Most dot-matrix printers have either 9 or 24 pins, with the 24-pin printer producing near "letter quality" text. The term *letter quality* references the quality to a daisy wheel printer that prints in the same manner as a typewriter by impacting raised characters onto a ribbon above the paper. The dot-matrix printer works in a similar fashion, with each impact of a pin producing a single dot (an electromagnet is used to move the pins to the paper and back).

Figure 1.6 illustrates how the 9-pin printhead forms letters as it moves horizontally across the paper. The top 7 pins form the capital letters, which are above the baseline; the 2 bottom pins form the tails of lowercase letters such as *y* and *p*. Because dots are positioned horizontally at half (dot) spaces as well as at full spaces, all letters can fit within five horizontal spaces. Note that the 24-pin printhead in figure 1.6 is shown with two staggered lines

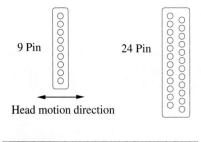

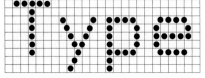

Figure 1.6 Printhead configurations of 9 and 24 pins, with an example of letters formed by a 9-pin printhead. The grid is for reference in locating the vertical and horizontal positions of the printed dots.

of pins so that printed dots will overlap for increased resolution and smoothness in forming characters. In addition to forming characters, the dots can represent a drawing or picture. Typically, the 9-pin printer will produce graphics at 70-dpi resolution and the 24-pin printer at 180 dpi. Most dot-matrix impact printers are monochrome, although some models add one or more colors to black by shifting to additional ribbons. Because of the speed at which the pins hit the ribbon, dot-matrix printers are usually noisy; the other printers and plotters described in this section are relatively quiet.

In recent years laser printers have replaced most daisy wheel and dot-matrix printers used for high-quality text. The standard resolution for a laser printer is 300 dpi, although 600-dpi printers are now available. Laser printer prices start at approximately $600. Practically all laser printers are monochrome at the present time; however, color models (at considerably higher prices) are becoming more common.

Figure 1.7 illustrates the optical system for a laser printer. A laser beam is modulated by data to be printed, and then reflected off a rotating polygonal mirror so that the beam scans along the axis of a rotating drum. The photoconductive coating of the drum is electrically charged, but loses the charge at points hit by the laser beam. In the remainder of the process (not shown in the figure), a black plastic powder (toner) is attracted to the remaining charge on the drum. The positively charged toner is then transferred to negatively charged paper, which moves across the back side of the drum. The toner is then melted into the paper to make the image permanent.

Monochrome ink-jet printers generally lie between dot-matrix and laser printers in price and resolution, whereas color ink jets are normally the least expensive option for full-color area fill applications. Most ink-jet printers for personal computers and workstations are drop-on-demand (impulse) systems in which a drop of ink is ejected from a small nozzle in response to a pressure pulse. Early systems were continuous devices in which a stream of ink breaks up into drops, which are then charged, and are either allowed to strike the paper or are deflected into a gutter, depending on whether or not a printed dot is desired at a given position on the paper.

Two common printer configurations for moving paper exist: the printhead containing ink-jet nozzles may follow the axial direction of a rapidly spinning drum to which the pa-

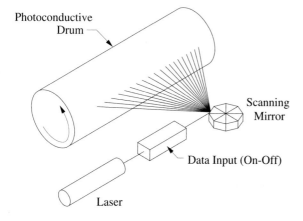

Figure 1.7 Optical system for a laser printer, adapted from the following article: J. A. Hall, "Laser Printing System Provides Flexible, High-Quality, Cost-Effective Computer Output," *Hewlett-Packard Journal*, pp. 3–8, June 1982.

per is attached, or the printhead may move back and forth across the paper, which moves up line by line. The latter configuration is most common and is the same as that used for a dot-matrix impact printer, except that the pin printhead is replaced by an ink-jet printhead. An ink-jet printhead typically contains 30 to 100 nozzles so that it can print rapidly as it sweeps across the page. The ink-jet printer is fast because the printhead can move continuously across the paper while ejecting drops; impact printers must move the pins to the paper and back before the printhead moves to the next position. In a third ink-jet configuration, a plotter pen is replaced by an ink-jet printhead; thus no time is needed to bring the pen to the paper at the beginning of a line and pick it up at the end.

The pressure pulse for drop-on-demand ink jets may be produced in two ways: the channel supplying ink may be squeezed (normally by a piezoelectric crystal), or a short power pulse may rapidly heat a resistor and produce a bubble that forces a drop of ink out of the nozzle. This latter method is called the thermal ink jet or bubble jet and is illustrated in figure 1.8.

Monochrome ink-jet printers offer almost the same resolution as laser printers at somewhat less cost. Color ink-jet printers mix dots of cyan, yellow, and magenta dyes to produce a relatively full range of colors by *dithering* (see chapter 6). Normally, a separate cartridge of black ink is provided to ensure a good black color for text and graphics (in theory black can be produced by equally mixing cyan, yellow, and magenta). Currently, color ink-jet printers are priced from $500 to $10,000 and produce resolutions of 300 to 400 dpi. Sometimes quality is reduced by the "banding" that results from the separate passes of the printhead across the paper and by lowered resolution for color shades produced by dithering. Color ink-jet printers often require special paper for the best output, whereas monochrome ink-jet printers often operate well with plain paper.

The above discussion applies to liquid ink jets that use water-based inks. At the high end of the ink-jet market are the solid or phase-change ink-jet printers, which can produce fully saturated colors on plain paper. These ink jets start with color wax sticks, which are melted and squirted as drops onto the paper. When the drops strike the paper, they cool and solidify.

Pen plotters excel at producing high-quality line drawings for CAD applications. Prices start at approximately $500, but typically range from $3,000 to $8,000 for plotters having eight pens and handling paper up to D or E size. Although pen plotters can fill areas by putting lines close together, such fill requires considerable time, so pen plotters work best on line drawings. Pen plotters operate with *vector* graphics; that is, a line is plotted by placing the pen at a starting point and drawing to the end point, just as you would do by hand. Early plotters were flat-bed plotters in which the paper lies flat and a bar carrying the pen moves in one direction across the paper while the pen moves along the bar in directions perpendicular to the bar motion. Most newer pen plotters move the paper in one direction while the pen moves in a perpendicular direction; see figure 1.9. This latter configuration permits the pen carriage to be lightweight, allowing higher accelerations and pen speeds while achieving high accuracy. The pen motion can be directly programmed, for example, by embedding into your program pen commands in HPGL or HPGL/2 (Hewlett-Packard Graphics Languages). Most CAD systems can directly output drawings to a plotter by using HPGL or HPGL/2.

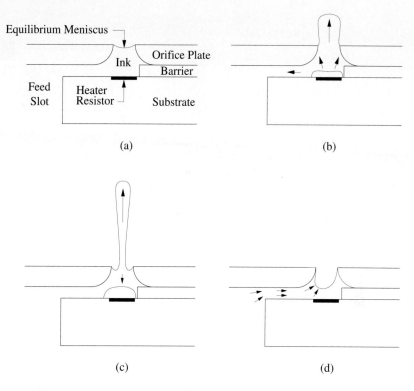

Figure 1.8 Stages of the thermal ink-jet cycle, showing a cross section along the axis of a nozzle region. (a) An ink meniscus forms across the nozzle orifice under equilibrium conditions (no ink motion) before the power pulse is applied to the heater resistor. (b) A bubble grows over the resistor a short time after the power pulse is applied. A drop starts to eject from the orifice, and there is some backflow toward the feed slot (arrows show the ink motion). (c) The ejected drop is nearly at the break-off point (when the menisci near the orifice join and the drop separates from the remaining ink). Because the power pulse is over and the resistor is cooling, the bubble starts to collapse. (d) The capillary forces exerted by the orifice meniscus (after drop ejection and bubble collapse) initiate refill. The refill period is the longest part of the cycle; it therefore determines the rate at which drops can be fired and thus the speed of the printer.

Because pen plotters are vector devices, with lines drawn one after another, plotting time is proportional to the number of lines in the drawing. In contrast, for raster output devices the actual drawing time is relatively independent of the drawing complexity because in every case the entire paper is scanned with dots placed at appropriate positions. Of course, in plotting with CAD software, particularly for 3-D drawings with hidden lines, much of the plotting time may be taken up by software computations that are strongly dependent on the complexity of the drawing. When using a pen plotter you should not plot too many lines through a single point or in a very small region on the paper because the pen can eat through the paper if a point is drawn over too frequently. This situation can occur easily with CAD software, in which a complex subpart of the drawing may shrink to nearly a

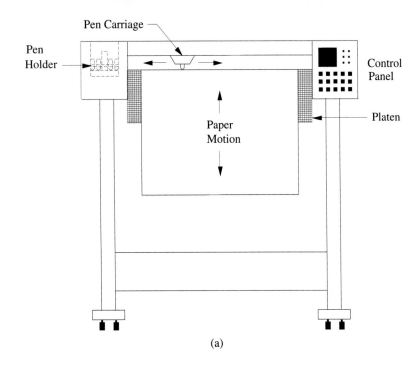

(a)

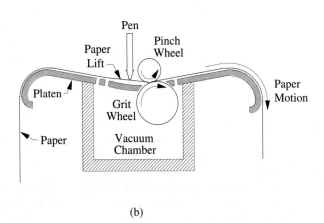

(b)

Figure 1.9   (a) An E-size pen plotter with the paper moving in one direction across a platen while the pen moves in a perpendicular direction. As the drawing is being executed, pens of different colors are exchanged from a rotating carousel holder. (b) Cross-section diagram showing the paper-moving mechanism for a plotter of the type shown in a, adapted from the following article: R. J. Kaplan and R. S. Townsend, "X-Axis Micro-Grip Drive and Platen Design," *Hewlett-Packard Journal*, pp. 33–36, November 1981. The paper is accurately moved between the grit and pinch wheels (drawn with exaggerated size) while the pen moves perpendicularly to the plane of this illustration. A vacuum chamber holds the paper to the platen, which is curved to prevent the paper from buckling. The amount of paper lift near the wheels determines how high the pen must be lifted between lines.

point on the scale of the overall drawing; therefore, you should carefully consider which portions of the drawing are to appear on the final pen plot. Some pen plotters also accept pencils, which are convenient when the user knows that part of the drawing will be erased later and modified by hand. Overall, pen plotters are very useful for providing line drawings of all sizes in a limited number (about eight) of colors.

Pen plotters are rapidly being replaced by raster plotters. For example, in 1994 Hewlett Packard is replacing its large pen plotters with its DesignJet raster plotters. Although the DesignJet plotters move paper in the same fashion as the pen plotter shown in figure 1.9, the plotting occurs in a raster mode at resolutions of 300 dpi and 600 dpi. The DesignJet increases the speed of plotting complex drawings by using the raster mode and by using ink jets (as noted previously, ink jets don't require the accelerations and decelerations associated with placing a pen on paper, drawing a line segment, and picking up the pen).

Color thermal printers produce high-quality pictures or drawings with area fill. These raster color printers start at approximately $2,000, and greatly differ from the inexpensive monochrome thermal printers that have been in existence for many years. Paper sizes are normally limited to A and B. Color thermal printers use either wax transfer or dye sublimation. The thermal wax-transfer printer uses a ribbon that contains alternating page-size layers of cyan, yellow, magenta, and sometimes black waxes. The ribbon lies between specially coated printing paper and a thermal printhead, and selectively applied heat from the thermal printhead melts colored wax onto the paper in small dots. The printer repeats the process for each color. Because colored wax is melted onto the paper, the output is smooth and glossy with relatively opaque, rich color. The thermal dye sublimation printer is similar to the wax-transfer printer except that dye pigments are not melted but are sublimated into gases that provide a slight spreading of color for near-continuous tone images. Therefore, the dye sublimation process, unlike wax transfer, does not require dithering to produce the very large number of colors needed for "near-photographic" images. Although dye-sublimation printers produce higher-quality images, they are more expensive than the wax-transfer printers.

As indicated at the beginning of this section, the electrostatic printer is at the high end of the printer/plotter market, with prices starting at approximately $15,000, and extending to $50,000 for E-size color output. These devices are especially useful for applications like map making or architectural rendering that require high quality, large sizes, and full-color fill. Electrostatic printers come in two resolutions: 200 dpi and 400 dpi. These printers are raster devices in which a writing head contains 1 to 3 rows of writing nibs or styli (400 nibs per inch for 400-dpi resolution). As specially coated paper passes over the nibs, a dot of electrostatic charge is deposited by each nib; the dots are then made visible as the paper passes over a toner applicator, where positively charged particles of liquid toner are attracted to the negatively charged dots on the paper. The toner particles are then dried and fixed to make them permanent. For color electrostatic printers, toner particles of cyan, magenta, yellow, and black are applied to the paper either in a single pass or in four successive passes.

A screen image can be readily captured on film when a standard camera is used to take a picture of the computer screen. However, the resulting image is limited by the screen resolution; the colors produced on the film will not be identical to those on the screen; and there will be some geometric distortion produced by the screen curvature and by the perspective view from the camera. Special computer output devices called film recorders circumvent these limitations. Desktop film recorder prices range from approximately $3,000 to $12,000. Also, there are slide service companies that use film recorders to produce slides, overhead transparencies, or prints from your CAD or graphics files saved in an appropriate format.

Film recorders may be either analog or digital. In an analog film recorder the red, green, and blue parts of a graphic image are separately projected onto a special monochrome flat-screen CRT (cathode-ray tube) in the recorder. The film is separately exposed to these three parts of the image through a color wheel with red, green, and blue filters to produce a composite image on the film that reproduces color accurately. A monochrome CRT increases the sharpness because it has no color mask to degrade image quality. Special 5-inch-diameter CRTs for film recorders can achieve resolutions of 3000 to 5000 dpi; however, for the analog film recorder the overall resolution is limited to the original monitor's screen resolution because the image information comes from that monitor. Because the digital film recorder obtains its information from the software data files, its resolution is not limited by the original monitor screen. Digital film recorders typically start with total image resolutions of 2000 × 2000 pixels and go to 8000 × 8000 pixels and higher.

1.3 SOFTWARE

An overview of the types of CAD software was presented in section 1.1. Here we will discuss graphics libraries available with common programming languages, as well as general CAD software. Software for combined 2-D and 3-D design on personal computers typically costs from $3,000 to $4,000. Popular software in this range includes AutoCAD, Cadkey, CADvance, Microstation, Personal Designer, and Versacad. These software packages integrate 2-D drafting with wireframe and surface modeling. Solid modeling is starting to be incorporated into these software packages; for example, AutoCAD includes solid modeling through its Advanced Modeling Extension® (AME®).

Most of the CAD software mentioned above was originally designed for personal computers. However, some software packages are PC versions of mainframe or workstation CAD systems. CAD software for mainframes and workstations is priced from about $10,000. These CAD packages are typically solid modelers that include (or can add) analysis software. Popular packages include ADAMS, ANVIL, CADAM, DADS, I-DEAS, and Hewlett-Packard's ME 30.

Language implementations on personal computers have a wide variety of graphics statements; table 1.1 lists some common ones. On the IBM PC and compatibles, the individual languages provide graphics libraries, although some versions have no graphics statements (FORTRAN implementations usually have no graphics statements, but third-party graphics libraries can be added). Macintosh users have the option of using QuickDraw graphics. Graphics libraries for workstations can be very extensive and often include advanced features such as 3-D transformations for fast display of graphics.

TABLE 1.1 GRAPHICS ROUTINES FOR PERSONAL COMPUTERS

Routine	Microsoft C or Visual C/QuickC[a]	Borland Turbo C[a]	Borland Turbo Pascal[a]	Microsoft QuickBASIC[a]	Macintosh QuickDraw[b]
Turn on a pixel	_setpixel()	putpixel()	PutPixel()	pset()	SetCPixel()[c]
Move to a point	_moveto()	moveto()	MoveTo()	preset()	MoveTo()
Line	_lineto()	lineto()	Line()	line()	LineTo()
Rectangle	_rectangle()	rectangle()	Rectangle()	line()[d]	FrameRect()
Ellipse (includes circle)	_ellipse()	ellipse()	Ellipse()	circle()	FrameOval()
Fill a polygon with color	_floodfill()	fillpoly()	FillPoly()	paint()	FillPoly()[e]
Arc	_arc()	arc()	Arc()	circle()	FrameArc()
Get color of pixel	_getpixel()	getpixel()	GetPixel()	point()	GetPixel()[e]
Set screen mode	_setvideomode()	initgraph()	InitGraph()	screen()	SetPort()[e]
Set color palette	_remappalette()	setrgbpalette()	SetRGBPalette()	palette()	NewPalette()
Clear the screen	_clearscreen()	cleardevice()	ClearDevice()	cls()	ScrollRect()
Set clipping rectangle	_setcliprgn()	setviewport()	SetViewPort()	view()	ClipRect()
Put image into memory	_getimage()	getimage()	GetImage()	get()	CopyBits()
Put image onto screen	_putimage()	putimage()	PutImage()	put()	CopyBits()

[a]For IBM PC compatible computers.
[b]For Macintosh implementations of C, Pascal, BASIC, and FORTRAN.
[c]For color only; for black and white, use other routines; e.g., FrameOval(), or Moveto() plus LineTo() for a single coordinate point.
[d]Use with the argument B for box.
[e]For color routines, use FillCPoly(), GetCPixel(), and OpenCPort().

Most of the program listings presented in this book use graphics statements from the QuickDraw library, such as MoveTo() or LineTo(), and from the Microsoft C library, such as _moveto() and _lineto(). (One exception is that SetPixel(), rather than QuickDraw function SetCPixel(), will be used to denote "turning on" a pixel regardless of whether we are using color or not.) Most QuickDraw graphics require integer arguments, although graphics functions for other systems often require floating-point numbers, or give the user the option to select from equivalent integer and floating-point routines. You should determine what graphics routines are available for your particular programming setup.

Table 1.1 shows that the Microsoft C or QuickC graphics functions all start with an underline as the first character. The Borland Turbo C and Turbo Pascal library functions have the same words, except that the Pascal functions include some uppercase letters. Note that the Macintosh QuickDraw library functions also include some uppercase letters (this is because the QuickDraw library was written in Pascal).

The procedure used in this book is to build up graphics algorithms starting with just the two most basic statements: turning pixels on with SetPixel() and obtaining the colors of pixels with GetPixel(). For example, in the next chapter algorithms for straight lines are implemented with the SetPixel() statement and are compared with QuickDraw lines constructed with MoveTo() and LineTo(). Then in chapter 3 the MoveTo() and LineTo() routines will be used to draw simple curves and to draw and fill polygons. Equivalent graphics commands on AutoCAD will be discussed along with the programming examples.

Instead of using the graphics library included in your computer language, you could construct your own graphics functions. The advantage of this approach is that your programs will include the definitions of all of the graphics functions, so they can be used with any implementations of your programming language. That is, by building your own graphics library, your programs can be ANSI (American National Standards Institute) standard. Note that all C functions used in this book are ANSI standard, *except* for the graphics functions. To build your own graphics library for IBM PC compatible computers, you can set your screen mode and form SetPixel() and GetPixel() functions in C by using the function int86() from the dos.h library. An example of using int86() to set the screen mode and write pixel functions is given in the book by Lindley (1992) listed in the bibliography at the end of this chapter. Because Microsoft C and Turbo C do not have functions for accessing mouse positions and button status, we have used the function int86() in appendix A at the end of this book to write a mouse subroutine for inputting points.

Although graphics routines may vary from one system to another, many of the implementations do largely follow recommended standards: GKS (*graphical kernel system*) and PHIGS (*programmer's hierarchical interactive graphics standard*). Conformity to these standards is more prevalent for implementations of graphics on workstations, leading to a greater portability of graphics software in the workstation environment.

Another type of graphics standard involves the interchange of drawing files between CAD systems. The IGES (*Initial Graphics Exchange Specification*) is supported by most professional CAD systems. Another format that has gained considerable popularity is DXF™, Autodesk's drawing interchange file format. In chapter 8 the DXF file format will be studied, with C programming being used to input data into AutoCAD as a DXF file.

1.4 REPRESENTING OBJECTS WITH 2-D AND 3-D DRAWINGS

Much design work is still being done with 2-D drawings. Such drawings represent true dimensions in the selected views; for example, top, front, and side views of the object. In the past many 3-D drawings were made so that viewers could readily picture an object in their minds. Three-dimensional drawings have also been useful for presenting an attractive picture (rendering) for display or sales purposes. Many designers feel that computer graphics has evolved to the state where objects should be modeled directly in three dimensions, with 2-D drawings produced as a by-product for views in specific directions.

The 2-D AutoCAD drawings in figure 1.10 illustrate features of a human-powered vehicle design. The top and middle figures show top and side views of the drive mechanism of the vehicle. At the bottom of the figure, blowup views show the gears and chain at two magnifications. These blowups illustrate that CAD systems can retain accuracy on a very large range of scales. AutoCAD saves dimensions to double-precision accuracy (16 places).

The movie camera drawing in figure 1.11 was constructed with AutoCAD's 3-D surface-modeling features. This 3-D drawing can be viewed from any direction—figure 1.11 shows an enlarged view from a general (axomometric) direction, along with front and side views. All three views in figure 1.11 were made from a single 3-D model, whereas each view in figure 1.10 represents a separate 2-D drawing.

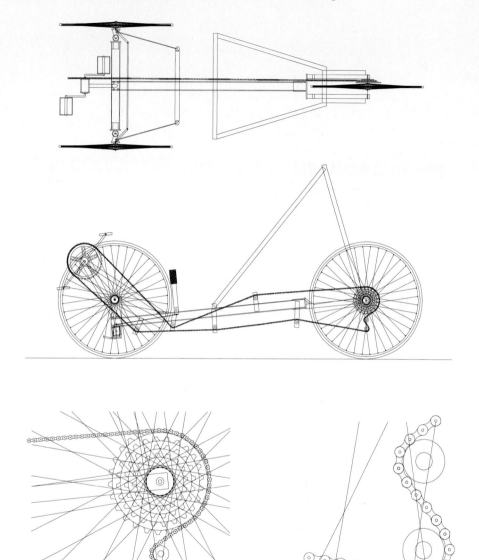

Figure 1.10 Two-dimensional drawings for a human-powered vehicle; drawn by Alan Payne.

Buildings and large structures such as the space station shown in figure 1.12 appear to be more realistic in perspective views. In a perspective view, the observer is at a finite distance from the object. Thus, the closer portion of the object appears larger than farther portions. In the perspective view of figure 1.12, the (closer) boom structure at the bottom

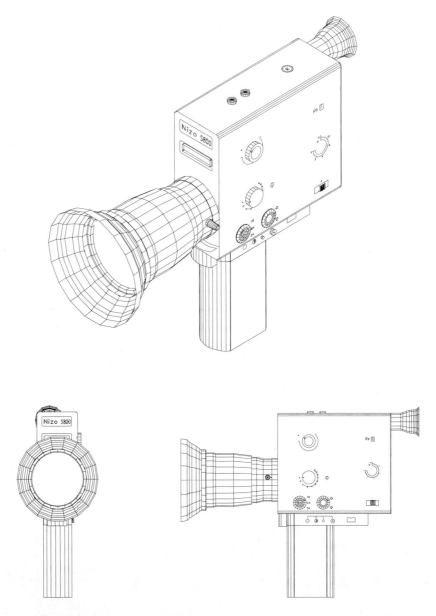

Figure 1.11   Three views of a three-dimensional representation of a movie camera; drawn by Gregory Stadler.

appears larger than the (farther) boom at the top, even though they have the same dimensions. Perspective viewing is discussed in chapter 11.

Figure 1.13 illustrates some ways in which an object can be represented in three dimensions. The picture on the left is a wireframe representation of a gear showing all edges of the faces that constitute the gear. The wireframe representation leads to confusion because it is difficult to distinguish edges on the back of the gear from those in front.

The second representation of the gear in figure 1.13 shows edges of faces, but a hidden-line algorithm is incorporated so that edges representing the back faces are not shown (same as for the movie camera in figure 1.11). Hidden-line algorithms require that an object be represented by a surface model or a solid model. Surface modeling is the subject of chapter 12, and solid modeling is discussed in chapter 13.

In the third picture of figure 1.13 the gear faces have been shaded to represent a light incident from above and from the left. The simple shading model that leads to this representation is discussed in chapter 14. Chapter 14 also describes the advanced rendering topics of ray tracing and texture mapping.

As mentioned above, the wireframe representation of 3-D objects can lead to confusion. For example, the wireframe object on the left in figure 1.14 can be interpreted as any of the other three objects on the right with hidden lines removed. Also, it is unclear whether or not the three objects on the right are solid or just surface representations. To illustrate this point, figure 1.15 shows the last object of figure 1.14 sectioned by a vertical plane. The three drawings on the right show how cross sections would appear for a wireframe, a surface representation, or a solid model. Obviously, the solid model represents the most complete

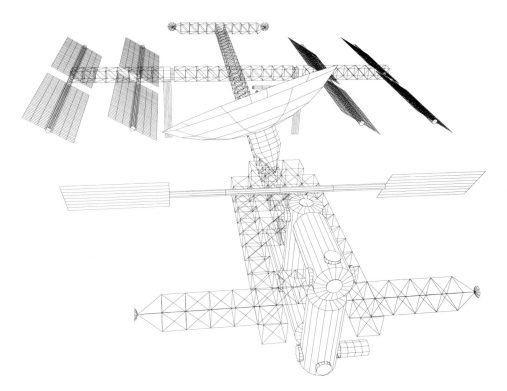

Figure 1.12   Perspective view of a 1985 space station design; drawn by Denise Barrera.

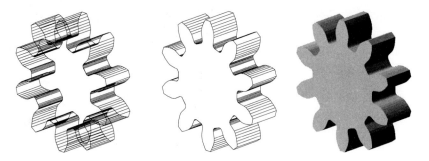

Figure 1.13   Three-dimensional representations of a gear.

description of the object, which can include material properties and thus enable the calculation of centers of gravity, moments of inertia, and other engineering properties.

One of the most popular methods of constructing a solid model is with CSG (constructive solid geometry). With CSG the solid is built up with Boolean operations of union, difference, and intersection. By finding the intersection of a completed group of solid parts, one can find out immediately if the design of the parts contains any overlap or tolerancing errors. Solid modeling is discussed in chapter 13 with examples from AutoCAD's Advanced Modeling Extension (AME).

1.5 AUTOCAD MENUS AND DRAWING EXAMPLE

An AutoCAD user may issue a command by typing on the keyboard or by picking the command from a menu on the screen or on a graphics tablet. The AutoCAD screen menus are illustrated in figure 1.16. In this figure the mouse cursor has been used to first select the As-

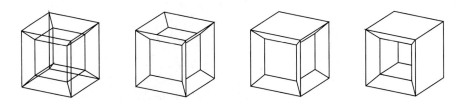

Figure 1.14   Different interpretations of a wireframe object consisting of concentric wire cubes joined at their vertices.

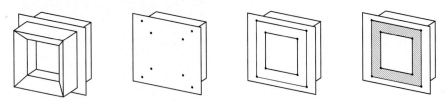

Figure 1.15   Cross sections illustrating wireframe, surface, and solid modeling.

sist pull-down menu item, then when Object snap is selected, another menu is displayed, from which the Endpoint option is selected. This example illustrates the nested character of some of the pull-down menu items. The top list of menu items appears when the cursor is placed along the top of the screen.

Almost all of the AutoCAD commands can be selected from the pull-down menus. Alternatively, these commands may be selected from the side menu. The side menu shown in figure 1.16 is the first one that appears in AutoCAD. Other menus appear on the side when items are selected, but one can always return to the original menu by selecting the word AutoCAD at the top of the side menu.

Different implementations of AutoCAD feature different menu designs. For Auto-CAD implementations on the Microsoft Windows and Apple Macintosh operating systems, many of the menu items are shown with icons rather than words; also, the Macintosh implementation features "tear-off" menus that can be placed anywhere for easy use. Menus are discussed in chapter 9 as part of the *graphical user interface,* or GUI.

AutoCAD commands can also be entered on a digitizing tablet. A tablet is convenient for CAD work because essentially all of the commands can be placed on its large area. The form of the AutoCAD template that overlays a digitizing tablet is shown in figure 1.17. The rectangular area with rounded corners to the right of the tablet center represents the monitor screen. In this area, points in the drawing region can be selected with a puck (like the one shown on the right of figure 1.4).

The remaining areas on the tablet contain the AutoCAD commands, which are grouped by type. The individual commands occupy small rectangular regions within these areas (the labels on the individual commands would be too small to show in this figure). Menu items are selected by placing the cross hairs of the puck over a command rectangle and pressing a button.

Figure 1.16   Nested pull-down menus in AutoCAD Release 12 for DOS.

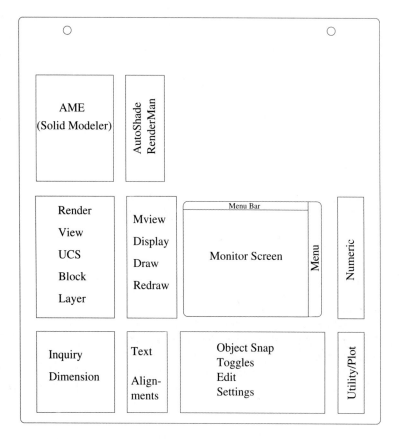

Figure 1.17   A schematic representation of the graphics tablet template for AutoCAD Release 12.

The tablet area to the left of the monitor screen area includes the same commands as in the pull-down menu DRAW; that is, commands for drawing entities such as line, polyline, arc, circle, ellipse, polygon, etc. In addition to DRAW, this area includes DISPLAY commands, such as zoom and pan, for changing the screen display. This area also includes the MVIEW command for setting up multiple views of a 3-D object, like those of the movie camera shown in figure 1.11.

The tablet area below the monitor screen area includes object snap modes for selecting particular points. These are the same snap modes shown in the pull-down menu in figure 1.16. That is, one can select Center for picking the center of an arc or circle, Endpoint for picking a line endpoint, Intersection for picking the intersection of two lines, etc.

The top third of the digitizing tablet is available for customizing, and for including templates for extensions and postprocessors. (Here a postprocessor is a program that works outside AutoCAD with a model and parameters that are set up in AutoCAD.) Figure 1.17 shows an area for AutoCAD Advanced Modeling Extension (AME), and for the postprocessor AutoShade/RenderMan. AutoShade® is Autodesk's original rendering program.

With release 12, AutoCAD includes some basic rendering within AutoCAD (this is the Render in the area at the far left in the middle of the tablet). The Autodesk RenderMan® part of the AutoShade/RenderMan package provides photorealistic rendering with ray tracing and texture mapping. AutoShade/RenderMan is discussed in chapter 14 along with AutoCAD's Render and other rendering programs.

As an example of using AutoCAD commands, consider the construction of the drawing border and title block shown in figure 1.18. CAD software provides many different ways of constructing a given drawing; the procedures listed below suggest only one way. After starting up a new drawing in AutoCAD, the GRID and SNAP commands may be used to enter grid and snap distances; say, 0.25 and 0.125 in. Alternatively, grid and snap distances may be entered by selecting Drawing Aids under the Settings pull-down menu. The grid is plotted over an area determined by the drawing limits, which can be set with the LIMITS command. The default values for the limits correspond to a 12×9-in. rectangle. Figure 1.18 illustrates a grid of dots extending over a 11×8.5-in. area, obtained by entering the coordinates (0,0) and (11,8.5) under LIMITS.

Both the grid and snap spacings may be toggled on and off. In the Drawing Aids menu you may also toggle blips on and off (or use the BLIPMODE command for this). Blips are small markers (crosses) placed at points you select when carrying out drawing operations. Like the the grid points, blips are drawing aids, not part of your drawing. Also, you can clean your screen with the command REDRAW, which fully erases and redraws your current drawing to eliminate blip marks and any leftover parts of erased or trimmed lines.

The lines for the border and title block may be drawn by typing LINE at the Command prompt, or by selecting LINE from one of the menus. The line is continued from point

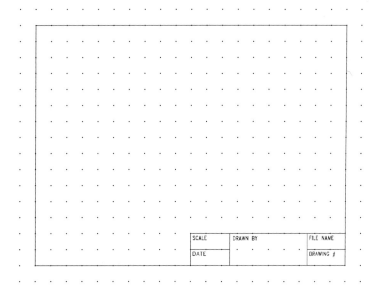

Figure 1.18   Completed title block example with grid marks.

to point until the RETURN key is pressed twice after entering a point. A point may be entered by moving the cursor to the desired position and pressing the mouse/puck button, using the grid and snap options to ensure exact placement. Alternatively, the point coordinates may be typed in from the keyboard; for example: 0.5,0.5 places a point at a distance a half inch to the right and a half inch up from the lower left corner of the drawing area (the drawing area size was selected during the setup). Successive points on a line may be entered in terms of relative distances by preceding the coordinate values with the @ symbol; for example, entering @ 9,0 places the second point on the border line at a distance of 9 in. to the right and 0 in. above the first point.

With CAD software there is no reason for lines not to be placed accurately; that is, closed lines should close, horizontal lines should be horizontal, etc. Every CAD program has a number of drawing features to help ensure accuracy. In AutoCAD you can toggle the ORTHO mode on to require the next line segment to be drawn only in the horizontal or vertical direction. While drawing a line, you can enter the letter C instead of coordinates to close the line; for example, enter C to return to the first point (0.5,0.5) on the border line. The following AutoCAD commands draw this border.

```
Command: LINE
First point: 0.5,0.5
Next point: @9,0
Next point: @0,7.5
Next point: @-9,0
Next point: C
```

To help select the next point on a line, Object snap modes may be selected from a menu or entered on the keyboard by typing the letters identified by capitals in the following examples: ENDpoint, which displays a box to place around a line endpoint; INTersection, to select the intersection of two lines; MIDpoint to select a point at the midpoint of a line segment; and CENter to select the center of an arc or circle. Also, because everyone makes mistakes, you will find it useful to ERASE, MOVE, or TRIM a line, as illustrated by the following prompts.

```
Command: ERASE
Select objects: (select with mouse)
Select objects: (RETURN)

Command: MOVE
Select objects: (select with mouse)
Select objects: (RETURN)
Base point or displacement: 0,0
Second point of displacement: (enter x and y distances)

Command: TRIM
Select cutting objects: (select with mouse)
Select cutting objects: (RETURN)
```

```
Select objects to trim: (select with mouse)
Select objects to trim: (RETURN)
```

The notation (RETURN) above represents a press of the return key (enter key), which is used here to terminate a repeated prompt. The response "select with mouse" can be carried out by placing a small box cursor on the object to select it and repeating to select all of the desired objects. If you have a large number of objects to select, you can type "W" to window around any number of objects on the screen. AutoCAD will prompt you for the window corners, as shown below.

```
First corner: (move cursor and press mouse button)
Second corner: (move cursor and press mouse button)
```

Alternatively, the letter "C" can be entered instead of "W" to select objects that cross the rectangular window in addition to those that are completely inside the window.

In constructing drawings on AutoCAD you will be changing the display by moving over the drawing surface and zooming in and out of regions on the drawing. The PAN and ZOOM commands carry out these functions. With the PAN command (typed or selected from a menu), you select a point on the drawing and then a second point on the screen to which you want the first point moved. PAN moves your view of the drawing; it does not move objects in the drawing relative to each other, as does the MOVE command. There are many options under the ZOOM command. One of the most useful options is to enter "W" after selecting ZOOM and windowing to the region you wish to display. If you wish to return to your previous view, enter "P" after ZOOM or select Zoom Previous from the pulldown or tablet menu.

After you have constructed the border and title block lines shown in figure 1.18, you are ready to type text into the drawing. First select Draw/Text/Set Style pull-down menu to choose the type and size of text font desired. For example, for the drawing in figure 1.18 the romand (roman with double strokes) font was selected with a height of 0.1 and a width-to-height ratio of 0.8. The specific text is inserted into the drawing by the TEXT command.

```
Command: TEXT
Start point or Align/Center/Fit/Middle/Right/Style:
     (select start point)
Height <0.1000>: (RETURN)
Rotation angle <0>: (RETURN)
Text: (type in desired text)
```

The return key was pressed in response to two of the above prompts in order to accept the default values presented in the <> brackets. The text height was previously set to the appropriate value with the Draw/Text/Set Style menu; this value became the current default value.

The completed title block drawing may be saved and used to frame drawings of objects that you construct later. The title block shown here is very simple. In engineering applications the title block usually includes many items, including the drawing number, sheet number, title, company name, company logo, scale, date, tolerances, record of revisions, and names of the drafter, checker, and supervisor. The following information may also be included for specific objects: material, weight, number required, surface characteristics, hardness, and heat treatment.

EXERCISES

1.1 For the particular compiler you are using, list the graphics statements that correspond to the routines listed in table 1.1. Also, list the graphics initialization statements required by your compiler/computer.

1.2 Determine how to produce graphics hard copy on your printer/plotter from your programming language or CAD software.

1.3 On your CAD system set up a border drawing similar to the one shown in figure 1.18.

BIBLIOGRAPHY

ALLEN, R. R., J. D. MEYER, AND W. R. KNIGHT, "Thermodynamics and Hydrodynamics of Thermal Ink Jets," *Hewlett-Packard Journal,* pp. 21–27, May 1985.

AutoCAD Release 12 Reference Manual. Sausalito, Calif.: Autodesk, Inc., 1992.

BAKER, J. P., D. A. JOHNSON, V. JOSHI, AND S. J. NIGRO, "Design and Development of a Color Thermal Inkjet Print Cartridge," *Hewlett-Packard Journal,* pp. 6–15, August 1988.

BOELLER, R. A., S. A. STODDER, J. F. MEYER, AND V. T. ESCOBEDO, "A Large-Format Thermal Inkjet Drafting Plotter," *Hewlett-Packard Journal,* pp. 6–15, December 1992.

HOHENSTEIN, C. L. *Computer Peripherals for Minicomputers, Microprocessors, and Personal Computers.* New York: McGraw-Hill Book Co., 1980.

LINDLEY, C. A., *Practical Ray Tracing in C.* New York: John Wiley & Sons, 1992.

PATTERSON, M. L., AND G. W. LYNCH, "Development of a Large Drafting Plotter," *Hewlett-Packard Journal,* pp. 3–7, November 1981.

ROONEY, J., AND P. STEADMAN, eds., *Principles of Computer-aided Design.* Englewood Cliffs, N.J.: Prentice Hall, 1987.

ZEID, I., *CAD/CAM Theory and Practice.* McGraw-Hill, Inc., 1991.

2

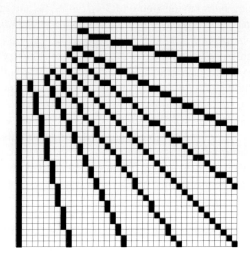

Pixels and Lines

In this chapter the elements of raster graphics are presented, starting with a description of the graphics screen in terms of pixels (picture elements). In section 2.2 line scan conversion is discussed; that is, fundamental algorithms for plotting straight lines on the raster graphics screen. In the above illustration a 40×40 pixel array is represented by open squares, with straight lines at various angles obtained by filling pixels close to the lines. On paper the black squares represent pixels that are filled (illuminated, lighted, turned on, or set), even though most software applications on computer monitors use a black background with graphics drawn with white or colored pixels. Graphics commands in programming languages usually assume that screen coordinates have an origin at the upper left-hand corner of the screen. So, for the above illustration the y-coordinate is measured downward, and the x-coordinate increases to the right. Particular lines were chosen for the illustration: the first horizontal line (slope equals 0) is represented by filled squares in the x-direction; the line below the horizontal line has a slope of 1/4 so that four squares are filled horizontally in the x-direction before shifting one square in the y-direction (downward); the next line of slope 1/2 has two horizontal squares filled at a time; and so forth for the remaining lines having slopes of 3/4 1, 4/3 2, 4, and infinity (vertical line). The algorithms specify which pixels should be filled for a straight line that is to be plotted between any two points on the screen.

Because of the finite size of the filled pixels, the lines have "jagged" edges. The appearance of the line can be smoothed by filling pixels with varying intensities (shades of gray) depending on how far they are from the true line position. This procedure is called *antialiasing,* which is the subject of section 2.3.

For objects to be drawn on the computer screen, dimensions must be transformed from real-world values to screen coordinates. Accordingly, simple scaling and translation transformations are discussed in section 2.4. Computations are carried out for line intersections, which are then used to *clip* lines at the boundary of a rectangle. In this way scaled drawings may be placed in *viewports.* The use of viewports in AutoCAD is described.

2.1 THE GRAPHICS SCREEN: PIXELS, INTENSITY, AND MEMORY

Nowadays practically all computer monitors are raster devices, on which lines and other graphic entities are displayed by means of illuminated pixels; earlier monitors had storage tubes or refresh devices on which a line could be drawn from essentially any point on the screen to any other point. The most common raster device is the cathode-ray tube (CRT), although laptop computers use liquid crystal displays (LCD) or plasma screens. The raster display may have a single level of intensity (black-and-white image) or many levels of gray or color.

On a CRT the image is composed of scan (raster) lines produced by an electron beam that impinges on phosphors coating the inside face of the picture tube. As illustrated in figure 2.1, plates in the CRT can deflect the electron beam in the horizontal and vertical directions to trace out an image on the phosphors that coat the tube face.

In a color CRT separate dots or stripes of red, green, and blue phosphors are illuminated by three separate electron guns. Figure 2.2 shows how shadow masks (thin metal

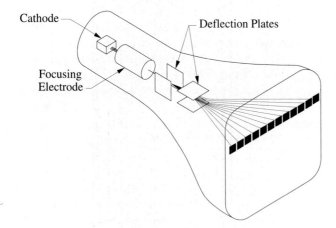

Figure 2.1 Main elements in a cathode-ray tube. Electrons are emitted from a heated cathode and are attracted to the positively charged anode inside the phosphor coating on the tube face. The electrons are focused to a beam, which is aimed by horizontal and vertical deflection plates. Pixels are illuminated as the beam scans across the phosphor coating on the tube face.

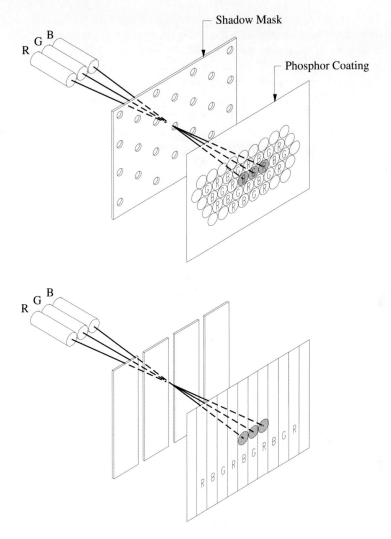

Figure 2.2   Two configurations for a shadow mask. The upper diagram illustrates a shadow mask with holes, and a phosphor coating with alternate blue, green, and red spots. The electron guns are labeled R, G, and B according to the phosphor color that their electrons hit. The bottom diagram illustrates an arrangement having a mask with long slots and a phosphor coating with alternating blue, green, and red stripes.

sheets with holes or slots) are aligned so that a given electron beam will strike phosphors of only one color. That is, the electron gun labeled R "sees" only the red phosphor spots (or stripes); the blue and green spots are in the "shadow" of the mask. The three electron guns are the same; only their position determines which color phosphor their electrons hit. Hereafter, references to an electron beam will mean the combined three-beam system for a color tube.

As the electron beam crosses the face of the CRT it traces out pixels. The pixel size should not be confused with the phosphor spot (or stripe) size. A single pixel consists of a number of spots (the three spots in figure 2.2 cover just part of the scanning beam of electrons). Figure 2.3 illustrates scan lines with pixels having a size equal to 4 × 4 spots. The illuminated spots for the letter G are shown as black, although in color the spots would be alternating in blue, green, and red. The original graphics mode for the IBM PC (CGA mode) had only 200-pixel resolution in the vertical and 640-pixel resolution in the horizontal, which produced rectangular pixels with a 5 × 12 aspect ratio. On this system the low vertical resolution yielded pronounced horizontal lines in the characters displayed on the monitor. Most graphics systems nowadays have greater vertical resolution, with equal horizontal and vertical resolutions producing square pixels.

On a raster CRT display the electron beam traces nearly horizontal lines (scan lines) across the tube face, and is turned off during overscans, horizontal retraces, and vertical retraces; see figure 2.4. The electron beam may trace either an interlaced or noninterlaced pattern. For the human eye to fuse together successive images (to avoid screen blinking), an image must be displayed every 1/50 or 1/60 second. Because of the large number of pixels that must be lighted for each full frame (complete image), the display requirements can be reduced by half if interlacing is used. With interlacing, only half of the scan lines of the full picture are drawn in 1/60 second; the other half are drawn in the next 1/60 second. That is, first the field of odd lines is traced, then the interlaced field of even lines. Because, in a normal analog video, the image intensity variations in the picture cover more than one scan line, the image is well fused by the eye, so there is no disconcerting blinking of the image. For images drawn in computer graphics, however, there can be a horizontal line of only one pixel height—such a line will appear with very noticeable blinking on an interlaced screen because it will be drawn only every 1/30 second. Therefore, higher-quality monitors for computer graphics are of the noninterlaced variety.

To understand the high information-transfer rates required by computer graphics, we must first look at the interlaced scan pattern produced by NTSC (National Television Standards Committee) video. For the NTSC video, 525 lines are drawn in 1/30 second, which

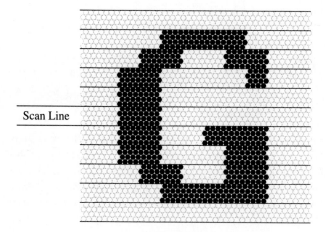

Scan Line

Figure 2.3 Spots lighted to form the letter G. The scan line is shown as one pixel in height, with each pixel containing 4 × 4 spots.

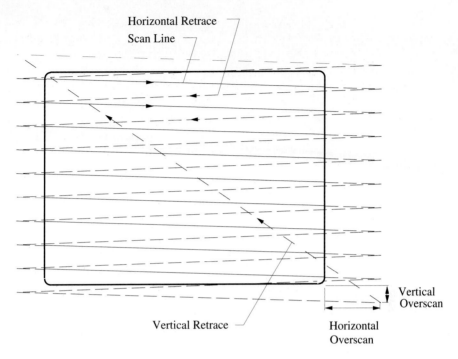

Figure 2.4   Noninterlaced raster scanning. The scan line is continuous and is drawn solid as it travels from left to right across the screen display (indicated as a heavy-line rectangle with rounded corners). The dashed portion of the scan line represents the overscan and retrace portions when the electron beam is turned off (blanked).

means that each line must be drawn in 63.5 μs (microseconds). However, some of this time (typically 10 to 17 percent) must be used for the horizontal and vertical retraces. Accordingly, most television monitors display fewer than 525 lines (often 480 lines or so), although some current video monitors approach the 525-line standard. Currently high-definition television (HDTV) is being developed with 1,125 lines compared with the NTSC standard of 525 lines. Also, HDTV will have a wider screen, probably a horizontal-to-vertical ratio of 16:9 compared with 4:3 for the standard video monitor.

On computer monitors each scan line is divided into pixels. Displays with high resolution (large numbers of pixels) and many levels of intensity or colors require large amounts of memory. The computer memory required for the graphics display is called the display buffer or frame buffer. For a black-and-white display each pixel requires one bit of computer memory to determine whether the bit is dark (value 0) or lighted (value 1). The display buffer can be schematically represented in terms of "bit planes," with each bit plane having a number of bits that is equal to the number of pixels in the screen display. A display buffer of N bit planes can provide the screen with 2^N intensity levels from 0 (dark) to $2^N - 1$, representing full intensity. Alternatively, 2^N different colors could be displayed. Figure 2.5a illustrates three bit planes with the selected pixel having an intensity level of 5 out of $2^3 = 8$ possible levels, or color number five out of eight possible colors. For a color

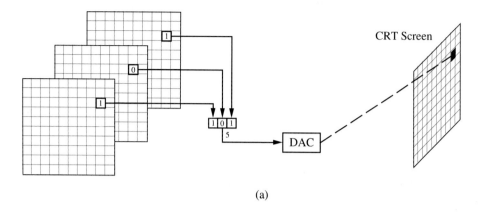

(a)

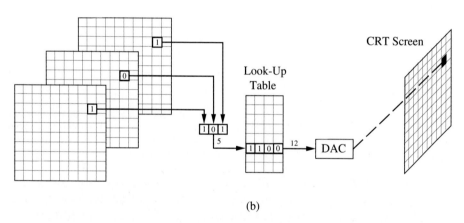

(b)

Figure 2.5   (a) Schematic representations of three bit planes with an intensity level of 5 on a particular pixel. The intensity level is transmitted to the screen through a digital-to-analog converter (DAC). (b) Three bit planes with a pixel intensity level of 12 obtained from a look-up table.

display, there could be an intermediate "look-up table" so the eight colors displayed simultaneously on the screen could be selected from a much larger palette of colors, as illustrated in figure 2.5b.

   Frame buffer memory requirements for some common graphics systems are listed in table 2.1. The number of bytes of memory required equals the total number of screen pixels times the number of bit planes divided by 8 (because there are 8 bits per byte). Table 2.1 shows that super VGA modes can be reached with PC graphics boards having one or two megabytes of memory. The continuous variation of shades needed for a high-quality rendering requires a very large number of colors, such as the 16.7 million colors available with 24 bit planes.

TABLE 2.1 SCREEN MODES

Screen mode	Pixels	Screen ratio	Colors	Bit planes	Memory (bytes)
CGA (medium res.)	320×200	4 : 3	4	2	16K
CGA (high res.)	640×200	4 : 3	1	1	16K
Macintosh (b&w)[a]	512×342	3 : 2	1	1	22K
EGA	640×350	4 : 3	16	4	112K
VGA	640×480	4 : 3	16/256	4/8	153K/307K
Super VGA (mode 1)	800×600	4 : 3	32K/16.7M	15/24	0.9M/1.5M
Super VGA (mode 2)	1024×768	4 : 3	256/65K	8/16	0.8M/1.6M
Workstations	1280×1024	5 : 4	1/16.7M	1/100[b]	164K/16.4M

[a]The Macintosh II series and Quadras have color starting with VGA resolution.
[b]Workstations can have bit planes for the Z-buffer, double-buffering, and transparency, in addition to color.

The CAD user benefits from a high-resolution display (such as the workstation standard listed in the table) because there is less confusion about lines that are in close proximity; therefore, the user can unambiguously see more of a complex drawing. Accordingly, a high-resolution display can reduce the number of times that a CAD user needs to use a ZOOM command to focus on a small part of the drawing.

2.2 LINE-DRAWING ALGORITHMS

As discussed at the beginning of this chapter, algorithms are used to plot pixels for the best representation of a straight line segment. Two algorithms that are essentially equivalent, but are conceptually different, will be discussed in this section. Figure 2.6 shows theoretical line segments as black lines and shaded rectangles illustrating the pixel representations of the lines on the computer screen. For convenience the standard mathematics convention of having positive y-direction point upward is used in this section. If you want the screen plotting to also have this convention, then the following simple translation and reflection transformation should be made in your program: $y_{screen} = y_{bottom} - y$, where y_{bottom} is the screen coordinate at the bottom of the screen. Simple two-dimensional translation and scaling (including reflection) is discussed in section 2.4, and a more complete discussion of two-dimensional transformations is the subject of chapter 10. Here we consider only screen coordinates because this is the coordinate system to which the line-drawing algorithms are applied, after transformation from world coordinates.

A line-drawing algorithm should light up only those pixels that are close to the theoretical line, and produce a line of relatively uniform intensity that does not vary greatly in intensity as its slope is changed. With only a black-and-white representation, lines cannot have constant intensity as the slope is changed; note that in the figure at the beginning of this chapter the horizontal and vertical lines have the greatest intensity per unit length, and the line with unit slope has the least intensity per unit length. A final criterion is that the

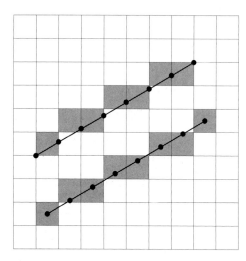

Figure 2.6 Pixel representations of line segments, with the y-coordinate increasing upward, and the x-coordinate increasing to the right.

line-drawing algorithm be efficient. The integer Bresenham algorithm is widely used in commercial systems because of its efficiency.

Figure 2.6 illustrates alternative representations of a line segment. For ease of interpretation, this figure is based on a normal mathematical coordinate system with y increasing in the upward direction, rather than downward as for screen coordinates. The top line uses the standard procedure in which points representing the pixel coordinates are drawn at the lower left-hand corner of the pixel, and pixels are set only if they lie between the line endpoints. Although this procedure of line representation usually appears in the computer graphics literature, commercial implementations often add an additional pixel at the end of the line. If we add an additional pixel and shift the line starting and ending points to pixel centers, then the representation shown by the bottom line is obtained; that is, the first and last pixels are set even though the line segment extends only to their centers.

The Digital Differential Analyzer (DDA) Algorithm

The simplest algorithm is the DDA, or digital differential analyzer, algorithm. Considering a straight line from the initial point (x_{start}, y_{start}) to the final point (x_{end}, y_{end}), the slope is $(y_{end} - y_{start})/(x_{end} - x_{start})$. If the line's horizontal distance is greater than its vertical distance, the line is drawn by increasing the horizontal coordinate x by one raster unit (pixel); otherwise, y is increased by one raster unit. In the program subroutine listed below, one variable is increased by one raster unit, the other variable is increased by a value less than one unit so that the ratio of the y-increment to the x-increment equals the line slope. The signs of the increments are determined by the relative placements of the line endpoints.

To illustrate this algorithm with equations, consider the special case of the *first octant*, for which $x_{end} > x_{start}$, $y_{end} > y_{start}$, and $length = (x_{end} - x_{start}) > (y_{end} - y_{start})$. The line slope is $(y_{end} - y_{start})/length$, and incremental points along the line segment are given by the following equations (for this case x is incremented by one raster unit).

$$x_{i+1} = x_i + \Delta x = x_i + 1$$

$$y_{i+1} = y_i + \Delta y = y_i + \frac{\Delta y}{\Delta x}\, \Delta x$$ (2.1)

$$= y_i + \frac{(y_{end} - y_{start})}{length}$$

Starting at the point (x_{start}, y_{start}), the incremental points lie exactly on the line segment. If the initial values are shifted by 1/2 pixel (the value 0.5 is added to x_{start} and y_{start} in the listing below), then evaluating integer values of x and y in the SetPixel() function represents rounding to the nearest integer, rather than truncating. The bottom line in figure 2.6 can represent the shifted line segment, with the dots representing the incremental points. In this figure a pixel will be set if an incremental point lies within the pixel boundaries.

The program subroutines presented in this book are written in the C programming language. For the benefit of readers who are unfamiliar with C, the first subroutine is also written in BASIC and in FORTRAN. In addition, appendix A provides a brief overview of C programs. In the appendix A programs, lines are drawn on the screen after endpoints have been entered and the graphics screen has been initialized.

The C program subroutine dda() uses the DDA algorithm to draw a line from (x_{start}, y_{start}) to (x_{end}, y_{end}), where the coordinates are of data type "double" (double-precision floating-point values), and the function dda is of "void" type because it returns no values to the main program (it just draws the line from the coordinates supplied by the main program). The function fabs() evaluates the floating-point absolute value of its argument; therefore the first *if* statement evaluates the absolute values of $(x_{end} - x_{start})$ and $(y_{end} - y_{start})$, and assigns *length* to the larger value. Because of the value assigned to *length,* the larger of *dx* and *dy* will be one raster unit.

The main loop of the subroutine is the *while* loop, with x increased by *dx*, y by *dy*, and i by 1 until i reaches the integer value of *length*. The floating-point value *length* is put into an integer form via the "type casting" function (int). The initial value of i has been set equal to 0 to add an additional pixel, as represented by the bottom line in figure 2.6. (The upper line in figure 2.6 corresponds to starting the *while* loop with $i = 1$.) Note that in the C programming language, statements end with a semicolon, and the individual statements belonging to an overall statement such as the *while* loop are enclosed in brackets {}. The SetPixel() function represents a function that turns on a pixel; specific functions for this purpose are listed in table 1.1 for some common systems.

```
void dda(double xstart,double ystart,double xend,double yend)
{
     double length,x,y,dx,dy;
     int i;

     if (fabs(xend-xstart) > fabs(yend-ystart))
          length = fabs(xend-xstart);
     else
          length = fabs(yend-ystart);
```

```
dx = (xend-xstart)/length;
dy = (yend-ystart)/length;

x = xstart + .5;
y = ystart + .5;
i = 0;

while (i <= (int) length)
{
    SetPixel((int) x, (int) y);
    x = x + dx;
    y = y + dy;
    i = i + 1;
}
}
```

In BASIC the DDA subroutine is very similar to the C version, except that BASIC does not require variable types to be declared, so type casting is unnecessary. Here the graphics statement that turns on a pixel has been written as the generic term SetPixel(), although most implementations of BASIC have the special function PSET() for this purpose.

```
DDA:
    IF ABS(xend-xstart) > ABS(yend-ystart) THEN
        length = ABS(xend-xstart)
    ELSE
        length = ABS(yend-ystart)
    END IF

    dx = (xend-xstart)/length
    dy = (yend-ystart)/length

    x = xstart+.5
    y = ystart+.5
    i = 0

    WHILE i <= length
        SetPixel (INT(x),INT(y))
        x = x + dx
        y = y + dy
        i = i + 1
    WEND
    RETURN
```

The following FORTRAN version of the subroutine is similar to the above versions. The line CALL SetPixel() is a generic representation for turning on a pixel; the specific statement depends on the graphics library for your system.

```
SUBROUTINE DDA(xstart,ystart,xend,yend)
REAL        length,x,y,dx,dy
INTEGER*2 i

IF (ABS(xend-xstart).GT.ABS(yend-ystart)) THEN
    length = ABS(xend-xstart)
ELSE
    length = ABS(yend-ystart)
ENDIF

dx = (xend-xstart)/length
dy = (yend-ystart)/length

x = xstart + .5
y = ystart + .5
i = 0

DO WHILE (i.LE.INT(length))
    CALL SetPixel(INT(x),INT(y))
    x = x + dx
    y = y + dy
    i = i + 1
END DO
RETURN
END
```

The Bresenham Algorithm

The Bresenham algorithm represents an optimized version of the DDA algorithm. In integer form the Bresenham algorithm is fast as well as accurate. Before the general integer form is discussed, the Bresenham procedure will be explained by considering the floating-point version in the first octant.

In the first octant x and y increase from (x_{start}, y_{start}) to (x_{end}, y_{end}), and $x_{end} - x_{start}$ is greater than $y_{end} - y_{start}$. Figure 2.7 presents lines plotted in the first octant with slopes of 0, 1/3, 2/3, and 1. Also shown is a dashed line of slope 1/2. The starting point (x_{start}, y_{start}) for the lines is placed at the center of the lower-left pixel. When x is increased by one pixel to the second column of pixels, the figure shows that the dots for the lower two lines lie within the bottom pixel, and those for the top two lines lie within the pixel above it. The dashed line is seen to cross through equal portions of the bottom two pixels. Therefore, the slope 1/2 of the dashed line is the slope that divides lines setting the bottom pixel from lines setting the pixel above it. The Bresenham algorithm can be interpreted in terms of these line slopes.

The floating-point Bresenham algorithm starts with a variable e called the error. The initial value of e is set equal to $-1/2$, and e is incremented by the line slope; that is,

$$e = e + \frac{\Delta y}{\Delta x} \tag{2.2}$$

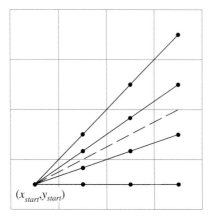

Figure 2.7 Lines starting at the point $(x_{start},\ y_{start})$, used to illustrate the Bresenham algorithm.

(x_{start}, y_{start})

If an incremented value of e is greater than or equal to zero, then y is increased by one raster unit. When y is increased, the value of e is reset by subtracting the value 1; that is $e = e - 1$ when $y = y + 1$; see the floating-point Bresenham subroutine listed below. For the lines in figure 2.7, the lower-left pixel is set because each line starts with $e = -1/2$. The zero slope line retains an e value of $-1/2$ for all x increments, so y is never increased, and the bottom row of pixels is set. For the line of slope 1/3, e has the value $-1/2 + 1/3 = -1/6$ after the first increment in x. Therefore, this line sets the bottom pixel in the second column of pixels. The next increment, to the third column of pixels, produces an e value of $-1/6 + 1/3 = +1/6$, which increases y so that the pixel above the bottom one is set. The errror e is then reset to $+1/6 - 1 = -5/6$. For the next increment (fourth column of pixels), the error is $-5/6 + 1/3 = -1/2$, so y is not increased, and the next to bottom pixel is set. You can step through the error increments for the other lines in figure 2.7 to show that the pixels with the dots will be set by the Bresenham algorithm. The dashed line of slope 1/2 has an error of zero after the first increment, so this is the smallest slope for which y is increased in the second column of pixels.

A C subroutine for the floating-point Bresenham algorithm in the first octant is shown below. Note that for this algorithm dx and dy are defined as the total horizontal and vertical lengths of the line segment. In the *for* loop $i++$ is an efficient way of writing $i = i + 1$. The index i is started at 0 so that pixels are set at both the starting and ending points.

```
void bresen(double xstart,double ystart,double xend,double yend)
{
    int i;
    double x,y,dx,dy,e;
    dx = xend - xstart;
    dy = yend - ystart;
    e = dy/dx - .5;
    x = xstart; y = ystart;
    for (i=0; i<=(int) dx; i++)
    {
```

```
      SetPixel( (int) x, (int) y);
      while (e >= 0)
      {
          y = y + 1.;
          e - e - 1.;
      }
      x = x + 1.;
      e = e + dy/dx;
}
```

The advantage of the Bresenham algorithm is that it can be transformed into an integer algorithm, which greatly increases its efficiency. The integer Bresenham normally will execute several times faster than the DDA algorithm. To change the floating-point equations into integer equations, e is redefined by multiplying the equations by $2dx$, to eliminate the 2 and dx terms in the denominators of the floating-point e equations. In the first octant, the integer Bresenham algorithm is

```
void bresen(int xstart,int ystart,int xend,int yend)
{
    int   i,x,y,dx,dy,e;
    dx = xend - xstart;
    dy = yend - ystart;

    e = 2*dy - dx;
    x = xstart; y = ystart;

    for (i=0; i<=dx; i++)
    {
        SetPixel(x,y);
        while (e >= 0)
        {
            y = y + 1;
            e = e - 2*dx;
        }
        x = x + 1;
        e = e + 2*dy;
    }
}
```

The integer Bresenham algorithm valid for lines in all directions uses the flag *change* that has the value 0 if the absolute value of $(x_{end} - x_{start})$ is greater than or equal to the absolute value of $(y_{end} - y_{start})$, otherwise *change* is 1. When *change* is 0, x is increased by *signx* $= \pm1$, which is the sign of $(x_{end} - x_{start})$. When *change* is 1, y is increased by *signy* $= \pm1$.

```
void bresen(int xstart,int ystart,int xend,int yend)
{
```

```
int i,x,y,dx,dy,e;
int signx,signy,change,temp;

signx = 1; signy = 1;
if (xend < xstart) signx = -1;
if (yend < ystart) signy = -1;
dx = signx*(xend - xstart);
dy = signy*(yend - ystart);

if (dy <= dx)
    change = 0;
else
{
    change = 1;
    temp = dx; dx = dy; dy = temp;
}

e = 2*dy - dx;
x = xstart; y = ystart;
for (i=0; i<=dx; i++)
{
    SetPixel(x,y);
    while (e >= 0)
    {
        if (change == 0)
            y = y + signx;
        else
            x = x + signx;
        e = e - 2*dx;
    }
    if (change == 0)
        x = x + signx;
    else
        y = y + signy;
    e = e - 2*dy;
}
}
```

Comparison of Line-Drawing Algorithms

You can compare the line algorithms discussed above with the line-drawing algorithm used by your compiler by using the different algorithms to draw lines in different colors between the same two points. Even with colors, however, the differences are hard to see, so a more effective comparison is to graphically enlarge the pixels by replacing each filled pixel with a square or circle covering a number of pixels. For the DDA and Bresenham algorithms this "big pixel" procedure corresponds to replacing the SetPixel() function in the algorithms with the construction of a finite square or circle, and incrementing x or y by an amount equal to (or greater than) the side of the square or the diameter of the circle.

You can reproduce a line drawn by your compiler in "big pixels" by first drawing a line segment with the MoveTo() and LineTo() statements (or the equivalent statements used by your compiler). Then choose a rectangular region that fully encloses the line segment; for example, the rectangle extending from $x_{start} - 1$ to $x_{end} + 1$ and from $y_{start} - 1$ to $y_{end} + 1$ for $x_{start} < x_{end}$ and $y_{start} < y_{end}$. This rectangle can be scanned with the GetPixel() function to determine which pixels are set, with the coordinates of the set pixels put into arrays as shown below. The coordinates can then be retrieved from the arrays and plotted as big pixels in the same manner as described in the preceding paragraph. In the program lines below (for $x_{start} < x_{end}$ and $y_{start} < y_{end}$), the integer k is increased by the value 1 each time a set pixel is found, with the coordinates of the pixel stored in the arrays $xpix[k]$ and $ypix[k]$.

```
k = 0;
for (y = ystart-1; y <= yend+1; y++)
{
    for (x = xstart-1; x <= xend+1; x++)
    {
        if (GetPixel(x,y) == TRUE)
        {
            k = k + 1;
            xpix[k] = x;
            ypix[k] = y;
        }
    }
}
kmax = k;
```

In the above subroutine the GetPixel() function for a black-and-white Macintosh screen returns TRUE if the pixel is set (black pixel on a white background). For color systems the equivalent GetPixel() function (for example, _getpixel() with Microsoft C) will return an integer representing the color index of the pixel.

The procedures described above were used to draw big pixel representations of the DDA algorithm, the integer Bresenham algorithm, and the Macintosh QuickDraw LineTo() (with MoveTo()) function. Figure 2.8 shows line segments drawn in two quadrant directions, with slopes having the same magnitudes as the lines in the diagram at the beginning of this chapter. (Similar results are obtained for the other two quadrant directions.)

As shown in figure 2.8, the three algorithms are in close agreement, with the only differences arising in borderline situations. For example, if the Bresenham algorithm is changed from the criterion $e >= 0$ to $e > 0$, then there is agreement between Bresenham and DDA lines for some cases in which they differed, but disagreement for other cases

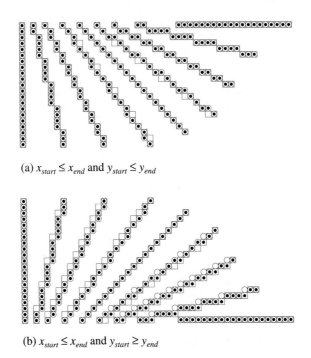

(a) $x_{start} \leq x_{end}$ and $y_{start} \leq y_{end}$

(b) $x_{start} \leq x_{end}$ and $y_{start} \geq y_{end}$

Figure 2.8 Comparison of line-drawing algorithms. Open squares designate pixels for the Macintosh QuickDraw routine; open circles, the Bresenham algorithm; small filled circles, the DDA algorithm.

where they previously agreed. Alternatively, the DDA algorithm presented can be slightly changed to give agreement with the Bresenham algorithm (this can be done by slightly perturbing the initial point; for example by adding $0.001*signx$ to the initial value $x_{start} + 0.5$, and $0.001*signy$ to $y_{start} + 0.5$, where $signx$ and $signy$ have the same definition as in the Bresenham algorithm).

2.3 ANTIALIASING OF LINES

The finite size of the screen pixels produces lines with a jagged or stepped appearance. The jagged effect can of course be reduced by increasing the screen resolution. Alternatively, the jagged appearance or *aliasing* of lines can be reduced by incorporating *antialiasing* into the line-drawing algorithm. Although a thorough understanding of antialiasing requires the use of filtering theory, it can be readily seen that aliasing can be reduced by using a range of pixel intensities to shade the pixels in proportion to their distance from the exact line vector. That is, a pixel will be at full intensity only if it is sufficiently close to the theoretical line. Pixels will fall off in intensity as they increase in distance from the line.

Antialiasing can considerably improve video images because video screens are of relatively low resolution, and the jagged edges of animated lines can be very noticeable as pixels are turned on and off while a line moves. Also, antialiasing techniques are incorporated into some new graphics systems for CAD, even though in the past they have not been used much because of the cost and loss of speed (antialiased lines typically take two or three times as long to draw as an ordinary line).

Figure 2.9 illustrates how intensities may be assigned to pixels. In this example the ordinary Bresenham algorithm would fill only the middle pixel (with full intensity, or black in this figure). With antialiasing the middle pixel will be at full intensity only if the pixel is sufficiently close to the exact line position. The triangular distribution function on the right of the figure determines the pixel intensities. Adjacent pixels have intensities that are separated by one-third the total vertical distance covered by the distribution function; that is, by two-thirds the distance from the maximum intensity to zero intensity.

Defining a parameter $\varepsilon = e/\Delta x$, where e is the error term in the integer Bresenham algorithm, the pixel intensities can be assigned by equations 2.3. In these relations i can be considered to be an intensity index number, with i_{min} and i_{max} representing the index numbers for minimum and maximum intensities. The range of intensities available depends on your computer graphics system. Chapter 6 includes a description of how to display different intensities and colors in various graphics modes by using the intensity index number i.

$$i_{1,2} = i_{min} + \frac{2}{3}(i_{max} - i_{min})\left(1 \pm \frac{\varepsilon}{2}\right)$$

$$i_3 = i_{min} \pm \frac{2}{3}(i_{max} - i_{min})\frac{\varepsilon}{2}$$

(2.3)

For $\varepsilon < 0$, the top equation gives intensities for the middle and bottom pixels (y increases downward in the figure), with the minus used for the middle pixel and the plus used for the bottom pixel. The bottom equation with the minus gives the intensity index number of the top pixel for $\varepsilon < 0$. For $\varepsilon \geq 0$, the top equation with the plus is used for the middle pixel, the bottom equation with the plus for the bottom pixel, and the top equation with the minus for the top pixel. The above equations apply for $-1 \leq \varepsilon \leq +1$. For $\varepsilon < -1$ or $\varepsilon > 1$ the intensity of the middle pixel should be set to the maximum, with the intensities of the other two pixels computed from the above formulas. In applying the above formulas you should compute ε just before the start of the *while* loop.

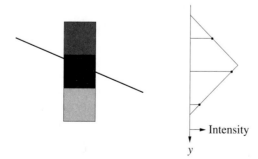

Intensity

y

Figure 2.9   The assignment of intensities to pixels for a Bresenham algorithm that incorporates antialiasing.

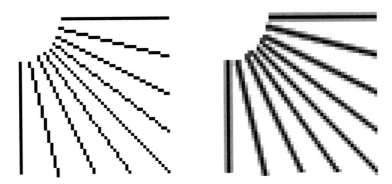

Figure 2.10   Lines drawn with the ordinary Bresenham algorithm (left) compared with
lines incorporating antialiasing (right).

Figure 2.10 presents antialiased lines on the right and ordinary Bresenham lines on
the left. The use of more than one pixel per position broadens the line somewhat but reduces
the jagged appearance. Also, it is easy to see that a moving line would undergo smoother
changes in the antialiased case because a given pixel would grow in intensity and then de-
cay as a line passes over it.

In the next chapter (section 3.3) a simple area antialiasing algorithm is considered for
use with filling or painting polygons. The area antialiasing algorithm can also be used for
lines by assigning finite widths to the lines.

2.4 SCALING, LINE INTERSECTIONS, AND CLIPPING

The lines described in this chapter have been drawn in screen coordinates. To represent lines
in various applications, we must consider scaling, line intersections, and clipping.

Scaling, along with translation, will enable us to use coordinates from the real world
and transform them into screen coordinates for plotting. Although scaling and translation
will be treated more thoroughly in chapter 10, where transformations will be put into matrix form, these topics are discussed briefly here to make line-drawing and plotting exercises easier in subsequent chapters.

Clipping and CAD operations such as trimming and drawing fillets depend on determining line intersections. Clipping appropriately trims lines at the edge of the plotting region (which could be the full monitor screen or a smaller area within the screen).

Scaling

For a drawing of a building, its actual coordinate values must be scaled down to fit on the
computer screen; for a drawing of a microchip, the values must be scaled up. The drawing
may also have to be moved horizontally or vertically to fit best on the screen. Therefore, to
properly place a drawing on the screen, transformations that scale and translate the real-
world coordinates to screen coordinates must be carried out. The following linear equations

transform a real-world point (x,y) to screen coordinates (x_{screen}, y_{screen}). The scale factors S_x and S_y will be equal for uniform scaling that preserves the real-world ratios of lengths in the horizontal (x) and vertical (y) directions. Of course, for plotting data, such as position versus time, the horizontal and vertical scale factors may be very different. From the equations below it is evident that when S_x and S_y each have the value two, the screen image is twice the size of the real image. The Δx_{transl} and Δy_{transl} terms are displacements representing translations in the x and y directions.

$$x_{screen} = S_x x + \Delta x_{transl}$$
$$y_{screen} = S_y y + \Delta y_{transl}$$
$$(2.4)$$

The remainder of this section will be devoted to line intersections and clipping in a normal mathematics coordinate system in which the y axis is positive upwards, measured from an origin at the lower left corner of the screen. Therefore, the screen x-coordinate remains the same, and the y-coordinate is transformed by the formula below.

$$x_{screen} = x$$
$$y_{screen} = -y + y_{bottom}$$
$$(2.5)$$

where y_{bottom} is the screen y-coordinate at the bottom of the screen. The scale factor $S_y = -1$ represents a reflection transformation that changes the positive direction for y from downward to upward.

Line Intersections

An infinite straight line in the xy-plane is represented by the linear equation

$$y = mx + b \qquad (2.6)$$

where the constant m represents the line slope and b represents the y-axis intercept. Here it is assumed that m is finite; that is, vertical lines can be treated as a special case.

Infinite straight lines in a plane will intersect at one point unless they are parallel. The above equation for two lines, with constants (m_1, b_1) and (m_2, b_2), will produce an equation for the x-coordinate of the intersection point (x_{int}) if the y-values for the two lines are equated. Then the y_{int} may be obtained by substituting x_{int} into the equation for either of the two lines. The following result is obtained.

$$x_{int} = \frac{(b_2 - b_1)}{(m_1 - m_2)}$$
$$y_{int} = m_1 x_{int} + b_1$$
$$(2.7)$$

The above equations hold except when $m_1 = m_2$, that is, for the case of equal slopes (parallel lines).

The above representation is for an infinite line; that is, it provides no information where a specific line segment starts or ends. For finite line segments in the xy plane, the following parametric representation is useful.

$$x = x_{start} + (x_{end} - x_{start})t$$
$$y = y_{start} + (y_{end} - y_{start})t \tag{2.8}$$

where t is a parameter that varies from 0 to 1 as the line is traced from its starting point (x_{start}, y_{start}) to its ending point (x_{end}, y_{end}). For this parametric representation, the intersection point obtained by equating x and y for two lines gives the following two equations involving the parameter t for line 1 and parameter s for line 2.

$$(x_{2,end} - x_{2,start})s + (x_{1,start} - x_{1,end})t = x_{1,start} - x_{2,start}$$
$$(y_{2,end} - y_{2,start})s + (y_{1,start} - y_{1,end})t = y_{1,start} - y_{2,start} \tag{2.9}$$

As long as the lines are not parallel, the above set of linear equations can be solved for s and t. The calculated intersection point will occur in the finite line segments only if $0 \le t \le 1$ and $0 \le s \le 1$; otherwise it will occur in the continuation of one or both of the line segments beyond their starting or ending points.

Clipping

As illustrated in figure 2.11, the start and end points of a line in screen coordinates may or may not be in the region covered by the clipping rectangle (which may also be termed the *viewport*). If both the start and end points are in the clipping area, then the entire line seg-

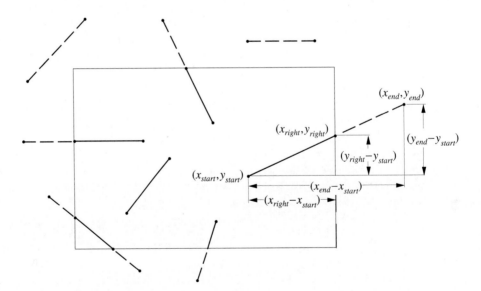

Figure 2.11   Clipping rectangle shown by thin solid lines. Line segments are dashed outside the clipping rectangle. Dots identify starting and ending points, as well as intersection points on the clipping rectangle. Either end of a line segment may be a starting or ending point.

ment may be plotted. If one point is within the area and the other outside, then the line segment must be appropriately trimmed at the boundary. If both points are outside the area, then the line segment may be totally outside (and therefore not plotted at all), or a part of the line may traverse the clipping area and require clipping at two boundaries. Although early implementations of line-drawing graphics statements did not incorporate clipping, nowadays almost all statements (such as MoveTo() and LineTo()) provide accurate clipping at the screen boundaries by default. Furthermore, most graphics libraries provide functions that provide clipping to an arbitrary rectangle within the screen area.

The similar triangles shown in figure 2.11 may be used to derive the equations that clip a line segment extending from a point (x_{start}, y_{start}) inside the rectangular area to a point (x_{end}, y_{end}) outside the right boundary. In these equations x_{right} and y_{right} are the endpoints on the right boundary to which the clipped line should be drawn. The coordinate x_{right} is simply the prescribed coordinate of the right clipping boundary, and y_{right} is determined by equation 2.10.

$$\left(\frac{y_{right} - y_{start}}{x_{right} - x_{start}}\right) = \left(\frac{y_{end} - y_{start}}{x_{end} - x_{start}}\right)$$

which reduces to

$$y_{right} = y_{start} + \left(\frac{y_{end} - y_{start}}{x_{end} - x_{start}}\right)(x_{right} - x_{start}) \tag{2.10}$$

Equations for clipping at other boundaries may be derived in a similar fashion, although development of the full clipping algorithm that considers all possible cases is rather tedious.

Graphics libraries often provide a function for clipping to a rectangular region, such as ClipRect() for Macintosh QuickDraw or _setcliprgn() for Microsoft C; see table 1.1. On CAD systems we can use a command such as TRIM on AutoCAD to trim lines at any "cutting edge." By using the boundary of a rectangle or other polygon as cutting edges we can clip a drawing so that it terminates at the edge of the polygon.

AutoCAD provides a VIEWPORTS (or VPORTS) command to divide the screen into a number of different rectangles, with lines clipped at the boundaries. Drawings of three-dimensional objects can then be viewed simultaneously from different directions in each of the viewports. Three viewports are set up by the following commands.

```
Command: VPORTS
Save/Restore/Delete/Join/SIngle/?/2/<3>/4: (RETURN)
Horizontal/Vertical/Above/Below/Left/<Right>: (RETURN)
```

The default values (in < > brackets) were used above to select three viewports with a large, vertical one on the right, as illustrated in figure 2.12. One can readily work in any of the viewports (for example, by moving the cursor to the viewport and clicking a mouse button). The screen can be divided into more than four viewports by selecting a viewport and using the VPORTS command to divide it into additional viewports.

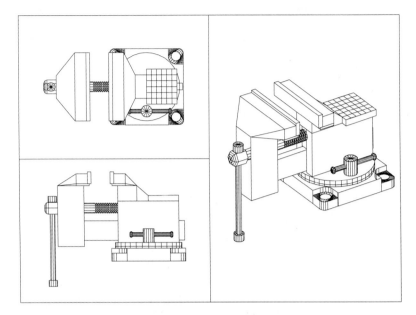

Figure 2.12 AutoCAD screen divided into three viewports, from a drawing by Samuel Massey. The object is shown with hidden lines removed, as it would appear after the HIDE command is used in each viewport.

A more versatile procedure for showing multiple views is provided by the AutoCAD MVIEW command, which must be applied in paper space. Paper space and the MVIEW command are discussed in section 13.2.

EXERCISES

2.1 Write a program that implements the DDA line-drawing algorithm by using the graphics command equivalent to SetPixel() in your programming language. The program should plot a line for initial and final points entered by the program user.

2.2 Write a program that implements the integer Bresenham line-drawing algorithm for initial and final points entered by the program user.

2.3 Instead of using a SetPixel() type of graphics command, draw a finite square or circle to produce "big pixels" in plotting out a line-drawing algorithm. If necessary, you may refer to chapter 3 for a discussion of circles and rectangles.

2.4 Compare your implementations of the DDA and Bresenham algorithms by plotting the same line segment in different colors for different algorithms or by plotting "big pixels" represented by finite squares for one algorithm and circles for the other.

2.5 Compare the line-drawing algorithm used by your compiler with the DDA or Bresenham algorithm. Use "big pixels" as described in section 2.2.

2.6 Program a loop to draw 200 long parallel lines using first the DDA algorithm and then the integer Bresenham algorithm. Verify the efficiency of the Bresenham algorithm by comparing the drawing times for these two algorithms.

2.7 Program a Bresenham circle algorithm; see, for example, Rogers (1985). Then plot "big pixels" like those below to show how the circle appears at different resolutions.

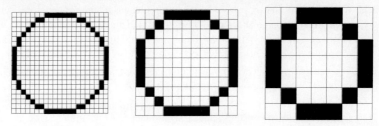

2.8 Implement the antialiasing algorithm discussed in section 2.3.

2.9 For practice in using the graphics commands corresponding to LineTo() and MoveTo() in your programming language, construct a program that produces graph paper. As illustrated below, the graph paper should include scales that are linear, log-linear, and log-log (your programming language should have a logarithmic function in its math library). You may wish to write this program in the manner of existing commercial software; that is, permit the program user to set scales, including total graph size, mesh size for the linear graph lines, and number of cycles for the log scales (two cycles were used on the plots below).

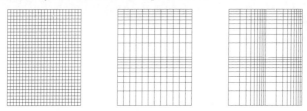

2.10 Use the line graphics commands in your programming language to plot the behavior of the partial sums for the following infinite series.

$$sum = 1 + \frac{1}{2} + \frac{1}{4} + \frac{1}{8} + \cdots + \frac{1}{2^n} + \cdots$$

$$sum = 1 + \frac{1}{2} + \frac{1}{3} + \frac{1}{4} + \cdots + \frac{1}{n} + \cdots$$

Your results should appear as below: the first vertical line on the left corresponds to sum = 0, with the next two lines being at the same positions in the two series because the sums are identical through these terms. As shown in the plots, the first series converges (its sum has a finite limit), while the second (harmonic) series diverges, with the line spacing becoming less than the line width (the plot was stopped after a large number of terms, but the sum would continue to add vertical lines to the right).

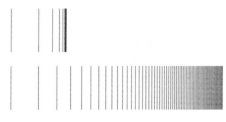

2.11 Write a program that will accurately clip lines from a bottom section of the screen; that is, all inputted lines should be trimmed at a prescribed screen coordinate y_{lower}.

2.12 If the graphics library in your programming language has a function that provides clipping to an arbitrary rectangular region, set up a plotting region centered in your screen that has half the length and width of your screen. Plot a number of lines to illustrate that lines are appropriately clipped at the boundaries of this rectangle.

2.13 Practice using the TRIM command on AutoCAD (or equivalent command on your system) by drawing a rectangular region, crossing its boundaries with a number of lines, and then trimming the lines at the boundaries.

2.14 Draw a simple 3-D object such as a wireframe cube on AutoCAD (or similar system), and set up four viewports for viewing the object from different directions.

BIBLIOGRAPHY

ANGEL, E., *Computer Graphics.* Reading, Mass.: Addison-Wesley Publishing Co., 1990.

AutoCAD Reference Manual, Release 12. Sausalito, Calif.: Autodesk, Inc., 1992.

BURGER, D., AND D. GILLIES, *Interactive Computer Graphics: Functional, Procedural and Device-Level Methods.* Reading, Mass.: Addison-Wesley Publishing Co., 1989.

FOLEY, J. D., A VAN DAM, S. K. FEINER, AND J. F. HUGHES, *Computer Graphics: Principles and Practice,* 2nd edition. Reading, Mass.: Addison-Wesley Publishing Co., 1990.

ROGERS, D. F., *Procedural Elements for Computer Graphics.* New York: McGraw-Hill Publishing Co., 1985.

3

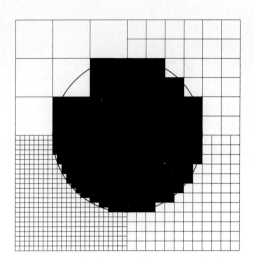

Simple Curves and Polygons

The straight line segments introduced in chapter 2 can be used to construct circles, ellipses, hyperbolas, parabolas, and other curves prescribed by simple algebraic relations. The theoretical curves are approximated by a number of connected straight line segments; that is, by polylines. Closed polylines are polygons. Algorithms can be used to fill polygons with solid color and patterns. The figure above illustrates solid black fill inside a circle, with different pixel resolutions shown in the four quadrants. Different line types and fill patterns can be constructed for use with AutoCAD.

3.1 CIRCLES AND SIMPLE CURVES

The most commonly used curves are the circle and circular arc. The other conic sections (ellipses, parabolas, and hyperbolas) are considered in this section along with some special plane curves. These curves can be expressed by algebraic formulas.

Circles

Most programming languages have a circle function that plots a circle by means of an algorithm similar to the Bresenham algorithm considered in the preceding chapter, except that the pixels which are filled are those closest to the theoretical position of a circular line rather than a straight-line segment. CAD software usually draws circles by means of connected straight-line segments that make up a polygon approximation to a circle.

Figure 3.1 shows that a regular polygon has the appearance of a circle if the polygon has a sufficient number of sides. The number of sides required depends on the size of the circle. The individual polygon segments are evident in the large inscribed polygons on the left of figure 3.1, but as the polygons become smaller they increasingly take on the appearance of a circle. The 32-sided polygon on the bottom is close to a circle at medium sizes; the 8-sided polygon approaches circular appearance only at very small sizes.

The Cartesian coordinates on a circle may be given parametrically in terms of the angle θ from the circle center (x_{center}, y_{center}) to a point (x, y) on the circle:

$$x = x_{center} + r\cos\theta$$
$$y = y_{center} + r\sin\theta$$

$$(3.1)$$

where r is the circle radius.

The circle could be programmed directly from equations 3.1 by incrementing the angle θ around the circle. Such a procedure, however, would have the disadvantage that the the sine and cosine functions would be evaluated at each increment. Because computing trigonometric functions takes time, this procedure would be time-consuming, particularly if a large number of circles were being drawn. Alternatively, one could express y as a function of x on the circle, and then increment x, but this procedure would result in an unattractive circle with unequal segment lengths.

An appropriate resolution to this problem lies in retaining a formulation that increments θ, but with the increment $\delta\theta$ algebraically separated out as shown below so that the trigonometric functions $\cos(\delta\theta)$ and $\sin(\delta\theta)$ need be evaluated only once, before the *for* loop begins. (For convenience the subscripted x and y values are identified with $x - x_{center}$ and $y - y_{center}$.)

$$x_{i+1} = r\cos(\theta_i + \delta\theta)$$
$$y_{i+1} = r\sin(\theta_i + \delta\theta)$$

$$(3.2)$$

which reduce to the following relations after the sums are expanded, with x_i and y_i being identified with $r\cos\theta_i$ and $r\sin\theta_i$, respectively:

$$x_{i+1} = x_i\cos\delta\theta - y_i\sin\delta\theta$$
$$y_{i+1} = x_i\sin\delta\theta + y_i\cos\delta\theta$$

$$(3.3)$$

For a circle approximated by n segments, the angle increment $\delta\theta$ is equal to $2\pi/n$.

The following C-program subroutine draws a circle by using equations 3.3. In this example the calculated circle points are stored in arrays $x[i]$ and $y[i]$, which can then be re-

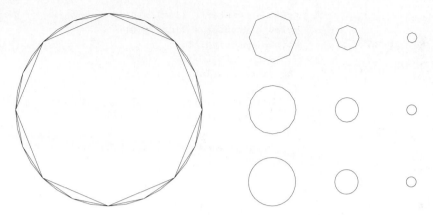

Figure 3.1 Circles approximated by regular polygons of 8, 16, and 32 sides.

called for drawing the circle for different center positions (x_{center}, y_{center}). At the beginning of the program, the *#define* directive is used to assign the value 3.141593 to the symbolic constant *PI*. The main part of the program is assumed to pass values for the circle center coordinates (x_{center}, y_{center}) and radius to the subroutine defined by the user-defined function circle(). The number of segments *num* ($= n$) is specified in the subroutine. Alternatively, the number of segments could be specified at the beginning of the program with a *#define* directive, where the number could be easily changed. Note that the arrays $x[i]$ and $y[i]$ must be dimensioned for a total number of elements *num*+1 (for C programs the arrays start with the subscript 0, so there are *num*+1 subscripts from 0 through *num*).

In the first part of the listing below, $\delta\theta$ is calculated, and cos$\delta\theta$ and sin$\delta\theta$ are evaluated outside the *for* loop so that the trigonometric functions need be evaluated only once. Then the screen coordinates of the first point are evaluated, and the current pen position is located there with a MoveTo() statement. Subsequent points on the circle are evaluated in the *for* loop, and line segments are drawn with the LineTo() statement.

```
#define PI 3.141593

void circle(int xcenter,int ycenter,double radius)
{
    int i, xplot, yplot;
    double x[65],y[65];
    double theta,dTheta,dCos,dSin,num;

    num = 64.;
    dTheta = 2.*PI/num;
    dCos = cos(dTheta);
    dSin = sin(dTheta);

    x[0] = radius;
    y[0] = 0.;
```

```
    xplot = xcenter + (int) x[0];
    yplot = ycenter + (int) y[0];
    MoveTo(xplot,yplot);

    for (i=0; i< (int) num; i++)
    {
        x[i+1] = x[i]*dCos - y[i]*dSin;
        y[i+1] = x[i]*dSin + y[i]*dCos;
        xplot = xcenter + (int) x[i+1];
        yplot = ycenter + (int) y[i+1];
        LineTo(xplot,yplot);
    }
}
```

A circle may be readily drawn with AutoCAD by specifying the center position and radius.

```
Command: CIRCLE
3P/2P/TTR/<Center point>: (enter center point coordinates
    or select with mouse)
Diameter <radius>: (enter radius value or pick point on
    circle with mouse)
```

Alternatively, a circle may be drawn by selecting three points on the circle, by selecting two endpoints on a diameter, or by selecting two tangent lines and a radius (the 3P, 2P, and TTR options in the first prompt above).

When circles are drawn with AutoCAD, the software selects the number of segments for each circle, with smaller circles having fewer (but at least eight) segments than the larger ones. If you zoom to a small region, the circles may have too few segments for a smooth appearance. In this situation you may change the number of segments in two ways. First, you may enter the command REGEN, which regenerates the drawing by selecting the number of circle segments appropriate for the current magnification. Second, by using the VIEWRES command you can change the number used by AutoCAD in its algorithm for selecting the number of circle segments.

```
Command: VIEWRES
Do you want fast zooms? <Y> (enter Y or N)
Enter circle zoom percent (1-20000) <100>: (enter value)
```

The default value for the "circle zoom percentage" is 100; greater values will increase the number of segments. For example, a circle zoom percentage of 1,000 will enable you to zoom in a factor of 10 and still have the same circle smoothness that a zoom percentage of 100 would have at the original magnification. Because increasing the number of segments increases the time required to draw circles, you may wish to keep the zoom percentage value low if you have many circles in your drawing, and increase the zoom percentage only when you need to for the final output or when you zoom in on a small circle. If you answer N on the first prompt above, then all ZOOM, PAN, and VIEW Restore commands will perform regenerations, that is, will require AutoCAD to regenerate the entire drawing and redraw the viewport. If you answer Y to the first prompt, then AutoCAD will maintain a large *virtual* screen, and normally will perform fast ZOOM, PAN, and VIEW Restore commands by redrawing from this virtual screen. Entering the REGEN command regenerates the drawing and sets up a new virtual screen with the new value for the zoom percentage. AutoCAD also has a REDRAW command that quickly redraws your drawing from the virtual screen.

Arcs

The program for a circle may be modified to draw a circular arc. For an arc determined by a starting angle θ_{start}, an ending angle θ_{end}, and a radius r, the angle increment $\delta\theta$ is equal to $(\theta_{end} - \theta_{start})/n$ where n is the number of segments in the arc. The above program listing for a circle is converted to an arc program by changing the equation for $\delta\theta$, and by changing the initial point to that determined by the initial angle, $x_0 = r\cos\theta_{start}$ and $y_0 = r\sin\theta_{start}$.

   In the arc subroutine listing below, the expression $y_{plot} = y_{bottom} - y_{plot}$ (written as $y_{plot} = YBOTTOM - y_{plot}$) transforms a point to screen coordinates from a user coordinate system with its origin at bottom left and y positive in the upward direction (see section 2.4). This y-coordinate transformation also enables angles to be measured by means of the standard mathematical convention: counterclockwise from the positive x-axis, as shown in figure 3.2. The value *YBOTTOM* of the screen-bottom coordinate is assumed to be assigned at the program beginning with a *#define* directive. The main part of the program is assumed to pass values for the following variables to the subroutine: *xcenter* (= x_{center}), *ycenter* (= y_{center}), *radius* (= r), *startTheta* (= θ_{start}), and *endTheta* (= θ_{end}).

```
void arc(int xcenter,int ycenter,double radius,
             double startTheta,double endTheta)
{
      int    i,xplot,yplot;
      double x[65],y[65];
      double theta,dTheta,dCos,dSin,num;
```

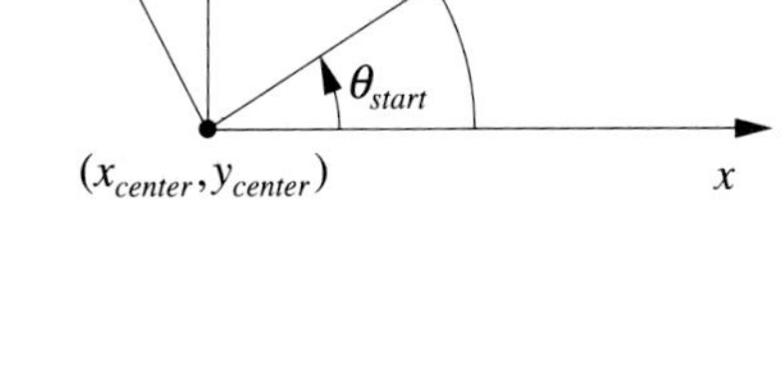

Figure 3.2   Notation for drawing a circular arc.

```
num = 64.;
dTheta = (endTheta - startTheta)/num;
dCos = cos(dTheta);
dSin = sin(dTheta);

x[0] = radius*cos(startTheta);
y[0] = radius*sin(startTheta);

xplot = xcenter + (int) x[0];
yplot = ycenter + (int) y[0];
yplot = YBOTTOM - yplot;
MoveTo(xplot,yplot);

for (i=0; i< (int) num; i++)
{
    x[i+1] = x[i]*dCos - y[i]*dSin;
    y[i+1] = x[i]*dSin + y[i]*dCos;
    xplot = xcenter + (int) x[i+1];
    yplot = ycenter + (int) y[i+1];
    yplot = YBOTTOM - yplot;
    LineTo(xplot,yplot);
}
}
```

AutoCAD provides an ARC command that permits an arc to be drawn in several different ways. In the following procedure, specification of the first and center points determines the arc radius and starting angle, and the sum of the starting angle and the included angle is the ending angle.

```
Command: ARC
Center/<Start point>: (enter start point coordinates or
     select with mouse)
Center/End/<Second point>: C
Center: (enter coordinates or select with mouse)
Angle/Length of chord/<End point>: A
Included angle: (enter value)
```

A slightly different way of entering the arc data is described for an example in section 5.3.

Fillets

Fillets are rounded corners, drawn as circular arcs tangent to two straight lines. We specify the fillet radius and the two lines to which the fillet arc must join. As shown in section 2.4, the intersection-point coordinates (x_{int}, y_{int}) may be readily calculated from the slopes (m_1, m_2) and y-intercepts (b_1, b_2) for the two lines. The fillet is drawn as an arc of radius R with a center (x_{center}, y_{center}) on the line that bisects the angle between the two lines to be filleted. From the geometry illustrated in figure 3.3, the following relations are evident:

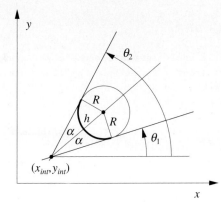

Figure 3.3   Geometry for drawing a fillet (heavy arc) between two intersecting lines.

$$\sin\alpha = \frac{R}{h}, \qquad \alpha = \frac{1}{2}(\theta_2 - \theta_1)$$

$$x_{center} = x_{int} + h\cos(\theta_1 + \alpha), \qquad y_{center} = y_{int} + h\sin(\theta_1 + \alpha) \tag{3.4}$$

where h is the distance between the intersection point and the arc center. After substitution for h and α, the arc center coordinates become

$$x_{center} = x_{int} + R\,\frac{\cos\left(\frac{1}{2}[\theta_1 + \theta_2]\right)}{\sin\left(\frac{1}{2}[\theta_2 - \theta_1]\right)}, \qquad y_{center} = y_{int} + R\,\frac{\sin\left(\frac{1}{2}[\theta_1 + \theta_2]\right)}{\sin\left(\frac{1}{2}[\theta_2 - \theta_1]\right)} \tag{3.5}$$

The angles are obtained from the line slopes, $\theta_i = \tan^{-1}(m_i)$ for $i = 1,2$. With the line orientations shown in figure 3.3, the fillet arc starting and ending angles are $\theta_{start} = \theta_2 + \pi/2$ and $\theta_{end} = \theta_1 + 3\pi/2$.

The program lines below calculate the quantities (x_{center}, y_{center}, θ_{start}, and θ_{end}) needed for input into the arc routine listed above. For line orientations different from those shown in figure 3.3, additional program lines would have to be added to differentiate between the four fillet positions that are possible with two intersecting lines. With the AutoCAD FILLET command, the particular fillet position is determined when the user chooses line segments on the appropriate side of the intersection point.

```
void fillet(double radius,double m1,double m2,
        double b1,double b2)
{
    int    xcenter,ycenter;
    double theta1,theta2,thetaBar,alpha,xint,yint;
    double startTheta,endTheta;

    theta1 = atan(m1);
    theta2 = atan(m2);
    thetaBar = 0.5*(theta1 + theta2);
    alpha = 0.5*(theta2 -theta1);
```

```
xint = (b2 - b1)/(m1 - m2);
yint = m1*xint + b1;

xcenter = (int) (xint + radius*cos(thetaBar)/sin(alpha));
ycenter = (int) (yint + radius*sin(thetaBar)/sin(alpha));
startTheta = theta2 + 0.5*PI;
endTheta = theta1 + 1.5*PI;

arc(xcenter,ycenter,radius,startTheta,endTheta);
}
```

With AutoCAD a fillet between intersecting lines is drawn with the following commands.

```
Command: FILLET
Polyline/Radius/<Select two objects>: R
Enter the fillet radius: (enter value)
Command: FILLET
Polyline/Radius/<Select two objects>: (select the lines)
```

Ellipses and Isometric Drawings

The procedure for drawing a circle can be easily modified for drawing an ellipse. The following form for the equations of an ellipse involves the parameter t, which—unlike the circle parameter θ—does not represent the angle around the center point. Equal increments in t from 0 to 2π trace out a polygon that approximates the ellipse in an efficient manner; namely, for a given number of segments the area of the resulting inscribed polygon is a maximum (closest to the ellipse area). With this procedure the polygon segments are smaller in regions of higher curvature, where greater resolution is needed.

$$x = x_{center} + a \cos t$$
$$y = y_{center} + b \sin t \tag{3.6}$$

where a is the semimajor axis and b is the semiminor axis, for an ellipse with its major axis in the x direction.

The procedure is the same as for a circle: an increment δt is added to the parameter t, with the trigonometric functions expanded to give the following segment coordinates around the ellipse center:

$$x_{i+1} = x_i \cos \delta t - \left(\frac{a}{b}\right) y_i \sin \delta t$$
$$y_{i+1} = \left(\frac{b}{a}\right) x_i \sin \delta t + y_i \cos \delta t \tag{3.7}$$

Unlike a circle, an ellipse has an orientation. Although 2-D rotation transformations are presented in more detail in chapter 10, for our current purposes the following equations will be used for rotating a point (x,y) counterclockwise an angle α to the position (x',y'):

$$x' = x \cos\alpha - y \sin\alpha$$
$$y' = x \sin\alpha + y \cos\alpha$$

(3.8)

In the subroutine listed below, the x- and y-coordinates are calculated in the first *for* loop, and then transformed by equations 3.8 as the segments are plotted in the second *for* loop.

```
void ellipse(int xcenter,int ycenter,double a,
             double b,double alpha)
{
    int    i,xplot,yplot;
    double x[65],y[65];
    double num,dt,dCos,dSin,sina,cosa,adivb,bdiva;

    num = 64.;
    dt = 2.*PI/num;
    dCos = cos(dt);
    dSin = sin(dt);
    sina = sin(alpha);
    cosa = cos(alpha);
    adivb = a/b;
    bdiva = b/a;

    x[0] = a;
    y[0] = 0.;

    for (i=0; i< (int) num; i++)
    {
        x[i+1] = x[i]*dCos - adivb*y[i]*dSin;
        y[i+1] = bdiva*x[i]*dSin + y[i]*dCos;
    }
    xplot = xcenter + (int) (x[0]*cosa - y[0]*sina);
    yplot = ycenter + (int) (x[0]*sina + y[0]*cosa);
    yplot = YBOTTOM - yplot;
    MoveTo(xplot,yplot);

    for (i=0; i< (int) num; i++)
    {
        xplot = xcenter + (int) (x[i+1]*cosa - y[i+1]*sina);
        yplot = ycenter + (int) (x[i+1]*sina + y[i+1]*cosa);
        yplot = YBOTTOM - yplot;
        LineTo(xplot,yplot);
    }
}
```

Ellipses can be drawn on AutoCAD in several different ways. First, the ellipse can be identified by specifying the endpoints of one axis, and the semiaxis distance (*a* or *b*) of the other axis.

```
Command: ELLIPSE
<Axis endpoint1>/Center: (enter coordinates or select with mouse)
Axis endpoint2: (enter coordinates or select with mouse)
<Other axis distance>/Rotation: (enter value or select with mouse)
```

If the Center option is selected on the first prompt, then the ellipse may be drawn with the following inputs.

```
Command: ELLIPSE
<Axis endpoint1>/Center: C
Center of ellipse: (enter coordinates or select with mouse)
Axis endpoint: (enter coordinates or select with mouse)
<Other axis distance>/Rotation: (enter value or select with mouse)
```

If Rotation is selected on the last prompt of the ellipse command, then the ellipse is drawn as the projection of a circle that has been rotated around the major axis by an angle from the viewing plane. The ratio of minor-to-major axes b/a equals the cosine of the rotation angle. (The limiting rotation angle 0° yields a circle, whereas 90° rotation produces a straight line because the circle is perpendicular to the viewing plane.)

```
<Other axis distance>/Rotation: R
Rotation around major axis: (enter value of angle)
```

The ellipses in the hand-drafting template shown in figure 3.4 are drawn for the rotation angle required by an isometric view, as derived below. In addition to this isometric case, templates exist for ellipse rotation angles in intervals of 5°, from 15° to 75°.

AutoCAD offers features for producing isometric drawings. In an isometric view the three coordinate axes are separated by equal angles (120°), so the drawn object appears to be in three dimensions, even though it is drawn with two-dimensional entities. That is, unlike the true three-dimensional AutoCAD constructs that will be considered later in this book, the isometric features described here produce a two-dimensional drawing (as with hand drafting) showing three planes of the object.

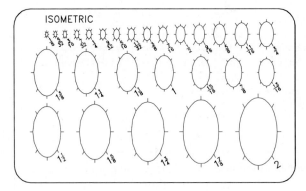

Figure 3.4   An isometric ($\theta_{rotation} =$ 54.736°) ellipse template for drafting.

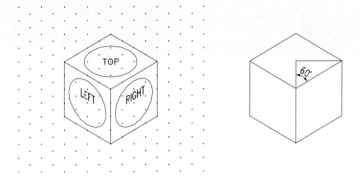

Figure 3.5   Isometric plots of a cube: the left diagram shows holes in the cube faces and grid points; the right diagram illustrates relative dimensions on the cube's top face.

Figure 3.5 shows an isometric cube, with the three *isoplanes* identified as the left, top, and right isoplanes. The isometric grid shown by the dots is set up after checking the *isometric* box in the Drawing Aids menu under the Settings heading in AutoCAD. Lines can be easily drawn on the isometric grid by using the snap option between grid points. Circles representing holes in the cube faces appear as ellipses. These isometric ellipses may be drawn on any of the three isoplanes by first selecting the isoplane and then using the Isocircle option under the ELLIPSE command.

```
Command: ISOPLANE
Left/Top/Right/<Toggle>: (enter isoplane desired or press
      the return key to toggle to next isoplane in the
      Left/Top/Right sequence)

Command: ELLIPSE
<Axis endpoint1>/Center/Isocircle: I
Center of Circle: (enter coordinates or select with mouse)
<Circle radius>/Diameter: (enter value or select with mouse)
```

Note that the ELLIPSE command now has an Isocircle option as a result of the fact that an isometric drawing was selected in the drawing aids menu. As illustrated by the triangle in the top cube face on the right of figure 3.5, the ratio of the horizontal half diagonal to the vertical half diagonal equals $\tan(60°)$ or $\sqrt{3}$. Therefore, an ellipse minor-to-major axis ratio b/a in this isoplane equals $1/\sqrt{3}$, which corresponds to the sine of the ellipse angle $\theta_{ellipse} = \sin^{-1}(1/\sqrt{3}) = 35.264°$, or a rotation angle $\theta_{rotation} = 90° - 35.264° = 54.736°$. Figure 3.6 shows isometric views of three objects.

Other Special Plane Curves

Parabolic curves passing through the origin can be calculated directly from the equation $y^2 = 4ax$, or by means of the parametric representation

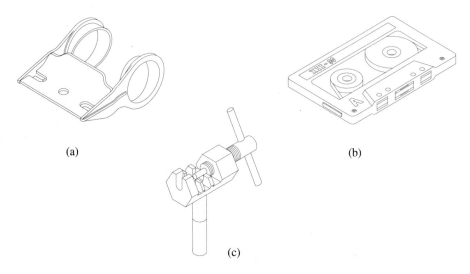

(a)   (b)

(c)

Figure 3.6 Isometric views of three objects drawn on AutoCAD: (a) an adhesive tape dispenser, drawn by Wei-Min Chiu; (b) a magnetic tape cassette, drawn by Paul Clark; (c) a bicycle chain tool, drawn by Joshua Brown.

$$x = at^2, \qquad y = \pm\, 2at \tag{3.9}$$

where a is a constant. This parametric representation yields the maximum inscribed area and involves only additions and multiplications as t is incremented. As discussed previously, translation and rotation can be included in calculations to put the curve at any position and orientation on the screen. The following parametric representation for a hyperbola yields the maximum inscribed polygon:

$$x = \pm a \, \cosh t, \qquad y = \pm b \, \sinh t \tag{3.10}$$

Incrementing t and expanding the hyperbolic functions with the $+$ signs gives the following incremental coordinate equations in the first quadrant:

$$x_{i+1} = x_i \cosh \delta t + \left(\frac{a}{b}\right) y_i \sinh \delta t$$
$$\tag{3.11}$$
$$y_{i+1} = \left(\frac{b}{a}\right) x_i \sinh \delta t + y_i \cosh \delta t$$

Because parabolic and hyperbolic curves are infinite in extent, the parameter t is incremented to a value appropriate to the desired extent of the figure. Figure 3.7 shows sample plots of parabolic and hyperbolic curves in the first and fourth quadrants. (The hyperbolic equations also have branches opening to the left in the second and third quadrants.) As $x \to \infty$, the slopes of the parabolic curves approach zero, whereas the slopes of the hyperbolic curves approach b/a (this ratio varies from 1/12 to 1/2 for the hyperbolas shown).

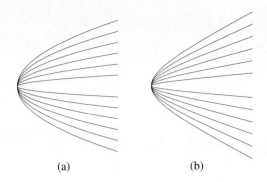

Figure 3.7 (a) Parabolas extending from $x = 0$ to $x = 360$, with $a = 1, 4, 9, 16, 25,$ and 36. (b) Hyperbolas extending from $x = 180$ to 540, with $a = 180$ and $b = 15, 30, 45, 60, 75,$ and 90.

(a)   (b)

Any curve can be plotted if it is represented algebraically as $y(x)$ or $x(y)$, or in parametric form as $y = y(t)$ and $x = x(t)$. The following generalization of the equation for an ellipse yields a family of curves called *superellipses*.

$$(x/a)^n + (y/b)^n = 1 \qquad (3.12)$$

To plot superellipse curves, one must put equation 3.12 into the parametric form shown in equations 3.13. The curves in figure 3.8a were computed directly from equations 3.13 by incrementing t in small steps from 0 to 2π (unlike the circle and ellipse cases, efficient incremental equations cannot be evaluated from the superellipse equations for arbitrary n). As shown in figure 3.8a, superellipse curves vary smoothly from a normal ellipse for $n = 2$ to a rectangle as $n \rightarrow \infty$. The following superellipse curves can be used to approximate cross sections in an airplane fuselage, and half curves can be used for boat hull cross sections (nowadays, however, such cross sections are usually described by curves fitted by means of the methods described in chapter 7).

$$x = a\,(\cos t)^{(2/n)}, \qquad y = b\,(\sin t)^{(2/n)} \qquad (3.13)$$

As another example, we consider a particular epitrochoidal curve that is used in chapter 10 for drawing the chamber for a rotary (Wankel) engine. This particular curve permits a triangular rotor to remain in contact with the chamber wall. The epitrochoid for the Wankel chamber is described parametrically by the following equations, with ε being the eccentricity (which is less than approximately 0.57 for the Wankel chamber):

$$x = 3\cos t - \varepsilon \cos(3t)$$
$$y = 3\sin t - \varepsilon \sin(3t) \qquad (3.14)$$

where t varies from 0 to 2π. Equations 3.12 are a special case of the following equations for a general epitrochoid:

$$x = \sigma \cos t - \varepsilon \cos\!\left(\frac{\sigma t}{\omega}\right) \qquad (3.15)$$

$$y = \sigma \sin t - \varepsilon \sin\!\left(\frac{\sigma t}{\omega}\right)$$

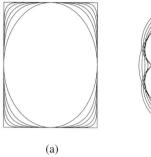 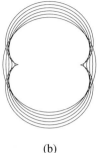

Figure 3.8 (a) Superellipse curves for n values of 2, 3, 4, 6, and 10, with the rectangle representing the limit of $n \to \infty$. In this example $b > a$. (b) Epitrochoidal curves for the eccentricity ε varying between 0 and 1 in steps of 0.2.

(a)   (b)

For the Wankel case, $\sigma = 3$ and $\omega = 1$.

Figure 3.8b presents plots of equations 3.14 curves for various values of the eccentricity ε. The curves vary from a circle for $\varepsilon = 0$ to a cusped figure for $\varepsilon = 1$.

3.2 POLYGONS AND AREA-FILL ALGORITHMS

In the preceding section, smooth theoretical curves were approximated by straight line segments. A collection of straight line segments is called a *polyline* if it is open at the ends or a *polygon* if it is closed.

Polylines and Polygons

A general polyline or polygon is drawn by moving to the first point, and then drawing lines to succeeding points. For instance, the subroutine drawLines() draws lines to form the boundary of the polygon shown below.

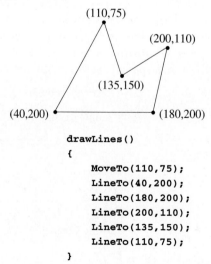

```
drawLines()
{
        MoveTo(110,75);
        LineTo(40,200);
        LineTo(180,200);
        LineTo(200,110);
        LineTo(135,150);
        LineTo(110,75);
}
```

Although the resulting drawing is a polygon shape, the above subroutine simply draws connected lines. Many programming languages have a polygon function that collects the line segments into an overall entity. As shown in the subroutine below, the Macintosh QuickDraw library provides the OpenPoly()/ClosePoly() functions to store a polygon geometry for use in drawing or filling this polygon.

```
drawPoly()
{
    oddPoly = OpenPoly();
        MoveTo(110,75);
        LineTo(40,200);
        LineTo(180,200);
        LineTo(200,110);
        LineTo(135,150);
        LineTo(110,75);
    ClosePoly();
    FramePoly(oddPoly);
}
```

In the above subroutine the polygon is drawn with the FramePoly(*oddPoly*) function, where *oddPoly* is a user-defined PolyHandle to use in referring to this particular polygon. If FillPoly(*oddPoly*,*black*) were used instead of FramePoly(*oddPoly*), then the polygon area would be filled with black. The polygon is illustrated in figure 3.9 with just the frame, and with the Macintosh fill patterns *ltGray*, *gray*, *dkGray*, and *black*. Instead of using the FillPoly(*oddPoly*,*gray*) function to fill the polygon with gray, one can use PaintPoly (*oddPoly*), which will fill the polygon with gray if that shade is the current pen pattern (set with the PenPat(*gray*) function). Later in this section fill algorithms will be discussed, and in chapter 6 shades of gray will be set up with dithered patterns.

If your programming language does not have a special polygon function, then you can readily create such a function by using one-dimensional coordinate arrays (or with structures in C, if you prefer). In the program lines listed below, the number of polyline points *nPts* and the coordinate arrays *xPt*[*i*] and *yPt*[*i*] are first set with coordinate values in the subroutine polyData(), and then the polygon is drawn in the subroutine framePoly().

```
void polyData(void)
{
    int nPts;
```

Figure 3.9   A polygon filled with shades of gray.

```
int xPt[] = {110,40,180,200,135,110};
int yPt[] = {75,200,200,110,150,75};

nPts = 6;

framePoly(nPts,xPt,yPt);
}

void framePoly(int n,int x[],int y[])
{
int i;

MoveTo(x[0],y[0]);
for (i=1; i<n; i++)
{
    LineTo(x[i],y[i]);
}
}
```

The LINE command in AutoCAD first requests the coordinates of the first point and then continues to request additional points until the command is terminated by an extra pressing of the return key. Thus the LINE command can provide a sequence of lines; these lines, however, are saved in the drawing database as individual lines (as will be shown in chapter 8). AutoCAD provides the POLYLINE (or PLINE) command to draw a polyline that is stored as such in the database. The AutoCAD polyline has many useful features, which we will employ in several different sections of this book. The polygon in figure 3.9 is drawn with the following PLINE inputs.

```
Command: PLINE
From point: 110,225
Current line width is 0.0000
Arc/Close/Halfwidth/Length/Undo/Width/<Endpoint of line>:
40,100
Arc/Close/.../Width/<Endpoint of line>: 180,100
Arc/Close/.../Width/<Endpoint of line>: 200,190
Arc/Close/.../Width/<Endpoint of line>: 135,150
Arc/Close/.../Width/<Endpoint of line>: C
```

For the above PLINE, the displayed y-coordinates are related to screen coordinates by $y = y_{bottom} - y_{screen}$, where we have chosen $y_{bottom} = 300$ (recall that y is measured downward with the screen coordinates and upward in an AutoCAD drawing). The response C for *Close* enters the coordinates of the first point (here 110,225) to close the polygon. The PLINE is completed when C is entered. To complete an open polyline, simply press the RETURN key when prompted for the next endpoint. As discussed in chapter 1, absolute coordinate values are not the only way to enter points in AutoCAD: relative coordinate values are entered by preceding the pair of numbers with an @ symbol; also, points can be selected with a mouse or other pointing device.

Thick Lines and Filled Rectangles

Lines of various thicknesses are used to enhance technical drawings; for example, the outline of an object stands out if it is of greater thickness than interior lines. Programming languages often provide a function that controls the thickness of a line. The Macintosh QuickDraw library provides the PenSize(w,h) function that produces a "rectangular pen tip" of width w and height h, measured in pixels. The PenSize() function is set before the line is drawn. When w and h are each set equal to the value 1, the normal line of "one pixel thickness" is drawn.

The top row of figure 3.10 shows lines of varying thickness: the first group has $h = 1$ with increasing w values; the second group has $w = 1$; and the last group is drawn with $w = h$. The bottom row shows thick lines with varying slopes along with a thick-lined polygon. The pointed line ends match up to produce polygon vertices having one, two, or three corners as the thick line changes direction.

The PenSize() function can be simulated by incorporating the rectangular pen tip directly into the Bresenham line-drawing algorithm. For example, we can replace the SetPixel() function in the Bresenham algorithm with a filled rectangle of width w and height h. As illustrated by the figure to the right of the subroutine listing, the rectangle is drawn below and to the right of the point (x,y). The filled rectangle may be drawn directly with a graphics library function, such as the QuickDraw function FillRect(), or lines may be drawn with the LineTo() function to fill the rectangle as shown in the listing below. (Instead of filling the rectangle with lines, one could fill the rectangular array of pixels by using a *for* double loop with the SetPixel() function.)

Figure 3.10   Lines of varying thickness drawn with Macintosh QuickDraw.

```
void fillRect(int x,int y,int w,int h)
{
    int i;

    for (i=0; i<h; i++)
    {
        MoveTo(x,y+i);
        LineTo(x+w-1,y+i);
    }
}
```

With AutoCAD, lines drawn with the PLINE or TRACE command can have specified widths. The top row of figure 3.11 shows AutoCAD PLINEs drawn with increasing widths and varying slopes. The bottom row shows three forms of a polygon drawn with a wide PLINE. The first form results when the PLINE or TRACE command is used with the last point given as the coordinates of the first point. The second form of the polygon results when the PLINE command is used with a *C* for *Close* to complete the polygon, instead of reentering the first point coordinates. The use of Close produces a mitered corner on the first vertex, similar to those on the other vertices. A FILL command can be toggled on and off to display PLINEs and TRACEs as solid or open, as illustrated in the third polygon. The FILL command toggles the fill of all PLINEs and TRACEs on and off; figure 3.11 is a composite of two drawings, since both filled and unfilled PLINEs cannot appear on the same drawing.

The line width on a PLINE is set by the Width or Halfwidth command, as in the following lines for the illustrated polygon.

```
Command: PLINE
From point: 110,225
Current line width is 0.0000
Arc/Close/Halfwidth/Length/Undo/Width/<Endpoint of line>: W
```

Figure 3.11   Wide lines drawn with AutoCAD's PLINE command.

```
Starting width <0.0000> 20
Ending width <20.0000> 20
Arc/Close/.../Width/<Endpoint of line>: 40,100
...
```

Note that the default line width is zero; that is, the line will be drawn as the thinnest line available on your monitor or printer/plotter. Once the line width is set, it applies to all subsequent PLINES until it is changed.

A program to simulate the width of a PLINE can be written by drawing lines at constant y-values across the interior of the rectangle representing the line. The theoretical line segment starts at the point (x_{start}, y_{start}) and ends at (x_{end}, y_{end}). If $y_{start} > y_{end}$, then y_{start} and y_{end} will be interchanged, so that only the two cases shown in figure 3.12 need to be considered. The wide line extends a halfwidth *HW* on either side of the line segment. For each case in figure 3.12, the rectangle representing the wide line may be filled by incrementing y by one pixel and filling a starting triangle, a parallelogram, and an ending triangle.

The sides of the wide line are parallel to the theoretical line segment of slope *m*, and may be expressed by the following equations for x in terms of y.

$$x = x_{start1} + (y - y_{start1})/m$$
$$x = x_{start2} + (y - y_{start2})/m$$

(3.16)

You can readily verify that for equations 3.16, $dy/dx = m$, with the top equation passing through the point (x_{start1}, y_{start1}) and the bottom equation through (x_{start2}, y_{start2}). The lines forming the ends of the wide line have slopes $-1/m$, and are given by the following equations.

$$x = x_{start1} - m(y - y_{start1})$$
$$x = x_{start2} - m(y - y_{start2})$$

(3.17)

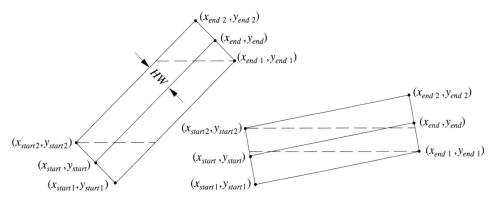

Figure 3.12   Rectangles representing wide lines.

Because consideration of the different cases results in a long listing for the subroutine wideLine(), this subroutine is given in appendix B as listing 3.1. This subroutine first interchanges y_{start} and y_{end} if $y_{start} > y_{end}$, then the coordinates of the endpoints and the halfwidth are passed on to separate subroutines for the cases of vertical, horizontal, and diagonal lines. The general diagonal case is further divided into the two cases shown in figure 3.12, depending on whether or not y_{start2} is less than y_{end1}. In the subroutine the quantities dx and dy are the projections of the line halfwidth hw ($= HW$) on the x- and y-axes, respectively. In the diagLine() subroutine, the value 0.5 is added to the y variable so that rounding occurs when integer values are computed.

In the subroutine wideLine(), the total line width is $2HW+1$ pixels, which reduces to one pixel for the special case of zero line halfwidth ($HW = 0$), similar to AutoCAD. The implementation of an algorithm to produce a mitered corner between two lines of equal widths is given as exercise 3.16 at the end of this chapter.

Ellipse-Fill Algorithm

With AutoCAD any polygon or bounded region, including an ellipse, can be filled with a HATCH pattern. The HATCH pattern may include a solid fill, which is constructed by a crosshatch of lines so close that their line widths overlap. For example, the ellipses of figure 3.13 were filled with the following AutoCAD commands.

```
Command: HATCH
Pattern (? or name/U, style): U
Angle for crosshatch lines <0>: (RETURN)
Spacing between lines <1.0000>: .002
Double hatch area? <N>: (RETURN)
Select objects: (select the ellipse with mouse)
Select objects: (RETURN)
```

In the first prompt above, a question mark will call up a list of the current available hatch patterns; a specific name may be entered for a previously defined pattern; or U may be entered to define a pattern "on the fly." In the above example horizontal lines are chosen sufficiently close that a solid pattern results; the value of line spacing required for a solid fill depends on the drawing scale and line thickness (pixels on the screen, or pen/line size on a plotter/printer). Double hatching would include lines at right angles to the original lines (un-

Figure 3.13   Filled ellipses and DONUTs drawn on AutoCAD.

necessary for solid fill). Here we consider just a solid fill pattern; other hatch patterns are discussed in section 3.4.

Pictured in figure 3.13 are a circular ring and a filled circle, which are drawn with the DONUT (or DOUGHNUT) command. The circular ring shown has the default diameters of 0.5 for the inner circle and 1.0 for the outer circle. The solid circle is a DONUT with an inner radius of zero and an outer radius of 1.0, as constructed with the following commands.

```
Command: DONUT
Inside diameter <0.5000>: 0
Outside diameter <1.0000>: (RETURN)
Center of doughnut: (select with mouse or enter coordinates)
Center of doughnut: (RETURN)
```

We can fill an ellipse by programming horizontal lines extending from its left side to its right side. The equation for an ellipse provides the following expression for the ends of a horizontal fill line.

$$x = x_{center} \pm a\left(1 - \frac{y^2}{b^2}\right)^{\frac{1}{2}} \qquad (3.18)$$

This equation provides the following subroutine for filling an ellipse.

```
void fillEllipse(int xcenter,int ycenter,double a,double b)
{
    int dx,yplot;
    double y;

    for (y=-b; y<=b; y=y+1.)
    {
        dx = (int) (a*sqrt(1-(y*y)/(b*b)));
        yplot = ycenter + (int) y;

        MoveTo(xcenter-dx,yplot);
        LineTo(xcenter+dx,yplot);
    }
}
```

For $a > b$ the major axis is horizontal, for $a = b$ a circle is obtained, and for $a < b$ the major axis is vertical, as in the second ellipse of figure 3.13.

Polygon-Fill Algorithms

There are two main types of polygon-fill algorithms. The edge-fill algorithm uses the polygon vertices to determine the polygon edges. Intersections of the polygon edges with horizontal scan lines then determine the lengths of fill lines in the polygon. The second algorithm type is a *flood*, or *seed*, fill. In this algorithm a seed point is specified somewhere inside the polygon. A horizontal fill line starts at the seed point and floods the entire polygon by turning back on a new line when it detects (via theGetPixel() function) the polygon edge.

The flood-fill algorithm has the advantage that the polygon need not be constructed as a separate entity. That is, the fill line will extend in all directions until it reaches boundary pixels. Figure 3.14 shows how a flood fill progresses as it fills a region bounded by an irregular polygon and several circles. The boundary of the fill region must be completely enclosed by boundary pixels; otherwise, the fill color will spill out of the region, just like water in a leaky container. Another problem that can arise with a flood fill is that a seed point may miss the interior of the fill region. If polygons on a 3-D wireframe object are seen nearly on edge, then care must be taken to ensure that a seed point is properly located inside the polygon for shading.

As illustrated by figure 3.14, the flood fill algorithm must properly check pixels near the boundary edges to determine if there are vertex points or interior regions that are "hiding" additional regions in the interior. The algorithm keeps track of these regions, so that they can be filled after the current section is completed. The top diagram in the figure shows the fill proceeding upward from a seed point near the bottom of the region. As shown in the remaining diagrams, the fill continues to the top of the region, but regions in the shadow of interior and boundary circles are omitted. The fill is then extended to the bottom boundary, and the "shadow" regions are filled one by one.

The edge-fill algorithm is illustrated in figure 3.15. The polygon vertex coordinates are sorted to determine the range of horizontal scan lines that can intersect the polygon. For

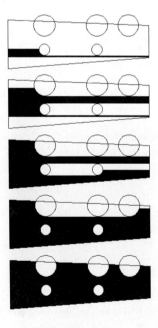

Figure 3.14 The progressive filling of a region by means of a flood-fill algorithm.

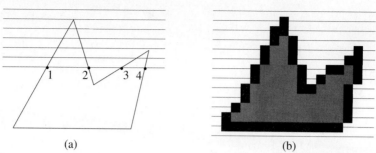

Figure 3.15   Edge-fill diagrams: (a) a scan line intersecting a polygon at four points; (b) completed fill represented by shaded pixels, surrounded by the boundary of black pixels.

each scan line in this range, intersection points are calculated with the polygon edges. When a scan line intersects two boundaries, then a fill line is drawn between the boundaries. If four intersections are detected, as illustrated by the bottom scan line in figure 3.15a, then a fill line will be drawn between the first and second intersections and between the third and fourth intersections, after the x-coordinates of the intersection points have been sorted.

For the edge-fill algorithm, special cases arise when the scan line intersects a horizontal line or a vertex point. These special cases considerably complicate an edge-fill algorithm that can handle general concave polygons. Convex polygons can be filled by using relatively simple procedures, similar to those described earlier for the special cases of rectangles and ellipses. Some graphics workstations have convex-fill algorithms in their hardware. On these systems a concave polygon should be broken up into two or more convex polygons, so that the speed of the convex algorithm in hardware can be used.

Rather than a C subroutine for a general polygon-fill algorithm, a four-sided polygon (quadrilateral) fill algorithm is presented below. This subroutine is useful for implementation with compilers (such as QuickC) that do not have a polygon-fill function in their graphics library. This subroutine can be used to fill faces on a 3-D object; see the painter's hidden line algorithm in section 12.9 and the rendering algorithm in section 14.2. For such applications a flood-fill function is inconvenient because the object faces may appear on edge, resulting in a vanishing target for the seed point required by the flood-fill function.

The geometry for the fillQuadrilateral() subroutine is shown in figure 3.16. In this subroutine, the index number of the bottom vertex is first found, and then relabeled as $v0$. The other vertices are numbered as $v1$, $v2$, and $v3$ while retaining their initial ordering relative to vertex $v0$. Next, the vertex numbers $v1$ and $v3$ are interchanged if it is necessary in order to ensure that vertex $v1$ lies below vertex $v3$. This vertex ordering procedure results in the possible configurations shown in figure 3.16.

As in the wideLine() subroutine described earlier, the three regions shown in each quadrilateral of figure 3.16 are to be filled with horizontal lines. The bottom triangular region will be filled by horizontal lines drawn in the first *if* statement of the subroutine fillQuadrilateral(). The second *if* statement fills the middle quadrilateral region. The top triangular region will be filled by one of the last two *if* statements, depending on whether vertex $v3$ lies below vertex $v2$ (top cases in figure 3.16) or above vertex $v2$ (bottom cases).

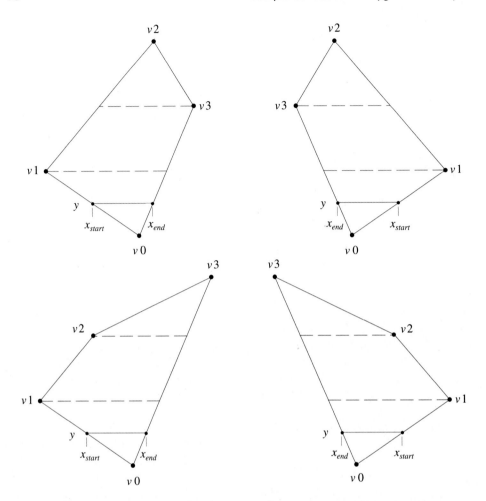

Figure 3.16 Geometry for filling a general quadrilateral defined by four vertices.

The subroutine fillQuadrilateral() is given as listing 3.2 in appendix B. In this subroutine, the starting and ending x-values of a scan line are calculated from the equation for a straight line between the two pertinent vertices. For example, in the first triangular region, the starting point for a scan line lies on the line segment extending between the points (x_{v0}, y_{v0}) and (x_{v1}, y_{v1}) and is given by the following equation.

$$x_{start} = x_{v0} + m_1(y - y_{v0}), \quad \text{with} \quad m_1 = (x_{v1} - x_{v0})/(y_{v1} - y_{v0}) \qquad (3.19)$$

In the above equation, m_1 is the reciprocal of the line slope. If the slope of the line between (x_{v0}, y_{v0}) and (x_{v1}, y_{v1}) is zero $(y_{v0} = y_{v1})$, then the triangular region disappears, and no lines are drawn in this region because an *if* statement in the subroutine is not satisfied (note also that m_1 diverges in this case, but is not evaluated because its computation lies within the *if* statement).

3.3 AREA ANTIALIASING

The hard, jagged edges of polygon fills can be softened by varying the pixel intensities near the edges. This procedure, called *area antialiasing,* is exhibited in the simple example shown in figure 3.17. To produce this figure, a large filled circle was drawn on the computer screen. Then the circle was scanned with "big pixels" comprising arrays of 8 × 8 screen pixels. On the top part of the large circle the big pixels were assigned a shade (intensity) proportional to their number of black (lighted) subpixels. Figure 3.17a shows three scan lines of big pixels, with shading in the first two scan lines from the top. At the circle edge, the third scan line shows a big pixel divided into the 64 subpixels, for use in determining its intensity.

In the bottom half of the circle the big pixels were assigned only black or white shades, depending on whether or not more than half of the subpixels were black. It may not be evident from this example, but area antialiasing can considerably improve images. Area antialiasing is often used when high-resolution graphics are transferred to a lower-resolution medium, such as video.

3.4 LINE TYPES AND FILL PATTERNS

Preparing drawings for engineering or architectural design often requires different line types or fill patterns. That is, it is useful to break up the continuous lines and solid fill into patterns that impart information about the edge or surface of an object. For example, a line made up of short dashes can identify an edge that is hidden from view, or a brick-fill pattern can indicate the construction material for a surface.

Line Types

The common types of lines used in design work are provided by AutoCAD; see the first nine line types illustrated in figure 3.18. The last line shown in the figure is an example of

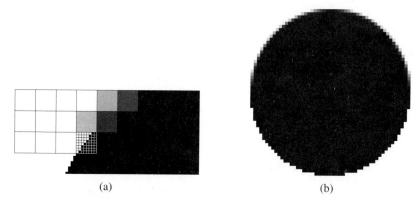

(a)   (b)

Figure 3.17   Area antialiasing: (a) close-up of the region near an edge; (b) filled circle with antialiasing on the top edge.

a user-created type. The user can readily change from one type of line to another, but it is often recommended that different line types be allocated to different layers. Assigning line types by layer provides the convenience of turning lines of a given type (such as hidden lines) on and off simply by turning the layer on and off.

The line type EXAMPLE in figure 3.18 was created by the following procedure in AutoCAD.

```
Command: LINETYPE
?/Create/Load/Set: C
Name of linetype to create: EXAMPLE
File for storage of linetype <ACAD>: (provide a file name)
Creating a new file
Descriptive text: EXAMPLE _____ _ . _
Enter pattern (on next line):
A, 1,-.25,.25,-.25,0,-.25,.25,-.25
New definition written to file.
?/Create/Load/Set: (RETURN)
```

The length scale of the line patterns shown in figure 3.18 can be changed by the LTSCALE command.

```
Command: LTSCALE
New scale factor <1.0000>: (enter new value)
```

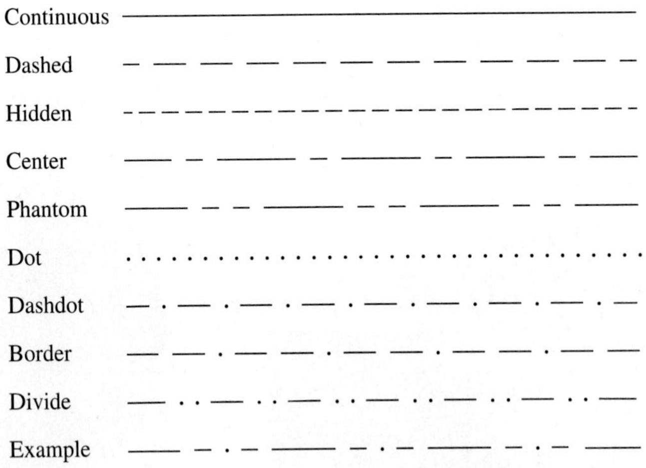

Continuous	────────────────
Dashed	─ ── ── ── ── ── ── ── ── ── ── ── ── ─
Hidden	─ ─ ─ ─ ─ ─ ─ ─ ─ ─ ─ ─ ─ ─ ─ ─ ─ ─ ─
Center	── ─ ── ─ ── ─ ── ─ ──
Phantom	── ─ ─ ── ─ ─ ── ─ ─
Dot	· ·
Dashdot	─ · ── · ── · ── · ── · ── · ── · ──
Border	── ── · ── ── · ── ── · ── ── · ──
Divide	── ·· ── ·· ── ·· ── ·· ── ·· ──
Example	── ─ · ─ ── ─ · ─ ── ─ · ─ ──

Figure 3.18 The top nine line types are the original ones offered on AutoCAD (additional standard line types are now available with AutoCAD). The bottom line was created as a custom line type.

LTSCALE is a global scale factor that will change the pattern scale for all of the lines. If you wish to simultaneously display two scales of dashed lines, you can use the HIDDEN line as well as the DASHED line. The only difference between these two line patterns is that the scale for the HIDDEN line is half the scale for the DASHED line.

The dashed lines on AutoCAD can be simulated with the program subroutine listed below. As illustrated in figure 3.19, the dashes are of length d, and the spaces of length $d/2$. The total line length is divided by the segment (dash plus space) length of $1.5d$ to obtain a maximum of s_{max} segments in the total length of the line. To form the dashed line, a total of $s_{max}-1$ segments are placed in the middle, with a length of one to two segments left over to form two dashes and one space at the ends. This makes the dash pattern symmetrical; the first and last dashes vary from $0.5d$ to $1.25d$ (depending on line length). Note that for these symmetrical patterns with dashes reaching the endpoints, separate dashed lines will join at a common point with a common dash length from d to $2.5d$.

The following program subroutine draws a dashed line between the points (x_1,y_1) and (x_2,y_2), with the length scale determined by the constant *LTSCALE*, which is assumed to be set in the program with a *#define* statement. This subroutine permits hidden lines to be plotted with half-size dash lengths when the flag *hidden* is nonzero.

```
void dashLine(double x1,double y1,double x2,double y2,
              int hidden)
{
      double x,y,d,dx,dy,dx1,dy1,length;
      int    s,smax;
```

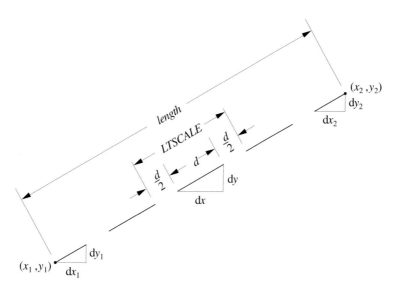

Figure 3.19   Diagram for constructing a dashed line program.

```
length = sqrt((x2-x1)*(x2-x1) + (y2-y1)*(y2-y1));

if (hidden == 0)
     d = 0.5*LTSCALE;
else
     d = 0.25*LTSCALE;

dx = (x2-x1)*d/length;
dy = (y2-y1)*d/length;
smax = (int) (length/(1.5*d));

dx1 = 0.5*((x2-x1) - (1.5*smax-1.)*dx);
dy1 = 0.5*((y2-y1) - (1.5*smax-1.)*dy);

MoveTo((int) x1, (int) y1);
LineTo((int) (x1+dx1),(int)  (y1+dy1));

for (s=0; s<smax-1; s++)
{
     x = x1 + dx1 + (1.5*s+0.5)*dx;
     y = y1 + dy1 + (1.5*s+0.5)*dy;

     MoveTo((int) x,(int) y);
     LineTo((int) (x+dx),(int) (y+dy));
}
MoveTo( (int) x2,(int) y2);
LineTo((int) (x2-dx1),(int) (y2-dy1));
}
```

Line types can also be constructed on a pixel basis within most programming environments. For example, Microsoft C has the function _setlinestyle(), in which the argument is a hexadecimal number that provides a 16-pixel pattern. Thus, any line drawn with _lineto() (or other line-drawing function) is constructed with the pattern given by the previous _setlinestyle() assignment; this pattern is repeated along the length of the line.

As an example of the Microsoft C line type, consider the 16-pixel pattern that consists of a space of four pixels, a dash of four pixels, a space of four pixels, and a dash of four pixels. This pattern can be represented by the binary number 0000 1111 0000 1111, with a 0 representing an empty (background color) pixel and 1 representing a filled pixel. Four binary digits represent the 16 decimal numbers 0 through 15 (because from left to right the binary digits represent 2^3, 2^2, 2^1, and 2^0). These 16 numbers may be represented by a single digit in the hexadecimal system; that is by 0, 1, 2, 3, 4, 5, 6, 7, 8, 9, A, B, C, D, E, and F.

For the example case of short dashes, the first four binary digits equal 0 in the hexadecimal system, the second four binary digits equal F, the third hex digit is 0, and the final hex digit is F. Thus the hex number for line type is given by 0x0F0F, where the leading 0x term denotes a hexadecimal number. Accordingly, with Microsoft C the function _setlinestyle(0x0F0F) sets the line type to short dashes. You can set up any repeating 16-pixel pattern; for example, longer dashes are set with the function call _setlinestyle(0x00FF).

Fill Patterns

In this section, fill patterns are considered for both AutoCAD and for a programming language (here the Microsoft C graphics library is considered; most other graphics libraries have a similar fill pattern feature). AutoCAD fill patterns, called HATCH patterns, are composed of line segments that can be scaled and rotated. The Microsoft C fill patterns are based on an 8×8 pixel template (called a fill mask) that restricts the patterns to small scale and to relatively simple designs.

AutoCAD includes a number of standard HATCH patterns, including some ANSI standard patterns for material surfaces; also, you may individually design patterns. As described for the ellipse-fill example in section 3.2, simple crosshatched fill patterns can be designed "on the fly" by entering U (for "you design") on the first prompt under the HATCH command. With the use of a word processor or editor, more detailed patterns may be designed and added to the AutoCAD file "acad.pat."

HATCH patterns were used to construct the brick designs in figure 3.20. The first pattern of stacked-bond bricks consists of solid horizontal and vertical lines. On the first line of the pattern file listed below, the asterisk precedes the pattern name, with a pattern description appearing after the comma. (The first lines of all patterns are listed on the screen when a question mark is entered on the first prompt under the HATCH.)

The pattern is described by the remaining two lines of the file. The first entry is the line direction (0° for horizontal lines and 90° for vertical lines). The next two numbers give

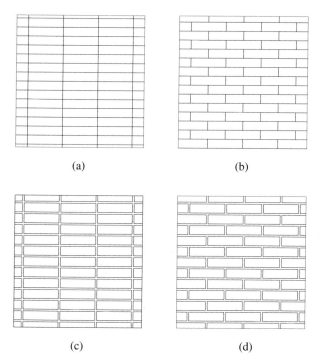

(a)   (b)

(c)   (d)

Figure 3.20 Hatch patterns for bricks: (a) stacked bond, (b) running bond, (c) stacked bond with grouted joints, and (d) running bond with grouted joints.

the coordinates of a point through which one of the parallel lines passes. The 0 in the next pair of numbers denotes that the parallel lines are not to be offset *along* their lengths. The last number (.25 for the horizontal lines and 1 for the vertical lines) represents the offset, or spacing, between the parallel lines. Note that all numbers in a HATCH file are separated by commas, and that spaces may be inserted for readability.

```
*s_brick,stacked-bond bricks
0,    0,0,    0,.25
90,   0,0,    0,1
```

The next example, shown in figure 3.20b, is the pattern for running-bond bricks. As shown in the file below, the horizontal lines are described by the same numbers as in the preceding example. Figure 3.20b shows that the vertical lines are dashed, separated by .5 units (half a brick length), and are offset in the vertical direction by .25 (a line starting with a dash is next to ones starting with a space). In the bottom line of the file, the pair of numbers .25,.5 give the vertical offset and the distance between lines. The last pair of numbers describes a dashed line in the same way as under the LINETYPE command. That is, .25,−.25 represents a dash of .25 units followed by a space of .25 units (you may consider positive numbers to mean "pen down" and negative numbers, "pen up").

```
*r_brick,running-bond bricks
0,    0,0,    0,.25
90,   0,0,    .25,.5,   .25,-.25
```

Figures 3.20c–d show the stack-bond and running-bond brick patterns with grouted joints. As shown in the files listed below, each of these designs is constructed by two horizontal dashed lines and two vertical dashed lines.

```
*sg_brick,stacked-bond, grouted bricks
0,    0,0,    0,.3,    1,-.05
0,    0,.25,  0,.3,    1,-.05
90,   0,0,    0,1.05, .25,-.05
90,   1,0,    0,1.05, .25,-.05

*rg_brick,running-bond,grouted bricks
0,    .05,0,    .525,.3,  1,-.05
0,    .05,.25,  .525,.3,  1,-.05
90,   0,0,      .3,.525,  .25,-.35
90,   .05,0,    .3,.525,  .25,-.35
```

The file named cane listed below produces a pattern that represents the weave in a cane chair. The numbers for this pattern were determined by first measuring dimensions from a chair, then drawing one section of the pattern on AutoCAD. Then the DIST command was used to measure the dash and space lengths along the lines in the drawing. Figure 3.21 shows four different horizontal lines. Two of the lines require two unequal dashes; that is, four numbers are needed to describe the line type. Similarly, four different vertical

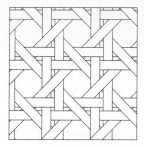 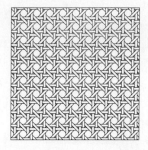

Figure 3.21   Weave pattern for a cane chair, plotted for two different scales.

lines appear in the file below. Only two 45° lines and two 135° lines are needed for the diagonals in the pattern. These lines require staggering (offsetting along their lengths), as determined by the nonzero values for the fourth numbers on the lines of the file.

```
*cane,Cane chair pattern
0,     .26,.1,      0,1.4,      .1562,-.3677,.6162,-.26
0,     0,.36,       0,1.4,      -.5238,.8762
0,     -.1,1.14,    0,1.4,      .8762,-.5238
0,     -.1,0,       0,1.4,      .6162,-.3677,.1562,-.26
90,    0,0,         0,1.4,      .6162,-.3677,.1562,-.26
90,    .26,0,       0,1.4,      .8762,-.5238
90,    1.04,.1,     0,1.4,      .5238,.8762
90,    1.3,.36,     0,1.4,      .1562,-.3677,.6162,-.26
45,    .7762,.36,   .98995,.98995,  1.1031,-.3677,.0707,-.4384
45,    1.1438,.36,  .98995,.98995,  1.1031,-.4384,.0707,-.3677
135,   1.04,.8762,  .98995,.98995,  1.1031,-.3677,.0707,-.4384
135,   .04,1.2438,  .98995,.98995,  1.1031,-.4384,.0707,-.3677
```

Although it would be tedious to directly program the cane pattern, a simpler version is presented as exercise 3.17, which provides practice drawing with thick, solid lines.

Programming languages often provide convenient ways of setting up raster patterns for use in filling polygons. These patterns are used in chapter 6 to produce gray shades by means of ordered dithering. An example of a brick fill pattern in Microsoft C is given below.

As mentioned at the beginning of this section, fill patterns in Microsoft C are based on an 8 × 8 template called a *fill mask*. Figure 3.22 shows the fill mask for a brick pattern. Note that the individual bricks cannot be longer that seven pixels (with the grout accounting for the eighth pixel in the horizontal direction). Thus the patterns are restricted to small scales.

As illustrated on the right of figure 3.22, the fill mask is expressed in terms of hexadecimal numbers for the rows of fill mask. These hexadecimal numbers can be determined by first forming binary numbers, with 1 representing a filled pixel and 0 and empty pixel. Each set of four binary numbers corresponds to the numbers 0 through 15 in the decimal system, which in turn can be expressed as a single hexadecimal digit 0 through F. (Recall that the hexadecimal digits are 0, 1, 2, 3, 4, 5, 6, 7, 8, 9, A, B, C, D, E, and F.) Thus, the top row of the fill mask shown in figure 3.22 is represented by the hexadecimal number 0xFF, which corresponds to eight filled pixels (each F equals the binary number 1111, corresponding to four filled pixels). The 0x denotes that a hexadecimal number follows.

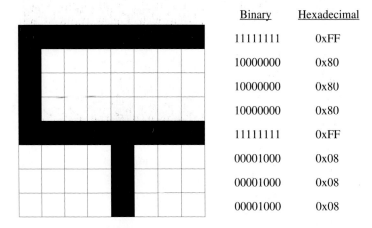

Binary	Hexadecimal
11111111	0xFF
10000000	0x80
10000000	0x80
10000000	0x80
11111111	0xFF
00001000	0x08
00001000	0x08
00001000	0x08

Figure 3.22   The Microsoft C fill mask for a brick pattern.

The brick pattern and fill mask are set up with the following Microsoft C statements.

```
unsigned char brickMask[] =
                {0xFF,0x80,0x80,0x80,0xFF,0x08,0x08,0x08};

        _setfillmask(brickMask);
```

The brick pattern will now appear when the function _floodfill() is used, or when _rectangle() and _ellipse() are used with the control variable _GFILLINTERIOR.

EXERCISES

3.1 Draw squares and 90° arcs arranged to form the spiral shown below. Use either programming or CAD software.

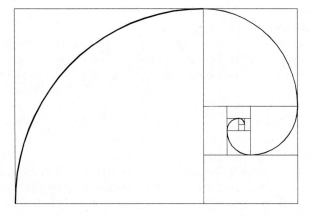

3.2 Use the line, arc, and fillet commands on your CAD system to construct the following illustration of a puck for a Hewlett-Packard drafting tablet (this is also illustrated in figure 1.4).

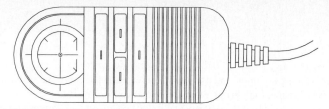

3.3 Draw the ellipse template shown below by using a programming language or a CAD system.

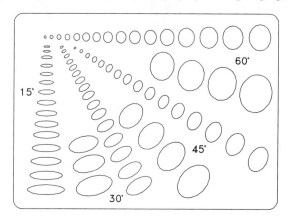

3.4 Use your CAD system to construct a template drawing similar to figure 3.4, but for ellipses with $\theta_{rotation} = 45°$.

3.5 Use the isometric drawing features of AutoCAD to produce the following: (a) the representation of a bolt shown below; (b) a measured object like one of those shown in Figure 3.6.

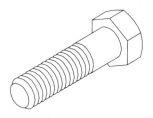

3.6 Use equations 3.12 to construct superellipse curves for the following two cases: (a) $a = b$, $n = 2, 3, 4$, and 10, and (b) $a = 2b$, $n = 2, 3, 4$, and 10.

3.7 Consider epitrochoidal curves given by equations 3.14 and 3.15.
(a) Use equations 3.14 to draw curves with $\varepsilon > 1$, as well as for $\varepsilon \le 1$.
(b) Use equations 3.15 to plot the curve for $\sigma = 4$, $\varepsilon = 3$, and $\omega = 2$.

3.8 Draw figures by using the rhodeonea (or rose) curve, $r = a \cos(m\theta)$, where r is the polar radius and $0 \le \theta \le 2\pi$ ($x = r \cos\theta$ and $y = r \sin\theta$). Draw curves for $m = 2, 3, 10$, and 11. There are m petals on the curve when m is odd and $2m$ petals for m even; pictured below are rhodonea curves for $m = 3, 4, 9$, and 10.

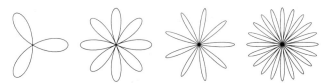

3.9 Write a program that will draw linear spirals according to Archimedes' formula $r = a\cos\theta$, where r is the polar radius, and the angle θ increases as the curve spirals outward from a starting angle θ_0 (related to the starting radius by $r_0 = a\cos\theta_0$). The Cartesian coordinates are related to polar coordinates by $x = r\cos\theta$ and $y = r\sin\theta$. The constant a determines the tightness of the spiral: the spiral on the left below was drawn for $a = 3$, and the one on the right for $a = 1.5$.

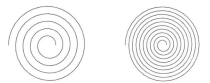

3.10 Construct a program that draws logarithmic spirals $r = \exp(a\theta)$, where r is the polar radius and the angle θ increases as the curve spirals outward from a starting angle θ_0, related to the starting radius by $r_0 = \exp(a\theta_0)$. The Cartesian coordinates are related to polar coordinates by $x = r\cos\theta$ and $y = r\sin\theta$. The constant a determines the tightness of the spiral: the spiral on the left below was drawn for $a = 0.14$, and the one on the right for $a = 0.07$. Note that the exponential in the relation for r produces a spiral that decreases its tightness as r increases, whereas the linear spiral in the preceding exercise retains the same tightness at all r values.

3.11 Use arrays to write a program that will draw the polygon shown below.

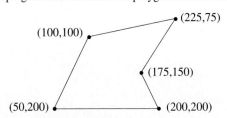

3.12 Write a program that draws the above polygon by using *relative* coordinates. Use this program to place the polyline at four different positions.

3.13 As outlined in section 3.2, write a program that draws with a rectangular pen tip by replacing the SetPixel() function in the Bresenham line-drawing algorithm with a subroutine that fills a rectangle having user-specified values for width and height.

3.14 Incorporate a circle-filling subroutine into the Bresenham algorithm to simulate a circular pen tip. Use your subroutine to draw some connected line segments like those illustrated in the following figure.

3.15 Implement a program that draws a line segment of halfwidth *HW*, having flat ends perpendicular to the line direction, as illustrated in figure 3.12.

3.16 Write a subroutine that connects two line segments (each of halfwidth *HW*) with a mitered corner (in the same fashion as the AutoCAD PLINE). As illustrated below, consider both the filled and open cases. Hint: Calculate the intersection points for lines displaced by halfwidths *HW* from the original line.

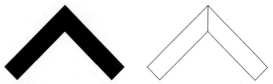

3.17 Construct the pattern below representing the weave for a cane chair. Program thick lines to draw this pattern.

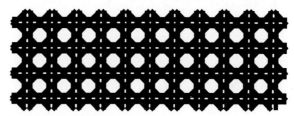

3.18 Implement the quadrilateral fill algorithm described in section 3.2 and presented as listing 3.2 in appendix B.

3.19 If the graphics library of your programming language has some default gray shades, colors, or patterns, fill the polygon of exercise 3.11 with these shades.

3.20 Set up the tile fill pattern shown below. This pattern can be stored as an AutoCAD hatch pattern consisting of three dashed lines.

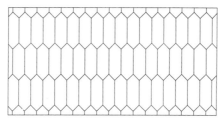

3.21 With both AutoCAD and Microsoft C (or other programming language) construct the tile pattern shown below (the AutoCAD version is on the left, and the Microsoft C version is on the right). That is, with an editor write an AutoCAD hatch pattern file, and then use this hatch pattern to fill a region in AutoCAD. For the second part of this exercise, construct an 8 × 8 pixel fill mask in Microsoft C for this tile pattern, and use it to fill a rectangle or other boundary.

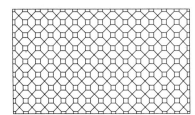 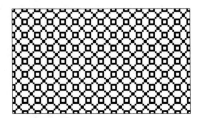

BIBLIOGRAPHY

AutoCAD Release 12 Reference Manual. Sausalito, Calif.: Autodesk, Inc., 1992.

FOLEY, J. D., A. VAN DAM, S. K. FEINER, AND J. F. HUGHES, *Computer Graphics: Principles and Practice,* 2nd ed. Reading, Mass.: Addison-Wesley Publishing Co., 1990.

LAWRENCE, J. D., *A Catalog of Special Plane Curves.* New York: Dover Publications, Inc., 1972.

ROGERS, D. F., *Procedural Elements for Computer Graphics.* New York: McGraw-Hill Publishing Co., 1985.

ROGERS, D. F., AND J. A. Adams, *Mathematical Elements for Computer Graphics,* 2nd ed. New York: McGraw-Hill Publishing Co., 1990.

THE WAITE GROUP, *Microsoft C Programming for the PC*, 2nd ed. Indianapolis: Howard Sams, 1990.

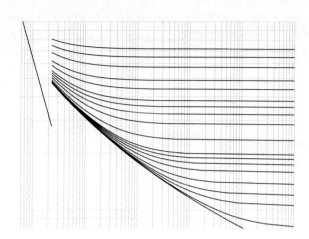

Technical Drawings and Graphs

In this chapter, the CAD features discussed in the preceding chapters are used to construct technical drawings. Also, the C programming techniques are used to draw graphs for engineering and scientific visualization.

Technical drawings for engineering and architecture can usually show all pertinent features and dimensions in orthographic views. For example, a simple mechanical object, such as the crank arm in section 4.3, may require just two views (front and side) for a full representation. More complex objects, like those shown in figures 4.1 and 4.2, require more views. In architecture, a plan view and elevations from the four sides are often sufficient to show a building's exterior.

Even when an object can be represented by orthographic views, a pictorial representation, such as an isometric view, is useful for visualizing the object. The AutoCAD isometric features discussed in the preceding chapter may be used to construct an isometric view as a 2-D drawing.

There are a large number of commercial programs for producing *presentation graphics*. Also, some programming languages (such as Microsoft C) have special library functions for presentation graphics. Most of the commercial programs are developed for business graphics (bar charts, pie charts, and simple line plots), but some good software packages have been developed specifically for more technical applications.

Even though technical graphics software is available, creating graphics from scratch from within your programs often increases your speed and flexibility. Programming languages give you control over size, font, and placement of numbers and labels. CAD software can also be useful for graphing, although sometimes you may need a programming interface for the CAD software to enter data efficiently; see chapter 8, section 8.2.

There are several levels of *scientific visualization*. The first level, considered in this chapter, is the representation of technical data in black-and-white 2-D plots. In the next level the display is enhanced with other visual attributes such as color (section 6.4), 3-D plots (section 12.6), animation, or the use of *glyphs* (small icons for marking regions of special interest).

An even higher level of scientific visualization results when a program can be used in a strongly interactive mode; that is, when a researcher can readily change the manner in which the data are viewed and can quickly change data to observe consequences. Ideally, scientific visualization software should be used as an integral part of the research process.

Software for *image analysis* can be used to enhance images through a number of procedures. Also, *virtual reality* hardware, such as head-mounted displays and data gloves, can

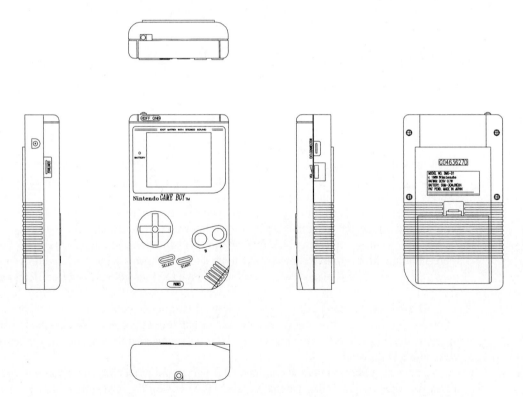

Figure 4.1   Views of a Nintendo Game Boy; drawn on AutoCAD by Stephanie Oba.

give the user the illusion of moving around in the data field and selecting items of interest; for example, walking through a computer model of a building or moving around a flow simulation for an aircraft or spacecraft to select regions for viewing streamlines.

4.1 TECHNICAL DRAWINGS

A relatively complex mechanical object may require all of the six orthographic views displayed below. These views are parallel projections along the positive and negative directions of the three coordinate axes (the coordinate origin is assumed to be inside the object).

```
                    top
     left side     front     right side     back
                  bottom
```

The drawing of the hand-held game in figure 4.1 illustrates the six views listed above, and the camera in figure 4.2 shows five of the six views.

Some objects may have important features on a plane that is not perpendicular to one of the three coordinate axes. These features can be shown with an *auxiliary* projection that

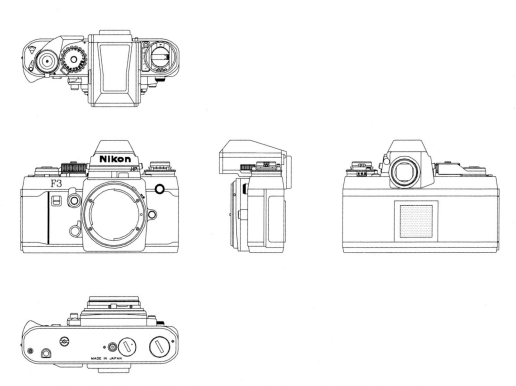

Figure 4.2   Views of a Nikon 35mm camera body; drawn on AutoCAD by Jamie Anderson.

is normal to the plane of interest. Books on engineering graphics, such as Spence 1988 or Ludzadder and Duff 1993, discuss 2-D drafting techniques for drawing auxiliary projections.

CAD systems can construct projections from a 3-D solid model. For example, in section 13.2 orthographic and axonometric (arbitrary direction) projections are produced from solid models. Although it is widely believed that in the future all design may be done with 3-D modeling, currently a large part of CAD use is for 2-D drafting.

The two orthographic views of the crank arm shown in figure 4.3a were constructed by using 2-D drafting procedures on AutoCAD. These views include dimension lines in-

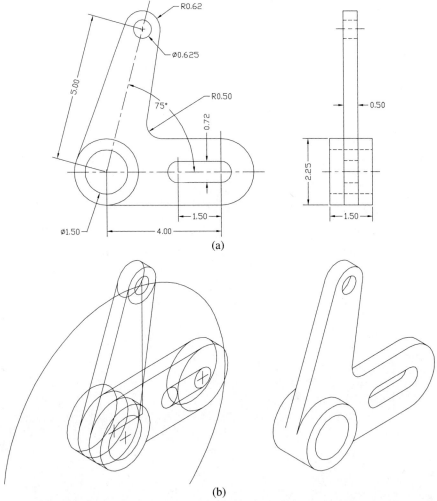

Figure 4.3   Views of a crank arm: (a) orthographic views; (b) isometric view on the right, with isometric circles and construction lines shown on the left. These views were drawn on AutoCAD, with dimensions obtained from an exercise in Warren J. Luzadder and Jon M. Duff, *Introduction to Engineering Drawing,* 2nd ed., © 1993, Exercise 4.7. By permission of Prentice-Hall, Englewood Cliffs, New Jersey.

serted with the AutoCAD DIM command. This command (and DIM1 for a single-dimension line) are described in section 9.4.

An isometric view of the crank arm is shown on the right-hand side of figure 4.3b. This isometric projection was constructed by using isometric circles and by measuring distances along the isometric axes. Isometric circles and construction lines used in drawing the isometric projection are illustrated on the left-hand side of figure 4.3b.

4.2 GRAPHS

As discussed in the book by Tufte (1983), considerable care must be taken to display data clearly and precisely. Truncating vertical scales to emphasize differences in data can be misleading if the truncation is not strongly indicated on the graph. Tufte shows that misrepresentation can result when the size of an effect shown in a graph is different from the size of the effect in the data.

Bar Graphs

Bar charts are useful for comparing a relatively small number of values; for example, truck durability of four manufacturers is shown in figure 4.4. The representation shown in 4.4a approximates a bar chart shown in a full-page advertisement on the back of a national magazine, with manufacturers' names replaced by the letters A–D (obviously the ad was paid for by manufacturer A).

Because the bars in figure 4.4a start at 95%, the small differences are greatly amplified. Plotting the same data on a scale from 0 to 100% shows that the great majority of all the trucks are still on the road after 10 years. A more meaningful comparison might be the durability of the trucks after 15 or 20 years (however, manufacturer A might not be the leader then).

Other factors besides the truncation of bars should be of concern when using bar graphs. For example, labels and tick marks should appear at easily readable intervals such as 1, 5, 10, 50, 100, etc., not 3, 4, 6, 7, etc. The bars should be the same color or shade, unless a different color is used to represent another factor. More than one color can be used on each bar when the bar is divided into parts to supply more information; for example, a bar representing all trucks on the road could be divided by color sections according to those

Percentage of trucks sold over the last 10 years that are still on the road

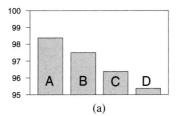
(a)

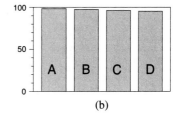
(b)

Figure 4.4   Two bar-graph representations of the same data on truck durability.

manufactured in the last 10 years, those manufactured 10 to 20 years ago, those manufac-tured 20 to 30 years ago, etc.

It is recommended that the bar widths be greater than the distance between adjacent bars. Examples of good and bad bar graphs are given by Dewey (1988).

There is a tendency to add "interest" to a bar graph by presenting pictorial bars. The use of pictures in portraying data can lead to misleading (or even incorrect) graphs. For ex-ample, the fictitious pictorial graph shown in figure 4.5 represents data by barrels of oil. In this barrel graph it is unclear whether the amount of oil is proportional to the barrel height as in a standard bar graph, or proportional to the volume of the barrel (or even proportional to the projected area of the barrel, as in a pie chart). Although choosing the amount of oil as proportional to the volume appears to be the best selection, even this representation makes it hard for a person to judge amounts by viewing container volumes. That is, you cannot easily determine that one container holds exactly 2 times as much as another, and not 1.9 or 2.1 times as much.

Figure 4.5 contains one more source of confusion: namely, the perspective makes the barrels seem to recede into the past. It is impossible to judge how much of a barrel's ap-parent size derives from this perspective effect.

Pie Charts

Pie charts provide a convenient form for illustrating fractions of a whole quantity. In figure 4.6, four representations of a pie chart show how the computer graphics market is divided. The areas of the pie sections are drawn in proportion to the fractional amount they repre-sent. For example, the pie section for CAD/CAM/CAE is drawn with an angle of $0.30 \times 360° = 108°$ because it represents the fraction 0.30 (or 30%) of the total pie area.

The data are well presented by the shaded and unshaded pie charts in figure 4.6a–b. Hatching in pie charts (as well as in bar graphs) is often distracting, as illustrated in fig-ure 4.6c.

Tilted pie charts have become increasingly popular. Although a tilted chart may save some space, it has the disadvantage that areas change shape with the tilt angle. For exam-ple, in figure 4.6d, it is not clear that the two 6% areas (mapping and architectural design) are the same size because the pie sections have different shapes. In fact, it is not immedi-ately obvious that visual communications (9%) is appreciably larger than mapping (6%),

Worldwide Oil Production

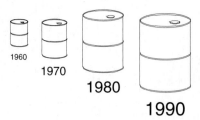

Figure 4.5 Fictitious graph illustrating the confusion that can arise when pictures are used as indicators of quantities.

The 1992 Worldwide Computer Graphics Market

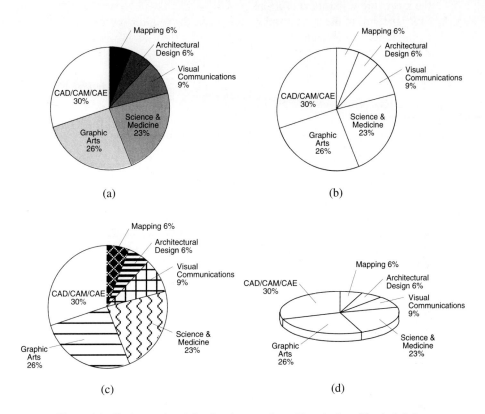

Figure 4.6   Four examples of showing the same data with a pie chart. The shaded chart (a) approximates the color pie chart that appears in the following article: J. Gantz, "The Market at Large," pp. 27–32, *Computer Graphics World,* January 1993.

although in figure 4.6a–b the difference in these areas is obvious. Thus, pie charts with large tilt angles are not recommended.

Examples of Engineering Graphs from Fluid Mechanics

Technical data is often plotted in terms of dimensionless quantities. For example, an exact solution of the Navier-Stokes equations of fluid mechanics provides a relation for the fluid velocity u in a vortex as a function of radius r and time t. The radius is measured from the center of the viscous core of the vortex. The streamlines are circles, with the velocity decreasing to zero as the radius approaches infinity. The viscous core diffuses outward with time and reduces the velocity near the vortex center.

For this vortex problem, a dimensionless radius R is formed by dividing by a reference radius r_0, $R \equiv r/r_0$. Similarly, a dimensionless velocity U is formed, $U \equiv u/u_0$, where the reference velocity is defined by the formula $u_0 \equiv \Gamma_0/(2\pi r_0)$, with Γ_0 being the total circulation around the vortex. The dimensionless time is given by $T \equiv 4vt/r_0^2$, with v being the kinematic viscosity coefficient.

In terms of the dimensionless quantities, the solution for the decaying vortex is given by the following formula.

$$U = \frac{\left[1 - \exp\left(-\dfrac{R^2}{T}\right)\right]}{R} \qquad (4.1)$$

The program subroutine listed below plots the curves shown in figure 4.7. The velocity curve for $T = 0$ (given by $U = 1/R$) is plotted separately because the argument of the exponential in equation 4.1 diverges at $T = 0$. Each curve is plotted by incrementing R in a *for* loop, with the leader line to the T value plotted as a straight line segment when the value $R = .5$ is reached (determined by an *if* statement).

Although not shown in this example, the main curves can be drawn on the screen with a thick line using the PenSize() function for Macintosh QuickDraw. For systems that do not have a thick-line function, one could use a Bresenham subroutine with a square "pen tip" as outlined in exercise 2.3.

The origin of the plot is specified by the values *xleft* and *ybottom*. These values along with the horizontal and vertical scale factors *sfx* and *sfy* determine the screen coordinates for any world coordinates R and U.

The programming language, through the use of the Macintosh QuickDraw command MoveTo(), allows text to be placed at any pixel location. With Microsoft C on the PC, graphics fonts may be used to place text at any pixel location, although the default text font can place text characters only on particular rows and columns (30 rows and 80 columns for the VGA mode). If your system requires that the text be placed only at specific row and column locations, you should choose your graph origin (*xleft, ybottom*) and scales (*sfx* and *sfy*) so that numbers can be placed close to axis tick marks.

The curves shown in figure 4.7 are relatively smooth. To produce smooth plots on a laser printer, one can reduce the size of the original plot when printing. Also, a printer smoothing option can provide further improvement.

```
void vortexCurves(void)
{
    int     xleft=120,ybottom=400;
    double u,r,t,sfx=250,sfy=120;

    for (t=0.1; t<=.5; t=t+.1)
    {
        MoveTo(xleft,ybottom);
        for (r=.025; r<=2.0; r=r+.025)
        {
            u = (1. - exp(-r*r/t))/r;
```

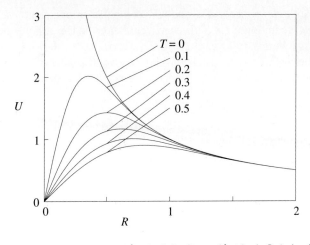

Figure 4.7 The dimensionless velocity U versus dimensionless radial distance R from the core of a vortex, plotted for different values of the dimensionless time T.

```
LineTo(xleft + (int) (sfx*r),ybottom - (int) (sfy*u));
if ((r>.49) && (r<.51))
{
    LineTo(xleft + (int) sfx,ybottom - (sfy*(2.5-2.*t)));
    MoveTo(xleft + (int) (sfx*r),ybottom - (int) (sfy*u));
}
    }
}
MoveTo(xleft + (int) (sfx/3.0),ybottom - (int) (sfy*3));
for (r=.35; r<=2.0; r=r+.025)
{
    u = 1./r;
    LineTo(xleft + (int) (sfx*r),ybottom - (int) (sfy*u));
    if ((r>.49) && (r<.51))
    {
        LineTo(xleft + (int) (sfx*.9),ybottom - (sfy*2.5));
        MoveTo(xleft + (int) (sfx*r),ybottom - (int) (sfy*u));
    }
}
    }
```

For another example, consider the Ekman solution for the boundary layer at the top of the ocean, given by the following equations (see White 1986):

$$u = V_0\, e^{-(\pi z/D)} \cos\!\left(\frac{\pi}{4} - \frac{\pi z}{D}\right) \qquad \text{and} \qquad v = V_0\, e^{-(\pi z/D)} \sin\!\left(\frac{\pi}{4} - \frac{\pi z}{D}\right) \qquad (4.2)$$

where the penetration depth D is determined by the kinematic viscosity of water v, the earth rotation rate ω, and the latitude angle ϕ:

$$D = \pi \sqrt{\frac{v}{\omega \sin\phi}} \qquad (4.3)$$

The dimensionless velocity components u/V_0 and v/V_0 computed from equation 4.2 are plotted to form the spiral curve in figure 4.8. This curve represents the locus of the tips of velocity vectors in the Ekman boundary layer at the top of the ocean. As shown in the figure, the water velocity at the surface is at an angle of 45° to the wind direction. The velocity vector decreases and rotates clockwise (in the Northern Hemisphere) with increasing distance z from the surface.

The velocity vectors in figure 4.8 were plotted for equal increments in the dimensionless depth; namely, for $z/D = 0, 0.1, 0.2, 0.3, \ldots, 1.5$. To keep the plot relatively clean, these values are not identified on the graph, but are described in the caption.

On the computer screen, the rotation of the labels "Wind" and "Surface" was performed by the bitmapping operation described in section 10.4.

The 2-D plot shown in figure 4.9 is the Moody chart, which is probably the most widely used graphic in the field of hydraulics. Almost every introductory textbook in fluid mechanics displays this plot, which presents the friction factor f for pipes as a function of the Reynolds number Re (based on pipe diameter D), and pipe roughness ratio ε/D. The semilog graph lines were muted by drawing them thinner than the data lines. The separate regions of laminar flow and turbulent flow are labeled on the plot. The curves were calculated from the formulas below. The laminar flow equation is an exact solution of the Navier-Stokes equations, and the turbulent formula is obtained by dimensional analysis and matching of expressions across the wall region, with constants empirically determined; see, for example, White (1986).

Laminar flow:

$$f = \frac{64}{Re_D}$$

(4.4)

Turbulent flow:

$$\frac{1}{f^{1/2}} = -2.0 \log\left(\frac{\varepsilon/D}{3.7} + \frac{2.51}{Re_D f^{1/2}}\right)$$

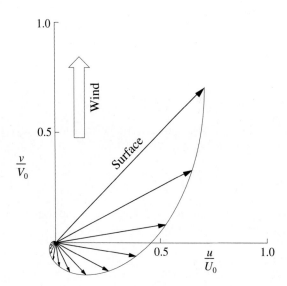

Figure 4.8 The Ekman spiral in the ocean, with velocity vectors plotted at equal increments of depth $\Delta z/D = 0.1$; that is, $z/D = 0, 0.1, 0.2, 0.3, \ldots, 1.5$.

Note that the friction factor f appears on both sides of the equal sign for the turbulent flow case. Accordingly, this equation was plotted by expressing Re in terms of f, and using an iteration procedure to find initial and final f values; see Olfe (1987).

As the Reynolds number Re is increased in pipe flow (for example, by increasing the flow velocity), the friction factor f decreases along the laminar curve, which is a straight line on this semilog plot. When the Reynolds number increases to a value somewhat above 2,000, transition to turbulent pipe flow takes place, and the friction f jumps up to the turbulent curve appropriate for the pipe roughness ratio ε/D. Because the transition depends on additional factors, there is no single curve or set of curves in the transition region, so this region is identified by the shaded area in figure 4.9. The lowest curve on the right corresponds to a smooth pipe; for small roughness values the friction factor initially follows this curve until the Reynolds number becomes sufficiently large that the curve for the appropriate roughness value separates from the smooth pipe curve and asymptotes to a horizontal line.

Examples of Graphs in Nonlinear Science

A new area of research in nonlinear science is described in a best-selling book by Gleick (1987). The new research focuses on the multiplicity of solutions to physical problems and the existence of chaotic behavior. This new perspective has produced important results in

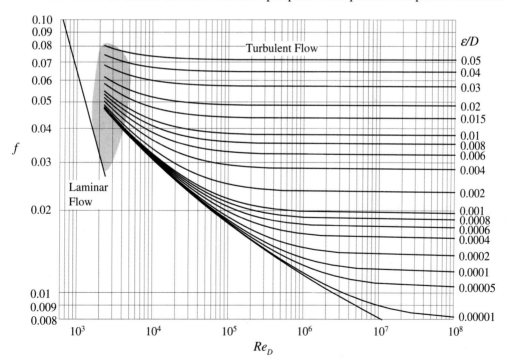

Figure 4.9   The Moody chart: pipe friction factor f as a function of the Reynolds number Re_D, for various values of the roughness ratio ε/D.

many fields, including biology, physics, chemistry, medicine, and engineering. Graphics is an important tool in nonlinear science, not only for displaying results, but also for understanding the complex behavior of the physical phenomena.

Surprisingly, the complex behavior leading to chaos can occur in very simple systems. An important example involves the following nonlinear equation for a variable x_{n+1} in terms of its value at the previous iteration x_n.

$$x_{n+1} = \mu x_n(1-x_n) \tag{4.5}$$

This equation has an interpretation in population dynamics; namely, x_{n+1} is the normalized population of a species in year $n+1$, calculated from the population in the previous year's population x_n. If x_n is small, then the right-hand side of the equation is approximately equal to μx_n, so that the population the following year is proportional to the species population x_n available for mating. The extra term $(1 - x_n)$ restrains the population when x_n is close to unity (x_n is the population normalized by its maximum possible value); therefore, this term models population-limiting factors such as food supply.

Equation 4.5 can be iterated many times to determine if there is a single steady-state solution for the population x. Figure 4.10 plots populations x that occur after a large number of iterations for each value of the rate coefficient μ. Finite solutions are obtained for

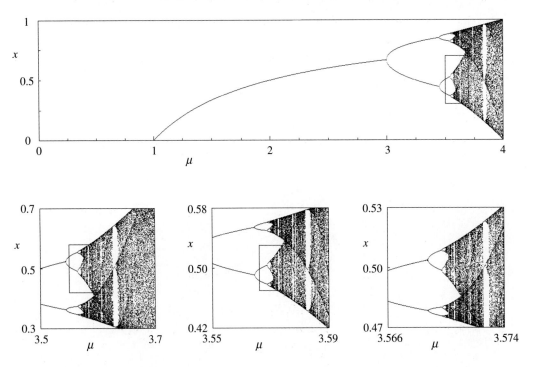

Figure 4.10   Population x as a function of the rate coefficient μ, with the lower plots showing increasingly smaller regions.

$\mu < 4$, with the full μ range from 0 to 4 being presented in the top plot. For $\mu < 1$ the species dies out, and for $1 < \mu < 3$, there is a single steady-state population that increases with μ. As μ increases above 3, two population values occur at large times, with the population shifting between these values every year (as will be shown below). The point at which the two solutions appear is called a *bifurcation* point. At larger μ values the two curves bifurcate to produce four solutions, then eight, and so forth. At many μ values there are an infinite number of solutions, with x chaotically changing from one value to another within a well-defined range of values. To obtain the top plot in figure 4.10, equation 4.5 was first iterated 1,000 times; then the next 100 values of x_{n+1} were plotted as points, with the calculation repeated as μ was incremented by one pixel (picture element) to cover the entire graph. The first 1,000 iterations were carried out before plotting so that the nature of the results would not depend on the initial value of x_n.

Below is a portion of the C program used in constructing the top plot in figure 4.10. The initial x value was chosen as 0.1, and the total length of the diagram was 1,000 pixels on the screen, over which μ (called *mu* in the program) varied from 0 to 4. In the listing below, $i++$ means $i = i+1$; X0 and Y0 are the coordinates of the lower left-hand portion of the diagram on the screen; *SFH* and *SFV* are horizontal and vertical scale factors (each equal to 250 for this case); and the operator (int) changes a floating-point quantity to an integer quantity for use in the SetPixel() function that plots a single point.

```
lengthDiagram = 1000.;
dmu = 4./lengthDiagram;

for (mu=0.; mu<4.; mu=mu+dmu)
{
    x=0.1;
    for (i=1; i<1001; i++)
    {
        x = mu*x*(1-x);
    }
    for (j=1; j<101; j++)
    {
        x = mu*x*(1-x);
        SetPixel((int)(X0+SFH*mu),(int)(Y0-SFV*x);
    }
}
```

The bottom three plots in figure 4.10 show the fine-scale details: the square on the lower left is a blowup of the small rectangular region in the top plot; the middle square plots the detail in the small rectangle shown in the left square; and the right square is a blowup from the middle square. Because the lower plots are focused on regions of decreasing size, more x_{n+1} values were calculated (beyond the initial 1,000 iterations) at each μ value, with only those values falling within the graph boundaries being plotted: 250 values of x_{n+1} were calculated for the lower left plot, 600 for the middle plot, and 1,400 for the right-hand plot.

The lower plots are remarkably similar, a fact that illustrates the nature of the phenomenon; namely, regions with a finite number of solutions continue to be embedded in regions of chaos regardless of how much we zoom in to look at the details. By measuring ratios of distances in the bifurcation regions on smaller and smaller scales, Feigenbaum (1980) was able to determine two universal constants that govern the asymptotic nature of this type of problem. These two Feigenbaum numbers do not depend on the specific form of equation 4.5; that is, different functions of x_n on the right-hand side of equation 4.5 yield the same two numbers.

Graphics is useful not only for mapping out the chaotic regions for equation 4.5, but also for helping us trace the iteration of the equation to better understand how two or more asymptotic solutions can arise. Figure 4.11 shows plots for four different μ values, with x_{n+1} plotted versus x_n for a number of iterations. An initial value $x_0 = 0.16$ was used in each plot, although the general nature of the solution is independent of this initial value. In these plots

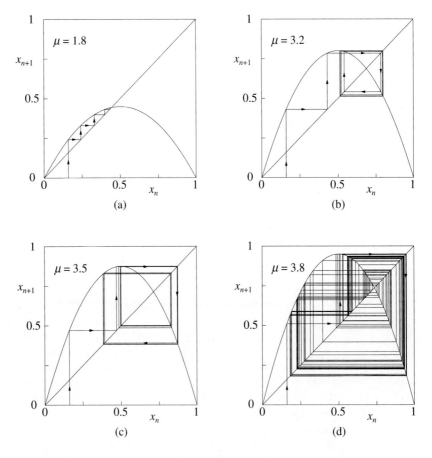

Figure 4.11   Iteration paths plotted for four different values of the rate coefficient μ, with x_{n+1} being the population at iteration $n+1$ and x_n the population at iteration n.

the dark lines are the parabola $y = \mu x(1-x)$, and the diagonal straight line $y = x$, with x and y representing distances along the horizontal and vertical axes.

The thin vertical and horizontal lines illustrate how iterations of equation 4.5 are obtained. From the initial value $x_0 = 0.16$, the vertical line intersection with the parabola provides the first iterated value x_1. Then the horizontal line intersection with the diagonal represents transferring x_1 to the right-hand side of equation 4.5. The next step is a vertical path up to the parabola to determine x_2. The top left plot in figure 4.11 shows that for $\mu = 1.8$ the paths approach a single solution corresponding to the intersection of the diagonal line with the parabola. The top right curve for $\mu = 3.2$ shows the paths quickly locking into a square configuration corresponding to a solution alternating between two values. The $\mu = 3.5$ plot illustrates a solution that cycles between four values, and the final plot illustrates the chaotic nature of the solution for $\mu = 3.8$, with the x_{n+1} values continuing to take on different values with time, but confined within a particular range of values.

EXERCISES

4.1 Draw and dimension the orthographic views of the crank arm shown in figure 4.3.

4.2 Construct the isometric projection of the crank arm, as illustrated in figure 4.3.

4.3 Measure a real object and draw the pertinent orthographic views.

4.4 Write an interactive program to draw bar charts, pie charts, or simple line plots. Labels should be placed in appropriate positions that depend on parameter values entered by the program user. Such programs are discussed in the textbook by Demel and Miller (1984).

4.5 Use a line plot to display technical data for application in your field of interest. Choose your text size and placement carefully, and, if appropriate, use different line widths or line shades of gray to enhance the display.

4.6 Carry out computations of equation 4.5 to produce plots similar to those shown in figure 4.10.

4.7 Select one or more of the following equations to calculate one-dimensional iterated maps similar to those shown in figure 4.10.

(a) $x_{n+1} = \mu x_n - x_n^3$

(b) $x_{n+1} = 1 - \mu x_n^2$

(c) $x_{n+1} = \mu e^{x_n}$

4.8 Compute and plot iteration path diagrams of the type shown in figure 4.11.

BIBLIOGRAPHY

DEMEL, J. T., AND M. J. MILLER, *Introduction to Computer Graphics*. Monterey, Calif.: Brooks/Cole Engineering Division, 1984.

DEWEY, B. R., *Computer Graphics for Engineers*. New York: Harper & Row, 1988.

FEIGENBAUM, M. J., "Universal Behavior in Nonlinear Systems," *Los Alamos Science*, pp. 4–27, Summer 1980.

FIREBAUGH, M. W., *Computer Graphics: Tools for Visualization*. Dubuque, Iowa: Wm. C. Brown Communications, Inc., 1993.

GLEICK, J., *Chaos: Making a New Science.* New York: Viking Penguin Inc., 1987.

LUZADDER, W. J., AND J. M. DUFF, *Fundamentals of Engineering Drawing: With an Introduction to Interactive Computer Graphics for Design and Production,* 11th ed. Englewood Cliffs, N.J.: Prentice-Hall, 1993.

OLFE, D. B., *Fluid Mechanics Programs for the IBM PC.* New York: McGraw-Hill, 1987.

RIETMAN, E., *Exploring the Geometry of Nature: Computer Modeling of Chaos, Fractals, Cellular Automata and Neural Networks.* Blue Ridge Summit, Pa.: Windcrest Books (Division of TAB Books, Inc.), 1989.

SPENCE, W. P., *Engineering Graphics,* 2nd ed. Englewood Cliffs, N.J.: Prentice-Hall, 1988.

THOMPSON, J. M. T., AND H. B. STEWART, *Nonlinear Dynamics and Chaos: Geometric Methods for Engineers and Scientists.* New York: John Wiley and Sons, 1986.

TUFTE, E. R., *The Visual Display of Quantitative Information.* Cheshire, Conn.: Graphics Press, 1983.

WHITE, F. M., *Fluid Mechanics,* 2nd ed. New York: McGraw-Hill, 1986.

5

Arrays of Graphical Elements

In this chapter we use repeated graphics elements in arrays. A relatively simple two-dimensional array of circles and squares is shown above; it is a copy of artist Vasarely's work *Canopus* (© 1994 Artists Rights Society [ARS], New York/ADAGP, Paris). More complex rectangular arrays in art and pattern design are described in section 5.1 below. Although it may seem disrespectful to reduce good works of art to programmed formulas, I find that this activity helps me more fully observe and appreciate the art.

Other sections in this chapter cover the circular array of teeth on a spur gear and examples of repeated elements in architectural design. AutoCAD methods are discussed in addition to programming examples.

This chapter considers only arrays of graphical elements. Procedures for using arrays in programs to store line and surface data are discussed in chapter 8.

5.1 RECTANGULAR ARRAYS IN ART AND PATTERN DESIGN

The above painting is relatively easy to construct as a program: a large black rectangle is overlaid with a smaller white rectangle; then two rectangular arrays of filled circles are drawn—a 3 × 2 array of black circles and a 3 × 3 array of white circles; and the work is completed with a 5 × 5 array of small black squares. Each rectangular array may be programmed as nested loops; for example, the following program lines construct the 3 × 2 array of circles at the top of the drawing (also shown below).

```
x0 = 200;
y0 = 50;
diameter = 20;
for (i=0; i<=2; i++)
{
    for (j=0; j<=1; j++)
    {
        x1 = x0 + i*diameter;
        y1 = y0 + j*diameter;
        x2 = x1 + diameter;
        y2 = y1 + diameter;
        SetRect(r,x1,y1,x2,y2);
        FillOval(r,black);
    }
}
```

In the above program fragment, $x0$ and $y0$ are the coordinates of the upper left part of the array (the vertical coordinate is positive in the downward direction), with the coordinates $x1,y1$ and $x2,y2$ defining a variable square (established by the SetRect() function) in which the filled circles are drawn with the function FillOval(). There are three circles in the horizontal direction because the entry $i++$ increments i by one unit from values 0 through 2.

The 3 × 2 array of filled circles could also be easily constructed with AutoCAD. A circle can be filled with a solid hatch pattern, or the DONUT (or DOUGHNUT) command can be used with the inner radius set equal to zero; see section 3.2. The resulting filled circle can then be put into a 3 × 2 array with the ARRAY command. Below is the set of Auto-CAD inputs that construct the same array of six filled circles as the C program fragment above. Here we start with the circle on the lower left, and recall that in AutoCAD the vertical coordinate is positive in the upward direction.

```
Command: DONUT
Inside diameter <0.5000>: 0
Outside diameter <1.0000>: 20
Center of doughnut: 210,80
Center of doughnut: (RETURN)

Command: ARRAY
Select objects: (Pick donut with mouse button)
Select objects: (RETURN)
```

```
Rectangular of Polar array (R/P): R
Number of rows (---) <1>: 2
Number of columns (|||) <1>: 3
Unit cell or distance between rows (---): 20
Distance between columns (|||): 20
```

In the AutoCAD commands above, default values appear in the < > brackets. The six filled circles could have been placed with the DONUT command by entering six sets of coordinates, rather than by terminating the command with the RETURN key. The ARRAY command is very convenient for large arrays of objects. (In the next section the polar array option will be used to construct a gear.)

Completion of *Canopus* requires drawing white filled circles in addition to the black filled circles (here we are considering the background color to be white; on your screen the background may be black, so for your screen image interchange black and white in the following discussion). The fill color may changed in a program; for example, by the Macintosh QuickDraw function FillOval(*r,white*). With AutoCAD the white circles in a black rectangle may be constructed by using the HATCH command. First, the outside of the bottom black rectangle is drawn with the LINE command, and then the outlines of the six circles are drawn with the CIRCLE and ARRAY commands. Next, the HATCH command is used with the U,N option for a user-defined hatch pattern in the normal style. The spacing between hatch lines may be selected sufficiently small to yield a black fill, and on the *select object* prompt the rectangle and six circles may be selected by entering W and windowing around the objects. AutoCAD then puts the black fill between the rectangle and the circles, and in the interior regions between circles. The final result is an array of white circles on a black rectangle.

An approximation of a more complex painting—*Supernovae* by Vasarely—is shown in figure 5.1. This figure was programmed by modifying squares and circles with empirical formulas as they are drawn on a 27 × 43 array. The modifications to the basic rectangular array include changing the sizes of the squares with horizontal and vertical distances in rows 4 through 12 from the top of the figure, distorting the square to a polygon on row 16 from the top, and at selected positions in the bottom part of the figure, replacing squares with circles that increase in size proportional to their horizontal position.

The shearing distortion of the square in row 16 of the painting *Supernovae* can be achieved by programming a polygon fill as discussed in section 3.2; for example, on the Macintosh, the polygon is first traced out between program lines that call the OpenPoly() and ClosePoly() functions, and then the polygon is filled using a FillPoly() or PaintPoly() function. With AutoCAD we could draw a polygon with a LINE or PLINE command and then fill it with a dense hatching. It is simpler, however, in this case to use the PLINE statement with a variable line thickness. For example, the sheared square shown below is drawn in AutoCAD with the following commands.

Figure 5.1   A computer graphics approximation of the oil painting *Supernovae* by the artist Vasarely; © 1994 Artists Rights Society (ARS), New York/ADAGP, Paris.

```
Command: PLINE
From point: 10,10
Current line width is 0.0000
Arc/Close/Halfwidth/Length/Undo/Width/<Endpoint of line>: W
```

```
Starting width <0.0000>:  (RETURN)
Ending width <0.0000>: 12
Arc/Close/Halfwidth/Length/Undo/Width/<Endpoint of line>: 20,20
Arc/Close/Halfwidth/Length/Undo/Width/<Endpoint of line>: W
Starting width <12.0000>:  (RETURN)
Ending width <0.0000>: 0
Arc/Close/Halfwidth/Length/Undo/Width/<Endpoint of line>: 30,30
```

The above statements draw, at 45°, a polyline that starts out with zero thickness, increases linearly to a thickness of 12 units, and then decreases to zero thickness. The above commands can produce the full range of polygons in row 16 of the painting; for example, a filled square would result if the maximum thickness were set equal to the total length of the polyline.

The representation of the painting *Supernovae* exhibits an optical illusion; namely, light gray circles seem to appear in the intersections of the white lines between the black squares. A more pronounced illusion appears in figure 5.2, where rows of alternating black and white squares are shifted by a half square. The straight horizontal lines separating the squares appear to slope and curve; this effect is called the café-wall illusion.

The rectangular arrays considered above are based on repetitive two-dimensional patterns. Designs that are almost, but not quite, repetitive may be produced by the simple program listed below. In this program the equation for a circle ($z = x^2 + y^2$ with z being the radius squared) is truncated to an integer. The point (x,y) is plotted as a black point if the truncated value of z is even; otherwise, the point is not plotted (left white). In this program the integer coordinates $x0$ and $y0$ simply set the upper left starting point on the screen.

```
for (i=1; i<101; i++)
{
    for (j=1; j<101; j++)
    {
        x =side*i/100;
        y = side*j/100;
        z = x*x + y*y;
        c = (int) z % 2;
        if (c == 0) SetPixel(x0+i,y0+j);
    }
}
```

Figure 5.2 Staggered filled squares produce the café-wall illusion. This illusion is discussed in an article by J. Walker, "The Café-Wall Illusion, in Which Rows of Tiles Tilt That Should Not Tilt at All," in The Amateur Scientist column, pp. 138–141, *Scientific American,* November 1988.

The modulus operator % returns the remainder after (int) z is divided by the number 2. If c is 0 then a black pixel is plotted with the SetPixel() function; otherwise, the pixel is left as white. The maximum values of i and j were set equal to 100 for the upper left-hand plot of figure 5.3; larger values would continue the pattern over a larger area.

In the above program the parameter *side* is divided by the value 100. If *side* = 100, the variable c alternates between even and odd values, yielding a uniform gray pattern of

Figure 5.3   Patterns produced by truncation of the equation for a circle.

black and white pixels. Similarly, if *side* divides evenly into 100 or into a small multiple of 100, a repetitive pattern will develop. For example, the middle row of figure 5.3 shows patterns for *side* = 10, 25, and 80, from left to right. The top row of the figure illustrates a nonrepetitive pattern for *side* = 87, with the right-hand side being a blowup of the lower-left corner (2 × 2 pixel squares are filled with black in the blowup).

At the bottom of figure 5.3 the quiltlike pattern was produced for *side* = 89 by replacing the parameter 2 with 3 after the modulus operator % in order to divide the pattern into three shades: black, gray, and white, corresponding to *c* values of 0, 1, and 2, respectively. Also, for this bottom pattern the shades were put into squares of 2 × 2 pixels. For color output, different colors can be assigned instead of shades of gray, and the modulus parameter can be increased above the value 3 to accommodate any desired number of colors. Color examples are given in an article by Dewdney (1986).

5.2 CIRCULAR ARRAY APPLICATION: THE SPUR GEAR

Spur gears have constant thickness, and the gear teeth normally have a shape that follows an involute curve. Figure 5.4 illustrates a spur gear, including definitions of geometric quantities. Two different procedures for drawing a spur gear will be described: first, programming the equations, and second, using AutoCAD for the drafting method outlined in mechanical engineering books (see, for example, Shigley and Mitchell 1983). For each method, a half tooth is constructed, then mirrored to form a whole tooth, and finally the tooth is arrayed around a circle to form the complete gear.

Gears mesh at their pitch circles, and, as illustrated in figure 5.4, the thickness of a tooth equals the width of space between teeth at the pitch circle. The involute curve form-

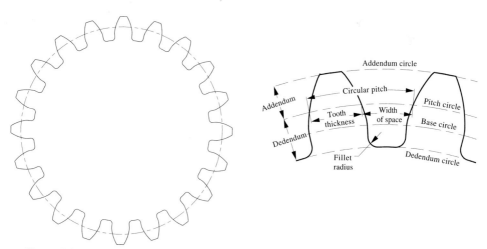

Figure 5.4   A drawing of a spur gear and a diagram defining parameters used in drawing the gear teeth.

ing a tooth starts at the base circle, which lies between the dedendum and pitch circle, and has a radius r_b related to the pitch circle radius r_p and a quantity ϕ_{press} called the *pressure angle*.

$$r_b = r_p \cos\phi_{press} \tag{5.1}$$

The curved (involute) part of the gear tooth extends from the base circle to the addendum circle at the top of the tooth. The tooth profile extends downward from the base circle along a radius until it meets a fillet that curves to the bottom of the space, which is a dedendum distance b below the pitch circle. For the gear shown in figure 5.4, the following values were used: pitch diameter $d = 1.0$ in., number of teeth $N = 20$, and pressure angle $\phi_{press} = 20°$. The pitch diameter d and the number of teeth N define the diametral pitch $P = N/d$, from which the remaining quantities are determined from formulas for standard interchangeable teeth: addendum $a = 1/P = 0.05$ in., dedendum $b = 1.25/P = 0.0625$ in., and fillet radius $r_{fillet} = 0.3/P = 0.015$ in.

Programming a Gear Drawing

An involute curve is the path that the end of a length of tape follows as it is stripped from the circumference of a circle. In figure 5.5 the straight length ρ of tape equals its length along the circle; therefore, the following relations hold:

$$\rho = r_b \tan\phi = r_b\theta$$

which gives

$$\phi = \tan^{-1}\theta \tag{5.2}$$

Equation 5.2 and the right triangle in figure 5.5 provide the following relation.

$$\theta = \tan\phi = \frac{\rho}{r_b} = \frac{\sqrt{r^2 - r_b^2}}{r_b} \tag{5.3}$$

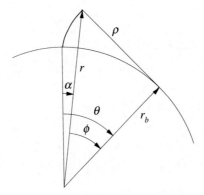

Figure 5.5 Variables used to calculate the involute curve for a gear tooth.

The angle α may be expressed in terms of θ.

$$\alpha = \theta - \phi = \theta - \tan^{-1}\theta \qquad (5.4)$$

The above equations are used to calculate the gear outline by the following procedures.

1. Divide the radius into 10 or so values between the base radius r_b and the tooth top at $r_a = r_p + a$, where a is the addendum distance.
2. Increment a loop over the r values, calculating θ from equation 5.3 and α from equation 5.4. The r and α values can be used to calculate x- and y-coordinates on the involute curve, and store the results in the following arrays: $x[i] = r\sin\alpha$ and $y[i] = r\cos\alpha$. See the first loop in the program fragment listed below, where i is incremented to a maximum value $imax = 10$ to obtain a smooth involute curve.
3. To start with the top tooth in a vertical position, as shown in figure 5.4, shift the angle α by the amount σ, which corresponds to the angle subtended by a tooth half-thickness plus the angle subtended by the portion of the involute curve between the base circle and the pitch circle (where tooth thickness is measured).

$$\sigma = \frac{t}{2r_p} + \tan(\phi_{press}) - \phi_{press} \qquad (5.5)$$

The first term on the right-hand side of equation 5.5 corresponds to the angle subtended by a half-tooth thickness; the last two terms represent the angle α subtended by the involute curve segment between radii r_b and r_p.

4. A loop over all n teeth is used to draw the involute curves corresponding to the curved left sides of the gear teeth by means of the formulas given in the program listing below; see the second loop over n values of j. The angle variable *ang* in the program gives the starting angle for the involute curve at each tooth, with the variables *xpt* and *ypt* of a point along a curve obtained in terms of $x(i)$, $y[i]$, and *ang* by a transformation representing the two-dimensional rotation about the gear center (such transformations are the subject of chapter 10).

```
dr = (ra-rb)/imax;
num = (double) n;

for (i=0; i<=imax; i++)
{
    r = rb+i*dr;
    theta = sqrt((r*r)/(rb*rb) - 1.);
    alpha = theta - atan(theta);
    x[i] = r*sin(alpha);
    y[i] = r*cos(alpha);
}
for (j=0; j<n; j++)
{
    ang = 2.*j*PI/num - sigma;
```

```
for (i=0; i<=imax; i++)
{
    xpt = x[i]*cos(ang) + y[i]*sin(ang);
    ypt = -x[i]*sin(ang) + y[i]*cos(ang);
    if (i == 0)
        MoveTo((int)(x0+sf*x),(int)(y0-sf*y));
    LineTo((int)(x0+sf*x),(int)(y0-sf*y));
}
}
```

In the above program listing, the $x0$ and $y0$ parameters determine the screen location of the gear, and *sf* is a scale factor that sets the size of the gear.

5. The curved right sides of the gear teeth are drawn by the same program lines as above, except with $x[i]$ replaced by $-x[i]$ and $-sigma$ replaced by $+sigma$.

6. The ends of the right and left involute curves at the addendum are connected to draw the tops of the gear teeth.

7. The end of each involute curve at the base circle is extended radially inward toward the gear center until it meets the start of the fillet at $r = r_p - b + r_{fillet}$.

8. The fillet radii are drawn as quarter circles, and their ends are connected to form the space bottom at the dendendum.

Parameters in the gear program can be readily changed to calculate a gear profile with different dimensions or a different number of teeth.

Constructing a Gear with AutoCAD Drafting Methods

Figure 5.6 illustrates the drafting method used to construct the involute curve for a gear tooth.

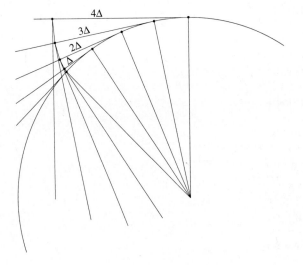

Figure 5.6   The base circle, radii, and tangent lines used to construct the involute curve for a gear tooth.

The gear can be drawn directly with AutoCAD by means of the following steps:

1. Draw a circle with the base radius.
2. Draw a vertical radius and a tangent to the radius.
3. Array these two lines for a total of five items over the included angle of 45° as shown in figure 5.6. Although the exact number is arbitrary, five radii are used to provide sufficient resolution for the involute curve; also, 45° is selected to ensure that the involute curve extends past the addendum circle.
4. Calculate the circumferential distance Δ between two radii, and offset the radii distances of Δ, 2Δ, 3Δ, and 4Δ as shown in figure 5.6. Note that Δ equals the base radius r_b times the angle (in radians) between adjacent radii.
5. Connect the offset intersections with a polyline (PLINE).
6. Use PEDIT with Fit to smooth the polyline.
7. Draw the addendum circle, and trim and erase unneeded lines.
8. Draw the pitch circle and determine the angular distance between the 45° radius and the polyline at the pitch circle.
9. Draw a mirror line as a radius through the tooth center, as determined by the half-tooth angular distance and the angular distance determined in the previous step.
10. Draw the dedendum circle.
11. Draw a radius to the bottom of the involute curve and construct the fillet between this radius and the dedendum circle.
12. Trim and erase unneeded lines and mirror the remaining lines across the tooth center.
13. Array the tooth around the gear.
14. Rotate the gear so that the top tooth is in a vertical position.

The ARRAY command can be used in step 3 to array lines around a circular arc.

```
Command: ARRAY
Select objects: (select lines with the mouse)
Rectangular or Polar (R/P): P
Center of array: (select gear center with mouse)
Number of items: 5
Angle to fill (+=CCW,-=CW): 45
Rotate objects as they are copied <Y>: (RETURN)
```

In step 6 above, the polyline edit command PEDIT is used to draw a smooth curve between the polyline vertex points. As will be discussed in chapter 7, this smooth curve is formed with two arcs placed between adjacent polyline vertices. Step 6 is carried out as follows.

```
Command: PEDIT
Select polyline: (select with mouse)
```

```
Close/Join/Width/Edit vertex/Fit curve/.../eXit <X>: F
Close/Join/Width/Edit vertex/Fit curve/.../eXit <X>: (RETURN)
```

In step 7, the AutoCAD command TRIM may be used to trim lines where they cross other lines; see section 1.5.

The small angular distance in step 8 can be measured with the DIST command, which displays the angle as well as the distance between two selected points. First, however, the UNITS command must be used to increase the number of fractional places for the angle display (for example, to 4) from the default value of 0. The first point selected below is the gear center, and the second is the pitch circle–polyline intersection. The resulting angle is subtracted from 135° because the 45° line is measured from the vertical, whereas the default reference direction for angles is counterclockwise from the horizontal direction.

```
Command: DIST
First point: (select with mouse)
Second point: (select with mouse)
Distance = (calculated distance displayed on screen)
```

The fillet in step 11 can be drawn directly by using the AutoCAD FILLET command discussed in section 3.1.

In step 12 the following MIRROR command is used.

```
Command: MIRROR
Select objects: W (Window the lines to be mirrored)
First point of mirror line: (select with mouse)
Second point: (select with mouse)
Delete old objects? <N> (RETURN)
```

In the final step the entire gear is rotated by the appropriate amount (as determined from the calculation of the mirror line angle) to put the top gear tooth in a vertical position. The ROTATE command performs this task.

```
Command: ROTATE
Select objects: W (window the entire gear)
Base point: (select gear center)
<Rotation angle>/Reference: (enter angle)
```

The entered angle should be negative for rotation in the clockwise direction.

In addition to rotating the gear, we can change its size with the SCALE command. Also, we could put the gear into a block and insert it at various locations with different scales and rotation angles. The BLOCK command is discussed in the next section. Unlike the programmed version of the gear, however, the number of teeth or other configuration parameters cannot be changed unless you reconstruct the gear from scratch. AutoLISP can be used to incorporate a programmed version of the gear into AutoCAD.

5.3 AUTOCAD METHODS FOR REPEATED DESIGN ELEMENTS IN ARCHITECTURE

The preceding sections presented methods for constructing rectangular and polar (circular) arrays of graphic entities. These methods can be used in architectural design; for example, figure 5.7 presents plan views as examples of polar arrays.

The cable dome on the left of the figure starts in the center with a tension ring drawn with the DONUT command and extends to a compression ring at the outer edge. The compression ring is drawn with a single straight PLINE segment (of appropriate thickness), which is put into a polar array around the dome center to produce a total of 16 segments. Ridge cables extend from the tension ring to the ends of the segments on the compression ring, with each ridge cable passing over three posts that are drawn with the DONUT command. Valley cables extend radially outward between the ridge cables.

The drawing on the right in figure 5.7 illustrates an upper-roof structure inside the interior pair of concentric circles, with the region between the inner and outer pairs of concentric circles representing a lower, annular roof structure that cantilevers outside the pavilion from an external compression ring. The column in the center flairs out at the ceiling to meet the ribs, which are drawn as circular arcs between the column and the pavilion wall (represented by the interior pair of concentric circles). The circular arcs representing the ceiling ribs may be drawn on AutoCAD with the ARC command by identifying the two end points and the arc radius. It is convenient to draw radial lines and an inner circle so the arc end points may be readily identified with intersection points.

```
Command: ARC
Center/<Start point>: (pick intersection point with mouse)
Center/End/<Second point>: E
End point: (pick intersection point with mouse)
```

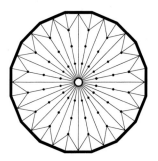 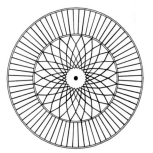

Figure 5.7   Left, plan view of the roof structure of the Seoul gymnastics stadium, designed by engineer David H. Geiger for the 1988 Olympics (AutoCAD drawing based on dimensions in "Structural Gymnastics for the Olympics," pp. 128–135 in *Architectural Record,* September 1988). Right, plan view of the Kursaal pavilion at Ostia Lido, Italy, designed by engineer Pier Luigi Nervi (AutoCAD drawing based on dimensions in P. L. Nervi, *Aesthetics and Technology in Building.* Cambridge, Mass.: Harvard University Press, 1965).

```
Angle/Direction/Radius/<Center point>: R
Radius: (input value)
```

The arcs shown in the figure have thickness. We can add this thickness by changing the arc to a polyline and setting the polyline thickness.

```
Command: PEDIT
Select polyline: (select arc with mouse)
Entity selected is not a polyline.
Do you want to turn it into one <Y>: (RETURN)
Close/Join/Width/Edit vertex/Fit curve/.../eXit <X>: W
Enter new width for all segments: (enter value)
Close/Join/Width/Edit vertex/Fit curve/.../eXit <X>: (RETURN)
```

The window shown in figure 5.8 can be used for practicing the rectangular and polar ARRAY commands, the MIRROR command, and the OFFSET command. With the latter command, one circular arc drawn at the top of the window may be used to construct the remaining arcs by simply selecting the arc and entering the offset distance. The arcs increase in size as they are offset to larger radii.

```
Command: OFFSET
Offset distance or Through <last>: T
Select object to offset: (select with mouse)
Side to offset: (select with mouse)
Through point: (select with mouse)
```

Figures 5.9 and 5.10 show additional plan views where OFFSET, MIRROR, and ARRAY commands can be used to greatly simplify the construction of the drawing. In figure 5.9 the stepped sides of the Mayan pyramid are drawn as right-angle corners that can

Figure 5.8   Window design by Sir Christopher Wren.

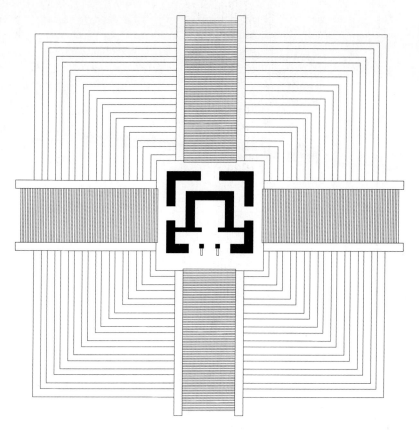

Figure 5.9   Plan view of a Mayan pyramid with temple building on top, at Chichén Itzá, Mexico (constructed A.D. 950). This AutoCAD drawing was adapted from an illustration in *Drawings of Great Buildings,* by W. Blaser and M. Stucky. Basel, Switzerland: Birkhäuser Verlag, 1983.

be constructed with the OFFSET command. In figure 5.10 the right-angle corners represent rows of seating at a convention center.

The AutoCAD command BLOCK is useful for a variety of purposes. With this command any drawing or part of a drawing can be identified and saved as a block. When designated as a block the selected parts are removed from the screen display. However, the block drawing may be inserted at any number of points. Furthermore, the block drawing may be rescaled in the *x, y,* and *z* directions and rotated as it is inserted. For example, the window of figure 5.8 may be put into a block and transformed into the windows shown in figure 5.11.

A drawing file can be considerably reduced in size if the BLOCK command rather than the ARRAY command is used to repeat a complex drawing element. The ARRAY command copies the elements and therefore repeats all of the drawing commands in the drawing file, whereas the BLOCK command saves the commands just once and gives the location, scale, and rotation of each occurrence or instance of the drawing element (in computer graphics

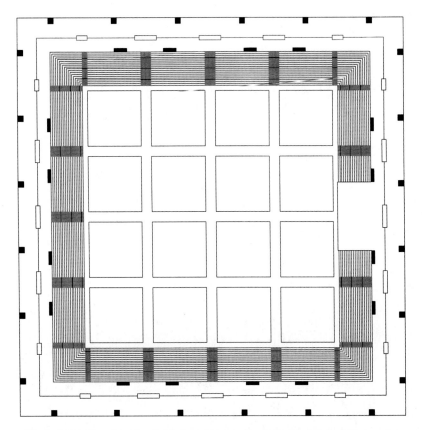

Figure 5.10 Plan view of a design for a Chicago Convention Center, by Mies van der Rohe (1953–1954). The dimensions for this AutoCAD drawing were obtained from the book *Mies van der Rohe* by D. Spaeth. New York: Rizzoli, 1985.

the term *instancing* is often used to describe the operation of repeating a graphic item at different locations). For example, the single window of figure 5.8 has a drawing file of 90K bytes, which reduces slightly to 77K when the window is put into a block. Using the block to insert the window at 20 locations increases the size of the drawing file only slightly, with the 20-window drawing still listed as 77K bytes in the computer memory. Using the ARRAY command on the window of figure 5.8 to produce 20 windows yields a drawing file of 1.4M bytes, which is almost 20 times as large as the file in which the BLOCK command was used. As noted above, this result was to be expected because with the ARRAY command the 1,860 individual drawing entities that make up the window are repeated and saved for each instance of the window, whereas with the BLOCK command the drawing entities are saved just once.

A block for the window shown in figure 5.8 is set up with the following commands.

```
Command: BLOCK
Block name (or ?): WinBlock
Insertion base point: (pick lower left corner with mouse)
```

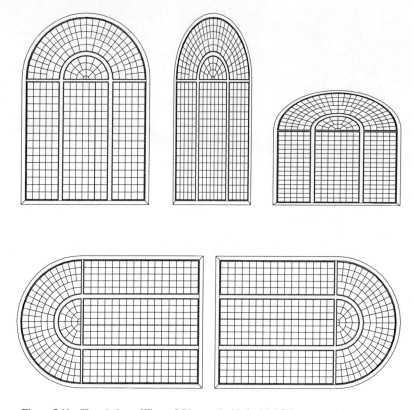

Figure 5.11   The window of Figure 5.8 inserted with the BLOCK command at various positions, with scaling and rotation.

```
Select objects: W (window around drawing)
 1860 objects found.
Select objects: (RETURN)
```

To insert the window block into an array of 20 windows, the multiple insert command MINSERT is used.

```
Command: MINSERT
Block name (or ?): WinBlock
 Insertion point: .75,7
 X scale factor <1>: 0.08
 Y scale factor (default = X): (RETURN)
 Rotation angle <0>: (RETURN)
Number of rows (---) <1>: 2
Number of columns (|||) <1>: 10
Unit cell or distance between rows (---): 1
Distance between columns (|||): 0.7
```

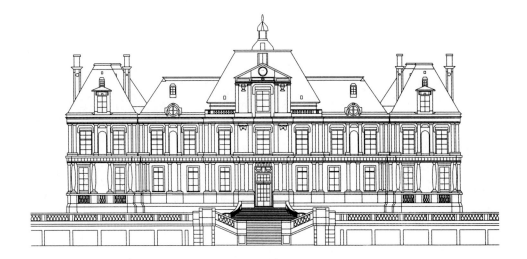

Figure 5.12   Building elevations drawn on AutoCAD. Top, Chateau of Maisons, drawn on AutoCAD by Michael Riley, from a photograph in the book *The World Atlas of Architecture*. London: Mitchell Beazley Publishers, 1984. Bottom, the National Theater, drawn on AutoCAD by Harbinder Singh Virdee.

With the BLOCK command the window made up of 1,860 objects (drawing entities) is put into a block named WinBlock. This block is scaled down by a factor of 0.08 so that it will fit onto the same size paper when it is inserted into a 10 × 2 rectangular array. The drawing of the 20 windows will have just 20 objects because each block insertion is just one object. If you wish to access individual drawing entities within a window drawing, you can use the EXPLODE command to free the drawing entities from their grouping as a block.

To insert one block at a time, use the INSERT command, which provides the same first five questions as the MINSERT command above. Figure 5.11 shows an example of using the INSERT command to distort the window block by specifying unequal X and Y scale factors, and to rotate it by specifying nonzero rotation angles.

The BLOCK and MINSERT commands can be used to considerably reduce the memory requirements for drawings such as the building elevations shown in figure 5.12.

EXERCISES

5.1 Use programming or CAD to produce the following array that suggests the 1964 painting *Night Wall* by artist Will Insley.

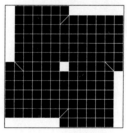

5.2 Select and reproduce a work of art that has repetitive simple shapes that can be readily programmed or drawn with CAD software.

5.3 Use programming or CAD to draw a gear with 10 teeth and a pitch diameter of 0.5 in. with the remaining quantities the same as the example in section 5.2.

5.4 Mesh the 10-tooth gear of exercise 5.3 with the 20-tooth gear drawn in section 5.2.

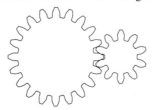

5.5 Use polar arrays to draw automobile wheels. Either copy the ones shown below, or construct some new ones.

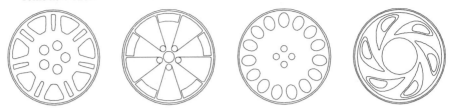

5.6 Draw one or both of the tree grates shown below.

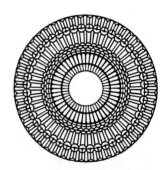

5.7 Reproduce on your CAD system one of the drawings shown in figures 5.7–5.10.

5.8 Find and reproduce an architectural plan or detail that has repeated elements in rectangular and/or polar arrays.

5.9 The diagrams below represent plan views of four pavilion roofs in a house designed by San Diego architect Wallace E. Cunningham. Reproduce these designs by using the POLYGON command in AutoCAD to draw an octagon; saving the octagon as a block; and inserting the block with reduced scale and rotation in order to draw the inscribed octagons. Because the half angle subtended at a side of an octagon is 22.5°, alternate inscribed octagons are rotated by 22.5°; also, the octagons decrease in scale from one to the next by the ratio $\cos(22.5°)$ = 0.92387953.

5.10 Use rectangular arrays to draw the keyboard of your computer. The following drawing by Darby Crow is two-dimensional, but has a 3-D appearance because it is drawn as an oblique view. After being arrayed, many of the individual keys in this drawing had to be trimmed to fit neatly behind adjacent keys.

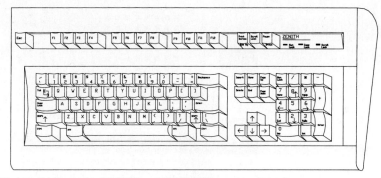

5.11 With AutoCAD use the BLOCK and MINSERT commands to draw a computer motherboard. The motherboard shown below was drawn by Marcus Chacon.

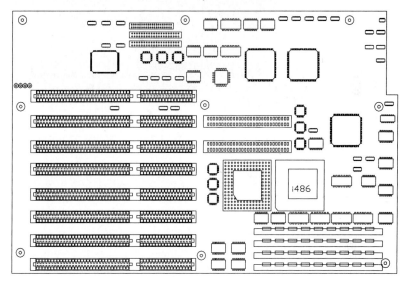

BIBLIOGRAPHY

AutoCAD Release 12 Reference Manual. Sausalito, Calif.: Autodesk, Inc, 1992.

DEWDNEY, A. K., "Wallpaper for the Mind: Computer Images That Are Almost, But Not Quite, Repetitive," in Computer Recreations column, *Scientific American,* pp. 14–23, September 1986.

MITCHELL, W. J., R. S. LIGGETT, AND T. KVAN, *The Art of Computer Graphics Programming: A Structured Introduction for Architects and Designers.* New York: Van Nostrand Reinhold, 1987.

SHIGLEY, J. E., AND L. D. MITCHELL, *Mechanical Engineering Design,* 4th ed. New York: McGraw-Hill Book Company, 1983.

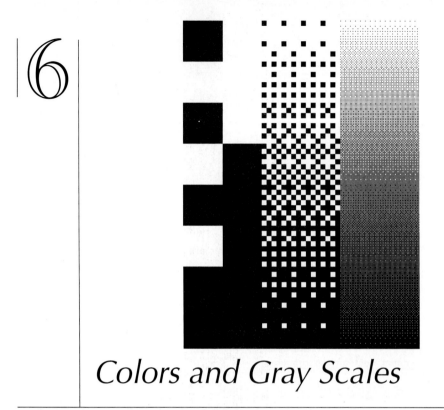

Colors and Gray Scales

Color is not one-dimensional or two-dimensional; it is three-dimensional. One way of visualizing the three dimensions is to separate color into *hue, saturation,* and *brightness.* Hue and saturation are the chromatic attributes of color, whereas brightness (similar to *lightness, value, intensity,* or *luminosity*) is achromatic. Hue is the spectral part of color; that is, hue determines whether the color is similar to red, yellow, green, blue, etc. Saturation determines the purity of the color. Colors of zero saturation are shades of gray, varying from black to white as brightness increases from zero to its maximum value.

The illustration at the top of this page shows how gray scales may be produced by ordered *dithering.* On the left side of the illustration, 4 nonwhite shades of gray are produced as black squares and are filled in a 2 × 2 matrix. In the middle part of the illustration, 16 nonwhite shades are produced in a 4 × 4 matrix. On the right, 64 shades result from an 8 × 8 matrix. Dithering is also useful for expanding the number of colors. For example, if your color graphics adapter is set to a mode that produces only 16 colors, then your rendering (on AutoCAD, AutoShade, AutoVision, or other software) will expand the number of colors to 256 by dithering a number of different hues.

Color is a complex subject because it involves human perception in addition to the physical characteristics of light. A given color does not require a unique formation; it can be constructed in a variety of ways by mixing three or more other colors. To quantify color mixing, the Commission Internationale de l'Eclairage (CIE) developed a chromaticity diagram in 1931. The CIE diagram was based on a large number of experiments in which subjects determined the amounts of three standard colors that combined to match any given color. New color-application tools relate color models for computers to color-perception models (CIE diagram) and to color characteristics of monitors and printers.

6.1 COLOR MODELS

The color models discussed in this section were developed for convenient visualization of the three-dimensional character of color. These models can be readily implemented into computer graphics systems. Transformations relate the three color variables of one system to the variables of any other system. Before the first color models (RGB and CMY color cubes) are considered, the concepts of additive and subtractive color mixing must be reviewed.

Color Mixing

Additive and subtractive color mixing are shown in figure 6.1 and color plate 1. Additive mixing corresponds to adding light sources, such as overlapping beams of colored lights. Also, additive mixing applies to the red, green, and blue dots (or lines) on a computer monitor. Although a magnifying glass will reveal individual colored dots on a computer screen, at normal viewing distances the human eye fuses the dots to form a full set of colors. With additive mixing, red and green produce yellow; green and blue yield cyan; blue and red combine to form magenta; and red, green, and blue produce white. Black corresponds to the absence of any light source.

Subtractive color mixing (filtering) applies to colors on paper illuminated by ambient white light. The colors may overlap, or they may be separate small dots. An example is the the small cyan, magenta, and yellow dots produced by an ink-jet printer. For subtractive mixing, cyan and magenta combine to form blue; magenta and yellow yield red; yellow and cyan form green; and cyan, magenta, and yellow produce black. The ink dyes subtract color from the ambient white light. For example, cyan filters out red in the ambient light, and magenta filters green; therefore cyan combined with magenta results in the

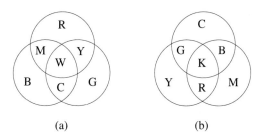

(a)   (b)

Figure 6.1 Diagrams illustrating (a) additive color mixing and (b) subtractive color mixing. The letters indicate the colors: R, red; G, green; B, blue, C, cyan; M, magenta; Y, yellow; W, white; and K, black.

color blue being reflected; see figure 6.2. Similarly, magenta together with yellow filters green and blue, with the result that white light reflects as red.

The RGB and CMY Color Cubes

The RGB color cube maps out color space by plotting red, green, and blue along perpendicular axes; see figure 6.3a. Colors are obtained by additive color mixing of the three primary colors (RGB). Accordingly, grays lie along the diagonal of the cube, from the origin (black) to the far corner (white). Along the cube face on which red = 0, green and blue combine, reaching saturated cyan at the corner corresponding to maximum amounts of green and blue. As illustrated in the figure, magenta and yellow lie on the corners of other faces.

The CMY cube in figure 6.3b is similar to the RGB cube, except that subtractive color mixing determines the colors in the cube. Grays occur along the cube diagonal, starting with white at the origin and ending with black at the far corner, corresponding to maximum amounts of cyan, magenta, and yellow.

The CMY values for a given color may be obtained from the RGB values by means of the following transformation, in which the CMY and the RGB colors are each normalized to a maximum value of 1.

$$
\begin{bmatrix} C \\ M \\ Y \end{bmatrix} = \begin{bmatrix} 1 \\ 1 \\ 1 \end{bmatrix} - \begin{bmatrix} R \\ G \\ B \end{bmatrix}
\tag{6.1}
$$

Equation 6.1 is given in terms of column vectors, presented in the form of 1×3 matrices; see appendix C for a review of matrix operations.

The above transformation may be readily interpreted for the cases shown in figures 6.2a–b. For example, figure 6.2a corresponds to $R = 0$, $G = 1$, and $B = 1$, which transform to $C = 1$, $M = 0$, and $Y = 0$. For figure 6.2b, $R = 0$, $G = 0$, and $B = 1$, which correspond to $C = 1$, $M = 1$, and $Y = 0$.

The columns in equation 6.1 may be transposed to provide the following transformation for normalized RGB values in terms of normalized CMY values.

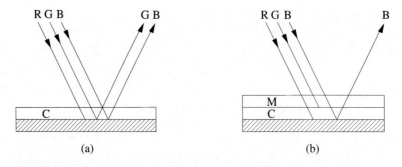

(a)   (b)

Figure 6.2   Diagrams illustrate the interaction of white light (W = R + G + B) incident on paper (cross-hatched layer) coated with the color cyan (C) in (a) and the colors cyan and magenta (M) in (b).

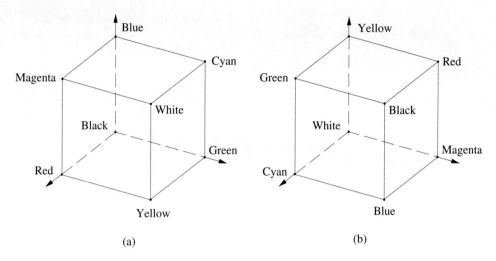

Figure 6.3   Color cubes: (a) the RGB cube for additive color mixing and (b) the CMY cube for subtractive mixing.

$$\begin{bmatrix} R \\ G \\ B \end{bmatrix} = \begin{bmatrix} 1 \\ 1 \\ 1 \end{bmatrix} - \begin{bmatrix} C \\ M \\ Y \end{bmatrix} \qquad (6.2)$$

Most color printers have four colors: black *(K)* is added to CMY because controlling the quality of a black produced by mixing cyan, magenta, and yellow inks is difficult. Also, black is the most frequently used color, so that for ink jets, for example, it is common to have one black ink cartridge, and one color cartridge that has separate bladders for the cyan, magenta, and yellow inks. For the CMYK system the amount of K (black) in a given color will equal the minimum of $C, M,$ and Y that would have been present if there were no black ink. Then the amount of the other components will be reduced by the amount of black. For example, if Y is the smallest component in a given color for the CMY system, then for CMYK, Y would be replaced by $K;$ C would be replaced by $C - K;$ and M would be replaced by $M - K.$

The HSV and HLS Color Models

As mentioned at the beginning of this section, the three-dimensionality of color space can be viewed in terms of hue (H), saturation (S), and value (V), with value being similar to lightness or brightness. It is easier for most people to select a color based on $H, S,$ and $V,$ than on $R, G,$ and B. That is, an HSV model is a more natural way for us to formulate colors. Although most programming languages require RGB values for setting a color on the computer monitor, a transformation from the HSV model to the RGB model can be used in software to select colors based on $H, S,$ and $V.$ For example, the Macintosh "color picker" illustrated in plate 2a permits the user to choose a color based on HSV values, as well as on RGB values.

The HSV color model is usually referenced to the hexcone shown in figure 6.4a. In the hexcone, hue is measured around the circumference of the hexagonal cross sections, with red at 0°, yellow at 60°, green at 120°, cyan at 180°, etc., as shown in the figure. Saturation varies from zero on the axis (center of the hexagonal cross sections) to a maximum value on the side surfaces of the hexcone. The value varies from zero (black) at the bottom vertex of the hexcone to a maximum (white) at the center of the top (hexagonal) face. The cylindrical representation illustrated in figure 6.4b corresponds to the Macintosh color picker, in which the circle showing the hue and saturation becomes black when the value (slider bar in plate 2a) is set equal to zero. The saturation and value variables are often given a maximum of 1, although the Macintosh picker displays maximum values of 65,553 for all color dimensions: H, S, V, R, G, and B.

Consider a normalized RGB system in which R, G, and B all vary between 0 and 1, and an HSV system with H varying from 0° to 360°, and with S and V ranging from 0 to 1. The value V can be identified with the maximum of R, G, and B.

$$V = \max(R,G,B) \tag{6.3}$$

Note that because R, G, and B are normalized to maximum values of 1, V has a maximum value of 1.

The saturation is given by the following relation.

$$S = \frac{\max(R,G,B) - \min(R,G,B)}{\max(R,G,B)} \tag{6.4}$$

Equation 6.4 reduces to appropriate limits: for gray shades, $S = 0$ occurs when $\max(R,G,B) = \min(R,G,B)$, which implies $R = G = B$. Also, S equals its maximum value of 1 when $\min(R,G,B) = 0$; that is, when one of the RGB colors is zero, a fully saturated color will occur somewhere on the side surfaces of the hexcone between the other two RGB values.

The relation between H and R, G, and B depends on whether the hue is nearest R (0°), G (120°), or B (240°). When H is near R, the hue is computed from the following equation.

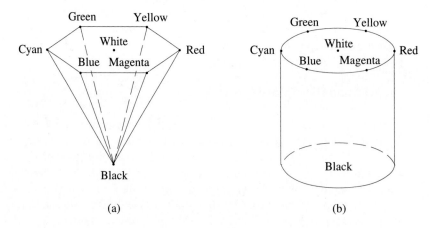

(a)   (b)

Figure 6.4   HSV color solids: (a) the hexcone, and (b) the circular cylinder.

$$H = \frac{60(G - B)}{\max(R,G,B) - \min (R,G,B)} \qquad (6.5)$$

When $G = B$, equation 6.5 reduces to $H = 0°$, that is, to a red, as expected. On the other hand, when $G = R$, a yellow hue results and equation 6.5 gives $H = 60°$. If $B = R$, then equation 6.5 yields magenta at $H = -60°$, and $360°$ must be added to the result to put the hue in the proper degree range ($0°$ to $360°$).

When H is nearest G or B, the hue is given by the following relations.

$$H = 120 + \frac{60(B - R)}{\max(R,G,B) - \min (R,G,B)} \qquad (6.6)$$

$$H = 240 + \frac{60(R - G)}{\max(R,G,B) - \min (R,G,B)} \qquad (6.7)$$

It is evident that the above equations reduce to the proper angles when the hue is yellow, green, cyan, blue, or magenta.

Equations 6.3 through 6.7 are implemented in the subroutine below. When the saturation $S = 0$, the hue is undefined, but for specificity it is assigned the value $H = 0$, as in the operation of the Macintosh color picker. In the subroutine it has been assumed that the variables in the RGB system can have values up to a maximum RGBMAX (given, for example, by a *#define* assignment in the main part of the program). In the first part of the subroutine the values *maxrgb* and *minrgb* are computed, corresponding to the quantities $\max(R,G,B)$ and $\min(R,G,B)$, respectively.

```
void rgb2hsv(double r,double g,double b)
{
    double maxrgb,minrgb,h,s,v,cr,cg,cb;

    r = r/RGBMAX; g = g/RGBMAX; b = b/RGBMAX;

    maxrgb = r;
    if (g > maxrgb) maxrgb = g;
    if (b > maxrgb) maxrgb = b;
    minrgb = r;
    if (g < minrgb) minrgb = g;
    if (b < minrgb) minrgb = b;

    v = maxrgb;
    if (v == 0.)
        s = 0.;
    else
        s = (maxrgb - minrgb)/maxrgb;
    if (s == 0.)
        h = 0.; /* actually, h is undefined */
    else
    {
        if (r == v) h = 60.*(g-b)/(s*v);
```

```
      if (h < 0) h = h + 360.;
      if (g == v) h = 120.+ 60.*(b - r)/(s*v);
      if (b == v) h = 240.+ 60.*(r - g)/(s*v);
   }
   Hue = h*HMAX/360.; Saturation = s*SMAX; Value = v*VMAX;
}
```

In the above subroutine, the calculations are performed with H measured in degrees, and S and V each normalized to a maximum value of 1. Then the calculated values are transferred to global variables *Hue, Saturation,* and *Value,* which have maximum values HMAX, SMAX, and VMAX.

We will often wish to specify HSV values to be displayed on a computer that works with RGB values. Therefore, the inverse of the above transformation is required. For this HSV to RGB transformation, the six angular regions (of 60° each) of the hexagon are considered by introducing the variable *hexRegion,* which takes on six integer values. In the following subroutine, the values are scaled by dividing H by HMAX/6, S by SMAX, and V by VMAX. The transformation then computes normalized r, g, and b values that are multiplied by any desired scale RGBMAX at the end to determine values for the global variables *Red, Green,* and *Blue.*

```
void    hsv2rgb(double h,double s,double v)
{
    double r,g,b,c,d,e,f;
    int    hexRegion;

    h = h*6./HMAX; s = s/SMAX; v = v/VMAX;

    if (s == 0.)
    {
        r = v; g = v; b = v;
    }
    else
    {
        hexRegion = (int) floor(h);
        c = h - floor(h);
        d = v*(1.- s);
        e = v*(1.- s*c);
        f = v*(1.- s*(1.- c));
        switch(hexRegion)
        {
            case 0:
                r = v; g = f; b = d;
                break;
            case 1:
                r = e; g = v; b = d;
                break;
            case 2:
```

```
                                r = d; g = v; b = f;
                                break;
                    case 3:
                                r = d; g = e; b = v;
                                break;
                    case 4:
                                r = f; g = d; b = v;
                                break;
                    case 5:
                                r = v; g = d; b = e;
            }
        }
        Red = r*RGBMAX; Green = g*RGBMAX; Blue = b*RGBMAX;
    }
```

   The above transformations are included as part of the Macintosh color-picker package as the functions RGB2HSV() and HSV2RGB(). Other transformations included with the Macintosh software are CMY2RGB(), RGB2CMY(), HSL2RGB(), and RGB2HSL(). The transformations between CMY and RGB are given above in equations 6.1 and 6.2. The HSL model is often called the HLS model, and involves hue (H), lightness (L), and saturation (S).

   Representations of the HLS model are shown in figure 6.5. The double hexcone is similar to the HSV hexcone, with hue being measured by the circumferential angle around hexagonal cross sections. Lightness is measured along the axis with black being at the bot-

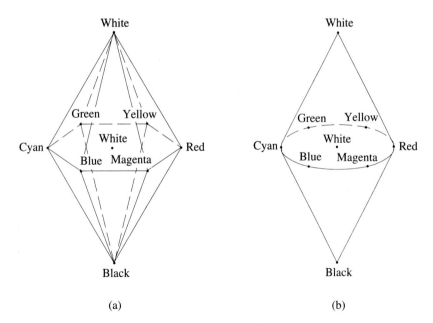

(a)   (b)

Figure 6.5   HLS color solids: (a) the double hexcone and (b) the double cone.

tom vertex and white at the top. Normally, black corresponds to $L = 0$, white to $L = 1$, and the hexagon that bisects the axis has a lightness $L = 0.5$. The double-cone representation of the HLS model corresponds to the Ostwald color space that was introduced in 1917. In the HLS model, saturation increases from the value 0 on the axis to the value 1 on the surface of the double hexcone or double cone.

Transformations for the HLS model are included in the books by Rogers (1985) and Watt (1989). Another important color model is the YIQ system adopted in 1953 by the National Television Standards Committee (NTSC) for color television broadcasting in the United States. Transformations between YIQ and RGB are given by Rogers (1985) and by Foley et al. (1990). In the next section, transformations will be studied that relate the RGB model to the tristimulus values XYZ and the CIE chromaticity diagram.

6.2 COLORIMETRY AND THE PERCEPTION OF COLOR

Colorimetry is the branch of color science that is concerned with the numerical specification of colors. Accurate representation of colors involves matching and mixing, which are very important in product design and manufacturing. Before we can describe colors by quantitative models, we must understand some basic facts about human visual perception.

The Perception of Color by the Human Eye

The human eye senses light by means of cone and rod cells. The rod cells are sensitive to low levels of light but cannot distinguish colors, only lightness or darkness. That is, when the ambient light is low at night or in the early morning, you cannot distinguish colors because only your rod cells, not your cone cells, can detect the low light levels—try picking out dark brown socks from black ones in ambient light at 6 a.m.

There are three types of cone cells in the human eye, with sensitivities peaking at long, medium, and short wavelengths within the visible spectrum. These cones are commonly called the red, green, and blue cones, although the red and green cones really have peak sensitivities in different parts of the yellow range of color. The fact that the cone cells have peak sensitivities in different parts of the spectrum enables us to distinguish colors. Furthermore, the three-dimensionality of color arises from the fact that there is visual stimulation from three different types of cone cells.

Our perception of a color, however, does not simply depend on the light spectrum from an object, but also on surrounding colors and conditions. Photographers know that different types of film are required for daylight and artificial light. The human eye compensates for these illumination differences to give us the impression that we are seeing the true colors of objects. Accordingly, our perception of colors depends on the physiology and psychology of vision, as well as on the physics of light.

To quantify color mixing, researchers performed a large number of experiments in which they asked people to determine the amounts of three standard colors that combined to match any given color. Each person viewed a projected spot of a given color and compared it with a color produced by mixing three standard colors (the three colors are projected on top of each other). Although visual perception varies among individuals, experiments with a large number of people have established results for a "standard observer." These experiments led in 1931 to the development of the widely used chromaticity diagram by the CIE.

Figure 6.6 illustrates the experiment used to establish color-matching functions $\bar{r}(\lambda)$, $\bar{g}(\lambda)$, and $\bar{b}(\lambda)$. At each wavelength λ, a monochromatic test color $E(\lambda)$ is matched by amount $\bar{r}(\lambda)$ of the red primary R, amount $\bar{g}(\lambda)$ of the green primary G, and amount $\bar{b}(\lambda)$ of the blue primary B. That is, the following linear relation holds between the monochromatic test color and the three primaries.

$$E(\lambda) = \bar{r}(\lambda)R + \bar{g}(\lambda)G + \bar{b}(\lambda)B \qquad (6.8)$$

In the above equation R, G, and B are primary stimuli of *unit* amounts, and $E(\lambda)$ is a monochromatic test color of *unit* radiant power.

For primaries R, G, and B consisting of monochromatic sources at wavelengths 700.0, 546.1, and 435.8 nm, respectively, the color-matching functions (also called tristimulus values) are plotted in figure 6.7. Although the linear relation (6.8) holds at every wavelength, in some wavelength regions one of the color-matching functions takes on negative values—primarily $\bar{r}(\lambda)$ between the wavelength of the blue and green primaries, 435.8 to 546.1 nm, although $\bar{g}(\lambda)$ and $\bar{b}(\lambda)$ take on small negative values in other wavelength regions. This result means that in the experiment, matching was achieved in the 435.8 to 546.1-nm wavelength region by adding the red primary to the monochromatic source, rather than to the green and blue primaries.

Equation 6.8 holds at each wavelength λ; therefore, a color with a spectral power distribution $P(\lambda)$ may be integrated over wavelength to obtain its total radiant power C. Integration of equation 6.8 over wavelength gives the following relation for C.

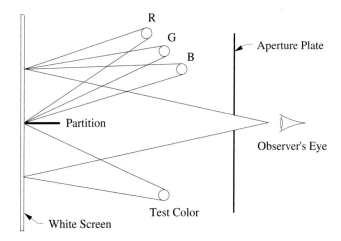

Figure 6.6   Experiment to determine color-matching functions. An observer views the superposition of three standard lights (R, G, and B) on one side of a partition and compares the resulting color with a test color projected on the other side of the partition.

$$C = rR + gG + bB$$

(6.9)

where

$$C = \int P(\lambda)\mathrm{d}\lambda, \qquad r = \int P(\lambda)\bar{r}(\lambda)\mathrm{d}\lambda, \qquad g = \int P(\lambda)\bar{g}(\lambda)\mathrm{d}\lambda, \qquad b = \int P(\lambda)\bar{b}(\lambda)\mathrm{d}\lambda$$

Color-matching functions for a different set of primaries can be obtained by a set of linear transformations from the above functions. Accordingly, a new set of functions was generated from the experimental data shown in figure 6.7. The new functions were the 1931 standard observer tristimulus values $\bar{x}(\lambda)$, $\bar{y}(\lambda)$, and $\bar{z}(\lambda)$. These new functions have no negative values, as shown in figure 6.8.

The three primaries corresponding to the CIE color-matching functions are designated as X, Y, and Z. The amounts of X, Y, and Z primaries needed to match a color light source having a spectral radiant power distribution $P(\lambda)$ are given by

$$X = k \int P(\lambda)\bar{x}(\lambda)\mathrm{d}\lambda, \qquad Y = k \int P(\lambda)\bar{y}(\lambda)\mathrm{d}\lambda, \qquad Z = k \int P(\lambda)\bar{z}(\lambda)\mathrm{d}\lambda$$

where

(6.10)

$$k = \frac{1}{\int P_w(\lambda)\bar{y}(\lambda)\mathrm{d}\lambda}$$

In the above equations the tristimulus values X, Y, and Z have been normalized by dividing by the integral of the spectral radiant power $P_w(\lambda)$ for a standard white light source multiplied by $\bar{y}(\lambda)$. Accordingly, a bright white light has a luminance Y of 1. (Sometimes a fac-

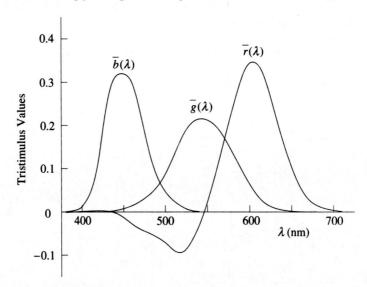

Figure 6.7   Color-matching functions (tristimulus values) for the experiment illustrated in figure 6.6. The R, G, and B primaries were monochromatic light sources at 700.0, 546.1, and 435.8 nm, respectively.

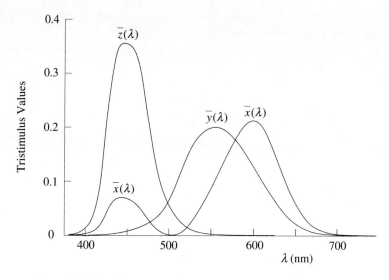

Figure 6.8   The CIE standard color-matching functions (tristimulus values).

tor of 100 is introduced into the equation for k to normalize a bright white light to a luminance of 100.) The primary Y has been set up to represent luminance (lightness, brightness, or value), and as shown below, the X and Y values will be further normalized to construct a chromaticity diagram that represents the chromatic aspects of color.

The CIE Chromaticity Diagram

The tristimulus values are divided by the sum $X + Y + Z$ to form the chromaticity coordinates x, y, and z.

$$x = \frac{X}{X + Y + Z}, \qquad y = \frac{Y}{X + Y + Z}, \qquad z = \frac{Z}{X + Y + Z} \qquad (6.11)$$

From the above equations, it may be readily shown that $z = 1 - x - y$. Therefore, z is not an independent parameter, and the luminance Y is used with the chromaticity coordinates x and y to specify a color.

The chromaticity diagram is shown in figure 6.9. Wavelengths are identified on the horseshoe-shaped curve that represents the bounds of visible colors, with the numbers from 400 to 700 representing the wavelengths in nanometers (nm) of the pure spectral colors. The straight line at the bottom connecting the limiting blue-violet (shortest visible wavelength) with the limiting red (longest wavelength) is called the line of purples. The colors along this straight line do not occur in the natural spectrum, but do occur as mixtures of red and blue-violet.

All points within the horseshoe-shaped curve represent visible colors, but only those within a triangle can be produced on a standard computer monitor. The red, green, blue, and white coordinates for the solid triangle are (Rogers 1985): $x_r = 0.628$, $y_r = 0.346$, $x_g =$

0.268, $y_g = 0.588$, $x_b = 0.150$, $y_b = 0.070$, $x_w = 0.313$, and $y_w = 0.329$. Color plate 3 illustrates the gamut of colors within the triangular region.

The triangular region of available colors depends on the particular monitor. The dashed triangle in figure 6.9 was determined from measurements on a Silicon Graphics monitor. The smaller, six-sided dashed polygon in figure 6.9 shows the color gamut for a color printer. Unlike colors on a monitor, the colors on a printer do not lie within a triangular region because they are determined by subtractive color mixing rather than by additive mixing. The dashed polygon for the printer was plotted by connecting measured coordinates for the six colors R, Y, G, C, B, and M. In general, a color hardcopy device has a much smaller gamut of colors than a color monitor.

Figure 6.10 illustrates some of the features of the chromaticity diagram. A straight line passing through the standard white source (W in the figure) connects complementary

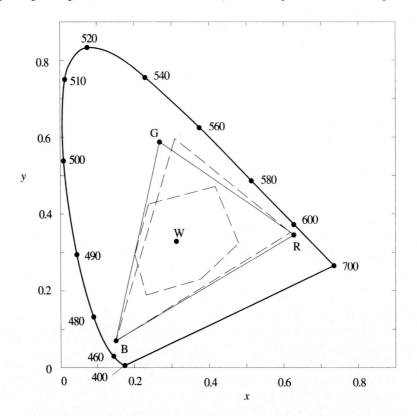

Figure 6.9 The CIE chromaticity diagram, with interior polygons showing color gamuts for two monitors and a printer. The triangle with the solid outline was plotted from monitor data given by Rogers (1985). The dashed polygons were plotted from data measured with a photometer by Michael Bailey (San Diego Supercomputer Center); the dashed triangle was measured on a Silicon Graphics 4D/320 VGX monitor; and the dashed, six-sided polygon was measured on hard copy from a Canon CLC-500 color copier/printer.

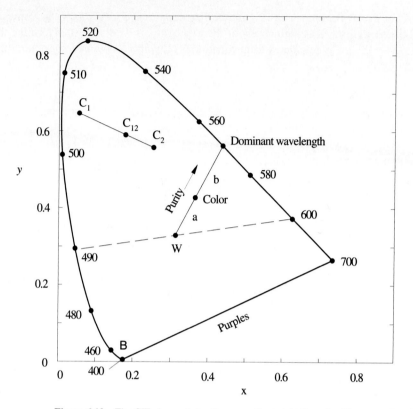

Figure 6.10   The CIE chromaticity diagram with straight lines that illustrate color characteristics and color mixing.

colors on opposite sides of the diagram. For example, the complement of the color corresponding to a 600-nm monochromatic light source is the color corresponding to a wavelength of approximately 490 nm (dashed line in the figure).

The chromatic character of a color may be described by the purity (similar to saturation) of the color and its dominant wavelength (similar to hue). In figure 6.10, a straight line is drawn from the white point W through a dot representing a given color to the dominant wavelength of the color at the boundary of the horseshoe curve. The purity of the color is defined as the distance a from W to the color divided by the distance $a + b$ between W and the dominant wavelength.

A straight line drawn between two colors (C_1 and C_2 in figure 6.10) contains all colors that may be obtained by mixing these two. From Grassman's laws for additive color mixture, two colors are mixed by summing their X, Y, and Z values. From the definition (6.11) of the chromaticity coordinates, the following relations are readily derived.

$$X + Y + Z = \frac{Y}{y}, \qquad X = x\frac{Y}{y}, \qquad Z = (1 - x - y)\frac{Y}{y} \qquad (6.12)$$

For the two colors C_1 and C_2, define $T_1 = Y_1/y_1$ and $T_2 = Y_2/y_2$. Then from equation 6.12 the sum of the XYZ primaries for the two colors is $T_1 + T_2$. After forming the sum $X_{12} = X_1 + X_2$, x_{12} is calculated from equation 6.11, with y_{12} obtained in a similar manner.

$$x_{12} = \frac{x_1 T_1 + x_2 T_2}{T_1 + T_2}, \qquad y_{12} = \frac{y_1 T_1 + y_2 T_2}{T_1 + T_2}, \qquad Y_{12} = Y_1 + Y_2 \qquad (6.13)$$

Note that T_1 is proportional to the luminance Y_1, and T_2 is proportional to Y_2. Therefore, when $Y_2 = 0$, the chromaticity coordinates reduce to those of color 1 ($x_{12} = x_1$ and $y_{12} = y_1$); similarly, if $Y_1 = 0$, then $x_{12} = x_2$ and $y_{12} = y_2$. When both Y_1 and Y_2 are nonzero, the chromaticity coordinates of the mixture lie on a line joining C_1 and C_2, as given by equations 6.13.

A mixture of three colors will be bounded by the triangle formed by connecting the colors with straight lines in the chromaticity diagram. The solid triangle shown in figure 6.9 and color plate 3 shows the colors (for a given luminance) that can be made by mixing the R, G, and B colors on a computer monitor.

The RGB color space of a monitor can be transformed to the CIE XYZ color space. The transformation may be written in the following form.

$$\begin{bmatrix} X \\ Y \\ Z \end{bmatrix} = \begin{bmatrix} X_r & X_g & X_b \\ Y_r & Y_g & Y_b \\ Z_r & Z_g & Z_b \end{bmatrix} \begin{bmatrix} R \\ G \\ B \end{bmatrix} \qquad (6.14)$$

The tristimulus values X_r, Y_r, and Z_r are normalized for unit values of the RGB primaries; for example, $R = 1$, $G = 0$, and $B = 0$ yield $X = X_r$, $Y = Y_r$, and $Z = Z_r$.

Equations 6.11 may be used to relate the X_r, Y_r, and Z_r terms to x_r and y_r, and to the quantity $C_r = X_r + Y_r + Z_r$. Along with similar relations for the other terms, equation 6.14 becomes

$$\begin{bmatrix} X \\ Y \\ Z \end{bmatrix} = \begin{bmatrix} x_r C_r & x_g C_g & x_b C_b \\ y_r C_r & y_g C_g & y_b C_b \\ (1 - x_r - y_r)C_r & (1 - x_g - y_g)C_g & (1 - x_b - y_b)C_b \end{bmatrix} \begin{bmatrix} R \\ G \\ B \end{bmatrix} \qquad (6.15)$$

The quantities C_r, C_g, and C_b can be evaluated by using the tristimulus values for white (X_w, Y_w, and Z_w, obtained from the chromaticity coordinates x_w and y_w, plus unit luminance $Y_w = 1$).

For the color monitor x- and y-values listed above for the colors red, green, blue, and white, the RGB to XYZ transformation (6.15) reduces to the following matrix equation (see Rogers 1985).

$$\begin{bmatrix} X \\ Y \\ Z \end{bmatrix} = \begin{bmatrix} 0.478 & 0.299 & 0.175 \\ 0.263 & 0.655 & 0.081 \\ 0.020 & 0.160 & 0.908 \end{bmatrix} \begin{bmatrix} R \\ G \\ B \end{bmatrix} \qquad (6.16)$$

After the above relation is used to obtain values for X, Y, and Z, the normalized chromaticity coordinates x and y may be obtained from equations 6.11.

The matrix equation 6.16 may be inverted to obtain the following relation (see appendix C for a matrix-inversion procedure).

$$
\begin{bmatrix} R \\ G \\ B \end{bmatrix} = \begin{bmatrix} 2.739 & -1.145 & -0.424 \\ -1.119 & 2.029 & 0.033 \\ 0.138 & -0.333 & 1.105 \end{bmatrix} \begin{bmatrix} X \\ Y \\ Z \end{bmatrix} \tag{6.17}
$$

The above matrix equations may be easily incorporated into subroutines, as shown below. In the subroutine rgb2cie(), x, y, and $ycap$ are assumed to be global variables; and in the subroutine cie2rgb(), *Red, Green,* and *Blue* are global variables.

```
void rgb2cie(double r,double g,double b)
{
    double   xcap,zcap;

    xcap = 0.478*r + 0.299*g + 0.175*b;
    ycap = 0.263*r + 0.655*g + 0.081*b;
    zcap = 0.020*r + 0.160*g + 0.908*b;

    x = xcap/(xcap + ycap + zcap);
    y = ycap/(xcap + ycap + zcap);
}


void cie2rgb(double x,double y,double ycap)
{
    double   xcap,zcap;

    xcap = x*ycap/y;
    zcap = (1.- x - y)*ycap/y;

    Red =    2.739*xcap - 1.145*ycap - 0.424*zcap;
    Green = -1.119*xcap + 2.029*ycap + 0.033*zcap;
    Blue =   0.138*xcap - 0.333*ycap + 1.105*zcap;
}
```

6.3 USE OF COLOR PALETTES

Workstations with 24-bit color are becoming more common, but many designers still are working with systems having only 4-bit or 8-bit color. On a 24-bit system, $2^{24} = 16,777,216$ colors can be displayed simultaneously on the computer screen. At the low end, only $2^4 = 16$ colors or $2^8 = 256$ colors can be displayed simultaneously. In between these color capabilities, graphics cards having 1M byte of memory can display $2^{15} = 32,768$ colors simultaneously on a screen of 800×600 pixels.

For line drawings, 16 or fewer colors may be enough to distinguish different parts or layers on the drawing. For scientific visualization, as discussed in the next section, approximately 256 colors are required to produce a fairly smooth variation in hue for color plots of a variable throughout a region. For photorealistic rendering, however, all three dimensions of color must be used to show appropriate variations in lighting, saturations, and hues. Accordingly, the best output for rendering can require up to 24 bits of color. When your system does not have the number of colors needed for rendering, the effective number of colors can be expanded by the use of dithering (at the expense of decreased resolution); see section 6.5.

As discussed in section 2.1, a color look-up table may be used to expand the number of colors available to your system. Although the number of colors that may be displayed simultaneously is not increased by a look-up table, the simultaneous colors can be selected from a much larger number of colors. That is, a look-up table makes it possible to change the *palette* of colors used for drawing on the screen.

The particular procedures for changing the color palette depend on your system. For Microsoft C on IBM PC compatibles, the functions that change the palette in VGA mode are _remappalette() and _remapallpalette(). In the VGA mode, 6 bits are used to assign the intensity of each of the RGB colors. Therefore, R, G, and B can each have $2^6 = 64$ different values, for a total number of $64 \times 64 \times 64 = 262,144$ colors. The standard VGA mode permits only 16 of these colors to appear on the screen at a time for 640×480 pixel resolution, or 256 simultaneous colors for 320×200 pixel resolution.

To illustrate the procedure for setting a palette color, the following Microsoft C subroutine uses the function _remappalette() to reset the color for one of the colors on the current palette (in contrast, _remapallpalette() resets all of the palette colors). In the subroutine, the integer *clrIndex* denotes one of the color numbers 0 to 15 in the 640×480 pixel mode, or a number 0 to 255 in the 320×200 pixel mode. The long integers *red*, *green*, and *blue* have values from 0 to 63.

```
void setPal(int clrIndex,long int red,
            long int green,long int blue)
{
    long int clr;

    clr = (blue<<16) | (green<<8) | red;
    _remappalette(clrIndex,clr);
}
```

In the above subroutine, the color red (0–63) is put into the first byte of the 4-byte long integer *clr*, the green into the second byte (shifted by 8 bits from the 6-bit red color), blue into the third byte, with the fourth byte being empty; see figure 6.11.

Color pickers programmed with Microsoft C are shown in color plates 2b–f. These programs use the hsv2rgb() subroutine given in section 6.1 along with the _remappalette()

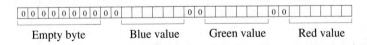

Empty byte   Blue value   Green value   Red value

Figure 6.11 Long-integer storage of a color value in the VGA mode for IBM PC compatibles.

function to continuously change a color in response to the user's mouse input. All of these color pickers are limited to a display of only 16 simultaneous colors, but a given color in the palette can be changed to any of 262,144 colors.

The color picker shown in plate 2b is similar to the Macintosh picker. It features a color wheel in which a dot can be dragged by the mouse cursor to change the hue and saturation. The Macintosh dot is less visible because it lies on top of the colors in the wheel—the color picker in plate 2b is limited by the 16-color display, so colors are placed only on the rim of the color wheel. In this color picker, slider (scroll) bars are used to change the color value (brightness) and also to directly change the amounts of red, green, and blue. A slider bar subroutine is discussed in chapter 9, section 9.5.

In plate 2c, hue and saturation levels are displayed by the dot location in the hexagonal region on the left, while the color is displayed around the rim of the color wheel on the right (this permits the color to be compared with many adjacent colors inside the wheel). The hue, saturation, and value levels are changed with the arrow buttons at the lower left.

To facilitate rapid selection of a color, the picker in plate 2d displays many colors close in hue to the one being changed (these colors can be selected at any time with the mouse). The center of this picker also displays a color wheel; the yellow radius can be dragged around the circle to change hue (which may also be changed by clicking on the + and − boxes). The angle between the cyan radii in the color wheel shows the range of hues for the colors displayed at the top (this range can be changed with the + and − boxes above the view range label). Value and saturation levels can be changed with the arrow buttons at the left; the horizontal and vertical yellow lines display the current levels (the saturation level is also displayed by the size of the inner yellow circle in the color wheel). Red, green, and blue levels can be changed directly with the buttons on the right.

The color pickers in plates 2e and f work effectively without color wheels. The color picker in 2e has slider bars that graphically display hue, saturation, and value. The cursor cross used for selection changes to a downward arrow when it is slid along one of these bars to change a color variable.

The color picker in plate 2f displays a bar chart of red, green, and blue amounts. By changing hue, saturation, and value levels with the + and − buttons on the left, the user can observe the rise and fall of the red, green, and blue bars. This display readily shows that one of the primary colors is reduced to zero as the saturation is increased to 100% (in this picker the maximum amounts of hue, saturation, and value are set at 360). Also, all bars move up when the value level is increased, and move down when the value is decreased.

6.4 COLOR FOR SCIENTIFIC VISUALIZATION

Color provides another dimension for the presentation of scientific and engineering data. A variable to be plotted can be color coded; that is, a spectrum of colors can represent a range of values. Plate 4 shows a color plot of the pressure coefficient C_p throughout the flow field surrounding an airfoil. A color key at the bottom of the plot identifies colors with C_p values.

The pressure coefficient plotted in plate 4 is defined by the equation

$$C_p = \frac{p - p_\infty}{\frac{1}{2}\rho_\infty V_\infty^2} = \frac{V_\infty^2 - V^2}{V_\infty^2} \tag{6.18}$$

in which p is pressure, ρ density, V velocity, and the subscript ∞ denotes freestream values far from the airfoil. Accordingly, C_p is a dimensionless parameter that is proportional to the difference between the local pressure p and the freestream pressure p_∞; alternatively, C_p may be expressed in terms of the difference between the square of the freestream velocity V_∞ and the square of the local velocity V. As observed from plate 4, the pressure coefficient is negative ($p < p_\infty$ and $V > V_\infty$) above the airfoil and positive over most of the region below the airfoil.

The color key at the bottom of plate 4 was selected by setting both the saturation S and value V of all the colors equal to their maximum amounts. Then the color spectrum was established by varying the hue H from red through violet (the range was extended to only about 82% of the maximum amount for hue, so that there would be sufficient difference between the colors of minimum and maximum hues, corresponding to minimum and maximum C_p values).

The color plot was then constructed by calculating C_p at the position of each pixel and setting the pixel color according to the color key. The calculation of C_p follows from the analytical solution for a Joukowski airfoil. With this solution, the airfoil thickness, camber (curvature), and angle of attack can be varied by the program user. Without color, individual line plots of C_p on the upper and lower airfoil surfaces can be drawn; on the other hand, color permits C_p to be plotted throughout the flow field near the airfoil, not just on the surface of the airfoil.

6.5 DITHERING

The printing industry uses a halftone process in which different gray scales or shades are produced by dots of different sizes. Although the halftone process can be simulated on a computer, most computer graphics software employs a dither pattern. Dither patterns are based on square cells composed of a matrix of $n \times n$ pixels, where the cell size n determines the number of gray shades that can be produced. (Dithering can also be used to increase the number of colors available with monitors and printers.)

The shade of gray produced by a dither pattern depends on the number of black pixels relative to the number of white ones in a cell. Gray values between white and black can be obtained by randomly distributing black pixels on a white background, as illustrated at the top of figure 6.12. Although this procedure can produce appropriate gray values, the overall effect of a *random* dither is to produce a "dirty" or "foggy" effect on the scene being rendered. A much better procedure is to use an *ordered* dither, which produces cleaner shading, as shown at the bottom of figure 6.12. In an ordered dither, pixels are turned on in a prescribed pattern to produce desired gray values.

The total number of required gray values determines the size of the cell needed. For example, a 2×2 pixel cell can produce five values of gray when 0, 1, 2, 3, or 4 of the pixels are filled; see figure 6.13. The order in which the pixels are filled is important; for ex-

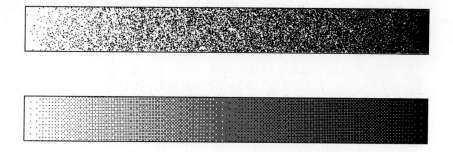

Figure 6.12   Gray scales produced by a random dither (top) and by an ordered dither (bottom).

Figure 6.13   The five gray shades available with a 2 × 2-pixel matrix.

ample, if we first fill the top pixels in a 2 × 2 cell, then at a 50% gray value, horizontal lines will be evident. Accordingly, a suitable procedure for filling the pixels is given by the dither matrix

$$[D_2] = \begin{bmatrix} 0 & 2 \\ 3 & 1 \end{bmatrix} \tag{6.19}$$

The numbers in the above equation provide the prescription for filling a matrix: first fill the upper left pixel, then the lower right pixel, followed by the upper right pixel, and finally the lower left pixel. The resulting five gray values (counting white with no filled pixels) are shown in figure 6.13; see also the left part of the figure at the beginning of this chapter.

A 3 × 3 pixel cell is filled by the prescription

$$[D_3] = \begin{bmatrix} 2 & 6 & 4 \\ 5 & 0 & 1 \\ 8 & 3 & 7 \end{bmatrix} \tag{6.20}$$

Dither matrices of higher order can be constructed from the formula

$$[D_n] = \begin{bmatrix} 4D_{n/2} & 4D_{n/2} + 2U_{n/2} \\ 4D_{n/2} + 3U_{n/2} & 4D_{n/2} + U_{n/2} \end{bmatrix} \tag{6.21}$$

in which $U_{n/2}$ stands for the unit matrix, which has the value 1 for every element. Therefore, the following $[D_4]$ matrix arises from equation 6.21 when equation 6.19 is used for $[D_2]$.

$$[D_4] = \begin{bmatrix} 0 & 8 & 2 & 10 \\ 12 & 4 & 14 & 6 \\ 3 & 11 & 1 & 9 \\ 15 & 7 & 13 & 5 \end{bmatrix} \tag{6.22}$$

The following matrix is used for the 5×5 pixel case:

$$[D_5] = \begin{bmatrix} 21 & 10 & 17 & 14 & 23 \\ 15 & 2 & 6 & 4 & 9 \\ 20 & 5 & 0 & 1 & 18 \\ 12 & 8 & 3 & 7 & 13 \\ 24 & 16 & 19 & 11 & 22 \end{bmatrix} \qquad (6.23)$$

With the above lower-order matrices, equation 6.19 can be used to generate dither matrices $[D_6]$, $[D_8]$, $[D_{10}]$, $[D_{12}]$, $[D_{16}]$, etc. The matrix $[D_8]$ is of particular interest because graphics libraries often feature convenient procedures for storing 8×8 pixel matrices. The Macintosh has a pixel editor for interactive use in creating patterns of 8×8 pixels, and Microsoft C for IBM PC compatibles has the function _setfillmask(*userArray*), in which *userArray* is the current fill pattern set up by the user as an 8-byte array. The bottom strip in figure 6.12 illustrates the range of gray scales that can be obtained by an 8×8 dither array (see also the right side of the figure at the beginning of the chapter).

Ordered dithering is very useful for increasing the range of colors in rendered images. Because rendering attempts to produce photorealistic images, a large range of colors is required for good results. For a low-end system that can display only 16 colors, dithering can expand the number of colors to 256. This procedure is used in renderings by AutoCAD and AutoShade with systems that can display only 16 colors in VGA (640×480 pixel) resolution. The disadvantage of using dithering is that the effective resolution is reduced, because shades are produced by pixel matrices rather than by intensity variations in a single pixel. Accordingly, for rendering it is usually better to set up your system for 320×200 pixel resolution with 256 colors at each pixel, rather than for 640×480 pixel resolution with only 16 colors at each pixel.

Dithering of colored pixels is important for printers, as well as for monitors. The printed quality of a rendering is enhanced by using the printer driver developed for your software (for example, the Hewlett-Packard PaintJet driver supplied with AutoShade). That is, the printer driver optimizes the dithering of the cyan, magenta, yellow, and black ink-jet dots on paper, so that the result is much better than a screen dump of the monitor pixels.

EXERCISES

6.1 If your system can display only 256 or fewer simultaneous colors, write a program to display its default palette as an array of filled rectangles.

6.2 Change the palette of your computer system's colors to gray scales and display the palette from white to black as thin rectangles from left to right across the screen. The result should resemble a shaded cylinder.

6.3 Write a program that displays the colors in a color cube as a series of cross sections along the red, green, or blue axis. If your system displays 256 colors, then retain the black color for the background and display $15 \times 15 = 225$ squares of color for each cross section. A total of 15 cross sections should be displayed while progressing along a given color axis (let the program user select the red, green, or blue color axis).

6.4 Design an RGB color picker. That is, write a program that changes the color palette of your system in response to values entered for red, green, and blue color components. The resulting color should be displayed and compared with other colors. Write your program so that colors can be changed quickly and efficiently.

6.5 Write a program for an HSV color picker; that is, have the user enter numbers for hue, saturation, and value. Display RGB values and HSV values along with the new colors and comparison colors.

6.6 Develop a generalized color picker with which the user can change any of the quantities H, S, V, R, G, or B. Values should be changed with a convenient user interface, such as slider bars. Examples are shown in plate 2, but your color picker should be of your own design.

6.7 For CIE diagram coordinates consider the statement "roses are $x = 0.441$, $y = 0.305$; violets are $x = 0.282$, $y = 0.218$." Check out these values by transforming to RGB values for a luminance $Y = 0.32 \times$ RGBMAX, where RGBMAX is the maximum value for RGB colors on your system. Display the resulting colors on your computer monitor.

6.8 Write a program that constructs a color plot for a solution to the heat-conduction equation in a rectangular region.

6.9 Write out (a) the 6×6 ordered-dither matrix $[D_6]$, and (b) the matrix $[D_8]$.

6.10 Set up an 8×8 ordered-dither matrix with your programming language. Check your results by printing out the 65 gray shades from white to black.

6.11 Write a program to produce a random dither of gray shades from white to black, similar to that shown in figure 6.12.

6.12 Look up three paintings of squares by Josef Albers and try to reproduce them on your computer screen (see, for example, *Albers*, by W. Spies, New York: Harry N. Abrams, Inc., 1970; *Josef Albers*, by J. Wissmann. Recklinghausen: Verlag Aurel Bongers, 1971). If you have a limited number of colors that can be displayed simultaneously on your monitor, change the palette to achieve a good match of colors with the painting. As illustrated below, Albers squares have sides of the following dimensions (arbitrary units): 8, 12, 16, and 20. The squares are separated by 2 units at their sides, 3 units at their tops, and 1 unit on the bottom.

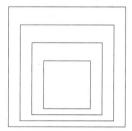

6.13 By referring to a book on the paintings of Frank Stella (for example, *The Prints of Frank Stella*, by R. H. Axsom, New York: Hudson Hills Press, 1983), produce on your computer screen an image that approximates a painting from his racetrack series (black-and-white example shown below). Try to match the colors in the painting.

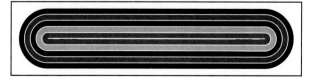

BIBLIOGRAPHY

BURGER, D., AND D. GILLIES, *Interactive Computer Graphics: Functional, Procedural and Device-Level Methods.* Reading, Mass.: Addison-Wesley Publishing Co., 1989.

FOLEY, J. D., A. VAN DAM, S. K. FEINER, AND J. F. HUGHES, *Computer Graphics: Principles and Practice,* 2nd ed. Reading, Mass.: Addison-Wesley Publishing Co., 1990.

HALL, R., *Illumination and Color in Computer Generated Imagery.* New York: Springer-Verlag, 1989.

MACADAM, D. L., *Color Measurement: Theme and Variations.* Berlin: Springer-Verlag, 1981.

MARK, D., *Macintosh C Programming: Volume II, Mastering the Toolbox Using THINK C.* Reading, Mass.: Addison-Wesley, 1990.

ROGERS, D. F., *Procedural Elements for Computer Graphics.* New York: McGraw-Hill Publishing Co., 1985.

ROSSOTTI, H., *Colour: Why the World Isn't Grey.* Princeton: Princeton University Press, 1983.

STONE, M. C., "Color Printing for Computer Graphics," pp. 79–127 in *Computer Graphics Techniques: Theory and Practice,* edited by D. F. Rogers and R. A. Earnshaw. New York: Springer-Verlag, 1990.

THE WAITE GROUP, *Microsoft C Programming for the PC,* 2nd ed. Indianapolis: Howard Sams, 1990.

WAITE, M., S. PRATA, B. COSTALES, AND H. HENDERSON, *Microsoft QuickC Programming,* 2nd ed. Redmond, Wash.: Microsoft Press, 1990.

WATT, A., *Fundamentals of Three-Dimensional Computer Graphics.* Reading, Mass.: Addison-Wesley Publishing Co., 1989.

WYSZECKI, G., *Color Science: Concepts and Methods, Quantitative Data and Formulae,* 2nd ed. New York: John Wiley & Sons, 1982.

7

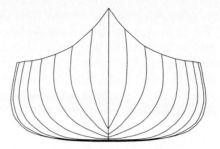

Splines and Other Curves for Data Fitting

The word *spline* originally referred to the flexible wood or metal strips used by draftspersons for drawing curves. These physical splines may be held in place with tacks or with lead weights called *ducks* that are used with large splines in boat and ship design. In the past, ship splines were laid out large loft rooms, and this drafting was called *lofting*.

The drawing at the top of this page shows vertical cross-section curves (ribs) for a canoe, along with a vertical line for the keel and two sheer lines. In chapter 12 these vertical cross-section lines will be connected to produce a surface representation of the canoe in three dimensions. Many of the curve types discussed in this chapter can be used to construct "patches" to represent surfaces in space, as developed in chapter 12.

In this chapter we consider a half-dozen of the common types of curves used for design purposes. These and other curves are analyzed more thoroughly in specialized books; see, for example, Bartels et al. (1987), Rogers and Adams (1990), and Farin (1990). One type of curve discussed below, the Bézier curve, was developed for the design of Renault automobiles.

Two general types of curves will be considered. The first type represents an *interpolation* between data points; the curve passes through each point. The second curve type is an *approximation* curve; it passes through few, if any, of the data points. In this latter case, the data points act as control points to shape the curve, rather than as points on the curve.

This chapter starts with a brief discussion of using high-order polynomials to fit data. This procedure, often described in calculus textbooks, is not useful for design purposes because the curve often has large oscillations between data points. Other interpolation schemes—which are useful for design work—are a circular-arc fit, parabolic blending, and the natural cubic spline. The natural cubic spline is the mathematical representation of the physical spline described above. Also in this chapter, various types of approximation curves are analyzed: uniform quadratic and cubic B-splines, nonuniform (nonrational and rational) B-splines of general order, general-order Bézier curves, and composite cubic Bézier curves.

Although high-order polynomials are discussed in the first section and in the general B-spline or Bézier cases, this chapter emphasizes curves that are constructed with segments described by second- and third-degree polynomials (quadratic and cubic equations), with the segments being connected at *joints* (also called *knots*). Note that the simplest curve fit is the linear case, considered in chapter 3 as a polyline that joins data points with straight-line segments.

The joints that connect curved-line segments may be classified according to the continuity of the derivatives at the joints. If the nth derivative is continuous at the joints, then the overall curve is said to be C^n continuous. The simple polyline is C^0 continuous because values match at the joints, but first derivatives do not. The circular-arc fit and parabolic blend are C^1 continuous, whereas the natural cubic spline is C^2 continuous. For the approximation curves, the quadratic B-spline and the composite cubic Bézier curve considered in this chapter have C^1 continuity, and the cubic B-spline is C^2 continuous.

7.1 HIGH-ORDER POLYNOMIALS

Consider n points at $y_i = f(x_i)$, where the x_i are monotonically increasing x-values. The following Lagrange interpolating polynomial of order $n-1$ passes through each of the n points.

$$y = \sum_{i=0}^{n-1} L_i(x)f(x_i) \tag{7.1}$$

where

$$L_i(x) = \prod_{j=0, j \neq i}^{n-1} \frac{x-x_j}{x_i-x_j}$$

Note that at a vertex point, say $x = x_k$, the polynomials $L_i(x)$ will equal zero for all vertices x_i except for $x_i = x_k$, where $L_k(x) = 1$. Therefore equation 7.1 reduces to $y = f(x_i)$ at the vertex points x_i.

The formula (7.1) is readily implemented by the following subroutine. The coordinates are in the units of screen pixels, and x is increased in steps of five pixels.

```
void highPolyFit(int n,double x[],double y[])
{
    int i,j;
    double xp,yp,L;

    MoveTo((int) x[0],(int) y[0]);
    for (xp=x[0]; xp<x[n-1]+.1; xp=xp+5.)
    {
        yp = 0.;
        for (i=0; i<n; i++)
        {
            L = 1.;
            for (j=0; j<n; j++)
            {
                if (j!=i) L = L*(xp-x[j])/(x[i]-x[j]);
            }
            yp = yp + L*y[i];
        }
        LineTo((int) xp,(int) yp);
    }
}
```

In the above listing, n points are passed to the subroutine by means of the arrays $x[]$ and $y[]$ for the horizontal and vertical coordinates. These arrays have elements $x[0]$ through $x[n-1]$. A horizontal point xp is incremented by a small amount (here five pixels), and the vertical coordinate yp is calculated from equation 7.1.

Although high-order polynomials pass through the vertex points, they usually oscillate too much between the vertex points. This result is not surprising because, for example, x to a large power n will increase rapidly when x is greater than unity. Figure 7.1 shows four different interpolation curves that pass through six vertex points representing data in which the first three points lie on a horizontal line and the last three points are on a higher (larger y-value) horizontal line. For this case the high-order (Lagrange) polynomial is a fifth-order polynomial.

The high-order polynomial shown as curve a in figure 7.1 oscillates widely between vertex points. Even higher oscillations can occur for other vertex configurations. Obviously, high-order polynomials are not suitable for approximating smooth curves in design applications. The other three curves in figure 7.1 interpolate the data in better ways.

A circular-arc fit (curve b) reduces to straight lines along the three colinear points at the beginning of the curve, and also at the end of the curve. It produces an s-shaped curve between the third and fourth vertex points.

Curve c in figure 7.1 represents a parabolic blend, which produces (between the third and fourth vertices) an s-shaped curve with much less deviation from the straight-line slope

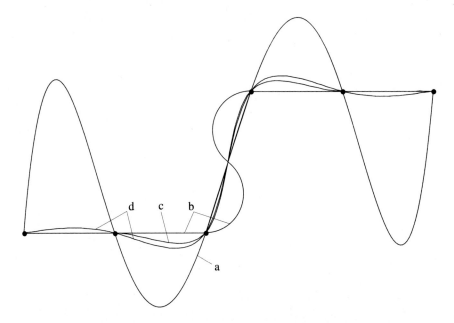

Figure 7.1 Interpolation curves drawn for six vertex points (dots), with y plotted in the vertical and x in the horizontal direction. Curves are shown for (a) a high-order polynomial fit, (b) a circular-arc fit, (c) a parabolic blend, and (d) a natural cubic spline.

than the circular-arc curve. Although this gentler s-shape may be more pleasing, it produces small oscillations in the curve between the other vertices (the deviation from the straight lines between the first two vertices and the last two is too small to be evident in the figure).

The natural cubic spline is represented by curve d in figure 7.1. It oscillates more between the first three and last three vertices than does the parabolic blend, but it has a less pronounced s-shape between the third and fourth vertices. Furthermore, the natural cubic spline has C^2 continuity (continuity of curvature) at the vertices, rather than only C^1 continuity like the circular-arc and parabolic-blend curves.

Figure 7.2 presents four approximation curves along with a polyline that connects the same six vertices as shown in figure 7.1. These approximation curves satisfy convex hull properties; for example, they all lie within the polygon that would be formed if a rubber band were stretched around all of the vertex points in figure 7.2. Accordingly, there are no oscillations in the curves between vertex points.

For approximation curves, the vertex points act as control points that attract the curve even though the curve does not normally pass through the vertex points. The general Bézier curve d is controlled at each point by all of the vertex points, whereas the other curves shown are controlled by the nearest three or four vertex points on any part of the curve. Therefore, for the general Bézier curve, a vertex point does not exhibit much local control over curve shape compared with the other three approximation curves. In figure 7.2 this lack of local control allows the curve to rise much more gradually between the lower and upper vertex points.

All of the curves in figures 7.1 and 7.2 are analyzed in this chapter.

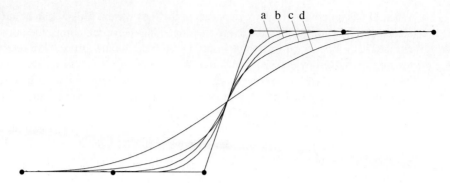

Figure 7.2   Approximation curves drawn for the same six vertex points shown in figure 7.1, with y plotted in the vertical and x in the horizontal direction. Curve a is the uniform quadratic B-spline; b the uniform cubic B-spline; c the composite cubic Bézier curve; and d the general (here fifth-order) Bézier curve.

7.2 CIRCULAR-ARC CURVE FIT

The interpolation curve fit used by AutoCAD consists of a pair of arcs drawn between each pair of vertex points. Because two arcs are used between vertices, this procedure is often called the *biarc method.* The biarc method was developed by Renner and Pochop (1981) for use in the design of BMW automobiles.

Use of the Circular-Arc Fit in AutoCAD

Any polyline drawn in AutoCAD (with the PLINE command) can be changed into a circular-arc fit of the data (vertex) points by using the FIT option under PEDIT. As discussed in chapter 5, polylines are edited as follows.

```
Command: PEDIT
Select polyline: (select with mouse)
Close/Join/Width/Edit vertex/Fit curve/
          Spline curve/Decurve/Undo/eXit <X>: F
Close/Join/Width/Edit vertex/Fit curve/
          Spline curve/Decurve/Undo/eXit <X>: (RETURN)
```

The response of "F" for fit immediately turns the polyline into a circular-arc curve fit. The curve may be changed back to a polyline by entering "D" for decurve.

After a polyline is drawn, the vertex points may be changed with the Edit vertex command under PEDIT.

```
Close/Join/Width/Edit vertex/Fit curve/
          Spline curve/Decurve/Undo/eXit <X>: E
Next/Previous/Break/Insert/Move/Regen/
          Straighten/Tangent/Width/eXit <N>: N
```

When "E" is entered a × symbol appears at the first vertex. This × can be moved to the next vertex by entering "N." After progressing along the vertex points, the polyline can be retraced in the opposite direction by inserting "P" for previous vertex. After selection, a vertex may be moved by entering "M," after which you will be asked for the coordinates of the new position. The edit vertex mode also permits new vertex points to be inserted when "I" is entered. The new vertex will appear between the selected vertex and the next vertex at coordinates specified under the insert option.

Vertex points may be eliminated by using the "straighten" option in the edit vertex mode. For example, the third and fourth vertex points on a polyline may be eliminated by entering "S" for straighten when the × symbol is on the second vertex. Then the × is moved to the fifth vertex, where "G" for go is entered. This action eliminates the third and fourth vertex points, and draws a straight polyline segment between the second and fifth vertex points (the fifth vertex is now the third vertex in the new polyline).

Manufacturing constraints often restrict mechanical parts and other objects to designs that have drawings consisting of straight lines and circular arcs. The crank arm drawn in figure 7.3 illustrates that the circular-arc fit is efficient for drawing these items (this is the same crank arm shown in figure 4.3). Five polylines are used to draw the entire crank arm: one for the entire outside edge, one for the slot that has semicircular ends, and three for the three circles.

Only eight points define the slot with semicircular ends. Because the circular-arc fit draws a straight line between any three colinear points, only three points are required for a straight line segment. Also, a circle is drawn through a closed polyline consisting of four vertex points lying anywhere on the circle (note that one of the three circles in the figure does not have all of its vertex points placed at opposite ends of diameters).

Because of the 75° angle in the crank arm, construction lines and circles were used to locate many of the polyline points in figure 7.3; however, the number of resulting polyline vertex points needed to complete the drawing is remarkably small. Other parts would be simpler to draw. For example, if the crank arm had a 90° angle, then the polylines could have been drawn directly on a rectangular grid.

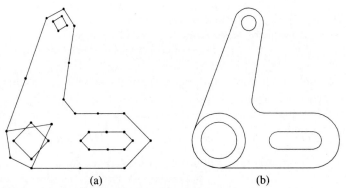

(a)   (b)

Figure 7.3   A crank arm drawn on AutoCAD with five polylines: (a) the polylines and vertex points and (b) the polylines after the circular-arc curve fit.

The warehouse ceiling structure shown in figure 7.4 was drawn with the circular-arc fit command in AutoCAD. The graceful concrete ribs are arrayed around the supporting columns, shown as filled squares in this plan view. First, one octant is drawn (figure 7.4a); then it is mirrored across a 45° line; then the resulting quadrant is put into a polar array around the column center; and finally all of the curves around one column are put into a rectangular array to produce the desired number of columns in the final illustration. (Of course, the BLOCK command could be used in place of the ARRAY command to save memory.) Proper matching along the 45° mirror line is achieved by using the Tangent option while in the Edit vertex mode of the PEDIT command. The tangents of the first and last

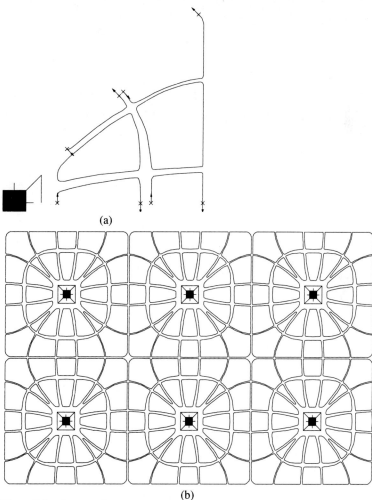

(a)

(b)

Figure 7.4   Concrete rib structure on the ceiling of a warehouse in Bologna, Italy, designed by engineer Pier Luigi Nervi: (a) the use of tangent lines at the boundary points of an octant drawn around a column and (b) the rib structure around six of the columns.

points ($\times$ marks) of the top polylines in figure 7.4a are set at $-45°$ and $135°$, respectively. Similarly, the tangents at the first and last vertex points on the bottom polylines are set at $\pm90°$ to match slopes when the first quadrant is put into a polar array.

Another drawing with the AutoCAD circular-arc fit is shown in figure 7.5. The cane weave on the chair seat was drawn with the hatch pattern developed in section 3.4.

The Circular-Arc Curve-Fit Algorithm

To draw a pair of arcs between each vertex pair, you must insert a new vertex point between each pair of data points. The RP (Renner-Pochop) method specifies the positions of the inserted vertices. This method also prescribes the curve tangents at each of the data points.

Consider n data points providing the coordinates (x_i,y_i) of n vertices $\mathbf{V}_i$, where the subscript i takes on values from 0 through $n-1$. A polyline through these points has $n-1$ segments, numbered 0 through $n-2$; see figure 7.6.

The first step in the curve-fitting routine is the calculation of vectors tangent to the curve at each of the vertices. Although in AutoCAD the user has the option of specifying tangent directions, most often only the vertex points are given, with the algorithm determining the tangents. The RP method prescribes the tangent vector $\mathbf{t}_i$ at vertex i as a weighted average of the unit vectors $\mathbf{e}_{i-1}$ and $\mathbf{e}_i$ on either side of the vertex. Weighting factors w_0 and w_1 are functions of the segment lengths l_{i-1} and l_i, and a shape factor s, with the value $s = -1$ being used by the AutoCAD Fit algorithm. Additional weighting factors A and B for interior vertices depend on the unit vectors $\mathbf{e}_{i+1}$ and $\mathbf{e}_{i-2}$, so the tangents at these vertices depend on the four nearest polyline segments.

$$\mathbf{t}_i = Aw_0\mathbf{e}_{i-1} + Bw_1\mathbf{e}_i \qquad (7.2)$$

where

$$w_0 = [(1 + s)l_{i-1} + (1 - s)l_i], \qquad w_1 = [(1 + s)l_i + (1 - s)l_{i-1}] \qquad (7.3)$$

$$\mathbf{e}_{i-1} = \frac{1}{l_{i-1}} [l_{x,i-1} \mathbf{i} + l_{y,i-1}\mathbf{j}], \qquad \mathbf{e}_i = \frac{1}{l_i} [l_{x,i} \mathbf{i} + l_{y,i}\mathbf{j}] \qquad (7.4)$$

Equation 7.2 holds for vertices with indices from $i = 1$ through $n-2$. For the two vertices adjacent to end points, $i = 1$ and $i = n-2$, the amplitude terms A and B each have the value 1. For the interior vertices, $i = 2$ through $n-3$, the amplitudes are computed by the following expressions.

$$A = \left|\mathbf{e}_{i+1} - \mathbf{e}_i\right|, \qquad B = \left|\mathbf{e}_{i-1} - \mathbf{e}_{i-2}\right| \qquad (7.5)$$

where the expressions within the absolute value symbols can be readily evaluated by formulas for the unit vectors of the form given in equations 7.4.

The tangent vector $\mathbf{t}_0$ at the first vertex is given by

$$\mathbf{t}_0 = 2(\mathbf{t}_1 \cdot \mathbf{e}_0)\mathbf{e}_0 - \mathbf{t}_1$$
$$= [w_0 + 2w_1\cos(\sigma_1 - \sigma_0)]\mathbf{e}_0 - w_1\mathbf{e}_1 \qquad (7.6)$$

where $\sigma_1 - \sigma_0$ is the angle between the directions of the first two polyline segments, obtained when equation 7.2 with $i = 1$ is used to expand the scalar product $\mathbf{t}_1\cdot\mathbf{e}_0$. The tangent vector

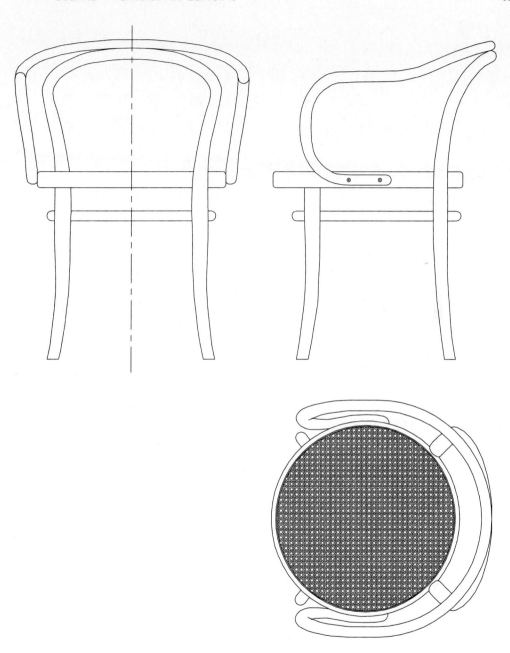

Figure 7.5 Bentwood armchair produced in 1870 by Gebrüder Thonet. Redrawn on AutoCAD from an illustration in *The Modern Chair: Classics in Production,* by Clement Meadmore, published by Van Nostrand Reinhold Co., 1975.

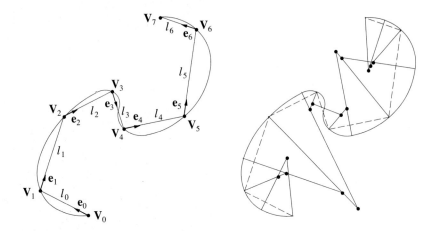

Figure 7.6   A polyline with eight vertex points V_0 through V_7. On the left, polyline segment lengths l_i and unit vectors e_i are shown, and on the right the arc centers and radii are drawn.

at vertex $i = n-1$ is calculated by a formula similar to that in equation 7.6, except with e_0, t_0, and t_1 replaced by e_{n-2}, t_{n-1}, and t_{n-2}.

The second step in the RP method is the calculation of the coordinates for the new vertices that are added between each pair of data points. Figure 7.7 shows three curve segments from figure 7.6, illustrating two different types of geometry. The first geometry, shown in 7.7a, arises when the tangent vectors t_i and t_{i+1} point to opposite sides of the segment (the figure shows a clockwise-turning polyline on the left and a counterclockwise polyline on the right). For this geometry the added point appears at the intersection of the lines that bisect the angles $2\alpha = \pm(\sigma_i - \phi_i)$ and $2\beta = \pm(\sigma_i - \phi_{i+1})$, which lie between the tangent vectors and the polyline segment (the $+$ sign in these angle relations is for the clockwise case, and the $-$ sign for the counterclockwise case).

As discussed in section 2.4, an intersection point may be readily calculated for two straight lines, which have equations of the form $y = mx + b$. The constants for the first line are determined by the fact that the line passes through the point $V_i = (x_i, y_i)$ and has a slope m equal to $\tan(\sigma_i \pm \alpha) = \tan\{(\phi_i + \sigma_i)/2\}$, whereas the second line passes through $V_{i+1} = (x_{i+1}, y_{i+1})$ and has a slope equal to $\tan(\phi_{i+1} \pm \beta) = \tan\{(\phi_{i+1} + \sigma_i)/2\}$. The intersection point for these two lines is obtained in the following form, after the $\tan()$ function is expressed as $\sin()/\cos()$, and multiplication by $\cos()$ is carried out to eliminate the divergences associated with the $\tan()$ functions when the argument is $\pm\pi/2$; that is, the following expressions hold for all orientations of the intersecting lines.

$$x_{int} = x_i + \frac{c_1[c_2(y_{i+1} - y_i) - s_2(x_{i+1} - x_i)]}{(s_1c_2 - s_2c_1)}$$

$$y_{int} = y_i + \frac{s_1[c_2(y_{i+1} - y_i) - s_2(x_{i+1} - x_i)]}{(s_1c_2 - s_2c_1)} \tag{7.7}$$

where $c_1 = \cos\{(\phi_i + \sigma_i)/2\}$, $s_1 = \sin\{(\phi_i + \sigma_i)/2\}$, $c_2 = \cos\{(\phi_{i+1} + \sigma_i)/2\}$, and $s_2 = \sin\{(\phi_{i+1} + \sigma_i)/2\}$.

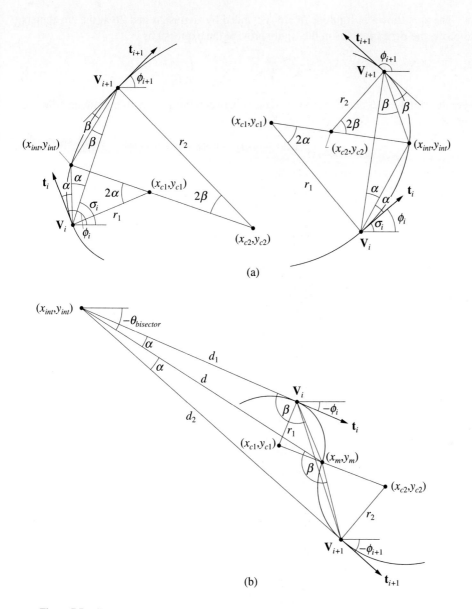

(a)

(b)

Figure 7.7   Geometry and nomenclature for calculating the coordinates of the added vertices and the arc centers. The case of tangent vectors pointing to opposite sides of the segment is shown in (a) with a clockwise-turning curve shown on the left, and a counterclockwise curve on the right. The diagram in (b) shows the case of the tangent vectors pointing to the same side of the segment, with the curve changing from clockwise to counterclockwise.

The arcs shown in figure 7.7a are subtended by angles 2α and 2β at the arc centers. Therefore, the right triangles in the figure provide the expressions

$$r_1 = \frac{d_1}{2|\sin\alpha|}, \qquad r_2 = \frac{d_2}{2|\sin\beta|} \qquad (7.8)$$

where the variables d_1 and d_2 are the distances between the intersection point and the segment ends

$$d_1 = [(x_{int} - x_i)^2 + (y_{int} - y_i)^2]^{1/2}, \qquad d_2 = [(x_{int} - x_{i+1})^2 + (y_{int} - y_{i+1})^2]^{1/2} \quad (7.9)$$

Because the distances in equations 7.9 are positive, the computed radii are ensured positive values because absolute values of the sine functions appear in equations 7.8.

The vector of length r_1 between (x_i, y_i) and the arc center (x_{c1}, y_{c1}) is perpendicular to the tangent vector $\mathbf{t}_i$, which lies in the direction ϕ_i to the horizontal. The vector of length r_2 between (x_{i+1}, y_{i+1}) and the arc center (x_{c2}, y_{c2}) is perpendicular to the tangent vector $\mathbf{t}_{i+1}$, which lies in the direction ϕ_{i+1}. Accordingly, the arc center coordinates may be calculated from the following relations.

$$x_{c1} = x_i - ccw\, r_1 \sin\phi_i, \qquad\qquad y_{c1} = y_i + ccw\, r_1 \cos\phi_i$$

$$x_{c2} = x_{i+1} - ccw\, r_2 \sin\phi_{i+1}, \qquad y_{c2} = y_{i+1} + ccw\, r_2 \cos\phi_{i+1} \qquad (7.10)$$

In equations 7.10, the multiplicative factor ccw takes on the value $+1$ for the counterclockwise case and the value -1 for the clockwise case.

The first arc is drawn from center (x_{c1}, y_{c1}) with radius r_1, with the radius starting in a direction perpendicular to $\mathbf{t}_i$; that is, $\theta_{start} = \phi_i - ccw\, \pi/2$, where again the ccw factor takes into account the clockwise and counterclockwise orientations. The first arc ends at $\theta_{end} = \theta_{start} + 2\alpha$. The second arc starts at the angle on which the first angle ends, and is drawn to subtend an angle 2β at (x_{c2}, y_{c2}).

The second case to be considered is the geometry shown in figure 7.7b, where the tangent vectors $\mathbf{t}_i$ and $\mathbf{t}_{i+1}$ point to the same side of the segment. The fitted curve along this segment will change orientation between clockwise and counterclockwise turning. The first step in calculating the position of the added vertex point is to determine the intersection point of lines extending along the tangent vectors at the segment ends. The coordinates (x_{int}, y_{int}) of this point are computed from equations 7.7, but with the arguments of the cosine and sine terms being equal to the angles of the tangent vectors; that is, $c_1 = \cos\phi_i$; $s_1 = \sin\phi_i$, $c_2 = \cos\phi_{i+1}$, and $s_2 = \sin\phi_{i+1}$.

The added vertex point (x_m, y_m) is measured along $\theta_{bisector}$, which represents the bisector of the angle between the tangent vectors. Along this bisector there is only one appropriate distance d to the point (x_m, y_m) such that the arcs meet with the same slope, as shown in figure 7.7b. Reference to the geometry in this figure shows that the triangle formed by points (x_{int}, y_{int}), (x_i, y_i), and (x_m, y_m) is similar to the triangle formed by (x_{int}, y_{int}), (x_m, y_m), and (x_{i+1}, y_{i+1}). Therefore the following equality exists between the ratio of triangle sides: $d/d_1 = d_2/d$. Thus, the distance d to the point (x_m, y_m) may be calculated from the equation

$$d = (d_1 d_2)^{1/2} \qquad (7.11)$$

Although for some orientations the bisector angle, $\theta_{bisector}$, equals the average of the tangent angles, $(\phi_i + \phi_{i+1})/2$; for other orientations ϕ_i and/or ϕ_{i+1} must be increased by π. Instead of dealing separately with different orientations, one can alternatively calculate the bisector angle from the positions of the arc centers relative to the intersection point. The following result is obtained for the added vertex point coordinates.

$$x_m = x_{int} + d\cos\theta_{bisector}, \quad y_m = y_{int} + d\sin\theta_{bisector} \tag{7.12}$$

where

$$\theta_{bisector} = \frac{1}{2}\left[\tan^{-1}\left(\frac{y_i - y_{int}}{x_i - x_{int}}\right) + \tan^{-1}\left(\frac{y_{i+1} - y_{int}}{x_{i+1} - x_{int}}\right)\right] \tag{7.13}$$

The coordinates (x_{c1}, y_{c1}) of the first arc center may be calculated from the top pair of equations 7.10. Because the turning orientation changes for the second arc (and the parameter ccw is determined by the first arc), the coordinates (x_{c2}, y_{c2}) are computed from the bottom pair of equations in 7.10, but with the $-$ sign changed to $+$ in the x_{c2} equation and $+$ changed to $-$ in the y_{c2} equation.

The two arcs may draw with angles starting at the data points and ending at the inserted vertex at (x_m, y_m).

First arc: $\theta_{start} = \tan^{-1}\left(\dfrac{y_i - y_{c1}}{x_i - x_{c1}}\right), \qquad \theta_{end} = \tan^{-1}\left(\dfrac{y_m - y_{c1}}{x_m - x_{c1}}\right)$

$$\tag{7.14}$$

Second arc: $\theta_{start} = \tan^{-1}\left(\dfrac{y_{i+1} - y_{c2}}{x_{i+1} - x_{c2}}\right), \qquad \theta_{end} = \tan^{-1}\left(\dfrac{y_m - y_{c2}}{x_m - x_{c2}}\right)$

The above equations, along with the function arc() from section 3.1, may be used to write a program subroutine arcFit() that fits two circular arcs between each pair of n data points. Because a number of different cases must be considered, the program subroutine arcFit() is rather long, so it is given in appendix B as listing 7.1.

7.3 PARAMETRIC REPRESENTATION OF CURVES

All of the curves described in the rest of this chapter have the same type of parametric representation. Consider the parameter $\bar{t}$, which starts with the value 0 at the vertex $\mathbf{V}_0$, increases to $\bar{t} = 1$ at vertex $\mathbf{V}_1$, then to $\bar{t} = 2$ at vertex $\mathbf{V}_2$, $\bar{t} = i$ at vertex $\mathbf{V}_i$, etc. With the variable $\bar{t}$ as the parameter, a point in two or three dimensions is presented as the row vector (matrix) $\mathbf{Q}_i(\bar{t})$. (Alternatively, column vectors may be used.)

$$\mathbf{Q}_i(\bar{t}) = [x(\bar{t}) \quad y(\bar{t})] \text{ for } \text{2-D}$$

$$\tag{7.15}$$

$$\mathbf{Q}_i(\bar{t}) = [x(\bar{t}) \quad y(\bar{t}) \quad z(\bar{t})] \text{ for } \text{3-D}$$

Parametric representation in terms of the variable $\bar{t}$ provides a convenient way to describe the curves, even when they have infinite slopes or turn back on themselves. Note that a nonparametric representation such as $y = y(x)$ requires special treatment when the slope becomes infinite and when the curve doubles back to give multiple values of y for a given x-value.

The curve data points are called vertex points and are designated by the vector $\mathbf{V}_i$.

$$\mathbf{V}_i = [x_i \quad y_i] \text{ for } 2\text{-D}$$
$$\mathbf{V}_i = [x_i \quad y_i \quad z_i] \text{ for } 3\text{-D} \qquad (7.16)$$

Two-dimensional curves are illustrated in figure 7.8.

It is convenient to transform to a new independent parameter t, which varies between 0 and 1 as the curve is traversed between each set of vertices $\mathbf{V}_i$ and $\mathbf{V}_{i+1}$. An appropriate transformation is $t = \bar{t} - i$, where i is the number of the vertex at the start of the curve segment. This is a *uniform* parametric representation, because t varies over the same range between each pair of vertices. Uniform parametric representations are considered in sections 7.4–7.6, and nonuniform representions in section 7.7.

Because vector equations are used, there is no difference in the formulation of the curve algorithms in two and three dimensions (this is an important benefit of the parametric representation). Although the following examples will be for two-dimensional cases, results for curves in three-dimensional space can be readily carried out by computing $z(t)$ in the same manner that the $x(t)$ and $y(t)$ coordinates are calculated.

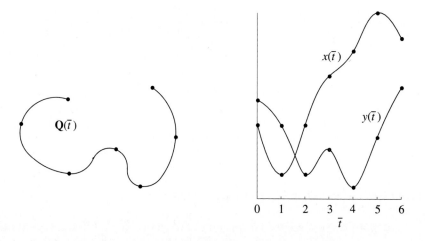

Figure 7.8 Parametric representation of a two-dimensional curve.

7.4 PARABOLIC BLEND

The curves developed in this section are produced by blending two parabolas, as illustrated in figure 7.9 (see Rogers and Adams [1990] for a more detailed derivation, and also for a generalized parabolic blend). The blended curve is shown as a dashed line between vertex points $\mathbf{V}_i$ and $\mathbf{V}_{i+1}$. The four vertices, $\mathbf{V}_{i-1}$ through $\mathbf{V}_{i+2}$, affect the shape of this dashed line by means of the formula

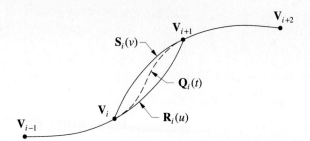

Figure 7.9   Configuration for parabolic blending.

$$Q_i(t) = V_{i-1}F_1(t) + V_iF_2(t) + V_{i+1}F_3(t) + V_{i+2}F_4(t)$$

$$= \sum_{k=-1}^{2} V_{i+k}F_{k+2}(t) \tag{7.17}$$

in which the variable t increases from 0 to 1 along the curve segment extending from the point V_i to the point V_{i+1}. That is, for this interpolation scheme, the overall curve comprises segments between the data points, which serve as joints or *knots* for the curve segments. In each curve segment the parameter t varies between 0 and 1.

In order to derive expressions for the functions F_1, F_2, F_3, and F_4 in equation 7.17, the individual parabolas shown in figure 7.9 are given the following parametric representations.

$$R_i(u) = [u^2 \quad u \quad 1][A]$$

$$S_i(v) = [v^2 \quad v \quad 1][B] \tag{7.18}$$

where $[u^2 \quad u \quad 1]$ represents a row vector (matrix) with three elements.

The first parabola is assumed to vary uniformly with the parameter u so that the points V_{i-1}, V_i, and V_{i+1} correspond to u values of 0, 1/2, and 1, respectively.

$$R_i(0) = V_{i-1} = [\,0 \quad 0 \quad 1\,][A]$$

$$R_i(1/2) = V_i = [1/4 \quad 1/2 \quad 1][A] \tag{7.19}$$

$$R_i(1) = V_{i+1} = [\,1 \quad 1 \quad 1\,][A]$$

The above equations can be written as a single matrix equation.

$$\begin{bmatrix} V_{i-1} \\ V_i \\ V_{i+1} \end{bmatrix} = \begin{bmatrix} 0 & 0 & 1 \\ 1/4 & 1/2 & 1 \\ 1 & 1 & 1 \end{bmatrix}[A] \tag{7.20}$$

Inverting the first matrix on the right of equation 7.20 produces the following expression for $[A]$:

$$[A] = \begin{bmatrix} 2 & -4 & -2 \\ -3 & 4 & 1 \\ 1 & 0 & 0 \end{bmatrix} \begin{bmatrix} V_{i-1} \\ V_i \\ V_{i+1} \end{bmatrix} \tag{7.21}$$

The same procedure is followed for $S_i(v)$, which crosses the points V_i, V_{i+1}, and V_{i+2} at the values $v = 0$, 1/2, and 1. The following value is obtained for the matrix $[B]$ of equation 7.18.

$$[B] = \begin{bmatrix} 2 & -4 & 2 \\ -3 & 4 & -1 \\ 1 & 0 & 0 \end{bmatrix} \begin{bmatrix} \mathbf{V}_i \\ \mathbf{V}_{i+1} \\ \mathbf{V}_{i+2} \end{bmatrix} \tag{7.22}$$

The blended curve $\mathbf{Q}_i(t)$ is obtained from $\mathbf{R}_i(u)$ and $\mathbf{S}_i(v)$ by linear interpolation.

$$\mathbf{Q}_i(t) = (1-t)\mathbf{R}_i(u) + t\mathbf{S}_i(v) \tag{7.23}$$

The blended curve vector $\mathbf{Q}_i(t)$ appropriately reduces to $\mathbf{R}_i(u)$ when $t = 0$ and to $\mathbf{S}_i(v)$ when $t = 1$. That is, the blended curve will reach the values and the slopes of the individual parabolas at each end of the curve segment.

Equations 7.18, 7.21, and 7.22 can be used to substitute for $\mathbf{R}_i(u)$ and $\mathbf{S}_i(v)$ in equation 7.23. The variables u and v are assumed to be linear functions of t. The linear expressions below result when it is required that at $\mathbf{V}_i$, $t = 0$, $u = 1/2$, and $v = 0$; and at $\mathbf{V}_{i+1}$, $t = 1$, $u = 1$, and $v = 1/2$. (These values are consistent with the analysis above and with figure 7.9.)

$$u = \frac{1}{2}(1 + t), \qquad v = \frac{1}{2}t \tag{7.24}$$

Substitution of the expressions for $\mathbf{R}_i(u)$ and $\mathbf{S}_i(v)$ into equation 7.23 yields the following result for $\mathbf{Q}_i(t)$.

$$\mathbf{Q}_i(t) = \begin{bmatrix} -\dfrac{t^3}{2} + t^2 - \dfrac{t}{2} & t^3 - t^2 - t + 1 & -\dfrac{t^3}{2} + \dfrac{t}{2} \end{bmatrix} \begin{bmatrix} \mathbf{V}_{i-1} \\ \mathbf{V}_i \\ \mathbf{V}_{i+1} \end{bmatrix}$$

$$+ \begin{bmatrix} \dfrac{t^3}{2} - \dfrac{3}{2}t^2 + t & -t^3 + 2t^2 & \dfrac{t^3}{2} - \dfrac{t^2}{2} \end{bmatrix} \begin{bmatrix} \mathbf{V}_i \\ \mathbf{V}_{i+1} \\ \mathbf{V}_{i+2} \end{bmatrix} \tag{7.25}$$

Multiplying the matrices and collecting terms in equation 7.25 yields a solution of the form of equation 7.17, with the following expressions for the F terms.

$$F_1(t) = -\frac{1}{2}(1 - t)^2 t$$

$$F_2(t) = \frac{1}{2}(3t^3 - 5t^2 + 2)$$

$$F_3(t) = \frac{1}{2}(-3t^2 + 4t + 1)t \tag{7.26}$$

$$F_4(t) = \frac{1}{2}(t - 1)t^2$$

The above F functions are used for all of the interior curve segments. For the end segments of an open curve, the curve may be continued along the individual parabolas that lead to the end points. For the first line segment, equations 7.18 and 7.21 are used for the parabola $R_i(u)$, with a new t defined by $t = 2u$, so that t varies from 0 to 1 and u varies from 0 to 1/2 along the first curve segment. The F_4 function is zero along this first segment, with the other F functions describing the parabola

$$F_1(t) = \frac{1}{2}(1 - t)(2 - t)$$

$$F_2(t) = (2 - t)t \qquad (7.27)$$

$$F_3(t) = \frac{1}{2}(t - 1)t$$

In a similar manner, equations 7.18 and 7.22 are used for calculations along the parabola representing the last segment of the curve. Along this last segment, t is defined by $t = (2v - 1)$, so that t varies from 0 to 1 while v varies from 1/2 to 1. Along this last segment, F_1 is zero, and the remaining functions are

$$F_2(t) = \frac{1}{2}(t - 1)t$$

$$F_3(t) = 1 - t^2 \qquad (7.28)$$

$$F_4(t) = \frac{1}{2}(t + 1)t$$

The C-program subroutine listed below calculates an open-ended parabolic blend curve fixed by n points having coordinate values passed to the subroutine by the arrays $x[]$ and $y[]$. The first *for* loop draws the curve for the first segment, the next double *for* loop draws the interior segments, and the last loop draws the last segment. In the *for* loops over the integer j, the parameter t is incremented by the operation $t+ = dt$ which equals the operation $t = t + dt$. The increment dt is determined by the parameter *nsegs,* which is the number of segments that make up the interval from $t = 0$ to $t = 1$.

```
void parBlend(int n,double x[],double y[])
{
    int     i,j,nsegs,xp,yp;
    double  t,dt,f1,f2,f3,f4;

    nsegs = 20; dt = 1./(double) nsegs;
    MoveTo((int) x[0],(int) y[0]);

    for (j=1,t=dt;j<=nsegs;j++,t+=dt)
    {
        f1 = .5*(1.-t)*(2.-t);
        f2 = (2.-t)*t;
        f3 = .5*(t-1.)*t;
        xp = (int) (f1*x[0]+f2*x[1]+f3*x[2]);
        yp = (int) (f1*y[0]+f2*y[1]+f3*y[2]);
```

```
      LineTo(xp,yp);
}
for (i=1;i<n-2;i++)
{
    for (j=1,t=dt;j<=nsegs;j++,t+=dt)
    {
        f1 = -.5*(1.-t)*(1.-t)*t;
        f2 = .5*(3.*t*t*t-5.*t*t+2.);
        f3 = .5*(-3.*t*t+4.*t+1)*t;
        f4 = .5*(t-1.)*t*t;
        xp = (int) (f1*x[i-1]+f2*x[i]+f3*x[i+1]+f4*x[i+2]);
        yp = (int) (f1*y[i-1]+f2*y[i]+f3*y[i+1]+f4*y[i+2]);
        LineTo(xp,yp);
    }
}
for (j=1,t=dt;j<=nsegs;j++,t+=dt)
{
    f2 = .5*(t-1.)*t;
    f3 = 1.-t*t;
    f4 = .5*(t+1.)*t;
    xp = (int) (f2*x[n-3]+f3*x[n-2]+f4*x[n-1]);
    yp = (int) (f2*y[n-3]+f3*y[n-2]+f4*y[n-1]);
    LineTo(xp,yp);
}
}
```

A *closed* parabolic blend curve may be constructed by adding three points with indices n, $n+1$, and $n+2$, having the same coordinates as points 0, 1, and 2, respectively. The program for the closed curve contains only the interior double *for* loop with the index *i* extending from 1 to n. The closed curve is drawn starting at the second point, as required by the blended-curve algorithm, and continues to point $n+1$, which has the same coordinates as the second point. The additional point $n+2$ is needed because, as shown by equation 7.17 and the program listing above, the algorithm for interior curve segments requires four points that define segments before and after the line segment being drawn.

7.5 NATURAL CUBIC SPLINE

Parametric representation of the natural cubic spline follows equations 7.15. Again t varies from 0 to 1 along each curve segment. For the natural cubic spline a cubic polynomial interpolates the curve between the data points, which serve as the segment joints or knots. The cubic polynomial provides a sufficient number of coefficients to match the segment values, slopes (first derivatives), and curvatures (second derivatives) at the knots.

As illustrated in figure 7.10, the *i*th segment extends between vertices (data points) V_i and V_{i+1}. Along this segment the curve is given by the formula

$$Y_i(t) = a_i + b_i t + c_i t^2 + d_i t^3 \tag{7.29}$$

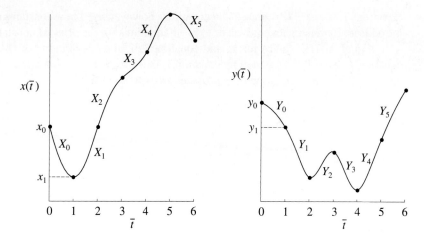

Figure 7.10   Notation for segments in a two-dimensional natural cubic spline curve.

where $Y_i(t)$ represents the $y(t)$ along the segment; a similar formula holds for $X_i(t)$ (and for $Z_i(t)$ in the 3-D case). Because t varies from 0 to 1 along each segment, $Y_i(t)$ reaches the ith vertex coordinate y_i when $t = 0$, and the vertex value y_{i+1} when $t = 1$. Similarly, $X_i(t) = x_i$ when $t = 0$ and $X_i(t) = x_{i+1}$ when $t = 1$; the coordinate values at the ends of the first segment are identified in figure 7.10.

The four unknown constants $(a_i, b_i, c_i,$ and $d_i)$ along each line segment will be determined by matching to the vertex values, requiring continuity of the first and second derivatives at the interior knots, and applying appropriate conditions at the curve ends. Along segment i, matching the vertex values y_i and y_{i+1} at the left and right ends of the segment gives the following equations.

$$Y_i(0) = y_i = a_i \tag{7.30}$$

$$Y_i(1) = y_{i+1} = a_i + b_i + c_i + d_i \tag{7.31}$$

The number of vertex points is n, with the segments numbered from 0 to $m = n - 1$. Matching vertex values provides 2 equations at each of the $m - 1$ interior knots plus 1 equation at each end of the total spline curve; therefore, matching values provides $2m$ equations involving the $4m$ unknown constants. Matching first and second derivatives at the $m - 1$ interior knots provides $2m - 2$ additional equations. The final two equations needed to solve for the $4m$ unknown constants are provided by requiring that the second derivatives vanish at the curve ends (this is the "natural" condition for a physical spline that is free at its ends).

Matching first derivatives at the interior knots provides $m - 1$ equations for the unknown constants. In solving for the unknown constants it proves useful to introduce new constants D_i representing the first derivatives at the vertex points. The first derivatives at the ends of segment i provide the equations

$$Y_i'(0) = D_i = b_i \tag{7.32}$$

$$Y_i'(1) = D_{i+1} = b_i + 2c_i + 3d_i \tag{7.33}$$

Equations 7.32 and 7.33 represent $2m$ equations; however, $m+1$ new constants D_i have been introduced, for a net gain equivalent to $m-1$ equations for the original constants.

Equation 7.30 solves for a_i, and equation 7.32 gives b_i in terms of D_i. Multiplying equation 7.31 by 3 and subtracting equation 7.33 leads to an expression for c_i, and 2 times equation 7.31 minus equation 7.33 provides an expression for d_i.

$$a_i = y_i \tag{7.34}$$

$$b_i = D_i \tag{7.35}$$

$$c_i = 3(y_{i+1} - y_i) - 2D_i - D_{i+1} \tag{7.36}$$

$$d_i = 2(y_i - y_{i+1}) + D_i + D_{i+1} \tag{7.37}$$

Matching the second derivatives at the $m-1$ interior knots, $Y_{i-1}''(1) = Y_i''(0)$, gives the following relation between the constants.

$$2c_{i-1} + 6d_{i-1} = 2c_i \tag{7.38}$$

After substitution from equations 7.36 and 7.37, the above equation reduces to the following expression for i values from 1 through $m-1$.

$$D_{i-1} + 4D_i + D_{i+1} = 3(y_{i+1} - y_{i-1}) \tag{7.39}$$

At the beginning of the curve the natural or free condition gives $Y_0''(0) = 2c_0 = 0$, which yields the following after equation 7.36 is used to substitute for c_0.

$$2D_0 + D_1 = 3(y_1 - y_0) \tag{7.40}$$

Similarly, the free boundary condition at the end of the curve gives $Y_{m-1}''(1) = 2c_{m-1} + 6d_{m-1} = 0$, which leads to the equation

$$D_{m-1} + 2D_m = 3(y_m - y_{m-1}) \tag{7.41}$$

The $m+1$ equations 7.39–7.41 for the $m+1$ first derivatives D_i may be put into matrix form (matrix operations are discussed in appendix C).

$$
\begin{bmatrix}
2 & 1 & & & & & \\
1 & 4 & 1 & & & & \\
 & 1 & 4 & 1 & & & \\
 & & \cdots & & & & \\
 & & & 1 & 4 & 1 & \\
 & & & & 1 & 4 & 1 \\
 & & & & & 1 & 2
\end{bmatrix}
\begin{bmatrix}
D_0 \\
D_1 \\
D_2 \\
. \\
D_{m-2} \\
D_{m-1} \\
D_m
\end{bmatrix}
=
\begin{bmatrix}
3(y_1 - y_0) \\
3(y_2 - y_0) \\
3(y_3 - y_0) \\
. \\
3(y_{m-1} - y_{m-3}) \\
3(y_m - y_{m-2}) \\
3(y_m - y_{m-1})
\end{bmatrix}
\tag{7.42}
$$

The first matrix on the left is tridiagonal; that is, all elements are zero except for three elements in each row centered about the diagonal.

The above matrix equation is simplified by first multiplying the top row by the factor $\gamma_0 = 1/2$. Then the element to the left of the diagonal (the value 1) in each of the remaining rows is eliminated by subtracting the row directly above it multiplied by an appropriate factor γ_i. These operations produce the matrix equation

$$
\begin{bmatrix}
1 & \gamma_0 & & & & & \\
& 1 & \gamma_1 & & & & \\
& & 1 & & & & \\
& & & \cdots & & & \\
& & & & 1 & \gamma_{m-2} & \\
& & & & & 1 & \gamma_{m-1} \\
& & & & & & 1
\end{bmatrix}
\begin{bmatrix}
D_0 \\ D_1 \\ D_2 \\ . \\ D_{m-2} \\ D_{m-1} \\ D_m
\end{bmatrix}
=
\begin{bmatrix}
\delta_0 \\ \delta_1 \\ \delta_2 \\ . \\ \delta_{m-2} \\ \delta_{m-1} \\ \delta_m
\end{bmatrix}
\tag{7.43}
$$

The parameters in equation 7.43 are given by the following relations.

$$\gamma_0 = 1/2$$

$$\gamma_i = 1/(4 - \gamma_{i-1}) \quad \text{for } i = 1 \text{ to } m-1 \tag{7.44}$$

$$\gamma_m = 1/(2 - \gamma_{m-1})$$

$$\delta_0 = 3(y_1 - y_0)\gamma_0$$

$$\delta_i = [3(y_{i+1} - y_{i-1}) - \delta_{i-1}]\gamma_i \quad \text{for } i = 1 \text{ to } m-1 \tag{7.45}$$

$$\delta_m = [3(y_m - y_{m-1}) - \delta_{m-1}]\gamma_m$$

Equation 7.43 may be readily solved by starting with the last row and stepping backwards to the first row.

$$D_m = \delta_m$$

$$D_i = \delta_i - \gamma_i D_{i+1} \quad \text{for } i = m-1 \text{ to } 1 \tag{7.46}$$

The above equations were used to write the subroutine natCubicSpline(), which is presented as listing 7.2 in appendix B. This subroutine plots a natural cubic spline interpolated between n data points having coordinates given by the arrays $x[]$ and $y[]$.

7.6 UNIFORM B-SPLINES

The simplest B-spline is the linear B-spline, which consists of straight lines drawn between the data points; that is, the linear B-spline is our standard polyline. The quadratic and cubic B-splines considered in this section are approximation curves rather than interpolation curves because these B-splines do not pass through the data points except at locations where there are multiple data points. The name B-spline arises from the basis (blending) functions used to describe the curves. At each point on a curve, the quadratic B-spline requires three basis functions, and the cubic B-spline requires four. These basis functions multiply the vertex point vectors in a manner similar to the $F_i(t)$ functions given in equation 7.17 for the parabolic blend.

Quadratic B-Spline

Figure 7.11a shows an open quadratic B-spline consisting of n vertex (control) points $\mathbf{V}_i$ and $n - 2$ curve segments $\mathbf{Q}_i(t)$. The tick marks delineate the interior knots joining curve segments, as well as the endpoints of the complete curve.

For the uniform B-splines considered in this section, the basis functions will have the same form along each curve segment. The open quadratic B-spline can be extended to the first and last control vertices by prescribing double points at these vertices. If these end-curve segments use the same basis functions as the interior segments, then the top end curves shown in figure 7.11b result. The bottom end curves result when the double end-points are treated as a nonuniform B-spline; see section 7.7. As will be shown later in this

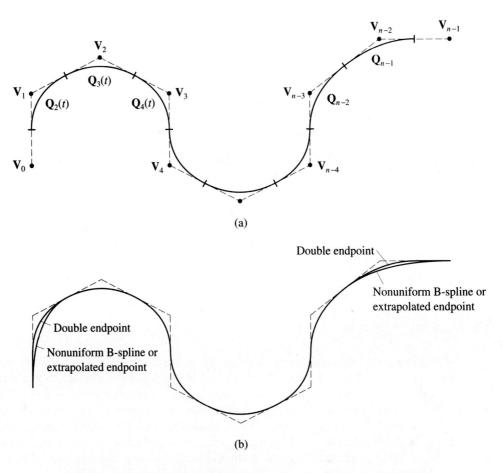

Figure 7.11 An open quadratic B-spline with the defining polyline (dashed): (a) curve for no special end conditions; (b) curve extended to the starting and ending control vertex points by means of two different procedures.

section, the bottom end curves can also be obtained by extrapolating the first and last control vertices to positions that relocate the curve ends to the original vertex positions.

The vector $\mathbf{Q}_i(t)$ for the coordinates along a quadratic B-spline may be expressed in terms of the three nearest vertex points $\mathbf{V}_{i-2}$, $\mathbf{V}_{i-1}$, and $\mathbf{V}_i$.

$$\mathbf{Q}_i(t) = \mathbf{V}_{i-2}B_{i-2}(t) + \mathbf{V}_{i-1}B_{i-1}(t) + \mathbf{V}_iB_{i-0}(t)$$

$$= \sum_{k=-2}^{0} \mathbf{V}_{i+k}B_{i+k}(t) \tag{7.47}$$

The three basis functions contributing to the curve segment between knots i and $i+1$ are illustrated in figure 7.12a. The bell-shaped curves peak at the vertex points, and spread across exactly three segments. As in the previous curve formulations, the parameter t increases from 0 to 1 along the curve segment.

The basis functions are quadratic in the parameter t within each curve segment.

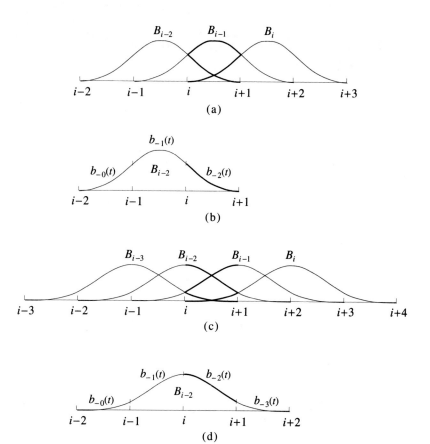

Figure 7.12   Basis functions for quadratic (a, b) and cubic (c, d) B-splines.

$$B_{i-2}(t) = a_j + b_j t + c_j t^2 \quad \text{for } i-2 \leq j \leq i \tag{7.48}$$

As illustrated in figures 7.12a and b, the basis function $B_{i-2}(t)$ extends across three segments, from knot $i-2$ to knot $i+1$, with t increasing from 0 to 1 along the curve from one knot to the next. Because the basis function coefficients are different in each curve segment, there are a total of 9 coefficients in equations 7.48. For the $B_{i-2}(t)$ curve shown in figure 7.12b, the quadratic polynomials 7.48 define a $b_i(t)$ function in each of the three segments.

$$b_{-0}(t) = a_{i-2} + b_{i-2}t + c_{i-2}t^2$$
$$b_{-1}(t) = a_{i-1} + b_{i-1}t + c_{i-1}t^2 \tag{7.49}$$
$$b_{-2}(t) = a_{i-0} + b_{i-0}t + c_{i-0}t^2$$

Because the shapes of the basis functions are the same, they may each be described as a composite of the three functions given in equations 7.49. Figure 7.12b shows that in the ith segment (between knots i and $i+1$), the basis function $B_{i-2}(t)$ contributes $b_{-2}(t)$, the function $B_{i-1}(t)$ contributes $b_{-1}(t)$, and $B_i(t)$ contributes $b_{-0}(t)$. Accordingly, equation 7.47 may be written as

$$\mathbf{Q}_i(t) = \mathbf{V}_{i-2}b_{-2}(t) + \mathbf{V}_{i-1}b_{-1}(t) + \mathbf{V}_i b_{-0}(t)$$
$$= \sum_{k=-2}^{0} \mathbf{V}_{i+k}b_k(t) \tag{7.50}$$

The single basis function $B_{i-2}(t)$ will now be considered. Because the curve is a superposition of the basis functions having the same shape, continuity of $B_{i-2}(t)$ will ensure continuity of the curve. The continuity requirement that $B_{i-2}(t)$ and its first derivative be zero at its boundary knots $i-2$ and $i+1$ gives the relations

$$a_{i-2} = 0$$
$$a_i + b_i + c_i = 0$$
$$b_{i-2} = 0 \tag{7.51}$$
$$b_i + 2c_i = 0$$

The first and third equations of 7.51 correspond to knot $i-2$, where the parameter t has the value 0 because the knot is approached from the right. The second and fourth equations are for knot $i+1$, where t has the value 1.

At the interior knots, $i-1$ and i, the basis function and its first derivative must be continuous (the quadratic B-spline has continuity C^1). This continuity provides a total of four relations. Because the derivative of $B_{i-2}(t)$ is $b_j + 2c_j t$, the following equations result.

$$a_{i-2} + b_{i-2} + c_{i-2} = a_{i-1}$$
$$a_{i-1} + b_{i-1} + c_{i-1} = a_i$$
$$b_{i-2} + 2c_{i-2} = b_{i-1} \tag{7.52}$$
$$b_{i-1} + 2c_{i-1} = b_i$$

The final equation needed to solve for the nine coefficients is provided by a normalization, which requires that the three basis functions contributing at any $t = 0$ sum to the value 1. Because each basis function has the same bell-shaped curve, normalization is provided by

$$b_{-0}(0) + b_{-1}(0) + b_{-2}(0) = 1$$

which gives   (7.53)

$$a_{i-2} + a_{i-1} + a_i = 1$$

The nine equations 7.51, 7.52, and 7.53 are solved for the nine coefficients, which upon substitution into equations 7.49, yield

$$b_{-0}(t) = \frac{1}{2}t^2$$

$$b_{-1}(t) = \frac{1}{2}(1 + 2t - 2t^2) \qquad (7.54)$$

$$b_{-2}(t) = \frac{1}{2}(1 - t)^2$$

Equations 7.54 substituted into equation 7.50 represents a solution for the quadratic B-spline curve. Values for the nine coefficients may be obtained by comparing equations 7.49 with equations 7.54. These coefficients can readily be shown to satisfy equations 7.51, 7.52, and 7.53. Also, the resulting expressions 7.54 satisfy the following normalizing condition at all t values.

$$b_{-0}(t) + b_{-1}(t) + b_{-2}(t) = 1 \qquad (7.55)$$

Because three basis functions are needed to describe the curve, the curve starts with the second segment. For an *open* curve, as shown in figure 7.11a, the curve starts midway between the first two vertex points (since $b_{-0}(0) = 0$ and $b_{-1}(0) = b_{-2}(0) = 1/2$), and ends midway between the last two vertices. The open quadratic B-spline is drawn by subroutine quadBSpline() listed below.

In the subroutine quadBSpline(), the outer *for* loop over index i extends over the *nisegs* $= n - 2$ curve segments. In the inner *for* loop over the integer j, the parameter t is incremented by the operation $t+ = dt$, which equals the operation $t = t + dt$. The increment dt is set by the parameter *ntsegs*, which is the number of segments that make the interval from $t = 0$ to $t = 1$.

```
void quadBSpline(int n,double x[],double y[])
{
    int i,j,nisegs,ntsegs;
    double t,dt,b0,b1,b2,xp,yp;

    nisegs = n - 2;
    ntsegs = 20; dt = 1./(double) ntsegs;

    for (i=2; i<= nisegs+1; i++)
    {
```

```
for (j=0,t=0.;j<=ntsegs;j++,t+=dt)
{
    b0 = .5*t*t;
    b1 = .5*(1.+2.*t-2.*t*t);
    b2 = .5*(1.-t)*(1.-t);
    xp = b2*x[i-2]+b1*x[i-1]+b0*x[i];
    yp = b2*y[i-2]+b1*y[i-1]+b0*y[i];
    if (i==2 && j==0)
        MoveTo((int) xp,(int) yp);
    else
        LineTo((int) xp,(int) yp);
    }
  }
}
```

The quadratic B-spline can be extended to the starting and ending control vertices by making these points double, that is, by placing one additional vertex at the location of the first vertex V_0 and placing an additional vertex at the last location V_{n-1}. Note that at $t = 0$ in the first segment, $b_{-0}(t) = 0$ and $b_{-2}(0)+b_{-1}(0) = 1$, therefore $Q_i(t)$ in equation 7.50 will equal V_{i-1} if it is a double point (since V_{i-2} equals V_{i-1} at the double point). A similar analysis shows that the curve will extend to a double point at the end of the curve.

If the functions 7.54 are used for $b_{-0}(t)$, $b_{-1}(t)$, and $b_{-2}(t)$ in the first and last curve segments (with the first and last vertices being double points), then the curves in these segments differ somewhat from those drawn by AutoCAD. The AutoCAD curves correspond to treating the double points as a nonuniform B-spline, as discussed in section 7.7. The first and last curve segments can be drawn by using the appropriate nonuniform B-spline expressions for $b_{-0}(t)$, $b_{-1}(t)$, and $b_{-2}(t)$. But the same curve segments can be programmed more simply by an equivalent procedure, namely, by extrapolating the first and last vertices to new positions, without adding any new vertices.

The extrapolation procedure for the first vertex V_0 consists of simply requiring that the new vertex position produce a curve that starts at the original vertex position. That is, using equation 7.50 at the beginning of the first curve segment ($i = 2$ and $t = 0$) produces the following condition:

$$x_0 = \frac{1}{2}x_0^{new} + \frac{1}{2}x_1, \qquad y_0 = \frac{1}{2}y_0^{new} + \frac{1}{2}y_1 \qquad (7.56)$$

Equations 7.56 give the following expressions for the new position of the starting vertex.

$$x_0^{new} = 2x_0 - x_1, \qquad y_0^{new} = 2y_0 - y_1 \qquad (7.57)$$

A similar extrapolation of the last vertex gives the expression

$$x_{n-1}^{new} = 2x_{n-1} - x_{n-2}, \qquad y_{n-1}^{new} = 2y_{n-1} - y_{n-2} \qquad (7.58)$$

Equations 7.57–7.58 can be used to provide the following program lines at the beginning of the subroutine quadBSpline() to produce beginning and ending curve segments that match those drawn by AutoCAD.

```
x[0] = 2.*x[0]-x[1]; y[0] = 2.*y[0]-y[1];
x[n-1] = 2.*x[n-1]-x[n-2]; y[n-1] = 2.*y[n-1]-y[n-2];
```

A *closed* quadratic B-spline can be constructed from the subroutine quadBSpline() by adding two vertex points to form a periodic set of vertices. For example, vertices $\mathbf{V}_n = \mathbf{V}_0$ and $\mathbf{V}_{n+1} = \mathbf{V}_1$ can be added, with the number of curve segments increased to *nisegs* = *n*. Also, arrays x[] and y[] should be dimensioned to handle $n + 2$ values. The additional vertices are added by placing the following lines at the beginning of the subroutine quadB-Spline().

```
x[n] = x[0]; y[n] = y[0];
x[n+1] = x[1]; y[n+1] = y[1];
```

B-spline curves can be drawn with AutoCAD by entering "S" for spline under the PEDIT command. The default spline is the cubic B-spline, but the quadratic spline can be drawn by changing the system variable SPLINETYPE from the value 6 (for the cubic B-spline) to the value 5. That is, enter SPLINETYPE, and then the number 5 (the command SETVAR may precede SPLINETYPE, but it is not necessary). Also, the following system variables can be changed: SPLFRAME can be changed from 0 to 1 to display the spline frame (polyline); SPLINESEGS may be increased from its default value of 8 to increase the number of segments used in drawing the spline curve.

Figure 7.13a shows some sample curves drawn with the quadratic B-spline option on AutoCAD. On the left of the figure, a vertical straight line appears because three sequential points were entered with the same x-values. In equation 7.50, the segment determined by these three points will have this same constant value of x because the $b_i(t)$ functions sum to the value 1. On the left of figure 7.13a it is also illustrated that when two points merge, the quadratic B-spline will pass through the double point, and the slope at the double point will be discontinuous.

The right side of figure 7.13a shows a closed quadratic B-spline drawn from four control points located at the corners of a square. When the upper-right-hand control point is changed to a double point, the curve passes through the double point and has a discontinuous slope at that point.

Cubic B-Spline

The cubic B-spline requires four basis functions at each point on the curve.

$$\mathbf{Q}_i(t) = \mathbf{V}_{i-3}B_{i-3}(t) + \mathbf{V}_{i-2}B_{i-2}(t) + \mathbf{V}_{i-1}B_{i-1}(t) + \mathbf{V}_iB_{i-0}(t)$$

$$= \sum_{k=-3}^{0} \mathbf{V}_{i+k}B_{i+k}(t) = \sum_{k=-3}^{0} \mathbf{V}_{i+k}b_k(t) \tag{7.59}$$

The open cubic B-spline curve shown in figure 7.14a for *n* control points has $n - 3$ line segments $\mathbf{Q}_i(t)$ (one less segment than the quadratic B-spline shown for the same con-

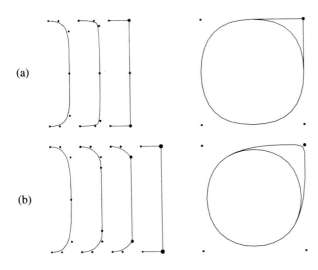

Figure 7–13 Sample B-spline curves drawn with AutoCAD: (a) the quadratic B-spline; (b) the cubic B-spline. The smallest dots represent single vertex points; the larger dots, double points; and the largest dots, triple points.

trol points in figure 7.11a). The index number i starts with $i = 3$ for the curve $\mathbf{Q}_i(t)$ in equation 7.59 because the first curve segment is controlled by the first four vertices: $\mathbf{V}_0$, $\mathbf{V}_1$, $\mathbf{V}_2$, and $\mathbf{V}_3$.

Figure 7.12c illustrates the four basis functions contributing to the curve segment between knots i and $i+1$. Each basis function extends across four curve segments, and is represented by a cubic polynomial in the parameter t. For example, the $B_{i-2}(t)$ function shown in figures 7.12c and d is given by the expression

$$B_{i-2}(t) = a_j + b_j t + c_j t^2 + d_j t^3 \quad \text{for } i - 2 \le j \le i + 1 \qquad (7.60)$$

The four coefficients in each of the four segments spanned by a basis function represent a total of 16 constants to be determined. Because the equations are now cubic, continuity of second derivatives can be required. Accordingly, 16 equations for the coefficients are obtained by requiring the following: values, first derivatives, and second derivatives are zero at the boundary knots $i-2$ and $i+2$ (6 equations); values, first derivatives, and second derivatives are continuous at the three interior knots $i-1$, i, and $i+1$ (9 equations); and normalization is prescribed at $t = 0$ (1 equation).

The above procedure yields the following expressions.

$$b_{-0}(t) = \frac{1}{6}t^3$$

$$b_{-1}(t) = \frac{1}{6}(1 + 3t + 3t^2 - 3t^3)$$

$$b_{-2}(t) = \frac{1}{6}(4 - 6t^2 + 3t^3) \qquad (7.61)$$

$$b_{-3}(t) = \frac{1}{6}(1 - t)^3$$

Equations 7.61 satisfy the following normalization at each value of t.

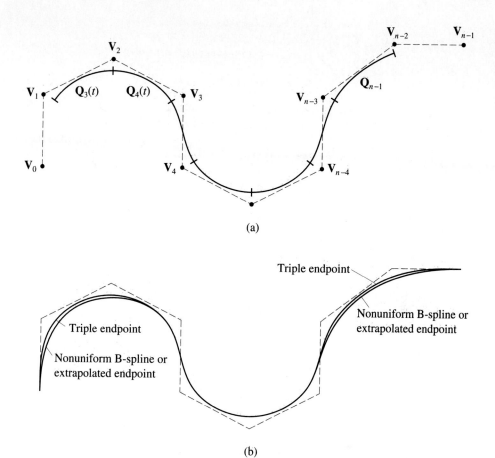

(a)

(b)

Figure 7.14   An open cubic B-spline with the defining polyline (dashed): (a) curve for no special end conditions; (b) curve extended to the starting and ending control vertex points by means of two different procedures.

$$b_{-0}(t) + b_{-1}(t) + b_{-2}(t) + b_{-3}(t) = 1 \tag{7.62}$$

In the open cubic B-spline subroutine given below, the outer *for* loop starts with index number $i = 3$ and extends to *nisegs*+2 so that a total number *nisegs* curve segments are drawn.

```
void cubicBSpline(int n,double x[],double y[])
{
    int i,j,nisegs,ntsegs;
    double t,dt,b0,b1,b2,b3,xp,yp;

    nisegs = n - 3;
    ntsegs = 20; dt = 1./(double) ntsegs;
```

```
for (i=3; i<= nisegs+2; i++)
{
    for (j=0,t=0.;j<=ntsegs;j++,t+=dt)
    {
        b0 = t*t*t/6.;
        b1 = (1.+3.*t+3.*t*t-3.*t*t*t)/6.;
        b2 = (4.-6.*t*t+3.*t*t*t)/6.;
        b3 = (1.-t)*(1.-t)*(1.-t)/6.;
        xp = b3*x[i-3]+b2*x[i-2]+b1*x[i-1]+b0*x[i];
        yp = b3*y[i-3]+b2*y[i-2]+b1*y[i-1]+b0*y[i];
        if (i==3 && j==0)
            MoveTo((int) xp,(int) yp);
        else
            LineTo((int) xp,(int) yp);
    }
}
```

The above subroutine will produce a cubic B-spline curve like the one shown in figure 7.14a. The curve can be extended to the starting and ending control vertices by making these points triple, that is, by placing two additional vertices at the location of the first vertex V_0, and placing two additional vertices at the last location V_n. When equations 7.61 are used for the $b_i(t)$ functions with each vertex in the triplets, the curves reach the starting and ending vertices as illustrated by the top curve in figure 7.14b. The bottom curve in 7.14b, which corresponds to the AutoCAD cubic spline, can be drawn by treating the triple points as a nonuniform B-spline (section 7.7), or by extrapolating vertices V_0, V_1, V_{n-1}, and V_n in the following manner.

The following conditions are obtained from equation 7.59 by requiring that V_0 be the starting point of the curve ($i = 3$ and $t = 0$ at the starting point).

$$x_0 = \frac{1}{6}x_0^{new} + \frac{2}{3}x_1^{new} + \frac{1}{6}x_2, \qquad y_0 = \frac{1}{6}y_0^{new} + \frac{2}{3}y_1^{new} + \frac{1}{6}y_2 \qquad (7.63)$$

In equations 7.63 both the first and second vertices are moved to new positions. An additional condition to be imposed is that the slope of the curve at V_0 be tangent to the line that connects the original vertices V_0 and V_1. This condition is imposed by the equations

$$\left(\frac{dx}{dt}\right)_{t=0} = -\frac{1}{2}x_0^{new} + \frac{1}{2}x_2 = \alpha(x_1 - x_0), \qquad \left(\frac{dy}{dt}\right)_{t=0} = -\frac{1}{2}y_0^{new} + \frac{1}{2}y_2 = \alpha(y_1 - y_0) \quad (7.64)$$

When the constant α in equation 7.64 is varied, different curves result, with $\alpha = 3$ giving curve segments that are identical to those drawn by AutoCAD and those given by the nonuniform B-spline. For $\alpha = 3$, equations 7.63 and 7.64 yield

$$x_0^{new} = x_2 - 6(x_1 - x_0), \qquad y_0^{new} = y_2 - 6(y_1 - y_0)$$

and

$$x_1^{new} = \frac{1}{2}(3x_1 - x_2), \qquad y_1^{new} = \frac{1}{2}(3y_1 - y_2) \qquad (7.65)$$

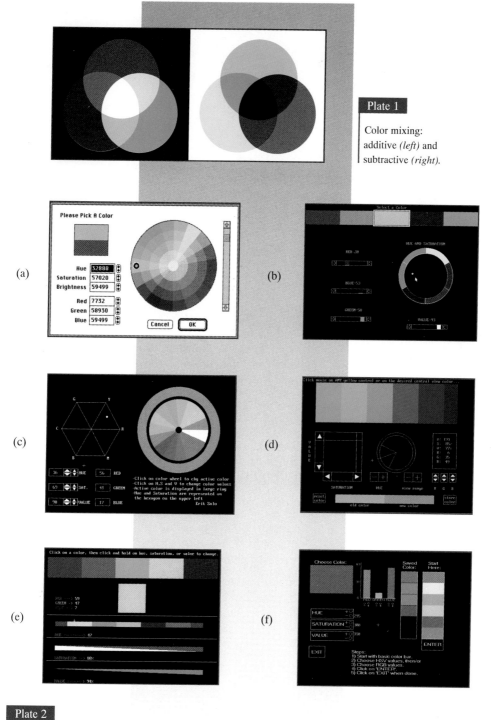

Plate 1

Color mixing: additive *(left)* and subtractive *(right)*.

Plate 2

Color pickers. (a) Macintosh color wheel dialog box (used with permission of Apple Computer, Inc.). Color picker designs for the PC, programmed by (b) Michael Rysdorp; (c) Erik Salo; (d) Joseph McKinley; (e) Jon Rucinski; and (f) Jason Frankson.

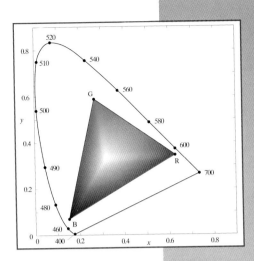

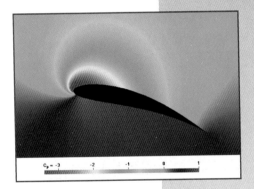

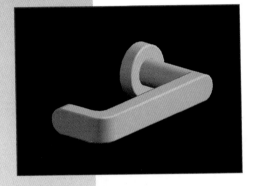

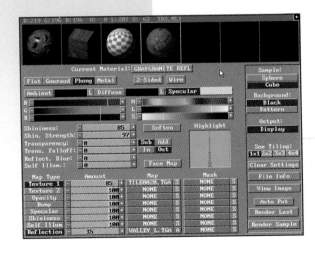

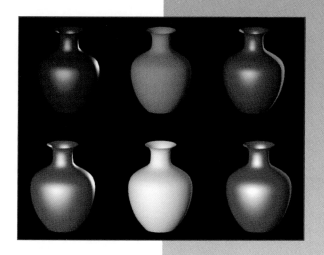

Plate 7

3D Studio renderings of a vase with metal shading and Phong shading. The two vases on the left have metal shading approximating copper (top) and stainless steel (bottom). The vases in the middle column were rendered with Phong shading with the same colors as the vases on the left (ambient and diffuse colors only). The right column shows Phong shading with material properties (including specular colors) adjusted to approximate metals.

(a)

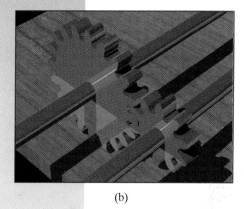

(b)

Plate 8

Renderings of gears above a wood table: (a) AutoVision image obtained with full ray tracing; (b) 3D Studio image obtained with reflection maps and ray-traced shadows.

Plate 9

3D Studio spheres: top row shows texture maps; middle row includes bump maps; and bottom row includes reflection maps.

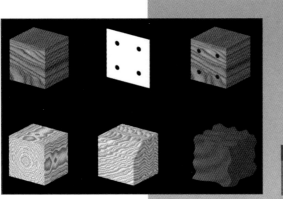

Plate 10

3D Studio opacity mapping (top row), and external processes (bottom row).

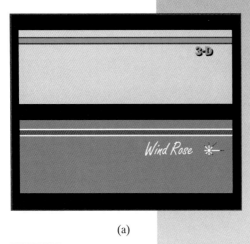

(a)

(b)

Plate 11

3D Studio texture maps applied to a yacht (hull surface model shown in figure 12.24b):
(a) Images used in the mappings; (b) Yacht hulls with mapped decals.

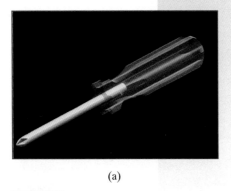

(a)

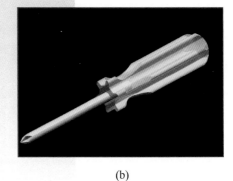

(b)

Plate 12

Screwdriver, with handle rendered at two different levels of transparency: (a) 90% transparent;
(b) 50% transparent. An AutoCAD solid model constructed by Stanley Peng and shown in figure 13.20a
was used for these renderings on AutoVision.

Because the x_1^{new} and y_1^{new} values do not depend on x_0 and y_0, the x_0^{new} and y_0^{new} values can be calculated first, as shown in the following program lines. These lines may be inserted into the subroutine cubicBSpline() to duplicate the AutoCAD open cubic B-splines. Note that this extrapolation procedure requires at least five control points ($n \geq 5$).

```
x[0] = x[2]+6.*(x[0]-x[1]); x[1] = 1.5*x[1]-.5*x[2];
y[0] = y[2]+6.*(y[0]-y[1]); y[1] = 1.5*y[1]-.5*y[2];
x[n-1] = x[n-3]+6.*(x[n-1]-x[n-2]);x[n-2] = 1.5*x[n-2]-.5*x[n-3];
y[n-1] = y[n-3]+6.*(y[n-1]-y[n-2]);y[n-2] = 1.5*y[n-2]-.5*y[n-3];
```

A *closed* cubic B-spline can be constructed from the subroutine cubicBSpline() by adding three vertex points to form a periodic set of vertices. For example, vertices $\mathbf{V}_n = \mathbf{V}_0$, $\mathbf{V}_{n+1} = \mathbf{V}_1$, and $\mathbf{V}_{n+2} = \mathbf{V}_2$ can be added, with the number of curve segments increased to *nisegs = n,* so that the curve closes on itself. Also, arrays $x[]$ and $y[]$ should be dimensioned to handle $n + 3$ values.

The behavior of cubic B-spline curves is illustrated in figure 7.13b. The first curve on the left of figure 7.13b has three colinear vertex points, but no straight segment exists in the spline curve. Four colinear points in the next spline curve do produce a straight-line segment. This result may be deduced from equation 7.59 because the curve segment determined by these four colinear vertex points will have a constant x-value (the four $b_i(t)$ functions sum to the value 1). Figure 7.13b also illustrates the merging of vertices to form double points and triple points. Although the cubic B-spline approaches close to a double point, it does not pass through it, and the first derivative remains continuous (but the second derivative does not). The curve does pass through a triple point, at which it has a discontinuous first derivative.

Figure 7.15 shows that cubic B-splines produce curves of considerable smoothness and flexibility. These curves are noticeably smoother than curves drawn with the circular-arc (biarc) fit. The circular-arc fit tends to produce some small-scale extraneous wiggles as arcs are fit between data points. Note that the circular-arc curves in figure 7.5 do not appear to be as smooth as the cubic B-spline curves in figure 7.15.

Smooth curves can be drawn with considerable efficiency with the cubic B-spline. As an example, consider the character fonts displayed in figure 7.16. The top part of the figure shows the spline frame; that is, a polyline through the vertex points. Each character is constructed with two or three B-splines, plus some short straight lines that form the serifs at the ends of the splines. Vertical straight segments on the splines forming the letters U and D are constructed with four colinear vertices.

Fonts can also be constructed from quadratic curves. For example, the TrueType font format developed for the Macintosh is based on quadratic B-spline curves. More vertex points are required for quadratic curves, but a quadratic curve can be computed and printed faster. The PostScript printing language for laser printers uses cubic curves; namely, composite cubic Bézier curves. In section 7.8, Bézier curves of general order are discussed along with composite cubic Bézier curves.

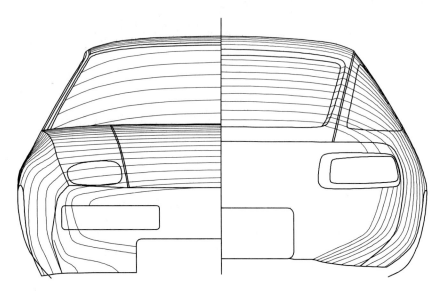

Figure 7.15 Vertical cross sections and some detail lines for a Porsche 928. These curves were drawn on AutoCAD with cubic B-splines.

Figure 7.16 Characters formed by cubic B-splines, with the spline frame shown at the top. The dots identify the locations of the vertex points.

7.7 NONUNIFORM B-SPLINES

Nonuniform rational B-splines (NURBS) are generalizations of the uniform B-splines considered in the preceding section. NURBS curves and surfaces form the basis of a number of CAD systems because they can represent free-form shapes as well as common analytic shapes such as conic sections (circles, ellipses, parabolas, and hyperbolas) and primitive surfaces like spheres, tori, cylinders, and cones. Although the basic AutoCAD release 12 software does not contain NURBS, AutoSurf™ release 2, which is an add-on package that works from within AutoCAD, is NURBS based.

The closed curves drawn in figure 7.17a show that the cubic uniform B-spline in a square polyline frame provides a rough approximation to a circle, while the quadratic uniform B-spline gives a poor approximation to a circle (the cubic B-spline is the inner solid curve, and the circles are shown with dashed lines). There is no way to accurately represent a circle with a uniform B-spline having a finite number of control vertices. On the other hand, NURBS curves have the flexibility to represent a continuous range of curves, as illustrated in figure 7.17b. For these NURBS curves, weights are assigned to each of the control vertices, which lie at the corners and side midpoints of the outer square. In figure 7.17b, the weights of the corner vertices are varied from 0 to ∞ to produce curves ranging from the inner rotated square to the outer square frame. When the weights of the corner vertices are √2/2 times the weights of the vertices on the square sides, the NURBS curve is a circle, as shown by the middle curve in figure 7.17b.

Before the theory of NURBS curves is developed in this section, nonuniform *nonrational* B-splines must be studied.

Nonuniform Nonrational B-Splines

The uniform B-splines described in the preceding section can be generalized by considering knots nonuniformly spaced along the parameter $\bar{t}$. Previously, the knots were considered to have equal spacing, with the $\bar{t}$ interval between knots being constant. The independent parameter t for the uniform B-splines described in section 7.6 varies between 0 and 1 and is related to the increasing parameter $\bar{t}$ by the relation $\bar{t} = i + t$, where i is the curve segment index number.

For convenience in the following discussion of nonuniform B-splines, the overbar is dropped from $\bar{t}$. The knots are placed along t as prescribed by the following knot vector $\mathbf{T}_{knot}$ having m elements t_0 through t_{m-1}.

$$\mathbf{T}_{knot} = [\; \underbrace{t_{min},\; t_{min},\; ...,\; t_{min}}_{k},\; t_k,\; ...,\; t_{m-k-1},\; \underbrace{t_{max},\; t_{max},\; ...,\; t_{max}}_{k} \;] \qquad (7.66)$$

The knot vector $\mathbf{T}_{knot}$ in equation 7.66 is appropriate for an open nonuniform B-spline of order k and degree $k-1$. Thus, an open quadratic nonuniform B-spline has a knot vector with $k = 3$ identical elements at the start of the curve ($t_0 = t_1 = t_2 = t_{min}$, where t_{min} is of-

(a) 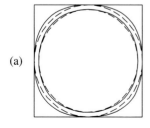   (b)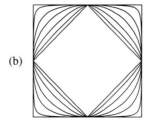

Figure 7.17 B-spline curves: (a) quadratic and cubic uniform B-splines, with control vertices at the corners of the square, and two circles (dashed lines); (b) quadratic nonuniform rational B-splines (NURBS), with the control vertices at the side midpoints having weights of 1.0, and the corner vertices having weights of 0.0, 0.1, 0.3, √2/2, 1.5, 5.0, and ∞.

ten set equal to 0) and $k = 3$ identical values at the curve end ($t_{m-3} = t_{m-2} = t_{m-1} = t_{max}$). The elements of the knot vector must be nondecreasing, $t_{min} \le t_k$, $t_i \le t_{i+1}$, and $t_{m-k-1} \le t_{max}$.

For the open nonuniform B-spline, the following relation holds between the number of knots m, the number of control points n, and the spline order k.

$$m = n + k \qquad\qquad (7.67)$$

Thus a quadratic spline ($k = 3$) will have three more knots than control points, and a cubic spline will have four more knots than control points.

AutoSurf can draw nonuniform B-splines with orders from 2 through 26. Because the order of the B-spline is limited by the number of control points, nine nonuniform B-splines (orders 2 through 10) can be drawn for the 10 control points shown in figure 7.18. Auto-Surf draws free-form splines as nonrational B-splines but constructs primitive curves like the circle shown in figure 7.17 with NURBS.

Splines are drawn in AutoSurf with the SPLINE3D command and are edited with the EDITSP command. These commands offer some advanced features not present in the PLINE and PEDIT commands of AutoCAD. For example, with SPLINE3D, points on the curve may be entered, and AutoSurf will determine appropriate control point positions.

Closed splines are drawn in AutoSurf by selecting "closed" in the advanced options dialog box, and entering points on the curve. AutoSurf then computes appropriate control point positions, including starting and ending control points that lie midway between two other control points. Thus, AutoSurf uses an "open" spline to represent the closed curve, in the same manner that the circle is represented in the next subsection. The EDITSP command can be used to move the first or last control point to "open up" closed curves including circles (circles and ellipses are drawn with the ELLIPSE3D command).

The EDITSP command in AutoSurf moves and adds control points like the AutoCAD PEDIT command, but with EDITSP, points can be moved dynamically by using the mouse to move the cursor, and points on the curve (as well as control points) can be selected for displacement.

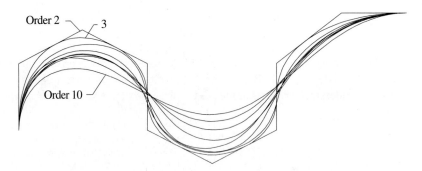

Figure 7.18   B-spline curves of orders 2 through 10 drawn with the AutoSurf SPLINE3D command. The control points are the same as those used in figures 7.11 and 7.14.

For the open nonuniform B-spline, the basis function of order k is represented with the notation $N_{i,k}(t)$, with the curve coordinates being represented by the vector $\mathbf{Q}(t)$.

$$\mathbf{Q}(t) = \sum_{i=0}^{n-1} \mathbf{V}_i N_{i,k}(t) \tag{7.68}$$

Although the form of equation 7.68 appears to be different from that of equations 7.47 and 7.59 for the uniform quadratic and cubic B-splines, the forms are comparable because for the quadratic case only three $N_{i,3}(t)$ functions will be nonzero along any curve segment, and only four $N_{i,4}(t)$ functions will be nonzero along a cubic B-spline curve segment. Thus the $N_{i,k}(t)$ functions for the nonuniform case correspond to the $B_i(t)$ functions of the uniform case.

The basis functions $N_{i,k}(t)$ of any order can be calculated from the Cox–deBoor recursion relation.

$$N_{i,k}(t) = \frac{(t - t_i)N_{i,k-1}(t)}{t_{i+k-1} - t_i} + \frac{(t_{i+k} - t)N_{i+1,k-1}(t)}{t_{i+k} - t_{i+1}} \tag{7.69}$$

To start the recursion relation 7.69, the following values are prescribed for the first-order basis functions.

$$N_{i,k}(t) = \begin{cases} 1 & \text{if } t_i \leq t < t_{i+1} \\ 0 & \text{otherwise} \end{cases} \tag{7.70}$$

As illustrated in figure 7.19a, each first-order basis function spans the distance between adjacent knots.

Although equations 7.69–7.70 can be directly programmed to provide a spline of any order, it is instructive to develop solutions algebraically for orders 2 and 3. First, when using equation 7.69 to calculate $N_{i,2}(t)$, note that $N_{i,1}(t)$ is nonzero only in the region $t_i \leq t < t_{i+1}$, and $N_{i+1,1}(t)$ is nonzero only in the region $t_{i+1} \leq t < t_{i+2}$. Thus, equation 7.69 yields the following result.

$$N_{i,2}(t) = \frac{(t - t_i)}{t_{i+1} - t_i} \quad \text{for } t_i \leq t < t_{i+1} \tag{7.71a}$$

$$N_{i,2}(t) = \frac{(t_{i+2} - t)}{t_{i+2} - t_{i+1}} \quad \text{for } t_{i+1} \leq t < t_{i+2} \tag{7.71b}$$

The fact that the second-order basis function $N_{i,2}(t)$ spans across two curve segments (from knot t_i to t_{i+2}) is illustrated in figure 7.19a.

An expression for $N_{i+1,2}(t)$ may be obtained by transforming $i \rightarrow i + 1$ in equations 7.71. The basis function $N_{i,3}(t)$ is then calculated from equation 7.69 by requiring that only $N_{i,2}(t)$ is nonzero in the region $t_i \leq t < t_{i+1}$, both $N_{i,2}(t)$ and $N_{i+1,2}(t)$ are nonzero in the region $t_{i+1} \leq t < t_{i+2}$, and only $N_{i+1,2}(t)$ is nonzero in the region $t_{i+2} \leq t < t_{i+3}$. The following result is obtained.

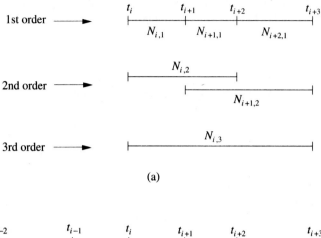

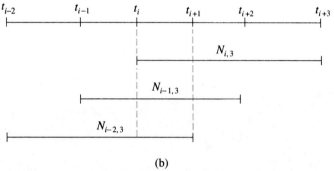

Figure 7.19 Basis function ranges for nonuniform B-splines: (a) the buildup of a third-order basis function from lower-order basis functions; (b) the three third-order basis functions that contribute to the B-spline in the region $t_i \leq t \leq t_{i+1}$.

$$N_{i,3}(t) = \frac{(t - t_i)^2}{(t_{i+2} - t_i)(t_{i+1} - t_i)} \quad \text{for } t_i \leq t < t_{i+1} \tag{7.72a}$$

$$N_{i,3}(t) = \frac{(t - t_i)(t_{i+2} - t)}{(t_{i+2} - t_i)(t_{i+2} - t_{i+1})} + \frac{(t_{i+3} - t)(t - t_{i+1})}{(t_{i+3} - t_{i+1})(t_{i+2} - t_{i+1})} \quad \text{for } t_{i+1} \leq t < t_{i+2} \tag{7.72b}$$

$$N_{i,3}(t) = \frac{(t_{i+3} - t)^2}{(t_{i+3} - t_{i+1})(t_{i+3} - t_{i+2})} \quad \text{for } t_{i+2} \leq t < t_{i+3} \tag{7.72c}$$

The above procedure for calculating $N_{i,3}(t)$ is summarized in figure 7.19a. The first-order basis functions $N_{i,1}(t)$ and $N_{i+1,1}(t)$ are used to form $N_{i,2}(t)$ by equation 7.69; $N_{i+1,1}(t)$ and $N_{i+2,1}(t)$ are used to form $N_{i+1,2}(t)$; then $N_{i,2}(t)$ and $N_{i+1,2}(t)$ are used to form $N_{i,3}(t)$.

Because the second-order basis functions each span two curve segments, a general point t will be covered by two second-order basis functions; see figure 7.20a. As shown by figure 7.20a and equations 7.71, second-order basis functions are linear in t. This results in a second-order spline consisting of straight-line segments connecting the control points.

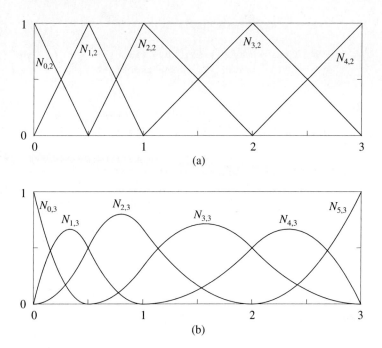

Figure 7.20   Basis functions for a nonuniform B-spline: (a) second-order basis functions for the knot vector $\mathbf{T}_{knot} = [\,0, 0, 0.5, 1, 2, 3, 3\,]$; (b) third-order basis functions for the same knot vector.

The third-order basis functions given by equations 7.72 cover three line segments, with the result that three third-order basis functions contribute at any t value. Third-order basis functions are shown in figure 7.20b for a particular nonuniform knot vector.

Figure 7.19b shows the three third-order basis functions that contribute for a value of t between knots t_i and t_{i+1}. The first is $N_{i,3}(t)$, which contributes a term (here called $b_{-0}(t)$ in analogy to the uniform B-spline case) determined by equation 7.72a; the second function is $N_{i-1,3}(t)$, which contributes a term $b_{-1}(t)$ calculated from 7.72b with i replaced by $i - 1$; and the third is $N_{i-2,3}(t)$, which contributes a term $b_{-2}(t)$ calculated from 7.72c with i replaced by $i - 2$. Thus, the curve coordinates along segment i may be calculated with a formula of the same form as for the uniform case in equation 7.50. Accordingly, the subroutine nonuQuadBSpln() given below is the same as the uniform quadratic B-spline subroutine quadBSpline(), except that a knot vector passed to the subroutine is used to calculate the $b_i(t)$ functions for the nonuniform B-spline.

```
void nonuQuadBSpln(int n,double x[],double y[],double tknot[])
{
    int i,j,nisegs,ntsegs;
    double t,dt,b0,b1,b2,xp,yp;
    double tn1,t0,t1,t2;

    nisegs = n - 2; ntsegs = 20;
```

```
for (i=2; i<=nisegs+1; i++)
{
    tn1 = tknot[i-1]; t0 = tknot[i];
    t1 = tknot[i+1]; t2 = tknot[i+2];
    if (t1 > t0)
    {
        dt = (t1-t0)/(double) ntsegs;
        for (j=0,t=t0;j<=ntsegs;j++,t+=dt)
        {
            b0 = (t-t0)*(t-t0)/((t2-t0)*(t1-t0));
            b1 = (t1-t)*(t-tn1)/((t1-t0)*(t1-tn1)) +
                        (t2-t)*(t-t0)/((t2-t0)*(t1-t0)));
            b2 = (t1-t)*(t1-t)/((t1-tn1)*(t1-t0));
            xp = b2*x[i-2]+b1*x[i-1]+b0*x[i];
            yp = b2*y[i-2]+b1*y[i-1]+b0*y[i];
            if (j == 0)
                MoveTo((int) xp, (int) yp);
            else
                LineTo((int) xp, (int) yp);
        }
    }
}
```

In the subroutine nonuQuadBSpln(), knots are related to the index i by the following notation: $tn1$ stands for "i negative 1", or knot number $i-1$; $t0$ for knot $i+0$; $t1$ for $i+1$; and $t2$ for $i+2$. Note that the first knot, $tknot[0]$, does not appear in the subroutine. Although $tknot[0] = t_0$ appears in equations 7.72a and b that represent $N_{0,3}(t)$, only equation 7.72c is used to represent $N_{0,3}(t)$ in the first curve segment. In a similar manner, the last knot is not used directly in the curve calculation.

As illustrated in figure 7.20b, the identical values (0) for the second and third knots produce the following basis functions at $t = 0$: $N_{0,3}(0) = 1$, $N_{1,3}(0) = 0$, and $N_{2,3}(0) = 0$. These values produce a curve that starts at the first control point. Similarly, the multiple knot values at the end of the knot vector force the curve to extend to the last control point.

When the knots are uniformly placed, the third-order basis functions $N_{i,3}(t)$ over interior line segments reduce to the uniform B-spline basis functions $B_i(t)$. That is, the three functions in equations 7.72a–c reduce to the three quadratic polynomials $b_i(t)$ given in equation 7.54 when the parameter t is replaced by $i + t$, where the new t varies from 0 to 1.

When t is replaced by $i + t$, the first curve segment is covered by parts of three basis functions: $N_{0,3}(t) \equiv b_{-0}(t)$ calculated by equation 7.72a with $i = 2$, $N_{1,3}(t) \equiv b_{-1}(t)$ calculated by equation 7.72b with $i = 1$, and $N_{2,3}(t) \equiv b_{-2}(t)$ calculated by equation 7.72c with $i = 0$. (Or equivalently, the value $i = 2$ for the first curve segment can be substituted in the formulas in the nonuQuadBSpln() subroutine.) This procedure was used to derive the following relations.

$$b_{-0}(t) = \frac{1}{2}t^2$$

$$b_{-1}(t) = \frac{1}{2}t\,(4 - 3t)$$ (7.73)

$$b_{-2}(t) = (1 - t)^2$$

In a similar manner, when t is replaced by $i + t$, the last curve segment yields the functions

$$b_{-0}(t) = t^2$$

$$b_{-1}(t) = \frac{1}{2}(1 + 2t - 3t^2)$$ (7.74)

$$b_{-2}(t) = \frac{1}{2}(1 - t)^2$$

The AutoCAD quadratic B-spline curves are reproduced when equations 7.73 are used for the first curve segment, equations 7.54 for the interior segments, and equations 7.74 for the last segment. As discussed in section 7.6 on uniform B-splines, equations 7.54 can be used with an extrapolation procedure on the first and last control points to produce the same first and last curve segments as equations 7.73 and 7.74.

The cubic (fourth order) nonuniform B-spline can be calculated by the same procedures as described above for the quadratic case. For the cubic case, four basis functions determine a portion of the curve. These fourth-order basis functions can be calculated from the third-order functions 7.72 by using the Cox–deBoor formula 7.69. (The implementation of the fourth-order nonuniform B-spline is left for exercises 7.17–7.19). When the knots are uniformly spaced, the uniform cubic B-spline discussed in section 7.6 is recovered.

Nonuniform Rational B-Splines (NURBS)

The term *rational* in NURBS signifies that a ratio of basis functions is formed. Specifically, the ratio is formed by dividing by the sum of the basis functions. Also, a weight w_i is assigned to each vertex. Thus, equation 7.68 is replaced by the following.

$$\mathbf{Q}(t) = \frac{\displaystyle\sum_{i=0}^{n-1} \mathbf{V}_i w_i N_{i,k}(t)}{\displaystyle\sum_{i=0}^{n-1} w_i N_{i,k}(t)} = \sum_{i=0}^{n-1} \mathbf{V}_i R_{i,k}(t)$$ (7.75)

In equation 7.75, the rational B-spline basis functions $R_{i,k}(t)$ are defined by

$$R_{i,k}(t) = \frac{w_i N_{i,k}(t)}{\displaystyle\sum_{i=0}^{n-1} w_i N_{i,k}(t)}$$ (7.76)

The weights w_i are often represented by the variable h_i because they can be interpreted geometrically in terms of homogeneous coordinates; see, for example, Rogers and Adams (1990), or Piegl (1991).

A subroutine for nonrational B-splines can be developed by passing to the subroutine an array w[] for the vertex weights and by using these weights in the calculation of the curve coordinates *xp* and *yp*. In particular, the subroutine nonuQuadBSpln() above can be modified for rational B-splines by replacing the two lines for *xp* and *yp* by the following three program lines, where the variable *bsum* is assigned a double data type.

```
bsum = b2*w[i-2]+b1*w[i-1]+b0*w[i];
xp = (b2*w[i-2]*x[i-2]+b1*w[i-1]*x[i-1]+b0*w[i]*x[i])/bsum;
yp = (b2*w[i-2]*y[i-2]+b1*w[i-1]*y[i-1]+b0*w[i]*y[i])/bsum;
```

For the closed curves shown in figure 7.17b, there are nine control points starting and ending at the midpoint of one of the sides of the outer square. The array for the weights has unit values at the side midpoints; that is, $w[0] = w[2] = w[4] = w[6] = w[8] = 1.0$, and the corner vertices are assigned equal weights: $w[1] = w[3] = w[5] = w[7] = w_c$, where the seven closed curves from the inner rotated square to the outer square are formed with w_c values of 0.0, 0.1, 0.3, $\sqrt{2}/2$, 1.5, 5.0, and ∞. A circle is formed for the value $w_c = \sqrt{2}/2$.

The curves of figure 7.17b are separated and replotted in figure 7.21, along with plots of the basis functions. The curve is an open curve that starts at one of the side control points (whose locations are shown on the square at the lower right of figure 7.21). Because of the double knot values, the curve always passes through the control points located at the side midpoints. When the corner control vertices have zero weight ($w_c = 0$), the curve reduces to straight line segments between the side control points. At the other limit, when $w_c \rightarrow \infty$, the curve extends all the way to the polyline frame defined by the control vertices.

In terms of the basis functions shown on the left of figure 7.21, the double knot values force one of the basis functions to peak at the value 1 (and the others to drop to 0) at each knot location ($t = 0, 1, 2, 3,$ and 4). These peaks force the curve to start at one of the side control points, then pass through the other three side control points, and end on the first side control point. The curves shown in figure 7.21 start on the control point at the middle of the bottom side of the square because the control points were given by the following vectors: $x[] = [1, 2, 2, 2, 1, 0, 0, 0, 1]$ and $y[] = [0, 0, 1, 2, 2, 2, 1, 0, 0]$.

Circles drawn on AutoSurf with the ELLIPSE3D command are formed as open B-splines, like the curves described above. When the EDITSP command is used to display control points, the square frame is shown, and the selection of control points starts and ends with a point at the middle of one side of the frame, indicating an open curve. Furthermore, if the starting or ending control point is moved (with the Pull option), displacement of the first or last control point opens up the curve and spline frame.

Alternatively, a circle could be represented by four 90° circular arcs, each drawn with three control points. For example, the lower-right quarter circle can be drawn with the following knot vector, weight vector, and control point coordinate vectors: $\mathbf{T}_{knot} = [\,0, 0, 0, 1, 1, 1\,]$, $\mathbf{w} = [\,1, \sqrt{2}/2, 1\,]$, $x[] = [1, 2, 2]$, and $y[] = [0, 0, 1]$.

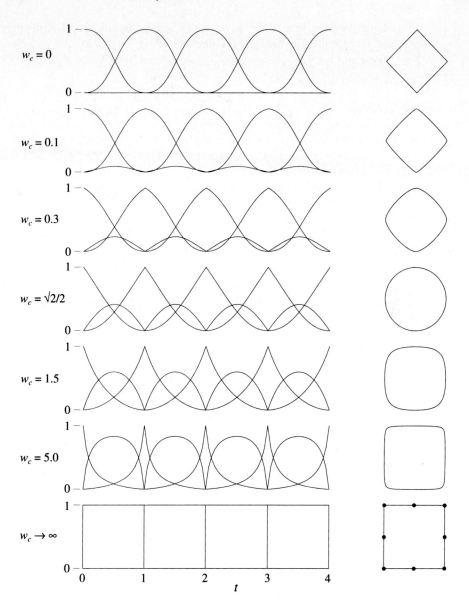

Figure 7.21 NURBS basis functions on the left, with the resulting closed curves on the right, calculated with the knot vector $\mathbf{T}_{knot} = [\,0, 0, 0, 1, 1, 2, 2, 3, 3, 4, 4, 4\,]$. The control vertices lie on the side midpoints and on the corners of the square shown on the lower right. The side vertices have a unit weight factor, and the corner vertices a weight of w_c, according to the weight vector $\mathbf{w} = [\,1, w_c, 1, w_c, 1, w_c, 1, w_c, 1\,]$.

A circular arc of any angle can be represented by a quadratic NURBS curve; see, for example, Rogers and Adams (1990). Three arcs of 120° each can form a circle, and combining these arcs into a single curve leads to the circle representation given in exercise 7.22.

7.8 BÉZIER CURVES

Two types of Bézier curves are considered below: first, the general Bézier curve of order $m = n - 1$, where n is the number of data points. This curve will start at the first vertex (data) point and extend to the last point, with the intermediate vertex points acting as control points. Each point on the curve is controlled by all of the vertex points, with the result that vertex points have very little local control of the curve when the Bézier curve is of high order. Although AutoCAD does not incorporate single Bézier curves, it does use Bézier surfaces defined by a mesh of Bézier curves of order determined by the number of data points. A discussion of Bézier surfaces is included in chapter 12.

The second type to be considered is a composite cubic Bézier curve, which is made up of cubic Bézier curves connected at inserted points. Such composite cubic Bézier curves are used to designate font shapes in PostScript software, which is widely used to produce high-quality characters on laser printers and typesetters.

General-Order Bézier Curve

The nonuniform B-spline curve reduces to the special case of a Bézier curve when the order $k = n$, where n is the number of vertices in the control polyline. The total number of knots given by equation 7.67 is $m = 2k = 2n$. Using the values $t_{min} = 0$ and $t_{max} = 1$, the knot vector for a Bézier curve is given by the equation

$$\mathbf{T}_{knot} = [\underbrace{0, 0, ..., 0,}_{k} \underbrace{1, 1, ..., 1,}_{k}] \tag{7.77}$$

The vector $\mathbf{Q}(t)$ for points along the curve is thus given by

$$\mathbf{Q}(t) = \sum_{i=0}^{d} \mathbf{V}_i P_{i,d}(t) \tag{7.78}$$

where d is the degree of the curve, which is related to the curve order k by the relation $d = k - 1 = n - 1$. The entire curve is drawn as t varies from 0 to 1.

Equation 7.78 is the same as equation 7.68, except that $P_{i,d}(t)$ has been used to denote the Bézier basis functions, which equal the nonuniform B-spline basis functions for the case $k = n$. The Bézier basis functions are given by the following Bernstein polynomials of order d.

$$P_{i,d}(t) = \binom{d}{i} t^i (1-t)^{d-i}, \qquad \binom{d}{i} \equiv \frac{d!}{i!(d-i)!} \tag{7.79}$$

The second of equations 7.79 defines the binomial coefficient.

The function $P_{i,d}(t)$ is given by equation 7.79 when $0 \le i \le d$; otherwise $P_{i,d}(t)$ is zero. Equations 7.79 can be used to derive the recursion relation for the Bernstein polynomials shown below.

$$P_{i,d}(t) = (1 - t)P_{i,d-1}(t) + tP_{i-1,d-1}(t) \tag{7.80}$$

Equation 7.80 can be proved by substituting equations 7.79 for the Bernstein polynomials and by collecting terms. When $i = 0$ in equation 7.80, the second term on the right is zero because for this case the subscript $i-1$ is less than zero (and thus outside of the subscript range for which $P_{i,d}(t)$ is nonzero). Similarly, when $i = d$ in equation 7.80, the first term on the right is zero because the subscript i is greater than the second subscript $d-1$.

Equations 7.78–7.80 can be programmed to provide the subroutine bezier() listed below. This subroutine plots a general Bézier curve, starting with the coordinates of n control points.

```
void bezier(int n,double x[],double y[])
{
    int i,j,k,d,nsegs;
    double t,dt;
    double p[20][20],xp,yp;

    d = n-1;
    nsegs = 50; dt = 1./(double) nsegs;
    MoveTo((int) x[0],(int) y[0]);

    for (j=1,t=dt;j<=nsegs;j++,t+=dt)
    {
        p[0][0] = 1.;
        for (k=1; k<=d; k++)
        {
            p[0][k] = (1.-t)*p[0][k-1];
            for (i=1; i<k; i++)
            {
                p[i][k] = (1.-t)*p[i][k-1] + t*p[i-1][k-1];
            }
            p[k][k] = t*p[k-1][k-1];
        }
        xp = 0.; yp =0.;
        for (i=0; i<=d; i++)
        {
            xp = xp + x[i]*p[i][d];
            yp = yp + y[i]*p[i][d];
        }
        LineTo((int) xp,(int) yp);
    }
}
```

For the general-order Bézier curve, each vertex point has an effect on every part of the curve. Therefore, there is little local control by an individual vertex point, especially for curves that have a large number of vertices. To achieve local control of the curve shape, cubic Bézier curves may be appropriately joined to form a composite cubic Bézier curve.

Composite Cubic Bézier Curves

PostScript printers use font outlines described by composite cubic Bézier curves. Because a cubic Bézier curve is determined by four vertex points, the overall curve is divided into segments that have four points each. Consider an even total number of data points greater than six. The open curve drawn by the subroutine cubicBezier() listed below is an approximation curve that passes through the first and last points, with the remaining data points acting as control points that influence the curve locally. Additional points are added at the curve joints. Therefore, an interior curve segment has two interior data points and two added vertex points at its ends, whereas an end segment has three data points and one added vertex point.

The curve segments will have matching slopes at the interior joints if the added vertices (joint positions) are colinear with the data points on either side. In the program listing below, C^1 continuity is achieved by placing the added vertex points at the midpoint of the line joining two data points; see figure 7.22a. This program subroutine was used to draw the letter S shown in figure 7.22b. In this figure, the original vertex points are shown as dots, and the added vertices are located where the tick marks cross the curves.

```
void cubicBezier(int n,double x[],double y[])
{
    int i,j,nsegs,m,remainder;
    double t,dt,p0,p1,p2,p3,xp,yp,xv[50],yv[50];

    m = 3*n/2 - 3;
    xv[0] = x[0]; yv[0] = y[0];
    j = 1;
    for (i=1; i<m; i++)
```

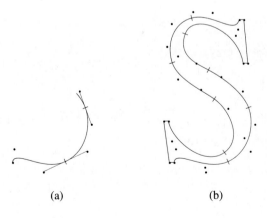

(a)   (b)

Figure 7.22 Composite cubic Bézier curves: (a) the first two curve segments at the bottom of the letter S, starting on the left, with the first joint (shown by a tick mark) located at the midpoint of a line joining the third and fourth data points, and the second joint at the midpoint of a line joining the fifth and sixth data points; (b) the completed letter S composed of two composite Bézier curves and six short line segments that form the serifs at the ends of the curves.

```
{
    remainder = i % 3;
    if (remainder == 0)
    {
        xv[i] = .5*(x[j]+x[j-1]);
        yv[i] = .5*(y[j]+y[j-1]);
    }
    else
    {
        xv[i] = x[j]; yv[i] = y[j];
        j++;
    }
}
xv[m] = x[n-1]; yv[m] = y[n-1];

nsegs = 50; dt = 1./(double) nsegs;
MoveTo((int) xv[0],(int) yv[0]);
for (i=0; i<m-2; i+=3)
{
    for (j=1,t=dt;j<=nsegs;j++,t+=dt)
    {
        p0 = (1.-t)*(1.-t)*(1.-t);
        p1 = 3.*t*(1.-t)*(1.-t);
        p2 = 3.*t*t*(1.-t);
        p3 = t*t*t;
        xp = p0*xv[i]+p1*xv[i+1]+p2*xv[i+2]+p3*xv[i+3];
        yp = p0*yv[i]+p1*yv[i+1]+p2*yv[i+2]+p3*yv[i+3];
        LineTo((int) xp,(int) yp);
    }
}
}
```

EXERCISES

7.1 Use the Lagrange interpolating polynomial formulation to implement the high-order polynomial curve-fitting method discussed in section 7.1. Apply your program to various polylines, and find cases for which large wiggles occur between data points.

7.2 Generalize the high-order polynomial curve fit of section 7.1 by incorporating a parametric representation for x and y following the discussion in section 7.3. Program your results and carry out a test on an open curve that first extends to larger x values and then turns back to smaller x values.

7.3 On your CAD system or with programming, reproduce the canoe cross sections shown at the beginning of this chapter. The data for these curves are given in table 12.3 in chapter 12.

7.4 On your CAD system, draw the curves representing the ceiling rib structure shown in figure 7.4.

7.5 Program the circular arc curve-fit developed in section 7.2. Extend the subroutine to include the cases of lines with two, three, and four points.

7.6 Write and test a program for a circular arc fit of *closed* curves.

7.7 Write a program to plot the parabolic blend for *closed* curves.

7.8 Use the subroutine given in section 7.5 to write a program for plotting natural cubic splines for open curves.

7.9 Implement the subroutines of section 7.6 to draw both open and closed quadratic uniform B-splines.

7.10 Implement the subroutine of section 7.6 to draw open cubic uniform B-splines.

7.11 Write a program for drawing *closed* cubic uniform B-splines.

7.12 Use AutoCAD to draw your initials in a particular font style (the Times Roman font was used for the example in figure 7.16). Draw the first letter with a circular-arc fit, the second letter with quadratic B-splines, and the third letter with cubic B-splines.

7.13 Use cubic B-splines to draw the automobile curves shown in figure 7.15.

7.14 Use cubic B-splines to draw the side view (shown below) of the bentwood rocker designed by Michael Thonet in 1860 (see, e.g., C. D. Gandy and S. Zimmermann-Stidham, *Contemporary Classics: Furniture of the Masters.* New York: Whitney Library of Design, 1981).

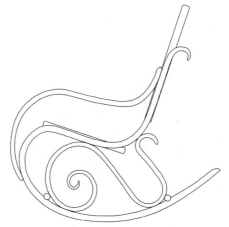

7.15 Use B-splines and arrays to draw the side view of a vehicle, like the Yamaha motorcycle below, drawn on AutoCAD by Nam Won Back.

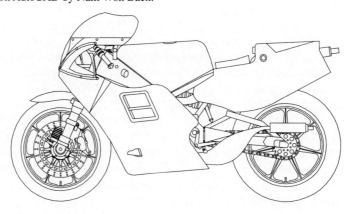

7.16 Implement the subroutine in section 7.7 to draw an open quadratic nonuniform B-spline.

7.17 Derive the algebraic expressions for the fourth-order (cubic) nonuniform B-spline basis function $N_{i,4}(t)$.

7.18 Write a program that draws fourth-order nonuniform B-splines.

7.19 For uniformly spaced knots, show that the fourth-order basis functions derived in exercise 7.17 reduce to the $b_i(t)$ expressions 7.61, except for the first two and last two segments along the curve. Derive the appropriate expressions for the $b_i(t)$ terms in the first two segments and in the last two segments.

7.20 Write a program to draw quadratic nonuniform rational B-splines from given control points, knot vector, and weight vector.

7.21 Write a quadratic NURBS program to produce the curves shown in figures 7.17b and 7.21.

7.22 Use the program of exercise 7.20 to plot a circle by using the seven control vertices located on the equilateral triangle shown below (the first and last control points lie at the midpoint of the equilateral triangle base). The following are the appropriate knot and weight vectors: $\mathbf{T}_{knot} = [\, 0, 0, 0, 1, 1, 2, 2, 3, 3, 3]$ and $\mathbf{w} = [\, 1, 0.5, 1, 0.5, 1, 0.5, 1]$.

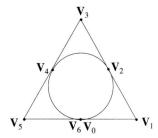

7.23 Implement the composite cubic Bézier curve subroutine of section 7.8, and then plot the curved portions of the letter *S* shown in figure 7.22b.

BIBLIOGRAPHY

ANAND, V. B., *Computer Graphics and Geometric Modeling for Engineers.* New York: John Wiley & Sons, Inc., 1993.

AutoCAD Release 12 Reference Manual. Sausalito, Calif.: Autodesk, Inc., 1992.

AutoSurf Release 2 Reference Manual. Sausalito, Calif.: Autodesk, Inc., 1993.

BARTELS, R. H., J. C. BEATTY, AND B. A. BARSKY, *An Introduction to Splines for Use in Computer Graphics and Geometric Modeling.* Los Altos, Calif.: Morgan Kaufmann Publishers, Inc., 1987.

FARIN, G., *Curves and Surfaces for Computer Aided Geometric Design: A Practical Guide,* 2nd ed. San Diego, Calif: Academic Press, Inc., 1990.

PIEGL, L. A., "Rational B-spline Curves and Surfaces for CAD and Graphics," pp. 225–269 in *State of the Art in Computer Graphics: Visualization and Modeling,* D. F. Rogers and R. A. Earnshaw, editors. New York: Springer-Verlag, 1991.

RENNER, G., AND V. POCHOP, "A New Method for Local Smooth Interpolation," pp. 137–147 in *Eurographics '81,* J. L. Encarnacao, editor. Amsterdam: North-Holland Publishing Co., 1981.

ROGERS, D. F., AND J. A. ADAMS, *Mathematical Elements for Computer Graphics,* 2nd ed. New York: McGraw-Hill Publishing Co., 1990.

8

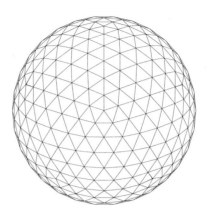

Data Structures
and Drawing Files

In previous chapters data points were represented by the coordinate arrays $x[i]$, $y[i]$, and $z[i]$, where the number of elements i in the array corresponds to the number of points being considered. A polyline was drawn by moving to the first point in the coordinate arrays, and then drawing line segments from point to point. In this chapter, alternative procedures are introduced for representing lines by arrays and by structure functions in the C programming language. Although structure functions have some advantages over arrays, arrays are used throughout this book because they can be represented in any programming language.

AutoCAD saves its drawing database in a compact file identified by the extension DWG; that is, a drawing named GEAR is stored in a file named GEAR.DWG. Most CAD programs cannot read or write DWG files. For the purpose of transferring a drawing database between different software products, two special file formats have been developed: the IGES (Initial Graphics Exchange Specification) format, and the DXF™ format developed by Autodesk. A drawing developed on one CAD software package can be ported to another CAD package by transferring the file in the IGES or DXF format. Also, a drawing developed on CAD software can be transferred to an analysis software package such as a finite-element program for calculations, and then ported back to the CAD package for display (for example, to display the calculated deflections of a structure). Still another use of drawing interchange files is to permit programmers to access the information in the drawing file, or to program information into the drawing.

Nonuniform rational B-splines (NURBS) are not currently supported by the DXF file format but are part of IGES. Therefore, a NURBS-based modeler, such as AutoSurf, must use the IGES format for transferring files to and from other NURBS-based CAD systems.

In this chapter the DXF file format is used to provide a programming interface to AutoCAD. This format was selected because it is easy incorporate into programs, and because it is becoming more widely supported by other graphics software (such as illustration and desktop publishing software).

The geodesic dome figure at the opening of this chapter was developed by programming a DXF file that was imported into AutoCAD with the DXFIN command and displayed with hidden lines removed (HIDE command). The dome is made up of 720 triangular faces, with 1,080 edges and 362 vertex points. Obviously, it would take a tremendous amount of time to enter the information directly by hand into AutoCAD (via the 3DFACE command). This example is one of the many situations in which programming DXF files can be very useful.

In addition to examples of reading and writing DXF files, this chapter also presents an AutoCAD script file. A script file is read by AutoCAD as a list of AutoCAD commands and values. Therefore, like the DXF file, the script file is useful for entering complex drawing entities or operations on entities into AutoCAD. Script files are also useful for setting parameters in AutoCAD: for example, a set of start-up conditions that you frequently use.

Other important file formats, although not analyzed in this chapter, should be mentioned here. Encapsulated PostScript (EPS) is frequently used by desktop publishing software. AutoCAD can import and export EPS files.

Pixel-based file formats are often used with paint programs in desktop publishing software. Important formats include TIFF (tagged image file format) for all systems, PICT for the Macintosh, and PCX for IBM PC compatibles. Other formats are discussed in connection with rendered images in chapter 14.

The pixel-based formats are used for storing optically scanned images. Special conversion programs (and some drawing or desktop publishing programs) can transfer the pixel-based file of a scanned image to a DXF file by the process of *auto tracing,* in which pixels of a certain threshold intensity are connected to form lines or polygons. Auto tracing is inexact, so that sometimes it is preferable to import a scanned image file directly into AutoCAD for use as a template with manual tracing (by using polylines and other drawing entities). Manual tracing is often necessary to produce a clean drawing without a number of short, unnecessary lines, particularly if the original image is not a simple line drawing. AutoCAD can directly import TIFF files for use with manual tracing.

The DXF and PostScript file formats are also useful for exporting AutoCAD drawings to desktop publishing software for the addition of special fonts, shading, and other features. Many of the figures in this book were enhanced by exporting AutoCAD drawings in the DXF format to Canvas. AutoCAD and other CAD programs are incorporating more desktop publishing capabilities with each new release, and desktop publishing and illustration programs are increasingly able to import CAD drawings.

8.1 REPRESENTATION OF LINES AND SURFACES IN PROGRAMS

Paint programs store pictures as arrays of pixel intensities or colors. A CAD program stores its drawing as a collection of various drawing entities. That is, a CAD drawing file can recognize different entities and reproduce them accurately (usually to double-precision accuracy). In section 8.2 the structure of the AutoCAD DXF file will be discussed; in this section different representations of drawing entities in C programs are given. In particular, the structuring of data for lines and surfaces is considered. In advanced CAD systems, objects are represented by solid modeling, which is discussed in chapter 13.

Lines

The term *line* is used to denote a single line segment, whereas *polyline* is used for connected line segments that are treated as a single entity. A drawing may have connected line segments stored as single lines; for example, when a number of coordinate pairs are entered sequentially under the AutoCAD LINE command.

A line segment may be identified by the coordinates of its starting and ending points: (x_{start}, y_{start}) and (x_{end}, y_{end}) in two dimensions, or $(x_{start}, y_{start}, z_{start})$ and $(x_{end}, y_{end}, z_{end})$ in three dimensions. The line may also have other attributes, such as color, type (continuous, dashed, dotted, etc.), or weight (thickness). The data structure for the line must include all of the pertinent information. Table 8.1 shows the data for four lines in two dimensions determined by their endpoint coordinates, color, and type. The entries in this table can be stored in the array *lines[i][j]*, where i represents the table row number (also the line number) and j the column number. The four lines are numbered 0 through 3 because arrays in C programs start with 0. In general, the number of lines will be given by the variable *nLines*, with individual lines numbered from 0 through $nLines - 1$.

The numbers in table 8.1 are presented as integers. Integer values are appropriate when dealing with screen coordinates (see section 9.1). The integer value for the $j = 4$ entry can represent the color index number, or it can be used as a flag in a program to set the color. Similarly, the $j = 5$ entry can be a flag value for setting the line type.

TABLE 8.1 DATA FOR LINE SEGMENTS, WITH *nLines* = 4

i	x_{start} $j = 0$	y_{start} 1	x_{end} 2	y_{end} 3	Color 4	Line type 5
0	50	50	150	80	1	1
1	150	80	500	200	1	1
2	300	250	300	400	1	3
3	0	500	250	250	2	1

As discussed in the next section, CAD data for line coordinates are stored as double-precision floating-point values. Thus for many applications the array *lines[i][j]* should be declared as the data type *double.*

In the programming examples in this book, data for lines and surfaces are stored in arrays, because arrays may be programmed in any of the common languages: FORTRAN, BASIC, C, or Pascal. The C and Pascal languages also offer structures (called records in Pascal) that permit the variable to be a function of quantities of different types. For example, the following program statements define a data type called *line.*

```
typedef struct
        {
           double xstart,ystart,xend,yend;
           int    color,type;
        } line;
```

Once the data type *line* has been defined, it can be used to declare an array *lines[i]* in the normal manner with the following statement.

```
line lines[100];
```

Line number *i* in the array of one hundred lines defined above has double-precision floating-point coordinates given by *lines[i].xstart, lines[i].ystart, lines[i].xend,* and *lines[i].yend.* The integer numbers for color and line type are *lines[i].color* and *lines[i].type.* Because of their versatility, structures are often used in C graphics programs.

Unlike line segments, polylines are described by an arbitrary number of coordinate points, not just starting and ending points. Thus, in section 9.3, where polylines are represented by the array *plines[i][j],* the integer *j* ranges from 0 to *2nVertices[i]* − 1, where *nVertices[i]* is the number of vertices in polyline number *i.* The x-coordinate values are stored with even values of *j,* and y-coordinates are stored with odd values. For the example given in section 9.3, there are no variables for color or line type. Alternatively, structures can be used to store polyline data.

Surfaces

A surface can be represented by connected faces (or facets), with each face having a number of edges meeting at vertices. This arrangement can be described by a tree structure in which the complete surface object is at the root, with succeeding levels from the root containing the following entities: faces, edges, vertices, and vertex coordinate values (see Zeid 1991).

A wireframe object may be drawn without reference to surfaces; for example, an array can provide a list of connected vertices to draw (see Demel and Miller 1984). But the use of surfaces provides a more complete representation of an object, and permits hidden line removal and rendering operations.

A face may be formed by three or more vertices lying in a plane. The face is drawn by moving to one of the vertices and then drawing lines to the other vertices and back to the original vertex to form the edges of the face. In AutoCAD, a single face is formed with

the 3DFACE command. As shown in the next section, a 3DFACE is represented by four
vertex points, which form a triangular face if two of the points are the same.

The first step in setting up a surface is to specify the 3-D coordinates for all of the
vertices in the surface. Table 8.2 gives coordinate values for the six vertices of the octahedron shown in figure 8.1. The entries in the table may be stored in the array $vert[i][j]$,
where $i = vnum$ is the vertex number, and $j = 0, 1,$ and 2 for the $x, y,$ and z coordinates.
That is, $vert[3][2]$ equals the z-coordinate of vertex number 3.

A face is defined by the edges that border it or by the vertices connected by those edges.
In table 8.3 the faces are specified by the vertices. For example, the face numbered 2 has
three vertex points, numbered 2, 3, and 4; see table 8.2 and figure 8.1. The information in
table 8.3 can be stored in the two-dimensional array $vn[i][j]$, where i is the face number and
j ranges over the vertex numbers appropriate for face i. Often, as in the 3DFACE example
in the next section, j starts and ends with the same vertex number. For example, for $vn[2][j]$,
j takes on the values 2, 3, 4, and 2. This arrangement can be used when drawing the wireframe representing the face; face 2 is drawn by moving to vertex 2, drawing a line to vertex
3, then to vertex 4, and back to vertex 2 to complete the three edges of the face.

TABLE 8.2 COORDINATE VALUES
FOR THE SIX VERTICES
OF AN OCTAHEDRON,
WHERE *vnum* IS THE
VERTEX NUMBER

vnum	*x*	*y*	*z*
0	0.5	0.5	0.0
1	−0.5	0.5	0.0
2	−0.5	−0.5	0.0
3	0.5	−0.5	0.0
4	0.0	0.0	0.7071
5	0.0	0.0	−0.7071

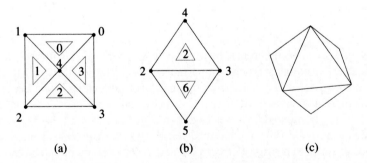

(a)   (b)   (c)

Figure 8.1   An octahedron shown in three views: (a) top, (b) front, and (c) axonometric
projection from above and to the left. The first two views show numbers for vertices and
faces. The coordinate values in table 8.2 are referenced to an origin in the center of the octahedron, with the x-axis extending to the right and the y-axis upward in the first view (a).

TABLE 8.3 VERTEX NUMBERS *vn*[*i*][*j*] FOR AN OCTA-
HEDRON, WHERE *i* IS THE FACE NUMBER

i	*j* = 0	*j* = 1	*j* = 2	*j* = 3
0	0	1	4	0
1	1	2	4	1
2	2	3	4	2
3	3	0	4	3
4	0	5	1	0
5	1	5	2	1
6	2	5	3	2
7	3	5	0	3

8.2 THE DXF DRAWING INTERCHANGE FILE

A DXF file is produced when the DXFOUT command is entered in AutoCAD. The DXF file has the extension DXF, and this drawing database may be inserted into a new drawing by entering the command DXFIN after the new drawing has been opened. The format of the DXF file was designed to facilitate access to the drawing information. Accordingly, a certain amount of redundancy was built into this format, with the result that a file with the DXF extension is longer than the same drawing in a DWG file. A DXF file may contain the entire database for the drawing, or it can be restricted to drawing entities selected by the user.

Table 8.4 illustrates the overall format of a DXF file. Every line in the file belongs to a group of two lines. The first line carries the group code number. For group codes 0–9 and 999–1009, the succeeding line has a string; for 10–59, 210–239, and 1010–1059, the succeeding line has a floating-point number; for 60–79 and 1060–1079, the succeeding line has an integer.

The header section of the DXF file holds the settings of the drawing variables. There are over 100 settings associated with items such as units, dimensioning variables, text variables, tolerances, coordinate systems, mesh parameters, drawing aids, and other drawing functions. The tables section of the DXF file supplies parameters and settings: LTYPE lists the line types; LAYER lists the names and status of the different layers used in the drawing; STYLE lists information on the text parameters; VIEW lists the view direction, target point, and other factors associated with viewing the drawn object; UCS lists the positioning of the user coordinate systems; VPORT lists the viewport configurations; DIMSTYLE lists the settings for dimension syles; and APPID is an application identification table used internally by AutoCAD. The BLOCKS section of the DXF file lists the blocks defined in the drawing, and includes the entities that make up the blocks.

The last section of the DXF file, ENTITIES, contains all of the drawing entities such as lines, points, circles, arcs, polylines, and 3Dfaces. One option provided by the DXFOUT command permits writing a DXF file that contains only the drawing entities. This abbrevi-

TABLE 8.4 SECTIONS IN A DXF FILE, FROM *AUTOCAD RELEASE 12 CUSTOMIZATION MANUAL,* 1992 (COURTESY OF AUTODESK, INC.)

```
  0                                    (Begin HEADER section)
SECTION
  2
HEADER
                    << Header variable items go here >>
  0
ENDSEC                                 (End HEADER section)
  0                                    (Begin TABLES section)
SECTION
  2
TABLES
  0
TABLE
  2
VPORT
(viewport table maximum item count)
                    << Viewport table items go here >>
  0
ENDTAB
  0
TABLE
  2
LTYPE, LAYER, STYLE, VIEW, UCS, and DWGMGR
  70
(Table maximum item count)
                    << Table items go here >>
  0
ENDTAB
  0
ENDSEC                                 (End TABLES section)
  0                                    (Begin BLOCKS section)
SECTION
  2
BLOCKS
                    << Block definition entities go here >>
  0
ENDSEC                                 (End BLOCKS section)
  0                                    (Begin ENTITIES section)
SECTION
  2
ENTITIES
                    << Drawing entities go here >>
  0
ENDSEC                                 (End ENTITIES section)
  0
EOF                                    (End of file)
```

ated file can be loaded into a drawing with the DXFIN command. As mentioned above, programs can readily be written to access the information in a DXF file, or to place information into a DXF file.

The following command produces a DXF entities file with 16 decimal places of accuracy.

```
Command: DXFOUT
Enter decimal places of accuracy (0 to 16)/Entities/Binary <6>: E
Select objects: (pick with mouse)
Select objects: (RETURN)
Enter decimal places of accuracy (0 to 16)/Binary <6>: 16
```

A lower decimal accuracy will reduce the size of the DXF file, but the full 16-place accuracy of the original AutoCAD file is preferable unless a smaller file is required and the extra accuracy is unnecessary.

The DXF File for a Line

The program listing below generates the DXF entity file shown on the next page for a single line segment. The file includes the x-, y-, and z-coordinates of the starting and ending points of the line. Lines containing multiple segments would repeat the section of the DXF file starting with 0, LINE, as given in the subroutine writeLine().

```c
#include <stdio.h>

void      writeStart(void),lineCoords(void);
void      writeLine(void),writeEnd(void);

FILE      *dxf;
double    xstart,ystart,zstart,xend,yend,zend;

main()
{
    dxf = fopen("dxf1Line.dxf","w");
    writeStart();
    lineCoords();
    writeLine();
    writeEnd();
    fclose(dxf);
}

void writeStart(void)
{
    fprintf(dxf,"%3d\n",0);
    fprintf(dxf,"SECTION\n");
    fprintf(dxf,"%3d\n",2);
    fprintf(dxf,"ENTITIES\n");
}
```

```
void lineCoords(void)
{
    xstart = 2.25;
    ystart = 1.0;
    zstart = 0.0;
    xend = 6.25;
    yend = 4.5;
    zend = 0.0;
}

void writeLine(void)
{
    fprintf(dxf,"%3d\n",0);
    fprintf(dxf,"LINE\n");
    fprintf(dxf,"%3d\n",8);
    fprintf(dxf,"0\n");
    fprintf(dxf,"%3d\n",10);
    fprintf(dxf,"%lf\n",xstart);
    fprintf(dxf,"%3d\n",20);
    fprintf(dxf,"%lf\n",ystart);
    fprintf(dxf,"%3d\n",30);
    fprintf(dxf,"%lf\n",zstart);
    fprintf(dxf,"%3d\n",11);
    fprintf(dxf,"%lf\n",xend);
    fprintf(dxf,"%3d\n",21);
    fprintf(dxf,"%lf\n",yend);
    fprintf(dxf,"%3d\n",31);
    fprintf(dxf,"%lf\n",zend);
}

void writeEnd(void)
{
    fprintf(dxf,"%3d\n",0);
    fprintf(dxf,"ENDSEC\n");
    fprintf(dxf,"%3d\n",0);
    fprintf(dxf,"EOF\n");
}
```

```
            DXF OUTPUT FILE

          0
          SECTION
          2
          ENTITIES
          0
          LINE
          8
          0
          10
          2.250000
          20
          1.000000
          30
          0.000000
          11
          6.250000
          21
          4.500000
          31
          0.000000
          0
          ENDSEC
          0
          EOF
```

In the DXF entities file, the code number 8 appearing after the entry LINE signifies that the name of the drawing layer will follow. Therefore the number 0 following the 8 is actually a string denoting that the line is on the layer named "0." Note that for any line, the DXF file will include the z-coordinate values, even when the line is drawn in AutoCAD as a 2-D line (which is on the $z = 0$ plane).

Of course, it is easier to draw a single line directly with the AutoCAD software, but direct programming of drawing entities into AutoCAD DXF files can be especially useful for objects that can be described by mathematical formulas. For example, the three-dimensional spiral of a screw thread can be easily described by a mathematical formula, but it is difficult to construct the spiral by directly inputting points or drawing entities in CAD software.

The program listing above can be readily expanded to provide a DXF file for a logarithmic spiral. Including the mathematics header file <math.h> in the C program and replacing the subroutine lineCoords() above with the subroutine listed below makes it possible to construct the DXF file for the spiral shown in figure 8.2. The left-hand side of the figure shows the spiral in the *xy* plane, and the right-hand side shows the spiral viewed at an angle of 20° to the surface of the *xy* plane (the VPOINT command in AutoCAD provides viewing from any angle). The spiral stretches into the positive z-direction as the radius *r* increases because the value *zend* for a line segment is set equal to *r* in the listing below.

```
void lineCoords(void) /* logarithmic spiral */
{
    double a,r,r0,theta,xcenter,ycenter;

    xcenter = 6.0; ycenter = 4.0;
    a = 15.0; r0 = 1.0;
    theta = a*log(r0);
    xend = xcenter + r0*cos(theta);
    yend = ycenter + r0*sin(theta);
    zend = r0;
    for (r=r0+.02; r<7.0; r=r+.02)
    {
        xstart = xend;
        ystart = yend;
        zstart = zend;
        theta = a*log(r);
        xend = xcenter + r*cos(theta);
        yend = ycenter + r*sin(theta);
        zend = r;
        writeLine();
    }
}
```

It is useful not only to write programs to generate DXF files but also to construct programs that read DXF files. In the following example, a DXF entities file for line segments

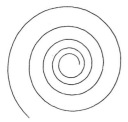 

Figure 8.2   Two views of a logarithmic spiral.

in a plane will be read by a program that then maps the lines onto a cylindrical surface. For this example, consider the characters UCSD in figure 7.16, which were drawn in AutoCAD with the cubic B-spline option under PEDIT. The B-spline curves representing the characters are first put into the form of connected small line segments by means of the EXPLODE command. Then the DXFOUT command is used in AutoCAD to make a DXF entities file.

    The program listed below reads this file and transforms the coordinates on the plane (*xplane, yplane,* and *zplane*) into coordinates on a cylindrical surface (*xcyl, ycyl,* and *zcyl*); see figure 8.3 for a diagram showing the geometry of the transformation. The results are shown in figure 8.4 for three different viewing angles. Note that in the bottom view (looking downward), the straight horizontal lines (serifs) at the top of the letter *U* extend a bit

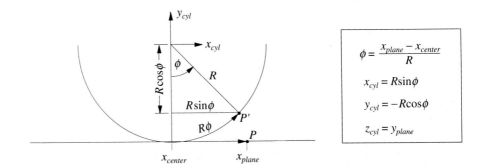

Figure 8.3   A view down on a cylindrical surface formed by curling up a planar surface at x_{center}. The point P at x_{plane} on the plane transforms to the point P' on the cylinder. Thus the distance $x_{plane} - x_{center}$ on the plane equals the curved distance $R\phi$ on the cylinder; this relation yields the top equation in the box to the right of the figure. The next two relations, for the distances x_{cyl} and y_{cyl} measured from the cylinder center, are illustrated in the figure. The coordinate $z_{cyl} = y_{plane}$ is directed out of the paper.

The box equations:

$$\phi = \frac{x_{plane} - x_{center}}{R}$$
$$x_{cyl} = R\sin\phi$$
$$y_{cyl} = -R\cos\phi$$
$$z_{cyl} = y_{plane}$$

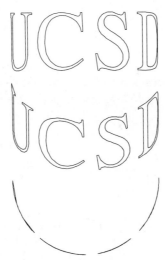

Figure 8.4   Three views of the characters UCSD mapped onto a cylindrical surface.

into the cylinder. This effect arises because only the ends of line segments are placed on the cylinder; the serifs could be divided into a number of shorter segments in order to place them closer to the cylinder.

```c
#include <stdio.h>
#include <math.h>

#define XCENTER    4.85
#define R          2.34
#define PI         3.141593

FILE      *dxfin,*dxfout;
int       code,code2,code3,i;
char      label[20];
double    xplane,yplane,zplane;
double    phi,xcyl,ycyl,zcyl;
void      newCoords(void);

main()
{
    dxfin = fopen("UCSD.dxf","r");
    dxfout = fopen("UCSDcyl.dxf","w");
    while ( strcmp( label, "EOF") != 0 )
    {
        fscanf(dxfin,"%3d\n",&code);
        fprintf(dxfout,"%3d\n",code);

        if (code <10)
        {
            fscanf(dxfin,"%s\n",label);
            fprintf(dxfout,"%s\n",label);
        }
        else
        {
            fscanf(dxfin,"%lf\n",&xplane);
            fscanf(dxfin,"%3d\n",&code2);
            fscanf(dxfin,"%lf\n",&yplane);
            fscanf(dxfin,"%3d\n",&code3);
            fscanf(dxfin,"%lf\n",&zplane);

            newCoords();
        }
    }

    fclose(dxfin);
    fclose(dxfout);
}
```

```
void newCoords(void)
{
    phi = (xplane - XCENTER)/R;
    xcyl = R*sin(phi);
    ycyl = -R*cos(phi);
    zcyl = yplane;

    fprintf(dxfout,"%lf\n",xcyl);
    fprintf(dxfout,"%3d\n",code2);
    fprintf(dxfout,"%lf\n",ycyl);
    fprintf(dxfout,"%3d\n",code3);
    fprintf(dxfout,"%lf\n",zcyl);
}
```

In the above program the file UCSD.dxf is read line by line, with each line being immediately copied to the file UCSDcyl.dxf unless the line represents a coordinate value. Coordinate values are transformed to the cylindrical surface before being written to the file.

DXF Files for 3DFACES

In AutoCAD a surface of arbitrary shape can be built up with the 3DFACE command, which constructs individual faces defined by three or more vertex points. Although 3DFACE is very versatile for constructing surfaces, specifying the coordinates of a large number of vertex points within AutoCAD is a tedious process. Thus, for many surfaces it is useful to compute or otherwise specify the vertex coordinates in a program that writes a DXF file. As an example, the DXF file for the icosahedron pictured on the left in figure 8.5 will be constructed from arrays of vertex points following the procedure outlined in section 8.1. After the icosahedron is constructed, a geodesic dome can be created by using each triangular face of the icosahedron to form four, nine, or more triangular faces on the dome; see the center and right-hand examples in figure 8.5.

The program that generates the DXF file for a single face is listed below along with the output DXF file. For this case, a triangular face is produced by entering the same co-

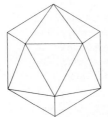  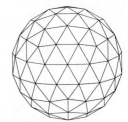

Figure 8.5 Objects constructed by programming DXF files, with an icosahedron on the left and geodesic domes in the center and on the right. The objects are displayed in a slightly downward view (12° below the horizontal) and with hidden lines removed (HIDE command in AutoCAD).

ordinates for the first and last vertices. A face with four vertex points can obtained by entering four different vertices; however, these four points must all be in the same plane (recall that three points determine a plane, so a fourth point must be constrained to be in the plane). In chapter 13 it will be shown that more than four vertex points can be used with the 3DFACE command, resulting in a single face if an invisible line option is used.

```
#include <stdio.h>

FILE *dxf;
void writeStart(void),vertexCoords(void),writeEnd(void);
void writeFace(double x[],double y[],double z[]);

main()
{
    writeStart();
    vertexCoords();
    writeEnd();
}

void writeStart(void)
{
    dxf = fopen("3dface.dxf","w");
    fprintf(dxf,"%3d\n",0);
    fprintf(dxf,"SECTION\n");
    fprintf(dxf,"%3d\n",2);
    fprintf(dxf,"ENTITIES\n");
}

void vertexCoords(void)
{
    double x[4] = {6.0,7.0,6.5,6.0};
    double y[4] = {5.0,6.0,4.0,5.0};
    double z[4] = {0.0,1.0,3.0,0.0};

    writeFace(x,y,z);
}

void writeFace(double x[],
               double y[],double z[])
{
    int i;

    fprintf(dxf,"%3d\n",0);
    fprintf(dxf,"3DFACE\n");
    fprintf(dxf,"%3d\n",8);
    fprintf(dxf,"%d\n",0);
```

```
         DXF OUTPUT FILE

             0
          SECTION
             2
          ENTITIES
             0
          3DFACE
             8
             0
            10
         6.000000
            20
         5.000000
            30
         0.000000
            11
         7.000000
            21
         6.000000
            31
         1.000000
            12
         6.500000
            22
         4.000000
            32
         3.000000
            13
         6.000000
            23
         5.000000
            33
         0.000000
             0
          ENDSEC
             0
           EOF
```

```
    for (i=0; i<4; i++)
    {
        fprintf(dxf,"%3d\n",10+i);
        fprintf(dxf,"%1f\n",x[i]);
        fprintf(dxf,"%3d\n",20+i);
        fprintf(dxf,"%1f\n",y[i]);
        fprintf(dxf,"%3d\n",30+i);
        fprintf(dxf,"%1f\n",z[i]);
    }
}


void writeEnd(void)
{
    fprintf(dxf,"%3d\n",0);
    fprintf(dxf,"ENDSEC\n");
    fprintf(dxf,"%3d\n",0);
    fprintf(dxf,"EOF\n");
    fclose(dxf);
}
```

To construct a DXF file for an object made up of a number of faces, the function vertexCoords() above can be replaced by a routine that loops through any number of faces. For example, the icosahedron pictured in figure 8.5 is constructed by replacing vertexCo-ords() by the function icosahedron() listed below. The program uses the two-dimensional arrays *vert[i][j]* and *vn[i][j]* discussed in section 8.1.

```
    void icosahedron(void)
    {
        int     i,faceNum,vnum;
        double  xp[4],yp[4],zp[4];

        double  vert[12][3] = {{0.0,0.0,0.9512},{0.0,0.8507,0.4253},
                    {0.8090,0.2629,0.4253},{0.5,-0.6882,0.4253},
                    {-0.5,-0.6882,0.4253},{-0.8090,0.2629,0.4253},
                    {-0.5,0.6882,-0.4253},{0.5,0.6882,-0.4253},
                    {0.8090,-0.2626,-0.4253},{0.0,-0.8507,-0.4253},
                    {-0.8090,-0.2629,-0.4253},{0.0,0.0,-0.9512}};

        int     vn[20][4] = {{0,1,2,0},{0,2,3,0},{0,3,4,0},{0,4,5,0},
                    {0,5,1,0},{1,7,2,1},{2,8,3,2},{3,9,4,3},
                    {4,10,5,4},{5,6,1,5},{1,6,7,1},{2,7,8,2},
                    {3,8,9,3},{4,9,10,4},{5,10,6,5},{6,11,7,6},
                    {7,11,8,7},{8,11,9,8},{9,11,10,9},{10,11,6,10}};

        for (faceNum=0; faceNum<20; faceNum++)
        {
            for (i=0; i<4; i++)
```

```
{
        vnum = vn[faceNum][i];
        xp[i] = vert[vnum][0];
        yp[i] = vert[vnum][1];
        zp[i] = vert[vnum][2];
    }
    writeFace(xp,yp,zp);
    }
}
```

On the icosahedron, all of the faces are equilateral triangles, and all of the vertices lie equidistant from the center, on a sphere called the circumsphere. One procedure for constructing a geodesic dome is to first divide each face of the icosahedron into smaller triangular faces (see Gasson 1983). The vertices of the small triangles are then translated radially to the surface of the circumsphere to form the geodesic dome. Although all of the vertices lie on the circumsphere, the triangles are not quite equilateral, nor are they all identical.

By including the math header file math.h at the beginning of the program, and replacing the loop over the faces in the icosahedron() function above with the program lines given in listing 8.1 of appendix B, a geodesic dome is formed by dividing each icosahedron face into n^2 triangles, as illustrated in figure 8.6. In the listing, $n = 3$, which corresponds to the dome on the right in figure 8.5. The middle dome in figure 8.5 has $n = 2$, and the dome pictured at the beginning of this chapter has $n = 6$. The total number of faces on a complete geodesic dome is $20n^2$.

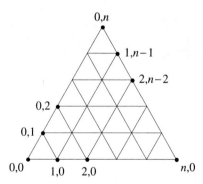

Figure 8.6 Notation for the 2-D array of vertex points that define n^2 triangles inside the triangular boundaries of the icosahedron face.

8.3 THE SCRIPT FILE

A script file is a list of AutoCAD commands and values, arranged in the exact order in which you would type them if you were running AutoCAD. The script file is executed by entering the command SCRIPT.

```
Command: SCRIPT      Script file <default>: enter name
```

The current file name is listed as the default. Script files have the extension SCR, but the name should be entered without the extension (it is assumed by the command).

In the following example, a script file inserts two blocks that have been saved as drawings (with the WBLOCK command) to produce the design shown in figure 8.7. The first block, named fillUCSD, consists of letters filled with a solid hatch, and the second block, openUCSD, has open letters. The second block is inserted at a continuously changing angle with a scale that steadily decreases. Because 20 block insertions are performed, it is easier to write a script file to perform these operations than to perform the operations by hand within AutoCAD.

```
#include <stdio.h>
#include <math.h>

#define SCALE_X0        0.5
#define RATIO           0.8
#define DELTA_THETA     -18.
#define INSERT_X        4.
#define INSERT_Y        8.

FILE        *script_out;
int     i;
double  scale_x,scale_y,theta;

main()
{
    script_out = fopen("rotation.scr","w");

    theta = 0.;
```

Figure 8.7   Rotation and scaling of a block by means of a script file.

```
for ( i=0; i<20; i++ )
{
    scale_x = (1.+ theta/360.)*SCALE_X0;
    scale_y = RATIO*scale_x;
    fprintf(script_out,"INSERT\n");

    if (i == 0)
    {
        fprintf(script_out,"fillUCSD\n");
    }
    else
    {
        fprintf(script_out,"openUCSD\n");
    }
    fprintf(script_out,"%lf,%lf\n",
      INSERT_X,INSERT_Y);
    fprintf(script_out,"%lf\n",scale_x);
    fprintf(script_out,"%lf\n",scale_y);
    fprintf(script_out,"%lf\n",theta);

    theta = theta + DELTA_THETA;
}

fclose(script_out);
}
```

```
SCRIPT OUTPUT FILE

INSERT
fillUCSD
4.000000,8.000000
0.500000
0.400000
0.000000
INSERT
openUCSD
4.000000,8.000000
0.475000
0.380000
−18.000000
INSERT
openUCSD
4.000000,8.000000
0.450000
0.360000
−36.000000
(+17 more insertions)
```

EXERCISES

8.1 Implement the program for writing a line to a DXF file and apply it to the logarithmic spiral example given in section 8.2. Then bring the DXF spiral entity into your CAD system and view it at different angles.

8.2 Write a program for a DXF file that draws a helix as line segments, with x and y tracing a circle many times while z steadily increases. View the helix in 3-D on your CAD system.

8.3 Study the DXF file format of a two-dimensional polyline (PLINE) by using the DXFOUT command in AutoCAD to produce an entity DXF file. Then write a program to construct a PLINE DXF file and use this program to draw an involute curve (defined in section 5.2 for application to gear-teeth profiles).

8.4 Write a program to construct a DXF file for a three-dimensional polyline (3DPOLY) and use this program to draw a helix.

8.5 Start with an AutoCAD drawing containing line segments in a plane. Then write a program to read the DXF output file and transform the drawing to the surface of a cylinder by using the mapping given in section 8.2.

8.6 Write a program to read the DXF file for a polyline drawn on your CAD system. After your program reads the vertex points for the polyline, insert these points into one of the curve-fitting subroutines from chapter 7 (parabolic blend, natural cubic spline, B-spline, etc.). Then place the short line segments from the curve fit into a new DXF entities file for lines. Bring this file into your original CAD drawing for the polyline and compare your curve fit with curve fits available on your CAD system (by using the same polyline vertices).

8.7 Write a program that reads line segments from the B-spline letters formed in AutoCAD and then maps them onto a sphere as illustrated below. Start in AutoCAD by adding vertices to any long sections that may occur along straight portions of your letters. Then use the EXPLODE command to separate the sections into individual line segments and output a DXF entities file. Your program then reads this DXF file and transforms the coordinates according to the following equations.

$$\phi = \frac{x_{plane} - x_{center}}{R}, \quad \theta = \frac{y_{plane} - y_{center}}{R}$$

$$x_{sph} = R\cos\theta\sin\phi, \quad y_{sph} = R\cos\theta\cos\phi, \quad z_{sph} = R\sin\theta$$

Two views of mapped letters are shown below. Mappings for three cases of y_{center} are shown, with the middle position of the letters corresponding to a y_{center} value equal to the y_{plane} value at the center of the letters.

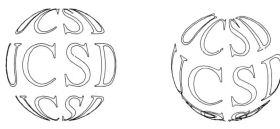

8.8 Write a DXF file for faces to construct the octahedron illustrated in section 8.1. The octahedron has six vertices and eight faces, with the vertex coordinates given in table 8.2, and face data in table 8.3.

8.9 Construct the DXF file for an icosahedron by using the subroutine given in section 8.2. View the icosahedron at various angles on your CAD system.

8.10 Starting with the icosahedron subroutine written in exercise 8.9, incorporate the subroutine 8.1 of appendix B that constructs geodesic domes.

8.11 Make a drawing of a geodesic dome house or pavilion by using the subroutines described in section 8.2 to construct a dome and then modifying it in your CAD system. For the example shown below in axonometric and perspective views, $n = 3$. Some faces on the original dome were erased, and others added so that all vertices on the ground plane lie on a circle (the use of colored lines helped in the selection of vertex points in this construction). Also, faces were added to form the entrance canopy at the opening.

8.12 Write an AutoCAD script file to rotate and shrink a planar object (similar to the example given in section 8.3).

8.13 Write a script file that incorporates the AutoCAD parameter settings that you commonly use at start-up.

BIBLIOGRAPHY

AutoCAD Release 12 Customization Manual, Chapter 11, "Drawing Interchange and File Formats." Sausalito, Calif.: Autodesk, Inc., 1992.

DEMEL, J. T., AND M. J. MILLER, *Introduction to Computer Graphics*. Monterey, Calif: Brooks/Cole Engineering Division, 1984.

GASSON, P. C., *Geometry of Spatial Forms: Analysis, Synthesis, Concept, Formulation and Space Vision for CAD*. Chichester, West Sussex, England: Ellis Horwood Limited, 1983.

JUMP, D. N., *AutoCAD Programming*. Blue Ridge Summit, Pa.: TAB Books, Inc., 1989.

MORTENSON, M. E., *Computer Graphics Handbook: Geometry and Mathematics*. New York: Industrial Press Inc, 1990.

SPROULL, R. F., W. R. SUTHERLAND, AND M. K. ULLNER, *Device-Independent Graphics*. New York: McGraw-Hill, Inc., 1985.

ZEID, I., *CAD/CAM Theory and Practice*. New York: McGraw-Hill, Inc., 1991.

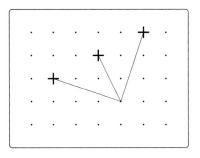

Interactive Features for Computer Graphics

Computer-aided design depends strongly on interactive features. Also, many other types of software are enhanced by interactive graphics. The success of the Apple Macintosh computer has largely resulted from its graphical user interface (GUI), which permits easy manipulation of files, windows, and other entities. The first four sections of this chapter deal with interactive features in CAD; the last section briefly discusses some GUI features for more general applications.

CAD software is useful not only because it offers a wide array of drawing entities but also because it provides interactive features for placing those entities precisely and easily. With AutoCAD, line endpoints may be placed with the help of options in an "assist" menu. These options have names that describe their functions; for example, END-POINT (snap to the endpoint of another line), INTERSECTION (snap to the intersection of lines), MIDPOINT, PERPENDICULAR, NEAREST, CENTER, and TANGENT. Interactive graphics also can modify drawing entities with commands such as TRIM, EXTEND, MOVE, FILLET, MIRROR, and OFFSET.

216

As pictured in the chapter opening figure, a mouse device is often used to place points in a drawing. In this chapter, a program is developed for using a mouse to accurately place line segments. To aid in accurate placement, the end of a line segment follows the mouse cursor as it moves across the screen—this *rubberbanding* is illustrated on the left, with the cursor being a cross (+) that appears in three positions on the screen as the mouse moves through the three positions shown. Additional drawing aids included in the program are the display of the cursor coordinates, the display of a rectangular array of grid points (as illustrated), an optional snap mode in which the cursor moves in finite increments, and an option that permits a snap to the endpoint of a previously drawn line.

Two program subroutines are presented for conveniently deleting lines. First, a single line may be deleted by placing a square cursor so that it intersects the line. Second, a group of lines can be deleted by windowing—drawing a rectangle by placing two corner points—and erasing all line segments lying completely within the rectangle.

Interactive editing of polylines is also discussed. After a polyline is drawn, its vertices can be moved, and the polyline can serve as a frame for an approximation or interpolation curve. The cubic B-spline curve is used for examples in this chapter, but other curves can be treated in exactly the same manner.

In addition to lines and curves, CAD drawings often contain dimension lines. This chapter presents a simple example of dimensioning. After a mouse has been used to pick the positions of the extension lines and the dimension line, these lines are automatically inserted along with arrowheads and a numeric label. All of the interactive subroutines described in the first four sections of this chapter simulate features in AutoCAD and other CAD software.

The final section of this chapter, on the graphical user interface, includes a discussion of the Macintosh GUI, as well as two programming examples for GUI features on the IBM PC. The programs consist of an interactive menu for the drawing subroutines given in this chapter, and a slider bar program. Slider bars are useful for color pickers and other applications requiring interactive changes of variables. When used on the side of a window, slider bars become scroll bars that scroll the text (or graphics) up and down in the window.

9.1 ADDING LINE SEGMENTS TO A DRAWING

To develop subroutines for interactive features, we must first set up a simple framework for a drawing program. As discussed in section 8.1, lines will be stored in a two-dimensional array called *lines[i][j]*, where *i* ranges over all of the line segments (from 0 through *nLines* − 1), and *j* holds the coordinates and any other information about the line. For the 2-D case considered here, *j* values of 0, 1, 2, and 3 correspond to x_{start}, y_{start}, x_{end}, and y_{end}, representing the starting and ending points of a line segment. (For this 2-D case, information about line color and line type could be included as the $j = 5$ and $j = 6$ elements.)

The flow chart in figure 9.1 shows the relations between the various functions presented in the first two sections of this chapter. This chart is simpler than it first appears. In the main() function, first the mouse and cursor are initialized by means of the mouseInit()

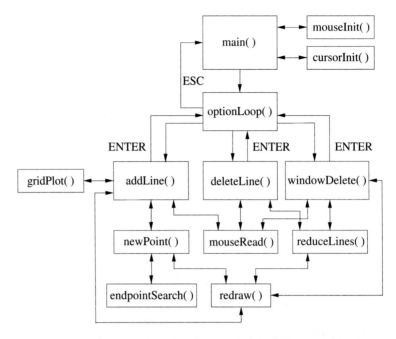

Figure 9.1   Flow chart for a drawing program that adds and deletes lines.

and cursorInit() functions. Program control then passes to the function optionLoop(), where the program user may choose from four options: adding line segments with the addLine() function; deleting segments line by line with deleteLine(); deleting a group of line segments by drawing a window around them with windowDelete(); and ending the program by exiting back to main() with the ESC key. Each of the three options for adding or deleting lines calls the mouseRead() function to read the current cursor position, the status of the left button on the mouse, and some particular key options. Also, each of these options returns to the optionLoop() when the RETURN (ENTER) key is pressed.

Under the addLine() option, a rectangular grid can be toggled on and off by calling the function gridPlot(). Also, within addLine() a snap option may be toggled on to force the cursor to move only in increments of the snap distance. The addLine() function calls the function newPoint() when a new vertex point is added (this becomes the last point of the current line segment and the first point of the next line segment). Also, addLine() provides an option for snapping to the endpoint of a previously drawn line segment; this option uses the endpointSearch() function to search through existing endpoint coordinates to find if an endpoint lies within the bounds of the square cursor.

The deleteLine() function deletes line segments one by one. When a line has been selected for deletion, the reduceLines() function is called to eliminate the particular line from the array $lines[i][j]$, with the lines renumbered so all the array elements are used from $i = 0$ to $i = nLines - 1$, where $nLines$ is the current number of lines. The reduceLines() function, along with addLine() and windowDelete(), calls the function redraw() to redraw all of the line segments existing at the particular time.

The windowDelete() function permits the program user to draw a rectangle around a group of line segments to be deleted. This function uses reduceLines() to eliminate any line segment with endpoints lying within the drawn rectangle.

The mouseInit() and mouseRead() functions are presented in appendix A, so they are not reproduced in this chapter. The functions main() and cursorInit() are listed below, (in Microsoft C), along with the header file list, the *#define* quantities, and global variables.

```c
#include <conio.h>
#include <stdio.h>
#include <stdlib.h>
#include <graph.h>
#include <dos.h>
#include <math.h>

#define ESC          27
#define RETURN       13
#define MOUSE        51
#define LEFT_BUTTON  1
#define GREEN        10
#define WHITE        15
#define BLACK         0

int     mouseInit(void),mouseRead(void);
void    cursorInit(void),optionLoop(void);
void    gridPlot(void),addLine(void);
void    newPoint(int),endpointSearch(int);
void    deleteLine(void),windowDelete(void);
void    redraw(int),reduceLines(int);

union REGS reg;
char far    *imageCursor,*imageCross,*imageBox;
int         nLines,lines[2000][4];
int         choice,endPt,endFound;
int         grid,gridFlag,snap,snapFlag;
int         x,y,button,mouseData;
int         xold=-1,yold=-1,xref=-1,yref=-1,buttonref=-1;
int         xmin=10,xmax=630,ymin=24,ymax=455;

void main(void)
{
    _setvideomode ( _VRES16COLOR );
    if (mouseInit() == 0)
    {
        printf ("Error, mouse isn't working\n");
        exit(1);
    }
    cursorInit();
    nLines = 0;
```

```
        grid = 20; gridFlag = 0;
        snap = 10; snapFlag = 0;

        optionLoop();

        _setvideomode (_DEFAULTMODE);
    }


    void cursorInit(void)
    {
        _setcolor(GREEN);
        _moveto(5,0);_lineto(5,10);
        _moveto(0,5);_lineto(10,5);
        imageCross = (char far *) malloc(
                            (unsigned) _imagesize(0,0,10,10));
        _getimage(0,0,10,10,imageCross);
        _putimage(0,0,imageCross,_GXOR);

        _moveto(0,0);_lineto(10,0);_lineto(10,10);
        _lineto(0,10);_lineto(0,0);
        imageBox = (char far *) malloc(
                            (unsigned) _imagesize(0,0,10,10));
        _getimage(0,0,10,10,imageBox);
        _putimage(0,0,imageBox,_GXOR);
        _setcolor(WHITE);
    }
```

In main(), the video mode is set; the mouse and cursor are initialized; and values are given for the initial number of lines (zero) and for the grid and snap parameters. Program control is then turned over to the optionLoop(). At the end of the program, the default video mode is restored.

Two types of cursors are set up in cursorInit(). First, a green cross, 11 × 11 pixels in size, is drawn and stored as *imageCross*. Next, a green 11 × 11-pixel square is constructed as *imageBox*. The cursor is placed and erased in the program with the _putimage() operation using the _GXOR action (which erases the cursor and restores the background to its original colors when the cursor is placed over a previously drawn cursor image).

In AutoCAD and other software programs, the initial cursor is a cross that extends all the way across the drawing screen rather than being confined within an 11 × 11 square. (With release 12, the AutoCAD cursor has been augmented with a small box, which can be used for entity selection before a command is entered.) The larger cross can be readily constructed from two line images; see the description and subroutine presented in appendix A. The small cross used in the above subroutine flickers less than does the large cross.

In optionLoop(), listed below, the program user can pick from four options by hitting keys: L for adding a line, D for deleting individual lines, W for deleting lines within a rectangle (window) drawn with the cursor, and ESC to exit the program.

```
void optionLoop(void)
{
    do
    {
        _settextposition(30,1);
        printf(" Line       Delete       Window delete      exit <ESC>  ");

        choice = getch();
        if ((choice == '1')  ||  (choice == 'L')) addLine();
        if ((choice == 'd')  ||  (choice == 'D')) deleteLine();
        if ((choice == 'w')  ||  (choice == 'W')) windowDelete();
    } while (choice != ESC);
}
```

When the key L is pressed to add a line, the function optionLoop() calls the function addLine(), listed below. To aid in placing the line, the grid and snap features may be toggled on and off; also the line may be attached to the end of a previously drawn line with the endpointSearch() routine.

Until the RETURN key is pressed, the mouse position and button, along with pressed keys, are continuously read in the *do while* loop in addLine(). The addLine() subroutine begins with the index number *i* being set equal to the current total number of lines *nLines*. Also, the flag parameter *endPt* is set equal to zero to indicate that the endpoint snap option is off. Next the cursor image is set as the cross image, and it is turned on with the _putimage() function. Then a menu is placed at the bottom of the screen, and the *do while* loop is entered.

As new cursor positions (*x,y*) are read by the mouseRead() function, they are immediately changed to snap positions if *snapFlag* = 1; that is, if snap is toggled on with the S key. Because *x* and *snap* are integer variables, (*x/snap*) is an integer; therefore, *snap**(*x/snap*) is an integral multiple of the value *snap*. Accordingly, this expression, and a similar one with *x* replaced by *y*, ensures that only coordinates at the snap points will be considered when the snap option is toggled on.

Next in the addLine() function, the cursor is erased at the old position (*xold,yold*), and the line from the last endpoint (*xlast,ylast*) to the old cursor position (*xold,yold*) is erased with a black line. Then the lines are redrawn with white by the function redraw(*i* – 1), which redraws the *i* lines numbered from 0 through *i* – 1. Figure 9.2a illustrates this procedure: line segment 1 is eroded when line 3 to the point (*xold,yold*) is erased with a black line. Redrawing lines 1 and 2 restores the eroded line so that all of its pixels are white. Thus the program keeps the drawing continuously "clean" by using frequent calls to redraw() and by erasing and redrawing the cursor at appropriate times. Alternatively, a program could be designed to clean up the drawing only when the user specifically requests a redraw (a procedure used by AutoCAD).

Within the *do while* loop of the addLine() function, the program user may initiate options by hitting the following keys: E sets the cursor to the square image, and sets the flag called *endPt* to 1 so that endpoint capture (snap) will be in effect; G toggles *gridFlag*

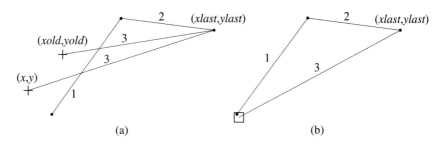

Figure 9.2 Representations of screen images for two procedures for adding line segments: (a) two cursor positions for adding line segment 3 across line segment 1; (b) the endpoint capture option for which the added segment 3 will snap to the endpoint of segment 1 when the left button of the mouse is pressed.

between the values 0 and 1 and calls the subroutine gridPlot(); and the key S toggles *snapFlag* between 0 and 1 to toggle the snap option off and on. Also, the current cursor x- and y-values are printed along the top right-hand part of the screen.

Next, an *if* statement handles operations that occur when the left button of the mouse is pressed. After the line from the last point to the cursor position is erased with a black line, the function newPoint(i) is called. This function adds a new vertex point at the end of line $i - 1$ and the start of line i. If endpoint capture is not in effect (*endPt* = 0) or if capture is in effect and the endpoint was found (*endFound* = 1), then the new total number of lines, *nLines* = i, is printed in the upper left corner of the screen, the index i is incremented, and the coordinates of the last vertex (*xlast,ylast*) are reset to (*x,y*). If endpoint capture was attempted (*endPt* = 1) but not achieved (*endFound* = 0), then i is not incremented. At the end of the *do while* loop the cursor coordinates (*xold,yold*) are reset to the values (*x,y*).

After the *do while* loop is exited by pressing the RETURN key, the line to the cursor is erased with a black line, and the total number of lines, *nLines,* is set equal to $i - 1$. This latter number represents the total number of completed line segments; note that if an endpoint capture failed during the last mouse button press, the line added in newPoint() is not counted because i was not incremented after newPoint() was called.

```
void addLine(void)
{
    int i,xlast,ylast;

    i = nLines; endPt = 0; imageCursor = imageCross;
    _putimage(xold-5,yold-5,imageCursor,_GXOR);
    _settextposition(30,1);
    printf(" Endpoint    Grid      Snap      finish line <RETURN>  ");

    do
    {
        mouseData = mouseRead();
        if (x < xmin) x = xmin; if (x > xmax) x = xmax;
        if (y < ymin) y = ymin; if (y > ymax) y = ymax;
```

```
if (snapFlag == 1)
{
    x = snap*(x/snap); y = snap*(y/snap);
}


_putimage(xold-5,yold-5,imageCursor,_GXOR);
if (i > nLines)
{
    _setcolor(BLACK);
    _moveto(xlast,ylast); _lineto(xold,yold);
    _setcolor(WHITE);
    _moveto(xlast,ylast); _lineto(x,y);
}
redraw(i-1);


if ((mouseData == 'e') || (mouseData == 'E'))
{
    imageCursor = imageBox;
    endPt = 1;
}
if ((mouseData == 'g') || (mouseData == 'G'))
{
    gridFlag = 1 - gridFlag;
    gridPlot();
}
if ((mouseData == 's') || (mouseData == 'S'))
    snapFlag = 1 - snapFlag;
_putimage(x-5,y-5,imageCursor,_GXOR);


_settextposition (1,40);
printf (" x=%3d y=%3d",x,y);


if (button == LEFT_BUTTON)
{
    if ((x != xlast) || (y != ylast))
    {
        _putimage(x-5,y-5,imageCursor,_GXOR);
        _setcolor(BLACK);
        _moveto(xlast,ylast); _lineto(x,y);
        _setcolor(WHITE);
        _putimage(x-5,y-5,imageCursor,_GXOR);

        newPoint(i);

        if ((endPt == 0) || (endFound == 1))
        {
            _settextposition(1,1);
            printf("nLines = %d  ",i);
```

```
            i++;
            xlast = x; ylast = y;
        }
        endPt = 0;
      }
    }
    xold = x; yold = y;
  } while(mouseData != RETURN);

  _putimage(x-5,y-5,imageCursor,_GXOR);
  _setcolor(BLACK);
  _moveto(xlast,ylast); _lineto(xold,yold);
  _setcolor(WHITE);
  nLines = i-1;
}
```

The following redraw() function draws i lines numbered from 0 through $i - 1$.

```
void redraw(int i)
{
    int k;

    for (k=0; k<i; k++)
    {
        _moveto(lines[k][0],lines[k][1]);
        _lineto(lines[k][2],lines[k][3]);
    }
}
```

The function gridPlot() plots a rectangular array of points (dots of one-pixel size) separated by the distance *grid* in the horizontal and vertical directions. The points are plotted as white dots if the parameter *gridFlag* equals 1; otherwise, they are plotted as black dots for erasure.

```
void gridPlot(void)
{
    int i,j;

    if (gridFlag == 0) _setcolor(BLACK);
    for (i=grid; i<640; i=i+grid)
    {
        for (j=grid; j<480; j=j+grid)
        {
            _setpixel(i,j);
        }
    }
    if (gridFlag == 0) _setcolor(WHITE);
}
```

The function newPoint(i) first checks to see if endpoint capture is in effect (*endPt* = 1). If so, then the subroutine endpointSearch(i) is called. If a line segment endpoint is found, then endpointSearch(i) changes the values (x,y) to these endpoint values. Next, if $i = nLines$, then the new point (x,y) is the start of a new series of connected line segments, so this point is set as the start of line i. If $i > nLines$ then the new point represents both the end of line $i-1$ and the start of line i. The array *lines[i][j]* is set accordingly.

```
void newPoint(int i)
{
    if (endPt == 1)
    {
        _putimage(x-5,y-5,imageCursor,_GXOR);
        endpointSearch(i);

        imageCursor = imageCross;
        _putimage(x-5,y-5,imageCursor,_GXOR);
    }
    if (i == nLines)
    {
        lines[i][0] = x;
        lines[i][1] = y;
    }
    else
    {
        lines[i][0] = lines[i-1][2] = x;
        lines[i][1] = lines[i-1][3] = y;
    }
    _putimage(x-5,y-5,imageCursor,_GXOR);
    redraw(i);
    _putimage(x-5,y-5,imageCursor,_GXOR);
}
```

The function endpointSearch(), below, checks to see if the point (x,y) is within a 10×10 square of either the beginning coordinates (*lines[j][0]*,*lines[j][1]*) or ending coordinates (*lines[j][2]*,*lines[j][3]*) of the line segments.

```
void endpointSearch(int i)
{
    int j;

    endFound = 0;
    for (j=0; j<i; j++)
    {
        if ((abs(lines[j][0]-x)<10) && (abs(lines[j][1]-y)<10))
        {
            x = lines[j][0]; y = lines[j][1]; endFound = 1;
        }
```

```
if ((abs(lines[j][2]-x)<10) && (abs(lines[j][3]-y)<10))
{
    x = lines[j][2]; y = lines[j][3]; endFound = 1;
}
        }
    }
```

9.2 DELETING LINE SEGMENTS

Lines can be deleted with the two procedures illustrated in figure 9.3. In the first procedure single line segments are deleted by placing a square cursor so that it intersects the line; in the second procedure a box is drawn around all lines to be deleted.

Single Line Deletion

To delete a single line with the square cursor, one must calculate the geometry for line intersection with a square. Figure 9.4 illustrates this geometry, where the line will be on an intersection path with the box (square) if the distance *dbox* to the box corner is greater than or equal to the distance *d* to the line. In figure 9.4a dashed lines are drawn through the center and corner of the box parallel to the line segment, which has a slope *m* equal to $\Delta y/\Delta x$.

The following relation is derived by referring to the two similar triangles in figure 9.4a.

$$dbox = (h + mh)\cos\alpha = \frac{h(1 + m)}{\sqrt{1 + m^2}} \tag{9.1}$$

Because computing of square roots is time-consuming, the square of distances will be compared in the line deletion subroutine. Thus, squaring equation 9.1 and substituting $m = \Delta y/\Delta x$ gives the result in equation 9.2.

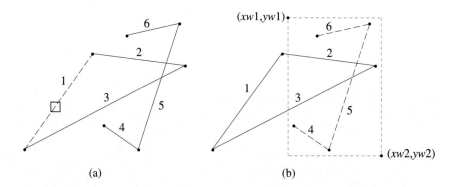

(a)   (b)

Figure 9.3 Line deletion by two procedures: (a) line segment 1 is deleted when the square cursor is placed on it and the left mouse button is pressed; (b) line segments 4, 5, and 6 are erased after placement of the window corner points ($xw1,yw1$) and ($xw2,yw2$).

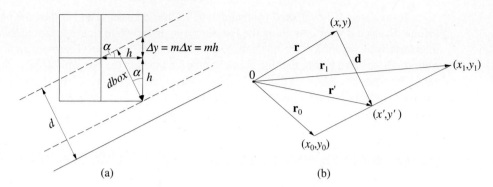

Figure 9.4   Single line deletion: (a) geometry for a cursor box of halfwidth h with its center a distance d from a line segment; (b) vector diagram with 0 denoting the origin, (x,y) the cursor box center, with (x_0,y_0) and (x_1,y_1) being the endpoints of the line segment. The distance vector $\mathbf{d}$ is normal to the line segment at the point (x',y').

$$(dbox)^2 = \frac{h^2(\varDelta x + \varDelta y)^2}{[(\varDelta x)^2 + (\varDelta y)^2]} \tag{9.2}$$

In the program subroutine, the quantities $\varDelta x$ and $\varDelta y$ in equation 9.2 are computed from the total line segment; that is, $\varDelta x = x_1 - x_0$ and $\varDelta y = y_1 - y_0$.

For computing the distance d from the box center to the line, consider the vector diagram shown in figure 9.4b. The line segment from $\mathbf{r}_0 = [x_0\ \ y_0]$ to $\mathbf{r}_1 = [x_1\ \ y_1]$ is given by the parametric relation below, in which t varies from 0 to 1. The notation $[x'\ \ y']$ represents a 2-D row vector having elements x' and y'. Here primed coordinates x' and y' are used to represent points along the line because the unprimed coordinates represent the center of the cursor box.

$$\mathbf{r}' = (1 - t)\,\mathbf{r}_0 + t\,\mathbf{r}_1$$

or
$$[x'\ \ y'] = (1 - t)\,[x_0\ \ y_0] + t[x_1\ \ y_1] \tag{9.3}$$

The distance d from the box center $\mathbf{r} = [x\ \ y]$ to the line is obtained by requiring that the distance vector $\mathbf{d} = \mathbf{r}' - \mathbf{r}$ be perpendicular to the line segment $\mathbf{r}_1 - \mathbf{r}_0$; see figure 9.4b.

$$(\mathbf{r}' - \mathbf{r})\cdot(\mathbf{r}_1 - \mathbf{r}_0) = 0 \tag{9.4}$$

The dot in equation 9.4 represents the scalar product. After substituting for $\mathbf{r}_1$, $\mathbf{r}_0$, and $\mathbf{r}$, and using equation 9.3 for $\mathbf{r}'$, equation 9.4 may be expressed as

$$[(1 - t)x_0 + t\,x_1 - x](x_1 - x_0) + [(1 - t)y_0 + t\,y_1 - y](y_1 - y_0) = 0 \tag{9.5}$$

The above expression may be readily solved for the parameter t at the point where the perpendicular distance vector $\mathbf{d}$ intersects the line that passes through $\mathbf{r}_0$ and $\mathbf{r}_1$.

$$t = \frac{(x - x_0)(x_1 - x_0) + (y - y_0)(y_1 - y_0)}{[(x_1 - x_0)^2 + (y_1 - y_0)^2]} \tag{9.6}$$

If the value of t computed from equation 9.6 lies between 0 and 1, then the perpendicular distance **d** intersects along the line segment, as shown in figure 9.4b; otherwise, it intersects a continuation of the line outside the region of the segment. Therefore, in the subroutine delete listed below, the first condition for intersecting the box with a line is that $0 \leq t \leq 1$. The second condition is that $d^2 \leq (dbox)^2$. The squared distance d^2 may be readily calculated from t and the coordinate values by evaluating the magnitude of $\mathbf{d} = \mathbf{r}' - \mathbf{r}$.

$$d^2 = [(x_0 - x) + t(x_1 - x_0)]^2 + [(y_0 - y) + t(y_1 - y_0)]^2 \qquad (9.7)$$

In the program subroutine deleteLine() listed below, $(dbox)^2$ is given the name $dbox2$, and d^2 is called $d2$. Therefore, the cursor box is considered to intersect the line segment if $0 \leq t \leq 1$ and $d2 \leq dbox2$. These two conditions are checked for all line segments until they are satisfied, at which time the flag *lineFound* is set equal to 1 and the line segment number (*jdelete*) is passed on to the subroutine reduceLines() so that this line segment can be eliminated from the line storage array.

It should be noted that the calculations for $dbox2$ and $d2$ are carried out with floating-point variables (here double-precision values xd, $xd0$, $xd1$, etc.). Calculations with integer variables will lead to serious errors in multiplication and division operations (multiplications involving large dx or dy quantities result in errors because the normal range of integer values is from $-32,768$ to $32,767$).

```
void deleteLine(void)
{
    int j,jdelete,lineFound;
    double xd,yd,xd0,yd0,xd1,yd1,dx,dy;
    double t,dbox2,d2,f1,f2;

    imageCursor = imageBox;
    _putimage(xold-5,yold-5,imageCursor,_GXOR);
    _settextposition(30,1);
    printf("                    Select line to delete.                    ");
    do
    {
        mouseData = mouseRead();
        if (x < xmin) x = xmin; if (x > xmax) x = xmax;
        if (y < ymin) y = ymin; if (y > ymax) y = ymax;

        _putimage(xold-5,yold-5,imageCursor,_GXOR);
        _putimage(x-5,y-5,imageCursor,_GXOR);

        if (button == LEFT_BUTTON)
        {
            lineFound = 0;
            for (j=0; j<nLines; j++)
            {
                if (lineFound == 0)
                {
```

```
                        xd0 = (double) lines[j][0];
                        yd0 = (double) lines[j][1];
                        xd1 = (double) lines[j][2];
                        yd1 = (double) lines[j][3];
                        xd = (double) x; yd =(double) y;
                        dx = xd1 - xd0; dy = yd1 - yd0;
                        t = ((xd-xd0)*dx + (yd-yd0)*dy)/(dx*dx+dy*dy);

                        if ((t >= 0.) && (t <= 1.))
                        {
                            f1 = fabs(dx)+fabs(dy);
                            f2 = dx*dx+dy*dy;
                            dbox2 = 25.0*f1*f1/f2;
                            f1 = xd0-xd+t*dx;
                            f2 = yd0-yd+t*dy;
                            d2 = f1*f1 + f2*f2;
                            if (d2 < dbox2)
                            {
                                lineFound = 1;
                                jdelete = j;
                                reduceLines(jdelete);
                            }
                        }
                    }
                }
            }
            xold = x; yold = y;
        } while(mouseData != RETURN);
        _putimage(x-5,y-5,imageCursor,_GXOR);
    }
```

In the function reduceLines(*jdelete*) listed below, the line segment number *jdelete* is eliminated from *lines*[*j*][*k*] by renumbering the arrays from *j* = *jdelete* through the last line, *j* = *nLines* − 1. This operation deletes the appropriate line segment, and renumbers the lines above it so there is no gap in the line storage array.

```
            void reduceLines(int jdelete)
            {
                int     j,k;

                _putimage(x-5,y-5,imageCursor,_GXOR);
                _setcolor(BLACK);
                redraw(nLines);
                nLines = nLines - 1;

                for (j=jdelete; j<nLines; j++)
                {
```

```
                    for (k=0; k<4; k++)
                    {
                        lines[j][k] = lines[j+1][k];
                    }
            }
            _setcolor(WHITE);
            redraw(nLines);
            _putimage(x-5,y-5,imageCursor,_GXOR);
            _settextposition(1,1);
            printf("nLines = %d  ",nLines);
    }
```

Window for Deleting Lines

If a number of line segments are to be deleted, then it is more efficient to select the lines by drawing a rectangle (window) around them. This windowing procedure can be used to select a group of entities in AutoCAD for many situations, not just for line deletion (AutoCAD ERASE command).

The first *do while* loop in the windowDelete() function listed below draws the window used for line deletion. The flag variable *corner* is set equal to 1 to identify the window's first corner. When the left mouse button is pressed, the corner coordinates $(xc1,yc1)$ are set equal to the cursor coordinates (x,y). Then with the flag set as *corner* = 2, rectangles are drawn and erased from $(xc1,yc1)$ to the changing cursor position (x,y), so that the program user can view a rectangle that has a second corner moving with the cursor. When the rectangle contains the desired line segments, depressing the left cursor button removes all lines within the rectangle. The first step in achieving this result is to identify the second selected point as $(xc2,yc2)$ and set the flag *corner* equal to the value 3.

When the first *do while* loop is exited, the selected window corner coordinates are ordered, with the rectangle now identified by an upper left corner $(xw1,yw1)$ and a lower right corner $(xw2,yw2)$; that is, $xw1 \le xw2$ and $yw1 \le yw2$. A second *do while* loop checks all of the line segments' end points and eliminates, with a call to reduceLines(), all of the line segments that have both endpoints lying within the window. That is, a line segment is erased if both endpoints have x-values between $xw1$ and $xw2$, and y-values between $yw1$ and $yw2$. The function windowDelete() ends by erasing the window rectangle with a black line and redrawing all line segments with white.

```
void windowDelete(void)
{
    int     j,xc1,yc1,xc2,yc2,xw1,yw1,xw2,yw2,corner;

    imageCursor = imageCross;
    corner = 1;
    _putimage(xold-5,yold-5,imageCursor,_GXOR);
    _settextposition(30,1);
```

```
printf("      Select first corner of window.                  ");
do
{
    mouseData = mouseRead();
    if (x < xmin) x = xmin; if (x > xmax) x = xmax;
    if (y < ymin) y = ymin; if (y > ymax) y = ymax;

    _putimage(xold-5,yold-5,imageCursor,_GXOR);
    if (corner == 2)
    {
        _setcolor(BLACK);
        _rectangle(_GBORDER,xc1,yc1,xold,yold);
        _setcolor(WHITE);
        _rectangle(_GBORDER,xc1,yc1,x,y);
    }
    _putimage(x-5,y-5,imageCursor,_GXOR);

    if (button == LEFT_BUTTON)
    {
        if (corner == 1)
        {
            xc1 = x; yc1 = y;
            corner = 2;
            _settextposition(30,8);
            printf ("      Select second corner of window.    ");
        }
        else
        {
            if ((x != xc1) && (y != yc1))
            {
                xc2 = x; yc2 = y;
                corner = 3;
            }
        }
    }
    xold = x; yold = y;
} while(corner != 3);

if (xc1 < xc2) {xw1 = xc1; xw2 = xc2;}
else {xw1 = xc2; xw2 = xc1;}

if (yc1 < yc2) { yw1 = yc1; yw2 = yc2;}
else { yw1 = yc2; yw2 = yc1;}

j = 0;
do
{
```

```
        if ((lines[j][0] >= xw1) && (lines[j][0] <= xw2) &&
            (lines[j][1] >= yw1) && (lines[j][1] <= yw2) &&
            (lines[j][2] >= xw1) && (lines[j][2] <= xw2) &&
            (lines[j][3] >= yw1) && (lines[j][3] <= yw2))
            reduceLines(j);
        else
            j++;
    } while (j < nLines);
    _putimage(x-5,y-5,imageCursor,_GXOR);
    _setcolor(BLACK);
    _rectangle(_GBORDER,xc1,yc1,xold,yold);
    _setcolor(WHITE);
    redraw(nLines);
}
```

9.3 EDITING CURVES

Interpolation and approximation curves can be drawn with the methods described in chapter 7. To use these curves in a CAD system, one must be able to quickly modify them. In AutoCAD, curves are modified with the PEDIT command. In this section the following features of PEDIT are modeled: a polyline is selected with a square cursor; a particular vertex is selected by moving an ✕-shaped cursor back and forth between vertices with the N key (for next vertex) and the P key (for previous vertex); a vertex is moved with the mouse after the M key (for move) is pressed; and a cubic B-spline curve is drawn from the polyline frame when the S key (for spline) is pressed.

The polyline data is stored in a global array *plines*[*i*][*j*], where *i* gives the polyline number, and *j* contains vertex x-coordinates as the even elements and the y-coordinates as the odd elements. The number of vertices in polyline *i* is defined by the array *nVertices*[*i*], where the polylines are numbered from $i = 1$ to *nPlines*.

First, the following function prototypes and global variables must be declared in order to include polylines and polyline editing in the previous program.

```
void addPline(void),newPlinePoint(int);
void findPline(void),pedit(void);
void cubicBSpline(int n,double x[],double y[]);

int     nPlines,nVertices[30],plines[20][60],plineNum;
char    far *imageX;
```

Next, the following lines for a polyline and editing options are inserted into the function optionLoop().

```
if ((choice == 'p') || (choice == 'P')) addPline();
if ((choice == 'e') || (choice == 'E'))
{
```

```
            findPline();
            pedit();
    }
```

Under optionLoop(), the words Pline and EditPoly should be added to the function printf() that prints the menu at the bottom of the screen. Also, in main(), the number of polylines should be initialized with the statement *nPlines* = 0.

   The addPline() function is similar to the addLine() function discussed in section 9.1, except that here only open polyline functions are considered, so the snap to endpoint option is not included. Also, a given polyline may have many vertices, so vertices are continuously added until the RETURN key is pressed. As shown in the listing below, only one polyline is added each time addPline() is called.

```
    void addPline(void)
    {
        int i,xlast,ylast;

        nPlines = nPlines + 1; imageCursor = imageCross;
        i = 0;
        _settextposition(30,1);
        _putimage(xold-5,yold-5,imageCursor,_GXOR);
        printf("   Grid         Snap         finish line <RETURN>          ");
        do
        {
            mouseData = mouseRead();
            if (x < xmin) x = xmin; if (x > xmax) x = xmax;
            if (y < ymin) y = ymin; if (y > ymax) y = ymax;

            if (snapFlag == 1)
            {
                x = snap*(x/snap); y = snap*(y/snap);
            }
            _putimage(xold-5,yold-5,imageCursor,_GXOR);
            if (i > 0)
            {
                _setcolor(BLACK);
                _moveto(xlast,ylast); _lineto(xold,yold);
                _setcolor(WHITE);
                _moveto(xlast,ylast); _lineto(x,y);
            }
            nVertices[nPlines] = i;
            redraw(nLines,nPlines);
            if ((mouseData == 'g') || (mouseData == 'G'))
            {
                gridFlag = 1 - gridFlag;
                gridPlot();
            }
```

```
    if ((mouseData == 's') || (mouseData == 'S'))
        snapFlag = 1 - snapFlag;
    _putimage(x-5,y-5,imageCursor,_GXOR);
    _settextposition (1,40);
    printf (" x=%3d y=%3d",x,y);

    if (button == LEFT_BUTTON)
    {
        if ((x != xlast) || (y != ylast))
        {
            newPlinePoint(i);
            _settextposition(1,1); printf("vertex = %d   ",i);
            i++;
            xlast = x; ylast = y;
        }
    }
    xold = x; yold = y;
}while(mouseData != RETURN);
_putimage(x-5,y-5,imageCursor,_GXOR);
_setcolor(BLACK);
_moveto(xlast,ylast); _lineto(xold,yold);
_setcolor(WHITE);
}
```

In the function addPline(), vertices are added by the call to the function newPline-Point(*i*), listed below. Because *i* begins with the value 0, the x-coordinate of the first vertex is stored as *plines*[*nPlines*][0], whereas the y-coordinate is stored as *plines*[*nPlines*][1]. Subsequent x- and y-coordinates are stored as even and odd values of the second subscript.

```
void newPlinePoint(int i)
{
    plines[nPlines][2*i] = x;
    plines[nPlines][2*i+1] = y;
    _putimage(x-5,y-5,imageCursor,_GXOR);
    redraw(nLines,i);
    _putimage(x-5,y-5,imageCursor,_GXOR);
}
```

In the above functions, both the lines and polylines are redrawn to restore all the white pixels in line segments that may be erased when the line to the cursor is erased with a black line. Accordingly, the function redraw() is changed so that it accepts two integer values: *i* represents the number of lines, and *j* represents the number of polylines.

```
void redraw(int i, int j)
{
    int k,n;
```

```
for (k=0; k<i; k++)
{
    _moveto(lines[k][0],lines[k][1]);
    _lineto(lines[k][2],lines[k][3]);
}
for (n=1; n<=j; n++)
{
    _moveto(plines[n][0],plines[n][1]);
    for (k=1; k<nVertices[n]; k++)
    {
        _lineto(plines[n][2*k],plines[n][2*k+1]);
    }
}
}
```

The function prototype for redraw() must be changed to the above form, and the calls to redraw() must be changed to the new form with appropriate arguments; that is, redraw(*i*–1,*nPlines*) in addLine(), redraw(*i,nPlines*) in newPoint(), and redraw(*nLines,nPlines*) in reduceLines() and in windowDelete().

Simulating the AutoCAD PEDIT Command

Polylines may be readily edited with the command PEDIT in AutoCAD. It is often necessary to edit polylines to produce a desired curve in design applications. The polyline editing features described at the beginning of this section (9.3) are initiated from optionLoop() when the E key is pressed.

First the function findPline() is called in order to find the polyline to edit, and then the function pedit() is called to carry out the editing. The function findPline() is given as listing 9.1 in appendix B.

The editing of polylines is illustrated in figure 9.5. After a polyline has been selected, an × cursor appears at the first vertex. This cursor may be advanced to the next vertex by pressing the N key. After the cursor has advanced, it may be returned to the previous vertex by pressing the P key. In addition, the M key may be pressed to move the vertex marked by the cursor. The cursor changes to a cross, which may be moved to the new cursor position, with the vertex position set by pressing the left button of the mouse. These operations are given in subroutine pedit(), which is presented as listing 9.2 in appendix B.

The pedit() subroutine permits a cubic B-spline to be drawn when the S key is pressed. Therefore, one may edit the polyline frame until the appropriate configuration is reached, and then plot a cubic B-spline by pressing the S key. The function cubicBSpline() is the same as that given in section 7.6. Other curve fits from chapter 7 may be substituted for cubicBSpline().

The above subroutines do not include erasing a cubic B-spline once it is drawn, although the spline frame may be changed and additional B-splines drawn. Dynamic dragging of the frame and B-spline is presented below to better illustrate the effect of moving the polyline frame on the resulting cubic B-spline.

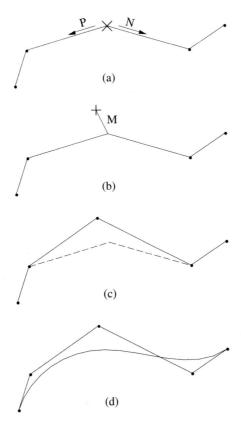

Figure 9.5 Polyline: (a) the $\times$ cursor is moved to the next vertex with the N key or to the previous vertex with the P key; (b) after the M key is pressed, the cross cursor appears and is moved to the new location for the vertex; (c) when the left mouse button is pressed, the new vertex position is set, and line segments are relocated to the new positions; (d) a cubic B-spline curve is drawn when the S key is pressed.

Dragging Polyline Vertices

Dynamic manipulation of drawing entities was introduced with release 12 of AutoCAD. This procedure involves the introduction of *grips,* which can be selected and dragged with the mouse. Grips appear if a drawing entity or block is selected with the small pick box (on the cross-hair cursor) before a command is given. Grips are identified by small squares, whose locations depend on the particular drawing entity selected. Grips are an example of *handles.* Handles have been used for many years by Macintosh CAD and drawing programs to provide a means for moving, stretching, scaling, and rotating drawing entities.

For a single line segment, three AutoCAD grips appear: one at the center of the line and one at each of the endpoints. If the center grip is selected with the mouse cursor, the line segment can be moved to a new location. Selection of the endpoint grips permits the line endpoints to be moved, thus changing the length and orientation of the line segment. After a grip selection has been made on the line segment or on another drawing entity, the RETURN key may be pressed to cycle through the following operations: stretch, move, rotate, scale, and mirror. After the operation on a drawing entity has been completed, the se-

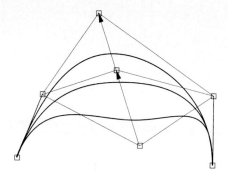

Figure 9.6   Multiple exposures of a cubic B-spline, where the third vertex point is dragged from the lower position to two new positions shown by the arrows. The three cubic B-spline curves shown are those determined by the three polyline frames. The small squares represent AutoCAD grips. The program peditDrag() produces a similar animation.

lected grip(s) can be de-selected by entering Control-C, and the grips can be turned off by entering Control-C again.

For a polyline, grips are located at the control vertices. When a grip is selected, it can be dragged, and the polyline will follow. Figure 9.6 illustrates three positions that occur when a polyline frame and its spline curve are dragged along with the selected vertex.

A program that drags B-spline curves with the mouse is obtained when the subroutine pedit() is replaced by peditDrag(). With peditDrag(), when key M for move is pressed, the vertex marked by the × cursor follows the mouse motion, and a cubic B-spline is continuously drawn and erased so that it follows the motion of the polyline frame. The resulting animation provides a good illustration of how the frame determines the cubic B-spline.

The subroutine peditDrag() is given as listing 9.3 in appendix B.

9.4 DIMENSIONING

A good computer-aided drafting system will enter dimensions on a drawing in a convenient and comprehensive fashion. For example, with AutoCAD a horizontal dimension can be entered by using the cursor to identify the origin points for the extension lines and the location of the dimension line (figure 9.7). The specific commands for horizontal dimension lines in AutoCAD are shown below.

```
Command: DIM1
Dim: HOR
First extension line origin or RETURN to select: (pick with mouse)
Second extension line origin: (pick with mouse)
Dimension line location: (pick with mouse)
Dimension text <measured value>: (RETURN)
```

One dimension line may be drawn with the DIM1 command. (Multiple lines can be drawn by entering the dimension mode by typing DIM, with the mode terminated by entering EXIT or Control-C.) A horizontal dimension line is started with the HORIZONTAL or HOR command; other options are initiated by typing VERTICAL, ALIGNED, ROTATED,

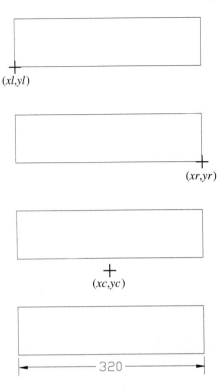

Figure 9.7 Placement of a horizontal dimension line after the following three points have been picked with the mouse cursor (cross): the left extension line origin, the right extension line origin, and the y-location of the dimension line. After these three points are picked, the dimension line with arrowheads and numeric text (label) appear as shown at the bottom of the figure.

ANGULAR, DIAMETER, or RADIUS (or their abbreviations VER, ALI, ROT, ANG, DIA, RAD). The two extension (witness) line origins are selected next, or existing extension lines may be used. After the dimension line location is selected, the measured value for the dimension line distance is displayed as the default value in the $<>$ brackets. This value may be selected by pressing the RETURN key, or a different value (or word) may be entered.

The horizontal dimension-line subroutine horDimLine() (given as listing 9.4 in appendix B) can be added to the program developed in this chapter. For text to be placed at any pixel location with Microsoft C, a font file (extension FON) must be present in the directory, and must be "registered" and "set." For example, for the Helvetica font, the following two commands may be placed at the beginning of the main() function.

```
if (_registerfonts("HELVB.FON")<0)
{
    _outtext("The font is not available!");
    exit(0);
}
_setfont("t'helv'h16w7b");
```

The above lines will warn you if the appropriate font file HELVB.FON is not in your subdirectory.

In the function _setfont(), *t'helv'* denotes the typeface Helvetica, *h*16 is the character height, *w*7 the width, and *b* denotes a bit-mapped character. If the exact character size requested does not exist, then Microsoft C will pick the closest size available.

For the dimension mode to be entered, the word HorDimLine should be added to the menu at the bottom of the screen, and the following line added to optionLoop().

```
if ((choice == 'h') || (choice == 'H')) horDimLine();
```

The subroutine is given in appendix B as listing 9.4.

The above subroutine draws horizontal dimension lines in the same fashion as Auto-CAD. Horizontal dimension lines may be placed quickly with this subroutine, especially when the snap option is used to locate the points; see figure 9.8 for sample dimension lines constructed with this subroutine. The subroutine presented here requires the numeric text to be placed in a space at the middle of the dimension line. Commercial drafting software, such as AutoCAD, provides other options when the dimension line is too short for the text to fit in the center of the line: the text can be placed to the side, above, or below a dimension line.

The construction of vertical dimension lines is presented as an exercise (9.15).

In this section dimensions are in integer pixel values. Dimensions in a CAD program are floating-point values that represent real (world) dimensions. In the next chapter an example for 2-D scaling treats lines and dimensions as double-precision floating-point values. Also, 2-D rotations are considered for rotated and aligned dimension lines.

AutoCAD provides over 40 dimensioning variables that may be changed to produce dimension lines in almost any format or syle. For example, the variable DIMASZ, similar to *asz* in program listing 9.4, changes the size of arrowheads. If you wish the tick marks favored by architects instead of arrowheads, then set the variable DIMTSZ to the tick size desired, and tick marks will be drawn instead of arrowheads (arrowheads are drawn only when DIMTSZ is set equal to zero).

AutoCAD and many other CAD systems provide *associative* dimensioning. An associative dimension is created as a single entity; that is, the extension lines, dimension line, arrowheads, and text constitute a single entity. Furthermore, the associative dimension entity can be edited with commands such as EXTEND, MIRROR, ROTATE, SCALE, STRETCH, and TRIM, with the numerical value of the text being adjusted automatically. The associative dimensioning feature is very useful for drawings that are frequently modified.

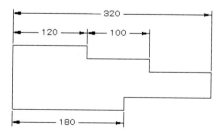

Figure 9.8 Horizontal dimension lines placed with the subroutine horDimLine(). This is a screen capture image with black and white colors reversed.

9.5 THE GRAPHICAL USER INTERFACE

The term *graphical user interface* (GUI) has become popular for describing graphics features used in application software packages. Construction of a user interface involves setting up rules and procedures, as well as designing graphics features such as the screen layout, menus, typography, icons, and color. Many GUIs are for special applications; others are for general use in computer operating systems or windows software.

Some applications permit an individual to design a GUI in a relatively short time; see figure 9.9, which illustrates a graphics interface developed by a student for a program that performs calculations for tape cartridge designs. The menu on the right leads to additional menus. The small cross on the right below the menu is the mouse cursor, which may be used to select menu items or to change parameters with the arrow buttons shown at the lower left. When the tape is moving forward, it travels from the left hub to the right one (in the figure only a small amount of tape has moved to the right hub). The menu item labeled "file" permits tape cartridge designs to be loaded and saved. Under the "animate" menu option, the tape may be moved forward or backward. The "modify" menu item changes the parameters to be modified with the arrow buttons at the lower left part of the screen. In addition to the tape properties shown, belt properties may be changed, as well as the positions of the hubs, pins, and rollers. The "data" menu item permits the user to select variables for display in the rectangular sections at the bottom center and right of the screen.

As described by Marcus (1992), a large development effort is required to design GUIs for operating systems, window systems, or complex applications. The Apple Macintosh op-

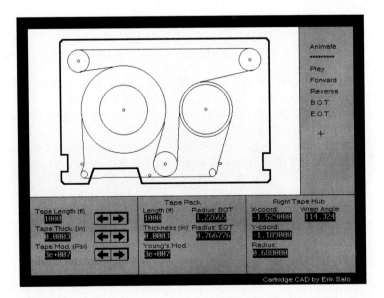

Figure 9.9   Screen image from the C program "Cartridge CAD," developed by Eric Salo.

erating system, introduced in 1984, was the first widely used example of a GUI. In 1988 NextStep, the operating system for the NeXT computer, introduced a three-dimensional appearance for its graphics items. (As illustrated in the figure for exercise 9.19, the rectangular region around a menu item can be shown as a 3-D beveled button by placing a highlight along the left and top edges, and a shadow along the right and bottom edges.) Other systems include Microsoft Windows™ for IBM PC compatible computers, OS/2 Presentation Manager (developed jointly by Microsoft and IBM for the PC), and the following UNIX-based systems for workstations: OPEN LOOK from Sun Microsystems Inc., Motif from Open Software Foundation, NewWave from Hewlett Packard, and DECWindows from Digital Equipment Corporation.

These operating and window systems use a graphical interface that resembles a desktop, with icons representing files, file folders, a trash can, and other items. Icons are manipulated with a mouse; for example, files (and file folders) can be opened by double-clicking (moving the mouse cursor to the file icon and pressing the mouse button twice), and files can be moved by dragging them with the mouse cursor (moving the cursor to the icon and holding the mouse button down while moving the mouse). When an application file is opened, it appears in a window that may be moved by dragging its frame with the mouse; the window size may be changed by clicking or dragging a size box on the frame; the text in the application may be moved with scroll bars; and the application may be closed by clicking on a close box located on the window frame. The use of graphics rather than typed commands usually makes a system faster and easier to use.

Well-designed menus are an important part of the graphical user interface. Menus may be fixed, pull down from the top of the screen, pull out from the side, or pop up (as with dialog boxes that pop up on the screen at appropriate times in a program).

The Macintosh User Interface

Macintosh GUI features can be incorporated into programs using the Toolbox, which may be accessed through any of the programming languages available for the Macintosh.

The QuickDraw (including Color QuickDraw) part of the Toolbox contains the graphics functions used for graphics programming—functions of the type listed in table 1.1; for example, MoveTo(), LineTo(), FrameRect(), and FillOval().

Another important part of the Toolbox is the Resource Manager. Resources are a concept developed for the Macintosh, but resources can be modeled on the IBM PC; see Rimmer (1992). The Resource Manager keeps track of resource files, which provide data for windows, menus, fonts, icons, and other items. The resources that are used by an application (program) are created and changed separately from the application code. This procedure simplifies the development of an application program.

A number of other "managers" are available in the Macintosh Toolbox. As their names indicate, the following managers are important for the Macintosh GUI: Dialog Manager, Menu Manager, Window Manager, Font Manager, Control Manager, Scrap Manager, Event Manager, File Manager, Color Manager, Palette Manager, Sound Manager, and Printing Manager. Even tasks that appear simple, such as activating a window by clicking on it, require a number of programming steps; see Mark and Reed (1989) and Mark (1990) for sample programs.

Although specific Macintosh programming examples will not be presented here, it is instructive to review some of the Macintosh GUI features. Detailed descriptions of the Macintosh Toolbox are given in *Inside Macintosh,* volumes I–V.

Figure 9.10a shows an example of a Macintosh screen. Several windows are displayed on the screen, but only the one highlighted with horizontal lines across its title bar (top of frame) is active. The active window is a Microsoft® Word document; namely, the

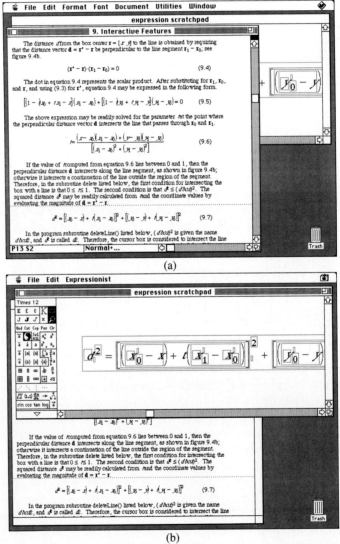

Figure 9.10 Overlapping windows, with a change in active window. Screen shots reprinted with permission from Microsoft Corporation.

present chapter identified with the title "9. Interactive Features" written on the title bar. The Word pull-down menus are at the top of the screen. Behind the active window lies an interactive window entitled "expression scratchpad," for the equation-writing utility Expressionist. This window may be made active by clicking on it, at which time its title bar becomes highlighted and moves to the front; see figure 9.10b, in which the window "expression scratchpad" has become the active window. The active window may be moved around on the screen by dragging the highlighted window frame.

Slider bars that act as scroll bars are important to the operation of a window. In figure 9.10a, the gray regions on the scroll bar at the right of the window indicate that there is more text above and below, which may be brought into the window by any of the following procedures: clicking on the up and down arrows, clicking on the gray regions, or moving the scroll (slider) box by dragging it. Similarly, the bottom scroll-bar controls can be used to view text to the right of the window. When all of the application lies in either the horizontal or vertical extent of the window, then the scroll bar becomes white and the scroll box disappears because scrolling is unnecessary in that direction; note that the right scroll bar in figure 9.10b is white because the entire vertical extent of the equation is encompassed by the window. A program for setting up scroll bars with Microsoft C on the PC is described at the end of this chapter.

An application may be closed by clicking on the close box in the upper-left corner of the frame. The size box on the lower-right corner may be dragged in any direction to continuously change the size and aspect ratio of the window. The size box in the upper-right corner toggles the window between two sizes: one that extends to the boundaries of the screen or application, and another that has been set by the application or by the user with the other size box.

A software package that is used on different computer operating systems may be designed so that it has the same GUI on each system, or it may be designed with different GUIs that take advantage of each operating system's special features. For the first approach, once a user has become proficient with the program on one system, he can readily use it on any system. With the second approach, the user may find the program easy to learn because it uses approaches similar to other software packages on his computer system. For example, Macintosh users can usually learn to use a new software package more quickly if it has an interface similar to the GUI for the Macintosh operating system.

Early releases of AutoCAD were almost identical on different computer systems, but now the AutoCAD GUI varies to take on the features of the operating system. Figure 9.11 shows menus on the Microsoft Windows and Macintosh operating systems. Along with other changes from the DOS version of AutoCAD, the Windows version features a floating menu called the toolbox, which can be dragged to any position on the screen. The toolbox can be turned on and off, and can be changed from a vertical bar to the nearly square rectangle shown in figure 9.11a.

The Macintosh version of AutoCAD shown in figure 9.11b features icon bars that can be vertical or horizontal, and dragged to any desired location. Also, some of the other pull-down menus are tear-off menus. A tear-off menu is one that has been torn off; that is, dragged to a convenient part of the screen, where it remains until its close box is selected. (Normal pull-down menus close up as soon as an item has been selected.) In figure 9.11b,

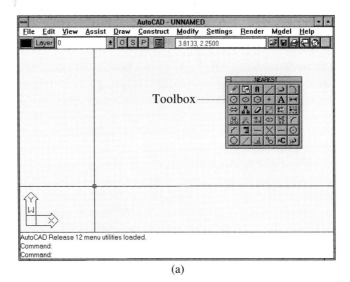

(a)

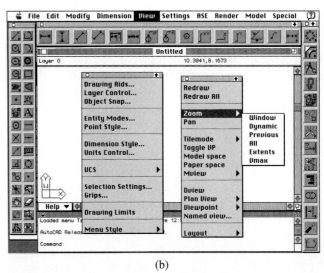

(b)

Figure 9.11   AutoCAD release 12 menus: (a) the Windows version; (b) the Macintosh version.

the torn-off "settings" menu is on the left, and the torn-off "view" menu is on the right. The "zoom" item has been selected from the "view" menu, and the zoom options are shown on the small, supplemental menu on the right.

On the Macintosh, an item is selected from a pull-down menu (which is not torn off) by dragging the highlight to the desired item and releasing the mouse button. With the DOS and Windows operating systems, pull-down menus require one press of the mouse button to open the menu (which remains open when the button is released), and then a second press to select a menu item.

Another feature of interest in figure 9.11 is the use of symbols or icons in place of words for the menu items. Some CAD systems use icons almost exclusively to make their user interface international, or language independent. Also, a user can recognize a well-designed icon as fast as or faster than a word. Although not evident from the monochrome illustrations in figure 9.11, the icons have colors to enhance their visibility.

A programming language may access the Macintosh Toolbox to create menus, buttons, check boxes, and scroll bars. The uses of these features, and of windows, are described by Mark and Reed (1989) and by Mark (1990), with programs written with THINKC. For IBM PC compatibles, windows and other GUI features are discussed by Rimmer (1992), with subroutines in Turbo C. The GUI subroutines for IBM PC compatibles described below are written with Microsoft C, but only minor changes would be required for Turbo C versions.

Programming Some GUI Features on IBM PC Compatibles

Two programming examples are given: first, a menu that uses the mouse to select options, and second, a slider bar for changing the values of a variable. The menu example considered is the menu that offers the various selections in the subroutine optionLoop(), used in sections 9.1–9.3.

The menu format is similar to that used by AutoCAD and other applications. The menu items are listed on the right-hand side of the screen. When the mouse cursor is in the drawing area, it appears as a cross; but when it is moved to the menu area, the cross disappears, and a menu item becomes highlighted. A specific menu item is selected by moving the mouse up and down to highlight the item, then the left mouse button is pressed to complete the selection. Figure 9.12 shows the menu screen with some of the coordinate values in the program listing.

The menu program requires that the function optionLoop() be changed, and that two new subroutines be declared by the function prototypes listed below. Also, two global coordinates for the menu are declared, along with two pointers to images. The images are a filled rectangle used for highlighting and an image of the menu itself.

```
void      menuInit(void),restoreMenu(void);

int       xmenu=551,ymenu=25;
char far *imageRect,*imageMenu;
```

The images are set up and stored in the subroutine menuInit() listed below.

```
void menuInit(void)
{
    int i,dx;
    int ylabel[9],xlabel[9],cursorFlag;
```

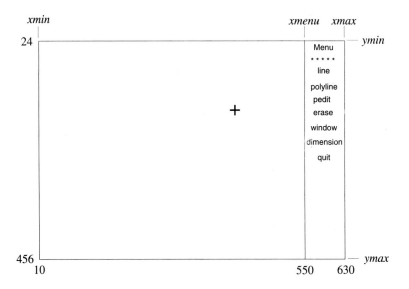

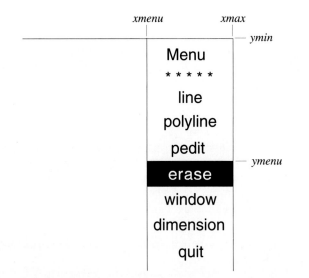

Figure 9.12   Menu screen with coordinate variables.

```
char *label[9] = {"Menu","* * * * *","line","polyline",
                  "pedit","erase","window","dimension","quit"};

_rectangle(_GFILLINTERIOR,0,0,78,24);
imageRect = (char far *) malloc(
                            (unsigned) _imagesize(0,0,78,24));
_getimage(0,0,78,24,imageRect);
_putimage(0,0,imageRect,_GXOR);
```

```
    _moveto(xmin-1,ymin-1); _lineto(xmax,ymin-1);
    _lineto(xmax,ymax+1); _lineto(xmin-1,ymax+1);
    _lineto(xmin-1,ymin-1);
    _moveto(xmenu-1,ymin); _lineto(xmenu-1,ymax);

    for (i=0; i<9; i++)
    {
        ylabel[i] = ymin+3+24*i;
        dx = _getgtextextent(label[i]);
        xlabel[i] = xmenu + (xmax-xmenu-dx)/2;
        _moveto(xlabel[i],ylabel[i]);
        _outgtext(label[i]);
    }
    imageMenu = (char far *) malloc(
            (unsigned) _imagesize(xmenu,ymin+1,xmax-1,ymin+216));
    _getimage(xmenu,ymenu,xmax-1,ymenu+216,imageMenu);
}
```

The above subroutine begins with data-type declarations, which include the placement of the menu entries in the character array *label*[]. Next, a filled rectangle is drawn and stored under the name *imageRect*. Lines are then drawn to enclose the drawing area and the menu; see figure 9.12. The menu entries are then placed midway between the vertical edges of the menu area. This centering of the menu entries is facilitated with the function _getgtextextent() to calculate the length of each entry in pixels. Finally, the _getimage() function is used to place the menu image in memory under the name *imageMenu*. Note that the lines defining the menu borders were placed just outside the menu image, so that in optionLoop() only the menu entries, not the border lines, will be erased and drawn with the _putimage() function.

In the subroutine optionLoop() listed below, the *do while* loop continues until the "quit" menu item is selected (this sets *quitFlag* equal to 1). When the cursor position is in the drawing area ($x <= xmenu$), the cursor appears as a cross; otherwise, it is replaced by the filled-box cursor that highlights a menu item (reverses the colors of the menu word and its background). The particular menu word to be highlighted is determined by calculating the variable *menuItem* from the y-position returned by the mouse.

When the left mouse button is pressed and *menuItem* f has one of the values 1 through 7, then a menu item has been selected; see the *if* statement in the last half of optionLoop(). After an item is selected, the highlight box is turned off with the first _putimage() function call, then the menu is erased with the second _putimage() call. Next, the cursor is constrained to remain in the drawing area by changing the boundary value *xmax* to *xmenu−2*. The particular menu options are performed in the switch() function. After an option other than "quit" has been carried out, the menu is restored, and another option may be selected.

```
    void optionLoop(void)
    {
        int i,ymenuOld,menuItem,quitFlag;

        quitFlag = 0;
```

```
do
{
    mouseData = mouseRead();
    if (x < xmin) x = xmin; if (x > xmax) x = xmax;
    if (y < ymin) y = ymin; if (y > ymax) y = ymax;

    if (x <= xmenu)
    {
        imageCursor = imageCross;
        endPt = 0;
        if (xold <= xmenu)
            _putimage(xold-5,yold-5,imageCursor,_GXOR);
        else
            _putimage(xmenu,ymenuOld,imageRect,_GXOR);
        _putimage(x-5,y-5,imageCursor,_GXOR);
    }
    else
    {
        menuItem = (y-ymin)/24 - 1;
        ymenu = ymin + (menuItem+1)*24;
        if (xold <= xmenu)
            _putimage(xold-5,yold-5,imageCursor,_GXOR);
        if ((xold > xmenu) && (ymenu != ymenuOld))
            _putimage(xmenu,ymenuOld,imageRect,_GXOR);
        if ((ymenu != ymenuOld) || (xold <= xmenu))
        {
            _putimage(xmenu,ymenu,imageRect,_GXOR);
            ymenuOld = ymenu;
        }
    }
    if (x <= xmenu)
    {
        _settextposition (1,40);
        printf (" x=%3d y=%3d",x,y);
    }
        else
    {
        _settextposition (1,40);
        printf ("                      ");
    }
    if ((button == LEFT_BUTTON) && (x > xmenu)
        && (menuItem > 0) && (menuItem < 8))
    {
        _putimage(xmenu,ymenuOld,imageRect,_GXOR);
        _putimage(xmenu,ymin+1,imageMenu,_GXOR);
        xmax = xmenu - 2;
```

```
                        switch(menuItem)
                        {
                            case 1:
                                addLine();
                                restoreMenu();
                                break;
                            case 2:
                                addPline();
                                restoreMenu();
                                break;
                            case 3:
                                findPline();
                                pedit();
                                restoreMenu();
                                break;
                            case 4:
                                deleteLine();
                                restoreMenu();
                                break;
                            case 5:
                                windowDelete();
                                restoreMenu();
                                break;
                            case 6:
                                horDimLine();
                                restoreMenu();
                                break;
                            case 7:
                                quitFlag = 1;
                        }
                    }
                    xold = x; yold = y;
                } while(quitFlag == 0);
                _putimage(x-5,y-5,imageCursor,_GXOR);
        }
```

To restore the menu after an option has been carried out, the program calls the function restoreMenu(). This function first resets the *xmax* value so that the menu area can be accessed. Then the menu is drawn with the _putimage() function, and the cursor that was used in the option is erased with _putimage(). Finally, the line at the bottom of the screen that displayed instructions for the option is erased with the printf() function.

```
        void restoreMenu(void)
        {
            xmax = 630;
```

```
_putimage(xmenu,ymin+1,imageMenu,_GXOR);
imageCursor = imageCross;
_putimage(xold-5,yold-5,imageCursor,_GXOR);
_settextposition(30,1);
printf("                                              ");
}
```

The final programming example is a slider bar, as pictured in figure 9.13. Slider bars are useful not only with windows, but also with any application in which values are selected over a continuous range. For example, some of the color pickers shown in color plate 2 use slider bars to change HSV and RGB values. For the example considered here, a variable *yval* will take on values from 0 to 100 as the slider box (also called the thumb) moves from its bottom position to its top position. The range values for *yval* were chosen arbitrarily, and can be changed for any application.

The slider bar makes it possible to change values in three ways. First, the cursor may be placed on the up or down arrow, with the left mouse button pressed to continuously increase or decrease *yval*. In the programming example, the *yval* values are printed out, and the slider box moves up and down according to the current value. The second way of using the slider bar is to click the cursor on the rectangular regions above and below the slider box to cause a jump in *yval* (the slider box also jumps). In the program the jump amount is 10; that is, *yval* is changed by +10 when the mouse is clicked above the slider box, and by −10 when clicked below. The third procedure is to place the cursor on the slider box, as shown in figure 9.13, and drag the box up or down to continuously change *yval*. This latter method provides a quick and accurate way of selecting any value between 0 and 100.

The program listing for the slider bar is presented in appendix B as listing 9.5. This program uses the standard mouse cursor pictured in figure 9.13 and discussed in appendix A. This mouse cursor is turned on and off with the functions cursorOn() and cursorOff(), given in appendix A. The mouseInit() function is identical to the one in appendix A, whereas mouseRead() has one important change from the function listed in appendix A; instead of setting *buttonref = button,* as in the appendix, the following assignment is now used.

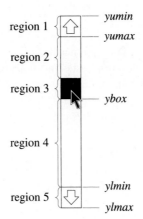

Figure 9.13 Slider bar diagram shows regions and variables used in the example program that appears as listing 9.5 in appendix B. The arrow cursor points to the slider box.

```
if (sliderFlag == 0)
    buttonref = -1;
else
    buttonref = button;
```

The above assignment causes the mouseRead() *do while* loop to be exited after one pass when *sliderFlag* equals 0. This means that *yval* can change continuously (and the slider box be moved continuously) while the left mouse button is held down. This operation is appropriate when the mouse cursor is in the arrow regions (regions 1 and 5 in figure 9.13). In the subroutine slider() that appears in listing 9.5 of appendix B, *sliderFlag* is set equal to 0 but is changed to 1 when the cursor is in regions 2 and 4. When the cursor is in region 2 or 4, then only one jump in the cursor box should occur each time the left button is pressed; thus, *sliderFlag* is set equal to 1 to ensure that the program stays in mouseRead() until the mouse position or button status changes. When the cursor is over the slider box (region 3), *sliderFlag* remains equal to 0 because *yval* and the box position change only when the mouse moves; thus the value of *sliderFlag* is immaterial.

EXERCISES

9.1 On your computer system, implement the program subroutines given in sections 9.1 and 9.2 for adding and deleting lines.

9.2 Change the cursorInit() function in section 9.1 so that the initial cursor is a cross that extends all the way across your drawing region. For example, for VGA resolution, set up an *image0* that represents a horizontal line 640 × 1 pixels and an *image1* for a vertical line 1 × 480 pixels. Then place both images at each point (x,y) where the cursor is drawn and erased.

9.3 Generalize the grid and snap options to the program in section 9.1 by permitting the program user to interactively change the values of the grid and snap distances. Also, permit the snap distance in the x-direction to be different from the value in the y-direction.

9.4 Simulate AutoCAD's ORTHO option by restricting line segments to be placed in only horizontal or vertical directions when the O key is toggled on and off. That is, the value of either the x- or y-coordinate of the ending point of a line segment is restricted to its value at the starting point. The program should show the cursor (with line from the starting point) in either the horizontal or vertical direction, depending on whether the change is greater in x or in y.

9.5 The AutoCAD Crossing option is similar to the Window option, except that entities that cross the window are selected in addition to those that are completely inside the window. Modify the program subroutine windowDelete() of section 9.2 to include the Crossing option.

9.6 Simulate AutoCAD's MOVE command by moving selected lines to new locations. Let the program user select lines with a small square cursor and with a window. The cross cursor should be used to pick a base point and a new point (these two points provide the coordinate value changes for selected lines).

9.7 Write a program that cuts off lines along a cutting edge in a manner similar to the TRIM command in AutoCAD. That is, the program user first selects cutting edges with a square cursor and then selects lines to trim. As illustrated on the next page, lines are trimmed on the left, middle, or right of two cutting edges depending on where the square cursor is placed when the program requests "lines to trim."

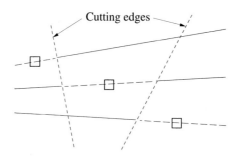

9.8 Construct an interactive program to extend a given line segment to a boundary line, similar to the EXTEND command in AutoCAD.

9.9 In the pedit() subroutine, include an option to delete (with the D key) a vertex point when the cross cursor rests on that vertex. That is, eliminate the vertex point from the plines[][] array and adjust the indices so that there are no gaps in the array (in a manner similar to that used in section 9.2 for deleting lines). The two line segments to the deleted vertex should be erased and replaced by a single segment between neighboring vertices.

9.10 Add the quadratic B-spline to the program described in section 9.3, with a flag called SPLINETYPE in the program determining which approximation curve is plotted (in AutoCAD SPLINETYPE = 5 gives the quadratic B-spline, and the value 6 gives the cubic B-spline).

9.11 Add an option called Fit to the menu of the program outlined in section 9.3. When the F key is pressed after a polyline has been selected, plot an interpolation curve, such as the circular-arc curve fit (used by AutoCAD), the parabolic blend, or the natural cubic spline.

9.12 For the dragged cubic B-spline program described in section 9.3, change the display of the spline frame to a display of just the control points for the selected polyline. Display a changing control point when it is selected for moving.

9.13 Write a subroutine that will select and delete entire polylines, and incorporate this subroutine into the drawing program of sections 9.1–9.3.

9.14 Add a subroutine to the drawing program of sections 9.1–9.3 that will read and write to DXF files. Then use this subroutine to store and retrieve drawing entities for line segments and polylines. Also, use this subroutine to exchange drawing entities with AutoCAD or another CAD system that reads DXF files.

9.15 Write a subroutine for vertical dimension lines similar to the one for horizontal dimension lines given in section 9.4. For the vertical dimension lines the text may be printed in the horizontal direction (which is the default option in AutoCAD, although it can be changed to print in the vertical direction).

9.16 Incorporate the data for drawing horizontal dimension lines into an array; for example, *horDim*[][], where (like plines[][]) the first array subscript is an index number (1,2,3, . . .) that identifies a particular dimension line, and the second subscript has the six coordinate values (*xl, yl, xr, yr, xc,* and *yc*) from which the dimension line may be calculated. Then write a subroutine that will select and delete dimension lines in a manner similar to the deletion of lines.

9.17 Simulate a feature of associative dimensioning by writing a subroutine that will start with the dimension array of exercise 9.16 and change either *xl* or *xr* to a new value selected by the mouse (this is similar to operating on a dimension line in AutoCAD with the EXTEND command). The value of the dimension distance displayed should change automatically.

9.18 Write a GUI for the drawing program of sections 9.1–9.3 similar to the one displayed in figure 9.12. That is, the program user should choose options by clicking on selection buttons or boxes in menus, rather than by pressing keys.

9.19 Draw a menu that simulates 3-D buttons; that is, draw highlights on the top and left edges of the buttons and shadows on the right and lower edges. In the right screen image below, one button image shows reversed colors after being picked with the standard arrow cursor. In this example, the button labeled *line* remains reversed until the *line* option is completed. The gray fill is drawn with the VGA default color number 7 (white), and the white with color number 15 (bright white).

9.20 Incorporate some or all of the options in your drawing program into a pull-down menu. This menu should drop down only after it is selected from a line of items at the top of the screen. You may wish to draw a "drop shadow" outside the bottom and right edges of the menu to give a 3-D effect.

9.21 Replace the words in your drawing program menu with icons.

9.22 Design an HSV color picker in which choices are made with selection boxes, slider bars, and other GUI features. Refer to color plate 2 for some ideas but make the design your own.

BIBLIOGRAPHY

AutoCAD Release 12 Reference Manual. Sausalito, Calif.: Autodesk, Inc., 1992.

DEMEL, J. T., AND M. J. MILLER, *Introduction to Computer Graphics.* Belmont, Calif.: Brooks/Cole Engineering Division of Wadsworth, Inc., 1984.

FOLEY, J. D., A. VAN DAM, S. K. Feiner, AND J. F. HUGHES, *Computer Graphics: Principles and Practice,* 2nd ed. Reading, Mass.: Addison-Wesley Publishing Co., 1990.

Inside Macintosh, volumes I-V. Apple Computer, Inc., Reading, Mass.: Addison-Wesley Publishing Co., 1985–1988.

MARCUS, A., *Graphic Design for Electronic Documents and User Interfaces.* New York: ACM Press, 1992.

MARK, D., *Macintosh C Programming Primer, Volume II: Mastering the Toolbox Using THINKC.* Reading, Mass.: Addison-Wesley Publishing Co., 1990.

MARK, D., AND C. REED, *Macintosh Programming Primer: Inside the Toolbox Using THINK's LightspeedC.* Reading, Mass.: Addison-Wesley Publishing Co., 1989.

RIMMER, S., *Graphical User Interface Programming.* Windcrest/McGraw-Hill, 1992.

10

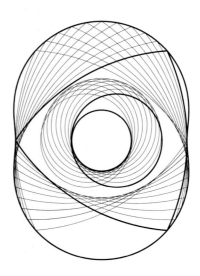

2-D Transformations

In this chapter two-dimensional transformations are presented for translation, scale, rotation, and reflection. Translation and scale were discussed in section 2.4, and a rotation transformation was used in section 5.2. Here the transformations are put into their standard matrix forms. Various combinations of these transformations are discussed.

Transformations can be applied in two situations. First, they can be used for viewing a drawing, as when one pans or zooms in AutoCAD to translate and rescale the drawing on the computer screen. Second, transformations can be applied to a drawing entity (or group of entities), as when one uses the AutoCAD commands MOVE, SCALE, and ROTATE to change an entity relative to others in a drawing. The reflection transformation corresponds to the AutoCAD MIRROR command, which produces mirror images. (MIRROR is often used to draw symmetrical objects by constructing half the object and mirroring to complete it.)

Transformations are often used in combination. For example, to rotate an object about a point that is not the origin, it is first necessary to translate the object so that the rotation point is at the origin, then rotate the object, and finally translate the rotation point back to its original position. Similarly, a combination of translation, rotation, and reflection across the x-axis is required to reflect an object across an arbitrary line.

Various applications of 2-D transformations are considered in this chapter. The translation and scale transformations are incorporated into the drawing program that was developed in chapter 9, so that world coordinates can be considered rather than just screen coordinates.

The rotation and scale transformations are used to rotate and resize numbers. Rotated numbers can be displayed in aligned dimensions in the drawing program.

Rotation and translation transformations with constraints are required for analyzing machinery designs, such as the rotary (Wankel) engine. The diagram at the opeing of this chapter illustrates a rotary engine, with the triangular rotor shown at various positions. As it rotates, the corners of this rotor fit exactly inside the epitrochoidal chamber.

10.1 MATRIX FORMS OF THE TRANSFORMATIONS

Translation

It is evident from figure 10.1 that translation of a point from $\mathbf{P}$ to $\mathbf{P}'$ yields the following relations between the coordinates (x',y') of $\mathbf{P}'$ and the coordinates (x,y) of $\mathbf{P}$. In equation 10.1 the notation $[x'\ y']$ represents the point vector $\mathbf{P}'$ as a row vector.

$$x' = x + \Delta x, \quad y' = y + \Delta y$$

or   (10.1)

$$[x'\quad y'] = [x\quad y] + [\Delta x\quad \Delta y]$$

The latter form of this equation can be written as $\mathbf{P}' = \mathbf{P} + \mathbf{T}$, where the translation vector $\mathbf{T}$ represents the last row vector in equation 10.1. This addition form of the translation transformation differs from the transformations for scale and rotation, which have the forms $\mathbf{P}' = \mathbf{P}[S]$ and $\mathbf{P}' = \mathbf{P}[R]$. These latter transformations have the form of 2×2 transformation matrices multiplied by the 1×2 row vector for the point $\mathbf{P}$.

It is convenient to formulate the transformations so that they all have the same multiplication form. To do this, one must use the method of *homogeneous coordinates*. With this method, 1×3 row vectors are introduced for the positions $\mathbf{P}'$ and $\mathbf{P}$ along with the

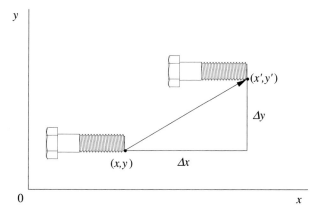

Figure 10.1 Translation of a bolt drawing, with the point (x,y) being transformed to the point (x',y').

following 3×3 translation matrix [T] (which may be written as $[T(\varDelta x, \varDelta y)]$ to display the variables $\varDelta x$ and $\varDelta y$).

$$
[x' \quad y' \quad 1] = [x \quad y \quad 1]\begin{bmatrix} 1 & 0 & 0 \\ 0 & 1 & 0 \\ \varDelta x & \varDelta y & 1 \end{bmatrix} \tag{10.2}
$$

The two scalar equations 10.1 result when matrices on the right of equation 10.2 are multiplied. A third scalar equation provided by the matrix equation 10.2 is just the identity $1 = 1$. These results can be checked by carrying out the matrix multiplication in equation 10.2. (Matrix multiplication is reviewed in appendix C.)

The matrix form (10.2) can be written as $\mathbf{P}' = \mathbf{P}[T]$. Although this format is common in computer graphics, the form $\mathbf{P}' = [T]\mathbf{P}$ is also used, in which case [T] is the transpose of the matrix given in equation 10.2. Also, column vectors, rather than row vectors, may be used for $\mathbf{P}'$ and $\mathbf{P}$.

Scale

Scaling an object consists of multiplying all x-coordinates by the scale factor S_x and all y-coordinates by the factor S_y. Thus, in figure 10.2 the rescaled bolt in the upper right has twice the length and twice the width of the original bolt at the lower left. In this case *uniform* scaling resulted because the factors S_x and S_y were equal. Two cases of unequal scaling are also shown in the figure.

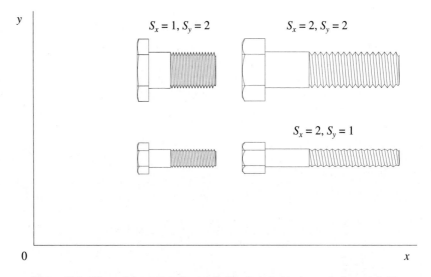

Figure 10.2 The scale transformation applied to the bolt drawing at the lower left. The scale factors S_x and S_y are listed above each scaled image.

In AutoCAD, uniform scaling of the screen image occurs when the ZOOM command is used to change the display. Also, the SCALE command can be used to uniformly change the absolute size of one or more entities, that is, to change their physical size in the drawing database, not just their displayed size. Nonuniform scaling in AutoCAD can be achieved by saving an object as a block and then specifying different values for the x- and y-scale factors on inserting the block (see the example in figure 5.11).

Scaling is described by the following formulas.

$$x' = S_x x, \quad y' = S_y y \tag{10.3}$$

Because the coordinates are changed linearly with the factors S_x and S_y, the size and shape of the transformed object does not depend on the distance from the origin; however, the final position does. For example, the original bolt drawing in figure 10.2 was placed sufficiently far from the origin so that the transformed images do not overlap the original drawing. Note that the origin is the only point that is unchanged by the transformation 10.3.

Equations 10.3 may be represented by the matrix equation

$$[x' \quad y'] = [x \quad y]\begin{bmatrix} S_x & 0 \\ 0 & S_y \end{bmatrix} \tag{10.4}$$

As discussed above, the translation matrix equation cannot be put into form 10.4, but it can be written in a homogeneous form with a 3×3 transformation matrix. The equivalent form for the scale transformation is

$$[x' \quad y' \quad 1] = [x \quad y \quad 1]\begin{bmatrix} S_x & 0 & 0 \\ 0 & S_y & 0 \\ 0 & 0 & 1 \end{bmatrix} \tag{10.5}$$

Rotation

Figure 10.3 illustrates the rotation of an object through an angle θ about the origin 0. A point (x,y) on the object before rotation can be expressed in terms of the angle α and the radius r.

$$x = r\cos\alpha, \quad y = r\sin\alpha \tag{10.6}$$

After rotation through the angle θ, the distance from the origin to the point (x',y') is still r, but the angle from the x-axis is now $\alpha + \theta$.

$$x' = r\cos(\alpha+\theta) = r\cos\alpha\cos\theta - r\sin\alpha\sin\theta$$
$$y' = r\sin(\alpha+\theta) = r\cos\alpha\sin\theta + r\sin\alpha\cos\theta \tag{10.7}$$

Substituting equations 10.7 into equations 10.8 yields the following transformation:

$$x' = x\cos\theta - y\sin\theta, \quad y' = x\sin\theta + y\cos\theta \tag{10.8}$$

Because the distance from the origin to the point does not change for this rotation, the distance between any two points on the object remains constant. Thus the object retains its

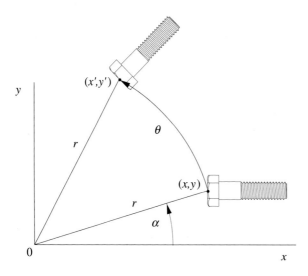

Figure 10.3   Rotation of an object through the angle θ about the origin 0. The point (x,y) at the top of the bolt head transforms into the point (x',y').

shape. (Here the rotation point is the origin; rotation about an arbitrary point is considered in section 10.2.) Figure 10.3 illustrates the fact that the angle of rotation θ of the object does not depend on its initial location, but that the object's position after rotation does depend on its distance from the origin.

Equations 10.8 may be put into the matrix form

$$[x'\ \ y'] = [x\ \ \ y]\begin{bmatrix} \cos\theta & \sin\theta \\ -\sin\theta & \cos\theta \end{bmatrix} \tag{10.9}$$

The following equivalent matrix equation has the same form as the translation transformation 10.2 and scale transformation 10.5:

$$[x'\ \ \ y'\ \ \ 1] = [x\ \ \ y\ \ \ 1]\begin{bmatrix} \cos\theta & \sin\theta & 0 \\ -\sin\theta & \cos\theta & 0 \\ 0 & 0 & 1 \end{bmatrix} \tag{10.10}$$

This equation can be written as $\mathbf{P}' = \mathbf{P}[R]$, where $[R]$ is the 3×3 rotation matrix.

Reflection

Mirror reflection about a line is a useful procedure for modifying a drawing on a CAD system. Often it is efficient to draw only half of a symmetrical object and then reflect with AutoCAD's MIRROR command to complete the object.

The reflection transformations are special cases of the scale transformation when one of the scale factors is negative. For example, reflection across the x-axis occurs when the y-coordinates of all points are reversed, whereas the x-coordinates remain the same. This result occurs when $S_x = 1$ and $S_y = -1$. Thus the scale equation 10.6 reduces to $\mathbf{P}' = \mathbf{P}[M_x]$, where $[M_x]$ is given below. A reflection across the y-axis is written as $\mathbf{P}' = \mathbf{P}[M_y]$, which corresponds to $S_x = -1$ and $S_y = 1$.

$$[M_x] = \begin{bmatrix} 1 & 0 & 0 \\ 0 & -1 & 0 \\ 0 & 0 & 1 \end{bmatrix}, \quad [M_y] = \begin{bmatrix} -1 & 0 & 0 \\ 0 & 1 & 0 \\ 0 & 0 & 1 \end{bmatrix} \qquad (10.11)$$

Figure 10.4 illustrates the reflection of an object across the x-axis and across the y-axis. If reflections were performed across both axes simultaneously, corresponding to a matrix with the first two diagonal elements equal to -1, then the final image would not be reversed, and the transformation would be equivalent to rotating the object through an angle of 180°.

Shear

Another useful primitive transformation is the shear transformation given by the following shear matrix:

$$[SH] = \begin{bmatrix} 1 & SH_y & 0 \\ SH_x & 1 & 0 \\ 0 & 0 & 1 \end{bmatrix} \qquad (10.12)$$

When $SH_y = 0$ in the shear matrix, a square is sheared in the x-direction, with the shear displacement proportional to the value of SH_x; see figure 10.5b. Similarly, when $SH_x = 0$, the square is sheared in the y-direction, as illustrated in figure 10.5c.

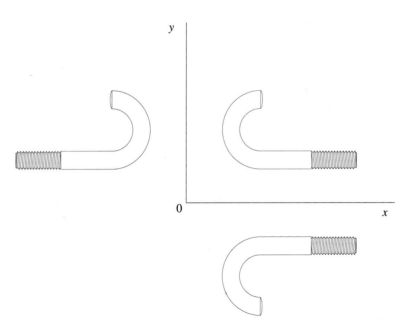

Figure 10.4 The hook bolt shown at the upper right is reflected across the x-axis to produce the image at the lower right, and across the y-axis to produce the image at the left. The reflected images are the reverse of the original image.

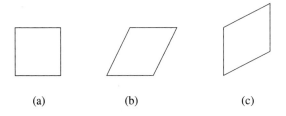

Figure 10.5 The shear transformation: (a) the original square; (b) shear in the x-direction ($SH_y = 0$); (c) shear in the y-direction ($SH_x = 0$).

(a)   (b)   (c)

10.2 COMBINATIONS OF TRANSFORMATIONS

Two transformations are commutative if the same result is obtained regardless of the order of operation; that is, $[T_1]$ and $[T_2]$ commute if $[T_1][T_2] = [T_2][T_1]$. The transformations in section 10.1 commute with themselves, and the rotation transformation commutes with the *uniform* scale transformation. No other combination of the transformations is commutative.

Multiplying out the matrices demonstrates that $[T(\Delta x_1, \Delta y_1)][T(\Delta x_2, \Delta y_2)] = [T(\Delta x_2, \Delta y_2)][T(\Delta x_1, \Delta y_1)] = [T(\Delta x_1 + \Delta x_2, \Delta y_1 + \Delta y_2)]$. This result is obvious; the total distance translated after two transformations is the vector sum of the two translated distances. The procedure for multiplying two 3×3 matrices is reviewed in appendix C.

Multiplication of the two scale transformations gives $[S(S_{x1}, S_{y1})][S(S_{x2}, S_{y2})] = [S(S_{x2}, S_{y2})][S(S_{x1}, S_{y1})] = [S(S_{x1} \cdot S_{x2}, S_{y1} \cdot S_{y2})]$. The product of two scale transformations is the same as a single transformation having products of scale factors. For example, if an object is uniformly scaled up by a factor of 2, and then scaled down by a factor of 1/2, the object returns to its original size. Also note that the reflection matrices are commutative because they are special cases of the scale transformation.

For rotations, $[R(\theta_1)][R(\theta_2)] = [R(\theta_2)][R(\theta_1)] = [R(\theta_1 + \theta_2)]$. As expected, rotation angles are additive.

A rotation commutes with a scale transformation if the scaling is uniform, but not otherwise. Consider the rotation and scale transformations shown below.

$$[x' \quad y' \quad 1] = [x \quad y \quad 1]\begin{bmatrix} \cos\theta & \sin\theta & 0 \\ -\sin\theta & \cos\theta & 0 \\ 0 & 0 & 1 \end{bmatrix}\begin{bmatrix} S_x & 0 & 0 \\ 0 & S_y & 0 \\ 0 & 0 & 1 \end{bmatrix}$$

$$= [x \quad y \quad 1]\begin{bmatrix} S_x\cos\theta & S_y\sin\theta & 0 \\ -S_x\sin\theta & S_y\cos\theta & 0 \\ 0 & 0 & 1 \end{bmatrix} \tag{10.13}$$

$$= [S_x(x\cos\theta - y\sin\theta) \quad S_y(x\sin\theta - y\sin\theta) \quad 1]$$

Equation 10.13 shows that when the rotation transformation is performed first, the transformed coordinate x' is the product of S_x times the rotated x-coordinate given by equation 10.9, and y' is equal to S_y times the rotated y-coordinate. When the scale transformation is applied before the rotation, the following result is obtained.

$$[x' \quad y' \quad 1] = [(S_x x\cos\theta - S_y y\sin\theta) \quad (S_x x\sin\theta + S_y y\cos\theta) \quad 1] \tag{10.14}$$

When $S_x \neq S_y$, equations 10.13 and 10.14 give different results, but for uniform scaling ($S_x = S_y$) they become identical. Considering the case $S_x = 2$ and $S_y = 1$, it is evident that when the scale transformation is second, the object in its final position is stretched in the x-direction; when scaling is first, the object ends up stretched in the direction corresponding to the angle of rotation. On the other hand, when $S_x = S_y$, the order of the transformations makes no difference, and the object is uniformly scaled at the rotated angle.

Rotation About an Arbitrary Point

When the ROTATE command is used in AutoCAD, the user is asked to locate a base point, which is the rotation point. Because the rotation matrix 10.11 carries out a rotation about the origin of the coordinate system, the object must first be translated so that the desired rotation point is at the origin. Figure 10.6 illustrates this procedure.

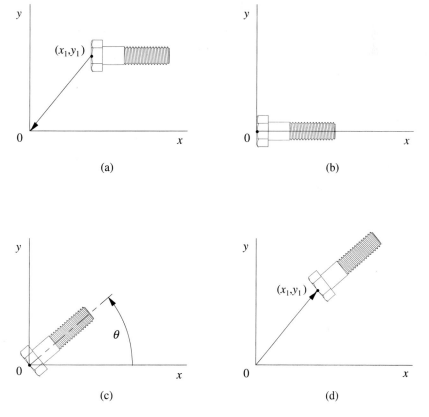

Figure 10.6   Steps required to rotate an object through angle θ about the point (x_1,y_1). Here the rotation point is located at the top center of a bolt head. Between (a) and (b) the bolt is translated to place the rotation point at the origin. In (c) the bolt has been rotated through the angle θ, and in (d) the rotation point has been translated back to (x_1,y_1).

With the rotation point identified as (x_1, y_1), the translation $[T(-x_1, -y_1)]$ is performed first. Negative values occur because the point moves from (x_1, y_1) to $(0,0)$. The rotation through a desired angle θ is then carried out with the transformation $[R(\theta)]$, and finally the rotation point is translated back to its original location with the transformation $[T(x_1, y_1)]$. Thus, rotation about the point is achieved with the following combination of transformations:

$$\mathbf{P'} = \mathbf{P}[T(-x_1, -y_1)][R(\theta)][T(x_1, y_1)] \tag{10.15}$$

Reflection Through an Arbitrary Line

As described in the gear-tooth example in section 5.2, AutoCAD's MIRROR command requires selection of a mirror line as well as selection of the object to be reflected. As illustrated in figure 10.7a, the mirror line can be in any position. To reflect the half gear tooth about the mirror line, the line can first be translated and rotated so that it lies on the x-axis. If the mir-

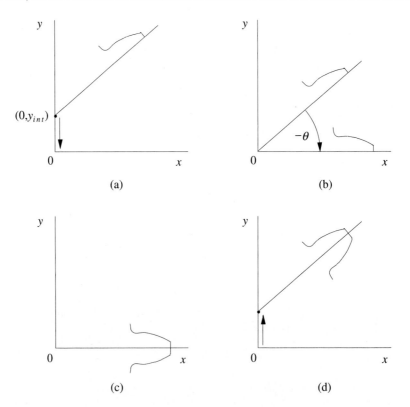

Figure 10.7 Steps required to reflect an object across an arbitrary line. Here the reflection line is a line of symmetry for a gear tooth. This line intersects the y-axis at the point $(0, y_{int})$. Between (a) and (b) the reflection line is translated downward until it intersects the origin. In (b) the reflection line is rotated down to the x-axis. In (c) the gear tooth profile is reflected across the x-axis. The gear tooth is returned to its original position in (d) after being rotated and translated upward.

ror line intersects the y-axis at y_{int}, then this point can be translated to the origin with $[T(0, -y_{int})]$. Assuming that the mirror line is at an angle θ to the x-axis, the rotation is given by $[R(-\theta)]$. Then the mirror reflection matrix $[M_x]$ can be used to reflect the half gear tooth across the x-axis (alternatively, the mirror line could be placed on the y-axis and $[M_y]$ used).

The reverse transformations $[R(\theta)]$ and $[T(0, y_{int})]$ must be applied to return the gear tooth and mirror line to their original positions. Thus the following sequence of operations reflects an object about an arbitrary line:

$$\mathbf{P'} = \mathbf{P}[T(0, -y_{int})][R(-\theta)][M_x][R(\theta)][T(0, y_{int})] \qquad (10.16)$$

In the example of section 5.2, the full gear tooth was arrayed in a circle to produce the gear. With somewhat more effort, the reflection transformation could also array the tooth: the gear center could be translated to the origin; the tooth could be rotated so that an end touches the x-axis, then reflected to produce a second tooth; and the operations could be repeated to produce four teeth, then eight teeth, etc.

Transformations can often be called directly on workstation software. For advanced graphics workstations, the transformations are performed in the hardware, which greatly speeds their execution. On personal computers, where normally the transformations must be written into the programs, it is more efficient to carry out the matrix multiplications by hand so that the program requires fewer math operations. For example, a program that uses the expressions for x' and y' from equation 10.14 requires fewer multiplications and additions than a program that performs the full matrix multiplications in equation 10.13.

10.3 IMPLEMENTING TRANSFORMATIONS IN A DRAWING PROGRAM

The transformations discussed in this chapter can be implemented in a drawing program in several ways. Here, two coordinate systems are set up to distinguish the world (or physical) space from the screen (or device) space. Then translation and scale transformations are used to pan and zoom in screen space for the drawing program developed in chapter 9.

Another way of implementing the transformations is to modify individual drawing entities. That is, objects can be moved, resized, and rotated in world space; see problems 10.10–10.12.

World and Screen Coordinates

Designs are created in coordinate systems appropriate to real objects. CAD systems permit users to specify units and overall size of the drawing area. In the preceding chapter, program subroutines were developed for drawing on a computer screen at a particular resolution (VGA resolution of 640 × 480 pixels). To have a convenient interface for design, the user must create objects in a world-coordinate system and view the results on the computer in screen coordinates.

A third set of 2-D coordinates, not considered here, is the normalized device coordinate (NDC) system defined by the coordinate space $0 \le x \le 1$ and $0 \le y \le 1$. The NDC system is specified by a graphics standard, the Graphical Kernel System (GKS), to provide a system useful for device-independent graphics. That is, software can be written for the NDC system, and then separate drivers can be written to transfer the graphics to specific devices such as screen displays and printers.

The translation and scale transformations may be used for transferring between world and screen coordinates. Below, the subscript s denotes screen, and w denotes world.

$$x_s = S_x x_w + \Delta x_{transl}, \ y_s = S_y y_w + \Delta y_{transl} \qquad (10.17)$$

Equations 10.17 are the same as equations 2.4, with slightly different notation. The screen coordinates start in the upper-left-hand corner of the display, with the y-coordinate increasing in the downward direction. The world-coordinate system should be set up in a manner preferred by designers: the origin should be at the lower left of the display, with y increasing upward. This result can be achieved by setting $S_y = -S_x$, $\Delta x_{transl} = 0$, and $\Delta y_{transl} = y_{bottom}$, where y_{bottom} is the screen coordinate value at the bottom of the drawing area.

To permit panning and zooming of the screen image, the translations x_{pan} and y_{pan} are included in Δx_{transl} and Δy_{transl}; also, S_x is set equal to sf, which is identified as the current scale factor in zoom operations. Thus the following equations will be included in drawing program subroutines.

$$x_s = sf\, x_w + x_{pan}, \ y_s = -sf\, y_w + y_{bottom} + y_{pan} \qquad (10.18)$$

In the drawing program developed in chapter 9, the data for line segments was stored in the integer array $lines[i][j]$, and the polyline data was stored in $plines[i][j]$. When world coordinates are introduced, the screen storage arrays are relabeled $slines[i][j]$ and $sPlines[i][j]$; world coordinates are stored in the floating-point (double) arrays $wlines[i][j]$ and $wPlines[i][j]$. Also, the program introduces parameters yb for y_{bottom}, rsf for the reciprocal of the scale factor sf, and the coordinates $(xcen, ycen)$ of the center of the screen drawing area. The listing below defines three function prototypes and the new global variables:

```
void sLinesUpdate(void),pan(void),zoom(void);

int     yb,xpan,ypan;
double  wlines[500][6],wPlines[20][40];
double  sf,rsf,xcen=280.0,ycen=240.0;
```

The function sLinesUpdate() is called when the screen coordinates are to be updated after the pan coordinates and scale factor are changed. As shown in the listing below, the current scale factor sf and and pan coordinates $(xpan, ypan)$ are used to calculate the screen array values from the world arrays.

```
void sLinesUpdate(void)
{
    int k,n;

    for (k=0; k<nLines; k++)
    {
        slines[k][0] = (int) (sf*wlines[k][0]) + xpan;
```

```
          slines[k][1] = (int) (-sf*wlines[k][1]) + yb + ypan;
          slines[k][2] = (int) (sf*wlines[k][2]) + xpan;
          slines[k][3] = (int) (-sf*wlines[k][3]) + yb + ypan;
     }
     for (n=1; n<=nPlines; n++)
     {
          for (k=0; k<nVertices[n]; k++)
          {
               sPlines[n][2*k] = (int) (sf*wPlines[n][2*k]) + xpan;
               sPlines[n][2*k+1] = (int) (-sf*wPlines[n][2*k+1]) + yb + ypan;
          }
     }
}
```

The storage arrays *wlines[i][j]* and *wPlines[i][j]* for world coordinates must be set up when line endpoints and polyline vertices are added under the functions newPoint() and newPlinePoint(). This is done by inverting equations 10.18, as in the following example for the starting point of a line segment. In the program subroutines the coordinates *x* and *y* represent the screen coordinates x_s and y_s.

```
          wlines[i][0] = (x-xpan)*rsf;
          wlines[i][1] = (yb-y+ypan)*rsf;
```

Implementing a Pan Operation

A pan operation is performed by selecting two points and moving the screen image from the first point to the second. This operation is achieved by the function pan(), which uses a mouse to select the two points. (With AutoCAD the points may either be selected by a mouse or entered on the keyboard.) In the listing below, the flag variable *panFlag* changes from the value 0 to 1 when the first point is selected, and then to the value 2 when the second point is selected. When panFlag equals 2, the *do while* loop is exited. Then all lines are erased with the color black; the pan coordinates (*xpan,ypan*) are calculated; the screen lines and polylines are updated with a call to sLinesUpdate(); and the lines are redrawn at their new position with redraw().

```
     void pan(void)
     {
          int i,k,n,xlast,ylast,panFlag,xpan1,ypan1,xpan2,ypan2;

          imageCursor = imageCross;
          panFlag = 0;
          _settextposition(30,1);
          _putimage(xold-5,yold-5,imageCursor,_GXOR);
          printf(" pan displacement:                          ");
          do
          {
               mouseData = mouseRead();
```

```
        if (x < xmin) x = xmin; if (x > xmax) x = xmax;
        if (y < ymin) y = ymin; if (y > ymax) y = ymax;

        _putimage(xold-5,yold-5,imageCursor,_GXOR);
        if (panFlag > 0)
        {
            _setcolor(BLACK);
            _moveto(xlast,ylast); _lineto(xold,yold);
            _setcolor(WHITE);
            _moveto(xlast,ylast); _lineto(x,y);
        }
        redraw(nLines,nPlines);
        _putimage(x-5,y-5,imageCursor,_GXOR);

        if (button == LEFT_BUTTON)
        {
            if ((x != xlast) || (y != ylast))
            {
                if (panFlag == 0)
                {
                    xpan1 = x; ypan1 = y;
                    panFlag = 1;
                    _settextposition(30,25);
                    printf("second point:");
                }
                else
                {
                    xpan2 = x; ypan2 =y;
                    panFlag = 2;
                }
                xlast = x; ylast = y;
            }
        }
        xold = x; yold = y;
    } while(panFlag != 2);
    _putimage(x-5,y-5,imageCursor,_GXOR);
    _setcolor(BLACK);
    _moveto(xlast,ylast); _lineto(xold,yold);
    _moveto(xpan1,ypan1); _lineto(xpan2,ypan2);
    redraw(nLines,nPlines);
    _setcolor(WHITE);
    xpan = xpan + xpan2-xpan1;
    ypan = ypan + ypan2-ypan1;
    sLinesUpdate();
    redraw(nLines,nPlines);
}
```

Three screen images are shown in figure 10.8: the top image appears after the first pan point has been selected, and the middle image after the second point has been selected and the screen image has moved. The bottom screen image appears after the drawing has been enlarged by a factor of two with the zoom() function.

The pan() function and zoom() functions can push part of the drawing out of the screen drawing area, as shown in figures 10.8b and c. The drawing will move onto the border and menu regions unless it is clipped to the drawing area. This clipping can be done by calling the Microsoft C function _setcliprgn(*xmin,ymin,xmenu*−2,*ymax*) at the beginning of the subroutine redraw(), and then returning to the full screen area at the end of the subroutine with _setcliprgn(0,0,639,479).

As the drawing is translated and rescaled with pan() and zoom(), lines and polylines can continue to be selected for the erase and pedit options if some minor additions and changes are made to the subroutines. First, floating-point errors may arise unless the coordinates xd0, yd0, xd1, and yd1 in deleteLine() and findPline() are computed from *wlines[i][j]* and *wPlines[i][j]*, rather than from *slines[i][j]* and *sPlines[i][j]*. For example, *xd0 = sf*wlines[j][0]* + (double) *xpan*. Second, the subroutine reduceLines() must include a renumbering for the world line storage array along with the renumbering of the screen line storage array; that is, the following program line must be added: *wlines[j][k]* = *wlines[j*+1*][k]*.

Implementing a Zoom Operation

The zoom operation is implemented by using the keyboard to enter a zoom factor zf. The new scale factor is then set equal to the product of zf times the old scale factor. A useful zoom operation should rescale the image relative to the center of the drawing area. That is, the zoom operation should not cause a centered image to pan toward the screen edges.

In order to rescale with respect to the screen center, the translation matrix must first be used to move the screen center to the origin. Then the points are rescaled with the zoom factor zf, and the point at the origin is moved back to the screen center. Thus, the screen coordinates are tranformed by the operations

$$\mathbf{P}' = \mathbf{P}[T(-x_{cen}, -y_{cen})][S(zf, zf)][T(x_{cen}, y_{cen})]$$

or

$$[x' \quad y' \quad 1] = [x \quad y \quad 1]\begin{bmatrix} 1 & 0 & 0 \\ 0 & 1 & 0 \\ -x_{cen} & -y_{cen} & 1 \end{bmatrix}\begin{bmatrix} zf & 0 & 0 \\ 0 & zf & 0 \\ 0 & 0 & 1 \end{bmatrix}\begin{bmatrix} 1 & 0 & 0 \\ 0 & 1 & 0 \\ x_{cen} & y_{cen} & 1 \end{bmatrix} \quad (10.19)$$

Equation 10.19 reduces to the following relations between the new screen coordinates (x', y') and the old ones (x, y).

$$x' = zf\, x + (1 - zf)x_{cen}$$
$$y' = zf\, y + (1 - zf)y_{cen} \quad (10.20)$$

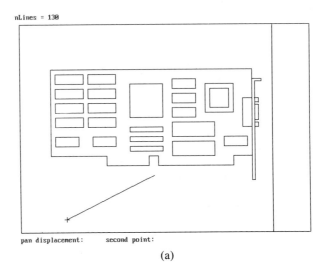

(a)

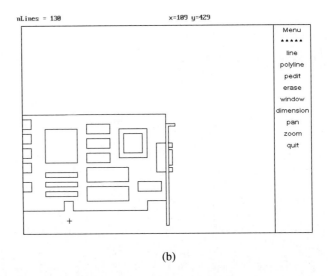

(b)

Figure 10.8 Screen images during pan and zoom operations: (a) after the first point has been selected, a line connects the first point with the cursor; (b) after the second point has been selected the image shifts; (figure continues next page)

After equations 10.18 are used to substitute for the old screen coordinates in equations 10.20, the following relations between screen and world coordinates are obtained:

$$x' = (sf)_{new}\, x_w + (x_{pan})_{new}$$
$$y' = -(sf)_{new}\, y_w + y_{bottom} + (y_{pan})_{new}$$

(10.21)

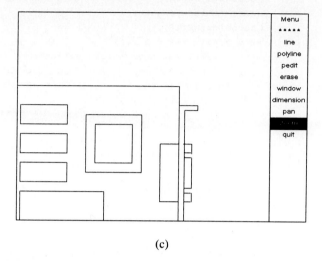

(c)

Figure 10.8 continued   (c) the image is enlarged after zooming by a factor of 2. In (a) the
menu is not displayed because the pan option has not been completed; in (b) the cursor rests
in the drawing area at the position corresponding to the coordinates displayed at the top; in
(c) the cursor rests on the highlighted zoom option in the menu. The images in (b) and (c)
have been clipped to the edges of the drawing area.

where

$$(sf)_{new} = zf\ sf$$

$$(x_{pan})_{new} = zf\ x_{pan} + (1-zf)x_{cen}$$ (10.22)

$$(y_{pan})_{new} = zf\ y_{pan} + (1-zf)(y_{cen} - y_{bottom})$$

The new scale factor $(sf)_{new}$ is just the old one multiplied by the zoom factor, while
the new pan coordinate values $(x_{pan})_{new}$ and $(y_{pan})_{new}$ ensure that the center of the screen
drawing remains fixed during the zoom operation. Figure 10.8c shows the screen after
zooming a factor of two from screen 10.8b.

The zoom operation is implemented with the subroutine zoom() listed below.

```
void zoom(void)
{
    double zf;

    _putimage(xold-5,yold-5,imageCursor,_GXOR);
    _settextposition(1,1);
    printf(" Enter the zoom factor: ");
    scanf("%lf",&zf);
    _settextposition(1,1);
    printf("                                         ");
```

```
        _setcolor(BLACK);
        redraw(nLines,nPlines);
        _setcolor(WHITE);
        sf = zf*sf; rsf = 1./sf;
        xpan = (int) (zf*xpan + (1.- zf)*xcen);
        ypan = (int) (zf*ypan + (1.- zf)*(ycen-yb));
        sLinesUpdate();
        redraw(nLines,nPlines);
    }
```

10.4 ROTATION AND SCALE OF TEXT CHARACTERS

Text characters can be constructed in several ways. As discussed in chapter 7, characters can be represented accurately by curves, such as the Bézier curves used by PostScript printers. Characters composed of curves can be scaled and rotated; see the example given in section 8.3.

A computer screen can display two types of characters: bitmap characters and vector (or stroke) characters. Bitmap characters are composed of arrays of filled pixels that approximate the shape of the character. Large characters contain a greater number of pixels than small characters; thus, large characters can be represented more accurately than small characters (see figure 10.9). Apple's first personal laser printer, the LaserWriter IIsc, uses a bitmapping technique to print out character fonts that are derived from fonts four times the size of the screen fonts. For example, the 12-point characters on the top right of figure 10.9 would be printed on paper in the greater resolution, 48-point fonts shown on the left. (On the computer screen the fonts do not appear quite so jagged as in figure 10.9 because the screen pixels are more blurred than the sharply defined squares used to construct the figure.)

Vector characters are composed of lines (vectors) that can easily be scaled. Figure 10.10 shows dimension lines using the simple default text font of AutoCAD. As illustrated, the text can be easily rotated for a more pleasing appearance.

Bitmap Characters

A bitmap character can be represented by an array that specifies the character's filled pixels. The bold and italic characters shown in figure 10.9 can be represented by their own arrays, or they can be derived from the plain text arrays. Note that a bold character can be produced from a plain character by reprinting the character after it has been displaced a short distance to the right (a technique used by old daisy-wheel and dot-matrix impact printers). In a similar manner, plain text arrays can be used to print bold text. Similarly, italic characters can be printed from plain text arrays by displacing filled pixels to the right by increasing amounts as the character is drawn from bottom to top; this corresponds to a shear transformation; see exercise 10.19. For example, the italic characters in figure 10.9 could be formed from the plain characters by displacing the filled pixels to the right by one additional pixel for every three pixels in the upward direction.

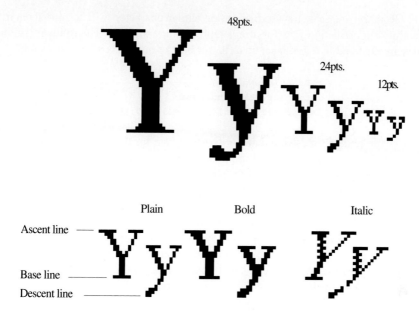

Figure 10.9   Text sizes and styles for bitmap characters. The top row illustrates three different sizes of characters, and the bottom row shows three different styles. Characters are drawn along the base line, with uppercase letters extending up to the ascent line (or cap height) and lowercase letters extending down to the descent line (or bottom line). These characters were drawn from the Macintosh Times font by locating filled pixels with the GetPixel() function and mapping them to larger filled rectangles for display in the figure.

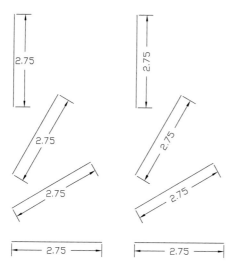

Figure 10.10   AutoCAD's simplest vector font in dimension lines at various angles of attack. The lines at the left were drawn with the default settings on the DIM command. The lines on the right were drawn with the dimension variable DIMTIH turned off (a similar variable DIMTOH controls text placed outside the extension lines). Text angle can also be changed with the TROTATE and TEDIT commands under the DIM command.

Rotation and scale transformations on bitmap characters will be carried out in the this section by constructing files for arrays representing numerals. The following global variables are declared in order to set up a file for bitmap numerals in the Times font:

```
FILE *timesNum;
int wchar,hchar,numchar;
int xpix[11][400],ypix[11][400],kmax[11];
```

A file named timesNum.data will contain data for the 10 numerals plus the period, which is used as the decimal point in floating-point numbers. The character width *wchar* is the same for each numeral. Except for particular fonts, such as the Courier font, the width of the period character is less. Although it has not been done here, a separate character width could be specified for the period.

The variable *numchar* is the total number of characters—11 in this example. The height of the characters, *hchar,* in this example is equal to 48, which is the pixel size on the screen and also the point size of the printed character. This height includes not only the height from the character's base line to the ascent line (figure 10.9), but also the space from the ascent line to the base line of the next row of text above. That is, text rows of full-size characters can be stacked vertically by placing them 48 pixels apart. The text at the bottom of figure 10.9 is plotted with a scale factor of one-half, producing characters having effective character or row heights of 24.

The program for bitmap characters was written on a Macintosh computer. After a graph port has been initialized and opened, the following lines in the main() function open a file, generate the character data, write the data to the file, and close the file.

```
timesNum = fopen("timesNum.data","w");
charData();
writeFile();
fclose(timesNum);
```

The character data comprise the number of characters, their height and width, and a list of all the filled pixels for each character. The arrays $xpix[n][k]$ and $ypix[n][k]$ denote the x- and y-coordinates of a filled pixel relative to the lower left corner of the character. The index number n denotes the character 0-9 for numerals 0–9, and 10 for the period. The index number k ranges from 1 through $kmax[n]$, which is the total number of filled pixels for character n. As shown in the subroutine below, use of the GetPixel() function in *for* loops over the pixel array for a character determines the coordinates of the filled pixels.

At the beginning of the subroutine charData(), Macintosh functions are used to set the font and size, and draw the characters.

```
void charData(void)
{
    int x,y,n,i,k;

    wchar = 25; hchar = 48; numchar =11;
```

```
TextFont(times); TextSize(hchar);
MoveTo(0,hchar);
DrawString("\p0123456789.");

for (n=0; n<numchar; n++)
{
    k = 0;
    for (i=0; i<wchar; i++)
    {
        x = wchar*n + i;
        for (y=1; y<=hchar; y++)
        {
            if (GetPixel(x,y) == TRUE)
            {
                k = k + 1;
                xpix[n][k] = x - wchar*n;
                ypix[n][k] = hchar - y;
            }
        }
    }
    kmax[n] = k;
}
}
```

The data generated by the charData() subroutine is written to the timesNum.data file by the following subroutine:

```
void writeFile(void)
{
    int n,k;

    fprintf(timesNum,"%3d\n",numchar);
    fprintf(timesNum,"%3d\n",hchar);
    fprintf(timesNum,"%3d\n",wchar);
    for (n=0; n<numchar; n++)
    {
        fprintf(timesNum,"%4d\n",kmax[n]);
        for (k=1; k<=kmax[n]; k++)
        {
            fprintf(timesNum,"%3d\n",xpix[n][k]);
            fprintf(timesNum,"%3d\n",ypix[n][k]);
        }
    }
}
```

The data file for the bitmap numerals can be read and transformed in your programs. Figure 10.11 shows rotated numerals from data files for Times, Helvetica, and Courier fonts. The plot for the Times font was generated by opening the data file timesNum.data,

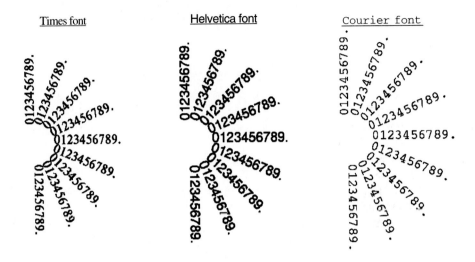

Figure 10.11   Bitmap characters plotted at different angles for three different font styles.

reading the data, and then rotating and plotting the character arrays. The global variables are the same as given above. The following program lines produce the plot:

```
timesNum = fopen("timesNum.data","r");
readData();
plotNumbers();
fclose(timesNum);
```

The data are read by the following subroutine:

```
void readData(void)
{
    int k,n;

    fscanf(timesNum,"%3d\n",&numchar);
    fscanf(timesNum,"%3d\n",&hchar);
    fscanf(timesNum,"%3d\n",&wchar);
    for (n=0; n<numchar; n++)
    {
        fscanf(timesNum,"%4d\n",&kmax[n]);
        for (k=1; k<=kmax[n]; k++)
        {
            fscanf(timesNum,"%3d\n",&xpix[n][k]);
            fscanf(timesNum,"%3d\n",&ypix[n][k]);
        }
    }
}
```

The plot of numbers uses the rotation transformation (10.9) along with a translation to a center of rotation located at $(x\,0, y\,0)$. Because $ypix[n][k]$ is measured upward and the screen coordinate y*plot* is measured downward, the transformed y-coordinate is subtracted from $y0$ in the listing below. For the standard Macintosh graph port (black and white), a SetPixel(x, y) operation is carried out with the combination MoveTo(x, y) and LineTo(x, y).

The subroutine plotNumbers() listed below plots the characters at 9 angles evenly divided between $\theta = -\pi/2$ and $+\pi/2$. Also, note that the trigonometric functions are evaluated outside the *for* loops over n and k; otherwise, the subroutine would run much more slowly.

```
void plotNumbers(void)
{
    int i,k,n,x0,y0,xplot,yplot;
    double theta,xd,yd,sf,cost,sint;

    x0 = 160; y0 =320; sf = .5;
    for (i=-4; i<5; i++)
    {
        theta = 3.141593*i/8.;
        cost = cos(theta); sint = sin(theta);
        for (n=0; n<numchar; n++)
        {
            for (k=1; k<=kmax[n]; k++)
            {
                xd = (double) (xpix[n][k] + wchar*(n+3));
                yd = (double) ypix[n][k];
                xplot = x0 + (int) (sf*(xd*cost - yd*sint));
                yplot = y0 - (int) (sf*(xd*sint + yd*cost));
                MoveTo(xplot,yplot); LineTo(xplot,yplot);
            }
        }
    }
}
```

Figure 10.11 shows that some loss of quality occurs when the character fonts are plotted in directions other than the horizontal or vertical. The segments of the characters that are vertical or horizontal align well with pixel locations when the characters are horizontal or vertical (note the vertical part of the uppercase *Y* in figure 10.9). Also, the bitmap representation was designed for horizontal characters, so that the selection of filled pixels was optimized for that orientation.

To improve the appearance of characters plotted at an angle, a scale factor $sf = 0.5$ was chosen for plotting figure 10.11. When $sf = 1$, the calculated pixel locations with angle rotation missed some pixels that were left unfilled in the middle of character lines. Reduction of the scale factor ensured that all appropriate pixels were filled, although some extra filled pixels appear to thicken the characters somewhat.

The above procedures show that bitmap characters can be transformed through translation, scale, and rotation. However, the plotting is slow, and results are not as good as for the vector characters considered below. Because vector characters are composed of lines, there is no limit on their scale, and they appear almost equally good at any angle. (Written with a pen plotter, vector characters would be of equal quality at any angle.)

Vector Characters

Text in AutoCAD consists of vector characters that are available in a number of different font styles. Figure 10.12 shows the numerals 0–9 plus the decimal point plotted in the AutoCAD font MONOTXT. The MONOTXT font is the simplest AutoCAD font and is the same as the default font TXT, but with equal character widths.

In addition to providing standard font styles, AutoCAD permits creation of your own fonts and symbols. A single character or symbol may be created by writing a shape file according to the format given in the AutoCAD manual. The shape file, which has the extension SHP added to its name, may be compiled from the AutoCAD main menu to produce a file with the extension SHX. Within AutoCAD, the SHX file may be loaded with the LOAD command, and then the character or symbol inserted with the SHAPE command. The shape character may be scaled and rotated before being placed anywhere in the drawing.

It is simpler to save a single font or symbol as a block than to create a shape file (also, a block can contain a much more complex drawing). However, shape files can be grouped together to form font files, with characters and symbols drawn directly from key strokes within the TEXT command.

An AutoCAD font file starts with a two-line header identifying the font style and giving pertinent information such as numerical values for the ascent and descent line distances from the base line. The font file header lines are followed by the shapes for the individual characters, which are identified by their ASCII code numbers. For example, the ASCII code number for uppercase A is 65, so the two-line entry for uppercase A starts with *65,11,uca. The first number is the ASCII number; the second number lists the number of data bytes required to describe the character; and the third entry is the shape name (here *uca* stands for uppercase *A*). The second line of the file for the character describes its shape with a list of vectors (the vector length and direction encoding is described in the AutoCAD manual).

To simulate the AutoCAD vector characters in a program, let each character be drawn as a single polyline, which is represented as an array, as in section 9.3. Also, the character height and width is specified to help place letters. Alternatively, one could construct a character by using several different polylines, with some prescription for "pen up" and "pen

0123456789.

Figure 10.12 Vector numerals from the MONOTXT font style in AutoCAD. The lower enlargement of the numeral 3 shows that the characters are based on line segments drawn within a 6 × 6 mesh.

down" (that is, for distinguishing MoveTo from LineTo operations). For example, negative numbers for coordinates could signify a move to the absolute values of the coordinates, with positive coordinates signifying a line to the coordinates. In the shape description of an AutoCAD character, the code number 1 denotes pen down and 2 denotes pen up. Also, the shape ends with a pen up move to the lower-right corner of the character, so that no separate specification of character width is required. In this section MONOTXT numerals are simulated with single polylines, with a specified height and width constant for all the characters.

In the program below, the polyline for character number n has a total number of vertices given by the array charVert[n]. As shown in the list of global variables below, the character 0 (corresponding to $n = 0$) has nine vertices, and the period ($n = 10$) is just a single line segment with two vertices. In a character array, the x-coordinates of the vertices are given by numChar[n][$2k$] and the y-coordinates by numChar[n][$2k+1$], where k ranges over the vertices, from 0 through charVert[n]-1.

The arrays are based on the 6×6 mesh drawn around the numeral 3 in figure 10.12. It may be readily confirmed that the fourth array under numChar[][] gives the coordinates for the numeral 3, as measured from the lower-left corner of the mesh in figure 10.12. The other arrays can easily be developed from AutoCAD plots of the characters.

```
int        numchar;
double     wchar,hchar;
double     charVert[] = {9,5,10,13,4,9,10,3,16,10,2};
double     numChar[11][32] = {{2,0,3,0,4,1,4,5,3,6,2,6,1,5,1,1,2,0},
     {1,0,3,0,2,0,2,6,1,5},{4,0,0,0,0,2,1,3,3,3,4,4,4,5,3,6,1,6,0,5},
          {0,1,1,0,3,0,4,1,4,2,3,3,2,3,3,3,4,4,4,5,3,6,1,6,0,5},
          {3,0,3,6,0,2,4,2},{0,1,1,0,3,0,4,1,4,3,3,4,0,4,0,6,4,6},
          {3,6,2,6,0,4,0,1,1,0,3,0,4,1,4,2,3,3,0,3},{0,6,4,6,1,0},
     {1,3,0,2,0,1,1,0,3,0,4,1,4,2,3,3,1,3,0,4,0,5,1,6,3,6,4,5,4,4,3,3},
          {4,3,1,3,0,4,0,5,1,6,3,6,4,5,4,2,2,0,1,0},{2,0,2,1}};
```

Because the vector characters specified in the above arrays are located within a 6×6 square; the values *wchar* and *hchar* are both equal to 6. For the scale factors *sx* and *sy* equal to 4 in the subroutine plotVectorNumbers() below, the character heights and widths equal 24 pixels. The subroutine plotVectorNumbers() draws numerals at various angles, just like the subroutine plotNumbers() above, except that the two scale factors have been retained as separate variables. The combination of a scale transformation (with separate x- and y-scale factors) followed by a rotation is given by equation 10.14.

```
void plotVectorNumbers(void)
{
    int i,k,n,x0,y0,xplot,yplot;
    double theta,xd,yd,sx,sy,cost,sint;

    x0 = 200; y0 =200;
    sx = 4; sy = 4;
    wchar = hchar = 6; numchar = 11;
```

```
for (i= -4; i<5; i++)
{
    theta = 3.141593*i/8;
    cost = cos(theta); sint = sin(theta);
    for (n=0; n<numchar; n++)
    {
        for (k=0; k<charVert[n]; k++)
        {
            xd = numChar[n][2*k] + wchar*(n+5);
            yd = numChar[n][2*k+1];
            xplot = x0 + (int) (sx*xd*cost - sy*yd*sint);
            yplot = y0 - (int) (sx*xd*sint + sy*yd*cost);
            if (k == 0) MoveTo(xplot,yplot);
            LineTo(xplot,yplot);
        }
    }
}
```

Figure 10.13 shows that a simple vector representation produces characters that retain their quality as they are scaled and rotated. Also, the plotting is considerably faster than for the bitmap vectors. Because the vector characters have the same representation as polylines, they can easily be included in a drawing program that performs pan and zoom operations.

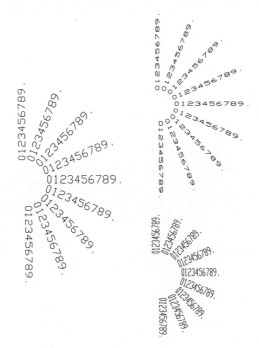

Figure 10.13 Vector characters drawn at different angles, with the following scale factors: $sx = sy = 24$ for the left plot; $sx = 12$ and $sy = 24$ for the top right plot; and $sx = 24$ and $sy = 12$ for the lower-right plot.

10.5 ROTATIONS FOR MACHINERY DESIGN: THE ROTARY ENGINE

The rotation transformation is useful for calculating the motion of parts for mechanical design. This analysis involves the study of kinematics, which is the study of motions subject to constraints, but without the consideration of forces (forces are included in the equations of dynamics). CAD software for mechanical design can include modules for kinematics and dynamics.

The rotary engine, developed by Felix Wankel, is a compact, high-performance engine used in a variety of applications. Although a number of automobile companies have used this engine, current automobile use is primarily in Mazda cars.

Figure 10.14 shows the main features of the rotary engine. A remarkable feature of this design is that the tips of the triangular rotor fit exactly inside the epitrochoidal chamber at all times. The figure at the beginning of this chapter illustrates a number of rotor positions. The rotor moves when its interior gear rotates around the fixed spur gear.

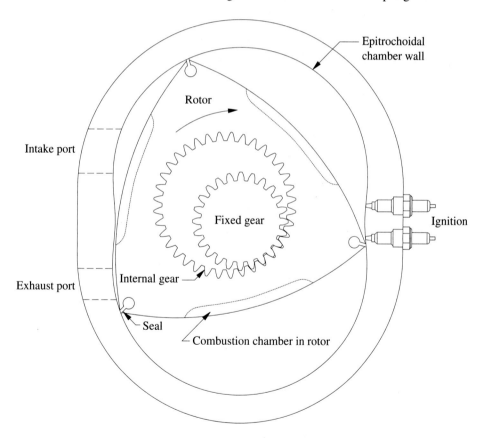

Figure 10.14 Rotary engine configuration typical of that found in some Mazda automobiles.

The engine operation can be explained in reference to figure 10.14. The cycle starts with the fuel-air mixture being drawn through the intake port on the upper left. The intake phase continues until the rotor face reaches the upper horizontal position, and the seal at the lower left in the figure moves up past the intake port. Then the fuel-air mixture is compressed as the face rotates to a position next to the spark plugs, at which time ignition occurs. Combustion begins in the small pocket or combustion chamber in the rotor face and continues into the main chamber as the rotor face moves downward. The exhaust phase begins when the rotor face moves past the lower horizontal position, and the seal moves past the exhaust port. For the three chambers defined by the rotor position in figure 10.14, the upper-left chamber is in the intake phase, the upper-right chamber is in the compression phase, and the lower chamber is near the end of the combustion phase just before the exhaust phase begins.

Two-dimensional transformations are useful for analyzing both the chamber and the rotor. First, the epitrochoidal shape of the chamber is explained geometrically as the curve generated by a circle rolling around the outside of a base circle that has a diameter twice that of the generating circle. Second, the motion of the rotor's internal gear around the fixed gear is analyzed by considering one circle rolling inside a base circle. In this particular case the generating circle has a diameter one and a half times that of the base circle, so it represents the interior gear rotating around the fixed gear (base circle).

Figure 10.15 shows the standard geometrical method for generating an epitrochoid. A generating circle rolls around a base circle of radius $r_b = 2r_g$. When the generating circle lies in its initial position to the right of the base circle, a point P is specified along a horizontal radius from the generating circle's center C. The distance d between C and P is some fraction ε of the radius; that is, $d = \varepsilon r_g$.

When the generating circle rolls to the next position shown, its center is at C', and the point P has moved to point P'. Because there is no slippage when the generating circle rolls

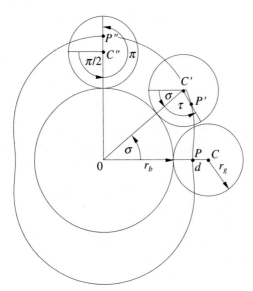

Figure 10.15   An epitrochoid generated by rolling a circle on a base circle.

to its new position, the distance $r_b\sigma$ along the base circle must equal the distance $r_g\tau$ along the generating circle (these distances represent the portions of the circles that were in contact when the generating circle rolled between the two positions). Thus the following relation exists between σ and τ:

$$r_g\tau = r_b\sigma, \quad \text{or } \tau = (r_b/r_g)\sigma = 2\sigma \qquad (10.23)$$

Our 2-D transformations can represent the rolling operation shown in figure 10.15. First, the generating circle is translated a horizontal distance $\Delta x = -(r_b+r_g)$ so that its center lies at the center of the base circle (which is selected as the origin of the coordinate system). Next, the generating circle is rotated counterclockwise through the angle $(\sigma + \tau)$, and then translated by $\Delta x = (r_b+r_g)\cos\sigma$ and $\Delta y = (r_b+r_g)\sin\sigma$, so that its center is at the point C'. Thus, any point on the generating circle may be computed from the following operations:

$$\mathbf{P'} = \mathbf{P}[T(-(r_b+r_g), 0)][R(\sigma+\tau)][T((r_b+r_g)\cos\sigma, (r_b+r_g)\sin\sigma)] \qquad (10.24)$$

Multiplying the matrices in equation 10.24 produces the following expressions for the coordinates (x',y') of point $\mathbf{P'}$ in terms of (x,y) at $\mathbf{P}$.

$$x' = x\cos(\sigma+\tau) - y\sin(\sigma+\tau) - (r_b+r_g)\{\cos(\sigma+\tau) - \cos\sigma\}$$
$$y' = x\sin(\sigma+\tau) + y\cos(\sigma+\tau) - (r_b+r_g)\{\sin(\sigma+\tau) - \sin\sigma\} \qquad (10.25)$$

For the point P in figure 10.15, $x = (r_b + r_g - d)$ and $y = 0$. Also, for the case of an epitrochoid, $\tau = 2\sigma$. After these relations are substituted into equations 10.25, and the results nondimensionalized by r_g, the following equations are obtained:

$$\frac{x'}{r_g} \equiv X = 3\cos\sigma - \varepsilon\cos3\sigma, \quad \frac{y'}{r_g} \equiv Y = 3\sin\sigma - \varepsilon\sin3\sigma \qquad (10.26)$$

Equations 10.26 for the nondimensional coordinates X and Y are the same as equations 3.14 given as an example of a special curve in chapter 3. The full epitrochoid is traced out as σ varies from 0 to 2π. The parameter ε changes the shape of the epitrochoid, with the value $\varepsilon = 0.45$ being used in figure 10.15.

Equations 10.26 may be used to compute the chamber's overall width $W = X(\pi) - X(0)$ and height $H = Y(\pi/2) - Y(3\pi/2)$, where the values in parentheses are σ values:

$$W = 2(3 - \varepsilon), \quad H = 2(3 + \varepsilon) \qquad (10.27)$$

The values given by equation 10.27 are evident from figure 10.15 because the chamber half-width is equal to $r_b + r_g - d$, which equals $(2+1 - \varepsilon) = W/2$ when nondimensionalized by r_g; the half-height in the figure is $r_b + r_g + d$ or $(2+1 + \varepsilon) = H/2$ in nondimensional form.

Figures 10.16a and b show the chamber dimensions W, along with the rotor dimension R measured from the rotor center to a tip. Figure 10.16a shows that for the horizontal orientation, R must equal the half-width $W/2$ plus the nondimensional radius R_p of the path traveled by the rotor center. For the vertical orientation, figure 10.16b shows that R equals the half-height $H/2$ minus R_p. These equations are listed below.

$$R = \frac{1}{2}W + R_p = \frac{1}{2}H - R_p \qquad (10.28)$$

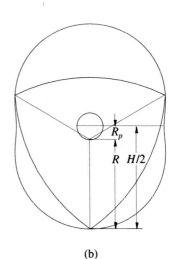

(a)

(b)

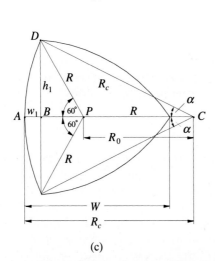

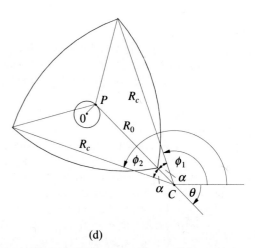

(c)

(d)

Figure 10.16 Rotary engine configuration: (a) and (b): the rotor at two positions in the chamber, with the circle indicating the path of the rotor's center; (c) variables used to calculate the radius of curvature for a side of the rotor; (d) rotor at an arbitrary position, with angles defined for the arc that represents the upper-left side of the rotor.

Equations 10.28 may be solved for R_p, which gives the following result after equations 10.27 are substituted for W and H:

$$R_p = \frac{1}{2}(H - W) = \varepsilon \qquad (10.29)$$

Substitution of the above relation for R_p into equation 10.28 shows that $R = 3$.

The path radius given by equation 10.29 is used below to calculate the sizes of the fixed and interior gears. However, first the curvature of the rotor's sides is calculated. Figure 10.16c shows a rotor at the same orientation as in 10.16a, but the variables are defined relative to the rotor so that the relations to be derived will be valid for any rotor orientation. The point P is the rotor center, which follows the path of radius R_p given by equation 10.29. Point C is the center from which the left arc is drawn with R_c, the radius of curvature.

From figure 10.16c it is evident that the distances AC and DC both equal R_c. As shown in the figure, the distance AB is defined as w_1, and equals $W - R - BP$. These relations lead to the following equations:

$$R_c = R_c\cos\alpha + w_1$$

where

$$w_1 = W - R - R\cos 60° = W - \frac{3}{2}R = \frac{1}{2}(3 - 4\varepsilon) \tag{10.30}$$

The above expression for w_1 uses equation 10.27 for W and the relation $R = 3$.

Equations 10.30 relate two unknowns, R_c and α. Another relation between these two variables results from the two right triangles that have h_1 as a vertical side in figure 10.16c.

$$h_1 = R_c\sin\alpha = R\sin 60° = R\frac{\sqrt{3}}{2} = \frac{3\sqrt{3}}{2} \tag{10.31}$$

Equations 10.30 and 10.31 may be combined as follows:

$$R_c^2\{(\sin\alpha)^2 + (\cos\alpha)^2\} = R_c^2 = \left(\frac{3\sqrt{3}}{2}\right)^2 + \{R_c - \frac{1}{2}(3 - 4\varepsilon)\}^2$$

which yields

$$R_c = \frac{9 - 6\varepsilon + 4\varepsilon^2}{3 - 4\varepsilon} \tag{10.32}$$

Also, figure 10.16c provides the following relation for the angle α.

$$\alpha = \tan^{-1}\left(\frac{h_1}{R_c - w_1}\right) \tag{10.33}$$

In the above equation, the values w_1, h_1, and R_c are given by equations 10.30–10.32.

The distance from the rotor center P to the arc center C in figure 10.16c is defined as R_0.

$$R_0 = R_c - w_1 - R\cos 60° = R_c - (3 - 2\varepsilon) \tag{10.34}$$

The rotation of the interior gear around the fixed spur gear is analyzed by considering one circle rolling inside another, as depicted in figures 10.17a and 10.17b. In the first figure the generating circle rolls inside the base circle; in the second figure the generating circle is larger, so the base circle is fixed inside it. The equations that are developed below apply equally well to either figure. The first figure applies to the calculation of the rotor

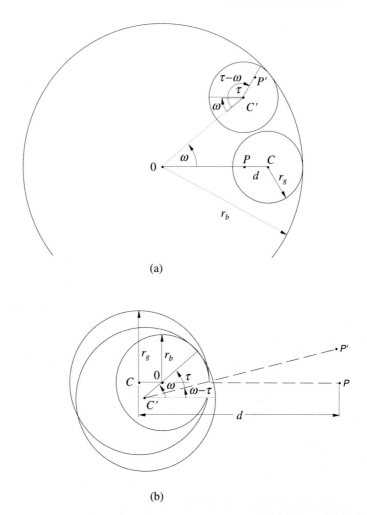

(a)

(b)

Figure 10.17 Rolling on the interior of a circle. For the configurations shown in
(a), $r_g = r_b/4$, with the generating circle rolling on the inside of the fixed base circle. For (b),
$r_g = 3r_b/2$, with the generating circle rolling around a base circle that is fixed in the interior
of the generating circle. The configuration in (b) corresponds to the rotary engine gears, for
which $d = 0$ when the motion of the generating circle's center is considered, and $d = -3$
when P represents a point at the rotor tip. Note that the horizontal distance d to point P is
positive when measured leftward from C, and negative when measured rightward, as in (b).

profile for a Roots blower, considered in problems 10.21 and 10.22; the second figure applies to the interior gear of the Wankel engine rotor moving around the fixed gear.

The rolling of the generating circle in figure 10.17 may be described by the following transformations: a horizontal translation of the generating circle by the amount $\Delta x =
-(r_b-r_g)$ so that its center lies at the origin; next a rotation through the angle $(\omega-\tau)$; and
then a translation of $\Delta x = (r_b-r_g)\cos\omega$ and $\Delta y = (r_b-r_g)\sin\omega$, so that the center generat-

ing circle lies on point C'. Thus any point (x',y') on the generating circle may be computed from the following operations:

$$\mathbf{P}' = \mathbf{P}[T(-(r_b-r_g), 0)][R(\omega+\tau)][T((r_b-r_g)\cos\omega, (r_b-r_g)\sin\omega)] \qquad (10.35)$$

By multiplying the matrices in equation 10.35, the following expressions are obtained for the coordinates (x',y') of point $\mathbf{P}'$ in terms of (x,y) at $\mathbf{P}$:

$$x' = x\cos(\omega-\tau) - y\sin(\sigma+\tau) - (r_b-r_g)\{\cos(\omega-\tau) - \cos\omega\}$$
$$y' = x\sin(\sigma+\tau) + y\cos(\omega-\tau) - (r_b-r_g)\{\sin(\omega-\tau) - \sin\omega\} \qquad (10.36)$$

For the point P in figure 10.17a, $x = (r_b - r_g - d)$ and $y = 0$. When these x- and y-values are substituted into equations 10.36, the following expressions are obtained:

$$x' = -d\cos(\omega-\tau) + (r_b-r_g)\cos\omega$$
$$y' = -d\sin(\omega-\tau) + (r_b-r_g)\sin\omega \qquad (10.37)$$

For the case of a Roots rotor profile, $d = r_g$, and $r_b = 4r_g$, which yield $\tau = (r_b/r_g)\omega = 4\omega$ and thus $\omega - \tau = -3\omega$. Then equations 10.37 reduce to the expressions given in exercise 10.22 at the end of this chapter.

For the rotary engine gears depicted in figure 10.17b, first consider $d = 0$ to find the path of the rotor center. It was determined earlier in this section that the nondimensional radius R_p of the path is equal to ε, which was defined by the epitrochoidal chamber (and not by the present d value). This path can be obtained by substituting $d = 0$ and $r_b - r_g = \pm\varepsilon$ into equations 10.37. If the negative sign is chosen for ε so that $r_g > r_b$, the following path expressions are given by equations 10.37:

$$x_p = -\varepsilon\cos\omega, \quad y_p = -\varepsilon\sin\omega \qquad (10.38)$$

For the rotary engine the appropriate radius ratio is $r_g/r_b = 3/2$. This ratio, along with the relation $r_b - r_g = -\varepsilon$ derived above, yields values for r_b and r_g.

$$r_b = 2\varepsilon, \quad r_g = 3\varepsilon \qquad (10.39)$$

To prove that the rotor tip follows the shape of the epitrochoidal chamber wall, use the value $d = -3$ in equations 10.37. As illustrated in figure 10.17b, this negative d value corresponds to a point P that is attached to the generating circle, but lies to the right beyond r_g. The particular value arises from figure 10.16a, where the right rotor tip is reached from the origin (corresponding to the base circle center in figure 10.17b) by measuring a distance $R_p = \varepsilon$ to the left and then a distance $R = 3$ to the right. Note that for the initial position $x_p = -\varepsilon$ and $y_p = 0$, as given by equations 10.38. Substitution of $d = -3$ and equations 10.38 into equations 10.36, and defining $v = \omega - \tau = \omega - (r_b/r_g)\omega = \omega/3$ produces

$$x' = 3\cos v - \varepsilon\cos 3v, \quad y' = 3\sin v - \varepsilon\sin 3v \qquad (10.40)$$

Equations 10.40 are exactly the same as equations 10.26 for the epitrochoidal chamber. In equations 10.40, x' and y' are in nondimensional form because the path radius was identified with the value ε. Equations 10.40 prove that the rotor tips follow the shape of the epitrochoidal chamber wall.

The formulas for the rotary engine are incorporated into the Microsoft C program given as listing 10.1 in appendix B.

Figure 10.18 shows five positions of the rotor drawn from the program. As ω (=w) passes through values from 0 to π radians, the rotor center travels on its circular path through π radians clockwise, but the rotor turns only one-third as much because its motion is determined by the angle $\nu = \omega - \tau = \omega/3$.

The value for the factor ε may be changed in the rotary engine program. Figure 10.19 shows the configurations for five different ε values. When ε approaches zero, the chamber reduces to a circle (base circle for the chamber), and the gear radii shrink to zero. When ε approaches a value of approximately 0.57, the interior gear radius intersects the rotor faces. Because greater ε values result in greater compression ratios, rotary engines are designed with the larger ε values (but far enough below 0.57 so that the rotor can be structurally sound).

Figure 10.18   Plots from the rotary engine program, calculated for $\varepsilon = 0.45$.

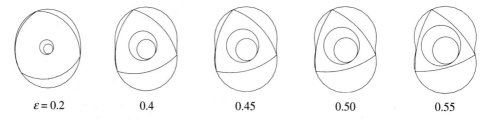

$\varepsilon = 0.2$ 0.4   0.45   0.50   0.55

Figure 10.19   Rotary engine configurations calculated for five different ε values.

EXERCISES

10.1 By multiplying matrices, prove that translation transformations are commutative, with the translated distance equaling the vector sum of the two distances. That is, show that $[T(\Delta x_1, \Delta y_1)][T(\Delta x_2, \Delta y_2)] = [T(\Delta x_2, \Delta y_2)][T(\Delta x_1, \Delta y_1)] = [T(\Delta x_1 + \Delta x_2, \Delta y_1 + \Delta y_2)]$.

10.2 Show that two scale transformations are commutative and lead to a multiplication of scale factors: $[S(S_{x1}, S_{y1})][S(S_{x2}, S_{y2})] = [S(S_{x2}, S_{y2})][S(S_{x1}, S_{y1})] = [S(S_{x1} \cdot S_{x2}, S_{y1} \cdot S_{y2})]$.

10.3 Multiply two rotation matrices to prove they are commutative and lead to a sum of the two angles: $[R(\theta_1)][R(\theta_2)] = [R(\theta_2)][R(\theta_1)] = [R(\theta_1 + \theta_2)]$.

10.4 Derive equation 10.14 by carrying out the multiplication of the scale and transformation matrices.

10.5 Show that translation and rotation transformations do not generally commute; that is, multiply matrices to show that $[R(\theta)][T(\Delta x,\Delta y)] \neq [T(\Delta x,\Delta y)][R(\theta)]$.

10.6 AutoCAD's SCALE command requires that a base point be identified. This base point is the origin for the scaling. Show that scaling about an arbitrary point can be achieved with a combination of translation and scale transformations. Write out the matrix products to achieve this result and multiply the matrices to find the resulting expressions of x' and y'.

10.7 Carry out the matrix multiplications in equation 10.15 to find expressions for x' and y' after a rotation of angle θ about the point (x_1,y_1).

10.8 Consider the rotating, shrinking square shown below. Draw this figure by applying equation 10.14 for the combined scale and rotation transformations. For this figure let f be the fractional distance that a vertex is displaced along the side of the previous (outer) square to construct the next square. The turning angle is then $\phi = \tan^{-1}(f/(1-f))$, and the scale factor $sf = S_x = S_x$ is obtained by comparing the side of a square with the side of the previous square: $sf = [f^2 + (1-f)^2]^{1/2}$. For the figure below, 22 squares were plotted for the value $f = 0.1$.

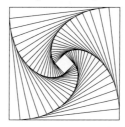

10.9 Starting with the drawing program developed in chapter 9, implement the pan and zoom operations described in section 10.3.

10.10 Write a subroutine that will select and translate lines or polylines in the drawing program of chapter 9.

10.11 Write a subroutine that will select lines or polylines and then resize them.

10.12 Write a subroutine that will rotate selected lines or polylines.

10.13 Implement the programs in section 10.4 that construct a file for bitmap characters, and plot the characters at various angles. To determine values for character height and width for a selected font style and size, you may need to draw some horizontal and vertical lines around characters printed on your monitor screen.

10.14 Create several characters or symbols of your own design to use with AutoCAD. You may wish to start by copying one of the existing AutoCAD font files under a new name, say MYTXT.SHP, and changing the shape vectors for some of the characters. The AutoCAD manual describes the procedures for specifying shape vectors. When you have completed changing the file, compile it in AutoCAD to form the SHX file, load this new font, and write out the new characters or symbols under the TEXT command.

10.15 Plot MONOTXT vector fonts at various angles by implementing the program given in section 10.4.

10.16 Use the MONOTXT vector fonts from problem 10.12 in an aligned dimensioning subroutine for the drawing program developed in chapter 9.

10.17 Write a program that plots a vector font selected from one of the font styles (other than the MONOTXT style) available on your CAD system.

10.18 Write a program for plotting vector fonts of your own design.

10.19 Apply a shear transformation to horizontal vector text, like the numbers given in the subroutine plotVectorNumbers() in section 10.4. The illustration below shows the normal text at the top and three cases with increasing shear below.

0123456789,

0123456789,

0123456789,

0123456789,

10.20 Multiply the matrices given in equation 10.24 to derive equations 10.25.

10.21 Show that equations 10.36 are obtained from the matrix products in equation 10.35.

10.22 The Roots blower is a compressor having two identical rotors. Show that the equations listed below are obtained for the profile of a rotor in a Roots blower. The rotor profile is constructed from two curves as illustrated below, with $r_b = 4r_g$ and $d = r_g$ for each case (generating circle rolling outside or inside the base circle).

$$X = 5\cos\sigma + \cos5\sigma, \qquad Y = 5\sin\sigma + \sin5\sigma$$

(outside the base circle: $\sigma = \pi/4$ to $3\pi/4$ and $5\pi/4$ to $7\pi/4$ radians)

$$X = 3\cos\sigma - \cos3\sigma, \qquad Y = 3\sin\sigma + \sin3\sigma$$

(inside the base circle: $\sigma = -\pi/4$ to $\pi/4$ and $3\pi/4$ to $5\pi/4$ radians)

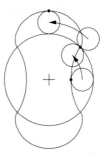

10.23 Use the Roots rotor profiles of exercise 10.22 to write a program to animate the Roots blower, as illustrated below. The arrows in the figure on the left show the rotation directions on the rotors and the gas flow into the blower at the bottom and out at the top. In the right figure, the rotors have advanced 45° ($\pi/4$ radians) relative to their positions in the left figure. The chamber wall is formed from two circular arcs.

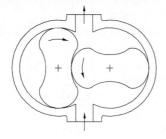
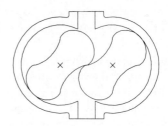

BIBLIOGRAPHY

AutoCAD Release 11 Reference Manual. Sausalito, Calif.: Autodesk, Inc., 1990.

FOLEY, J. D., A. VAN DAM, S. K. FEINER, AND J. F. HUGHES, *Computer Graphics: Principles and Practice,* 2nd ed. Reading, Mass.: Addison-Wesley Publishing Co., 1990.

Inside Macintosh, volume I. Apple Computer, Inc., Reading, Mass.: Addison-Wesley Publishing Co., 1985.

NORBYE, J. P., *The Wankel Engine.* Philadelphia: Chilton Book Co., 1971.

PAUL, B., *Kinematics and Dynamics of Planar Machinery.* Englewood Cliffs, N.J.: Prentice-Hall, 1979.

ROGERS, D. F., AND J. A. ADAMS, *Mathematical Elements for Computer Graphics,* 2nd ed. New York: McGraw-Hill Publishing Co., 1990.

SPROULL, R. F., W. R. SUTHERLAND, AND M. K. ULLNER, *Device-Independent Graphics, with Examples from IBM Personal Computers.* New York: McGraw-Hill Publishing Co., 1985.

11

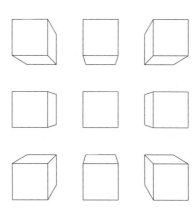

3-D Transformations

Three-dimensional transformations may be used in several different ways: to transform individual objects, to transform from one coordinate system to another, and to view objects.

Transformations of objects in 3-D may readily be developed from the 2-D procedures of chapter 10. Objects can be translated, scaled, and rotated with respect to the three axes.

Transformation between the world-coordinate system and a user-coordinate system makes it possible to use the procedures for constructing surface and solid models at any location or orientation. For example, the AutoCAD command REVSURF can be applied in a user-coordinate system to generate a surface of revolution at any angle relative to the world-coordinate axes.

Objects in 3-D can be viewed with parallel or perspective projections. A parallel projection corresponds to viewing from an infinite distance because rays traveling from the object to the viewer do not converge. For the perspective projection, rays from the object converge to the observer's position, which is located at a finite distance from the object. A perspective projection of nine cubes is shown above; in a parallel projection, all of the cubes would be the same (squares, if viewed from the front). At an appropriate viewing angle, the three-point perspective transformation reduces to the two-point projection favored by architects.

11.1 TRANSLATION, SCALE, AND ROTATION IN 3-D

The first transformations to be considered are the three-dimensional forms of two-dimensional transformations considered in chapter 10: translation, scale, and rotation.

Translation

Translation in 3-D is a function of the displacements Δx, Δy, and Δz. In order to put translation into multiplicative form, $\mathbf{P}' = \mathbf{P}[T(\Delta x, \Delta y, \Delta z)]$, the translation matrix $[T]$ must be a 4×4 matrix, and $\mathbf{P}'$ and $\mathbf{P}$ are 1×4 matrices.

$$[x' \quad y' \quad z' \quad 1] = [x \quad y \quad z \quad 1] \begin{bmatrix} 1 & 0 & 0 & 0 \\ 0 & 1 & 0 & 0 \\ 0 & 0 & 1 & 0 \\ \Delta x & \Delta y & \Delta z & 1 \end{bmatrix} \tag{11.1}$$

The product of the 1×4 row vector and the 4×4 matrix is carried out by the procedure described in appendix C. For example, the first element in the product matrix equals the product of the four elements of the 1×4 row vector with the four elements in the first column of the 4×4 matrix. Thus, equation 11.1 is equivalent to $x' = x + \Delta x$, $y' = y + \Delta y$, and $z' = z + \Delta z$.

Scale

The form of the scale transformation $\mathbf{P}' = \mathbf{P}[S(S_x, S_y, S_z)]$ is a simple generalization of equation 10.6 for 2-D scaling:

$$[x' \quad y' \quad z' \quad 1] = [x \quad y \quad z \quad 1] \begin{bmatrix} S_x & 0 & 0 & 0 \\ 0 & S_y & 0 & 0 \\ 0 & 0 & S_z & 0 \\ 0 & 0 & 0 & 1 \end{bmatrix} \tag{11.2}$$

After matrix multiplication, equation 11.2 yields the scaling relations $x' = S_x x$, $y' = S_y y$, and $z' = S_z z$.

Reflection transformations are special cases of the scale transformation: for reflection through the $x = 0$ plane, $S_x = -1$, $S_y = 1$, and $S_z = 1$; for reflection through the $y = 0$ plane, $S_x = 1$, $S_y = -1$, and $S_z = 1$; and through the $z = 0$ plane, $S_x = 1$, $S_y = 1$, and $S_z = -1$. With AutoCAD, reflection through an arbitrary plane can be carried out with the MIRROR command after the coordinate system has been changed to a user-coordinate system (UCS) in which the plane appears as a line. Procedures for setting up the UCS are discussed in section 11.2.

Rotation

A rotation matrix is defined for each of the three axes. A rotation in the xy-plane is described by matrix $[R_z(\psi)]$, where ψ is the angle rotated about the z-axis. The rotations about the y- and x-axes are expressed as $\mathbf{P}' = \mathbf{P}[R_y(\theta)]$ and $\mathbf{P}' = \mathbf{P}[R_x(\phi)]$. The complete forms of the matrices are shown below.

$$[R_z(\psi)] = \begin{bmatrix} \cos\psi & \sin\psi & 0 & 0 \\ -\sin\psi & \cos\psi & 0 & 0 \\ 0 & 0 & 1 & 0 \\ 0 & 0 & 0 & 1 \end{bmatrix}$$

$$[R_y(\theta)] = \begin{bmatrix} \cos\theta & 0 & -\sin\theta & 0 \\ 0 & 1 & 0 & 0 \\ \sin\theta & 0 & \cos\theta & 0 \\ 0 & 0 & 0 & 1 \end{bmatrix} \qquad (11.3)$$

$$[R_x(\phi)] = \begin{bmatrix} 1 & 0 & 0 & 0 \\ 0 & \cos\phi & \sin\phi & 0 \\ 0 & -\sin\phi & \cos\phi & 0 \\ 0 & 0 & 0 & 1 \end{bmatrix}$$

The rotation angles ψ, θ, and ϕ are pictured in figure 11.1, where they are identified with the yaw, pitch, and roll angles associated with aircraft motions.

Combinations of Transformations

A drawn object can be placed in an arbitrary position by combining a translation with rotations about two axes. For example, the following combination of transformations will

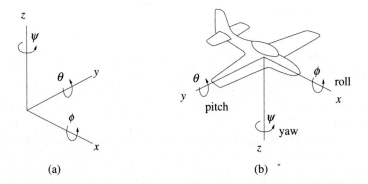

(a)   (b)

Figure 11.1 Two orientations for axes showing rotation angles: (a) the z-axis pointing upward; (b) the z-axis pointing downward from the airplane's center of gravity, with the rotation angles ϕ, θ, and ψ identified as the pitch, roll, and yaw angles about the x-, y-, and z-axes, respectively.

place the object at an arbitrary position, with an initial point **P** on an object being moved to point **P′**:

$$\mathbf{P}' = \mathbf{P}[T(\Delta x, \Delta y, \Delta z)][R_y(\theta)][R_x(\phi)] \qquad (11.4)$$

Of course, the combination 11.4 is not unique. The same result could be obtained by an appropriate translation after the rotations, or by a different combination of rotations.

The product of the 4×4 matrices in equation 11.4 is evaluated by multiplying row and column elements in the manner described in appendix C. Namely, the element c_{ij} of a product matrix $[C] = [A][B]$ equals the sum of the products of the elements in the ith row of [A] with the elements of the jth column of [B]: $c_{ij} = a_{i1}b_{1j} + a_{i2}b_{2j} + a_{i3}b_{3j} + a_{i4}b_{4j}$.

Equation 11.4 gives the transformed coordinates in terms of the original coordinates. In some situations it is desirable to express the original coordinates in terms of the transformed coordinates. To obtain this result, equation 11.4 is inverted by multiplying the equation from the right by the following product: $[R_x(\phi)]^{-1}[R_y(\theta)]^{-1}[T(\Delta x, \Delta y, \Delta z)]^{-1}$. The notation $[M]^{-1}$ denotes the inverse of the matrix [M]; that is, $[M][M]^{-1} = [I]$, with [I] being the identity matrix. After multiplication, equation 11.4 yields the following result:

$$\mathbf{P} = \mathbf{P}'[R_x(\phi)]^{-1}[R_y(\theta)]^{-1}[T(\Delta x, \Delta y, \Delta z)]^{-1} \qquad (11.5)$$

The procedure given in appendix C may be used to calculate matrix inverses in order to determine the coordinates of point **P** from the **P′** coordinates. Alternatively, one can first multiply the matrices in equation 11.4 to obtain three equations for x', y', and z' in terms of x, y, and z, and then solve these three equations for x, y, and z in terms of x', y', and z'.

Objects drawn with AutoCAD can be translated, scaled, and rotated with the commands MOVE, SCALE, and ROTATE. Also, transformations between coordinate systems are essential to the operation of CAD systems. First, a transformation between the world coordinates and a user-defined coordinate system can greatly facilitate the construction of a 3-D object. Second, transformation to a viewing coordinate system is required for displaying 3-D objects.

11.2 TRANSFORMATIONS BETWEEN WORLD- AND USER-COORDINATE SYSTEMS

Translation and rotation transformations such as those given in equation 11.4 make it possible to set up a user-coordinate system (UCS) at any position and orientation relative to the world-coordinate system (WCS). In AutoCAD, a user-coordinate system is set up with the UCS command.

Figure 11.2 shows a ladle (consisting of a cup and handle) constructed with AutoCAD. An icon denoting the world-coordinate system (labeled W) lies in the horizontal plane, showing axis directions with x and y arrows. The origin of the coordinate system is at the center of the icon cross, and the z-axis is perpendicular to the xy-plane (upward in the figure to form a right-handed coordinate system).

In figure 11.2a, a UCS has been set up with its y-axis pointing upward; that is, in the z-direction of the WCS. To aid in viewing the icons, the UCS origin has been translated to

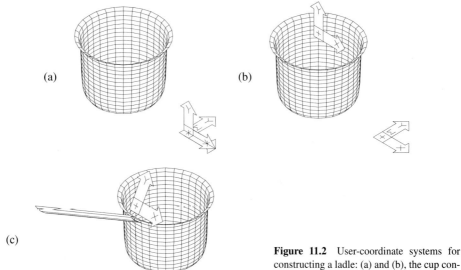

(a)

(b)

(c)

Figure 11.2 User-coordinate systems for constructing a ladle: (a) and (b), the cup constructed as a surface of revolution about an axis in the y-direction of a UCS; (c) the handle extruded along the z-direction of a UCS.

the cup axis position in figure 11.2b, although this translation is not necessary for constructing the cup with AutoCAD's REVSURF command. (The REVSURF command is discussed in chapter 12). Thus the user-coordinate system appropriate for constructing the cup can be set up by rotating the world system 90° about its x-axis. This +90° rotation of the axes is equivalent to rotating objects by −90° with the last of equations 11.3. Let a point $\mathbf{P}'$ on an object in the UCS correspond to the point $\mathbf{P}$ in the WCS. Then the transformation between the coordinate systems may be written as $\mathbf{P}' = \mathbf{P}[R_x(-90°)]$, which is written out below after using $\sin(-90°) = -1$ and $\cos(-90°) = 0$.

$$[x_u \quad y_u \quad z_u \quad 1] = [x_w \quad y_w \quad z_w \quad 1] \begin{bmatrix} 1 & 0 & 0 & 0 \\ 0 & 0 & -1 & 0 \\ 0 & 1 & 0 & 0 \\ 0 & 0 & 0 & 1 \end{bmatrix} \qquad (11.6)$$

The above matrix equation reduces to

$$x_u = x_w, \qquad y_u = z_w, \qquad z_u = -y_w \qquad (11.7)$$

For example, a unit distance along the z-axis in the WCS corresponds to $(x_w, y_w, z_w) = (0,0,1)$, which by equations 11.7 corresponds to the UCS values $(x_u, y_u, z_u) = (0,1,0)$. For this case of a 90° rotation, the correctness of relations 11.7 is evident from figure 11.2a. Note that for this rotation, it is a trivial matter to invert equations 11.7 so that x_w, y_w, and z_w are expressed as functions of x_u, y_u and z_u.

The handle shown in figure 11.2c is constructed by extruding line segments in the z-direction of a UCS that is rotated 60° from the WCS (so that the handle extends upward at an angle of 30° from the horizontal). That is, in the UCS, line segments were attached to the cup and then given a thickness with the CHANGE command (thickness is one of the properties of a line that can be changed—the default thickness is zero). This extrusion of the handle does not require the translation of the UCS origin shown in figure 11.2c, just a rotation given by [$R_x(-60°)$]. The following relations between the coordinate values may be obtained.

$$x_u = x_w, \qquad y_u = \frac{1}{2}y_w + \frac{\sqrt{3}}{2}z_w, \qquad z_u = -\frac{\sqrt{3}}{2}y_w + \frac{1}{2}z_w \qquad (11.8)$$

With AutoCAD a user-coordinate system can be set up easily with the command UCS. The following statements set up a UCS rotated 90° around the x-axis from the WCS position, as shown in figure 11.2a.

```
Command: UCS
Origin/ZAxis/3point/Entity/View/X/Y/Z/Prev
                    /Restore/Save/Del/?/<World>: X
Rotation angle about the X axis <0.0>: 90
```

After the UCS command is entered, AutoCAD offers a number of options. In addition to the X, Y, and Z options for rotation about the x-, y-, and z-axes, the Origin option translates the origin to any entered point. Other options for rotating the axes include the ZAxis option for aligning the z-axis in the UCS, the Entity option for aligning the UCS with a selected drawing entity, and the View option for setting the xy-plane of the UCS perpendicular to the current view direction (as established from the view or display menu).

Another option for setting the UCS position is the 3point option illustrated in figure 11.3. The first selected point (P1) sets the origin, then the second point (P2) determines the location of the x-axis, and the third point (P3) determines the xy-plane. Figure 11.3a shows

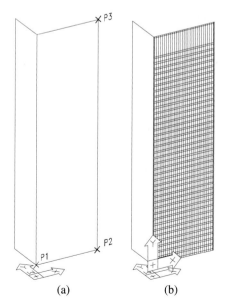

Figure 11.3   A user-coordinate system on a face: (a) three points on the face to set the origin, the x-axis, and the xy-plane; (b) the UCS icon on the face, with arrays of lines drawn in the xy-plane.

(a)   (b)

two rectangular faces drawn with the 3DFACE command, with the three corners picked from the assist menu with the mouse. As shown in 11.3b, a UCS icon is established on the selected face, and two-dimensional drafting techniques can be used to construct lines on this face (here arrays of lines are drawn to represent windows on a building; see figures 11.15 and 11.21 for views of the resulting building). That is, the x- and y-coordinates for 2-D drawing operations refer to the x- and y-values in the UCS.

Other options listed above under the UCS command include Prev for setting the UCS to the previous one; the Save option for saving the UCS under a name that can be recalled under the Restore option; the ? option for a list of all UCS names saved under the current drawing; the Del option for deleting UCS names from the list; and the World option to go back to the WCS. Once a UCS has been selected, entries in the view menu permit quick switching to plan views in the UCS and the WCS.

The coordinate system icons can be controlled with the UCSICON command.

> **Command: UCSICON**
> **ON/OFF/All/Noorigin/Origin <current ON/OFF state>:**

The default setting of the UCS icon is ON with Noorigin; that is, the icon is shown in the lower-left corner of the viewport (drawing area). (If a UCS has not been set up, then the UCS defaults to the WCS.) Selection of the option Origin adds the cross to the icon, and places the center of the cross at the origin of the UCS while that origin is in the viewport. When a pan operation moves the origin off the screen, the icon moves to the lower-left corner of the viewport, and the cross is erased. The All option applies changes to the icons to all viewports, rather than to just the active viewport.

11.3 VIEWING WITH PARALLEL PROJECTIONS

With AutoCAD, viewing with parallel projections is done with the command VPOINT.

> **Command: VPOINT**
> **Rotate/<View point> <0.000,0.000,1.000>: 2,4,3**

The default viewpoint given above is the current viewpoint (which is the plan view in this example). That is, the viewpoint is located on the positive z-axis because the first two default entries are zero. To view from along the positive x-axis, the values 1,0,0 could be entered. The viewpoint given above (2,4,3) is illustrated in figure 11.4. For the parallel projections considered here, the absolute distance of the point is unimportant; only its direction is important. Thus, the view for point (3,0,0) is the same as for (1,0,0), and (4,8,6) gives the same view as (2,4,3).

In the above VPOINT command, the letter *R* may be entered for the rotate option. Under this option, two angles are entered: the azimuth angle in the xy-plane and the elevation

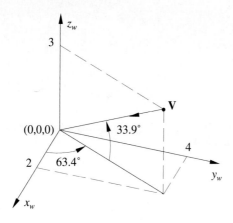

Figure 11.4   A view direction in AutoCAD, specified by the viewpoint **V** having coordinates 2,4,3. The origin (0,0,0) is the default target point.

angle from the xy-plane. The viewpoint in figure 11.4 can be entered by specifying the angle 63.4° in the xy-plane and the angle 33.9° from the xy-plane. Because of this reference to the xy-plane, the selection of views is greatly facilitated if vertical direction for an object points in the z-direction. (For objects with their verticals not in the z-direction, it is very difficult to pick a direction in which the object appears untilted.) AutoCAD provides a graphic menu display for quick selection of particular views (views at 45° intervals in the xy-plane, with a scale for the elevation angle from the xy-plane).

It should be noted that the VPOINT command defaults to directions measured in the world-coordinate system (WCS). To change VPOINT to directions measured in the current user-coordinate system (UCS), one must change the system variable WORLDVIEW from its default value of 1 to the value 0. Therefore, it is recommended that objects be constructed with their verticals in the z-direction of the WCS, as illustrated in figures 11.2 and 11.3.

Special Viewing Directions and Projections

Drawings of engineering and architectural designs are usually presented as *orthographic* projections, that is, as parallel projections in directions that will present an object in top (or plan), front (or front elevation), side, bottom, and back views. Because most items are designed in rectangular shapes, orthographic projections often show features in true lengths that can be readily dimensioned.

Orthographic views may be drawn as separate 2-D drawings, as in figure 1.10, or they may be displayed as special views of a 3-D CAD object, as in figures 1.11 and 2.12. Because they may be hard to visualize from orthographic projections, complex objects are often presented in projections that provide a 3-D representation, such as an *isometric* projection, an *oblique* projection, or the more general *axonometric* projection. As discussed in section 3.1, AutoCAD provides features that use 2-D drafting techniques to construct isometric drawings.

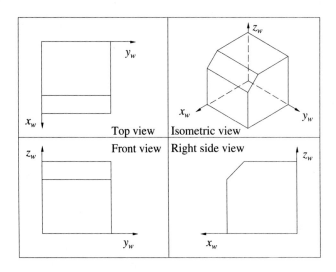

Figure 11.5 Multiviews of a cube with a beveled top front edge.

A multiview representation of a cube with a beveled (chamfered) edge is presented in figure 11.5. Coordinate axes are included in the three orthographic views and in the isometric view. These views are produced by parallel projection.

Figure 11.6a illustrates the parallel projection of the right side of the beveled cube onto a plane perpendicular to the y-axis. This side view would be seen by an observer looking in the negative y-direction from a viewpoint that approaches an infinite distance along the positive y-axis. For an observer at a finite distance, the projection lines converge, producing the perspective projection shown in figure 11.6b.

The perspective projection in figure 11.6b shows the left-side face with dashed lines because it is behind the larger projection of the right side. As the viewpoint **V** moves closer to the cube, the difference between the two side-face projections becomes greater; that is, there is a greater effect of perspective. The placement of the projection plane affects only the size of the image, not the perspective. Perspective projections are the subject of section 11.4.

For programming applications, the different projections can be calculated from algebraic formulas that represent transformations from the 3-D space of the object to the 2-D projection plane of the computer screen or plotter paper. For the top view of the beveled cube, figure 11.7 illustrates the transformations between the screen coordinates (x_s, y_s) and the world coordinates (x_w, y_w); also illustrated are plotting coordinates (x_{plot}, y_{plot}) with an origin at the lower-left corner of the plotter paper.

The following transformations are illustrated by figure 11.7:

$$x_s = sf\, y_w + x_0, \qquad y_s = sf\, x_w + y_0 \tag{11.9}$$

$$x_{plot} = sf\, y_w + x_0, \qquad y_{plot} = -sf\, x_w + y_0 \tag{11.10}$$

The same scale factor sf is used in both the x- and y-directions to preserve the same proportions as in the world coordinates. The values x_0 and y_0 represent the translation distances to the origin for the world coordinates; note that y_0 is measured from the top for the screen coordinates, but from the bottom for the plot coordinates.

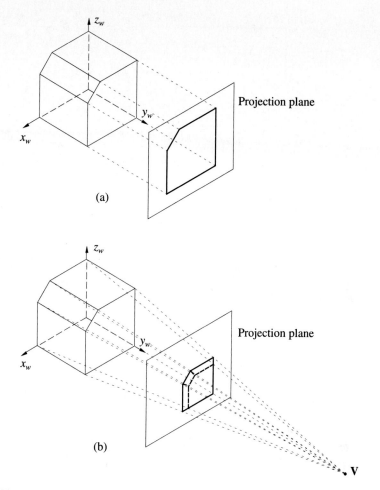

Figure 11.6   Projections onto a plane perpendicular to the y-axis in the world-coordinate system: (a) parallel projection; (b) perspective projection.

The transformation given by equation 11.9 may be expressed in the following matrix form as a combination of an orthographic projection, a scaling, and a translation.

$$[x_s \quad y_s \quad 0 \quad 1] = [x_w \quad y_w \quad z_w \quad 1]\begin{bmatrix} 0 & 1 & 0 & 0 \\ 1 & 0 & 0 & 0 \\ 0 & 0 & 0 & 0 \\ 0 & 0 & 0 & 1 \end{bmatrix}\begin{bmatrix} sf & 0 & 0 & 0 \\ 0 & sf & 0 & 0 \\ 0 & 0 & sf & 0 \\ 0 & 0 & 0 & 1 \end{bmatrix}\begin{bmatrix} 1 & 0 & 0 & 0 \\ 0 & 1 & 0 & 0 \\ 0 & 0 & 1 & 0 \\ x_0 & y_0 & 0 & 1 \end{bmatrix}$$

$$(11.11)$$

The matrix equation 11.11 may be written in the following form.

$$\mathbf{P}_s = \mathbf{P}_w[P_z][S(sf,sf,sf)][T(x_0,y_0,0)] \qquad (11.12)$$

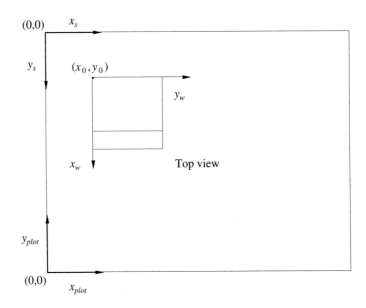

Figure 11.7 Screen coordinates (x_s, y_s) and plot coordinates (x_{plot}, y_{plot}) compared with world coordinates (x_w, y_w) for the top view of a beveled cube.

Thus, a point $\mathbf{P}_s$ in screen coordinates is obtained from point $\mathbf{P}_w$ in world coordinates by applying a projection matrix $[P_z]$, a uniform scaling matrix $[S(sf, sf, sf)]$, and a translation matrix $[T(x_0, y_0, 0)]$. The matrix $[P_z]$ represents a projection on the $z = 0$ plane, with a form given by the first 4×4 matrix in equation 11.11. The form of the projection matrix depends on the orientation of world axes in figure 11.5; here the world z-axis was placed in the vertical direction and the x-axis points to the front (another common orientation has the y-axis in the vertical and the z-axis pointing to the front).

Transformation 11.10 for the plot coordinates has a negative sign in the equation for y_{plot}. One may include a negative sign in a matrix equation by using the matrix $[M_y]$ for a mirror reflection across the $y = 0$ plane. Thus equations 11.10 may be written in the following matrix form:

$$\mathbf{P}_{plot} = \mathbf{P}_w[P_z][M_y][S(sf, sf, sf)][T(x_0, y_0, 0)] \qquad (11.13)$$

The mirror-reflection matrix $[M_y]$ has the same form as the scale matrix $[S(S_x, S_y, S_z)]$ in equation 11.2, but with $S_x = 1$, $S_y = -1$, and $S_z = 1$.

The transformations for the orthographic projections for the front and side faces illustrated in figure 11.5 may be derived in a similar fashion; see exercises 11.4–11.7.

Isometric drawings of the beveled cube are shown in figures 11.5 and 11.6. The coordinate axes in an isometric drawing have equal angular spacing around the origin; that is, an angle of 120° separates adjacent axes in an isometric drawing. The isometric transformation may be derived by reference to figure 11.8, where x, y, and z are projections of the world coordinates x_w, y_w, and z_w.

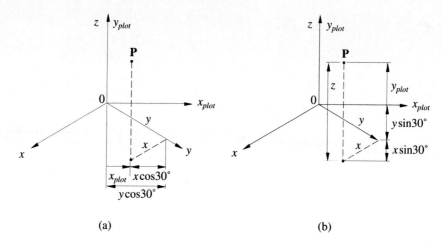

(a)   (b)

Figure 11.8   Geometry for deriving equations for plot coordinates (x_{plot}, y_{plot}) in terms of the coordinates (x, y, z) along the isometric axes.

In section 3.1 it was shown that the top face of a cube aligned with the world axes in an isometric view makes an angle of $\sin^{-1}(1/\sqrt{3}) = 35.264°$ with the horizontal. Because this cube face is perpendicular to the world z-axis, the world axes intersect the isometric projection plane at this same angle. Therefore, the ratio of the projected distances x, y, and z to the world distances is $\cos(35.264°) = \sqrt{(2/3)} = 0.816$. With hand drafting, true distances are measured along the isometric axes. But when an isometric projection is obtained as a special case of the general axonometric projection, the factor 0.816 arises naturally. Of course, an isometric drawing can be scaled by any factor desired.

In figure 11.8, the x- and y-axes lie at angles 30° below the horizontal, whereas x_{plot} lies in the horizontal direction, and y_{plot} lies in the vertical direction along with z. A point **P** with coordinates (x, y, z) may be reached in the projection plane by starting at the origin 0, moving a distance y along the y-axis, a distance x along the x-axis, and a distance z along the z-axis. Figure 11.8a shows that x_{plot} equals the distance $y \cos 30°$ minus the distance $x \cos 30°$. Similarly, figure 11.8b illustrates that y_{plot} equals the distance z minus the sum of $y \sin 30°$ and $x \sin 30°$. Substituting $\sin 30° = 1/2$ and $\cos 30° = \sqrt{3}/2$ yields the transformation

$$x_{plot} = \frac{\sqrt{3}}{2}y - \frac{\sqrt{3}}{2}x, \qquad y_{plot} = z - \frac{1}{2}x - \frac{1}{2}y \qquad (11.14)$$

With the relations $x/x_w = y/y_w = z/z_w = \sqrt{(2/3)}$, and rearrangement of the order of the terms, equation 11.14 yields

$$x_{plot} = -\frac{1}{\sqrt{2}}x_w + \frac{1}{\sqrt{2}}y_w, \qquad y_{plot} = -\frac{1}{\sqrt{6}}x_w - \frac{1}{\sqrt{6}}y_w + \frac{2}{\sqrt{6}}z_w \qquad (11.15)$$

The isometric projection may be expressed in the following matrix form:

$$\mathbf{P}_{plot} = \mathbf{P}_w[\mathbf{P}_{iso}] \qquad (11.16)$$

or

$$[x_{plot} \quad y_{plot} \quad 0 \quad 1] = [x_w \quad y_w \quad z_w \quad 1] \begin{bmatrix} -\dfrac{1}{\sqrt{2}} & -\dfrac{1}{\sqrt{6}} & 0 & 0 \\[2mm] \dfrac{1}{\sqrt{2}} & -\dfrac{1}{\sqrt{6}} & 0 & 0 \\[2mm] 0 & \dfrac{2}{\sqrt{6}} & 0 & 0 \\[2mm] 0 & 0 & 0 & 1 \end{bmatrix} \quad (11.17)$$

It will be shown later that the isometric projection matrix $[P_{iso}]$ given by the 4 × 4 matrix in equation 11.17 is a special case of the general axonometric projection; namely, the projection corresponding to a viewpoint at a 45° angle from the x_w axis in the xy-plane and 35.264° from the xy-plane.

The geometry for calculating an *oblique* projection is shown in figure 11.9. For this projection, dimensions in world yz-planes (front planes) are shown with true lengths, and lengths along the world x-axis are drawn at an oblique angle α to the horizontal. The oblique transformation can be derived from figure 11.9, and it also can be derived as a parallel projection when projection lines that are not perpendicular to the projection plane are used (see Rogers and Adams 1990).

Oblique projections for the beveled cube are shown in figure 11.10. Two common choices for the oblique angle are $\alpha = 30°$ and $\alpha = 45°$. The oblique projection is called a Cavalier projection when x-distances are drawn with true lengths along the oblique angle. As observed from the left part of figure 11.10, the Cavalier projection results in a drawing that appears to exaggerate an object's depth. Thus the oblique projections often are drawn as *cabinet* projections, for which the x-distances along the oblique angle are drawn with half of their true values. Cabinet projections are shown on the right of figure 11.10, and also in figure 11.11, which shows a file cabinet of the type used to store drawings. Obviously,

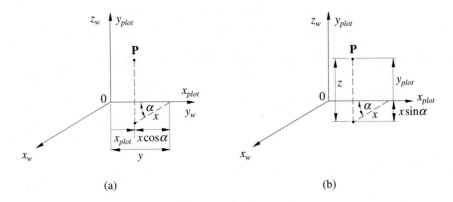

Figure 11.9 Geometry for the oblique projection.

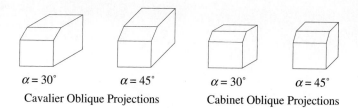

$\alpha = 30°$ | $\alpha = 45°$ | $\alpha = 30°$ | $\alpha = 45°$

Cavalier Oblique Projections   Cabinet Oblique Projections

Figure 11.10   Oblique projections of a beveled cube.

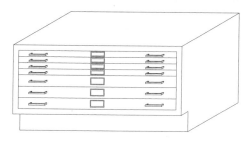

Figure 11.11 A file cabinet represented with a cabinet oblique projection for $\alpha = 30°$.

objects such as cabinets that have most of their detail in front faces are well represented by cabinet oblique drawings.

The coordinate transformation for the Cavalier oblique projection may be written down by referring to the geometry of figure 11.9a for x_{plot} and figure 11.9b for y_{plot}.

$$x_{plot} = y_w - x_w \cos\alpha, \qquad y_{plot} = z_w - x_w \sin\alpha \qquad (11.18)$$

Equations 11.18 for the Cavalier projection can be generalized by multiplying the x_w variable by the parameter f, which assumes a value of 1 for the Cavalier projection and a value of 1/2 for the cabinet projection.

After introducing the f factor, equations 11.18 can be written as

$$x_{plot} = -f x_w \cos\alpha + y_w , \quad y_{plot} = -f x_w \sin\alpha + z_w \qquad (11.19)$$

or,

$$[x_{plot} \quad y_{plot} \quad 0 \quad 1] = [x_w \quad y_w \quad z_w \quad 1] \begin{bmatrix} -f\cos\alpha & -f\sin\alpha & 0 & 0 \\ 1 & 0 & 0 & 0 \\ 0 & 1 & 0 & 0 \\ 0 & 0 & 0 & 1 \end{bmatrix} \qquad (11.20)$$

The above matrix form may be written as $\mathbf{P}_{plot} = \mathbf{P}_w[P_{obl}]$, where $[P_{obl}]$ is the 4×4 matrix for the oblique projection, as given in equation 11.20. The oblique projection matrix can be written in terms of an orthogonal projection matrix and a 3-D shear matrix: see exercise 11.9.

General Viewing Direction: The Axonometric Projection

For an axonometric projection, the viewpoint or camera-coordinate system shown in figure 11.12 is used. This (x_c, y_c, z_c) coordinate system is left-handed, with its z-axis pointing to-

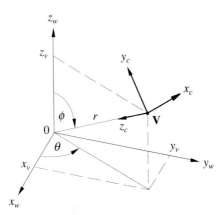

Figure 11.12   Camera-coordinate system (x_c, y_c, z_c) based at the viewpoint **V**.

ward the origin of the world-coordinate system; recall that $(x_w, y_w, z_w) = (0,0,0)$ is the target point for axonometric views in AutoCAD.

The transformation from the world-coordinate system to the camera-coordinate system may be achieved by combining a translation, two rotations, and a reflection. These transformations are illustrated in figure 11.13.

First, a translation of the origin from $(x_w, y_w, z_w) = (0,0,0)$ to $(x_w, y_w, z_w) = (x_v, y_v, z_v)$ is achieved by the matrix operator $[T(-x_v, -y_v, -z_v)]$. Here x_v, y_v, and z_v are the coordinates of the viewpoint **V** in the world-coordinate system, as illustrated in figures 11.12 and 11.13a. Negative signs are used in the translation matrix because moving the coordinate system from $(0,0,0)$ to (x_v, y_v, z_v) is equivalent to moving the objects from $(0,0,0)$ to $(-x_v, -y_v, -z_v)$.

From the geometry shown in figure 11.12, the following expressions may be derived between the Cartesian coordinates (x_v, y_v, z_v) and the spherical coordinates (r, θ, ϕ) of the viewpoint **V**.

$$x_v = r \sin\phi \cos\theta, \qquad y_v = r \sin\phi \sin\theta, \qquad z_v = r \cos\phi \qquad (11.21)$$

After the origin is translated to (x_v, y_v, z_v), a rotation is used to bring the y-axis into a plane that contains both the z-axis and the line joining **V** and the origin of the world coordinates. That is, the y-axis of the camera-coordinate system is rotated about the z-axis by the amount $90° - \theta$ in the clockwise direction; see figure 11.13b. This rotation is achieved by the matrix $[R_z(90° - \theta)]$. Although the rotation matrices in equations 11.3 are defined for counterclockwise rotation angles, the direction is reversed here because rotating a coordinate system in the clockwise direction is equivalent to rotating the objects counterclockwise.

Next, a rotation about the x-axis is performed to point the camera z-axis toward the world origin; see figure 11.13c. This rotation angle is $180° - \phi$ in the counterclockwise direction, which is achieved by the matrix operator $[R_x(\phi - 180°)]$.

Finally, the mirror-reflection operator $[M_x]$ is used to reflect the x-axis across the $x = 0$ plane to form the left-handed coordinate system shown in figures 11.12 and 11.13d. As noted in section 11.1, the matrix $[M_x]$ is given by the scale matrix 11.2 with $S_x = -1$, $S_y = 1$, and $S_z = 1$.

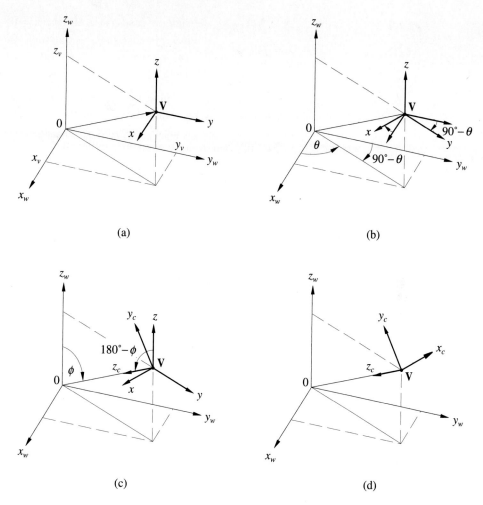

(a)   (b)

(c)   (d)

Figure 11.13   Transformation from world coordinates to camera coordinates: (a) translation of the origin from (0,0,0) to (x_v, y_v, z_v); (b) clockwise rotation by angle $90° - \theta$ about the z-axis; (c) counterclockwise rotation by angle $180° - \phi$ about the x-axis; (d) reflection of the x-axis.

The complete transformation between the world-coordinate system (x_w, y_w, z_w) and the camera-coordinate system (x_c, y_c, z_c) is given by

$$\mathbf{P}_c = \mathbf{P}_w \, [T(-x_v, -y_v, -z_v)][R_z(90° - \theta)][R_x(\phi - 180°)][M_x] \qquad (11.22)$$

The matrix products in equation 11.22 yield the result shown in equation 11.23. The following relations were used: $\sin(90° - \theta) = \cos\theta$, $\cos(90° - \theta) = \sin\theta$, $\sin(\phi - 180°) = -\sin\phi$, and $\cos(\phi - 180°) = -\cos\phi$.

$$[x_c \ \ y_c \ \ z_c \ \ 1] = [x_w \ \ y_w \ \ z_w \ \ 1] \begin{bmatrix} -\sin\theta & -\cos\phi\cos\theta & -\sin\phi\cos\theta & 0 \\ \cos\theta & -\cos\phi\sin\theta & -\sin\phi\sin\theta & 0 \\ 0 & \sin\phi & -\cos\phi & 0 \\ 0 & 0 & r & 1 \end{bmatrix} \quad (11.23)$$

Because the xy-plane is perpendicular to the viewing direction, an axonometric projection defined by the angles ϕ and θ may be obtained from equation 11.23 by setting $x_{plot} = x_c$, $y_{plot} = y_c$. Also, all terms involved in the equation for the z_c coordinate are set equal to zero because they are not relevant to the axonometric projection.

$$[x_{plot} \ \ y_{plot} \ \ 0 \ \ 1] = [x_w \ \ y_w \ \ z_w \ \ 1] \begin{bmatrix} -\sin\theta & -\cos\phi\cos\theta & 0 & 0 \\ \cos\theta & -\cos\phi\sin\theta & 0 & 0 \\ 0 & \sin\phi & 0 & 0 \\ 0 & 0 & 0 & 1 \end{bmatrix} \quad (11.24)$$

Equation 11.24 may be written in the form $\mathbf{P}_{plot} = \mathbf{P}_w\,[\mathbf{P}_{ax}]$, with $[\mathbf{P}_{ax}]$ being the axonometric 4×4 matrix. Special cases may be readily studied. When $\phi = \theta = 0°$, equation 11.24 reduces to $x_{plot} = y_w$ and $y_{plot} = -x_w$. This case corresponds to viewing downward on the xy plane toward the world origin (see figures 11.7 and 11.12).

Another case of special interest is $\theta = 45°$ and $\phi = 90° - 35.264°$. For this case, $\sin\theta = \cos\theta = 1/\sqrt{2}$, $\sin\phi = 2/\sqrt{6}$, and $\cos\phi = 1/\sqrt{3}$. Substituting these values into equa-

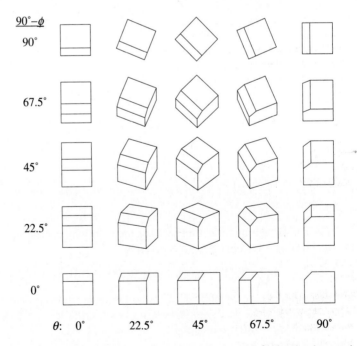

Figure 11.14 Axonometric projections of a beveled cube, with θ being the view rotation angle in the xy-plane, and $90°-\phi$ being the rotation angle *from* the xy-plane.

tion 11.24 shows that the $[P_{ax}]$ matrix reduces to the isometric matrix $[P_{iso}]$ given in equation 11.17. That is, an isometric view of an object is obtained for a viewpoint determined by a 45° rotation in the xy-plane and a 35.264° rotation *from* the xy-plane.

Axonometric projections of a beveled cube are shown in figure 11.14, for equal intervals in ϕ and θ. Note that $90° - \phi$ corresponds to the angle from the xy-plane.

Three axonometric views of a building are shown in figure 11.15. Because axonometric views are constructed by parallel projection, any upward axonometric view will show the bottom of the building. Accordingly, an upward view of a building is called a worm's-eye view. A downward axonometric view will always show the building's top, and is called a bird's-eye view.

In the next section, the perspective transformation will be used to produce more realistic images of this building. With a perspective projection, the building is viewed from a finite distance, and when the viewpoint is at human eye level, neither the top nor the bottom of the building is in view.

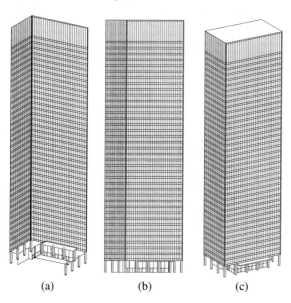

(a)   (b)   (c)

Figure 11.15 Axonometric projections of the 39-story tower of the Seagram Building designed by Mies van der Rohe and Philip Johnson (New York 1954–58): (a) an upward, or worm's-eye view; (b) a horizontal view; (c) a downward, or bird's-eye, view.

11.4 VIEWING WITH PERSPECTIVE PROJECTIONS

Vanishing points are used to construct perspective projections in hand drafting. As illustrated in figure 11.16, the edges of a cube in an axonometric projection are represented by parallel lines. With one-point perspective, four edges point toward one vanishing point. One-point perspective is often used in paintings: for example, a church interior viewed with the main building axis pointing toward the vanishing point, or a road that vanishes at the horizon.

The two-point perspective has two vanishing points, but vertical edges are retained as parallel lines; see figure 11.16. With three-point perspective none of the lines representing the cube edges are parallel. In CAD systems, perspective views are three-point per-

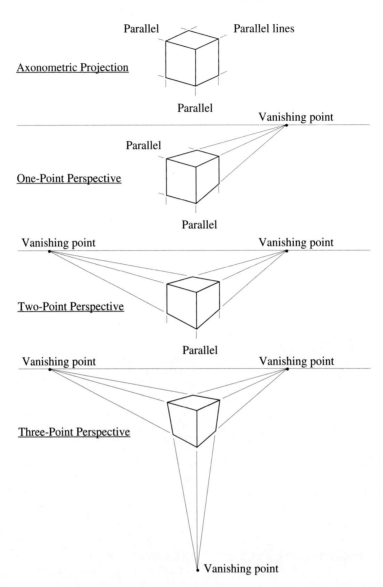

Figure 11.16   A cube viewed by axonometric and perspective projections.

spective views. Although special transformations can be used to produce two-point perspective views, such a procedure is unnecessary because two-point views can be produced from the general three-point transformation by setting the target point at the same height as the viewpoint.

    For the axonometric views considered in the preceding section, the target point was set at the origin of the world-coordinate system. In the axonometric case, moving the target point would correspond to a simple panning of the fixed image across the screen or drawing area. For perspective views, the relative position of the target point and viewpoint affects the shape of the image, not just its position on the screen or paper.

The Three-Point Perspective Projection

The DVIEW command in AutoCAD provides perspective viewing. This command can be used by itself to provide a wireframe or hidden-line perspective view, and it is also used with AutoCAD Render to render scenes (see chapter 14).

The following options appear under the DVIEW command:

```
Command: DVIEW
Select objects: <pick with mouse>
CAmera/TArget/Distance/POints/PAn/Zoom/TWist/CLip
                                 /Hide/Off/Undo/<eXit>:
```

The term DVIEW stands for dynamic view because selected objects rotate as the mouse moves. For example, under the CAmera option, objects selected immediately after the DVIEW command are rotated on the screen in response to movement of the mouse. Left–right mouse motion changes the viewing angle in the xy-plane, and forward–backward mouse motion changes the viewing angle *from* the xy-plane. Angles are selected by pressing the mouse button. Alternatively, angles can be entered from the keyboard. Once the angles have been selected, the view is changed for all objects in the drawing, not just those selected.

When the DVIEW command starts from an axonometric view, the CAmera option provides angles for the axonometric view, and the PAn and Zoom options have their usual meanings (PAn simply moves an unchanged image to different positions on the screen, and Zoom resizes the drawing based on a scale factor).

A perspective view requires a camera (observer) distance. When the Distance option is selected under the DVIEW command, the screen image becomes a perspective view. Also, the effects of other options change once this perspective mode is entered. When PAn is selected after a Distance has been entered, PAn changes the camera position, and thus changes the shape of the image, not just its position on the screen. The Zoom option continues to change only the image size, but instead of a scale factor, a lens size for a 35mm camera is entered.

The lens size determines the viewing angle subtended by the image as viewed by the camera. Figure 11.17a illustrates the horizontal viewing angle α, which encloses the portion of the scene that is projected onto the film. (The viewing angle α should not be confused with the view angles θ and ϕ that determine the *direction* in which the camera is pointing.) The default lens is 50mm, which corresponds closely to the viewing angle of the human eye.

An expression can be derived to relate the viewing angle to the focal length. As illustrated in figure 11.17a, the tangent of the viewing half-angle $\alpha/2$ equals the halfwidth of the image $w/2$ divided by the focal length f. Thus the horizontal viewing angle α may be computed from the formula

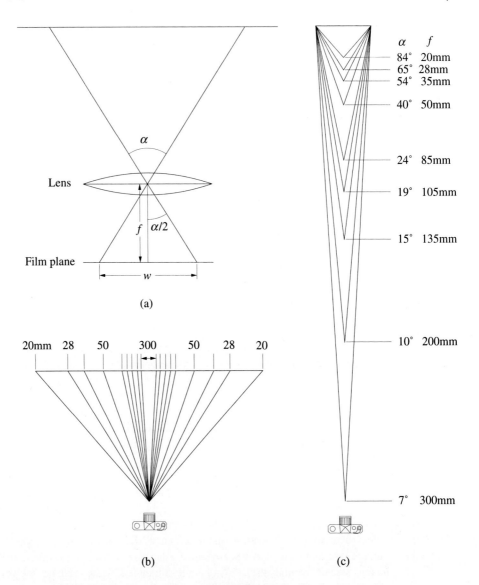

Figure 11.17   Horizontal viewing angle α subtended by the image: (a) camera geometry; (b) viewing angles for different lens focal lengths, with a fixed camera distance; (c) angles and camera distances for viewing a fixed object size.

$$\alpha = 2\tan^{-1}\left(\frac{w}{2f}\right) \tag{11.25}$$

At the back of a 35mm camera, a 36×24mm rectangle is exposed on the film. When $w = 36$mm in the above formula, the horizontal viewing angle may be calculated as a function of focal length f. The vertical viewing angle may be calculated from equation 11.25 if w is replaced by the image height h = 24mm. In photography, the total angular field or angle of view is referenced to the image diagonal, d = [(36)² + (24)²]¹/² = 43.3mm, which may be substituted for w in equation 11.25.

As illustrated in figure 11.17c, the 50mm lens has a horizontal viewing angle of 40°; telephoto lenses (small viewing angle) have large focal lengths, and wide-angle lenses have small focal lengths. Figure 11.17b shows that for a fixed camera distance, increasing the focal length decreases the amount of the object that is in view. Alternatively, the camera distance may be changed to include the same portion of the scene for different focal lengths. As illustrated in figure 11.17c, closer distances correspond to the smaller focal lengths, and result in a greater perspective effect.

The perspective projection may be viewed with the picture plane placed at different locations, as illustrated in figure 11.18. A camera has a picture plane (film plane) placed at position 1 in figure 11.18. Position 1 is on the side of the viewpoint away from the object, so the image becomes inverted as it passes through the viewpoint (the viewpoint in this case corresponds to the camera lens). When the picture plane is placed between the viewpoint and the object (position 2), the image has the same orientation as the object, and it is smaller than the object—the image ranges from zero size to the object's size as the picture plane moves from the viewpoint to the object. When the picture plane is placed beyond the object (position 3 in the figure), the image is larger than the object.

Because the projection lines are straight from the object through the viewpoint, the image does not change shape when the picture plane is moved; only the size changes. To eliminate inverted images, a front clipping plane may be placed in the view direction in front of the viewpoint (camera position). The front clipping plane eliminates all objects behind the plane from the view. If a perspective view is programmed without a front clipping plane, then as the viewpoint passes through the object, an inverted image appears when the

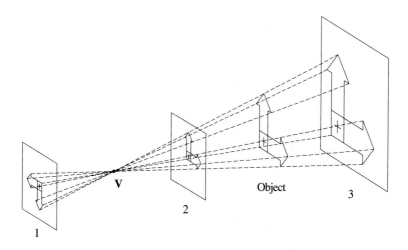

Figure 11.18   An object (flat arrows) projected on to three different picture planes in a perspective view. Projection lines from the object's vertices converge at the viewpoint **V**.

object is behind the viewpoint (for example, an inverted image appears when the view is toward picture plane 1 in figure 11.18). With the AutoCAD DVIEW command, the front clipping plane is placed at the viewpoint until it is changed by the CLip option. Also, a back clipping plane may be placed with the CLip option. Of course, four other clipping planes (left, right, top, bottom) occur along the edges of the viewport's drawing area.

The geometry for the perspective projection illustrated in figures 11.6b and 11.18 is reproduced in figure 11.19 for a view toward the front face of a beveled cube. Here the target point is the origin of the world-coordinate system, located at the lower-left rear corner of the cube.

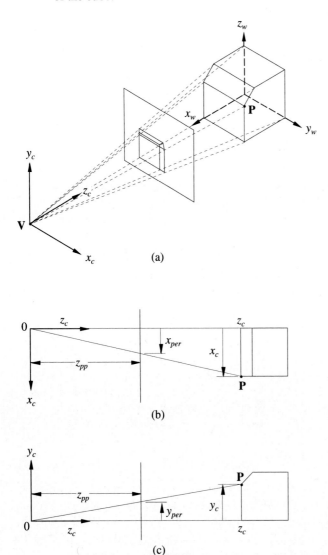

Figure 11.19 Geometry for a perspective projection: (a) isometric view shows the camera- and world-coordinate systems; (b) top view shows the projection line from point **P**; (c) side view of projection line from **P**.

From the top view of the projection (figure 11.19b), similar triangles provide the following relation between the projection distance x_{per} on the picture plane and the coordinate value x_c of point **P** on the object, as measured with the camera-coordinate system based at the viewpoint **V**:

$$\frac{x_{per}}{x_c} = \frac{z_{pp}}{z_c}, \quad \text{or} \quad x_{per} = \frac{x_c z_{pp}}{z_c} \tag{11.26}$$

Similarly, figure 11.19c provides the following relation for y_{per}.

$$y_{per} = \frac{y_c z_{pp}}{z_c} \tag{11.27}$$

Equations 11.26–27 show that the size of the perspective image is proportional to the picture-plane distance z_{pp} divided by the distance z_c to the object point, both measured from the viewpoint. These equations may be put into the form of a perspective-projection matrix $[P_{per}]$, which is similar to the scaling matrix with a scale factor z_{pp}/z_c. That is, the projection coordinates (x_{per}, y_{per}) may be obtained from the axonometric coordinates (x_c, y_c, z_c) by the transformation $\mathbf{P}_{per} = \mathbf{P}_c\,[P_{per}]$, which is written as

$$[x_{per} \quad y_{per} \quad 0 \quad 1] = [x_c \quad y_c \quad z_c \quad 1]\begin{bmatrix} \dfrac{z_{pp}}{z_c} & 0 & 0 & 0 \\ 0 & \dfrac{z_{pp}}{z_c} & 0 & 0 \\ 0 & 0 & 0 & 0 \\ 0 & 0 & 0 & 1 \end{bmatrix} \tag{11.28}$$

When the viewpoint lies at the same z-coordinate as the object point **P**, $z_c = 0$, which leads to a divergence in equations 11.26–28. Thus a floating-point error can occur when programming a perspective projection, unless a front clipping plane is used to restrict z_c to finite values.

The transformation 11.28 may be used to plot perspective views, like those in figure 11.20. Wireframe views of the beveled cube are shown in this figure to illustrate the effect of perspective; namely, that the faces closest to the viewpoint appear larger than the more distant faces. Thus perspective helps the observer determine the proper orientation of an object. The view angles presented in figure 11.20 are also shown in figure 11.14 for axonometric views (where hidden edges were eliminated to avoid confusion—in an axonometric view, a wireframe object appears the same when the view direction is reversed).

The Two-Point Perspective Projection

For architectural photography, a two-point perspective image can be obtained by tilting the back of a view camera so that the film plane is parallel to the vertical edges of the building. (Also, some 35mm cameras offer special perspective-control lenses for architectural photography.) Tilting a view camera back is equivalent to the computer operation of restricting the viewing to horizontal directions (perpendicular to the building's edges).

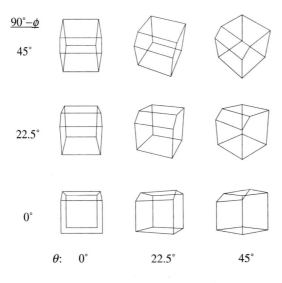

Figure 11.20 Perspective projections of a beveled cube, with θ being the view rotation angle in the xy-plane, and $90° - \phi$ being the rotation angle *from* the xy-plane.

When the view is in the horizontal direction, as in figure 11.19, the z_c distance is constant along the entire length of a vertical edge. Thus the scale factor z_{pp}/z_c for the perspective transformation remains constant, yielding a constant perspective distance x_{per} (because x_w and y_w are constant along a vertical line, x_c is constant in equation 11.26). Therefore, vertical edges on the object are plotted as parallel vertical lines in the perspective view if the view direction is horizontal.

Figure 11.21 shows four perspective views of the Seagram Building, which may be compared with the axonometric views in figure 11.15. In figure 11.21a the view angle is upward and in 11.21b it is downward, with the result that the building's edges converge toward the top in 11.21a and toward the bottom in 11.21b. Placing the target points at the same height as the camera, rather than at the building's center, produces the two-point perspective images shown in figures 11.21c and d. That is, the only difference between 11.21a and c (and between 11.21b and d) is the placement of the target point.

With AutoCAD's DVIEW command, the target point is in the center of the screen, so that the Zoom option may be required to display the entire image when the target point is placed at camera level near the bottom or top of the building. Note that the Zoom option changes only the size of the image, not its shape, whereas the PAn option changes the shape for a perspective view because PAn changes the camera position. For plotting an image on paper, the Extents plotting option may be used to ensure that the entire image is placed on the paper, even when it is not fully displayed on the computer screen.

Interactive Viewing

AutoCAD's DVIEW command permits dynamic viewing, with the camera position (viewpoint) changed by mouse motions. The Microsoft C program listed below simulates the CAmera option under DVIEW. In the subroutine moveViewpoint(), the view angle θ in the xy-plane is changed when the mouse x-coordinate is changed, and the angle ϕ from the

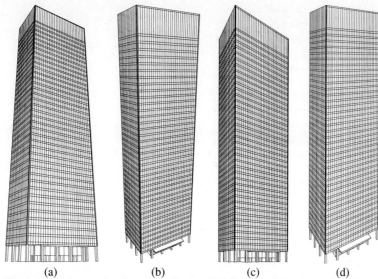

(a)	(b)	(c)	(d)

Figure 11.21   Perspective views of the Seagram Building designed by Mies van der Rohe and Philip Johnson: (a) and (b) target point at the building's center; (c) and (d) target point at the same height as the camera, which is just above ground level in (a) and (c) and at about 80% of the building's height in (b) and (d).

z-axis is changed with the mouse y-coordinate. The algebraic relations given in the subroutine drawCube() incorporate the axonometric transformation (11.23), followed by the perspective transformation (11.28). The wireframe image of the cube in perspective appears on the screen as depicted in figure 11.20.

The functions mouseInit() and mouseRead() are the same functions defined in appendix A. The minimum values *xmin* and *ymin* read by the mouse are set to $-32,000$, and the maximum values *xmax* and *ymax* are set to 32,000. These large values permit mouse motion to produce a large number of rotations in any direction. The large range of mouse x- and y-values is even more important for the last program in this section, which involves movement through a scene in the xy-plane; small values for *x* and *y* limits, such as those used previously, would restrict the simulated motion to only part of the total scene.

The line segments that represent the wireframe for a beveled cube are specified in the declaration of the global data type for the array *lines*[*i*][*j*]. The first index *i* in *lines*[*i*][*j*] is the line number, and the second index *j* includes six values representing the world coordinates (*xw,yw,zw*) for the start and end of the line segment.

The radius *r* given in the subroutine moveViewpoint() is the camera-to-target distance, as pictured in figure 11.12 for a target at the origin of the world-coordinate system. To treat a target at an arbitrary point (*xt,yt,zt*), one must subtract the target coordinates from the vertex coordinates to give world coordinates (*xw,yw,zw*) that have their origin at the target point; see the subroutine drawCube(). The effect of perspective is determined by the value for camera-to-target distance *r,* which can be changed in the program. Alternatively, the program could be enhanced to permit *r* values to be entered by the program user; see exercise 11.16.

```
#include <conio.h>
#include <stdio.h>
#include <graph.h>
#include <dos.h>
#include <math.h>

#define ESC          27
#define RETURN       13
#define MOUSE        51
#define LEFT_BUTTON 1
#define PI           3.141593

int     mouseInit(void),mouseRead(void);
void    moveViewpoint(void),drawCube(void);

union   REGS reg;
int     x,y,dx,dy,button,mouseData;
int     xold=-1,yold=-1,xref=-1,yref=-1, buttonfref=-1
int     xmin=-32000,xmax=32000,ymin=-32000,ymax=32000;
int     nLines=15;
double  xw,yw,zw,xt,yt,zt,r,theta,sint,cost,phi,sinp,cosp;
double  lines[15][6] ={{100,0,0,100,100,0},
    {100,100,0,100,100,75},{100,100,75,100,0,75},{100,0,75,100,0,0},
    {100,0,0,0,0,0},{0,0,0,0,0,100},{0,0,100,75,0,100},
    {75,0,100,100,0,75},{100,100,0,0,100,0},{0,100,0,0,100,100},
    {0,100,100,75,100,100},{75,100,100,100,100,75},
    {75,0,100,75,100,100},{0,0,100,0,100,100},{0,0,0,0,100,0}};

void main(void)
{
    _setvideomode ( _VRES16COLOR );
    if (mouseInit() == 0)
    {
        printf ("Error, mouse isn't working\n");
        exit(1);
    }

    moveViewpoint();

    _setvideomode ( _DEFAULTMODE);
}

void moveViewpoint(void)
{
    xold = 320; yold = 240;
    xt = 50; yt = 50; zt = 50;
    r = 300;
    theta = 0; phi = PI/2;
    do
```

```
        {
            mouseData = mouseRead();
            dx = x - xold; dy = y - yold;
            theta = theta + .01*dx; phi = phi + .01*dy;
            sint = sin(theta); cost = cos(theta);
            sinp = sin(phi); cosp = cos(phi);

            _clearscreen(_GCLEARSCREEN);
            drawCube();
            xold = x; yold = y;
        } while(mouseData != ESC);
    }


void drawCube(void)
{
    int     i,j;
    double xc,yc,zc,xper,yper,zpp=500;

    for (i=0; i<nLines; i++)
    {
        for (j=0; j<=3; j=j+3)
        {
            xw = lines[i][j] - xt; yw = lines[i][j+1] - yt;
            zw = lines[i][j+2] - zt;
            xc = -xw*sint + yw*cost;
            yc = -xw*cosp*cost - yw*cosp*sint + zw*sinp;
            zc = -xw*sinp*cost - yw*sinp*sint -zw*cosp + r;
            xper = xc*zpp/zc; yper = yc*zpp/zc;
            if (j==0)
                _moveto(320 + (int) xper,240 - (int) yper);
            else
                _lineto(320 + (int) xper,240 - (int) yper);
        }
    }
}
```

A transformation is made to screen coordinates for drawing the image with the Microsoft C _moveto() and _lineto() functions. This transformation includes translation to the screen center (320,240) and reflection of the y-coordinate, but no scale factor is used because the scale has been adjusted by selecting an appropriate picture plane distance z_{pp}.

Because the viewpoint is moving in the above program, the cube turns in a direction opposite to the mouse motion. Thus the user feels that he is "flying" around the cube on a sphere of radius r. (Of course, programming a flight simulator requires consideration of translations as well as rotations; see Penna and Patterson 1986.)

In the next example, motion along the radius r is considered along with rotation in the xy-plane. In the subroutine moveViewpoint() listed below, the radius is incremented by changes in the mouse y-position (downward motion increases r), and the angle θ in the xy-plane is changed with the mouse x-position. Because motion is restricted to the xy-plane, which corresponds to $\phi = 90°$, the angle ϕ does not explicitly enter into the transformation given in the new drawCube() subroutine listed below.

```
void moveViewpoint(void)
{
    xold = 320; yold = 240;
    xt = 50; yt = 50; zt = 50;
    r = 300; theta = 0;
    do
    {
        mouseData = mouseRead();
        dx = x - xold; dy = y - yold;
        theta = theta + .01*dx;
        r = r + dy;
        sint = sin(theta); cost = cos(theta);

        _clearscreen(_GCLEARSCREEN);
        drawCube();
        xold = x; yold = y;
    } while(mouseData != ESC);
}


void drawCube(void)
{
    int     i,j;
    double xc,yc,zc,xper,yper,zpp=500;

    for (i=0; i<nLines; i++)
    {
        for (j=0; j<=3; j=j+3)
        {
            xw = lines[i][j] - xt; yw = lines[i][j+1] - yt;
            zw = lines[i][j+2] - zt;
            xc = -xw*sint + yw*cost;
            yc = zw;
            zc = -xw*cost - yw*sint + r;
            xper = xc*zpp/zc; yper = yc*zpp/zc;
            if (j==0)
                _moveto(320 + (int) xper,240 - (int) yper);
            else
                _lineto(320 + (int) xper,240 - (int) yper);
        }
    }
}
```

The perspective transformation (11.28) assumes that the viewpoint is outside the cube. When the viewpoint is moved inside, additional lines appear. When the viewpoint travels all the way through the cube, the image appears inverted. This inverted image corresponds to the configuration given by picture plane position 1 in figure 11.18, where the object is behind the direction of view.

A clipping plane may be placed in front of the viewpoint to eliminate the inverted image and the extra lines that appear when the viewpoint is inside the object. Object edges are clipped at this front plane, ensuring that all clipped lines have endpoints lying in front of the viewpoint.

In the above subroutines, the translation of the viewpoint was constrained to the radius connected to the target point. To permit arbitrary motion in the xy-plane, the subroutine walkThrough() in appendix B (listing 11.1) replaces the moveViewpoint() subroutine

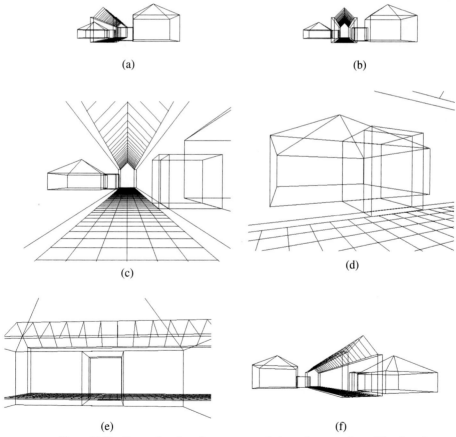

Figure 11.22   Perspective views from a program that uses the mouse for walking through a scene.

above. Listing 11.1 of appendix B also includes the subroutine drawScene(), which replaces the drawCube() subroutine. The subroutine drawScene() includes front plane clipping, so that the viewpoint may pass through objects in the scene.

The walkThrough() and drawScene() subroutines in listing 11.1 may be used with the lines[][] data for the beveled cube. However, a fuller scene provides a more interesting test of the program. The subroutine loadLines() given in listing 11.1 uses 230 line segments to construct a rough approximation to a house, based on the gallery house designs of Cesar Pelli.

Some images from the above program are presented in figure 11.22. The initial viewpoint and target point provided in the subroutine walkThrough() yield the scene shown in figure 11.22a. In this initial scene, the viewpoint is situated in front and to the right of the gallery entrance, but the initial view angle is parallel to the main axis of the gallery. Thus, without depressing the mouse button, mouse movement leads to the gallery entrance and down the corridor, as depicted in figures 11.22b and c.

Once the entrance to the room on the left is reached, the mouse button may be depressed to turn into the room as shown in 11.22d. Figure 11.22e shows the gallery as viewed from inside the room, and 11.22f shows a rear view of the house.

EXERCISES

11.1 Derive equations 11.8 by carrying out the matrix multiplication for a $-60°$ rotation about the x-axis. Also, invert equations 11.8 to obtain x_w, y_w, and z_w as functions of x_u, y_u, and z_u.

11.2 Draw a building similar to the one shown in figure 11.15. To draw windows on a 3dface of the building, set up a UCS on the face and draw line arrays, as illustrated in figure 11.3.

11.3 By writing out the matrices and multiplying them, verify that the matrix equation 11.11 yields the algebraic relations 11.9.

11.4 For the front view of the beveled cube shown in figure 11.5, write down the algebraic relations between screen coordinates (x_s, y_s) and the world coordinates (y_w, z_w). Then, express these relations in terms of the product of reflection, orthographic projection, scale, and translation matrices. The reflection matrix is needed in this case because the direction of positive y_s is opposite to the direction of positive z_w.

11.5 Carry out the analysis of problem 11.4 for the plot coordinates (x_{plot}, y_{plot}) rather than for the screen coordinates (x_s, y_s).

11.6 For the right-side view of the beveled cube shown in figure 11.5, write down the algebraic relations between plot coordinates (x_{plot}, y_{plot}) and the world coordinates (x_w, z_w). Then, express these relations in terms of the product of reflection, orthographic projection, scale, and translation matrices.

11.7 Carry out the analysis of problem 11.6 for the screen coordinates (x_s, y_s) rather than for the plot coordinates (x_{plot}, y_{plot}).

11.8 Write a program that draws the orthographic and isometric projections of the beveled cube shown in figure 11.5.

11.9 The oblique projection presented in section 11.3 can be represented by a shearing followed by an orthogonal projection; that is, $\mathbf{P}_{plot} = \mathbf{P}_w[\mathrm{SH}_x][\mathrm{P}_x]$. The shear and orthogonal projection matrices are

$$[SH_x] = \begin{bmatrix} 1 & SH_{xy} & SH_{xz} & 0 \\ 0 & 1 & 0 & 0 \\ 0 & 0 & 1 & 0 \\ 0 & 0 & 0 & 1 \end{bmatrix}, \quad [P_x] = \begin{bmatrix} 0 & 0 & 0 & 0 \\ 1 & 0 & 0 & 0 \\ 0 & 1 & 0 & 0 \\ 0 & 0 & 0 & 1 \end{bmatrix}$$

The shear matrix leaves the x-coordinates unchanged, but increases the y-coordinates by the amount $SH_{xy}x$ and increases the z-coordinates by $SH_{xz}x$. Reference to figure 11.9 shows that the shear terms are $SH_{xy} = -f\cos\alpha$ and $SH_{xz} = -f\sin\alpha$, where the factor f equals 1 for the Cavalier projection shown in figure 11.9. Evaluate the product of $[SH_x]$ and $[P_x]$ to show that it equals the oblique projection matrix $[P_{obl}]$ given in equation 11.20.

11.10 Write a program that draws the oblique projections of the beveled cube shown in figure 11.10.

11.11 On your CAD system construct a cabinet oblique view with $\alpha = 30°$ of a stereo cabinet, or a file cabinet such as the one shown in figure 11.11.

11.12 Derive equation 11.23 by substituting matrices into equation 11.22 and carrying out the matrix multiplications.

11.13 Write a program that simulates the AutoCAD VPOINT command. The program should display an axonometric view based on data supplied as viewpoint coordinates, or as two angles representing rotations in the xy-plane and from the xy-plane. Use a beveled cube as the test wireframe object and check your views with the ones shown in figure 11.14.

11.14 On your CAD system construct a beveled cube either with lines for a wireframe object or with 3DFACES as an object with surfaces. Then view this object at several of the angles shown in figure 11.14.

11.15 Implement the program given in section 11.4 for dynamic viewing of an object. That is, the rotation of a beveled cube around two axes is determined by mouse movement in two directions.

11.16 Generalize the dynamic viewing program of section 11.4 to include user input of the camera-to-target distances r from the keyboard, along with the angle changes entered by the mouse motion.

11.17 Repeat exercise 11.15 with rotation out of the xy-plane replaced by motion forward and backward along lines toward a target at the cube's center.

11.18 Repeat exercise 11.17 with the target for rotation in the xy-plane occurring a fixed distance ahead in the direction of motion, so that the beveled cube may be "walked around," as described in section 11.4.

11.19 Repeat one of the exercises 11.15–11.18 with the beveled cube replaced by a wireframe representation of a computer monitor, as illustrated below.

11.20 Implement the walkThrough() and drawScene() subroutines given in listing 11.1 of appendix B. Use the array lines[][] for the beveled cube as your scene.

11.21 Implement walkThrough() and drawScene() with the house data provided by the subroutine loadLines() given in listing 11.1 of appendix B.

11.22 Improve the house scene by adding more blocks to represent windows in the gallery walls (for detailing in the gallery houses by Pelli, see the book *Cesar Pelli: Buildings and Projects*

1965–1990. New York: Rizzoli, 1990). Also, use colors to differentiate the various parts of the house.

BIBLIOGRAPHY

AMMERAAL, L., *Programming Principles in Computer Graphics.* Chichester, West Sussex, England: John Wiley & Sons, 1986.

ANAND, V. B., *Computer Graphics and Geometric Modeling for Engineers.* New York: John Wiley & Sons, 1993.

ANGEL, E., *Computer Graphics.* Reading, Mass.: Addison-Wesley Publishing Co., 1990.

AutoCAD Release 12 Reference Manual. Sausalito, Calif.: Autodesk, Inc., 1992.

DEMEL, J. T., AND M. J. MILLER, *Introduction to Computer Graphics.* Belmont, Calif.: Brooks/Cole Division of Wadsworth, Inc., 1984.

FOLEY, J. D., A. VAN DAM, S. K. FEINER, AND J. F. HUGHES, *Computer Graphics: Principles and Practice,* 2nd ed. Reading, Mass.: Addison-Wesley Publishing Co., 1990.

PENNA, M. A., AND R. R. PATTERSON, *Projective Geometry and Its Applications to Computer Graphics.* Englewood Cliffs, N. J.: Prentice-Hall, 1986.

ROGERS, D. F., AND J. A. ADAMS, *Mathematical Elements for Computer Graphics,* 2nd ed. New York: McGraw-Hill Publishing Co., 1990.

12

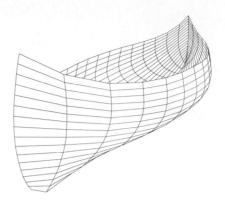

Surface Modeling

At the end of the preceding chapter, 3-D views were constructed for wireframe objects composed of line segments. Although suitable for simple objects, wireframe images can become cluttered with lines when used to represent complex objects. Complex objects should be displayed by means of a surface or solid representation.

Solid modeling (treated in chapter 13) provides the most complete representation. A solid model describes an object's material properties as well as its shape, including filled interior regions. A solid model of a mechanical part can be sent to numerically controlled machinery to construct the part.

Although less complete than a solid model, a surface model can represent objects accurately and realistically. A surface representation permits implementation of a hidden-line algorithm for more clearly displaying the object. Furthermore, textures can be mapped onto surfaces for use in rendered scenes with full color, lighting, reflections, and shadows. (Rendering is discussed in chapter 14.)

Figure 12.1 illustrates the basic procedures used by AutoCAD for generating surfaces. The simplest procedures consist of giving thickness to lines and curves by extruding them in the normal direction (z-direction), or by extruding them in an arbitrary direction with the TABSURF command. These extrusion procedures are the subject of section 12.1.

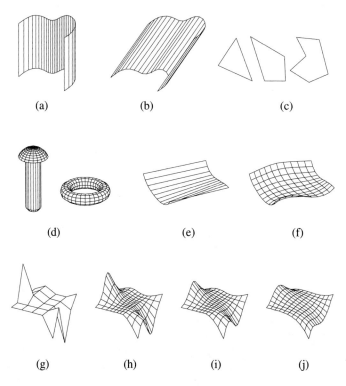

Figure 12.1 Examples of AutoCAD surfaces: (a) a polyline extruded with the Thickness option under the CHPROP command; (b) a polyline extruded in an arbitrary direction with the TABSURF command;(c) individual faces constructed with 3DFACE or PFACE; (d) surfaces of revolution drawn using REVSURF; (e) a ruled surface constructed with RULESURF; (f) a Coons patch constructed with EDGESURF; (g) a rectangular mesh drawn using the 3DMESH command, with three smoothing options to produce a quadratic B-spline surface (h), a cubic B-spline surface (i), and a Bézier surface (j).

In chapter 8 triangular faces were programmed into a DXF file representing surfaces built up with the 3DFACE command. Section 12.2 presents further study of the 3DFACE command, along with the command PFACE for more general polygon faces (figure 12.1c). Because the 3DFACE and PFACE commands build up faces one by one, they are normally used with programming, such as AutoLISP subroutines or programmed DXF files like the ones in sections 8.2 and 12.2. Also, 3Dfaces and pfaces can be used to connect, or stitch together, other surface meshes.

The PFACE command creates a general polygon mesh, whereas the 3DMESH command creates a topologically rectangular mesh. The 3Dmesh can be edited with the PEDIT command, but the topological complexity of the general polygon mesh precludes editing. For a 3Dmesh, the PEDIT command makes it possible to move vertices and smooth surfaces. In the three smoothing options available in AutoCAD, the mesh is used as a frame to generate a Bézier surface, a quadratic B-spline surface, or a cubic B-spline surface.

Rectangular meshes can be generated not only with the 3DMESH command, but also with the AutoCAD commands TABSURF, REVSURF, RULESURF, and EDGESURF. Surfaces generated with these commands can be edited with PEDIT.

In section 12.3 a program is given for generating a surface of revolution. This program simulates the AutoCAD REVSURF command. As illustrated in figure 12.1d, useful surfaces can be generated from open or closed curves. With REVSURF, a vertex point on the curve is rotated around an axis to place surface vertices on a circle (that is, equidistant from the axis). In section 12.3, a more general rotational sweep is programmed to place vertices on a "superellipse" rather than on a circle. This program produces surfaces with cross sections that can vary continuously from rectangular to elliptical shapes. Another program is used to construct a helical tube as an example of a rotational sweep around a curved axis.

In section 12.4, ruled surfaces are discussed. As an example, the simple canoe hull shown on page 323 is constructed with the command RULESURF. The ruled lines (like boards on a wood canoe) extend between adjacent cross sections.

Although a ruled surface is used to construct a ruled surface between two curved lines, a bicubic Coons patch is used (section 12.5) to represent a surface connecting four curves in space that meet at their endpoints; see figure 12.1f. The Coons patch, implemented in AutoCAD with the EDGESURF command, is useful for making connections between surfaces. Also, Coons patches can be joined to provide smoother surfaces than those constructed from ruled surfaces (note the discontinuous slopes at the joints between ruled surface sections in the canoe figure).

The generation of 3Dmeshes is described in section 12.6, followed by sections analyzing the smoothed surfaces, such as those produced by using the AutoCAD PEDIT command on meshes. The smoothed surfaces discussed in section 12.7 are constucted from uniform B-splines, and the surfaces described in section 12.8 are formed from nonuniform rational B-splines (NURBS).

Some advanced features used by the NURBS-based surface modeler AutoSurf® are discussed in section 12.9. AutoSurf capabilities include creating general swept surfaces, joining and trimming surfaces, finding surface intersection lines, blending surfaces, and forming surface fillets.

As noted above, when objects with surfaces are modeled, hidden lines can be removed from a scene. In section 12.10 examples of simple hidden-line algorithms are developed.

12.1 EXTRUDED LINES AND CURVES

Extrusion in the Z-Direction: Thickness of Lines and Curves

As illustrated in figure 12.2, lines and curves may be extruded to produce surfaces in AutoCAD. Line segments, polylines, circles, arcs, and other 2-D drawing entities are extruded in the z-direction of the current user coordinate system (UCS) when the Thickness option is selected under the CHPROP (change properties) command. That is, after a line segment or other entity is drawn, it is extruded by the following statements:

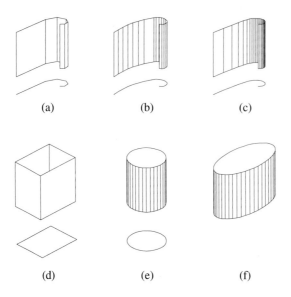

(a)   (b)   (c)

(d)   (e)   (f)

Figure 12.2 Examples of 2-D drawing entities being extruded by giving them thickness with the CHPROP command. Views are at an angle of 30° to the xy-plane in which the following 2-D entities lie: (a) a polyline and extruded surface shown above it; (b) the polyline smoothed with the Fit option; (c) the polyline smoothed with the Spline option; (d) a closed polyline with its extrusion representing the side walls of an open box; (e) circle with its extrusion exhibiting a top face; (f) the circle inserted from a block with different x and y scale factors.

```
Command: CHPROP
Select objects: (select with mouse)
Change what property (Color/Elev/LAyer/LType/Thickness)? T
New thickness <0.0000>: 3.25
Change what property (Color/Elev/LAyer/LType/Thickness)? (RETURN)
```

This operation can also be performed with the CHANGE command, which adds the prompt

```
                    Properties/<Change point>.
```

The Change point option may be used to change a circle radius, a line endpoint, the position and rotation angle of an inserted block, and text characteristics (font style, height, rotation angle, and new text).

Changing the thickness of lines and curves is a very simple and effective way of generating surfaces. For example, walls of a house drawn in a plan view can be given thickness to produce walls for elevation and axonometric views.

The lines (generatrices) in the z-direction that generate the surface from the unsmoothed polyline (figure 12.2a) will originate at each vertex of the polyline. Polylines that are smoothed with the Fit or Spline options will have generatrices determined by the number of line segments in the smoothed curves (this number will change with the value of the system variable VIEWRES). As illustrated in figures 12.2b–c, the smoothed polylines with thickness are drawn with the most generatrices where the curvature is greatest. This result is in contrast to the uniform spacing of generatrices produced by the other AutoCAD commands (TABSURF, REVSURF, RULESURF, and EDGESURF).

All surfaces discussed in this chapter will cover lines behind them with the HIDE command (or with the hidden-line option selected during plotting). It should be noted that giving thickness to closed curves and polygons produces only surfaces around the edges, with no top surfaces spanning the closed curves or polygons (see the rectangle in figure 12.2d). One exception to the preceding statement is circles, which hide objects behind them (figures 12.2e–f).

Thickness can be specified as a positive or negative value to produce a surface generated from the curve in the positive or negative z-direction. The surfaces in figure 12.2 were generated with positive thickness values (the curves below the surfaces are included to illustrate the starting curve shape at the bottom of each surface—the actual curve for the surface is at the bottom of the surface). The cylinder with elliptic cross section shown in figure 12.2f was not generated from an ellipse, but was produced from the circular cylinder in 12.2e (which was saved as a block and inserted at a rotated angle and with different x and y scaling). Note that the top face of this elliptic cylinder hides the lines behind it.

Extrusion in an Arbitrary Direction: Tabulated Surfaces

A curve is extruded in an arbitrary direction with the AutoCAD TABSURF command. The curve may be a line, circle, arc, 2-D polyline, or a 3-D polyline. The extrusion direction and length are determined by selecting a line that has been drawn in the desired direction. The surface starts with the curve (called *path curve* in AutoCAD) and has a length equal to the length of the selected direction line, with its extrusion being in the direction of the longest part of the line from the point picked. That is, for the surfaces in figures 12.3a–f,

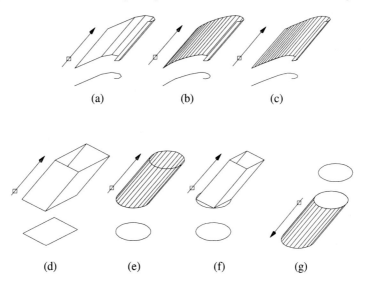

Figure 12.3 Examples of 2-D drawing entities being extruded along an arbitrary direction with the TABSURF command. Views are at an angle of 30° to the xy-plane containing the following entities: (a) an unsmoothed polyline; (b) the polyline smoothed with the Fit option; (c) the polyline smoothed with the Spline option; (d) a closed polyline; (e) and (f), a circle with the direction vector pointing toward the upper right; (g) the circle with the direction vector pointing toward the lower left.

the direction line shown on the left of each surface was selected near its bottom (pick box shown on direction line), whereas the direction line in 12.3g was selected near its top in order to extrude the path curve downward (the arrow on a direction line shows the extrusion direction).

The tabulated surface is generated by the following statements.

```
Command: TABSURF
Select path curve: (select with mouse)
Select direction vector: (select with mouse)
```

For an unsmoothed polyline (figure 12.3a), the generatrices originate at each vertex of the polyline to bound the faces on the tabulated surface. Note that the number of faces formed equals the number of generatrices minus one (if the original polyline has n vertices, then there are $n-1$ faces). For smoothed polylines, arcs, and circles, the number of faces is determined by the system variable SURFTAB1. To reset the value of SURFTAB1, the word SURFTAB1 can be entered on the command prompt, and then a new value entered. (Alternatively, the SETVAR command can be used first when resetting system variables, but this is unnecessary if you already know the variable name). SURFTAB1 was set to 16 for figures 12.3b–c, to 24 for 12.3e and g, and 4 for 12.3f.

When the value of SURFTAB1 is changed, surfaces previously constructed retain the number of faces with which they were constructed. Thus any tabulated curved surface in a drawing can have any desired number of faces. However, the number of faces on a surface generated by giving thickness to a curve is controlled by the system variable VIEWRES, and the number of faces shown on the surface will change any time VIEWRES is changed.

Note that unlike the circle with thickness in 12.1e, the circle is not translated to the end of the tabulated surface. If the direction line points downward, as in figure 12.3g, then the original circle appears at the top and will hide lines behind it. Of course, a circle could be easily drawn at the top of the tabulated surface in figure 12.3e to form a top face.

12.2 POLYGON FACES

Polygon faces are constructed in AutoCAD with the 3DFACE and PFACE commands. Individual faces can be joined to form surfaces of almost any shape.

The 3DFACE command was used in section 8.2 to construct triangular faces. In this section quadrilateral 3Dfaces will be constructed. Also, polygons of more than four sides are formed by multiple 3Dfaces joined at invisible edges. The 3DFACE command permits the user to specify which edges are invisible. Even though the 3DFACE command may be used to construct any group of polygons, the PFACE command is more convenient when constructing complex polygons. With the PFACE command, all the vertices in an arbitrary polygon net are numbered as their coordinates are entered, and then the faces are defined by specifying the vertex numbers for each face.

Building Surfaces with the 3DFACE and BLOCK Commands

The 3DFACE command is most useful in constructing triangular or quadrilateral faces one by one. Consider a unit cube with its diagonal extending from the origin (0,0,0) to the point (1,1,1). The top face of the cube may be constructed with the following AutoCAD statements.

```
Command: 3DFACE
First point: 0,0,1
Second point: 1,0,1
Third point: 1,1,1
Fourth point: 0,1,1
Third point: (RETURN)
```

The four sets of coordinate values given for the above 3DFACE command determine the square face at the top of the cube. Pressing the RETURN key at the end completes the face. If additional coordinates were entered at the final "Third point" prompt, then a second face adjoining the first face would be started. An edge will be invisible (not drawn) if the letter i is entered before coordinates are entered for the first vertex on the edge.

The DXF file for a quadrilateral face will have the same form as shown in section 8.2 for a triangular face. For the triangular face, four sets of vertex coordinates are given, with one set being the duplicate of another; for a quadrilateral face, all four sets of coordinates are distinct. Thus the triangular face may be considered to be the equivalent of a quadrilateral face in which two of the vertices have the same coordinates. This conclusion is consistent with the fact that a triangular face is entered with the same number of entries as shown above, except that the RETURN key is pressed on the last two prompts, thereby giving the fourth point the same coordinates as the third point. (Alternatively, a triangular face may be constructed by entering four sets of coordinates, but with the coordinates of one vertex duplicating the coordinates of an adjacent vertex.)

The cube may be completed by using the 3DFACE command to construct the remaining five faces. Alternatively, a unit square in the world plan view may be given unit thickness to construct the four sides, with only the top and bottom faces constructed with the 3DFACE command. Of course, the top and bottom faces could also be constructed by giving thickness to lines, but this requires changing to a user-coordinate system having its z-axis in the extrusion direction for the top and bottom faces.

AutoCAD also permits construction of some basic 3-D objects with an AutoLISP subroutine accessed from an AutoCAD menu item labeled "3D objects." The objects included under this menu item are a box, pyramid, wedge, dome (upper hemisphere), sphere, cone, torus, dish (lower hemisphere), and mesh. Although some time may be saved by constructing these objects from the menu, they can readily be constructed from the main AutoCAD surface commands discussed in this chapter (see exercise 12.11).

The unit cube constructed from 3Dfaces (or by other means) can be very useful if it is saved with the BLOCK command. As discussed in section 5.3, the INSERT command permits the block to be placed anywhere in a drawing, with any desired scaling. In three dimensions, the unit cube saved as a block called UCUBE is inserted into the drawing with the following operations.

```
Command: INSERT
Block name (or ?): UCUBE
 Insertion point: 0.25,1.08,0
X scale factor <1>/Corner/XYZ: XYZ
X scale factor <1>/Corner: 0.1
Y scale factor <default=X>: 2.15
Z scale factor <default=X>: 5.17
Rotation angle <0>: (RETURN)
```

To illustrate this block insertion procedure, the unit cube was inserted with scaling in order to represent boards that make up the chair shown in figure 12.4. The data for the chair were measured from an illustration showing orthographic views in the book by Meadmore (1975). The coordinates of a corner point and dimensions for each board are given in table 12.1 in arbitrary units (which depended on the measuring scale and picture size). Because the cube is of unit size, the scale factors in the three directions are exactly the board lengths in those directions. Inserting the cube with the appropriate coordinate and scaling data was efficient; it required less time than measuring the orthographic views for the construction of the table.

Using 3Dfaces to Build Fractal Mountains

Fractal geometry involves patterns that repeat on smaller and smaller scales, often with random variations introduced at each scale. In computer graphics, fractal geometry is often used to produce natural objects, such as plants and mountains. In this section, a mountain surface is described by a simple fractal model based on a triangular planform.

Figure 12.5 illustrates the triangular planform of the mountain, which is divided into increasingly smaller triangular elements. The single triangle, called level 0 in this proce-

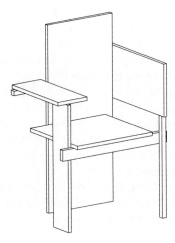

Figure 12.4 Axonometric view of the Berlin chair, designed by Gerrit Rietveld in 1923.

TABLE 12.1 BLOCK DATA FOR RIETVELD'S BERLIN CHAIR

No.	Insertion point	Length Δx	Length Δy	Length Δz
1	0.25, 1.08, 0	0.1	2.15	5.17
2	0, 0.12, 3.5	2.2	0.96	0.1
3	1.58, 0.38, 0	0.72	0.1	3.5
4	2.3, 0.12, 2.03	0.13	3.46	0.3
5	0.35, 0.48, 2.33	2.25	2.5	0.1
6	0.1, 3.23, 2.85	2.7	0.1	1.45
7	0.12, 0, 3.37	0.13	2.8	0.13
8	2.43, 3.33, 0	0.13	0.13	3.67

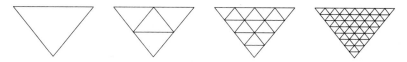

Figure 12.5 Plan views of a triangular fractal mountain, starting with a single triangle at level 0; 4 triangles at level 1; 16 triangles at level 2; and 64 triangles at level 3.

dure, is divided into 4 triangles at level 1, then each of these triangles is divided into 4 triangles to give a total of 16 triangles at level 2. This procedure may be continued to produce 64 triangles at level 3; 256 at level 4; 1,024 at level 5; etc. The total number of triangles at any level n may be computed from the formula $n_{triangles} = 4^n$.

The program given as listing 12.1 in appendix B builds a fractal mountain by carrying out random vertical displacements at each level of the base triangle subdivision, as illustrated in figure 12.6. That is, the three vertices of the level 0 triangle are first given random vertical displacements, then the four triangles of level 1 are displaced, then the 16 triangles of level 2, etc. The random displacements can be given different parameters to obtain different realizations of a fractal mountain; see figure 12.7. The parameters and program features are explained in listing 12.1.

Using 3Dfaces with Invisible Edges

For the next 3Dface example, consider the dodecahedron pictured in figure 12.8a. The dodecahedron surface is composed of pentagonal faces, from which five triangles can be constructed to form the geodesic dome shown in figure 12.8b. (Further refinement of the geodesic dome requires dividing each triangle into smaller triangles, similar to the procedure described in section 8.2.)

A single pentagon may be drawn with the 3DFACE command by entering two or three vertices in one direction, next entering the letter i followed by two vertices that are endpoints of an invisible edge across the polygon, and then entering the remaining vertices in the reverse direction. This procedure is illustrated by the following statements that construct a single pentagonal face at the top of the dodecahedron, as pictured at the right of the commands (with the invisible edge shown as a dashed line).

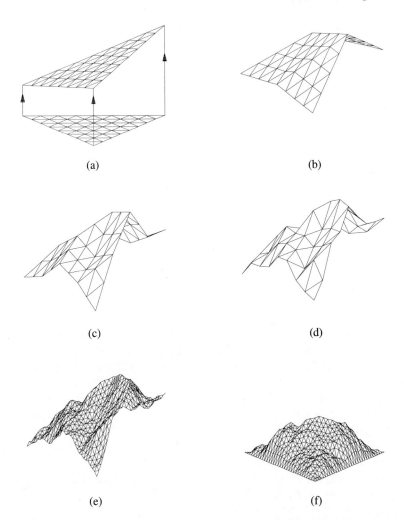

(a)   (b)

(c)   (d)

(e)   (f)

Figure 12.6   Generation of random displacements in a triangular surface viewed at an angle of 20° to the xy-plane, with 64 faces for *numLevel* = 3 in (a–d) and 1,024 faces for *numLevel* = 5 for (e) and (f): (a) initial displacement ($n = 0$) with arrows showing the vertical distance of the three boundary corners from the xy-plane; (b) surface after the $n = 1$ displacements of the 4 triangles containing 16 elements each; (c) after the $n = 2$ displacements of the 16 triangles containing 4 elements each; (d) after the $n = 3$ displacements of the 64 triangular elements; (e) surface of 1024 faces; (f) surface of 1024 faces with zero displacement at its triangular boundary.

```
Command: 3DFACE
First point: 0,0.8507,1.1135
Second point: 0.809,0.2629,1.1135
Third point: i (RETURN)
   0.5,-0.6882,1.1135
```

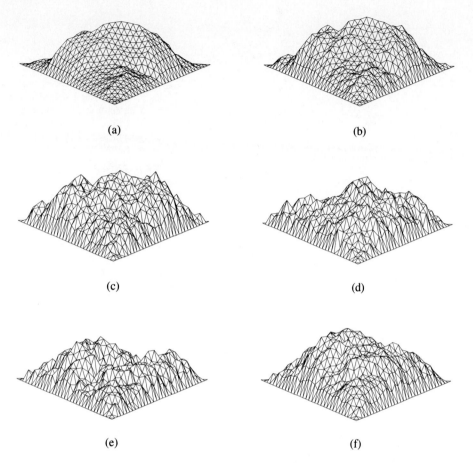

(a)   (b)

(c)   (d)

(e)   (f)

Figure 12.7   Mountain surfaces viewed at an angle of 20° to the xy-plane, with 1,024 faces for *numLevel* = 5: *(a)* displacement proportional to $0.3(dRows)^{1.5}$, with a random seed number of 5195; (b) displacement proportional to $0.8dRows$, with seed = 5195; (c) displacement proportional to $1.8(dRows)^{0.5}$, with seed = 5195; (d) displacement proportional to $1.8(dRows)^{0.5}$, with seed = 14242; (e) displacement proportional to $1.8(dRows)^{0.5}$, with seed = 24929; (f) mound added to a random displacement proportional to $1.2(dRows)^{0.5}$, with seed = 24929.

```
Fourth point: -0.809,0.2629,1.1135
Third point: -0.5,-0.6882,1.1135
Fourth point: (RETURN)
Fifth point: (RETURN)
```

The DXF entities file for the above pentagon face is shown in table 12.2. (To save space the DXF file is displayed in two columns, even though the file is one long continuous column of entries.) The pentagon is composed of two 3Dfaces, one with four edges, the other with three. The first face has vertices 1 through 4 in the above figure, with the third edge from 3 to 4 being invisible. At the end of the first column below, the code number 70 signifies

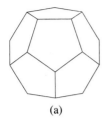

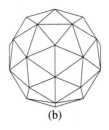

Figure 12.8 Surfaces constructed with 3Dfaces: (a) the dodecahedron; (b) a geodesic dome constructed by replacing each pentagonal face on the dodecahedron with five triangular faces.

(a)   (b)

TABLE 12.2 THE DXF FILE FOR A SINGLE
PENTAGONAL FACE

0	0
SECTION	3DFACE
2	8
ENTITIES	0
0	10
3DFACE	0.5
8	20
0	−0.6882
10	30
0.0	1.1135
20	11
0.8507	−0.809
30	21
1.1135	0.2629
11	31
0.809	1.1135
21	12
0.2629	−0.5
31	22
1.1135	−0.6882
12	32
0.5	1.1135
22	13
−0.6882	−0.05
32	23
1.1135	−0.6882
13	33
−0.809	1.1135
23	70
0.2629	1
33	0
1.1135	ENDSEC
70	0
4	EOF

that at least one edge is invisible, and the number 4 that follows specifies that only the third edge is invisible. The second face has the same coordinates for the third and fourth vertices because this face is a triangle. The number 1 follows the code number 70 near the end of the second column because only the first edge of the face, from vertex 3 to vertex 4, is invisible.

The number following code 70 specifies the invisible edges according to the following binary format: $2^0 = 1$ if only the first edge is invisible, $2^1 = 2$ if only the second edge is invisible, $2^2 = 4$ for the third edge, and $2^3 = 8$ for the fourth edge. If the number 0 follows code 70, then all edges are visible. Multiple invisible edges are designated by adding the numbers for the particular edges; for example, $1 + 4 = 5$ if the first and third edges are invisible, and $1 + 2 + 4 + 8 = 15$ if all edges are invisible.

To write a DXF file for the dodecahedron shown in figure 12.8a, one must enter a single pentagonal face as two faces having three and four edges, and joined along invisible edges. The subroutine dodecahedron() listed below is similar to the icosahedron() subroutine in section 8.2, except that it writes two 3Dfaces to represent a pentagonal face. Also, the writeFace() subroutine listed below now includes a flag to write the DXF lines that specify the invisible edges.

```
void dodecahedron(void)
{
    int      i,faceNum,vnum,flag;
    double   xp[4],yp[4],zp[4];

    double   vert[20][3] =
             {{0.0,0.8507,1.1135},{0.8090,0.2629,1.1135},
              {0.5,-0.6882,1.1135},{-0.5,-0.6882,1.1135},
              {-0.8090,0.2629,1.1135},{0.0,1.3769,0.2605},
              {1.3095,0.4255,0.2605},{0.8093,-1.1139,0.2605},
              {-0.8093,-1.1139,0.2605},{-1.3095,0.4255,0.2605},
              {0.8090,1.1139,-0.2605},{1.3095,-0.4255,-0.2605},
              {0.0,-1.3769,-0.2605},{-1.3095,-0.4255,-0.2605},
              {-0.8093,1.1139,-0.2605},{0.5,0.6882,-1.1135},
              {0.8090,-0.2629,-1.1135},{0.0,-0.8507,-1.1135},
              {-0.8090,-0.2629,-1.1135},{-0.5,0.6882,-1.1135}};
    int      vn[12][6] =
             {{0,1,2,4,3,3},{0,5,10,1,6,6},{1,6,11,2,7,7},
              {2,7,12,3,8,8},{3,8,13,4,9,9},{4,9,14,0,5,5},
              {10,15,16,6,11,11},{11,16,17,7,12,12},
              {12,17,18,8,13,13},{13,18,19,9,14,14},
              {14,19,15,5,10,10},{15,16,17,19,18,18}};

    for (faceNum=0; faceNum<12; faceNum++)
    {
        flag = 1;
        for (i=0; i<4; i++)
        {
            vnum = vn[faceNum][i+2];
            xp[i] = vert[vnum][0];
```

```
                    yp[i] = vert[vnum][1];
                    zp[i] = vert[vnum][2];
            }
            writeFace(xp,yp,zp,flag);

            flag = 4;
            for (i=0; i<4; i++)
            {
                    vnum = vn[faceNum][i];
                    xp[i] = vert[vnum][0];
                    yp[i] = vert[vnum][1];
                    zp[i] = vert[vnum][2];
            }
            writeFace(xp,yp,zp,flag);
    }
}
void writeFace(double x[],double y[],double z[],int visFlag)
{
    int m;

    fprintf(dxf,"%3d\n",0);
    fprintf(dxf,"3DFACE\n");
    fprintf(dxf,"%3d\n",8);
    fprintf(dxf,"%d\n",0);

    for (m=0; m<=3; m++)
    {
        fprintf(dxf,"%3d\n",10+m);
        fprintf(dxf,"%f\n",x[m]);
        fprintf(dxf,"%3d\n",20+m);
        fprintf(dxf,"%f\n",y[m]);
        fprintf(dxf,"%3d\n",30+m);
        fprintf(dxf,"%f\n",z[m]);
    }
    if (visFlag != 0)
    {
        fprintf(dxf,"%3d\n",70);
        fprintf(dxf,"%6d\n",visFlag);
    }
}
```

3Dfaces with invisible edges can be used to build complex surfaces. Figure 12.9 shows a gear represented with and without the invisible edges drawn. (Invisible edges are drawn on the screen or in a plot when the system variable SPLFRAME is changed from its default value of zero to a nonzero value.)

The four different types of 3Dfaces used to construct the gear are labeled 1–4 in figure 12.9a. The gear edges are made up of rectangular faces with all four edges visible. The 3Dfaces on the front of the gear teeth are quadrilaterals with their top and bottom edges in-

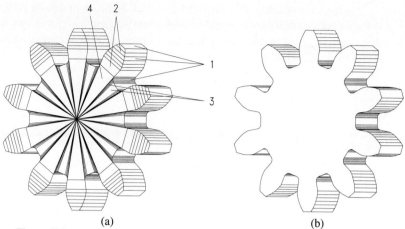

Figure 12.9   A gear constructed with 3Dfaces: (a) the system variable SPLFRAME set
equal to a nonzero value to draw the invisible lines; (b) with SPLFRAME set equal to zero.

visible. The 3Dfaces that extend from the center of the gear's front to the troughs between
the teeth are triangles with two edges invisible.

Beneath each gear tooth there is a triangle (numbered 4 in figure 12.9a) with all edges
invisible, and extending from the center of the gear front to points on either side of the tooth.
Although its edges are not visible when SPLFRAME is zero, this triangle is necessary for
hiding lines behind it when the HIDE command is in effect.

Once the DXF file is constructed for the four types of 3Dfaces described above, gears
of different sizes and placements can be constructed, as illustrated in figure 12.10. The gear
shafts in this figure can be added in AutoCAD with the REVSURF command, or they can
be included in the program for the DXF file by constructing them from rectangular 3Dfaces.

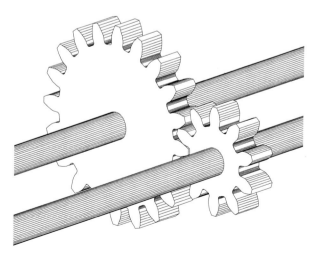

Figure 12.10   Meshed gears of 10 and 20
teeth, with the gears and shafts constructed
from a DXF file for 3Dfaces.

A simpler construction of the front gear face is shown in middle of figure 12.11b for a half tooth. This construction, which uses primarily triangular elements with two invisible sides, could be constructed with 3Dfaces. However, it will be used as an example of construction with the PFACE command.

Building Surfaces with the PFACE Command

Although the 3DFACE command can build almost any polygon surface, the PFACE command is more useful for building complex surfaces from within AutoCAD. For example, the front face on the half gear tooth shown in figure 12.11b was constructed by starting at the gear center and then selecting points continuously around the half tooth using the object snaps Endpoint and Nearest from the AutoCAD menu. Unlike the 3DFACE command, in which the user must insert all the invisible lines and reverse directions around the profile (as in the pentagon example above), the PFACE command automatically inserts the invisible lines to the first point as vertices are entered in one direction around the polygon.

Although the invisible lines are not drawn when the system variable SPLFRAME is equal to zero, they exist because the read-only system variable PFACEMAX is set to the value 4. That is, a complex polygon face constructed with PFACE is automatically divided into faces designated by three or four vertices (just like 3Dfaces). After a surface has been built with the PFACE command, the EXPLODE command can be used to break it up into the equivalent representation in 3Dfaces. (If a face exists with only one or two vertex points, then the EXPLODE command turns it into a point or line, respectively.)

To enter the top pentagonal face on the dodecahedron discussed above, enter the vertex points in one direction around the pentagon, and then enter the vertex numbers associated with this face.

```
Command: PFACE
Vertex 1: 0,0.8507,1.1135
Vertex 2: 0.809,0.2629,1.1135
Vertex 3: 0.5,-0.6882,1.1135
Vertex 4: -0.5,-0.6882,1.1135
Vertex 5: -0.809,0.2629,1.1135
Vertex 6: (RETURN)
Face 1, vertex 1: 1
Face 1, vertex 2: 2
Face 1, vertex 3: 3
Face 1, vertex 4: 4
Face 1, vertex 5: 5
Face 1, vertex 6: (RETURN)
Face 2, vertex 1: (RETURN)
```

The PFACE command automatically inserts an invisible edge to divide the pentagon into a quadrilateral and a triangle, connected along the invisible edge. If a face has more than five edges, then the PFACE command continues to add triangles by inserting invisible edges that lead back to the first vertex; see figure 12.11a.

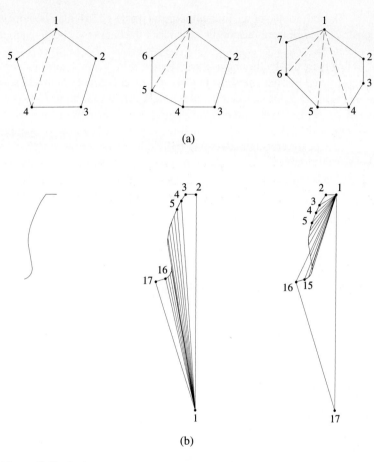

(a)

(b)

Figure 12.11   Surfaces constructed with the AutoCAD PFACE command: (a) polygons
with 5, 6, and 7 boundary edges, with internal invisible edges shown as dashed lines; (b) a
face constructed on the front of a half gear tooth, starting with the tooth profile shown on
the left (this is also the front view of the surface when invisible edges are not drawn). In (b)
the middle figure shows the invisible edges extending to vertex 1 placed at the center of the
gear; and the right figure shows that the invisible edges extend outside the tooth if the first
vertex is incorrectly placed.

In addition to the invisible edges automatically inserted by the PFACE command, you
may wish to designate some of the boundary edges as invisible. To do this, enter the vertex
number with a negative sign. For example, the half gear tooth shown in 12.11b was constructed with 17 vertices, with the vertex number for the first vertex entered as -1 and for
the last vertex as -17, to make the two edges extending to the center of the gear invisible.
In this case the first vertex must be at the center; otherwise, the invisible lines extending to
the first vertex would pass through regions external to the gear tooth, producing a surface
that is not properly fitted to the gear tooth (see the figure on the right of 12.11b).

The half tooth shown in the middle of figure 12.11b may be mirrored and arrayed to construct the full front face of the gear. Also, thickness may be given to the tooth profile to complete the gear.

As indicated by the above entries for the PFACE command, a complete polygon mesh is constructed by first entering all of the vertex coordinates and then specifying the vertex numbers for each face. Because a pface mesh can have arbitrary topology, it is used by the AutoCAD SOLMESH command to cover a solid model for the purpose of producing a surface display of the solid (solid modeling is discussed in the next chapter).

Except for erasing and adding individual faces, a pface mesh cannot be edited. The AutoCAD commands described in the remainder of this chapter form rectangular meshes, which can be edited with the PEDIT command.

12.3 SURFACES OF REVOLUTION

With the AutoCAD REVSURF command, a curve is swept around a straight line to form the standard surface of revolution that has circular (or circular-arc) cross sections. After examples of the REVSURF command are given below, this command is simulated with a C program. Also, two extensions of the program are considered: first, the circular cross section is generalized to a "superellipse" cross section; second, the straight axis is changed to a helical axis to produce a surface representing a helical tube.

The REVSURF Command in AutoCAD

The objects in figure 12.12 were constructed in AutoCAD by first drawing a polyline (shown above each surface) and rotating it 360° around a straight line representing the axis. The surface in figure 12.12a represents a washer, which was generated by rotating a rectangle around an axis. The other three surfaces represent a vase or pitcher constructed from an open polyline, with the polyline unsmoothed in 12.12b and smoothed with a cubic B-spline fit in 12.12c. (A separate straight line from the bottom of the polyline to the axis is used to construct the bottom of the vase.) In figure 12.12d, the PEDIT command has been used to move vertices at the top of the vase to construct a spout, turning the vase into a pitcher.

After a polyline (or other suitable curve) and an axis line have been drawn, the surface of revolution is constructed in AutoCAD with the following REVSURF command.

```
Command: REVSURF
Select path curve: (select with mouse)
Select axis of revolution: (select with mouse)
Start angle <0>: (return)
Included angle (+=ccw,-=cw) <Full circle>: (RETURN)
```

The path curve selected for the REVSURF command may be any line, arc, circle, 2-D polyline (PLINE), or 3-D polyline (3DPOLY). In the above example of the REVSURF command, default angles were accepted by pressing the return key to produce a full surface of revolution. Examples with less than a 360° rotation angle are given in figure 12.13.

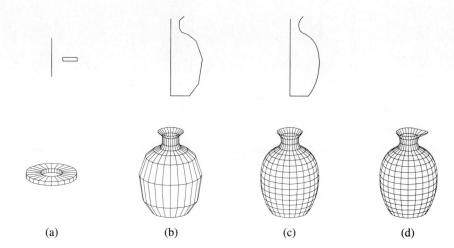

Figure 12.12 Surfaces constructed with the AutoCAD REVSURF command: (a) a washer constructed from the rectangle (path curve) and axis shown above the washer; (b) a vase constructed from an unsmoothed polyline (plus a separate line segment for the bottom) shown above the vase; (c) a vase constructed from the same polyline smoothed with a cubic B-spline under PEDIT; (d) a spout added to the vase to form a pitcher, constructed by moving vertices under PEDIT. The system variables were set to the following values for these drawings: SURFTAB1 = 24 and SURFTAB2 = 16.

The number of face elements, or meshes, in the circumferential direction is equal to the value of the system variable SURFTAB1. Because the default value of SURFTAB1 is 6, you may wish to change it to a larger value.

```
Command: SURFTAB1
New value for SURFTAB1 <6>: 24
```

In the AutoCAD nomenclature, there are M meshes in the circumferential direction and N meshes in the direction of the axis of revolution. Thus M equals SURFTAB1.

If the path curve is a polyline that has *not* been smoothed with the PEDIT option Fit curve or Spline curve, the number of face elements, or meshes, in the axial direction is determined by the points entered on the polyline. That is, mesh lines are drawn at the ends of the straight line segments of the polyline. Thus if there are nb points that determine the polyline, there will be $N = nb - 1$ faces (or meshes) in the axial direction.

If the path curve is an arc, circle, line segment, or polyline that has been smoothed, then the number of faces or meshes in the axial direction equals the value of the system variable SURFTAB2. Of course, the value of SURFTAB2 can be changed with the SURFTAB2 command. When SURFTAB2 determines the number of axial meshes, the path curve is divided into meshes of equal size. The third surface of revolution shown in figure 12.12 was constructed from a smoothed polyline and may be contrasted with the second surface, which was constructed from the same polyline, but unsmoothed.

Figure 12.13 shows AutoCAD representations of the two largest greenhouse roofs on the Lucille Halsell Conservatory, designed by Emilio Ambasz. The plants in the conserva-

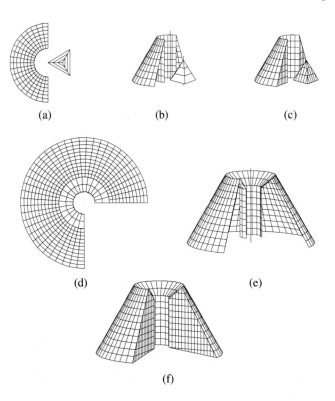

(a)   (b)   (c)

(d)   (e)

(f)

Figure 12.13   AutoCAD representations of the two largest greenhouse roofs on the Lucille Halsell Conservatory in San Antonio, Texas, designed by Emilio Ambasz. Surfaces
constructed with REVSURF are shown with plan views in (a) and (d), and with axonometric views in (b) and (e). Flat faces and lines are added in the completed roof structures shown
in (c) and (f).

tory are sheltered by earth berms, and light enters through the geometric roof structures.
The structures are shown with hidden lines removed, as they would appear with reflected
light. Plotting without the HIDE option would represent views with transmitted light when
the back frames are visible.

The roof shown in figures 12.13a–c consists of a structure having two half surfaces
of revolution (180° included angle) plus a three-sided pyramid (tetrahedron). The roof
frame is included as meshes, with SURFTAB1 = 20 and SURFTAB2 = 7 for the outer
surface generated from a line segment that slopes upward at 60° from the horizontal.
The inner, vertical, half-circular cylinder was constructed with SURFTAB1 = 10 and
SURFTAB2 = 7.

The flat vertical surfaces shown at the ends of the cylindrical structure in figure
12.13c were constructed with the 3DFACE command. The horizontal and vertical lines representing the frame are placed on the surface, after the drawing is put into the plan view of
a user-coordinate system (UCS) based on the surface. After one flat face with lines is constructed, it can be mirrored to produce the second face.

The pyramid in figures 12.13a–c is constructed from a line segment with SURFTAB1 = 3 and SURFTAB2 = 3. The three sides are equilateral triangles constructed from rotating a line segment of slope $\sqrt{2}$ to three positions around the vertical axis. To complete the frame lines shown in figure 12.13c, vertical lines are placed on a UCS attached to the pyramid faces.

The drawing of the largest roof structure, shown in figures 12.13d–f, was constructed by using REVSURF to revolve three line segments about an included angle of 270°. The outer surface slopes upward at 60° and has a frame represented by SURFTAB1 = 40 and SURFTAB2 = 11. The middle (roof) surface has SURFTAB1 = 20 and SURFTAB2 = 2; the vertical inner surface has SURFTAB1 = 10 and SURFTAB2 = 8. Note that the bottom of the inner surface lies on a platform that is one mesh above the bottom level of the outer surface. The flat end surfaces shown in figure 12.13f are constructed with the 3DFACE command, with horizontal and vertical lines representing the frame drawn in user-coordinate systems based on the vertical end surfaces.

Programming a Surface of Revolution

A surface of revolution may be easily programmed. Figure 12.14 shows a simple surface of revolution, with vertices and faces numbered in the bottom (plan) view. The surface is generated by rotating a curve about an axis. In the case presented here, the axis is assumed to be along the world z-axis, with points on the curve provided by the arrays *xcurve*[] and *zcurve*[]. Thus *xcurve*[] gives distances from the axis of revolution, and *zcurve*[] gives heights along the axis of revolution. Generalization to an arbitrary axis orientation is presented as an exercise (12.9).

The number of boundary points on the curve is *nb,* and the number of elements (faces) in the direction of rotation is *ne* (which corresponds to the SURFTAB1 variable in AutoCAD).

The program subroutine revSurf() listed below calculates the coordinates and connectivity of the vertices on the surface of revolution, and plotSurface() draws the edges of faces. The values of *nb, ne, xcurve*[], and *zcurve*[] are set by global data-type statements, and the value of PI (= 3.141593) is set with a *#define* declaration at the beginning of the program.

The subroutine revSurf() is assumed to be called in main(), like the calcVertices() subroutine in the mountain program presented earlier. The plotSurface() subroutine is not listed because it is the same as that given in the mountain program, except that the faces are now quadrilaterals rather than triangles. Thus the vertex number *k* loops over five values rather than four values (recall that the first vertex number occurs at both the beginning and the end of the *for* loop, so that a quadrilateral requires five vertex numbers). Also in plotSurface(), the scale factor *sf* and the bottom coordinate *yb* for the transformation to screen coordinates should be set to appropriate values; for example, *sf* = 6 and *yb* = 300 are suitable values for the simple surface of revolution given in the program below.

As illustrated in figure 12.14b, the vertices are numbered continuously from zero, starting at the bottom and continuing to the second level after all the vertices on the bottom have been numbered. The faces follow a similar numbering scheme.

The vertices are ordered in the vertex-number array *vn*[*m*][*q*] so that they progress in the counterclockwise direction as viewed from the outside surface of a face. If this same or-

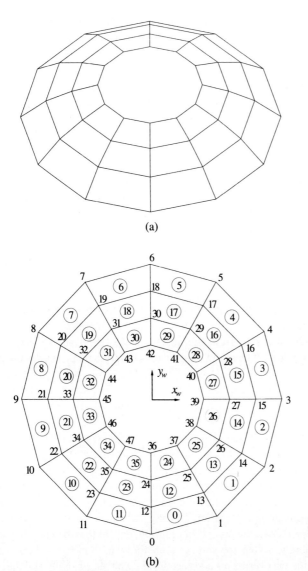

(a)

(b)

Figure 12.14 A shell structure created as a surface of revolution: (a) axonometric view; (b) top view with numbered vertices and faces.

dering procedure is established for each face, it will be easy later to calculate outward normals to the faces for use in hidden-line and rendering algorithms.

The vertex numbers are calculated in the last half of the subroutine revSurf(). The first vertex number equals the face number m; that is, $vn[m][0] = m$. The next vertex number equals $m+1$ unless it is on the last face around the circumference at its level (faces numbered 11, 23, and 35 in figure 12.14b), in which case the vertex number is $m+1-ne$, where ne is the number of faces around the circumference. The third vertex number is on the next higher level, so it jumps to the value $m+1+ne$, unless the vertex is on a last face on the circumference, in which case the vertex number is $m+1$. The fourth vertex number is $m+ne$, and the fifth vertex number returns to m, which is the starting vertex number.

The vertex number formulas can be confirmed for the faces in figure 12.14b, for which $nb = 4$ and $ne = 12$. For the simple surface shown in this figure, the arrays were dimensioned with the global data-type declarations vert[48][3] and vn[36][5] because the total number of vertices is $nb{\cdot}ne = 48$ and the total number of faces is $nb{\cdot}(ne-1) = 36$. (Because complex surfaces can require very large arrays, an alternative calculational procedure that does not require these arrays is presented in the next subsection.)

In the circumferential direction, the surface of revolution is divided into ne elements. From a world-coordinate system based at the axis of revolution, as shown in figure 12.14b, the angular distance $\varDelta\theta$ (dtheta in the program) between vertices is $2\pi/ne$ radians. In the subroutine revSurf() below, the index j steps from one vertex to the next in the circumferential direction, and the index i steps in the vertical from one level of ne vertices to the next. Thus, $i = 2$ and $j = 3$ give the vertex number 27 in figure 12.3b, and in general the vertex number k is given by $k = i*ne + j$.

The path curve, given by the arrays $xcurve[i]$ and $zcurve[i]$, has nb points that correspond to index i values from 0 through $nb-1$. The vertical coordinate $vert[k][2]$ of a vertex point k is equal to the vertical coordinate value $zcurve[i]$ of the path curve. The x-coordinate value $vert[k][0]$ of the vertex point equals the x-axis projection of the horizontal curve coordinate $xcurve[i]$ as it is incremented in angle by the amount $dtheta$ to form the surface of revolution. Thus $vert[k][0]$ equals $xcurve[i]*cos(theta)$ in the revSurf() subroutine below, where $theta$ is the angle in the xy-plane measured from the x-axis. The y-coordinate value $vert[k][1]$ is given by the same expression, but with cos($theta$) replaced by sin($theta$).

```
int numFaces,vn[36][5],nb=4,ne=12;
double vert[48][3];
double xcurve[] = {30,24,18,12},zcurve[] = {0,5,8,10};

void revSurf(void)
{
    int i,j,k,m;
    double theta,dtheta;

    dtheta = 2*PI/ne;
    for (i=0; i<nb; i++)
    {
        for (j=0; j<ne; j++)
        {
            k = i*ne+j;
            theta = -0.5*PI + j*dtheta;
            vert[k][0] = xcurve[i]*cos(theta);
            vert[k][1] = xcurve[i]*sin(theta);
            vert[k][2] = zcurve[i];
        }
    }
```

```
for (i=0; i<nb-1; i++)
{
    for (j=0; j<ne; j++)
    {
        m = i*ne+j; /* m is the face number */
        vn[m][0] = m; vn[m][4] = m;
        if (j == (ne-1))
        {
            vn[m][1] = m+1-ne;
            vn[m][2] = m+1;
        }
        else
        {
            vn[m][1] = m+1;
            vn[m][2] = m+1+ne;
        }
        vn[m][3] = m+ne;
    }
}
numFaces = (nb-1)*ne;
plotSurface();
}
```

Programming Objects Having Noncircular Cross Sections

The surface-of-revolution program given above can be improved in three ways. First, a hidden-line algorithm can be added, or alternatively, the program can write a DXF file to port 3Dfaces to AutoCAD (or other CAD program), which can incorporate hidden-line options along with the other standard display features. Second, the program can be changed so that the face edges are drawn (or 3Dfaces written) "on the fly" without the use of the arrays *vert*[][] and *vn*[][]. Although these two-dimensional arrays are useful for understanding the construction of the surface, they require a lot of memory, and will limit the number of meshes that can be drawn. The third improvement is changing the radius as it rotates around the axis. That is, a more general rotational sweep can generate cross sections that are not circular.

As an example of a more general rotational sweep, consider a cross section that can vary between an ellipse and a rectangle. The equation for this cross section is the superellipse given by the parametric equations 3.12, which are reproduced below.

$$x = a\,(\cos t)^{(2/n)}, \qquad y = b\,(\sin t)^{(2/n)} \tag{12.1}$$

Equations 12.1 reduce to the equations for a circle when $a = b = r$ and the exponents are $2/n = 1$. To generalize the surface-of-revolution program above to produce superellipse cross sections, two arrays are introduced: *yratio*[i] and *expon*[i], with the index i representing the cross section (which is equivalent to the index i that numbers the vertices along the polyline used for generating the surface). The array *yratio*[i] specifies the ratio b/a of the cross-section y-axis intercept to the x-axis intercept. In the following program, the x-axis intercept is given by *xcurve*[*i*], as in the program above. The array *expon*[*i*] provides values for the exponent 2/n at each cross section *i*.

The program listing below produces the DXF file for the bottle shapes in figure 12.15. The axis and polyline given by the path curve (*xcurve*[], *zcurve*[]) are shown in figure 12.15a. The values shown in the global variable declarations for *expon*[] and *yratio*[] in the program correspond to the right-hand bottle shape in figure 12.15b, which is the same as the middle bottle in figure 12.15c.

In figure 12.15b the elements of *expon*[] are all equal to 1 for the left-hand bottle, have a minimum value of 0.5 for the middle bottle, and a minimum value of 0.25 for the right-hand bottle. In figure 12.15c the elements of *yratio*[] are all equal to 1 for the left-hand bottle, have a maximum value of 1.5 for the middle bottle, and a maximum value of 2 for the right-hand bottle. For both *expon*[] and *yratio*[], the last three elements are each equal to 1 to ensure that the bottle top is axisymmetric.

More complex sweep surfaces can be generated by sweeping a variable curve around an axis and by sweeping a cross section along an arbitrary curve; see the examples in the book by Choi (1991).

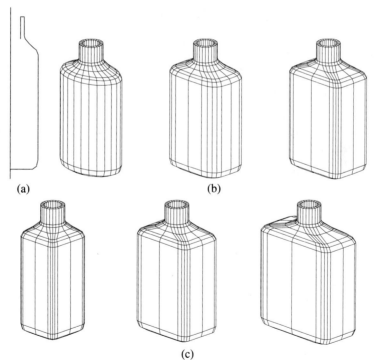

(a)   (b)

(c)

Figure 12.15   Bottle shapes with superellipse cross sections: (a) the starting polyline and axis; (b) squaring off the cross section by varying *expon*[*i*]; (c) stretching the bottle in the y-direction by varying *yratio*[*i*].

```c
#include <math.h>
#include <stdio.h>

#define PI 3.141593

FILE    *dxf;
void    writeStart(void),revSurfDXF(void),writeEnd(void);
void    calcVert(int,int);
void    writeFace(double x[], double y[],double z[]);

int     nb = 13, ne = 24;
double  xcurve[] = {0,2.4,2.85,3,3,2.8,2.5,2,1.6,1.5,1.5,1.1,1.1};
double  zcurve[] = {0,0,0.3,1,12,12.5,12.75,13.2,
                                      13.7,14,16,16,13.7};
double  expon[] = {.25,.25,.25,.25,.25,.25,.25,.5,.9,1,1,1,1};
double  yratio[] = {1.5,1.5,1.5,1.5,1.5,1.5,1.5,1.25,1.05,1,1,1,1};
double  dtheta,xw,yw,zw,xp[4],yp[4],zp[4];

void    main()
{
    writeStart();
    revSurfDXF();
    writeEnd();
}

void revSurfDXF(void)
{
    int i,j,k,ivert,jvert;
    double sf = 20;

    dtheta = 2*PI/ne;

    for (i=0; i<nb-1; i++)
    {
        for (j=0; j<ne; j++)
        {
            ivert = i; jvert = j;
            calcVert(ivert,jvert);
            xp[0] = xw; yp[0] = yw; zp[0] = zw;

            ivert = i;
            if (j == (ne-1))
                jvert = j+1-ne;
            else
                jvert = j+1;
            calcVert(ivert,jvert);
            xp[1] = xw; yp[1] = yw; zp[1] = zw;
```

```
                        ivert = i+1;
                        if (j == (ne-1))
                                jvert = j+1-ne;
                        else
                                jvert = j+1;
                        calcVert(ivert,jvert);
                        xp[2] = xw; yp[2] = yw; zp[2] = zw;

                        ivert = i+1;
                        jvert = j;
                        calcVert(ivert,jvert);
                        xp[3] = xw; yp[3] = yw; zp[3] = zw;
                        writeFace(xp,yp,zp);
                }
        }
}


void calcVert(int i,int j)
{
    double theta,sint,cost;

    theta = j*dtheta;
    sint = sin(theta); cost = cos(theta);
    if (cost < 0)
        xw = -xcurve[i]*pow(-cost,expon[i]);
    else
        xw = xcurve[i]*pow(cost,expon[i]);
    if (sint < 0)
        yw = -yratio[i]*xcurve[i]*pow(-sint,expon[i]);
    else
    yw = yratio[i]*xcurve[i]*pow(sint,expon[i]);
    zw = zcurve[i];
}
```

Programming Objects with a Rotational Sweep around a Curved Axis

The objects considered above were generated by a rotational sweep of *variable* radius around a *straight* axis. In this section the objects considered are generated by a rotational sweep of a *constant* radius around a *curved* axis. Although the same procedure can be applied to other curves, the only curve considered here is the helix. This curve is used to generate the helical tube shown in figure 12.16.

A helix is generated by a point that moves with a constant velocity in the z-direction while it traces out circles in the xy-plane. The following equations give the helix coordinates x_h, y_h, and z_h in terms of the angle α and helix radius r_h, with the helix axis being the world z-axis, as illustrated in figure 12.17.

$$x_h = r_h \cos\alpha, \qquad y_h = r_h \sin\alpha, \qquad z_h = c\alpha \qquad (12.2)$$

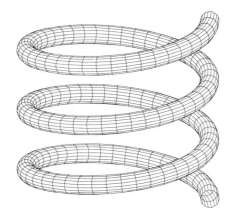

Figure 12.16 A helical tube viewed in AutoCAD at an angle $-90°$ from the x-axis in the xy-plane, and at an angle $18°$ above the xy-plane.

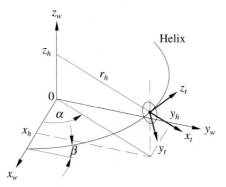

Figure 12.17 Geometry of the tube axes (x_t, y_t, z_t) on a helix, and the world axes (x_w, y_w, z_w).

A helix is traced out by equations 12.2, starting with $\alpha = 0$ and continuing to $\alpha = 2\pi N$ radians, where N is the number of coils in the helix. When $\alpha \to 0$, the upward slope of the helix is given by $(dz_h/d\alpha)/(dy_h/d\alpha)$, which equals c/r_h. Thus the constant c equals r_h times $\tan\beta$, where β is the angle that the helix makes with the horizontal plane (see figure 12.17).

Vertices on a tube surface surrounding the helix are located in planes perpendicular to the helix curve. Figure 12.17 shows a tube-coordinate system (x_t, y_t, z_t) with its origin on the helix, and its z-axis along the curve so that its xy-plane is perpendicular to the curve (its x-axis is in the radial direction). In the tube-coordinate system, the vertices are placed on a circle of radius r_t; that is, placed at points with $x_t = r_t \cos\theta$ and $y_t = r_t \sin\theta$, where the angle θ is incremented to produce n_e vertices around each circle.

Because the z-axis in the tube coordinate system points along the helix curve, it is directed at an angle β above the horizontal. Thus to move the tube axes (x_t, y_t, z_t) so that they are coincident with world axes, the tube axes must first be rotated through the angle $90° - \beta$ about the (tube) x-axis in order to place z_t parallel with z_w. Next, a rotation through angle $-\alpha$ about the z-axis brings x_t parallel with x_w and y_t parallel with y_w. Finally, a translation $(-x_h, -y_h, -z_h)$ brings the origin tube axes to the origin world axes. As discussed in chapter 11, moving a point in one direction corresponds to moving the axes in an opposite direction, thus the following transformation relates the world coordinates of a point $\mathbf{P}_w$ to its tube coordinates $\mathbf{P}_t$.

$$\mathbf{P}_w = \mathbf{P}_t[R_x(\beta - 90°)][R_z(\alpha)][T(x_h, y_h, z_h)] \tag{12.3}$$

After the matrix forms in section 11.1 are substituted into equation (12.3), and the matrix products are evaluated, the following expressions for points on the tube surface are obtained. (Recall that the tube's cross section is described by points on the circle: $x_t = r_t \cos\theta$, $y_t = r_t \sin\theta$, and $z_t = 0$.)

$$x_w = x_h + r_t(\cos\alpha \, \cos\theta - \sin\beta \, \sin\alpha \, \sin\theta)$$

$$y_w = y_h + r_t(\sin\alpha \, \cos\theta - \sin\beta \, \cos\alpha \, \sin\theta) \tag{12.4}$$

$$z_w = z_h - r_t\cos\beta \, \sin\theta$$

The values of the helix coordinates (x_h, y_h, z_h) in equations 12.4 are computed from equations 12.2.

A program to write a DXF file for a helical tube follows the same procedures as the preceding program, but with the subroutine revSurfDXF() replaced by the subroutine helicalTube(), and the calcVert() subroutine changed as shown below to include transformations 12.4. Also, the new global variables are listed below. The values listed in the program correspond to figure 12.16, which shows three coils, with angle $\beta = 6°$, and $r_t/r_h = 0.1$.

```
int     nb = 128, ne = 18, n = 3;
double  dalpha,beta,sinb,cosb,tanb,rh = 2,rt = 0.2;

void    helicalTube(void)
{
    int         xplot,yplot,xcen=250,yb=360;
    int         i,j,k,ivert,jvert;

    dtheta = 2*PI/ne, dalpha = 2*PI*n/(nb-1);
    beta = 6*PI/180;
    sinb = sin(beta); cosb = cos(beta); tanb = tan(beta);

    for (i=0; i<nb-1; i++)
    {
        for (j=0; j<ne; j++)
        {
            ivert = i; jvert = j;
            calcVert(ivert,jvert);
            xp[0] = xw; yp[0] = yw; zp[0] = zw;

            ivert = i;
            if (j == (ne-1))
                jvert = j+1-ne;
```

```
            else
                jvert = j+1;
            calcVert(ivert,jvert);
            xp[1] = xw; yp[1] = yw; zp[1] = zw;

            ivert = i+1;
            if (j == (ne-1);
                jvert = j+1-ne;
            else
                jvert = j+1;
            calcVert(ivert,jvert);
            xp[2] = xw; yp[2] = yw; zp[2] = zw;

            ivert = i+1;
            jvert = j;
            calcVert(ivert,jvert);
            xp[3] = xw; yp[3] = yw; zp[3] = zw;
            writeFace(xp,yp,zp);
        }
    }
}

void calcVert(int i,int j)
{
    double theta,sint,cost;
    double alpha,sina,cosa,xh,yh,zh;

    theta = j*dtheta;
    sint = sin(theta); cost = cos(theta);

    alpha = i*dalpha;
    sina = sin(alpha); cosa = cos(alpha);
    xh = rh*cosa; yh = rh*sina; zh = rh*tanb*alpha;

    xw = xh + rt*(cosa*cost-sinb*sina*sint);
    yw = yh + rt*(sina*cost+sinb*cosa*sint);
    zw = zh - rt*cosb*sint;
}
```

12.4 RULED SURFACES

The RULESURF Command in AutoCAD

A ruled surface is constructed by placing quadrilateral surfaces between two curves, like
the boards extending from one rib section to another on a wooden boat (see the canoe pictured in figure 12.18). The AutoCAD RULESURF command constructs a ruled surface,

with the system variable SURFTAB1 determining the number of surface elements. The ruled surface elements have straight edges representing a linear interpolation between points on the two curves.

A simple example of ruled surfaces is provided by the hull for a canoe, constructed from the data given in table 12.3. This canoe is symmetrical from front to back, so that only the left-front quarter has been constructed; the right side and the rear can then be produced by "mirroring."

The first step in constructing the canoe is to change to a user-coordinate system (UCS) that has its z-axis along the world x-axis. (After a UCS has been established, you can display the plan view in this UCS with the PLAN command.) Then a polyline (PLINE) is constructed from the data at each cross section 0–7 in table 12.3, with the section elevation (world x-value corresponding to the UCS z-value) being set with the ELEV command. The polyline is constructed with the world y- and z-values entered as UCS x- and y-values at the given cross-section elevation.

The data from table 12.3 is conveniently entered by setting the dimension mode to feet and inches by choosing architectural units under the UNITS command, with 32 selected as the smallest fraction to display. Then the last entry for cross section 0 in table 12.2 can be entered as inches or as feet and inches: 14-23/32,13-1/2 or as 1′2-23/32,1′1-1/2. Although the double quote (") can be used after the inch values, it is not necessary.

Figures 12.18a–b show two views of the polylines for sections 0–7 constructed at elevations from 0′ to 7′. Also shown is the bow/stern section constructed at zero elevation on a new UCS that has its y-axis located along the world z-axis.

To construct ruled surfaces on the canoe, the polylines representing the cross sections are first smoothed with the Fit option under PEDIT. Next the system variable SURFTAB1

TABLE 12.3 DATA FOR THE VERTICAL CROSS SECTIONS AND THE BOW/STERN SECTION OF THE PETERBOROUGH CANOE

Section 0 (x = 0 ft)		Section 1 (x = 1 ft)		Section 2 (x = 2 ft)		Section 3 (x = 3 ft)		Section 4 (x = 4 ft)		Section 5 (x = 5 ft)		Section 6 (x = 6 ft)		Section 7 (x = 7 ft)		Bow/Stern section (y = 0 ft)	
y in.	z in.	y	z	y	z	y	z	y	z	y	z	y	z	y	z	x in.	z in.
0	$1\frac{7}{32}$	0	$1\frac{9}{32}$	0	$1\frac{3}{8}$	0	$1\frac{7}{16}$	0	$1\frac{5}{8}$	0	$1\frac{7}{8}$	0	$2\frac{5}{16}$	0	$3\frac{3}{16}$	90	$5\frac{5}{8}$
2	$1\frac{7}{32}$	2	$1\frac{9}{32}$	2	$1\frac{3}{8}$	2	$1\frac{15}{32}$	2	$1\frac{23}{32}$	2	$2\frac{9}{16}$	2	$3\frac{13}{16}$	$\frac{1}{2}$	4	92	$7\frac{9}{16}$
4	$1\frac{9}{32}$	4	$1\frac{11}{32}$	4	$1\frac{13}{32}$	4	$1\frac{17}{32}$	4	$2\frac{1}{8}$	4	$3\frac{7}{16}$	$3\frac{15}{16}$	6	$1\frac{17}{32}$	6	$93\frac{1}{2}$	10
6	$1\frac{3}{8}$	6	$1\frac{7}{16}$	6	$1\frac{1}{2}$	6	$1\frac{11}{16}$	6	$2\frac{25}{32}$	6	$4\frac{13}{16}$	$5\frac{5}{8}$	8	$2\frac{1}{4}$	8	$94\frac{9}{32}$	12
8	$1\frac{19}{32}$	8	$1\frac{21}{32}$	8	$1\frac{25}{32}$	8	$2\frac{1}{4}$	$8\frac{1}{8}$	4	$8\frac{3}{32}$	8	$5\frac{13}{16}$	10	$2\frac{3}{4}$	10	$94\frac{19}{32}$	14
10	$1\frac{15}{16}$	10	2	10	$2\frac{11}{32}$	$10\frac{11}{16}$	4	$9\frac{15}{16}$	6	$8\frac{21}{32}$	10	$6\frac{1}{16}$	12	$2\frac{15}{16}$	12	$94\frac{1}{2}$	16
12	$2\frac{1}{2}$	12	$2\frac{3}{4}$	12	$3\frac{1}{2}$	$12\frac{1}{4}$	6	$10\frac{3}{4}$	8	$8\frac{23}{32}$	12	6	14	$2\frac{31}{32}$	14	$94\frac{3}{32}$	18
14	$3\frac{11}{16}$	14	$4\frac{1}{8}$	$13\frac{27}{32}$	6	$12\frac{13}{16}$	8	$11\frac{1}{32}$	10	$8\frac{9}{16}$	14	$5\frac{3}{4}$	$16\frac{1}{16}$	$2\frac{7}{8}$	16	$93\frac{15}{32}$	20
$15\frac{3}{8}$	6	$14\frac{31}{32}$	6	$14\frac{9}{32}$	8	$12\frac{7}{8}$	10	$10\frac{15}{16}$	12	$8\frac{1}{2}$	$14\frac{13}{16}$			$2\frac{21}{32}$	18	$92\frac{5}{8}$	22
$15\frac{5}{8}$	8	$15\frac{9}{32}$	8	$14\frac{5}{32}$	10	$12\frac{9}{16}$	12	$10\frac{3}{4}$	$14\frac{1}{8}$					$2\frac{9}{16}$	$18\frac{3}{4}$		
$15\frac{3}{8}$	10	$15\frac{1}{16}$	10	$13\frac{13}{16}$	12	$12\frac{1}{4}$	$13\frac{27}{32}$										
15	12	$14\frac{23}{32}$	12	$13\frac{1}{2}$	$13\frac{11}{16}$												
$14\frac{23}{32}$	$13\frac{1}{2}$	$14\frac{7}{16}$	$13\frac{9}{16}$														

Source: *Canoecraft* by Moores and Mohr (1983).

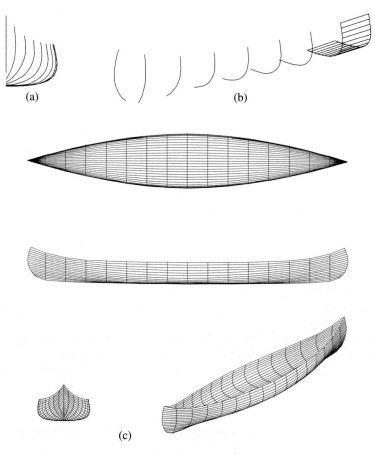

(a)

(b)

(c)

Figure 12.18   Construction of the Peterborough canoe from the data in table 12.3: (a) the
front left cross sections viewed from the front; (b) application of a ruled surface between
adjacent cross sections; (c) views of the completed canoe.

is set at a suitable value (a value of 16 was used for the canoe surface in figure 12.18). Then
the ruled surface is constructed between adjacent cross-section polylines with the following statements.

```
Command: RULESURF
Select first defining curve: (select with mouse)
Select second defining curve: (select with mouse)
```

Figure 12.18b shows the first ruled surface that has been applied to the canoe cross
sections. The next ruled surface cannot be immediately applied because the first ruled surface covers a cross section that must be selected. Therefore, the first ruled surface should

be moved (with the MOVE command) a fixed distance away from the cross sections. Then the RULESURF command can be applied to construct the next surface. This second surface is then moved by the same distance as the first, so that it joins up with the first surface. In this way the cross sections serve as a frame, or template, for the construction of the entire surface. After the surface has been constructed, the frame of cross sections can be erased.

Figure 12.18c shows the orthographic views and an axonometric view of the completed canoe. A perspective view of this same canoe was shown at the beginning of this chapter.

When using the RULESURF command, one must carefully identify which portions of the two curves are to be connected. Figure 12.19a shows two cases that can occur when RULESURF is used to connect two canoe cross sections. In the right-hand case, the "bowtie" surface results because the top of one cross-sectional curve and the bottom of the other curve were selected.

For closed curves, the ruled surface is not affected by the location of the pick points on the curves. As shown by the left-hand figure in 12.19b, the ruled edges will join points at similar angles on two circles or donuts (a donut with equal inner and outer radii was used in the figure so that only a circular curve results rather than a filled circle). The remaining ruled surfaces in figure 12.19b are constructed by rotating the top donut by different amounts before applying the RULESURF command. These latter figures represent hyperbolic shells, often used for natural-draft cooling towers. The hyperbolic shell is a good structural shape because the two different curvatures increase strength, and also because the shell can be constructed with straight-line elements (the straight edges of the ruled surface elements).

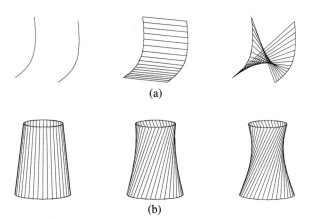

(a)

(b)

Figure 12.19   Surface construction with the RULESURF command: (a) the surface in the middle figure is obtained when points are selected at the same ends of the canoe rib sections shown on the left, and the "bow-tie" surface on the right is obtained by selecting a point near the top of one rib and a point near the bottom of the other rib; (b) ruled surfaces between two donuts (circular curves), with the top donut rotated by 0°, 60°, and 90° in the three figures.

Programming a Ruled Surface

For a programming example, two 3-D B-spline curves are connected with a ruled surface, as illustrated in figure 12.20. The two sides formed by the B-splines are calculated by extending the subroutine cubicBSpline() of section 7.6 to include z-coordinates. These sides are divided into *ne* equal lengths to determine the vertices for the faces of the ruled surface (The number of elements *ne* corresponds to the AutoCAD system variable SURTAB1.) The vertex numbers for each face may be determined from figure 12.20.

The complete program for the ruled surface is given as listing 12.2 in appendix B, which includes a detailed description of the program features.

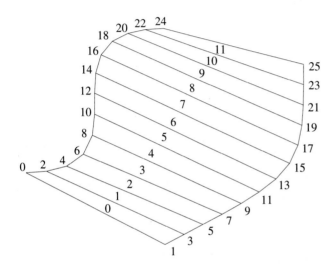

Figure 12.20 Vertex and face notation for the ruled surface given in the program listing (appendix B). The vertices for the 3-D polyline on the left start with *splNum* = 0; the vertices on the right polyline start with *splNum* = 1. There are 12 faces, numbered 0 through 11.

12.5 BICUBIC COONS PATCHES

In the preceding section, a ruled surface was constructed between two curves. The faces on a ruled surface have straight edges extending from one curve to the other. When two ruled surfaces join along a common curve, as in the canoe example, the surface slope is discontinuous from one side of the joining curve to the other.

In the present section, a bicubic Coons patch will be formed between four curves that are joined at their endpoints. Bicubic Coons patches can be joined along a common curve, with the surface slope being continuous across the joining curve. Thus Coons patches may be used to construct surfaces that are smoother than ruled surfaces.

The EDGESURF Command in AutoCAD

AutoCAD's EDGESURF command constructs a surface between four curves that are joined at their endpoints. Figure 12.21 shows a Coons patch connecting four 3-D polylines,

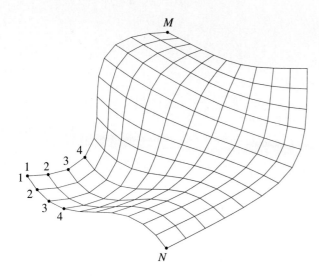

Figure 12.21   A Coons patch constructed between four 3-D polylines. This surface was constructed with the EDGESURF command, with the number of faces in the two directions determined by the system variables SURFTAB1 = 12 and SURFTAB2 = 10.

with two of the polylines being the same as those used for the ruled surface in figure 12.20. The EGESURF command is used to produce a Coons patch in the following manner.

```
Command: EDGESURF
Select edge 1: (pick with mouse)
Select edge 2: (pick with mouse)
Select edge 3: (pick with mouse)
Select edge 4: (pick with mouse)
```

The number of faces distributed along the direction of the first curve selected is equal to the value of the system variable SURFTAB1 (corresponding to M = SURFTAB1 + 1 vertices along the curve). The number of faces in the direction of the second curve equals the value of SURFTAB2 (with N = SURFTAB2 +1 vertices). Thus a rectangular mesh of $M \times N$ vertices and SURFTAB1 $\times$ SURFTAB2 faces is formed. In figure 12.21, the vertices are numbered from 1 to M along the first curve and from 1 to N along the second curve.

Figures 12.22a–b show Coons patches constructed with EDGESURF. Four semicircles produce a dome surface in figure 12.22a. In 12.22b, a pipe T-connector is constructed by first forming a surface between two quarter circles and two straight lines. This surface is mirrored across a vertical line, with the resulting surface mirrored across a horizontal line (the mirror lines are shown in figure 12.22b). Then the back half of the connector is constructed from a frame that consists of two semicircles joined by two straight lines. Finally, the T-connector is completed by adding three short circular cylinders at the circular openings. The semicircular and circular cylinders were constructed with EDGESURF, although they can also be constructed with REVSURF or RULESURF.

The AutoCAD EDGESURF command is also useful for constructing free-form shapes such as the hand grip and bottle shown in figure 12.23. Here a single Coons patch is used to form a quarter section of the object, with continuous slopes set up at the patch joints.

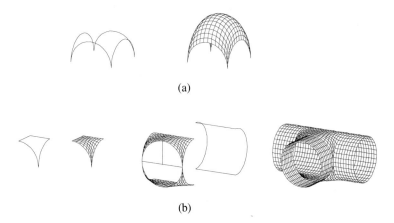

(a)

(b)

Figure 12.22   Use of EDGESURF to construct a T-connector for piping.

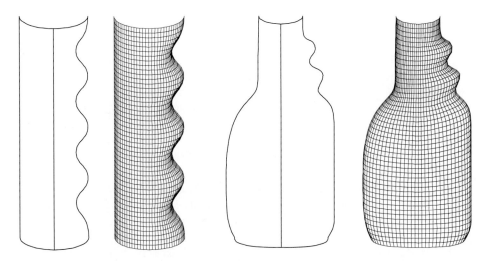

Figure 12.23   Sections of a hand grip and a bottle constructed with the AutoCAD EDGESURF command.

The boat hulls shown in figure 12.24 were drawn with the EDGESURF command after using cubic B-spline smoothing on the 2-D and 3-D polylines that form the boundaries of the Coons patches. Because the EDGESURF command requires that the boundary curve ends meet, 3-D polylines (3DPOLY command) were used for the sheer line (top of hull) and the cross-section lines so that the curve ends could be moved in any direction to snap to adjacent boundary curves.

The canoe in 12.24a illustrates that the Coons patches provide smooth curves with matching slopes from one patch to the next. In contrast, the canoe with a ruled surface (pic-

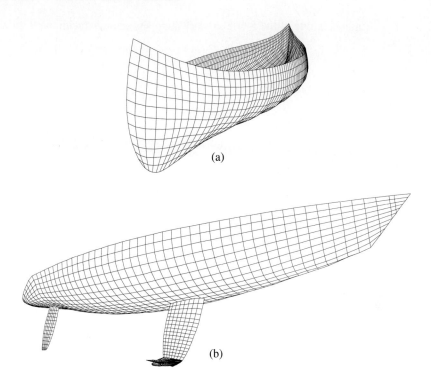

(a)

(b)

Figure 12.24   Boat hulls drawn with AutoCAD's EDGESUF command: (a) the Peterborough canoe, constructed from the curve data in table 12.2; (b) the Nauta 70 yacht, designed
by Bruce Farr, with this drawing constructed from curves and photographs given in the design journal *Domus*.

tured at the beginning of this chapter and in figure 12.18) has straight lines with discontinuous changes in slope between sections. The canoe surface in figure 12.24a does produce some
waviness along the side because of variations of the cross-sectional data. This waviness was
more noticeable when a circular-arc fit to the keel 2-D polyline was used rather than the cubic B-spline fit. In section 12.6, a smooth canoe surface without noticeable waviness will
be drawn by using a mesh that covers an entire canoe side to construct a B-spline surface.

The cross-sectional data for the yacht hull shown in 12.24b was smoothed before the
Coons patches were constructed, with the result that the surface does not exhibit noticeable
waviness. The rudder and winged keel on the yacht hull were also constructed with the
EDGESURF command.

Programming a Bicubic Coons Patch

The Coons patch extends between four 3-D curves shown as $P(0,v)$, $P(u,0)$, $P(1,v)$, and
$P(u,1)$ in figure 12.25. The variables u and v range between 0 and 1, with the result that
curves meet at the four corner points: $P(0,0)$, $P(1,0)$, $P(1,1)$, and $P(0,1)$.

Cubic blending of the four boundary curves is achieved with the following formula.

$$\mathbf{P}(u,v) = F_1(v)\,\mathbf{P}(u,0) + F_2(v)\,\mathbf{P}(u,1) + F_1(u)\,\mathbf{P}(0,v) + F_2(u)\,\mathbf{P}(1,v)$$

$$- [F_2(v)\,\mathbf{P}(0,1) + F_1(v)\,\mathbf{P}(0,0)]F_1(u)$$

$$- [F_2(v)\,\mathbf{P}(1,1) + F_1(v)\,\mathbf{P}(1,0)]F_2(u)$$

where   (12.5)

$$F_1(v) = 2v^3 - 3v^2 + 1, \qquad F_1(u) = 2u^3 - 3u^2 + 1$$

$$F_2(v) = -2v^3 + 3v^2, \qquad F_2(u) = -2u^3 + 3u^2$$

It may be readily shown that the function in equation 12.5 reduces to the boundary curves; that is, $\mathbf{P}(u,v) \rightarrow \mathbf{P}(0,v)$ as $u \rightarrow 0$, $\mathbf{P}(u,v) \rightarrow \mathbf{P}(u,0)$ as $v \rightarrow 0$, $\mathbf{P}(u,v) \rightarrow \mathbf{P}(1,v)$ as $u \rightarrow 1$, and $\mathbf{P}(u,v) \rightarrow \mathbf{P}(u,1)$ as $v \rightarrow 1$. Similarly, it can be shown from equation 12.5 that the slopes of the surface patch will match the curve slopes; thus Coons patches will join smoothly along smooth curves. This mathematical result shows why the Coons patches constructed on the yacht hull (with EDGESURF) in figure 12.24b join smoothly with no change in slope.

The program for the bicubic Coons patch is given as listing 12.3 in appendix B, for which the Coons patch is bounded by four cubic B-spline curves. Vertices on the curves are placed by ruling off *tab*1 equal intervals in one direction and *tab*2 equal intervals in the other direction, as illustrated in figure 12.25. (The parameters *tab*1 and *tab*2 represent the Auto-CAD variables TABSURF1 and TABSURF2.) The surface vertex coordinates are calculated from equation 12.5, and the vertices are numbered according to the scheme shown in figure 12.25.

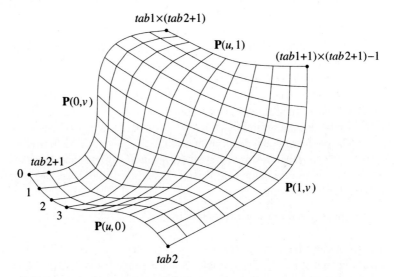

Figure 12.25 Notation for a Coons patch constructed between four 3-D polylines. This surface was constructed using the EDGESURF command, with the number of faces in the two directions determined by the system variables SURFTAB1 = 12 and SURFTAB2 = 10.

12.6 MESH GENERATION

The surfaces in the preceding sections were constructed with meshes that were automatically generated with the surfaces. The surfaces constructed with the TABSURF, REVSURF, RULESURF, and EDGESURF commands have 3Dmeshes that can be edited with the PEDIT command. In addition, meshes for use with PEDIT can be generated directly with the 3DMESH command. Like the 3Dfaces discussed in sections 8.2 and 12.2, complex 3Dmeshes may be constructed by programming DXF files.

With PEDIT, vertex points on a mesh can be moved, and the mesh can be used as a frame to generate the following smoothed surfaces: a Bézier surface, a quadratic B-spline surface, and a cubic B-spline surface. The mathematical formulations for these surfaces are presented in sections 12.7 and 12.8.

3-D Plots of Mathematical Functions from DXF Files for Meshes

The viewing and hidden-line features of CAD systems make them useful for presenting 3-D plots in engineering and scientific applications. For example, figure 12.26a shows a plot of cylindrical surface waves generated at a single point, and 12.26b shows the interference pattern that results when waves originate from two points. These AutoCAD plots were drawn from the DXF file written by the program given below.

The writeStart() function writes the beginning of the DXF file shown in the box on the right of the program listing. The coordinate data are written in the form of polyline vertices. The value 16 after the code number 70 indicates that this is a 3Dmesh. The number 100 after the code number 71 specifies that there are 100 vertices in the M-direction (here the y-direction), and the 160 after code 72 specifies 160 vertices in the N-direction (here the x-direction).

The subroutine writeMesh() consists of an outer *for* loop over the 100 y-coordinate values and an inner *for* loop over the 160 x-coordinate values. The subroutine zCalc() is called to calculate the wave height at each vertex point.

For the surface waves shown in figure 12.26, the wave height z is proportional to the Bessel function $J_0(kr)$, which corresponds to the $j0$ variable in the program. The variable r is the distance from the wave center, and k is a constant. The index number i in the subroutine zCalc() takes on the value 0 for the first group of waves (with centers at $x = 50$ and $y = 50$), and $i = 1$ for the second group of waves (with centers at $x = 110$ and $y = 50$). The two wave groups calculated by the program produce figure 12.26b; the single wave group shown in figure 12.26a results when the index i is limited to just the value 0.

In the function zCalc(), the Bessel function $j0$ is calculated to high accuracy by using two series expansions, one when $kr < 8$, the other when $kr \geq 8$.

```
#include <stdio.h>
#include <math.h>

#define PI 3.141593
```

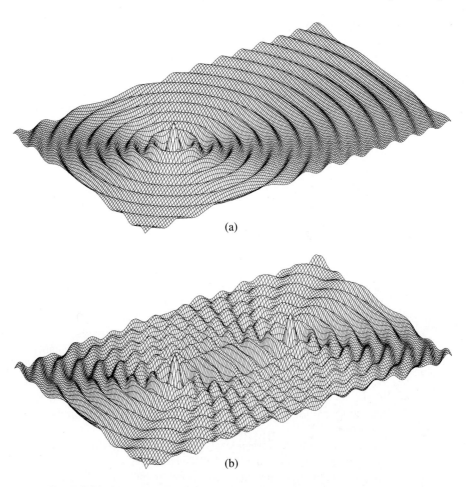

Figure 12.26   Three-dimensional plots of Bessel functions representing cylindrical waves
from one point (a) and from two points (b). The vertical coordinate can represent the surface elevation for waves on a liquid surface, or alternatively, a variable such as pressure for
acoustic waves.

```
void writeStart(void),writeMesh(void),zCalc(void);
void writeVertex(void),writeEnd(void);

FILE *dxf;
double x,y,z;

main()
{
    dxf = fopen("meshplot.dxf","w");
    writeStart();
```

```
      writeMesh();
      writeEnd();
      fclose(dxf);
}

  void writeStart(void)
  {
      fprintf(dxf,"%3d\n",0);
      fprintf(dxf,"SECTION\n");
      fprintf(dxf,"%3d\n",2);
      fprintf(dxf,"ENTITIES\n");
      fprintf(dxf,"%3d\n",0);
      fprintf(dxf,"POLYLINE\n");
      fprintf(dxf,"%3d\n",8);
      fprintf(dxf,"0\n");
      fprintf(dxf,"%3d\n",66);
      fprintf(dxf,"%6d\n",1);
      fprintf(dxf,"%3d\n",10);
      fprintf(dxf,"%f\n",0.0);
      fprintf(dxf,"%3d\n",30);
      fprintf(dxf,"%f\n",0.0);
      fprintf(dxf,"%3d\n",30);
      fprintf(dxf,"%f\n",0.0);
      fprintf(dxf,"%3d\n",70);
      fprintf(dxf,"%6d\n",16);
      fprintf(dxf,"%3d\n",71);
      fprintf(dxf,"%6d\n",100);
      fprintf(dxf,"%3d\n",72);
      fprintf(dxf,"%6d\n",160);
  }

  void writeMesh(void)
  {
      for (y=0.; y<100.; y=y+1.)
      {
          for (x=0.; x<160.; x=x+1.)
          {
              zCalc();
              writeVertex();
          }
      }

  }

  void zCalc(void)
  {
```

```
        0
    SECTION
        2
    ENTITIES
        0
    POLYLINE
        8
    0
       66
            1
       10
      0.0
       20
      0.0
       30
      0.0
       70
            16
       71
           100
       72
          160
```

```c
    int i;
    double kr,s,j0;

    z = 0;
    for (i=0; i<=1; i++)
    {
        if (i == 0)
            kr = 0.75*sqrt((x-50)*(x-50)+(y-50)*(y-50));
        else
            kr = 0.75*sqrt((x-110)*(x-110)+(y-50)*(y-50));
        s = kr*kr;
        if (kr < 8.)
        {
            j0 = (3830.2-s*(878.6336-s*(40.90045-s*(.62287452
                    -s*.00300211587)))) /(3831.3+s*(77.00291+s));
        }
        else
        {
            j0 = sqrt(2./(PI*kr))*(1.0-.07/s)*cos(kr-.25*PI)
                                    -(.125/kr)*sin(kr-.25*PI);
        }
        z = z + 12.*j0;
    }
}

void writeVertex(void)
{
    fprintf(dxf,"%3d\n",0);
    fprintf(dxf,"VERTEX\n");
    fprintf(dxf,"%3d\n",8);
    fprintf(dxf,"0\n");
    fprintf(dxf,"%3d\n",10);
    fprintf(dxf,"%f\n",x);
    fprintf(dxf,"%3d\n",20);
    fprintf(dxf,"%f\n",y);
    fprintf(dxf,"%3d\n",30);
    fprintf(dxf,"%f\n",z);
    fprintf(dxf,"%3d\n",70);
    fprintf(dxf,"%6d\n",64);
}

void writeEnd(void)
{
    fprintf(dxf,"%3d\n",0);
    fprintf(dxf,"SEQEND\n");
    fprintf(dxf,"%3d\n",8);
    fprintf(dxf,"0\n");
    fprintf(dxf,"%3d\n",0);
    fprintf(dxf,"ENDSEC\n");
```

```
fprintf(dxf,"%3d\n",0);
fprintf(dxf,"EOF\n");
}
```

Smoothing 3Dmeshes

Figure 12.27 shows that a 3Dmesh can act as a control grid for three types of smoothed surfaces: a quadratic B-spline surface, a cubic B-spline surface, and a Bézier surface. In
AutoCAD, a 3Dmesh is smoothed with the PEDIT command. The type of smooth surface
that results is determined by the system variable SURFTYPE. This variable can be reset at
the command line by entering SURFTYPE, and then the number 5 for a quadratic B-spline
surface, 6 for a cubic B-spline surface, or 8 for a Bézier surface.

For a 3Dmesh, the PEDIT command performs smoothing in the following manner.

```
Command: PEDIT
Edit vertex/Smooth surface/Desmooth/Mclose/Nclose/Undo/eXit <X>: S
Edit vertex/Smooth surface/Desmooth/Mclose/Nclose/Undo/eXit <X>: (RETURN)
```

As shown by the options under the PEDIT command, the vertices of the 3Dmesh can be
edited, and the mesh can be closed in the *M* and *N* directions.

The smoothed surfaces in figure 12.27 show that the quadratic B-spline surface lies
closest to the control vertex points in the 3Dmesh; next closest is the cubic B-spline; and the
Bézier surface lies the farthest from the 3Dmesh. This ordering of surfaces occurs because
each point on a quadratic B-spline surface is determined by the closest 9 vertices of the
3Dmesh; a cubic B-spline surface point is determined by 16 vertices; and a Bézier surface

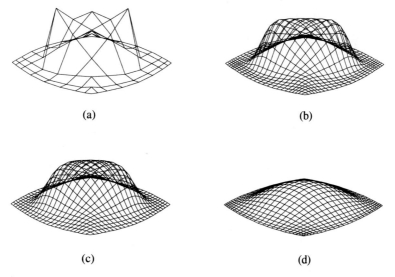

(a)   (b)

(c)   (d)

Figure 12.27   Smoothing of a 3Dmesh: (a) the original control 3Dmesh; (b) quadratic
B-spline surface; (c) cubic B-spline surface; (d) Bézier surface.

point is determined by all of the 3Dmesh vertices. In AutoCAD, Bézier surfaces can be
formed only for 3Dmeshes that contain 11 or fewer vertices in the *M* and *N* directions. Also,
the minimum size of the control mesh is 3 × 3 vertices for the quadratic B-spline and 4 × 4
vertices for the cubic B-spline.

Although all points are defined on smoothed surfaces, they are displayed by a rectangular mesh determined by the system variables SURFU and SURFV. By entering
SURFU and the command line, the number surface lines can be specified for the *M* direction. Similarly, the value of SURFV determines the number of surface lines in the *N* direction. In figure 12.27, the original control vertices are given by a 9 × 9 3Dmesh (with
SURFTAB1 = SURFTAB2 = 8), and the smoothed surfaces are displayed with a 25 × 25
mesh of vertices determined by the values SURFU = 24 and SURFV = 24.

As shown in figure 12.28, the cubic B-spline surface in figure 12.27c can be rotated
to approximate the wireframe seat of the classic Bertoia diamond chair. This chair seat rests
on a steel frame (not shown) that forms the chair legs.

Figure 12.29a shows a mesh constructed over an entire side of a canoe by placing vertices on the cross sections given in section 12.4. This mesh is smoothed to a quadratic B-
spline surface in figure 12.29b, and to a cubic B-spline surface 12.29c. This mesh cannot
be smoothed to a Bézier surface in AutoCAD because the mesh contains more than eleven
vertices along the length of the canoe.

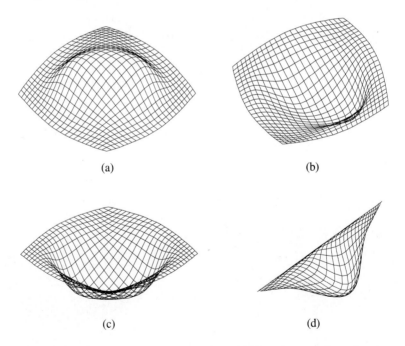

(a)   (b)

(c)   (d)

Figure 12.28   The cubic B-spline surface of figure 12.27, used to approximate the wireframe seat for the Bertoia diamond chair (see, for example, Larrabee, E., and M. Vignelli,
Knoll Design, New York: H. N. Abrams, Inc., 1981). Three orthographic views are shown,
along with an axonometric view.

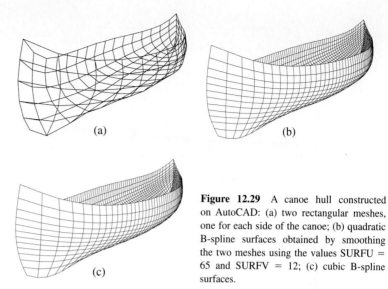

(a)

(b)

(c)

Figure 12.29 A canoe hull constructed on AutoCAD: (a) two rectangular meshes, one for each side of the canoe; (b) quadratic B-spline surfaces obtained by smoothing the two meshes using the values SURFU = 65 and SURFV = 12; (c) cubic B-spline surfaces.

12.7 UNIFORM B-SPLINE SURFACES

The quadratic and cubic B-splines of section 7.6 can be used to form surface patches that correspond to the AutoCAD smoothing operations on 3Dmeshes.

Quadratic B-Spline Surfaces

The vertices of a rectangular mesh (such as the AutoCAD 3Dmesh described above) are used as control points for quadratic B-spline surfaces. For example, the 16 vertices in the vertex mesh shown in figure 12.30a describe a quadratic B-spline surface consisting of four patches (separated by dashed lines in the figure). Because a quadratic B-spline requires 3 control points along a curve segment, a single quadratic B-spline patch requires an array of 3×3 vertices. Thus the lower-left patch in figure 12.30a is determined by vertices $\mathbf{V}_{0,0}$, $\mathbf{V}_{1,0}$, $\mathbf{V}_{2,0}$, $\mathbf{V}_{0,1}$, $\mathbf{V}_{1,1}$, $\mathbf{V}_{2,1}$, $\mathbf{V}_{0,2}$, $\mathbf{V}_{1,2}$, and $\mathbf{V}_{2,2}$.

In figure 12.30 the vertices are on a rectangular geometric grid in the xy-plane—this is a special case, of course, because the grid is required to be only topologically rectangular, not geometrically rectangular. That is, the spatial positions of the vertices can vary, as long as the vertices are connected topologically in the same rectangular manner.

A quadratic B-spline surface can be calculated from the following formula:

$$\mathbf{Q}_{i,j}(u,v) = \sum_{r=-2}^{0} \sum_{s=-2}^{0} \mathbf{V}_{i+r,j+s} b_r(u) b_s(v) \qquad (12.6)$$

In equation 12.6 the parameters u and v lie along the mesh directions (see figure 12.30a), and vary between 0 and 1 in each surface patch. At each point on the surface, the

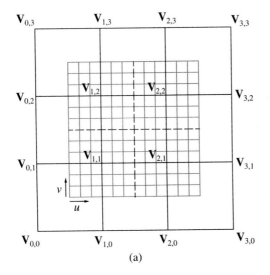

(a)

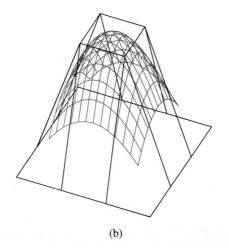

(b)

Figure 12.30   Views of a quadratic B-spline surface: (a) plan view showing the surface (gray lines) and control mesh (black lines), with dashed lines dividing the four surface patches; (b) axonometric view of the surface and control mesh.

double summation in equation 12.6 produces contributions from the nine nearest vertices. For example, the lower-left surface patch in figure 12.30 is traced out when $i = 2$ and $j = 2$ (in this case equation 12.6 includes the nine vertices shown in the lower-left portion of figure 12.30a). The lower-right patch is computed from equation 12.6 when $i = 3$ and $j = 2$; the upper-left patch when $i = 2$ and $j = 3$; and the upper right patch when $i = 3$ and $j = 3$.

The $b_r(u)$ and $b_s(v)$ functions in equation 12.6 have the same form as the $b_i(t)$ function in section 7.6; that is, $b_r(u)$ is given by equation 7.54, but with t replaced by u, and $b_s(v)$ is given by the same equation with t replaced by v. The continuity of the $b_i(t)$ functions and their slopes between curve segments ensures similar continuity in the products $b_r(u)b_s(v)$ in both the u and v directions, as may be verified by direct computation from equation 12.6. Thus the surface has the same continuity (C^1) as its component quadratic B-spline curves.

The control vertices on the boundary can be assigned as double points to extend the quadratic B-spline surface to the corner control points. Alternatively, the procedure used here is to extrapolate the vertices on the surface boundary in a manner similar to that used for the B-spline curves in section 7.6. The subroutine quadBSplSurf() given in listing 12.4 of appendix B uses this extrapolation procedure. This program was used to calculate the surface shown in figure 12.31, which duplicates the surface obtained by smoothing a 3Dmesh with AutoCAD (using PEDIT with SURFTYPE = 5 for the quadratic B-spline surface).

In listing 12.4 for quadBSplSurf(), corner vertices are extrapolated in both the u and v directions after the other boundary vertices have been extrapolated in either the u or the v direction. For example, for the vertices in figure 12.30a, $V_{0,0}$ is extrapolated downward and to the left after $V_{1,0}$ has been extrapolated downward and after $V_{0,1}$ has been extrapolated to the left. This procedure ensures that the corners of the surface are located at the orig-

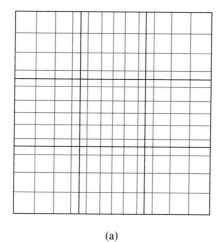

(a)

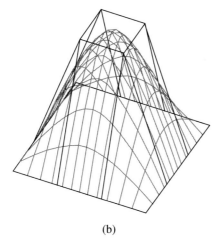

(b)

Figure 12.31 Views of a quadratic B-spline surface that has been extended to the corner control vertices: (a) plan view showing the surface (gray lines) and control mesh (black lines); (b) axonometric view of the surface and control mesh.

inal positions of the corner vertices. Extrapolation of the boundary control vertices was omitted from the program in order to calculate the surface shown in figure 12.30.

Equation 12.6 was used in the subroutine quadBSplSurf() to calculate the vertex coordinates of the faces that are drawn to display the surface. The number of faces is determined by the program parameters *surfu* and *surfv* that correspond to AutoCAD system variables SURFU and SURFV.

Cubic B-Spline Surfaces

The treatment of cubic B-spline surfaces is identical to the quadratic B-spline surfaces discussed above, except that any point on the surface is determined by the nearest 4×4 array of control vertices rather than by the nearest 3×3 array. Thus the 5×5 array of control

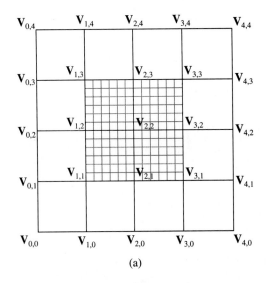

(a)

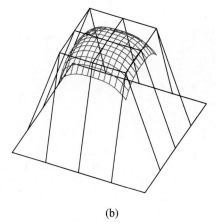

(b)

Figure 12.32 Views of a cubic B-spline surface: (a) plan view showing the surface (gray lines) and control mesh (black lines); (b) axonometric view of the surface and control mesh.

vertices shown in figure 12.32 produces a surface with four patches (in the plan view, the four patches lie in the four center meshes).

The coordinates of the cubic B-spline surface are determined by the formula

$$\mathbf{Q}_{i,j}(u,v) = \sum_{r=-3}^{0} \sum_{s=-3}^{0} \mathbf{V}_{i+r,j+s} b_r(u) b_s(v) \tag{12.7}$$

where now the $b_r(u)$ and $b_s(v)$ functions are given by equation 7.61 for the cubic B-spline.

The cubic B-spline surface has the same continuity (C^2) as its component spline curves; that is, values, first derivatives, and second derivatives are continuous along the entire surface.

The subroutine cubicBSplSurf() given in listing 12.5 of appendix B extends the surface to the control mesh corners by using the extrapolation procedure described in section

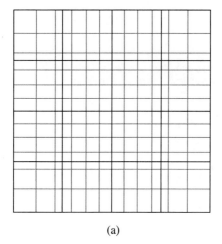

(a)

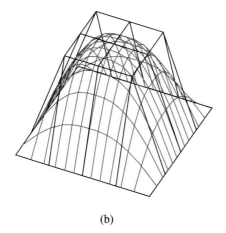

(b)

Figure 12.33   Views of a cubic B-spline surface that has been extended to the corner control vertices: (a) plan view showing the surface (gray lines) and control mesh (black lines); (b) axonometric view of the surface and control mesh.

7.6, rather than by using triple control points along the mesh boundary. When the extapo-
lation lines of code are omitted from the program, the surface shown in figure 12.32 is calculated; otherwise the surface shown in figure 12.33 is obtained. The arrays giving the
contol vertex coordinates can be changed to describe any topologically rectangular mesh,
as long as there are at least five control vertices in each direction (as required by the extrapolation procedure).

The subroutine cubicBSplSurf() duplicates the AutoCAD cubic B-spline surface obtained with PEDIT (with SURFTYPE = 6). This agreement can be verified by using
cubicBSplSurf() to program a DXF file to bring the programmed surface into AutoCAD;
see exercise 12.19.

12.8 NONUNIFORM B-SPLINE SURFACES

A nonuniform B-spline surface is formed by summing over the products of the nonuniform
basis functions $N_{i,k}(u)$ and $N_{j,l}(v)$ (for the examples given in this section, both basis functions are third order, $k = l = 3$). Again, u and v are the variables in the two directions along
the surface. The following formula is used to calculate the surface formed from n control
vertices in the u-direction and m vertices in the v-direction:

$$Q(u,v) = \frac{\sum\limits_{i=0}^{n-1}\sum\limits_{j=0}^{m-1} V_{i,j}w_{i,j}N_{i,k}(u)N_{j,l}(v)}{\sum\limits_{i=0}^{n-1}\sum\limits_{j=0}^{m-1} w_{i,j}N_{i,k}(u)N_{j,l}(v)} = \sum_{i=0}^{n-1}\sum_{j=0}^{m-1} V_{i,j}w_{i,j}S_{i,j}(u,v) \qquad (12.8)$$

where

$$S_{i,j}(u,v) = \frac{w_{i,j}N_{i,k}(u)N_{j,l}(v)}{\sum\limits_{i=0}^{n-1}\sum\limits_{j=0}^{m-1} w_{i,j}N_{i,k}(u)N_{j,l}(v)} \qquad (12.9)$$

The above equations describe nonuniform *rational* B-spline surfaces because they include the summations in the denominators, along with the weighting factors $w_{i,j}$. For the
nonrational case, each weight $w_{i,j} = 1$, and the double summation in the denominators is
also equal to one.

At a point (u,v) in a quadratic B-spline surface ($k = l = 3$), only the nine nearest vertices $V_{i,j}$ in a 3×3 array around the point will contribute (the product $N_{i,k}(u)N_{j,l}(v)$ will be
zero for the other vertices). Thus the surface may be calculated from a formula like equation 12.7, but with weight factors $w_{i,j}$, and with the b_i terms computed from the appropriate
$N_{j,k}$ terms. Listing 12.6 in appendix B carries out this procedure in the program subroutine
quadNURBSurf().

The mesh given in listing 12.6 is the same as that used for the uniform quadratic B-
spline case shown in figures 12.30–31. The left-hand smoothed surface in figure 12.34 was
calculated for all weighting factors equal to one—this gives a surface that duplicates the
surface in figure 12.31 that was calculated with extrapolated control vertices. As may be

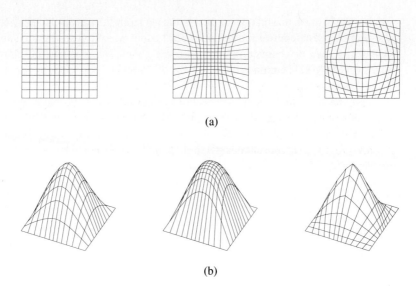

(a)

(b)

Figure 12.34   Mesh smoothed with a nonuniform rational B-spline. The mesh is the same as that used for the uniform splines in figures 12.30–31: (a) plan view; (b) axonometric view. The figures on the left correspond to the nonrational case (weight equals one at all vertices); the middle figures were computed for the weights of the four interior vertices being five times the weights at the other vertices; and the right-hand figures were calculated for weights at the four interior vertices being one-fifth the weights at the other vertices.

verified by bringing these surfaces into AutoCAD via DXF files, these results agree with the AutoCAD quadratic spline smoothing of a mesh (the u and v lines fall on the AutoCAD lines even when a view is zoomed for close inspection).

When the weight factors $w_{i,j}$ are increased by a factor of five for the four interior mesh vertices, the surface shown in the middle column of figure 12.34 is obtained. For this case, which corresponds to the weight vector given in listing 12.6, the surface is drawn closer to the four interior vertices. This produces a broader peak, but does not change the maximum height at the center. The center height of the surface remains the same for this mesh geometry because only the four interior vertices contribute to this center point; see exercise 12.20.

The right-hand views show that the mesh is drawn to the boundary vertices when the weights for the four interior vertices are smaller than the those for the boundary vertices. This produces a peak that is narrower, and a base that is pushed closer to the zero height of the boundary vertices.

As shown in the example surfaces of figure 12.34, weight factors can be use to shape a free-form NURBS surface, but they are limited in producing large displacements for free-form surfaces. Accordingly, some modelers such as AutoSurf rely primarily on control-point displacements for changing free-form surfaces. (The interactive displacement of free-form surfaces and curves in AutoSurf produces changes in the control vertices, even though it appears to the user that he is directly moving points on the surface or curve.)

Weight factors are essential when NURBS surfaces are used for precise representations of primitive surfaces such as the sphere. Sections of a sphere can be produced from a simple control mesh in a manner similar to the way a circle was produced by NURBS curves in section 7.7. The control mesh, knot vectors, and weight vector in the subroutine quad-NURBSurf() can be changed to form primitive sphere sections like those produced by the AutoSurf PRIMSF command. (The PRIMSF command has options for a sphere, cone, cylinder, and torus.)

Figure 12.35 shows spherical sections produced by the subroutine quadNURBSurf(), which duplicates the sphere option under the AutoSurf command PRIMSF. The mesh, shown in both the plan and the axonometric views, has an array of 3×5 control points. Accordingly, the vertex coordinates given in quadNURBSurf() must be changed to represent this new geometry. The upper left-hand illustration in figure 12.35 shows that the x- and y-coordinate values are calculated from trigonometric functions of θ, where θ is the angle of the sphere section. The radius of the sphere is assumed to equal one, with the bottom at $z = 0$ and the top at $z = 2$ (because the mesh points come together at the top and bottom, these locations each have three mesh points). As shown in the axonometric views of the meshes, the other three vertex locations in the xy-plane each have three separate points at

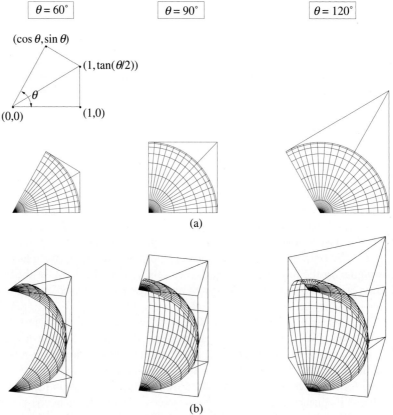

Figure 12.35 Sections of a spherical surface calculated from nonuniform rational B-splines: (a) plan views; (b) axonometric views.

$z = 0$, 1, and 2. For the 60° case, evaluation of the trigonometric functions $\cos\theta$, $\sin\theta$, and $\tan(\theta/2)$ gives the following control point coordinates:

```
double x[3][5] = {{0,1,1,1,0},{0,1,1,1,0},{0,.5,.5,.5,0}};
double y[3][5] = {{0,0,0,0,0},{0,.5773503,.5773503,.5773503,0},
                  {0,.866025,.866025,.866025,0}};
double z[3][5] = {{0,0,1,2,2},{0,0,1,2,2},{0,0,1,2,2}};
```

In the u-direction (planes of constant z), the three control points produce a circular arc for the knot vector *uknot*[] given below. In the v-direction, the five control points produce a semicircle with the knot vector *vknot*[] given below (this knot vector may be interpolated from the full-circle and quarter-circle knot vectors given in section 7.7).

```
double uknot[] = {0,0,0,1,1,1};
double vknot[] = {0,0,0,1,1,2,2,2};
```

The weights at the control vertices for the surface correspond to the product of the weights for the arcs in the u-and v-directions. In the v-direction, the weights are the same as for the circle and quarter-circle; thus for the semicircle the weights are 1, $\sqrt{2}/2$, 1, $\sqrt{2}/2$, and 1. As discussed in Rogers and Adams (1990), three control points form a circular arc of angle θ if the three weights are 1, $\cos(\theta/2)$, and 1. For $\theta = 60°$, $\cos(\theta/2) = 0.8660254$; thus the product of $\sqrt{2}/2 = 0.7070707$ and $\cos(\theta/2)$ equals 0.6123724. Accordingly, the product curve weights at the 3×5 surface mesh are given by the following vector:

```
double w[3][5] = {{1,.7070707,1,.7070707,1},
                  {.8660254,.6123724,.8660254,.6123724,.8660254},
                  {1,.7070707,1,.7070707,1}};
```

Substitution of the above vectors into the subroutine quadNURBSurf() of listing 12.6 yields the spherical section shown on the left of figure 12.35. The surfaces shown for $\theta = 90°$ and 120° were calculated in a similar manner after the trigonometric functions were calculated for these angles. For an angle greater than 180°, the spherical shell can be constructed with a 180° section (or two 90° sections) plus a section less than 180°. These component sections can be observed in AutoSurf by selecting ON under the EDITSF command to display the surface control points.

12.9 ADVANCED SURFACE-MODELING FEATURES WITH AUTOSURF

AutoSurf release 2 operates from within AutoCAD release 12AS. It is a NURBS-based surface modeler that provides some advanced features not available in the basic version of AutoCAD.

Three types of surfaces can be constructed in AutoSurf: primitive surfaces, free-form surfaces, and derived surfaces. Five primitive surfaces are available: cone, cylinder, sphere, torus, and planar. These primitives are formed with the PRIMSF command, except for planar surfaces, which are formed with the PLANESF. The NURBS representation of the sphere was discussed in the preceding section and is displayed in figure 12.35. Similar quadratic NURBS representations exist for the cone, cylinder, and torus.

Free-form surfaces can be extruded, revolved, ruled, swept, lofted, and tubular (formed with the commands EXTRUDESF, REVOLVESF, RULESF, SWEEPSF, LOFTSF, and TUBESF). In addition, a meshed surface can be constructed from two sets of curves (u,v curves) with the MESHSF command.

The free-form surfaces are nonrational, except for those surfaces formed with REVOLVESF and TUBESF. These latter surfaces are rational because their circular cross sections require the weight factors $w_{i,j}$ available with rational B-splines. The AutoSurf primitive surfaces are rational, with the exception of surfaces constructed with PLANESF. This result is to be expected from the fact that the cone, cylinder, sphere, and torus have circular cross sections.

The third type of surface is derived from existing NURBS surfaces. These consist of blended, fillet, corner, and offset surfaces, formed with the commands BLENDSF, FILLETSF, CORNERSF, and OFFSET. The CORNERSF command creates a blended fillet at the intersection of three fillets, and allows different radii at each surface edge. The OFFSET command creates a new surface that is offset normal to an existing surface by a specified distance.

AutoSurf also has advanced editing features for modifying surfaces to a desired shape. For example, surfaces can be trimmed in several different ways. A polyline can be projected onto a surface (with the PROJECTSF command) to cut a hole in the surface or to form a new edge of the surface along the polyline. Also, trimming can be performed at the intersection of two surfaces with the INTERSF command. An example surface-intersection calculation is presented in section 13.3 of the next chapter—this calculation applies equally to intersections in AutoSurf and to the AutoCAD AME solid modeling discussed in chapter 13. Trimming also occurs automatically when the FILLETSF command is used to create a fillet at the edge formed by two intersecting surfaces, and when the CORNERSF command is used to create a fillet in the corner formed by three intersecting surfaces.

Several display options are available with AutoSurf. In addition to other information, the command LISTAS identifies whether a surface is rational or nonrational. The DISPSF command permits the user to control the display of surfaces. The number of u and v lines in the display can be set, and the surface can be covered by a polyface mesh (triangular 3Dfaces) for rendering or for removing hidden lines with the HIDE command. The DISPSF command also enables the user to change the length of a displayed vector that is normal to the surface. The "show all normals" option displays a surface normal on each patch in the total surface. The number of separate patches that constitute a surface can be changed with the REFINESF command.

Free-form surfaces are normally of order 4 (cubic) with continuity C^2. The order and continuity can be changed from these default conditions at the time the surface is formed by entering "??" to use "advanced options."

The AutoSurf EXTRUDESF, REVOLVESF, and RULESF commands are similar to their corresponding AutoCAD commands TABSURF, REVSURF, and RULESURF. The EXTRUDESF and REVOLVESF commands generate surfaces by sweeping along a straight line and along a circular arc. Although these two sweep operations can be combined (as shown in figure 13.6 for the corresponding sweeps in solid modeling), they cannot generate the more complex surfaces that require the more general sweep features of the SWEEPSF command.

With the AutoSurf SWEEPSF command, an arbitrary sweep trajectory can be specified by one or two curves called rails. Figure 12.36a shows how a screw thread is swept by placing a polyline between two helical rails. The end of a bolt is formed by intersecting a plane primitive with the thread surface and using the INTERSF command. The bolt is completed by adding a cylinder primitive surface, and a bolt head is constructed with EXTRUDESF, PLANESF, and INTERSF commands.

SWEEPSF can also constuct a surface between several cross sections distributed on a single rail. Figure 12.36b shows how a duct is constructed using SWEEPSF with three polylines for cross sections on a spiral rail.

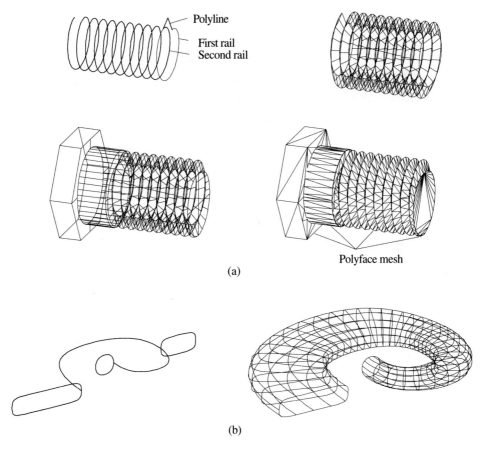

Polyline

First rail
Second rail

Polyface mesh

(a)

(b)

Figure 12.36   General sweep operations with the AutoSurf SWEEPSF command: (a) a screw thread constructed with a polyline traveling along two helical rails (one helix is shifted and rotated relative to the other one); (b) a duct formed from three polyline cross sections placed at appropriate locations along a spiral rail.

The LOFTSF command performs lofting, which is named after the lofts in which boat hulls were designed. LOFTSF is similar to RULESF, except with LOFTSF the number of polylines spanned by the surface is not limited to two. For figure 12.37, the LOFTSF command automatically generated a smooth canoe surface after all of the polylines in the top illustration were selected. The DISPSF command was used to change the number of surface lines from the values $u = 5$ and $v = 3$ shown in figure 12.7b to the values $u = 48$ and $v = 12$ in figure 12.37c. In figure 12.37d, the profile lines for both sides of the canoe were drawn with the PROFSF command (which is similar to SOLPROF discussed in section 13.2), and on the nearest side of the canoe, the SECTSF command was used to form horizontal section lines (water lines) and vertical (buttock) section lines.

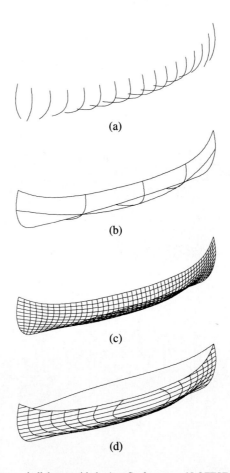

(a)

(b)

(c)

(d)

Figure 12.37   A canoe hull drawn with the AutoSurf command LOFTSF: (a) the cross sections and bow/stern sections; (b) the u and v lines on the surface hull after application of the LOFTSF command; (c) an increased number of u and v lines; (d) section lines (buttock and water lines) for the near side of the canoe, and profile lines for both sides of the canoe.

12.10 HIDDEN-LINE REMOVAL

Hidden lines can be removed in AutoCAD with the HIDE command, or with the Hide Lines/Hideplot options when plotting. A clear representation of a surface model is presented as a line drawing when hidden lines are removed—see the student drawings shown in figure 12.38. For a more realistic representation than can be provided by a line drawing, a rendering with shading can be carried out as discussed in chapter 14. To provide a hidden-line option for line drawings or to provide shading, the software must implement "hidden-line" algorithms.

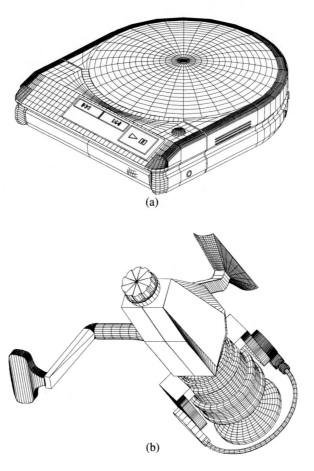

(a)

(b)

Figure 12.38 Surface models with hidden lines removed: (a) Sony compact disc player, drawn by Barry Nisly; (b) fly-casting fishing reel, drawn by Neal Wanket; (continued on next page)

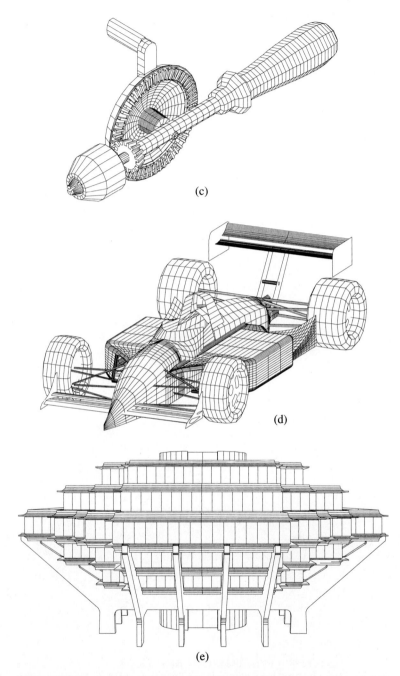

Figure 12.38 (continued) Surface models with hidden lines removed: (c) hand drill, drawn by Chris Hasse; (d) Indy race car, drawn by Jeff Klompus; (e) the University Library, UCSD, drawn by Christopher Casey.

General Hidden-Line Algorithms

The term *hidden-line removal* is used here in a general sense to include methods based on hidden-surface removal, such as the algorithm for convex objects given in the next subsection. Also, it should be noted that there are important pixel-based algorithms, such as ray tracing for rendered images (discussed in section 14.3), and the z-buffer algorithm (see Rogers, 1985; Foley et al., 1990).

A general hidden-line removal scheme may be implemented by first dividing the polygonal faces of all surfaces into their component triangles. Then, for a given observer position (viewpoint), a particular triangle can be compared with every other triangle in the scene to determine if the triangle is fully visible, invisible (hidden by the other triangles), or partially visible. To determine the visibility of a triangle, one must calculate line intersections. A detailed algorithm of this type is discussed and programmed by Ammeraal (1986).

Although general algorithms may be conceptually simple, implementation can be tedious; for example, Ammeraal (1986) considers six separate tests for line intersections. Furthermore, the simplest implementations are often the slowest, so that a variety of procedures are used to speed up the computations. Effort can lead to considerable improvement in hidden-line algorithms; for example, changes in the AutoCAD hidden-line algorithm in release 12 resulted in an order-of-magnitude speed-up in the HIDE operation.

A Hidden-Line Algorithm for Convex Surfaces

For convex volumes, hidden lines may be removed by simply plotting only those faces with normal vectors directed toward the observer (that is, pointing into the hemispherical solid angle toward the observer). Some common objects are convex volumes; for example, a closed box and a sphere are convex. However, most objects are not convex; that is, part of their volumes are concave. The algorithm considered here will not work by itself for concave volumes, which usually require a general algorithm like those discussed above. However, as part of a general algorithm, this procedure can be used to eliminate all faces with normals facing away from the observer. For example, the preferences dialog box for Auto-CAD Render lets you check a "discard back faces" button to speed up the rendering process by eliminating consideration of all faces with backward-facing normals.

Figure 12.39a shows a convex box in which only the three faces pointing toward the observer are plotted. The notched box shown in figure 12.39b is concave, with the result that for the view direction shown, one of the four faces pointing toward the observer is mostly obscured by other faces. Thus for a concave volume, a face may be partially or fully obscured even though its normal vector points toward the observer. On the other hand, for a convex volume, all faces pointing toward the observer are fully visible.

To remove hidden lines on a convex volume, the requirement that a face's normal vector point toward the observer is imposed by requiring that the scalar (dot) product of the normal vector and the vector from the face to the viewpoint be positive. Faces seen on edge will have a scalar product of zero but need not be plotted because the edge will be plotted as part of adjacent visible faces.

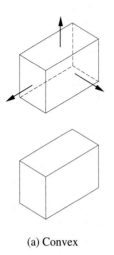

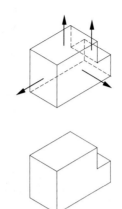

(a) Convex   (b) Concave

Figure 12.39 Convex and concave volumes as seen from the observer's viewpoint. In the top figures, only the normal vectors pointing toward the observer are drawn. The bottom figures represent the objects after hidden lines have been removed.

A vector normal to a face may be found by calculating the vector (cross) product of two vectors lying in the face. Any face has at least three vertices, so that two vectors lying in the face are given by the vector difference between the first and second vertex points, and by the vector difference between the first and third vertex points. The normal vector $N = n_x\mathbf{i} + n_y\mathbf{j} + n_z\mathbf{k}$ is calculated from equation 12.10 below by using vectors $A = a_x\mathbf{i} + a_y\mathbf{j} + a_z\mathbf{k}$ and $B = b_x\mathbf{i} + b_y\mathbf{j} + b_z\mathbf{k}$ that lie in the face.

The normal N to a face may be calculated from the equation

$$\mathbf{N} = \mathbf{A} \times \mathbf{B} = (a_y b_z - a_z b_y)\mathbf{i} + (a_z b_x - a_x b_z)\mathbf{j} + (a_x b_y - a_y b_x)\mathbf{k} \qquad (12.10)$$

Here the components of A and B can be identified with face vertex points as described above: a_x is the x component of the vector between the first and second vertex points; that is, for face number k, $a_x = vert[vnum1][0] - vert[vnum0][0]$, where $vnum1 = vn[k][1]$ and $vnum0 = vn[k][0]$. Similarly, $a_y = vert[vnum1][1] - vert[vnum0][1]$, $a_z = vert[vnum1][2] - vert[vnum0][2]$. Also, $b_x = vert[vnum2][0] - vert[vnum0][0]$, where $vnum2 = vn[k][2]$, etc.

The condition that the normal vector is directed toward the observer may be expressed by the relation $\mathbf{N}\cdot\mathbf{V} > 0$, where $\mathbf{V} = v_x\mathbf{i} + v_y\mathbf{j} + v_z\mathbf{k}$ is the vector from the face to the observer viewpoint. For perspective views, V can be expressed as the difference between a vector to the observer position and a vector to the face (any vertex point on the face is suitable). For an axonometric view, the viewpoint is at an infinite distance from the object and V may be any vector parallel but opposite to the view direction. The axonometric view is often set up along the negative z-axis, in which case V can be replaced by the unit vector $\mathbf{k}$ in the z-direction, and the criterion for a visible face reduces to $(a_x b_y - a_y b_x) > 0$.

The implementation of the hidden-line algorithm for convex volumes by the above procedures is relatively simple and is covered in exercises 12.25–12.27.

The Painter's Hidden-Line Algorithm

The painter's algorithm hides background objects by "painting" over them. That is, faces on surfaces are filled from back to front in the scene. For a wireframe representation with hidden lines removed, a face is first filled with the background color, and then the face edges are drawn with the object color. Thus edges from previously drawn faces are covered by the fill operation. This procedure can also be used for rendering; see section 14.2.

The difficult part of implementing this algorithm is ordering the faces from the back of the scene to the front. In this section only two special cases are considered; in these the face ordering can be simply prescribed (figure 12.40).

Figure 12.40a shows the face ordering for surfaces based on a rectangular grid in the xy-plane, like the mathematical functions displayed in figure 12.26. For this case, the face numbering starts with the face that is at the far corner from the viewer.

The painter's algorithm can be easily applied to a surface of revolution, with faces numbered from back to front as illustrated in figure 12.40b.

A program for a surface of revolution with hidden lines contains the same subroutine revSurf() as given in section 12.3, except with the faces on the right of the surface renumbered as shown in figure 12.40b. This renumbering is achieved by replacing the face number m by $m2$ in the array elements $vn[m][]$.

The subroutine revSurf() listed below calls the function plotHideSurface(), which first fills each face with the background color (BLACK) and then draws the face edges with WHITE (colors are assumed to be set by #define directives). The subroutine plotHideSurface() is written using the Microsoft C graphics functions, with a face being filled by the fillQuadrilateral() function given as listing 3.2 in appendix B. (Some graphics libraries, such as the Macintosh QuickDraw library, have their own functions for filling polygons.)

In the subroutine, the screen coordinates of the vertex points for a face are assigned to both ($xvert[4]$,$yvert[4]$) and to ($xpt[4]$,$ypt[4]$) because the points ($xvert[4]$,$yvert[4]$) become reordered in fillQuadrilateral() and are therefore not useful for plotting the face edges. (Recall that arrays are passed to subroutine functions by address; thus the values of $xvert[4]$ and $yvert[4]$ are reordered in plotHideSurface() after the function fillQuadrilateral() is called.)

```
void revSurf(void)
{
    int     i,j,j0,k,m,m2;
    double theta,dtheta;

    numFaces = (nb-1)*ne; dtheta = 2*PI/ne; j0 = ne/2 - 1;
    for (i=0; i<nb; i++)
    {
        for (j=0; j<ne; j++)
        {
            k = i*ne+j;
            theta = -0.5*PI + j*dtheta;
```

11	10	9	8	7	6	5	4	3	2	1	0
23	22	21	20	19	18	17	16	15	14	13	12
35	34	33	32	31	30	29	28	27	26	25	24
47	46	45	44	43	42	41	40	39	38	37	36
59	58	57	56	55	54	53	52	51	50	49	48

View direction   (a)

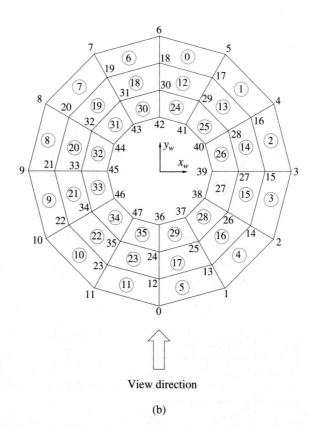

View direction

(b)

Figure 12.40 Surfaces with numbered faces showing the plotting order for implementing the painter's hidden-line algorithm; (a) a rectangular mesh for plotting a function like those shown in figure 12.26; (b) a surface of revolution.

```
                    vert[k][0] = xcurve[i]*cos(theta);
                    vert[k][1] = xcurve[i]*sin(theta);
                    vert[k][2] = zcurve[i];
            }
    }
    for (i=0; i<nb-1; i++)
    {
        for (j=0; j<ne; j++)
        {
            m = i*ne+j;
            if (j <= j0)
                m2 = m + j0 - 2*j;
            else
                m2 = m; /* m2 is the face number */
            vn[m2][0] = m;
            if (j == (ne-1))
            {
                vn[m2][1] = m+1-ne; vn[m2][2] = m+1;
            }
            else
            {
                vn[m2][1] = m+1; vn[m2][2] = m+1+ne;
            }
            vn[m2][3] = m+ne; vn[m2][4] = m;
        }
    }
    plotHideSurface();
}


void plotHideSurface(void)
{
    int     m,k,vnum,xcen=320,yb=350;
    double phi,sinp,cosp,sf = 6.0;
    double xw[4],yw[4],zw[4],xvert[4],yvert[4],xpt[4],ypt[4];

    phi = 70*PI/180; sinp = sin(phi); cosp = cos(phi);
    for (m=0; m<numFaces; m++)
    {
        for (k=0; k<4; k++)
        {
            vnum = vn[m][k];
            xw[k] = vert[vnum][0]; yw[k] = vert[vnum][1];
            zw[k] = vert[vnum][2];
            xvert[k] = xpt[k] = xcen + (int) (sf*xw[k]);
            yvert[k] = ypt[k] = yb - (int) (sf*(yw[k]*cosp+zw[k]*sinp));
        }
        _setcolor(BLACK);
        fillQuadrilateral(xvert,yvert); /* fill a face with black */
```

```
_setcolor(WHITE);
for (k=0; k<4; k++) /* plot the edges of a face */
{
    if (k == 0)
        _moveto((int) xpt[0],(int) ypt[0]);
    else
        _lineto((int) xpt[k],(int) ypt[k]);
}
_lineto((int) xpt[0],(int) ypt[0]);
}
}
```

EXERCISES

12.1 Use the 3DFACE command to construct a cube and then attach letters as shown below. The letters may be constructed with B-splines, as in section 7.6. Placement of the letters on a cube face is facilitated by placing a user-coordinate system on the face.

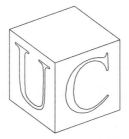

12.2 Construct a cube and save it as a block. Then insert the block with points and scales from table 12.1 to construct Rietveld's Berlin chair, shown in figure 12.4.

12.3 Implement the fractal mountain program given in listing 12.1 of appendix B. Use this program to experiment with different values for parameters in the formula for the random vertical displacements.

12.4 Write the fractal mountain program so that it produces a DXF file for input into your CAD program. Then view a fractal mountain at various angles with hidden lines removed.

12.5 Implement the program for a dodecahedron DXF file listed in section 12.2. Bring the dodecahedron into your CAD program and view it with hidden lines removed.

12.6 Write a subroutine that divides the pentagons of a dodecahedron into triangles in a manner similar to the way triangles were divided in section 8.2. Incorporate this subroutine into the dodecahedron program of section 12.2 to produce the geodesic dome pictured in figure 12.8b.

12.7 With AutoCAD, produce a cylinder of elliptical cross section which hides lines with its top and bottom surfaces, as well as with its side surface. To do this give thickness to a circle, save it as a block, and then insert it into the drawing with different x and y scale factors.

12.8 Program a surface of revolution following the procedures described in section 12.3.

12.9 Generalize the surface-of-revolution program so that it can treat an axis at any orientation. You can do this by using the translation and rotation transformations of chapter 11 to transfer to a coordinate system in which the axis of rotation is coincident with the z-axis. Then transform back to the world coordinates before plotting the surface.

12.10 Incorporate the surface-of-revolution program of section 12.1 into an interactive program in which points on the curve are selected by a mouse (similar to the polyline curves of section 9.3), and the resulting surface may be rotated around two angles (as in section 11.4). Consider both axonometric and perspective views.

12.11 Use the 3DFACE, PFACE, REVSURF, and 3DMESH commands to construct the following simple 3-D objects (these objects are those available from an AutoLISP program accessed from the AutoCAD menu): a box, cone, dish, dome, mesh, pyramid, sphere, torus, and wedge.

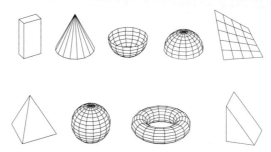

12.12 Use your CAD software to produce a ruled surface representation of the Peterborough canoe from the data given in table 12.3.

12.13 Use RULESURF to construct the two hyperbolic shell structures in figure 12.19b.

12.14 Implement the program for the ruled surface given in listing 12.2 of appendix B.

12.15 Implement the program for the Coons patch given in listing 12.3 of appendix B.

12.16 Write a program that implements the subroutine quadBSplSurf() described in section 12.7 and given in listing 12.4 of appendix B.

12.17 Write a program that generates a DXF file from the subroutine quadBSplSurf() given in listing 12.4 of appendix B. Bring this file into AutoCAD and show that it duplicates the surface obtained by smoothing a mesh (with SURFTYPE = 5) containing the same control points and SURFU and SURFV values as the program.

12.18 Write a program that implements the subroutine cubicBSplSurf() described in section 12.7 and given in listing 12.5 of appendix B.

12.19 Write a program that generates a DXF file from the subroutine cubicBSplSurf() given in listing 12.5 of appendix B. Bring this file into AutoCAD and show that it duplicates the surface obtained by smoothing a mesh (with SURFTYPE = 6) containing the same control points and SURFU and SURFV values as the program.

12.20 Consider the control mesh given in listing 12.6 of appendix B that was used to calculate the quadratic NURBS surfaces shown in figure 12.34. Use equations 12.8–9 to calculate the surface height at its center, and show that this height is independent of the weighting factors.

12.21 Program a control mesh like the one shown below, for which the control points in the u-direction (azimuthal direction) are the same as those for a circle with variable corner weights (as described in section 7.7). Carry out NURBS surface calculations to obtain examples like those shown below (for these illustrations the surfaces were brought into AutoCAD with a DXF file).

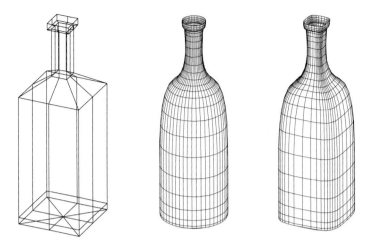

12.22 On your CAD system construct a surface model of a mechanical object like those shown in figures 12.38b–c.

12.23 Construct a surface model of an automobile or an airplane. The aircraft surface models shown below were constructed by Chris Shultz (top) and Stephan Emmenegger (bottom).

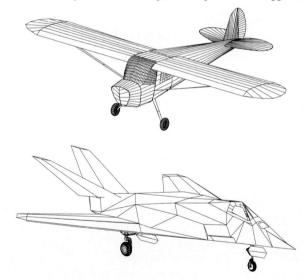

12.24 From plan and elevation views, construct a 3-D surface model of a building, like the one shown in figure 12.38e, or a house like the following one (drawn by Chris Jonas).

12.25 Write a program that uses the hidden-line algorithm for a convex surface given in section 12.10. Consider axonometric views of a box.

12.26 Write a program that uses the hidden-line algorithm for perspective views of a box.

12.27 Write a program that uses the hidden-line algorithm for perspective views of a geodesic dome (see section 8.2 for a discussion of geodesic domes).

12.28 Implement the painter's hidden-line algorithm for a surface of revolution, as given in the program subroutine in section 12.10.

12.29 Plot the Bessel function shown in figure 12.26a directly to the screen from a program by using the painter's hidden-line algorithm (see figure 12.40 for the ordering of faces).

BIBLIOGRAPHY

AMBASZ, E., *The Poetics of the Pragmatic.* New York: Rizzoli International Publications, Inc., 1988.

AMMERAAL, L., *Interactive 3D Computer Graphics.* Chichester, West Sussex, England: John Wiley & Sons, 1988.

AMMERAAL, L., *Programming Principles in Computer Graphics.* Chichester, West Sussex, England: John Wiley & Sons, 1986.

ANGELL, I. O., AND G. GRIFFITH, *High-resolution Computer Graphics Using FORTRAN 77.* New York: Halsted Press Book, John Wiley & Sons, 1987.

AutoCAD Release 12 Reference Manual. Sausalito, Calif.: Autodesk, Inc., 1992.

AutoSurf Release 2 Reference Manual. Sausalito, Calif.: Autodesk, Inc., 1993.

BARTELS, R. H., J. C. BEATTY, AND B. A. BARSKY, *An Introduction to Splines for Use in Computer Graphics and Geometric Modeling.* Los Altos, Calif.: Morgan Kaufmann Publishers, Inc., 1987.

BEACH, R. C., *An Introduction to the Curves and Surfaces of Computer-Aided Design.* New York: Van Nostrand Reinhold, 1991.

"Bruce Farr e Nauta Yachts Nauta 70". *Domus,* vol. 740, pp. 74–79, July/August, 1992.

CHOI, B. K., *Surface Modeling for CAD/CAM.* Amsterdam: Elsevier, 1991.

FARIN, G., *Curves and Surfaces for Computer Aided Geometric Design: A Practical Guide,* 2nd ed. San Diego, Calif.: Academic Press, Inc., 1990.

FOLEY, J. D., A. VAN DAM, S. K. FEINER, AND J. F. HUGHES, *Computer Graphics: Principles and Practice,* 2nd ed. Reading, Mass.: Addison-Wesley Publishing Co., 1990.

GASSON, P. C., *Geometry of Spatial Forms: Analysis, Synthesis, Concept, Formulation and Space Vision for CAD.* Chichester, West Sussex, England: Ellis Horwood Limited, 1983.

Meadmore, C., *The Modern Chair: Classics in Production.* Van Nostrand Reinhold, 1975

MOORES, T., AND M. MOHR, *Canoecraft: A Harrowsmith Illustrated Guide to Fine Woodstrip Construction.* Camden East, Ontario, Canada: Camden House Publishing, 1983.

Peitgen, H.-O., and D. Saupe, *The Science of Fractal Images.* New York: Springer-Verlag, 1988.

Piegl, L. A., "Rational B-spline Curves and Surfaces for CAD and Graphics," pp. 225–269 in *State of the Art in Computer Graphics: Visualization and Modeling,* D. F. Rogers and R. A. Earnshaw, editors. New York: Springer-Verlag, 1991.

Rogers, D. F., *Procedural Elements for Computer Graphics.* New York: McGraw-Hill Publishing Co., 1985.

Rogers, D. F., and J. A. Adams, *Mathematical Elements for Computer Graphics,* 2nd ed. New York: McGraw-Hill Publishing Co., 1990.

Zeid, I., *CAD/CAM Theory and Practice.* New York: McGraw-Hill Publishing Co., 1991.

13

Solid Modeling

Solid modeling provides the most complete representation of an object. Besides describing the geometry of an object, a solid model includes material properties, so that quantities such as mass, center of gravity, and moments of inertia can be readily calculated. The data available from a solid model can be used by numerically controlled machinery to physically construct prototypes or finished parts.

A number of different schemes have been used to represent solids. The overview below briefly describes the following schemes: primitive instancing, cell decomposition, sweep representations, constructive solid geometry (CSG), and boundary representation. These methods are not mutually exclusive; in fact, currently most commercial solid modelers, such AutoCAD AME (Advanced Modeling Extension) use constructive solid geometry together with boundary representation. Also, AME uses sweep representations to construct primitives for use with the CSG operations.

Solid modeling is computationally intensive, so that efficient methods of model construction are needed to reduce computing time and memory requirements. Several examples of solid model construction are presented that use AutoCAD AME (AutoCAD Designer, a newly released product, offers similar solid-modeling capabilities along with parametric design features). The mechanical part shown at the opening of this chapter was constructed with AME by using sweep primitives consisting of solids of revolution and extrusion. Two graphical representations are illustrated in the figure: on the left the solid is covered with a polygon mesh to permit hidden-line viewing; on the right, profile lines are plotted (with the addition of hatching on the sectioned surfaces).

Early development of solid modeling methods was called computer-aided geometric design (CAGD), which is based on computational geometry. In this chapter, examples in computational geometry include surface intersection curves and mass property calculations.

13.1 AN OVERVIEW OF SOLID MODELING METHODS

Primitive Instancing

Primitive instancing is useful for specialized situations where objects have only a few different topological configurations. The dimensions of a primitive solid can be changed to construct other members of the same topological family. For example, starting with a solid cube as a primitive, the solid version Rietveld's Berlin chair can be constructed in the same manner that the surface version was formed in section 12.2. Thus the solid boards of varying dimensions are "instances" of the primitive solid cube.

The different instances of a cube shown in figure 13.1a can represent boards, posts, and beams, depending on their dimensions. The objects in figure 13.1a were constructed by saving a solid cube (SOLBOX) as a block, and inserting it with dimensions determined by the x, y, and z scaling factors.

A slightly more complex case of primitive instancing consists of the I-beam shown in figure 13.1b. In this case there are five parameters that may be varied (l, h_1, h_2, w_1, and w_2) compared with the three dimensions of a board formed from a cube.

When saved as a block, the I-beam can be inserted with different scaling factors, shown by the first two objects in figure 13.1c. Because only three parameters (x, y, and z scaling) can be varied when a block is inserted, the thicknesses h_2 and w_2 of these objects are changed in proportion to changes in the overall dimensions h_1 and w_1. A solid modeler that incorporates primitive instancing for I-beams must permit separate specification of the thickness h_2 and w_2, as illustrated by the last two objects in figure 13.1c, in which the thicknesses h_2 and w_2 remain constant when the overall dimensions h_1 and w_1 are changed.

More complex examples of primitive instancing are provided by the sample API (advanced programming interface) C programs supplied with AutoCAD AME. For example, the program design.c provides solid models for six different mechanical objects: a gear, wheel, shaft, bearing bracket, bolt, and nut. The program is loaded with the AutoLISP command: (xload "design"). Also, if it has not already been loaded, AME should be loaded with the command (xload "ame"). Then instances of the six objects can be inserted with the following commands: SOLGEAR, SOLWHEEL, SOLSHAFT, SOLBEAR, SOLBOLT, and SOLNUT. Figure 13.2 shows instances of these objects, and the parameters that determine each object are listed in the figure caption.

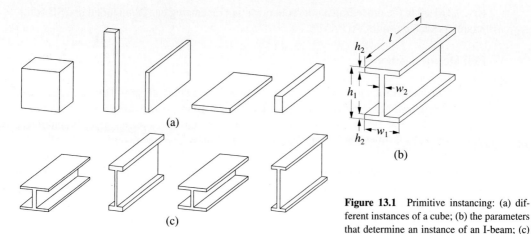

Figure 13.1 Primitive instancing: (a) different instances of a cube; (b) the parameters that determine an instance of an I-beam; (c) different instances of an I-beam.

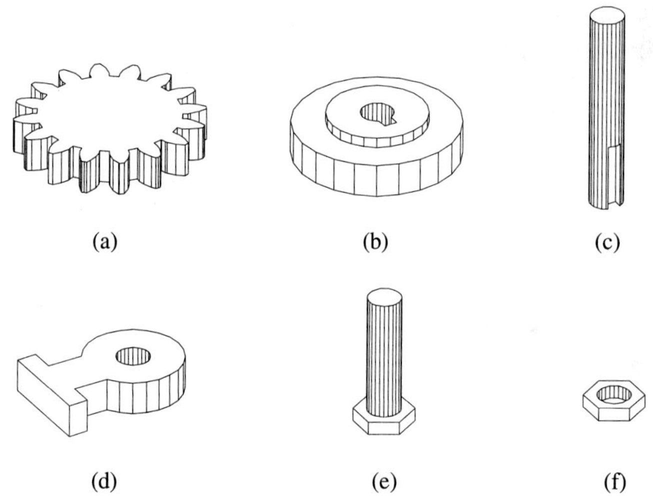

(a)

(b)

(c)

(a)

(b)

(c)

(d)

(e)

(f)

Figure 13.2 Primitive instances for mechanical objects in the sample program design.c: (a) a gear, specified by its pitch-circle diameter, number of teeth, thickness, and pressure angle (quantities defined in section 5.2); (b) a wheel, specified by its diameter, thickness, hub diameter, hub-extrusion thickness, hole diameter, keyway depth, and keyway width; (c) a shaft, specified by its diameter, length, keyway depth, keyway width, and keyway length; (d) a bearing bracket, specified by its diameter, thickness, hole diameter, distance from base to hole center, base height, and base width; (e) a bolt, specified by its head diameter, head height, screw diameter, and screw length; (f) a nut, specified by its diameter, height, and hole diameter.

By itself, primitive instancing can be an efficient solid modeling method when only a few types of solids are required, for example, a structure that requires only boards and I-beams, or a mechanical object constructed from the parts in design.c. On the other hand, the more general solid modelers discussed below must be able to represent any real 3-D object. As noted in the preceding paragraph, primitive instancing can be included in CSG solid modelers such as AutoCAD AME.

Cell Decomposition

The cell-decomposition procedure starts with the complete solid object and divides space into small cells in order to identify which cells the object occupies. The accuracy of this procedure depends on the cell size; cells may be made smaller until a desired accuracy is achieved.

Figure 13.3 illustrates cell division for a 2-D region. The tree diagram in figure 13.3c describes the cell-division procedure. The diagram is an upside-down tree, with the root at the top representing a bounding rectangle (here a square) around the complete 2-D object. At the first level below the root, there are four nodes representing the four cells (squares) that divide the bounding square.

At level 1, cell 5 contains no material, so it is divided no further, and this node is drawn as an unfilled square on the tree diagram. The other three nodes at level 1 are drawn as circles because they represent cells that must be further divided (at level 2) into four cells each. This tree diagram is called a quadtree because 2-D cell subdivision produces four cells at each branching node.

For the simple object (right-angle ruler) considered here, the tree diagram terminates at level 2 because at this level all of the cells are either entirely filled with material or en-

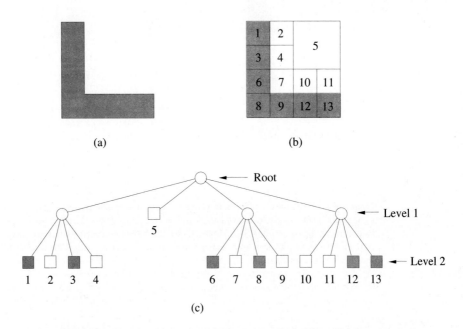

Figure 13.3 Cell decomposition for a 2-D region: (a) the object to be represented is a right-angle ruler; (b) the object is circumscribed by a bounding square, which is divided into increasingly smaller cells until each cell is either fully occupied by material or completely empty; (c) the cell decomposition is represented by a quadtree.

tirely empty. In figure 13.3c the nodes representing filled cells are shaded and are numbered so that they can be identified with the cells shown in figure 13.3b.

For more complex 2-D objects, such as those with sloping or curved boundaries, the cell-decomposition procedure will not provide an exact representation with a finite number of decomposition levels. As an example, a circular boundary is shown in figure 13.4 with three levels of decomposition. In this figure the circle boundary still passes through cells, which may be further divided to provide a more accurate representation of the boundary. Because further divisions of the cells will still result in partially filled cells, the material inside the boundary cannot be exactly described with a finite number of cell subdivisions. Thus, except for the simplest objects, cell decomposition is an approximate procedure, which is carried out to enough levels to describe the object with sufficient accuracy.

Cell division for a 3-D solid is illustrated in figure 13.5. The bounding cube around the 3-D object (here a simple bracket) is divided into eight cubes. Because branching nodes produce eight cells (cubes), 3-D cell decomposition is described by an octree graph, as shown in figure 13.5c.

Sweep Representations

Solids can be constructed by sweeping an area through a path. The simplest paths are straight lines for generating extruded solid objects, and circles for generating solids of revolution.

The three objects shown in figure 13.6 were generated with the same cross section—a thin rectangle topped by a circle. In figure 13.6a, the cross section is extruded along a straight line with the AutoCAD AME command SOLEXT. With AME, the cross section need not be a surface; that is, the cross section can be represented by a PLINE forming its outline.

The wheel in figure 13.6b was constructed by sweeping the cross section 360° around an axis with the SOLREV command. Figure 13.6c consists of a combination of extrusions and revoluions (of 90° and 45°); this figure could represent a railing that first travels horizontally, then turns and slopes downward before leveling out and turning back. This latter figure approximates a more general sweep along an arbitrary path, which is a procedure not yet available in AME.

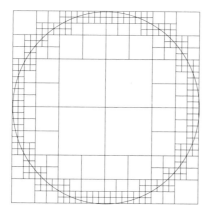

Figure 13.4 Cell decomposition for a circular boundary, with the object's material being inside the circle.

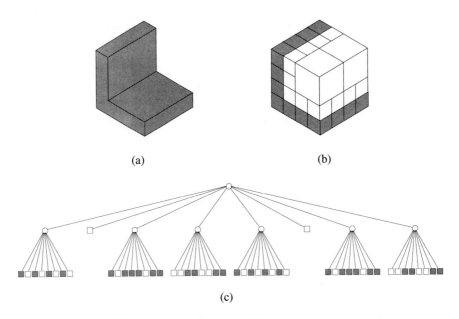

(a)   (b)

(c)

Figure 13.5   Cell decomposition for a solid described by an octree graph.

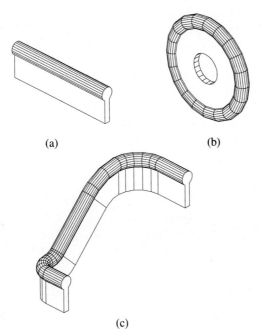

(a)   (b)

(c)

Figure 13.6   Sweep representations generated from a common cross section: (a) an extruded solid constructed by sweeping along a straight line; (b) a surface of revolution (wheel) constructed by sweeping around an axis; (c) a combination of extrusions and solids of revolution.

The sweep operations in AME produce primitives that are displayed initially as wire-frames. To produce hidden-line views, one should use the SOLMESH command to cover the object with a polyface mesh (pface), and then use the HIDE command. The number of lines represented in the wireframe and mesh views is determined by the value of the solid-wire-density parameter, which can be changed by the SOLWDENS command. For figure 13.6, SOLWDENS was set equal to 5; larger values (up to the maximum value of 12) would use more lines to more accurately represent curved surfaces.

The solids produced by sweep procedures in AutoCAD AME can be used as primitives for constructing more complicated objects by using the operations of constructive solid geometry (CSG).

Constructive Solid Geometry (CSG)

Objects are built up with CSG by starting with simple objects called *primitives* and combining them with Boolean operations. The three Boolean operations are union (or addition), difference (or subtraction), and intersection. These operations may be applied to solids that result from previous Boolean operations.

Figure 13.7 illustrates the CSG method starting with 2-D primitives for circular and rectangular areas (the figure may also be considered as a top view of 3-D cylinder and box solids). The union operation is described by the symbol $\cup$, the difference operation by the subtraction symbol $-$, and the intersection operation by the symbol $\cap$.

The union and intersection operations are commutative, but the difference operation is not. That is, for combining solid A with solid B, $A \cup B = B \cup A$, $A \cap B = B \cap A$, but $A - B \neq B - A$.

With AutoCAD AME, the CSG Boolean operations are given by the commands SOLUNION, SOLSUB, and SOLINT. These operations may be applied to any combination of 2-D regions or to any combination of 3-D solids, but not to a mixture of 2-D regions and 3-D solids. However, a 2-D region can be turned into a 3-D solid with the sweep operations SOLEXT and SOLREV, and then combined with other solids.

The SOLIDIFY command may be used to construct region primitives from the areas enclosed by 2-D entities such as polylines, polygons, ellipses, circles, and donuts. For ex-

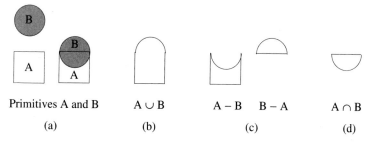

Primitives A and B	$A \cup B$	$A - B \quad B - A$	$A \cap B$
(a)	(b)	(c)	(d)

Figure 13.7   The Boolean operations of constructive solid geometry (CSG): (a) the circle primitive labeled B being placed along the top edge of the rectangle primitive A; (b) the union operation $A \cup B$; (c) the difference operations $A - B$ and $B - A$; (d) the intersection operation $A \cap B$.

ample, a complex primitive region can be constructed in the following manner: first, use 2-D drafting techniques to draw the region's outline; next, turn the outline into a polyline with the PEDIT command; and then form the region by picking the polyline after the SOLIDIFY command has been entered.

The basic primitives available for 3-D solid modeling with AutoCAD AME are the box, wedge, cylinder, cone, sphere, and torus illustrated in figure 13.8. The figure lists the commands for the primitives and also aliases, which are alternate names that may be entered to execute the command. After the command for a primitive has been entered, its location and dimensions must be specified. In figure 13.8, note that the cylinder and cone primitives can have elliptical cross sections. Also, the torus primitive can assume a football shape if a negative value is entered for its major radius.

In addition to the basic primitives shown in figure 13.8, additional primitives may be formed by the sweep operations of SOLEXT and SOLREV discussed in the preceding subsection. Also, fillet and chamfer edge primitives can be formed with the SOLFILL and SOLCHAM commands. The SOLFILL and SOLCHAM commands produce separate solids that are added (for internal fillets and chamfers) or subtracted (for external fillets and chamfers) from the existing solid.

Primitive Command	Aliases
SOLBOX	BOX
SOLWEDGE	WEDGE, WED
SOLCYLINDER	CYLINDER, CYL
SOLCONE	CONE, CON
SOLSPHERE	SPHERE, SPH
SOLTORUS	TORUS, TOR

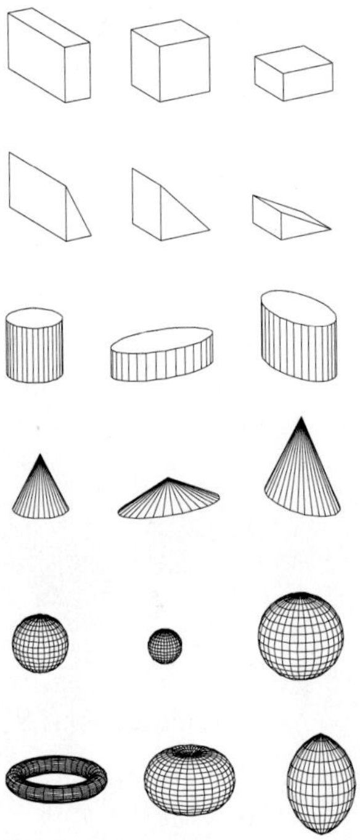

Figure 13.8   Basic primitives available with AutoCAD AME.

The Boolean operations used to construct an object may be illustrated with a binary tree structure. Table 13.1 shows the binary tree of a simple object (bracket) printed in text form when the Tree option is selected under the AME command SOLLIST. A pictorial representation of this same tree is shown in figure 13.9a.

Each object in the binary tree is identified by a "handle" in the form of a hexadecimal number, which is assigned by AME. The primitives are at the bottom (ends or leaves of each branch). A single Boolean operation (union, difference, or intersection) occurs between two objects at the tree nodes until the final object is completed.

TABLE 13.1 THE CSG TREE (EQUIVALENT TO THE PICTORIAL TREE
IN FIGURE 13.9A) PRINTED FROM THE SOLLIST
COMMAND

Object type = SUBTRACTION   Handle = 91
Component handles: 6C and 35
Area not computed Material = MILD_STEEL
Representation = WIREFRAME   Render type = CSG\

.... Object type = SUBTRACTION   Handle = 6C
....   Component handles: 4B and 32
....   Area not computed   Material = MILD_STEEL
....   Representation = WIREFRAME   Render type = CSG\
....   Node level = 1

.... Object type = UNION   Handle = 4B
....   Component handles: 26 and 15
....   Area not computed   Material = MILD_STEEL
....   Representation = WIREFRAME   Render type = CSG
....   Node level = 2

.... Object type = BOX(2.000000, −0.350000, 2.000000)   Handle = 26
....   Area not computed   Material = MILD_STEEL
....   Representation = WIREFRAME   Render type = CSG
....   Node level = 3

.... Object type = BOX(2.000000, −2.000000, 0.350000)   Handle = 15
....   Area not computed   Material = MILD_STEEL
....   Representation = WIREFRAME   Render type = CSG
....   Node level = 3

.... Object type = CYLINDER(0.200000, 0.200000, 0.500000)   Handle = 32
....   Area not computed   Material = MILD_STEEL
....   Representation = WIREFRAME   Render type = CSG
....   Node level = 2

.... Object type = CYLINDER(0.200000, 0.200000, 0.500000)   Handle = 35
....   Area not computed   Material = MILD_STEEL
....   Representation = WIREFRAME   Render type = CSG
....   Node level = 1

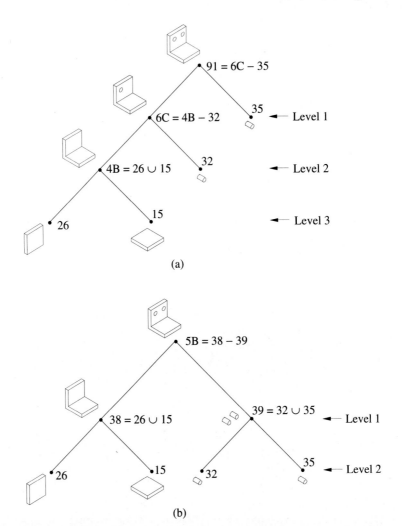

Figure 13.9 CSG trees illustrating the Boolean operations used in constructing a simple bracket.

For the bracket described by the tree structure given in table 13.1 and figure 13.9a, two boxes (handles 26 and 15) were first combined to form an object identified by handle 4B. Next a cylinder (handle = 32) was subtracted from the combined object to form the first hole. Finally, the bracket was completed by subtracting another cylinder (handle = 35) to form the second hole.

With AME, all of the Boolean operations needed to construct the bracket can be carried out with a single SOLSUB command. After SOLSUB is entered, the two boxes are selected for union, and the two cylinders are selected for subtraction. The AME software performs the Boolean operations in an order that minimizes the number of levels in the CSG tree. For example, AME selected the tree structure shown in figure 13.9b, which has only two levels below the root compared with the three levels shown in 13.9a. Note that in figure 13.9b two cylinders are combined to form a single object (handle = 39) even though the cylinders do not touch each other.

Boundary Representation (B-rep)

A solid may be defined by providing a representation of its boundary (with the solid occurring inside this boundary). The boundary may be an approximate one, made up of faces (faceted boundary), or it may be defined precisely by formulas. For example, the equation for the surface of a sphere provides an exact boundary representation of a sphere.

An object may be drawn as a wireframe representation of the boundary. The wireframe segments represent edges separating faces, with the edges joined at vertices. A wireframe box is shown in figure 13.10a, and the simplest wireframe representation of a cylinder is shown in 13.10b.

A consistency check on the boundary representation is provided by the Euler-Poincaré formula, which relates the number of vertices V, edges E, faces F, hole loops H, multiplicity M, and genus G of the object. A hole loop is formed in a face when a hole extends into the object or when a cylinder or other object protrudes from a face; see figure 13.10c. The multiplicity M is the number of separate parts that constitute the object; $M = 1$ when all parts of the object are connected as one piece. The genus G of the object equals the number of handles or holes that extend through the object; for example, $G = 1$ for a coffee cup with a single handle, and $G = 0$ for a cup with no handles.

The Euler-Poincaré formula is given by equation 13.1.

$$V - E + F - H = 2(M - G) \tag{13.1}$$

It is readily shown that the Euler-Poincaré formula is satisfied for the box illustrated in figure 13.10a, for which $V = 8$, $E = 12$, $F = 6$, $H = 0$, $M = 1$, $G = 0$. The simplest representation of the cylinder also satisfies equation 13.1 with the following values: $V = 2$, $E = 3$, $F = 3$, $H = 0$, $M = 1$, and $G = 0$.

Figure 13.11a shows AME wireframe representations for a cylinder and sphere with increasing values of the solid-wire-density parameter determined by the command SOLWDENS.

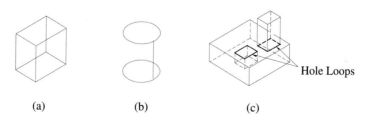

(a)   (b)   (c)

Figure 13.10   Wireframe representations: (a) solid box; (b) cylinder; (c) solid box with a rectangular hole and a rectangular extrusion.

The hidden-line representations in figure 13.11b were obtained by using the HIDE command after covering the objects with a polygon mesh by using the command SOLMESH. Except at its lowest values, increasing values of the SOLWDENS parameter increase the number of faces in the polygon mesh.

An object can be returned to its wireframe representation with the SOLWIRE command. Both the wireframe and mesh representations must satisfy the Euler-Poincaré formula.

The coffee mug shown in figure 13.12 was constructed from the union of a torus with a cylinder, followed by the subtraction of a cylinder to form the inside of the cup. The hole through the cup handle produces the value $G = 1$, and $H = 3$ results from the three hole loops (two where the handle meets the cup, and one where the cup's inside hole meets the top of the cup). Exercise 13.5 demonstrates that the Euler-Poincaré formula is satisfied by the wireframes shown in figure 13.12.

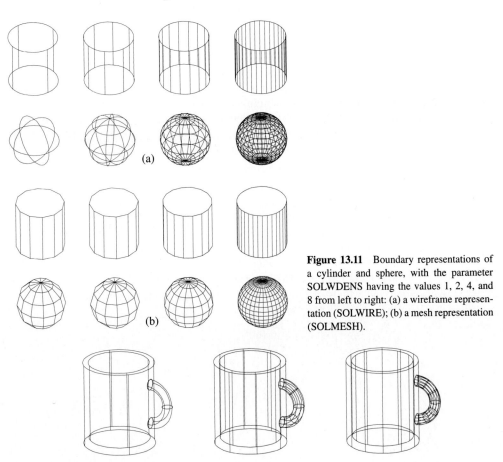

Figure 13.11 Boundary representations of a cylinder and sphere, with the parameter SOLWDENS having the values 1, 2, 4, and 8 from left to right: (a) a wireframe representation (SOLWIRE); (b) a mesh representation (SOLMESH).

Figure 13.12 Wireframe representations of a coffee mug, with the parameter SOLWDENS having the values 1, 2, and 3 from left to right.

13.2 EXAMPLES OF SOLID MODELING WITH AUTOCAD AME

The AutoCAD AME software was developed from Autodesk's AutoSolid, which in turn originated from a solid modeler developed by University of Rochester researchers using their Parts and Assembly Description Language (PADL). Many of the algorithms that were written in PADL have been translated to the C language.

AME contains two parts: a region modeler for 2-D areas and a solid modeler for 3-D solids. The Boolean operations of CSG may be used on regions or on solids, but the operations cannot be performed on a mixture of regions and solids. However, as illustrated by the examples below, regions can be turned into solids by the sweep operations of extrusion and revolution.

As described earlier, the CSG tree may be displayed on AutoCAD AME with the SOLLIST command. Furthermore, primitive objects at any level of the tree may be changed with the SOLCHP command. An object of even moderate complexity requires considerable computer memory because all of the information on the primitive objects in the CSG tree is stored. A user may release some of this memory with the SOLPURGE command, which can also reduce the drawing file size.

Individual drawing files may be kept small by using the XREF command to set up external references (Xrefs). With Xrefs, a solid model consisting of several parts may be drawn with each part on a separate drawing. Only the drawing opened as the current drawing can be modified, but the referenced drawings can be viewed along with the current drawing, and the referenced drawings can be used for object snaps and plots.

Regions and Their Extrusions

The SOLIDIFY command is used to turn single 2-D drawing entities (polylines, polygons, ellipses, circles, and donuts) into planar surfaces called regions. This is a much simpler procedure than the use of the PFACE or 3DFACE commands described in section 12.2. The primary limitation on the use of the SOLIDIFY command to form regions from a 2-D polyline is that the polyline cannot have more than 500 vertices.

It should be noted that the HIDE command will remove hidden lines from a scene containing regions only after the SOLMESH command has been used to cover the regions with a polygon mesh; that is, the use of SOLIDIFY together with SOLMESH will provide the same polygon mesh on a planar surface as does the PFACE command. To combine regions using CSG, the SOLWIRE command must be used to remove any polygon meshes covering regions.

The sweep operations SOLEXT and SOLREV may be used on regions to form 3-D objects. To construct a simple solid without interior holes or extrusions, it is easier to sweep the original polyline (or other entity) to form the solid, rather than to use a region. Regions with interior loops are useful for constructing solids with interior holes and/or interior extrusions.

Figures 13.13a–c show axonometric views of the construction of a region and its extrusion. This object represents a cover plate (or base plate) for a container, with four screw holes and two reinforcing ribs. The two ribs and the edge of the plate are constructed by forming three large holes that are extruded only part way through the material.

Figure 13.13a shows a polyline drawn to form the plate outline, three large polyline loops in the interior, and four small circles near the plate corners. All of these polylines are turned into regions with the SOLIDIFY command, and all of the interior regions are subtracted from the outer region with the command SOLSUB to form the single region shown in figure 13.13b.

A single extrusion operation forms the solid shown in figure 13.13c. The extrusion is in the negative z-direction, with the three large interior loops being extruded to only half the height of the object extrusion. The keyboard input for this extrusion operation is listed below.

```
Command: SOLEXT
Select regions, polylines and circles for extrusion...
Select objects: (pick region with mouse)
Select objects: (RETURN)
Height of extrusion: -0.3
Extrusion taper angle <0>: (RETURN)
Extrude loops to different heights <N>: Y
```

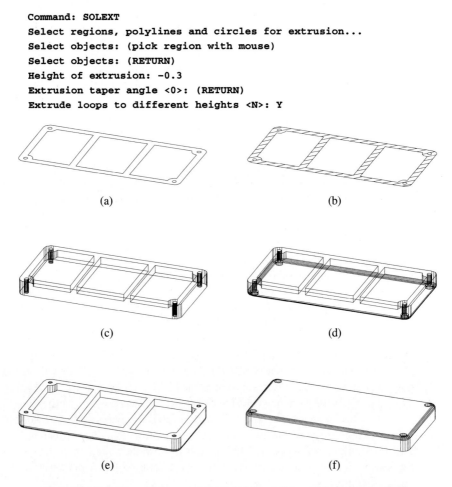

Figure 13.13 Solid model for a cover plate: (a) 2-D polylines and circles forming the object boundary and inner loops; (b) the region formed by subtracting the inner regions from the outer one; (c) extrusion with a smaller height for the three large inner loops; (d) inclusion of filleting and counterbore cylinders; (e) hidden-line view; (f) hidden-line view of the reverse side.

```
Pick loops for new height (press ENTER when done): (pick large
                                            loops with mouse)
Height of extrusion: -0.15
Extrusion taper angle <0>: (RETURN)
Pick loops for new height (press ENTER when done): (RETURN)
```

With this single SOLEXT command, the three large loops in figure 13.13 were selected for an extrusion height that was smaller than the object's extrusion height, while the
four small circles were extruded as holes completely through the object because they were
not selected for special consideration. For this example the extrusion heights are negative
to produce extrusion along the negative z-direction. The SOLEXT command permits specification of a taper angle, although for the examples in figure 13.13 the default value of zero
taper angle is selected.

Figures 13.13d–f show the completed cover plate, after the edges have been filleted
with the SOLFILL command, and after the screw holes have been counterbored by subtracting cylinders with the SOLSUB command.

Figure 13.14a shows a TV remote-control device constructed by extruding a region's
inner loops (the keys) in a direction opposite to the main extrusion. That is, the region was
given a negative extrusion height, while the inner loops were given a small positive extrusion height to produce the raised keys.

An example of inner loops within an inner loop is shown in figure 13.14b. Here the
combined region shown on the left is formed by subtracting the large loop from the outer
boundary and then adding (union) all of the small inner regions representing the keys. To
construct the 3-D device shown on the right, the overall region is given a negative extru-

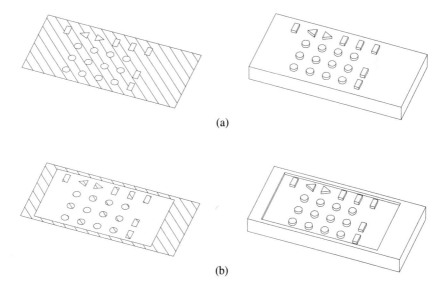

(a)

(b)

Figure 13.14   Extrusion of the regions shown on the left to produce the 3-D remote control devices on the right.

sion height. Then the large inner loop is given a small negative extrusion height to produce the indented area. Finally, the small loops for the keys are given a negative extrusion height equal to or greater than that for the large inner loop. That is, the small inner loops are extruded as keys that extend down to the bottom of the indented area.

Solid Modeling

Solid model construction can require considerable processor time and computer memory. Both time and memory can be saved with efficient construction methods, such as a minimum number of Boolean operations.

For example, the simple door handle shown in figure 13.15 starts with the extrusion of a single polyline, rather than the union of two boxes with filleting on two edges. The main part of the door handle is completed by a union of the extruded part with two cylinders, each with its axis perpendicular to the extrusion direction. The mounting plate included in figure 13.15c is constructed by subtracting one cylinder from another.

Three coordinate systems are used in constructing the door handle: the extrusion is formed in the world-coordinate system (WCS); the first cylinder is constructed in a user-coordinate system (UCS) that has its z-axis along the WCS y-axis; and the remaining cylinders are formed in a UCS having its z-axis along the WCS x-axis.

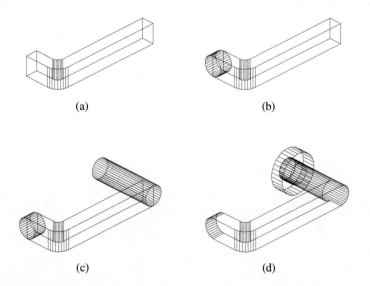

(a)   (b)

(c)   (d)

Figure 13.15   Solid model of a door handle: (a) extrusion in the z-direction; (b) addition of a cylinder with its axis in the y-direction; (c) addition of a cylinder with its axis in the x-direction; (d) union of the extrusion with the two cylinders, plus the addition of the mounting plate formed by subtracting one cylinder from another.

Presenting Views of a Solid in Paper Space

AutoCAD's paper space provides a convenient format for presenting views of a solid model. To enter paper space the TILEMODE command is used to toggle the tilemode variable to the value 0 (its default value is 1).

When paper space is entered, the image of the drawn object disappears. To restore the object to the screen, the MVIEW command is used to set up multiple views. The following keyboard input sets up four views that fill the screen.

```
Command: MVIEW
ON/OFF/Hideplot/Fit/2/3/4/Restore/<First Point>: 4
Fit/<First Point>: F
```

The same view of the object appears in each of the four viewports set up by MVIEW. To change the views in the viewports, the MSPACE command must be used to move to model space. While in model space, the mouse may be clicked on a viewport area to enter it, and the VPOINT command may be used to change the viewpoint in that viewport. Other commands, such as ZOOM and PAN may also be used to adjust the image in the viewport. After the views are set in each viewport, the PSPACE command may be used to return to paper space. Figure 13.16 shows the screen image after the door handle views have been adjusted in each of the viewports. The paper space icon in the lower-left corner of figure 13.16 shows that the PSPACE command has been used to return to paper space.

The MVIEW command is much more versatile than the older VPORTS command. MVIEW provides many options that are useful for producing hardcopy (paper) output; for

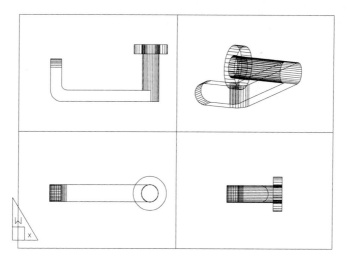

Figure 13.16   Wireframe representation of a door handle shown in paper space with four viewports set up with the MVIEW command.

example, the viewports can be independently dragged around in paper space for any desired positioning (including overlapping viewports). Also, titles and other text can be added in the paper space outside the viewports. The Hideplot option under the MVIEW command is used (in paper space) to pick which viewports should plot with hidden lines removed.

To produce hardcopy views of the door handle, it is useful to enter each of the viewports in model space and use the AME command SOLPROF. This command produces the solid profile lines shown in figure 13.17. The profile lines are not immediately evident after using the SOLPROF command, because these lines are covered by the wireframe image of the object. To make it possible to view the profile lines, the layer containing the solid model can be frozen.

The profile lines may be drawn on different layers when the SOLPROF command is used in each viewport.

```
Command: SOLPROF
Select objects: (pick with mouse)
Select objects: (RETURN)
Display hidden profile lines on separate layer? <Y>: (RETURN)
Project profile lines onto a plane? <Y>: (RETURN)
Delete tangential edges? <Y>: (RETURN)
```

The layers set up by AME can be viewed by using the LAYER command or the layer-control dialog box. AME sets up two layers for each viewport with assigned names of PV-viewport handle and PH-viewport handle, where the viewport handle is a hexadecimal number. The V in PV stands for visible, and H in PH stands for hidden. In the upper-right viewport of figure 13.17, the layer containing the hidden lines was frozen in order to elim-

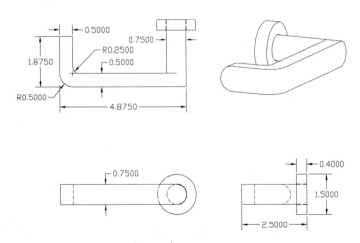

Figure 13.17   Profile lines obtained from a solid model of a door handle, plotted from paper space.

inate hidden lines from the plot. In the other viewports the linetype for the PH layers was set to HIDDEN.

The dimensions in figure 13.17 were drawn in model space on the appropriate PV layer for each viewport, with the UCS set to the view direction.

The door handle can be refined by using the SOLFILL command to fillet the edges of the handle and mounting plate as illustrated in figure 13.18. The SOLFILL command should be applied to an entire continuous edge in one operation, so that the fillets properly join around bends and corners. For the door handle, the SOLFILL command was applied three times: first to the entire closed edge on the outside of the handle, next to the inside edge of the handle before it was joined to the shaft, and then to the outside edge of the mounting plate.

When the SOLPROF command was applied to the filleted door handle, a "no" response was given to the question "Delete tangential edges?" because the tangential edges of the fillets are required to define the handle edges. These tangential edges can be edited if desired; for example, in the bottom representation in figure 13.18, some of the tangential edges were erased after the EXPLODE command was used to separate the individual edges.

Another example of a simple solid model is the crank arm shown in figure 13.19. This is the same crank arm configuration shown in sections 4.1 and 7.2. The solid model of the

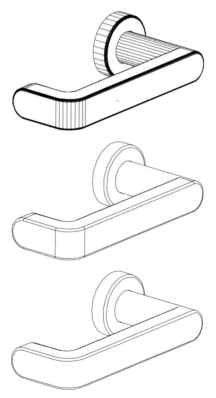

Figure 13.18 Door handle with filleted edges.

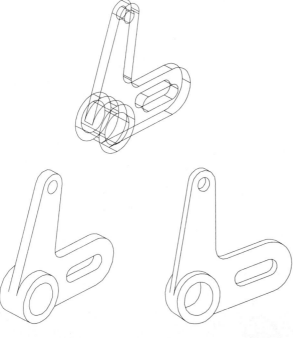

Figure 13.19 Crank arm solid model (top) and profile lines (bottom).

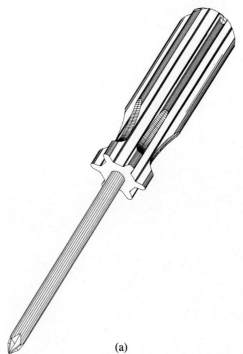

(a)

Figure 13.20 Solid models: (a) a screwdriver, drawn by Stanley Peng; (continued)

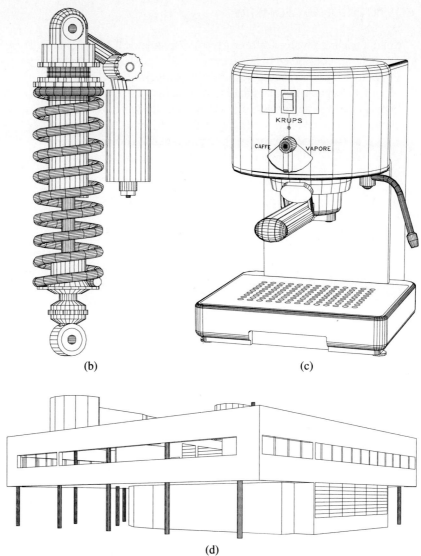

(b)   (c)

(d)

Figure 13.20 (continued)   Solid models: (b) a shock absorber, drawn by Ryan Strathearn;
(c) a Krups espresso coffee maker, drawn by Benjamin Thompson; (d) Le Corbusier's Villa
Savoye (constructed 1928–29), drawn by Michael Rysdorp.

crank arm can be formed entirely from cylinder, box, and wedge primitives, or more simply by extruding the main 2-D outline, and then adding and subtracting cylinders and a box.
The SOLPROF command is used to obtain the two views at the bottom of figure 13.19. The
human effort required to construct the crank arm solid model and profile views was less
than it was to draw the 2-D isometric view shown in figure 4.3.

More complicated solid models constructed by students are shown in figure 13.20.

13.3 COMPUTATIONAL GEOMETRY

Solid modeling involves different types of geometrical computations. Three example calculations are considered in this section. In the first example, the boundary polyline around the union of two rectangular regions is computed with a C program.

The second computational example in this section considers the case of two cylinders intersecting at an angle. Here the 3-D intersection curve is calculated with a C program and compared with the intersection curves drawn by AutoCAD AME.

The third example consists of a program that computes the mass properties of an object consisting of the union of two spheres. The calculated results are compared with those obtained with the AME command SOLMASSP.

Boundary Representation for the Union of Two Rectangles

The union, difference, and intersection operations of CSG require considerable computational effort. In this subsection, only the simplest 2-D example is considered: the union of two nonrotated rectangles; see figure 13.21. Boolean operations on more complex 2-D shapes and on 3-D objects require a more general programming approach to handle the very large number of configurations that can arise. Even the simple case considered here leads to nine separate configurations: this result hints at the complexity of the more general problem.

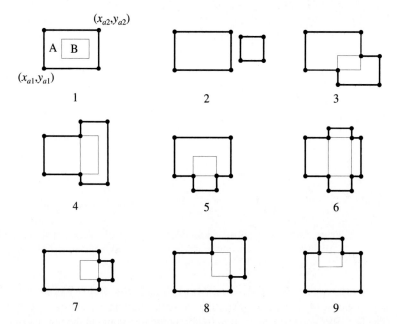

Figure 13.21 Nine configurations for calculating the boundary representation of the union of two rectangles. In each case the rectangle on the left is rectangle A, defined by its lower-left corner (x_{a1},y_{a1}) and its upper-right corner (x_{a2},y_{a2}). The second rectangle (B) changes size and orientation relative to the fixed rectangle A.

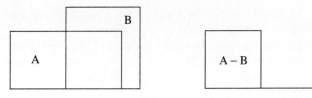

Figure 13.22   Illustration of a dangling edge or face resulting from the difference $A - B$.

Here the special case of one rectangle having an edge in common with another is neglected. These boundary points (edge on a rectangle or face on a box) can produce problems if they are not handled carefully. For example, the difference between two rectangles (or side views of two boxes) shown in figure 13.22 results in a dangling edge or face. With CAD software, dangling faces and other problems are avoided by properly accounting for small regions near boundaries where floating point round-off errors could cause difficulties. Therefore, with AutoCAD AME you can perform differences (SOLSUB) and other operations even when faces coincide.

Consider two rectangles A and B, with A specified by its lower-left corner (x_{a1}, y_{a1}) and its upper-right corner (x_{a2}, y_{a2}), and B specified by its corners (x_{b1}, y_{b1}) and (x_{b2}, y_{b2}). Assuming that the left side of rectangle A lies to the left of rectangle B, nine possible configurations for the union of A and B are pictured in figure 13.21.

The boundary representation for the union of rectangles A and B is described by a closed polyline consisting of *nPts* vertex points with coordinates specified by the arrays *xBrep[i]* and *yBrep[i]*. The calculation of this boundary polyline is given by the subroutine unionBoundary() presented as listing 13.1 in appendix B. Because nine cases must be considered, the subroutine is rather long. For more complex 2-D shapes, or for 3-D solids, the computations required to combine two objects can be lengthy.

Intersection Curves for the Union of Cylinders

The geometry for two intersecting cylinders is depicted in figure 13.23. A horizontal cylinder of radius r_1 has its axis along the world x-axis, and an inclined cylinder of radius r_2 has

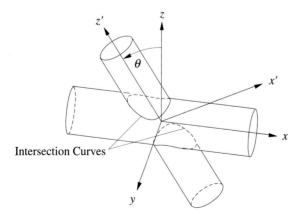

Figure 13.23   Geometry for calculating the intersection of two cylinders.

its axis along the z'-axis, which is at an angle θ to the world z-axis. The axes of the two cylinders are assumed to be coplanar.

AME plots of the union of two cylinders are illustrated in figure 13.24, where intersection curves are shown along with wireframe representations of the cylinders. In the top illustrations of 13.24, the cylinders are perpendicular ($\theta = 0°$), and for the bottom illustrations $\theta = 45°$.

As observed from figure 13.23, the intersection curve on the underside of the horizontal cylinder corresponds to the upper intersection curve mirrored across the $x = 0$ and $z = 0$ planes. Accordingly, only the upper intersection curve is considered in the following analysis.

The surfaces of the two cylinders are described by the following equations.

$$y^2 + z^2 = r_1^2, \qquad x'^2 + y^2 = r_2^2 \tag{13.2}$$

A rotation of angle θ around the y-axis is described by the transformation matrix given in equation 11.3. This matrix relates the surface coordinate x' to the world coordinates x and z.

$$x' = x \cos\theta + z \sin\theta \tag{13.3}$$

In order to draw the closed curve representing the intersection, the angle α about the z' axis is used as a parameter that varies from 0 to 2π radians. Thus the coordinates x' and y may be expressed by the relations

$$x' = r_2 \sin\alpha, \qquad y = r_2 \cos\alpha \tag{13.4}$$

After y is obtained from equation 13.4, the coordinate z is calculated from the first of equations 13.2.

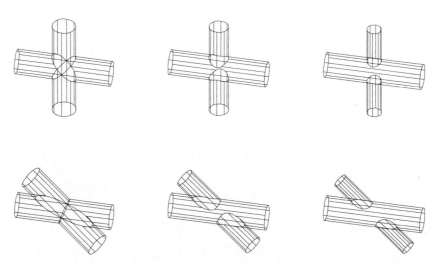

Figure 13.24 Axonometric views of unions of two cylinders constructed with AutoCAD AME. On the top row the cylinders intersect at 90°; on the bottom row the intersection angle is 45°. The ratio of the radius of vertical (or diagonal) cylinders to the radius of horizontal cylinders is 1.0 for the left figures, 0.8 for the middle figures, and 0.6 for the right figures.

$$z = (r_1{}^2 - y^2)^{1/2} \qquad\qquad (13.5)$$

Finally, x is obtained by inverting equation 13.3.

$$x = (x' - z\sin\theta)\sec\theta \qquad\qquad (13.6)$$

The subroutine IntersectCyl() has been set up to send line segment coordinates $(x_{start}, y_{start}, z_{start})$ and $(x_{end}, y_{end}, z_{end})$ to the subroutine writeLine(), which is contained in a program that writes a DXF file (as described in section 8.2). Alternatively, one could write a plotLine() subroutine to directly plot these line segments.

In the for loop contained in the subroutine below, the angle alpha ($\equiv \alpha$) is incremented by a small amount dalpha ($\equiv \varDelta\alpha$). The subroutine variables *yend, zend, xprime,* and *xend* correspond to the variables y, z, x', and x in equations 13.4–13.6. The starting coordinates for a line segment equal the ending coordinates of the preceding line segment (except for the first segment, which has its starting coordinates set on the program line above the *for* loop).

Intersection curves calculated by the C program are shown in figure 13.25 for the same conditions (and view) as shown for AME unions in figure 13.24.

```
#define PI 3.141593

void IntersectCyl(void)
{
    int     i,nsegs;
    double  r1 = 0.5,r2 = 0.3,theta = 0.25*PI;
    double  xprime,sint,sect,alpha,dalpha,sina,cosa;
    double  xstart,ystart,zstart,xend,yend,zend;

    sint = sin(theta); sect = 1.0/cos(theta);
    nsegs = 40; dalpha = 2.*PI/(double) nsegs;

    xstart = -sqrt(r1*r1 - r2*r2)*sint*sect;
    ystart = r2; zstart = sqrt(r1*r1 - r2*r2);
```

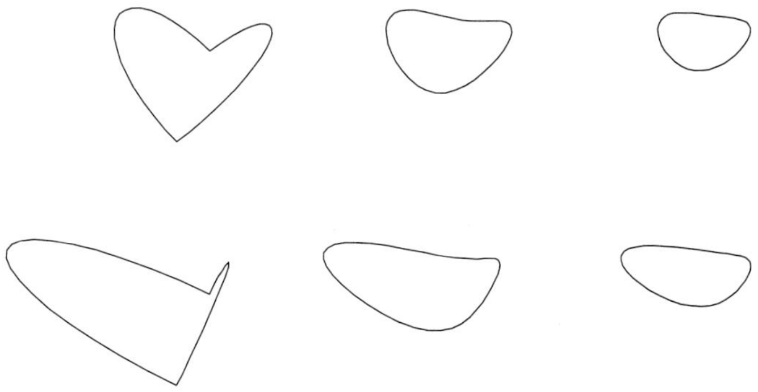

Figure 13.25   Intersection curves computed from the C program. These intersection curves are the same as those determined by AutoCAD AME in figure 13.24.

```
for (i=1,alpha=dalpha; i<=nsegs; i++,alpha+=dalpha)
{

    sina = sin(alpha); cosa = cos(alpha);
    yend = r2*cosa;
    zend = sqrt(r1*r1 - yend*yend);
    xprime = r2*sina;
    xend = (xprime - zend*sint)*sect;
    writeLine(xstart,ystart,zstart,xend,yend,zend);
    xstart = xend; ystart = yend; zstart = zend;

}

}
```

Calculation of Mass Properties for Intersecting Spheres

The union of two spheres is illustrated in figure 13.26a for three different distances between sphere centers of equal radii r. With the distance between given by the variable d, the spheres lie exactly on top of each other when $d = 0$, and they separate when $d = 2r$. In this section a program is developed to calculate the mass properties of the solid resulting from the union of the two spheres when $0 < d < 2r$.

The mass properties of an object may be computed in AutoCAD AME with the command SOLMASSP. The accuracy of the property values depends on the level of subdivision, which is determined by the parameter *solsubdiv*, which can be set to values from 1 to 8 with the command SOLSUBDIV. This parameter determines the density of a mesh

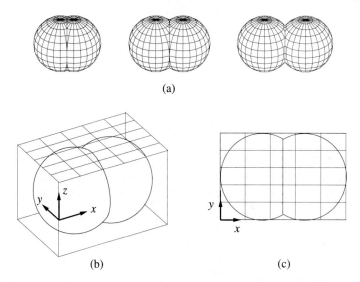

Figure 13.26   The union of two spheres having equal radii: (a) front view at an elevation angle of 30° above the xy-plane, for ratios of distance d between sphere centers to sphere radius r of $d/r = 0.5$, 1.0, and 1.5; (b) and (c) axonometric and top views of intersection spheres (for $d/r = 1.0$), with axes and a 5×5 mesh of cells for mass property computations.

of cells used to determine mass properties by a ray-casting procedure. The total number of cells n_{cell} in the mesh is related to the parameter *solsubdiv* by the formula

$$n_{cell} = (2^{solsubdiv} + 1)^2 \qquad (13.7)$$

For *solsubdiv* = 1, n_{cell} = 9, *solsubdiv* = 2 yields n_{cell} = 25, *solsubdiv* = 3 yields n_{cell} = 81, etc., up to *solsubdiv* = 8, which yields 66,049 cells. A mesh with n_{cell} = 25 is pictured in figures 13.26b–c.

Table 13.2 shows an AME printout of mass properties for an object consisting of the union of two spheres of radius 3cm, placed with centers 3cm apart (corresponding to the middle object in figure 13.26a). The values in the table were calculated for ray casting along the z-axis (set with the SOLDECOMP command), with the level of subdivision (*solsubdiv*) set equal to the value 7. Error estimates are provided with the values for the volume, centroid, moments of inertia, and products of inertia.

To explain the ray-casting procedure used to calculate the mass properties, the union of two spheres is analyzed with the subroutine rayCasting(). This subroutine calculates the

TABLE 13.2 THE MASS PROPERTIES FOR THE UNION OF TWO SPHERES OF EQUAL RADII

```
Ray projection along Z axis, level of subdivision: 7.
Mass:              1500.057 gm
Volume:            190.8469 cu cm (Err: 0.5407224)

Bounding box:         X: 0 -- 9 cm
                      Y: 0 -- 6 cm
                      Z: -3 -- 3 cm

Centroid:             X: 4.499567 cm (Err: 0.02246439)
                      Y: 2.999612 cm (Err: 0.01409811)
                      Z: -4.927523e-19 cm (Err: 1.301031e-18)

Moments of inertia:   X: 19233.6 gm sq cm (Err: 113.1008)
                      Y: 40330.73 gm sq cm (Err: 274.219)
                      Z: 53826.4 gm sq cm (Err: 297.6135)

Products of inertia: XY: 20244.76 gm sq cm (Err: 130.4956)
                     YZ: -3.221014e-15 gm sq cm (Err: 6.301522e-15)
                     ZX: -1.017922e-14 gm sq cm (Err: 9.639937e-15)

Radii of gyration:    X: 3.58077 cm
                      Y: 5.185185 cm
                      Z: 5.990235 cm

Principal moments(gm sq cm) and X-Y-Z directions about centroid:
                      I: 5736.578 along [0 1 0]
                      J: 9959.079 along [0 0 1]
                      K: 9959.079 along [1 0 0]
```

mass, the volume, the x and y centroids, the moment of inertia about the z-axis, the xy product of inertia, the z radius of gyration, and the moment of inertia about a principal axis. The computation starts with given values for the sphere radius r, the distance d between sphere centers, and the mesh subdivision level given by the parameter *solsubdiv*. This program calculates only properties associated with rays cast in the z-direction; the remaining quantities could be calculated in a similar fashion with rays cast in the other directions.

The total volume of the combined spheres is computed by summing the individual material volumes contained in the cells. Each cell has a width w_{cell} and height h_{cell}. The depth of material in cell number i determined by ray casting is identified by the variable Δz_i. The volume V and mass M of the combined solid are determined by the following formulas, where ρ is the density of the material:

$$V = \sum_i w_{cell}h_{cell}\Delta z_i = w_{cell}h_{cell}\sum_i \Delta z_i \tag{13.8}$$

$$M = \rho V$$

The summation in the formula covers all of the cells, with the cell number i varying from 0 to $n_{cell} - 1$. In the subroutine rayCasting(), the material depth Δz_i is written as dz, and the summation over the depths is written as *sumdz*.

The material depth Δz_i is calculated along a ray cast in the z-direction at the location (x,y) in a cell. The surfaces of the two spheres are described by the equations

$$(x - r)^2 + (y - r)^2 + z^2 = r^2, \qquad (x - r - d)^2 + (y - r)^2 + z^2 = r^2 \tag{13.9}$$

A ray cast in the z-direction at the point (x,y) will intersect the first sphere when

$$0 \le x \le r + \frac{1}{2}d \quad \text{and} \quad (x - r)^2 + (y - r)^2 \le r^2$$

and will intersect the second sphere when

$$r + \frac{1}{2}d \le x \le 2r + d \quad \text{and} \quad (x - r - d)^2 + (y - r)^2 \le r^2$$

The ray cast along the z-axis will intersect the spheres at $\pm$ values of z obtained by solving equations 13.9, yielding the following total lengths Δz_i of the ray inside the spheres:

$$\Delta z_i = 2[r^2 + (x - r)^2 + (y - r)^2]^{1/2} \quad \text{for } x < r + \frac{1}{2}d$$

and $\tag{13.10}$

$$\Delta z_i = 2[r^2 + (x - r - d)^2 + (y - r)^2]^{1/2} \quad \text{for } x \ge r + \frac{1}{2}d$$

The ray coordinates (x,y) are computed by considering random displacements in each cell about the center point; the center point of cell number i is labeled (x_i,y_i) in equations 13.11–13 and is called *(xcenter,ycenter)* in the program. In the program, the random number generated by the function rand() is normalized to form the random fraction *rnd* that varies between 0 and 1. Different sequences of random numbers can be generated by changing the argument of the random seed function srand() at the beginning of the subroutine.

The x and y centroids are computed from the formulas

$$x_{centroid} = \frac{w_{cell}h_{cell}}{V}\sum_i \Delta z_i\, x_i, \qquad y_{centroid} = \frac{w_{cell}h_{cell}}{V}\sum_i \Delta z_i\, y_i \qquad (13.11)$$

The z and xy moments of inertia are prescribed by the equations

$$I_z = \rho w_{cell}h_{cell}\sum_i \Delta z_i(x_i^2 + y_i^2), \qquad I_{xy} = \rho w_{cell}h_{cell}\sum_i \Delta z_i\, x_i y_i \qquad (13.12)$$

The principal moments of inertia are computed for a coordinate system having an origin at the centroid and oriented to produce maximum and minimum values for the moments of inertia. For the present case of intersecting spheres, the coordinates may be simply translated to the centroid, with the moment of inertia about the z-axis being the maximum. Because the object's configuration is identical relative to both the y-axis and the z-axis located at the centroid, this maximum value calculated can be identified with both I_j and I_k; the minimum moment of inertia I_i is not determined here. A formula for $I_j = I_k$ may be obtained from the first of equations 13.12 by replacing x_i by $x_i - x_{centroid}$ and y_i by $y_i - y_{centroid}$. After expanding the products, and using equations 13.11 for the centroid coordinates, the following result is obtained.

$$I_j = I_k = \rho w_{cell}h_{cell}\sum_i \Delta z_i[(x_i - x_{centroid})^2 + (y_i - x_{centroid})^2]$$

$$= I_z - M(x_{centroid}^2 + y_{centroid}^2) \qquad (13.13)$$

```
#define PI 3.141593


void rayCasting(double r,double d,int solsubdiv)
{
    int      i,j,ncell;
    double   density,vol,mass,wbox,hbox;
    double   wcell,hcell,x,y,xcenter,ycenter,r2,len2,dz,sumdz,rnd;
    double   xcentroid,ycentroid,xcentroidFactor,ycentroidFactor;
    double   zMomentFactor,zMomentInertia,zRadiusGyration;
    double   xyProductFactor,xyProductInertia,kMomentInertia;

    density = 7.860; /* mild steel density in gm/cu_cm */
    wbox = 2.*r + d; hbox = 2.*r;
    ncell = pow(2,solsubdiv) + 1;
    wcell = wbox/ncell; hcell = hbox/ncell;
    r2 = r*r;
    sumdz = 0; xcentroidFactor = 0; ycentroidFactor = 0;
    zMomentFactor = 0; xyProductFactor = 0;
    srand(5223);
```

```
for (i=0; i<ncell; i++)
{
    for (j=0; j<ncell; j++)
    {
        xcenter = (i+.5)*wcell; ycenter = (j+.5)*hcell;
        rnd = ((double) rand())/32767; x = (i+rnd)*wcell;
        rnd = ((double) rand())/32767; y = (j+rnd)*hcell;
        if (x<(r+.5*d))
            len2 = (x-r)*(x-r) + (y-r)*(y-r);
        else
            len2 = (x-r-d)*(x-r-d) + (y-r)*(y-r);
        if (len2<r2)
            dz = 2.*sqrt(r2-len2);
        else
            dz = 0.0;
        sumdz = sumdz + dz;
        xcentroidFactor = xcentroidFactor + dz*xcenter;
        ycentroidFactor = ycentroidFactor + dz*ycenter;
        zMomentFactor = zMomentFactor +
                        dz*(xcenter*xcenter+ycenter*ycenter);
        xyProductFactor = xyProductFactor+dz*xcenter*ycenter;
    }
}
vol = wcell*hcell*sumdz; mass = density*vol;
xcentroid = wcell*hcell*xcentroidFactor/vol;
ycentroid = wcell*hcell*ycentroidFactor/vol;
zMomentInertia = density*wcell*hcell*zMomentFactor;
xyProductInertia = density*wcell*hcell*xyProductFactor;
zRadiusGyration = sqrt(zMomentInertia/mass);
kMomentInertia = zMomentInertia -
            mass*(xcentroid*xcentroid + ycentroid*ycentroid);

printf("\nCombined mass = %lf gm\n",mass);
printf("Combined volume = %lf cu cm\n",vol);
printf("xcentroid = %lf cm, ycentroid = %lf cm\n",
                                    xcentroid,ycentroid);
printf("z moment of inertia = %lf gm sq cm\n",zMomentInertia);
printf("xy product of inertia = %lf gm sq cm\n",
                                    xyProductInertia);
printf("z radius of gyration = %lf cm\n",zRadiusGyration);
printf("Principle moment of inertia K = %lf gm sq cm\n",
                                    kMomentInertia);
}
```

To indicate the accuracy of mass-property calculations, the volumes computed by AME for two ray-casting directions and different values of *solsubdiv* are shown in table 13.3. Results from the C subroutine rayCasting() are also included for three different values of the seed number for the random function rand().

The actual error for the volume calculated by the ray-casting procedure is obtained by comparison with the exact volume, which is readily calculated by integrating over the volume contained within the union of the two spheres.

$$V_{exact} = \frac{4}{3}\pi r^3 \left[1 + \frac{3}{4}\left(\frac{d}{r}\right) - \frac{1}{16}\left(\frac{d}{r}\right)^3 \right] \qquad (13.14)$$

In the above fomula, the volume increases from the value for one sphere when $d = 0$ for completely overlapping spheres, to a value equal to the sum of the two sphere volumes when the spheres separate at $d = 2r$.

The accuracy of the calculations increases with an increase in the number of cells (increasing *solsubdiv*). For the present object, table 13.3 shows that generally the estimated error is slightly less for rays cast in the x-direction, because in this direction the object's cross section is smaller, yielding small cells and increased accuracy. The inaccuracies of calculating the amount of material along the ray direction will generally be less than the inaccuracies produced by the finite cell size.

For small values of *solsubdiv*, the cell division is very crude, and the actual error can vary greatly, with the estimated error giving only a rough approximation of the actual error. For the crude cell division occurring for small *solsubdiv* values, the random placement of rays greatly affects the error; note the large variation of errors calculated for the differ-

TABLE 13.3 THE ACCURACY OF THE VOLUME COMPUTATION FOR DIFFERENT VALUES OF THE CELL SUBDIVISION PARAMENTER *SOLSUBDIV*

solsubdiv	1	2	3	4	5	6	7	8
AME								
x-direction								
volume	147.302	211.816	192.739	188.738	190.223	190.789	190.929	190.862
est. error	23.074	12.892	5.941	3.862	1.895	0.949	0.471	0.235
error	−43.550	20.964	1.887	−2.114	−0.629	−0.063	0.077	0.010
z-direction								
volume	148.623	196.471	195.470	189.532	191.090	190.828	190.847	190.845
est. error	24.731	11.742	8.924	4.384	2.108	1.069	0.541	0.270
error	−42.229	5.619	4.618	−1.320	0.238	−0.024	−0.005	−0.007
C program								
(z-direction)								
seed = 1111								
volume	200.212	191.453	193.685	189.241	190.852	190.798	190.871	190.852
error	9.360	0.601	2.833	−1.611	0.000	−0.054	0.019	0.000
seed = 2222								
volume	137.854	204.115	189.745	190.441	190.271	190.922	190.855	190.854
error	−52.998	13.263	−1.107	−0.411	−0.581	0.070	0.003	0.002
seed = 6789								
volume	161.464	192.928	195.478	190.504	190.518	190.725	190.818	190.853
error	−29.388	2.076	4.626	−0.348	−0.334	−0.127	−0.034	0.001

For AutoCAD AME, the estimated error and the actual error are given for ray casting in both the x-direction and in the z-direction. For the C program, the ray casting is in the z-direction, and results are given for three different values of the random seed number.

ent seed values in the C program. The three seed numbers for the table were chosen arbitrarily; the sequence of random numbers depends not only on the seed number, but also on the particular C compiler being used.

When *solsubdiv* is large, the actual errors for this example are less than the estimated errors; that is, the estimated errors are conservative. The table shows that the volume calculated by the C program is more accurate, probably because the boundary points pierced by the rays were calculated by an exact analytical representation (sometimes called an A-rep), rather than by an approximate boundary representation (B-rep).

EXERCISES

13.1 Write an interactive program in which the user specifies the material and dimensions for a set of I-beams. The program should show scaled drawings of the I-beams along with their masses and moments of inertia.

13.2 Write a program similar to that described in exercise 13.1, but consider angle beams with four variable dimensions, *h, l, w,* and *t,* as illustrated below.

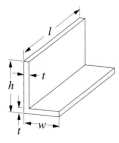

13.3 Use instances of the primitive solids SOLGEAR, SOLSHAFT, and SOLBEAR provided with AutoCAD's API sample program design.c to construct the gear train shown below.

13.4 Show that Euler-Poincaré formula is satisfied for the first two cylinders and spheres shown in figure 13.11a.

13.5 For each wireframe representation of the coffee cup in figure 13.12, list the values for V, E, F, H, M, and G, and show that Euler-Poincaré formula is satisfied.

13.6 Write a program to calculate the intersection curve for the union of a cylinder and a sphere, as pictured on the left below.

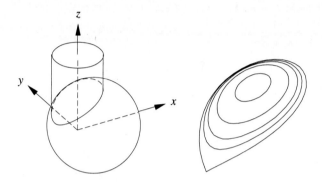

Consider a cylinder of radius r_2 and sphere of radius r_1 displaced a positive distance x_0 from the cylinder axis, as described by the following equations (with $r_2 + x_0 \leq r_1$).

$$x^2 + y^2 = r_2^2, \qquad (x - x_0)^2 + y^2 + z^2 = r_1^2$$

The intersection curves shown on the right above were calculated for $x_0/r_1 = 0.4$, and $r_2/r_1 = 0.2, 0.4, 0.5, 0.55,$ and 0.6.

13.7 Write a program to calculate the intersection curve for the union of a cylinder and a cone with parallel axes, as illustrated on the left below.

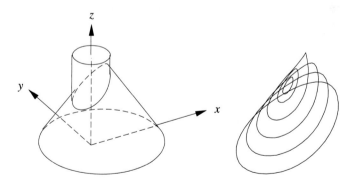

Consider a cylinder of radius r_2, and a cone of height h and base radius r_b with its axis placed a positive distance x_0 from the cylinder axis, as described by the following equations (with $r_2 + x_0 \leq r_b$).

$$x^2 + y^2 = r_2^2, \quad (x - x_0)^2 + y^2 = r_b^2\left(1 - \frac{z}{h}\right)^2$$

The intersection curves shown in the right figure were calculated for $h/r_b = 1.5$, $x_0/r_b = 0.2$, and $r_2/r_b = 0.05, 0.1, 0.2, 0.3, 0.4,$ and 0.5. The intersection curve for the case $r_2 = x_0$ passes through the apex of the cone, producing a corner in this curve.

13.8 Implement the C program given in section 13.3 for calculating mass properties for the union between two spheres. Compare the accuracy of the moments of inertia computed with this program with values obtained with AutoCAD AME.

13.9 As a project, construct a solid model from measurements taken from an object (appliance, instrument, tool, sports equipment, etc.). Examples are given by the fishing reel below, drawn by Gerard Hanley, and the objects shown in figures 13.20a–c.

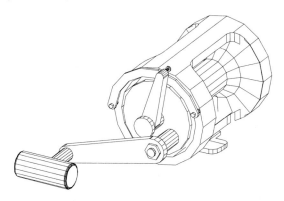

BIBLIOGRAPHY

Advanced Modeling Extension: Release 2.1 Reference Manual. Sausalito, Calif.: Autodesk, Inc., 1992.

GASSON, P. C., *Geometry of Spatial Forms: Analysis, Synthesis, Concept, Formulation and Space Vision for CAD.* Chichester, West Sussex, England: Ellis Horwood Limited, 1983.

HOFFMANN, C. M., *Geometric and Solid Modeling: An Introduction.* San Mateo, Calif.: Morgan Kaufmann Publishers, Inc., 1989.

JARED, G. E. M., AND J. R. DODSWORTH, "Solid Modelling," pp. 153–177 in *Principles of Computer-aided Design,* J. Rooney, and P. Steadman, editors. Englewood Cliffs, N.J.: Prentice Hall, 1987.

LEIGH, R. W., *Solid Modeling with AutoCAD: Second edition for AME 2.0 & 2.1.* Chapel Hill, N. C.: Ventana Press, 1992.

MÄNTYLÄ, M., *An Introduction to Solid Modeling.* Rockville, Md.: Computer Science Press, 1988.

MORTENSON, M. E., *Geometric Modeling.* New York: John Wiley & Sons, 1985.

ZEID, I., *CAD/CAM Theory and Practice.* New York: McGraw-Hill, Inc., 1991.

14

Rendering

Rendering is very useful for showing how a design will appear to the human eye. A rendered object can be placed in a scene to produce a photorealistic image.

Quite realistic images of objects can be formed with a simple rendering model that treats only diffuse and specular reflection from an opaque surface. The standard simple shading model for diffuse and specular reflection is described in section 14.1. In the simplest application, a flat face on a surface is shaded with uniform color. Improvements beyond this flat shading case are made by applying Gouraud and Phong smoothing across faces.

More than a dozen software packages provide renderings for models developed on CAD systems. In section 14.2, the implementation of the simple shading model is considered for the following software: AutoCAD Render, AutoShade/RenderMan, 3D Studio®, and AutoVision™. 3D Studio was used to render the boat hull shown above, with a wireframe surface assigned to the back and a simple shading (including Phong smoothing) assigned to the front.

Advanced features for photorealistic rendering are discussed in section 14.3. Ray tracing forms the basis of scene imaging, and it is required for particular effects such as the mirrored images in a smooth surface, the change of light as it is transmitted through a translucent material, and the formation of shadows.

Surface properties may be represented by texture mapping that permits scanned or drawn images to be mapped onto the surfaces of objects. Bump mapping may be used to give surface textures an embossed effect; that is, the appearance of more depth. Also, programming interfaces such as RenderMan shaders and 3D Studio external processes provide more versatility in defining surfaces; for example, 3-D textures can be defined, and surfaces can be displaced to produce prescribed patterns such as waves, grooves, or screw threads.

Animation is the subject of the last section in this chapter. After a brief discussion of slide presentations in AutoCAD, animation using keyframing in 3D Studio is described. Two animation examples for design applications are described: a robot arm and an architectural walkthrough.

14.1 THE SIMPLE ILLUMINATION AND REFLECTION MODEL

To a good approximation, light reflected from a surface may be represented by the sum of separate diffuse and specular components. In the diffuse case, the incident radiation is reflected equally in all directions, whereas for the specular case the incident radiation is reflected in a narrow beam about the ideal reflection direction.

Figure 14.1 shows how an increase in surface roughness changes reflection from being nearly specular to nearly diffuse. Two angles ($10°$ and $45°$) of incidence are considered, with the reflected intensity plotted over a wide range of angles. The reflectances plotted near the specular peaks lie in the plane of the incident and perfect reflection directions. Away from these peaks, the reflectance merges with a nearly constant diffuse background (the background reflectance was plotted from experimental data both in and out of the plane containing the incident and perfect reflection directions).

Ambient Intensity

Any real scene usually contains ambient illumination that results from natural or artificial light being reflected in all directions throughout the scene. By definition, the ambient intensity is equal from all directions; that is, from the entire solid angle of 4π steradians. Because the ambient intensity incident on a surface is equal in all directions, the reflected intensity will also be equal in all directions, regardless of the diffuse or specular nature of the surface. Accordingly, the reflected intensity is constant, given simply as the product of the incident ambient intensity I_a and the reflection coefficient k_a.

$$I = I_a k_a \tag{14.1}$$

Because the ambient illumination provides only a constant reflected intensity, it gives an object the appearance of a solid fill between its boundary edges; see figure 14.2a.

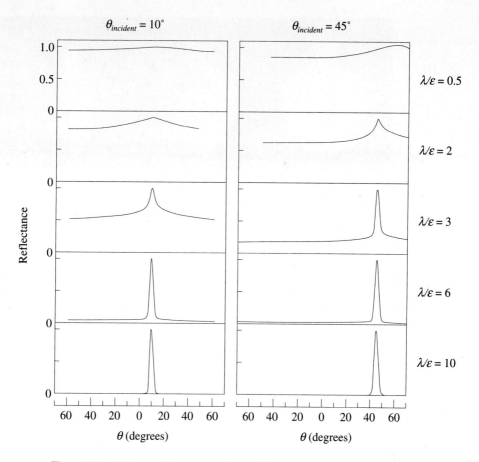

Figure 14.1   Reflectance from a magnesium oxide ceramic surface, redrawn from the experimental data shown in an article by K. E. Torrance and E. M. Sparrow: "Biangular Reflectance of an Electric Nonconductor as a Function of Wavelength and Surface Roughness," *Journal of Heat Transfer* **C87**, 283–292 (1965). When the light wavelength λ becomes large compared with the rms (root-mean square) roughness height ε, the surface appears smooth to the light, and reflection is concentrated in a narrow beam around the perfect reflection angle $\theta_{reflection} = \theta_{incident}$.

Diffuse Reflection

As discussed above, the reflection from a surface can be divided into a diffuse reflection component and a specular component. The diffusely reflected intensity will be independent of direction in the hemispherical region on the illuminated side of the reflecting surface. Thus the intensity for diffuse reflection is independent of the viewing direction, provided that the illuminated side of the surface is visible.

The diffuse reflection case is illustrated in figure 14.3, where a light is assumed to provide radiation that strikes the surface at an angle θ to the surface normal. Because a

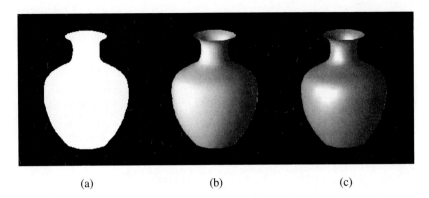

(a)   (b)   (c)

Figure 14.2   A surface of revolution rendered for three different shading cases: (a) ambient illumination only; (b) ambient illumination plus a single distant light with diffuse reflection; and (c) ambient illumination plus a single distant light with diffuse and specular
reflection.

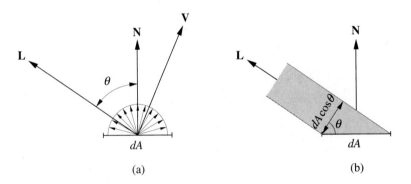

(a)   (b)

Figure 14.3   Geometry for reflection from a diffuse surface: (a) short vectors showing
light reflected equally in all directions from the top of area dA, and long vectors showing
the light source location **L**, viewpoint **V**, and surface normal **N**; (b) incident beam of radiation with cross-sectional area $dA \cos\theta$.

surface of area dA intersects the beam of light (intensity I_l) of cross section $dA \cos\theta$, the incident intensity (radiation per unit area) is $I_l \cos\theta$. Thus, for a diffuse reflection coefficient
k_d, the reflected intensity is given by the formula

$$I = I_l k_d \cos\theta \tag{14.2}$$

Equation 14.2 is appropriate for a directed light source, that is, light that is collimated
in a parallel beam (for example, by a parabolic reflector behind the light). For a point light
source having a beam that spreads out, the light will attenuate geometrically with distance
from the source. An ideal point light source has an intensity that decreases as the square of
the distance d from the light source (as the light travels outward it spreads out over a spherical surface of area $4\pi d^2$ around the source). Because an intensity decrease as d^2 is often

too rapid when viewed on a computer monitor, a linear decrease with d is often used. Thus, rendering software products often implement the following attenuation factor:

$$I = f_{att}I_lk_d\cos\theta, \quad \text{where } f_{att} = \frac{1}{c_0 + c_1d + c_2d^2} \qquad (14.3)$$

Equation 14.3 reduces to the case of a directed light source for $c_1 = c_2 = 0$, and to an ideal point source for $c_0 = c_1 = 0$. With most rendering software, a user can select c_i values to achieve a desired light fall-off for a given rendering.

As illustrated in figure 14.3, θ is the angle between the surface normal vector $\mathbf{N}$ and the light vector $\mathbf{L}$. Thus, $\cos\theta$ can be calculated directly from the scalar product of $\mathbf{N}$ and $\mathbf{L}$ according to the following equation.

$$\cos\theta = \frac{\mathbf{N} \cdot \mathbf{L}}{|\mathbf{N}| \, |\mathbf{L}|} \qquad (14.4)$$

For a directed light source, the beam is considered to originate a large distance from the scene, so that all objects in the scene are illuminated with parallel rays. In this case only the direction of $\mathbf{L}$ is important, not its magnitude (note that $\mathbf{L}$ appears in the normalized form $\mathbf{L}/|\mathbf{L}|$ in equation 14.4). Thus, for computations, the light vector $\mathbf{L} = L_x\mathbf{i} + L_x\mathbf{j} + L_x\mathbf{k} = 2\mathbf{i} + \mathbf{j} + \mathbf{k}$ gives the same results as the vector $\mathbf{L} = 4\mathbf{i} + 2\mathbf{j} + 2\mathbf{k}$. For the directed light source the same vector $\mathbf{L}$ may be used at each face in the scene.

The normal vector $\mathbf{N}$ is computed for each face on a surface to be rendered. This normal vector can be constructed (as in section 12.9) by forming the cross product of two vectors that lie in the face. Two vectors $\mathbf{A}$ and $\mathbf{B}$ lying in a face can be formed from the first three vertex points $(x_{w,i}, y_{w,i}, z_{w,i})$ defining the face.

$$\begin{aligned}
\mathbf{A} &= a_x\mathbf{i} + a_y\mathbf{j} + a_z\mathbf{k} = (x_{w,1} - x_{w,0})\mathbf{i} + (y_{w,1} - y_{w,0})\mathbf{j} + (z_{w,1} - z_{w,0})\mathbf{k} \\
\mathbf{B} &= b_x\mathbf{i} + b_y\mathbf{j} + b_z\mathbf{k} = (x_{w,2} - x_{w,0})\mathbf{i} + (y_{w,2} - y_{w,0})\mathbf{j} + (z_{w,2} - z_{w,0})\mathbf{k}
\end{aligned} \qquad (14.5)$$

A vector normal to the face can be formed as the cross product of $\mathbf{A}$ and $\mathbf{B}$.

$$\mathbf{N} = \mathbf{A} \times \mathbf{B} = (a_yb_z - a_zb_y)\mathbf{i} + (a_zb_x - a_xb_z)\mathbf{j} + (a_xb_y - a_yb_x)\mathbf{k} \qquad (14.6)$$

In equation 14.6 the coefficients a_i and b_i can be expressed in terms of the vertex coordinates by means of relations 14.5.

Specular Reflection

Specular reflection is concentrated in a narrow beam around the ideal reflection angle. As indicated by figure 14.1, the specular component of the reflected radiation increases and becomes focused into a narrow beam as the surface becomes smooth (with the roughness height becoming small relative to the light wavelength).

A simple model for the specular reflection was developed by Phong, who used the following formula:

$$I = f_{att} I_l k_s \cos^n \alpha \qquad (14.7)$$

In equation 14.5, α is the angle between the ideal reflection direction $\mathbf{R}$ and the view direction $\mathbf{V}$, as illustrated in figure 14.4a. The function $\cos^n \alpha$ is plotted in figure 14.4b for several values of the exponent n—the beam narrows as n increases.

The angle α between the reflection vector $\mathbf{R}$ and the view direction $\mathbf{V}$ can be calculated with the help of the vector diagram in figure 14.5. The two vector triangles in the figure give the following relations: $\mathbf{S} = \mathbf{N}' - \mathbf{L}$ and $\mathbf{R} = \mathbf{N}' + \mathbf{S} = 2\mathbf{N}' - \mathbf{L}$. The vector $\mathbf{N}'$ is directed along the surface normal and has a magnitude equal to $\mathbf{n} \cdot \mathbf{L}$, where $\mathbf{n} = \mathbf{N}/|\mathbf{N}|$ is the normalized surface normal vector. Thus $\mathbf{R}$ can be calculated from the equation

$$\mathbf{R} = 2\mathbf{n}(\mathbf{n} \cdot \mathbf{L}) - \mathbf{L} \qquad (14.8)$$

The factor $\cos\alpha$ can be calculated from the scalar product of vectors $\mathbf{R}$ and $\mathbf{V}$.

$$\cos\alpha = \frac{\mathbf{R} \cdot \mathbf{V}}{|\mathbf{R}| \, |\mathbf{V}|} \qquad (14.9)$$

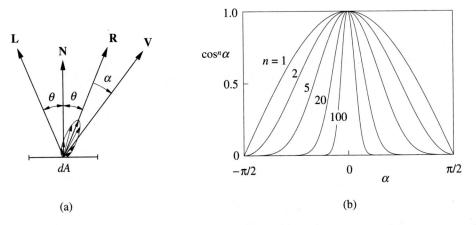

(a)   (b)

Figure 14.4 The specular reflection model of Phong: (a) the light source location $\mathbf{L}$, viewpoint $\mathbf{V}$, surface normal $\mathbf{N}$, and ideal reflection direction $\mathbf{R}$; (b) the distribution of light intensity in the reflected beam, as determined by the factor $\cos^n \alpha$.

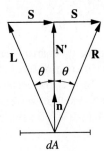

Figure 14.5 Vector diagram for calculating the reflection direction $\mathbf{R}$.

Thus, with specified directions for the light source **L** and the view direction **V**, **R** can be calculated from equation 14.8 and $\cos\alpha$ from equation 14.9.

Multiple Lights

In a general situation there will be ambient illumination along with illumination from more than one light. At a surface illuminated by N_l lights, the simple shading model developed above provides the following formula for the reflected intensity:

$$I = I_a k_a + \sum_{j=1}^{N_l} I_{l,j} \frac{(k_d \cos\theta_j + k_s \cos\alpha_j)}{(c_0 + c_1 d_j + c_2 d_j^2)} \tag{14.10}$$

The rendering applications discussed in the next section require that the user provide the data for the parameters in equation 14.10. For example, the surface finishes are distinguished by inputted values for the reflection coefficients k_a, k_d, and k_s.

In applications, light sources can be designated as directed (or distant), with parallel rays corresponding to zero fall-off of light intensity ($c_0 = 1$ and $c_1 = c_2 = 0$ in equation 14.10). For point light sources, the light fall-off coefficients c_i must be specified.

Programming Example: Uniform Shading over Faces

The illumination model described above can be readily implemented into a program; for example, the subroutine shadeSurface() listed below uses the diffuse shading model given by equation 14.2 to render a surface of revolution for a single directed light source. In the subroutine shadeSurface(), each face on the surface is given a single shade (intensity) as illustrated in figure 14.6a. Figures 14.6b–c show that greater realism can be achieved by varying the shading over a face with the Gouraud and Phong smoothing algorithms, considered in sections below.

For the general case of uniform shading over a face, the intensity is determined by equation 14.10 with the vector normal to the face computed by equation 14.6. Thus, only one intensity is determined for each face. This intensity is used to fill the polygon that forms the face(with fillQuadrilateral() from listing 3.2 in appendix B).

For a surface of revolution, the painter's hidden-line algorithm can be used in the same manner as in section 12.10, except for this shading case the color is proportional to the intensity given by equation 14.10. Thus, first the color palette is reset to grays ranging from black for color number 0 to the brightest white for the largest color index number. (The procedure for resetting the color palette in Microsoft C was described in section 6.3.)

After the color palette has been set, the function revSurf() is called. The revSurf() function is the same as that given in section 12.10, except that at its end the function shadeSurface() below is called rather than the function plotHideSurface().

The parameter MAXSHADE in the subroutine below is set with a *#define* directive to a value just below the maximum number of gray shades (say 15.999999999 for the VGA high-resolution mode or 63.999999999 for the VGA medium-resolution mode for Microsoft C). This results in the full range of color index numbers *icolor* being available (0 to 15, 0 to 63, or higher, depending on your system graphics mode).

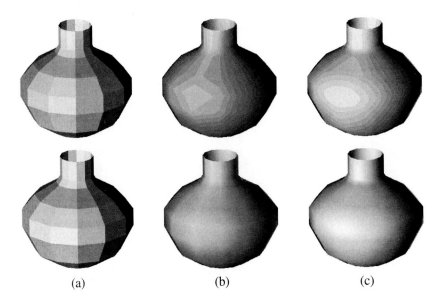

(a)   (b)   (c)

Figure 14.6   Shading for a surface of revolution: (a) constant intensity across each face; (b) Gouraud shading; and (c) Phong shading. The top row of figures was formed with 16 gray shades, and the bottom row with 64 shades. These figures were computed from a C program with a SuperVGA graphics adapter.

```
void shadeSurface(void)
{
    int     icolor,m,k,vnum,xcen=220,yb=350;
    double  phi,sinp,cosp,xw[4],yw[4],zw[4],sf = 6.0;
    double  ax,ay,az,bx,by,bz,nx,ny,nz,nv;
    double  lx=-1,ly=-2,lz=0.5,sum,cosnl,cosnv;

    phi = 70*PI/180; sinp = sin(phi); cosp = cos(phi);
    sum = sqrt(lx*lx + ly*ly + lz*lz);
    lx = lx/sum; ly = ly/sum; lz = lz/sum; /* normalization */

    for (m=0; m<numFaces; m++)
    {
        for (k=0; k<4; k++)
        {
            vnum = vn[m][k];
            xw[k] = vert[vnum][0]; yw[k] = vert[vnum][1];
            zw[k] = vert[vnum][2];
            xv[k] = xcen + (int) (sf*xw[k]);
```

```
      yv[k] = yb - (int) (sf*(yw[k]*cosp+zw[k]*sinp));
    }
    ax = xw[1]-xw[0]; ay = yw[1]-yw[0]; az = zw[1]-zw[0];
    bx = xw[2]-xw[0]; by = yw[2]-yw[0]; bz = zw[2]-zw[0];
    nx = ay*bz-az*by; ny = az*bx-ax*bz; nz = ax*by-ay*bx;
    cosnv = nz*cosp-ny*sinp;
    cosnl = (lx*nx+ly*ny+lz*nz)/sqrt(nx*nx+ny*ny+nz*nz);
    if ((cosnl > 0 && cosnv > 0) || (cosnl < 0 && cosnv < 0))
        icolor = (int) floor(MAXSHADE*fabs(cosnl));
    else
        icolor = 0;
    _setcolor(icolor);
    fillQuadrilateral();
  }
}
```

Gouraud Shading

In the above programming example, a constant intensity (shade) was used to fill a given face on the surface. The resulting shading produces a faceted appearance, as shown in figure 14.6a. A bilinear interpolation of the intensity across each face produces Gouraud shading, which is illustrated in figure 14.6b. This smooth shading yields a greatly improved image, except along the object's edges, where the flat face boundaries are evident. That is, in figure 14.6b the object has the appearance of a much more finely divided surface than in figure 14.6a.

The top figures in 14.6 were produced from a palette of 16 colors (shades of gray), and the bottom figures were produced from 64 shades of gray. On the PC, the VGA video mode can produce these images at resolutions of 640 × 480 pixels for 16 colors, and 320 × 200 pixels for 256 colors (which can produce 64 gray shades). Figure 14.6 was produced at a SuperVGA resolution of 1024 × 768 pixels available with a 1 MB graphics adapter.

From figures 14.6a and 14.6b it is apparent that considerable banding occurs with only 16 shades, whereas 64 shades produce a much more smoothly varying intensity, although 256 or more shades would be required to completely eliminate perception of separate bands of intensity.

The first step in implementing Gouraud shading is to calculate intensity values at each vertex. This is done by averaging the intensities of the faces surrounding the vertex. The 3-D world coordinates of a vertex i are transformed to the 2-D screen coordinates (x_{vk}, y_{vk}). In figure 14.7, the quadrilateral face on a surface is determined by four sets of screen coordinates (x_{vk}, y_{vk}) with $k = 0, 1, 2,$ and 3.

The fill line shown in figure 14.7 occurs in the region $y_{v0} < y < y_{v1}$, with a starting intensity I_{start} and an ending intensity I_{end}. The intensity I_{start} is obtained by a linear interpolation between vertex intensities I_{v0} and I_{v1}, whereas I_{end} is a linear interpolation between I_{v0} and I_{v2}. The interpolation distance can be measured along the line joining the two vertices or, as given below, along the vertical coordinate.

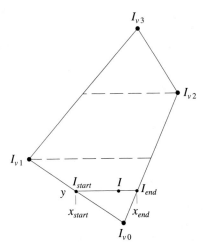

Figure 14.7   Geometry for Gouraud shading.

$$I_{start} = uI_{v1} + (1 - u)I_{v0}, \quad where\ u = \frac{y - y_{v0}}{y_{v1} - y_{v0}}$$

$$(14.11)$$

$$I_{end} = vI_{v2} + (1 - v)I_{v0}, \quad where\ v = \frac{y - y_{v0}}{y_{v2} - y_{v0}}$$

The following equation gives a linear interpolation for the intensity I at an arbitrary point (x,y) along the fill line that extends from x_{start} to x_{end}.

$$I = wI_{end} + (1 - w)I_{start}, \quad where\ w = \frac{x - x_{start}}{x_{end} - x_{start}} \qquad (14.12)$$

To implement Gouraud shading for a surface of revolution, one must set up a procedure to calculate the intensities at the vertex points. First, the subroutine revSurf() of section 12.9 is modified to include an array $fn[m][j]$ that numbers the faces surrounding a vertex. The array $fn[m][j]$ specifies four j values giving the face numbers for the faces surrounding the vertex m. The last *for* loop in the subroutine revSurf() listed below considers the top and bottom edges of the surface, where the array $fn[m][j]$ for vertex m is given only two different values over the four values of j because only two faces bound vertices on the surface edges.

The same shadeSurface() subroutine given above for flat face shading is called from the subroutine revSurf(). However, instead of calling fillQuadrilateral(), the subroutine shadeSurface() now calls gouraudFill() listed on page 438. In the subroutine gouraudFill() the intensities at interior vertices are determined by averaging four surrounding faces, and vertex intensities along the bottom and top edges of the surface of revolution are computed as the average of intensities from two faces.

A program for Gouraud shading of surface of revolution can be constructed by modifying the revSurf() subroutine of section 12.10 and the shadeSurface() subroutine given above. After setting the video mode and setting up a palette of gray shades, the program calls the function revSurf(), which sets up the face number array $fn[m][j]$, along with the vertex number array $vn[m2][j]$. The subroutine shadeSurface(), which is called at the end of revSurf(), uses the function gouraudFill() to fill the quadrilateral faces according to the Gouraud shading algorithm.

The first group of program lines below calculates the face number array $fn[m][j]$. These lines are to be added at the subroutine revSurf(), after the calculation of the vertex number array $vn[m2][j]$. The first set of *for* loops fills the $fn[m][j]$ arrays for the interior vertices. That is, $fn[m][j]$ gives the four face numbers that surround vertex m. The last *for* loop gives the face numbers for vertices on the top and bottom edges of the surface, where each face is counted twice because only two faces surround an edge vertex. After these program lines are added to revSurf(), the function shadeSurface() is called.

```
for (i=1; i<nb-1; i++)
{
    for (j=0; j<ne; j++)
    {
        m = i*ne+j; /* m is the vertex number */
        if (j <= j0) /* m2 is the face number */
            m2 = m+j0-2*j+1;
        else
            m2 = m;
        if (j == 0)
        {
            fn[m][0] = m2+j0; fn[m][1] = m2-1;
            fn[m][2] = m2-1-ne; fn[m][3] = m2+j0-ne;
        }
        if (j == (j0+1))
        {
            fn[m][0] = m; fn[m][1] = m-j0-1;
            fn[m][2] = m-j0-1-ne; fn[m][3] = m-ne;
        }
        if ((j != 0) && (j != (j0+1)))
        {
            fn[m][0] = m2; fn[m][1] = m2-1;
            fn[m][2] = m2-1-ne; fn[m][3] = m2-ne;
        }
    }
}
for (j=0; j<ne; j++)
{
    m3 = j+numFaces;
    if (j <= j0)
        m2 = j0-j+1;
    else
        m2 = j;
    if (j == 0)
    {
        fn[j][0] = fn[j][3] = m2-1;
        fn[m3][0] = fn[m3][3] = m2-1+numFaces-ne;
    }
```

```
                    fn[j][1] = fn[j][2] = ne-1;
                    fn[m3][1] = fn[m3][2] = numFaces-1;
            }
            if (j == (j0+1))
            {
                    fn[j][0] = fn[j][3] = j0+1;
                    fn[m3][0] = fn[m3][3] = numFaces-j0-1;
                    fn[j][1] = fn[j][2] = 0;
                    fn[m3][1] = fn[m3][2] = numFaces-ne;
            }
            if ((j != 0) && (j != (j0+1)))
            {
                    fn[j][0] = fn[j][3] = m2;
                    fn[m3][0] = fn[m3][3] = m2+numFaces-ne;
                    fn[j][1] = fn[j][2] = m2-1;
                    fn[m3][1] = fn[m3][2] = m2-1+numFaces-ne;
            }
    }
    shadeSurface();
```

The function shadeSurface() given previously is modified below to include calculation of vertex intensities *ivert*[] as the average of the intensities *iface*[] of the surrounding faces. Then in a *for* loop over the faces, the subroutine gouraudFill() is called to fill each face, starting with the global arrays for screen vertex coordinates (*xv*[], *yv*[]) and the vertex intensities *iv*[] calculated in shadeSurface().

```
void shadeSurface(void)
{
    int i,j,k,vnum;
    double phi,sinp,cosp,xw[4],yw[4],zw[4];
    double sf = 6.0,xcen=320.,yb=350.;
    double ax,ay,az,bx,by,bz,nx,ny,nz,nv;
    double lx=-1,ly=-2,lz=0.5,sum,cosnl,cosnv;

    phi = 70*PI/180; sinp = sin(phi); cosp = cos(phi);
    sum = sqrt(lx*lx + ly*ly + lz*lz);
    lx = lx/sum; ly = ly/sum; lz = lz/sum; /* normalization */

    for (m=0; m<numFaces; m++) /* m is a global variable */
    {
        for (k=0; k<4; k++)
        {
            vnum = vn[m][k];
            xw[k] = vert[vnum][0]; yw[k] = vert[vnum][1];
            zw[k] = vert[vnum][2];
        }
        ax = xw[1]-xw[0]; ay = yw[1]-yw[0]; az = zw[1]-zw[0];
```

```
        bx = xw[2]-xw[0]; by = yw[2]-yw[0]; bz = zw[2]-zw[0];
        nx = ay*bz-az*by; ny = az*bx-ax*bz; nz = ax*by-ay*bx;
        cosnv = nz*cosp-ny*sinp;
        cosnl = (lx*nx+ly*ny+lz*nz)/sqrt(nx*nx+ny*ny+nz*nz);
        if ((cosnl > 0 && cosnv > 0) || (cosnl < 0 && cosnv < 0))
            iface[m] = floor(MAXSHADE*fabs(cosnl));
        else
            iface[m] = 0;
    }
    for (i=0; i<nb; i++)
    {
        for (j=0; j<ne; j++)
        {
            m = i*ne+j;
            ivert[m] = 0;
            for (k=0; k<4; k++)
            {
                ivert[m] = ivert[m] + 0.25*iface[fn[m][k]];
            }
        }
    }
    for (m=0; m<numFaces; m++)
    {
        for (k=0; k<4; k++)
        {
            vnum = vn[m][k];
            xw[k] = vert[vnum][0]; yw[k] = vert[vnum][1];
            zw[k] = vert[vnum][2];
            xv[k] = xcen + sf*xw[k];
            yv[k] = yb - sf*(yw[k]*cosp+zw[k]*sinp);
            if (iface[m] == 0)
                iv[k] = 0;
            else
                iv[k] = ivert[vnum];
        }
        gouraudFill();
    }
}
```

The gouraudFill() subroutine is similar to the fillQuadrilateral() subroutine given as listing 3.2 in appendix B, except that the fill occurs pixel by pixel, rather than by drawing horizontal line segments across the quadrilateral. That is, the intensity is calculated at each pixel along the horizontal fill line shown in figure 14.7, and the pixel is filled with this intensity by means of the Microsoft C functions _setcolor() and _setpixel(). Because the starting point on the fill line may be to the left or right of the ending point, the pixel position is incremented by the amount *dx*, which equals $+1$ when *xend* $>$ *xstart* and equals -1 when *xend* $<$ *xstart*.

```
void gouraudFill(void)
{
    int i,   imin,icolor,j,v0,v1,v2,v3,vd;
    double  x,xd,dx,xstart,xend,y,yd,ymax;
    double  m1,m2,u,v,w,ivd,istart,iend;

    imin = 0;
    for (i=1; i<=3; i++)
    {
        if (yv[i] < yv[imin]) imin = i;
    }
    v0 = imin % 4; v1 = (imin+1) % 4;
    v2 = (imin+2) % 4; v3 = (imin+3) % 4;
    if (yv[v3] < yv[v1]) /* exchange v1 & v3 */
    {
        vd = v1; v1 = v3; v3 = vd;
    }
    if (yv[v0] < yv[v1]) /* bottom triangle */
    {
        m1 = (xv[v1]-xv[v0])/(yv[v1]-yv[v0]);
        m2 = (zv[v3]-xv[v0])/(yv[v3]-yv[v0]);
        for (y = yv[v0]     +1.; y<yv[v1]; y=y+1.)
        {
            xstart = xv[v0] + m1*(y-yv[v0]);
            xend = xv[v0] + m2*(y-yv[v0]);
            u = (y-yv[v0])/(yv[v1]-yv[v0]);
            v = (y-yv[v0])/(yv[v3]-yv[v0]);
            istart = u*iv[v1] + (1.-u)*iv[v0];
            iend = v*iv[v3] + (1.-v)*iv[v0];
            dx = (xend-xstart)/fabs(xend-xstart); x = xstart - dx;
            do
            {
                w = (x-xstart)/(xend-xstart);
                icolor = (int) (w*iend + (1. - w)*istart);
                _setcolor(icolor); _setpixel((int)   x, (int) y);
                x = x + dx;
            } while (fabs (x-dx-xend) > 1.);
        }
    }
    if (yv[v1]<yv[v2] && yv[v1]<yv[v3]) /* middle quadrilateral */
    {
        if (yv[v3] < yv[v2])
            ymax = yv[v3];
        else
            ymax = yv[v2];
        m1 = (xv[v2]-xv[v1])/(yv[v2]-yv[v1]);
        m2 = (xv[v3]-xv[v0])/(yv[v3]-yv[v0]);
        for (y=yv[v1]; y<ymax; y=y+1.)
```

```
        {
            xstart = xv[v1] + m1*(y-yv[v1]);
            xend = xv[v0] + m2*(y-yv[v0]);
            u = (y-yv[v1])/(yv[v2]-yv[v1]);
            v = (y-yv[v0])/(yv[v3]-yv[v0]);
            istart = u*iv[v2] + (1.-u)*iv[v1]);
             iend = v*iv[v3] + (1.-v)*iv[v0];
             dx = (xend-xstart)/fabs(xend-xstart); x = xstart - dx;
             do
             {
                 w = (x-start)/(xend-xstart);
                 icolor = (int) (w*iend + (1.-w)*istart);
                 _setcolor(icolor); _setpixel((int) x, (int) y);
                 x = x + dx;
             } while (fabs(x-dx-xend) > 1.);
        }
    }
    if (yv[v3] < yv[v2]) /* top triangle */
    {
        m1 = (xv[v2]-xv[v1])/(yv[v2]-yv[v1]);
        m2 = (xv[v2]-xv[v3])/(yv[v2]-yv[v3]);
        for (y=yv[v3]; y<yv[v2]; y=y+1.)
        {
            xstart = xv[v1] + m1*(y-yv[v1]);
            xend = xv[v3] + m2*(y-yv[v3]);
            u = (y-yv[v1])/(yv[v2]-yv[v1]);
            v = (y-yv[v3])/(yv[v2]-yv[v3]);
            istart = u*iv[v2] + (1.-u)*iv[v1];
            iend = v*iv[v2] + (1.-v)*iv[v3]);
            dx = (xend-xstart)/fabs(xend-xstart); x = xstart - dx;
            do
            {
                w = (x-xstart)/(xend-xstart);
                icolor = (int) (w*iend + (1.-w)*istart);
                _setcolor(icolor); _setpixel((int) x, (int) y);
                x = x + dx;
            } while (fabs(x-dx-xend) > 1.);
        }
    }
    if (yv[v3] > yv[v2]) /* top triangle */
    {
        m1 = (xv[v3]-xv[v0])/(yv[v3]-yv[v0]);
        m2 = (xv[v3]-xv[v2])/(yv[v3]-yv[v2]);
        for (y=yv[v2]; y<yv[v3]; y=y+1.)
        {
            xstart = xv[v0] + m1*(y-yv[v0]);
            xend = xv[v2] + m2*(y-yv[v2]);
            u = (y-yv[v0])/(yv[v3]-yv[v0]);
```

```
        v = (y-yv[v2])/(yv[v3]-yv[v2]);
        istart = u*iv[v3] + (1.-u)*iv[v0];
        iend = v*iv[v3] + (1.-v)*iv[v2];
        dx = (xend-xstart)/fabs(xend-xstart); x = xstart - dx;
        do
        {
            w = (x-xstart)/(xend-xstart);
            icolor = (int) (w*iend + (1.-w)*istart);
            setcolor(icolor); _setpixel((int) x, (int) y);
            x = x + dx;
        } while (fabs(x-dx-xend) > 1.);
    }
  }
}
```

Phong Shading

Phong shading uses a bilinear interpolation for the normal vector **n**, instead of the bilinear interpolation of the intensity *I* used for Gouraud shading. That is, for Phong shading the *I* terms in equations 14.11–12 are replaced by corresponding normal vector terms. Thus, a subroutine shadeSurface() for Phong shading passes vertex normal components $nvx[k]$, $nvy[k]$, and $nvz[k]$ to a phongFill() subroutine, as compared with Gouraud shading where the vertex intensities $iv[k]$ are passed to the gouraudFill() subroutine.

After bilinear interpolation in the phongFill() subroutine, the components of the normal vector at each point in the quadrilateral are used to calculate cosines for determining the intensity *i*color of a pixel. Because three components of the normal vector and the cosine functions are calculated at each point, the Phong shading model requires a longer computation time than the Gouraud model. However, the Phong model smooths surfaces more realistically because it is interpolating the normal vector, not just intensities determined from the normal vectors to flat faces.

The tops of figures 14.6b–c show that Gouraud shading produces a discontinuous slope for the intensity at the edges of faces, whereas for Phong shading intensity varies smoothly across the edges of faces. The higher number (64) of shades used in the bottoms of figures 14.6b–c shows that Gouraud shading gives the appearance of lighter edges. These lighter-appearing edges are an optical illusion, called *Mach bands*, which occur when the slope (rate-of-change) of intensity abruptly changes.

14.2 SIMPLE SHADING WITH RENDERING SOFTWARE

Beginning with AutoCAD Release 12, basic rendering (shading) capabilities have been provided by an external application called AutoCAD Render. AutoCAD Render runs from within AutoCAD. Previously, a postprocessor, such as Autodesk's AutoShade, was required for rendering.

AutoShade was the first AutoCAD rendering product. Release 2 of AutoShade is combined with RenderMan to offer capabilities beyond simple shading. That is, the RenderMan part of the Autodesk AutoShade/RenderMan software package provides advanced capabilities for photorealistic rendering. (RenderMan was first developed by Pixar as a rendering interface, with separate rendering packages for workstations and for the Macintosh computer.)

Another Autodesk product, 3D Studio, has become very popular for rendering models produced with AutoCAD, or produced with the modeling capabilities contained within 3D Studio. Although its rendering capabilities are not quite as complete as those of Render-Man, 3D Studio is versatile, fast, easy to use, and has good photorealistic rendering capabilities. In addition to still rendering, 3D Studio also provides advanced animation features.

Recently, another Autodesk product, AutoVision, has been introduced to provide advanced rendering capabilities from within AutoCAD. AutoVision incorporates many of the rendering features of 3D Studio, and also has ray-tracing capabilities.

In this section, the rendering software products are described with respect to how they implement the basic shading methods discussed in the preceding sections. More advanced rendering topics, such as ray tracing and texture mapping, are described in section 14.3.

AutoCAD Render

AutoCAD Render is initialized with the RENDER command (or by selecting the pull-down Render menu). Objects are rendered from the current viewpoint, that is, from the view set up with the VPOINT command or with the CAmera option under the DVIEW command. Lighting of the scene is achieved by setting up lights with the LIGHT command.

The LIGHT command displays a dialog box that permits the user to set the ambient light intensity (I_a in equation 14.10) and to set up new lights and modify or delete existing lights. The intensity $I_{l,j}$ of each new light may be specified, and a light may be either a distant light or a point light.

A distant light illuminates all objects from the same direction with no light fall-off (geometric attenuation). To specify this direction, target and light locations are entered. For the distant light source, only the direction of the vector from the light to the target is important, not the particular target and light locations.

A point light source sends out rays in all directions. Thus the direction of a light ray incident on an object depends on the light's location, as well as on the object's location. Because light is sent out in all directions, there is no target location for a point light source. Thus, for a point light source only the light's location is specified. With AutoCAD Render, the light fall-off for a point light can be specified as one of the following three options: none, inverse linear, or inverse square (thus determining the c_i coefficients in equation 14.10).

The reflective properties of a surface are specified in AutoCAD Render with the FINISH command, which displays a dialog box. In this dialog box, the finish color and reflective properties are specified. The reflection coefficients (k_a, k_d, and k_s in equation 14.10) are specified directly, and a surface roughness value is specified. The specular exponent n in equation 14.10 varies inversely as the roughness (recall that the reflected light beam narrows with decreasing roughness). After the user has specified and named a finish, it may be attached to surface or solid entities.

The preferences dialog box (selected under the Render menu) has a number of options, including a box to toggle smooth shading on and off. Smooth shading is an implementation of the Gouraud shading algorithm discussed above.

Figure 14.2 was constructed with AutoCAD Render using ambient illumination and a single distant light of equal intensity ($I_a = I_l$), with the smooth (Gouraud) shading option turned on. The three finishes shown in figure 14.2 have the following reflectivities: (a) $k_a = 1$, $k_d = k_s = 0$; (b) $k_a = 0.25$, $k_d = 0.75$, $k_s = 0$; and (c) $k_a = 0.25$, $k_d = 0.50$, $k_s = 0.50$. A roughness value of 0.06 was chosen for the specular component in figure 14.2. A distant light has no attenuation with distance; thus it corresponds to the values $c_0 = 1$ and $c_1 = c_2 = 0$ in equation 14.10.

Plate 5 shows an AutoCAD Render image of a door handle constructed with solid modeling in the manner described in section 13.2.

AutoShade/RenderMan

Renderings with AutoShade/RenderMan are formed from scenes that are set up in Auto-CAD. A number of different scenes can be constructed in an AutoCAD drawing; each scene has lights, surface finishes, and a camera. After lights, finishes, cameras, and scenes have been added, the AutoCAD drawing is saved with the FILMROLL command—this produces a file with the extension FLM. This filmroll file can be loaded after AutoCAD is exited and the AutoShade program is started.

The AutoCAD Render dialog boxes may be used to set up scenes for AutoShade. Alternatively, scenes may be set up in AutoCAD by loading AutoShade support files with the command (load "ashade"), where the parentheses and quotation marks are part of the command. Also, parameters for use with RenderMan may be set up with the AutoCAD Render dialog boxes, or by loading RenderMan support files with the command (load "rman").

Within the AutoShade program, the camera position and field of view (lens focal length) can be changed. Lights cannot be moved in AutoShade (although intensities can be changed)—the user must go back to AutoCAD to move lights. The parameters for surface finishes can be changed in AutoShade. In AutoCAD, surface finishes are attached to objects by means of their color, with the result that two objects in AutoShade have the same finish if their colors are the same (this is in contrast to AutoCAD Render, where finishes may be attached directly to objects).

AutoShade provides for separate input of the individual light intensities $I_{l,j}$. However, unlike AutoCAD Render (and RenderMan operating within AutoShade), AutoShade by itself does not provide for the direct entry of values for the ambient intensity I_a. Instead, it is assumed that I_a in equation 14.10 equals the sum of the N_l light intensities $I_{l,j}$, with the reflected ambient intensity controlled by the surface reflectivity k_a. That is, because the ambient reflected intensity occurs as the product $k_a I_a$, an appropriate choice for k_a can produce any desired amount of ambient reflection from an object.

The shading model dialog box in AutoShade provides different options for light falloff, including constant, inverse linear, and inverse square options. If finishes have not been provided in the filmroll, then the surface reflection coefficients can be supplied in the shading model dialog box (these values are the same for all surfaces without applied finishes).

Display options in AutoShade include a plan view for checking lights and camera positions, and a wireframe view from the camera position for a quick preview of the scene. In addition to the final, most accurate rendering provided by a *full shade* option, a preview of the rendering is provided by approximate, faster options called *quick shade* and *fast shade*. AutoShade provides rendered scenes similar in appearance to the AutoCAD Render displays shown in figure 14.2. AutoShade provides a smooth shading (Gouraud shading) option under the Expert selection in the Settings menu.

In addition to being displayed on the monitor (framebuffer), rendered scenes may be sent to a hardcopy device or saved to a file. The Autodesk file format for a rendering has the extension RND, but an AutoShade/RenderMan image also may be saved as a Targa file (TGA extension) or in the tagged image file format (TIFF file with the extension TIF).

The RenderMan software can be used to go beyond the simple shaded renderings provided by AutoCAD Render and by AutoShade. RenderMan is a programming interface that extends from a description of the model through the complete rendering of the scene. In the AutoShade/RenderMan package, RenderMan is run from within the AutoShade program. To carry out renderings with RenderMan, a RIB file must be constructed. This file format (extension RIB) was developed for RenderMan to provide a versatile format for programmers.

Normally RenderMan parameters are first set in AutoCAD. This includes applying surface shaders to objects with the RMPROP command and setting overall rendering parameters with the RMSETUP command. Icons for the surface shaders and for the setup are placed in the AutoCAD drawing along with the icons for the camera, lights, AutoShade finishes, and scenes. The shaders take the place of AutoShade finishes, and can represent surface properties in much more detail than AutoShade finishes or simple texture maps. (If RenderMan surface shaders are not assigned in AutoCAD, then they can be assigned to AutoShade finishes or AutoCAD colors in AutoShade; also, the RenderMan setup parameters can be set in AutoShade).

In addition to point and directed lights, RenderMan also has spotlights, which provide a cone of light. Spotlights are specified by a direction, cone angle, and the fall-off of light near the outer edge of the cone. Spotlights can be specified in AutoCAD after the RenderMan support files have been loaded.

3D Studio

3D Studio has five parts: the 2D Shaper, the 3D Lofter, the 3D Editor, the Materials Editor, and the Keyframer. The 2D Shaper is used to draw 2-D polygons, which can then be turned into 3-D surfaces in the 3D Lofter module. (The 3D Lofter can "loft" the polygon along a variety of paths to produce extrusions, surfaces of revolution, and more complicated surfaces.) In most design situations, it is preferable to build the 3-D model on more precise, full-featured CAD software, such as AutoCAD, and then bring the model into 3D Studio in the DXF file format. 3D Studio saves files in its own format, which has the extension 3DS.

The 3D Editor module of 3D Studio is used to set up and carry out the rendering process. First, the model is loaded from a DXF file or constructed with the 2D Shaper and

3D Lofter modules. Then lights and a camera are added to the scene. Surface properties are assigned to surfaces in the 3D Editor module, but new surface properties are created in the Materials Editor. The rendering operation is carried out in the 3D Editor module. The Keyframer module constructs and plays animations, as described in section 14.4.

Plate 6 shows a screen from the Materials Editor. Different colors may be entered for the ambient, diffuse, and specular parts of the reflectivities from a surface. That is, separate red, green, and blue reflectivities are entered for the ambient, diffuse, and specular components. Thus, nine surface reflectivities are entered ($k_{a,r}$, $k_{a,g}$, $k_{a,b}$, $k_{d,r}$, $k_{d,g}$, $k_{d,b}$, $k_{s,r}$, $k_{s,g}$, and $k_{s,b}$). This procedure provides an accurate modeling of surfaces; for example, colored plastics or glazed ceramics usually have white specular highlights, whereas metals normally have specular highlights with the same color as their ambient and diffuse components. In 3D Studio, the width of the specular beam is controlled by a shininess value, which varies from 0 for the broadest reflected beam to 100 for the narrowest, most concentrated beam. Release 3 of 3D Studio displays a small plot of the specular highlight function; see plate 6. Also, a separate slider bar permits the shininess strength (intensity) to be changed.

The Materials Editor in plate 6 shows the following buttons for surface shading models: flat, Gouraud, Phong, and metal. The flat shading option provides a uniform shade over a face on the surface mesh, like the shading in figure 14.6a. Higher levels of shading are provided by the Gouraud and Phong models described in section 14.1.

The highest level of shading is provided by metal shading, which incorporates the illumination model of Cook and Torrance (1982). The Cook-Torrance model contains several features particular to metal surfaces, including an increased contrast for the specular highlight, and brighter highlights for glancing light beams. Plate 7 illustrates the differences between metal shading and Phong shading. The two vases on the left of plate 7 have metal shading. The vases in the middle column were rendered with Phong shading for the same colors as the vases on the left. The right column shows Phong shading with material properties adjusted to approximate the metals (ambient, diffuse, and specular colors were changed in addition to the shininess and shininess strength). The Phong-shaded vases on the right approximate the metal-shaded vases on the left for the light incident from the front (upper-left front); however, the glancing light from the back that is reflected from the right sides of the vases is not well approximated by the Phong model. That is, the metal-shading model is needed if reflections on metallic surfaces at glancing incidence are to be accurately represented.

Light sources in 3D Studio may be omni (point) lights or spotlights. For a spotlight, the bright cone of light (hotspot) and the light fall-off region at the cone's edge can be readily changed. The ambient intensity can be specified as any color (any R, G, and B values) in contrast to AutoCAD Render and AutoVision, which permit only the intensity for white ambient light to be assigned.

Light attenuation (fall-off with distance) may be included for point lights and spotlights. With attenuation enabled, the light intensity falls from its full value at an inner radius to zero at an outer radius (for radii entered by the program user).

3D Studio can save and view rendered images in a large variety of bitmap formats, including the Targa format (extension TGA), the tagged image file format or TIFF (extension TIF), the Microsoft Windows format (BMP), the format of the Joint Photographic Experts Group (JPG), the graphics interchange format (GIF) developed by the CompuServe

Information Service, and the flic file format for animation (FLC and FLI extensions). The Materials Editor can define mappings with files in the preceding formats, as well as with cel files (CEL extension) produced by Animator Pro and Autodesk Animator, and with solid pattern external process files (SXP extension).

AutoVision

AutoVision works from within AutoCAD. After installation, AutoVision replaces Render in the AutoCAD menu. This enables mappings and ray tracing to be carried out from within AutoCAD. AutoVision can exchange files with 3D Studio (files with the extension 3DS) by means of the 3DSIN and 3DSOUT commands.

   Although the material dialog box in AutoVision is much smaller than the 3D Studio Material Editor, it provides many of the same features. Separate red, green, and blue colors are entered for the ambient, diffuse, and specular parts of the reflectivities from a surface. Thus, nine surface reflectivities are specified ($k_{a,r}$, $k_{a,g}$, $k_{a,b}$, $k_{d,r}$, $k_{d,g}$, $k_{d,b}$, $k_{s,r}$, $k_{s,g}$, and $k_{s,b}$). AutoVision supports flat and Phong shading (but not Gouraud or metal shading).

   In addition to the point and spotlight options like those provided by 3D Studio, Auto-Vision provides distant light sources. (In 3D Studio, a distant light must be approximated by a spotlight that is far from the target point.) AutoVision has a distant light of particular interest to architects: this is the sun light, for which azimuth and elevation angles are calculated automatically after the user specifies a date, time of day, and latitude (or location on a map).

   AutoVision point and spotlights have the standard options for light attenuation: none (constant intensity), inverse linear, and inverse square. The intensity of the ambient light can be changed but not its color.

   Bitmaps used in AutoVision materials must have the TGA format; however, AutoVision can save and replay rendered images in the TGA, TIF, GIF, and RND formats.

14.3 ADVANCED RENDERING TOPICS

Photorealistic rendering is based on ray-tracing methods and incorporates special procedures for representing surface properties. These procedures are used to represent surface textures, surface bumps, reflections, and the opacity (or transparency) of the surface.

Ray Tracing

In the physical world, a scene is viewed with light rays that originate from various light sources and are reflected from objects before they are directed to our eyes. It is beyond our computing power to follow a sufficient number of rays starting from light sources in order to determine which rays ultimately end up at our eyes (or camera). But because the laws of geometric optics are reversible (apply equally backward along a ray), the problem can be simplified by calculating rays starting from the eye and traveling out into the scene to see what objects they strike.

   The simple illumination model of section 14.1 considered only opaque surfaces with diffuse and specular reflection. Ray-tracing procedures provide a more realistic model that includes shadows, mirror-reflection effects, and transparency. The ray-tracing method determines shadowing by sending out "shadow feelers" directed toward the light sources to determine which sources illuminate a given surface point. For surfaces with specular reflection, reflected rays are traced back to their origins to calculate reflected images. Also, rays are traced through partially transparent objects to portray the transmission of the background scene through the object.

In the simplest ray-tracing computation, one ray is selected for each pixel to be colored in the image. Figure 14.8a shows a ray starting from the eye point, passing through a pixel in the image picture plane, and traveling out into the scene until it hits a sphere. The sphere is considered to be partially transparent and partially reflective. For the case considered in the figure, the transmitted ray T_1 intersects the back wall, while the reflective ray R_1 intersects the tile floor.

The back wall is considered to be opaque and nonreflective; therefore the transmitted ray is traced no further. In this simple example, refractive effects at the ray's entrance and exit points on the sphere are neglected; however, refractive effects could be included in a more comprehensive model. In this example, the back wall intersection point is illuminated by only light #1 because shadow feeler S_3 reaches this light, but shadow feeler S_4 to light #2 is blocked by an opaque cube. The contribution of the transmitted ray to the picture-plane pixel is thus determined by the color of the wall at the intersection point, weighted by the transparency of the sphere.

The ray R_1 reflected from the sphere intersects a floor tile, which in turn is partially reflective. Ray R_2 from the floor tile reflects back to the side wall. The intersection points on the sphere, floor tile, and side wall are all illuminated by both light sources, because shadow feelers S_1, S_5, and S_7 reach light #1, and shadow feelers S_2, S_6, and S_8 reach light #2.

The intersection points on the sphere, floor tile, and side wall all contribute color to the picture-plane pixel in amounts determined by the reflectivities of the sphere and tile.

The rays traced in figure 14.8a are summarized by the ray tree shown in 14.8b. There are shadow feelers to the lights at each node except the root node (eye viewpoint).

A ray-traced image of gears produced with AutoVision is shown in color plate 8a. This full ray tracing shows shadows; reflections of the wood table in the gear shafts, teeth, and faces; and reflections between the gear shafts, teeth, and faces. The gears and shafts were constructed as surface models; see the discussion in section 12.2 and figures 12.9–12.10. Antialiasing is used to smooth the edges of ray-traced images by appropriately averaging intensities over an array of pixels (see section 3.3). AutoVision offers the following antialiasing options: none, horizontal, 2×2, 3×3, and 4×4 pixel arrays. The increase in rendering quality offered by increasing the size of the pixel array increases the rendering time.

Although full ray-tracing calculations ensure complete realism for reflected images, these calculations can be time-consuming. Unlike other versions of RenderMan, Autodesk RenderMan does not include a full ray-tracing capability for reflected images; instead, reflected images are produced by reflection maps (also called environmental maps). 3D Studio also uses reflection maps.

Plate 8b shows the gears rendered with 3D Studio by means of the automatic reflection map mode. Reflection mapping in 3D Studio reproduces ray-traced shadows and reflections

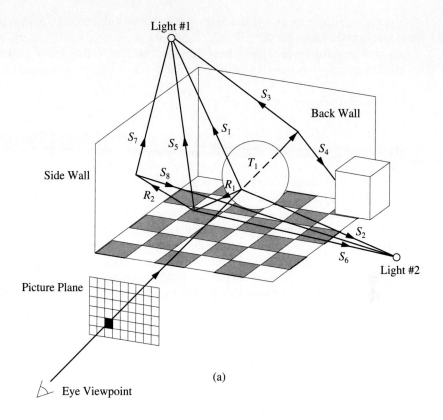

(a)

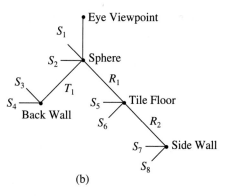

(b)

Figure 14.8   Diagram illustrating ray-tracing: (a) a ray passing through the picture plane and intersecting a sphere, where it is transmitted as ray T_1 and reflected as ray R_1 (R_1 is further reflected in the floor tile as R_2); (b) a ray tree showing the configuration of rays in the top figure.

of the wood table in the gear shafts, teeth, and faces. Also, the gear shafts are reflected in the flat faces of the gears, but the gear faces are not reflected in the shafts, nor are the gear teeth reflected in each other (as in the full ray tracing in plate 8a). The differences between the images in plates 8a–b is analyzed further after reflection mapping is discussed below.

Reflection Mapping

The Materials Editor for 3D Studio shown in color plate 6 provides buttons for texture maps, opacity maps, reflection maps, and bump maps. An opacity map affects the transparency of an object. Color plate 9 shows sphere surfaces with texture, bump, and reflection maps. The spheres shown in the bottom row of plate 9 have bitmap images reflected in the surface finishes. These are fixed images entered into the 3D Studio Materials Editor; for example, the editor screen shown in plate 6 lists a reflection image from the file VALLEY_L.TGA mapped at 35%, as indicated to the right of the reflection map button. This reflected image is combined with an 85% granitelike texture map from the file TILE0020.TGA to produce the surface shown on the last sphere in the bottom row of plate 9. The reflection map in this example is a mountain valley scene with a large tree and blue sky. This same image is shown as a 93% reflection map on a chromelike surface (without a texture map) on the next to last sphere in the bottom row of plate 9.

Bitmap images (for texture, opacity, reflection, and bump maps) can be placed on objects using planar, cylindrical, or spherical projections. The equations and a program subroutine for a cylindrical projection are given in section 8.2, and the equations for a spherical projection are given in exercise 8.7. In 3D Studio the bitmaps may be moved, rotated, and scaled before projection onto an object.

In addition to using fixed images, reflection maps can be determined from the actual scene. The lower camera in figure 14.9 represents the camera viewpoint for rendering a scene consisting of objects and a wall with a mirror section (heavier horizontal line). To determine the image reflected in the mirror, a camera is set up at the reflection point, which is the point at which the lower camera would appear to be when reflected in the mirror plane. The camera at the reflection point can sight through the mirror opening to take a "snapshot" of the objects in the scene. This snapshot can then be projected onto the mirror surface from the back to be seen by the lower camera. Thus the camera in figure 14.9 at the viewpoint sees a reflection map in the mirror (on the left of its view angle) along with a direct view of the objects on the right of its view angle.

For the flat surface reflection shown in figure 14.9, only one camera snapshot at the reflection position is required. The image reflected in a general curved surface may be approximated from a superposition of six snapshots taken along the orthogonal directions (perpendicular to the faces of an imaginary cube placed around the reflection point).

In Autodesk RenderMan, reflection mapping can be done manually, whereas 3D Studio has an automatic mode for reflection mapping. This automatic mode is set by clicking on the small "A" button at the far right of the reflection map buttons in the 3D Studio Materials Editor (see color plate 6). After the "A" button is pressed, the mirror can be specified as flat (or not flat), and other parameters can be set.

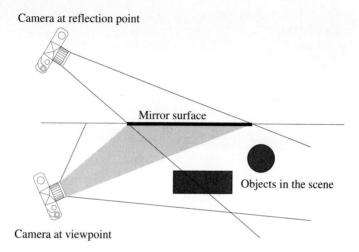

Camera at reflection point

Mirror surface

Objects in the scene

Camera at viewpoint

Figure 14.9   Plan view showing how a reflection map of a scene is created in a flat surface (mirror drawn as a heavier line). The camera creating the reflection map is placed at the reflection point of the viewpoint camera. The shaded region extending from the viewpoint camera shows the portion of the viewing angle subtended by the mirror, and the outer lines extending from this camera represent the total viewing angle.

The gear faces in plate 8b were specified as automatic flat reflection surfaces, whereas the gear edges and shafts were specified as automatic nonflat reflection surfaces. The gear faces are not reflected in the shafts because 3D Studio calculates cubic reflection maps for the nonflat surfaces before it calculates the flat reflection maps for the gear faces. Because the cubic reflection maps are created before the flat reflection maps, there are no gear faces in the scene while the cubic maps for the shafts are being calculated. Similarly, there are no gear-tooth (edge) surfaces in the scene while the reflection maps for the gear-tooth surfaces are being created. Thus the gear faces are not reflected in the shafts, nor are the gear-tooth edges reflected in each other. Although plate 8b does not reproduce all of the reflections, it is a realistic image—the missing reflections would probably go unnoticed if a more realistic image like the one in plate 8a were not available for comparison.

Texture Mapping

Surfaces with texture maps only are shown in the top row of spheres of color plate 9. The spheres in the second row have both texture and bump mapping, and the last sphere in the third row has texture and reflection maps. Texture maps start with an image and map it onto an object with a planar, cylindrical, or spherical projection.

A planar projection can be performed in any direction, producing a texture map that extends throughout the solid object. The woodgrain image shown in the top block of plate 10 was projected perpendicular to the front face, and thus the projection is parallel to the side faces, where the woodgrain appears as parallel lines. For this case, a more realistic

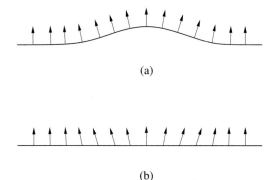

(a)

Figure 14.10   A surface bump: (a) the displaced surface and normal vectors; (b) a flat surface with its normal vectors tilted to represent the bump displacement shown in (a).

(b)

grain pattern can be obtained by projecting the woodgrain image at an oblique angle (not parallel to any face).

The 3-D grain pattern shown on the bottom block was not produced by a simple map of a 2-D texture image, but rather by a 3D Studio program called an external process. External processes in 3D Studio, along with RenderMan shaders, are discussed in the subsection Programming Interfaces (page 452).

Plate 11 illustrates texture mapping used to paint the hull of the yacht constructed with surface modeling (figure 12.24). First, the image to be mapped is drawn and saved as an image file (plate 11a), and then the image is mapped onto the boat hull (plate 11b). Release 3 of 3D Studio permits two separate textures to be mapped onto a surface; thus, the boat name could be saved as a separate texture map, and mapped onto the hull using the decal mode (the decal mode maps a single image, as compared with the tile mode, which repeats the image in a tile pattern over the entire surface).

Bump Mapping

With texture mapping, a pattern simply resides on the surface and has no appearance of depth. Bump mapping can give the pattern the appearance of depth. It achieves this by using the bitmap to tilt the surface normals used in the shading calculation.

Figure 14.10a illustrates how the surface normal vectors have their directions tilted over a bump in the surface. These changes in normal vector directions will produce the shading along the bump that the eye expects to see; for example, if light is incident from the left, then the left side of the bump will be brighter than the right side. This bump shading is reproduced by the mapping of the surface normals shown in 14.10b, even though the surface itself is not displaced; that is, the shading calculations use tilted vectors in place of the normals to the flat surface. Thus bump mapping gives the appearance of surface displacements, except it does not produce the bump displacement profile when the surface is viewed on edge.

The second row of spheres in color plate 9 incorporates bump mapping along with texture mapping. In most cases the bitmap used for bump mapping is the same as that used for texture mapping; for example, the woodgrain and granite textures shown by the last two spheres in the second row are the same as those of the last two spheres in the first row, except that bump maps of these same textures have been added.

3D Studio uses the brightness of the bitmap to determine the amount that normal vectors are tilted to simulate surface displacement: brighter regions appear to be raised, and darker regions seem depressed from the surface. Bump maps can be added to texture maps in any percentage from 0 to 100% to increase the magnitude of the simulated displacements. In the second row of plate 9, the wood sphere has a 10% bump map, and the granite sphere a 6% bump map (the spheres on the top row correspond to 0% bump maps).

Transparency, Opacity Mapping, and Refraction

The surfaces discussed so far have opaque finishes; that is, all incident light is either absorbed or reflected. The 3D Studio Editor has a transparency slider bar that permits transparency to vary from 0% (opaque) to 100% (completely transparent). In color plate 12, the screwdriver shaft is clearly visible where it penetrates a handle that is 90% transparent, but it is less visible when the handle is 50% transparent.

In addition to uniform transparency, 3D Studio permits an increase or decrease in transparency between the center and edges of the object (set with a transparency fall-off button). A solid, partially transparent object will be more transparent near its edges, where it is thinner, whereas a glass bowl will be thicker and less transparent near its edges.

In 3D Studio, an image can have 24-bit color; that is, 8 bits (256 colors numbered from 0 to 255) each for red, green, and blue. There are also 8 bits available in an *alpha channel* for storing the transparency information (from 0 for complete transparency to 255 for opaque). Thus an image that includes transparency information is stored as a 32-bit image. Also, transparency is assigned to pixels when antialiasing is turned on to smooth the edges of objects.

Transparency of an object can also be modified by using an opacity map. In an opacity bitmap, the transparency is determined by the gray scale of the bit, with black being opaque, and white transparent. Opacity maps may be combined with texture maps. In the the top row of plate 10, the wood texture on the first box is combined with the opacity map at the center to give the appearance of holes drilled in the box as shown on the right. Opacity maps may be used in this fashion to represent windows and other features on the side of a building (see exercise 14.6). For other applications, opacity maps with smoothly varying gray scales can be used to change the transparency of an object in a continuous fashion.

Ray-tracing programs can account for refraction effects at the surface of transparent solids. Snell's law of optics states that a light ray will be bent toward the surface normal vector as it enters a medium having a higher index of refraction n. The angle θ' between a light ray and the inward normal in a solid ($n > 1$) is related to the angle θ between the ray and the outward normal in air ($n = 1.00$) according to Snell's formula $\sin\theta' = \sin\theta/n$. Because the equations of geometric optics are reversible, this same formula is also valid for the ray as it leaves the transparent solid.

Figure 14.11 shows images from the AutoVision ray tracer. Three vertical cylinders lie behind a sphere that is 75% transparent. When the index of refraction of the solid sphere is 1.00, the images of the cylinder pass straight through the sphere; that is, no light rays are refracted at the surface. When $n > 1$, the sphere behaves like a thick lens, and the cylinder images are distorted by refraction effects that depend strongly on the value of n.

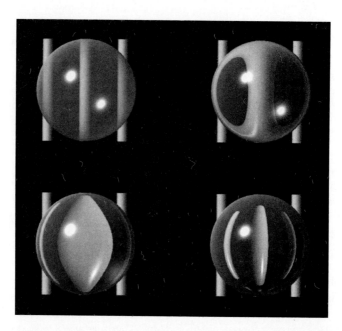

Figure 14.11 Refraction in sold glass spheres, each having 75% transparency. Produced with AutoVision with a single distant light directed from the upper-left front (in addition to the upper-left highlight, the top images also show a highlight from the reflected beam at the lower-right back of the sphere). The index of refraction n has the following values (from upper-left to lower-right image): $n = 1.00, 1.20, 1.58,$ and 2.29.

Other Mappings

In addition to the maps discussed above, Release 3 of 3D Studio provides specular maps, shininess maps, and self-illumination maps.

The specular and shininess maps affect the highlights on a material surface. The specular map affects the color of the highlight, and the shininess map affects the intensity of the highlight.

The self-illumination map increases the intensity (luminance value) on a surface based on the intensity of the pixels in a bitmap. The closer a bitmap pixel is to white, the greater the self-illumination effect. This appearance of self-illumination is useful for rendering objects such as automobile headlights, light bulbs, and stained-glass windows.

Programming Interfaces

Programming interfaces include shaders in RenderMan, external processes in 3D Studio, and three special solid patterns in AutoVision (for granite, marble, and wood 3-D textures).

RenderMan shaders are programs that describe the appearance of surfaces. Although a programmer can write his own shader (see Upstill 1990), one can use the shaders supplied with Autodesk RenderMan. The parameters in these shaders can be changed by the user.

For example, parameters can be changed in a wood grain to modify the light color in the grain pattern, the dark color, the specular highlight color, the spatial orientation of the grain, the scale of the grain patterns, and other parameters.

There are three types of shaders: surface, displacement, and atmosphere. The term *light shaders* is also used, but this simply refers to the light sources. Surface shaders determine the colors and textures of surfaces. Also, special shaders are supplied for mapping user-supplied textures with both decal and tile projection procedures.

The programming interface for 3D Studio is provided by several types of external process C programs. These are given the acronym IPAS3: I is for image processing (programs with extension IXP), P for procedural modeling (PXP), A for animated stand-in (AXP), S for solid pattern (SXP), and 3 for additional external processes added with Release 3 (KXP, Keframer external process; BXP, bitmap external process).

Two types external processes are illustrated with the objects shown at the bottom of color plate 10. The bottom left and middle blocks show a solid wood pattern. This pattern is 3-D, in contrast to the normal 2-D texture obtained by the planar mapping of a wood pattern bitmap (as in the top blocks). The 3-D wood texture mapping was produced by the solid pattern external process in the file WOOD.SXP. Another SXP program is DENTS.SXP, which produces a 3-D bump mapping to give objects a dented or aged appearance.

The second type of external process illustrated in plate 10 was produced by the procedural modeling programs GRID.PXP and RIPPLE.PXP. First, a grid on the surface of a cube is set up with GRID.PXP, then RIPPLE.PXP is used to produce ripples on the cube, as shown at the bottom right of plate 10. The magnitude and center of these ripples are set by the program user. Procedural modeling programs also construct gears, produce waves (different from ripples) on a surface, introduce randomness (jumble) in a collection of elements, and perform other operations.

14.4 ANIMATION

Programs with animation were presented as examples of 2-D and 3-D transformations in chapters 10 and 11. In section 10.5, the motion of a rotary engine was programmed; and in section 11.4, a walkthrough of a wireframe structure was programmed for interactive viewing using the computer's mouse device.

Within AutoCAD a slide presentation of wireframe and "simply" shaded scenes may be constructed with a script file, as described in the next subsection below. The playback of slides is not sufficiently fast for a true animation effect, but slide presentations are useful for showing different views of a product, scenes in an architectural walkthrough, and for other design applications.

As mentioned in section 2.1, approximately 50 or 60 frames per second must be displayed to give the sensation of continuous motion without noticeable screen flicker. Television frames are transmitted at 60 frames per second in the United States and at 50 frames per second in Europe; movies are shown at 48 frames per second. To reduce the requirements on the rate of transmission of information, television is transmitted with interlaced images so that in the United States only 30 separate full images are transmitted each second. Although movies are shown at 48 frames per second, each image is shown twice so that only 24 different images are shown each second.

Fully rendered scenes, in addition to AutoCAD slides, can be placed into an animation sequence with AutoFlix, which is software that is included in Autodesk's AutoShade/RenderMan package. AutoFlix procedures are not discussed here; instead, 3D Studio is used in this chapter for the animation of fully rendered scenes constructed with the concept of keyframes. The last two subsections of this chapter contain two animation applications: the motion of a robot arm and an architectural walkthrough.

With 3D Studio the frames can be saved in file formats that can be transferred to videotape, or the frames can be played back for direct viewing on the computer monitor. The frames can be played back at 60 frames per second if the images are of low resolution and if your computer is sufficiently fast; otherwise, your computer will require more time to display the images. Rates as low as 10 or 15 frames per second can provide the sensation of continuous motion, although the images will flicker very noticeably at these low rates.

Slide Presentations in AutoCAD

Within AutoCAD there is no procedure for animating fully rendered scenes, but wireframe and simple shaded scenes may be saved as slides and played back as a "slide presentation."

The command MSLIDE saves a "snapshot" of the screen image in a file with the extension SLD. This command works on wireframe scenes, with or without the lines hidden with the HIDE command, and also with wireframe scenes that are filled in with the SHADE command. The SHADE command provides flat shading across the entire surface, with no lighting effects, and with a superimposed wire frame of the background color (black in most cases). The color of the surface is the same as the color assigned to the original wireframe representation.

Some example views from an architectural slide show are shown in figure 14.12. Each perspective view was set up with the DVIEW command, and a slide was made with the MVIEW command.

A script file was written to play back the slides. The script file listed in table 14.1 plays back the four slides shown in figure 14.12. The slide show is started with the SCRIPT command in AutoCAD. Because in this case the command RSCRIPT has been used to continually repeat the slide show, the show can be stopped by entering Ctrl-C.

In the script file shown in table 14.1, the first slide is viewed with the VSLIDE command followed by the name of the slide (without the SLD extension). When the command VSLIDE is used with an asterisk (*) preceding the name of the second slide, the slide is preloaded, but not displayed. The second slide is displayed when the VSLIDE command is given again, without the slide name. This procedure ensures an exact timing between slides, regardless of the amount of time required for loading. That is, the loading of slide 2 occurs during the delay time of 2,000 (2,000 milliseconds, or 2 seconds) specified for viewing slide 1, with the display of slide 2 starting immediately after the delay time.

A presentation containing a large number of slides can be organized by setting up a slide library, as described in the *AutoCAD Customization Manual* (1992). Also, one could write a program that uses a *for* loop to write the commands in a large script file; see exercise 14.7.

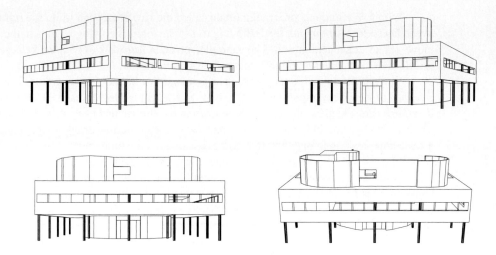

Figure 14.12   Four views from an AutoCAD slide show. The views were formed from a solid model of Le Corbusier's Villa Savoye drawn by Michael Rysdorp; see figure 13.20d.

TABLE 14.1 SCRIPT FILE FOR PLAYING FOUR SLIDES, WITH COMMENTS ON THE RIGHT

`VSLIDE BLDG1`	Begin slide show with slide 1 named BLDG1
`VSLIDE *BLDG2`	Preload slide 2
`DELAY 2000`	Delay time to permit view of slide 1
`VSLIDE`	Display slide 2
`VSLIDE *BLDG3`	Preload slide 3
`DELAY 2000`	Delay time
`VSLIDE`	Display slide 3
`VSLIDE *BLDG4`	Preload slide 4
`DELAY 2000`	Delay time
`VSLIDE`	Display slide 4
`DELAY 3000`	Delay time
`RSCRIPT`	Repeat the slide show

Animations with Keyframing in 3D Studio

With animation software that uses keyframing, a sequence of important scenes (keyframes) is first constructed, and then the remaining scenes are determined by the software. That is, the computer renders intermediate scenes to fill the gaps between the key scenes set up by the program user. This procedure follows that used for hand-drawn movie cartoons, where the chief designers set up the keyframes for the cartoon action, and then a room full of lesser-paid artists drew the frames connecting the keyframes.

As multimedia presentations have become more popular, software packages have added animation to their rendering capabilities. Here we refer to the animation features of 3D Studio, although most other animation software is based on similar keyframing features.

Within 3D Studio, a program module called the Keyframer can fill in the frames between keyframes set up with the following transformations involving objects in the scene: move, rotate, scale, and morph. The examples given in *Autodesk 3D Studio Release 3 Tutorials* (1993) include several different types of animations.

One type of animation is represented by a ball that bounces on a surface. The model consists of a sphere representing the ball and a flat plate representing the surface. Keyframes are set up by moving the ball down to the surface and back up. Additional realism is added by squashing the ball on impact (with a squash transformation that consists of a scale compression in one direction and expansions in the other normal directions). Spin can also be added to the ball with the rotate transformation.

A second example type involves the motion of a robot arm, in which the appropriate constraints on translations and rotations are achieved by a hierarchical linking of the objects (arm sections). This motion appropriately represents the kinematics of the motion. Special kinematics software for mechanical engineering exists for designing linkages such as robot arms, cams, gears, and other mechanisms. Some computer modeling also includes dynamics. The dynamics may be included as solutions of the exact equations of motion that involve the appropriate forces and masses of the components. Often the application is too complex for an exact dynamical representation, so an approximate "physical-based" model is used (see Badler et al. 1991; Barzel 1992). The hierarchical linkages in the robot arm are covered in more detail by a 3D Studio example given in the next subsection.

The morph transformation (called morphing) is used in a third type of animation given in the 3D Studio tutorials. "Morph" is derived from the word *morphosis,* which is defined as the manner in which an organism changes form. Thus in a morph transformation the shape of an object is changed in small steps from the shape given in one keyframe to the shape given in the next keyframe. Morphing has recently become popular in animated parts of movies and television advertisements.

A fourth type of animation, an architectural walkthrough, moves the camera along a path (and rotates it) through a fixed scene. This latter type of animation is described in the last subsection below for a walkthrough of a building.

Hierarchical Linkages for a Robot Arm

Animation in 3D Studio is set up with the Keyframer program module. The Keyframer has a Hierarchy/Link option that is used to control the mechanical linkages between the components of the robot arm. Figure 14.13 shows a robot arm composed of six named parts: Base, V-Shaft (a vertical shaft), Hinge, H-Arm (a horizontal arm), H-Shaft (a horizontal shaft), and Hand.

Hierarchical linkages are described in terms of a family tree with children linked to parents. For the robot arm, the V-Shaft is selected with the Hierarchy/Link menu item, and the Base is selected as its parent. Similarly, the V-Shaft is selected as the parent of the Hinge, the Hinge the parent of the H-Arm, the H-Arm the parent of the H-Shaft, and the H-Shaft the parent of the Hand. When the Show Tree menu item is selected, all objects are listed, as

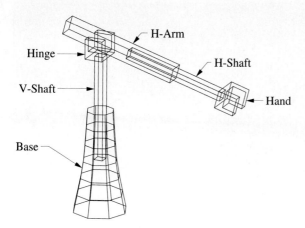

Figure 14.13   A robot arm with its labeled
components (courtesy of Autodesk, Inc.).

TABLE 14.2 HIERARCHICAL TREE
DISPLAYED FOR THE
ROBOT ARM

```
Camera01.target
Camera01
Base*
     V-Shaft*
          Hinge*
               H-Arm*
                    H-Shaft*
                         Hand*
Light01
```

shown in table 14.2. The camera, its target, and a light are listed in the display along with
the parts of the robot. The robot component names are indented to show the tree structure
(the asterisks signify that they are master objects rather than instances of master objects).
In this tree, each parent has only one child, although in general a parent object can have any
number of children.

Thus when the Base is moved, the V-Shaft moves with it because it is the child of the
Base. The constraints for the motion of the V-Shaft relative to the Base are set in the Key Info
dialog box shown in figure 14.14. In this dialog box the the V-Shaft is locked in the x- and z-
directions, but not in the y-direction (upward). The V-Shaft is also locked to prevent all rotations (the x-, y-, and z-axis rotations are locked). In a similar manner the Key Info dialog box
is used to set the appropriate constraints between the remaining components: the Hinge has
a fixed position and rotates only around the y-axis (relative to the V-Shaft); the H-Arm has
a fixed position and rotates only around the x-axis; the H-Shaft moves only in the z-direction and does not rotate; and the hand has a fixed position and rotates only around the z-axis.

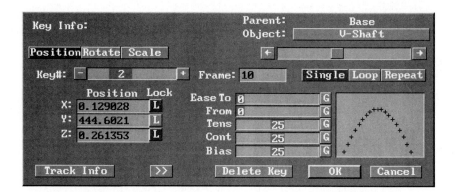

Figure 14.14   The Key Info dialog box for setting the constraints on the V-Shaft (courtesy of Autodesk, Inc.).

Next, the total number of frames is specified, and the keyframes are set up. For example, if 60 total frames are specified, then you may wish to set the robot configurations at frames numbered 10, 20, and 30. After using arrow buttons to move to a particular frame in the main Keyframer screen, the robot components may be moved and rotated (within their constraints) to any desired positions with the object/move and object/rotate menu items.

The Track Info dialog box shown in figure 14.15 may be used to view the operations performed at each keyframe. For this robot example, black dots show the keyframes for which positions and rotations have been set. The dialog box in figure 14.15 is for the V-Shaft and its subtree, which corresponds to all of the robot components except the base. In this dialog box the dots at frame 0 have been copied to the last frame—number 60—in order that all components return to their original positions so that the motion appears smooth when the animation repeats the 60 frames.

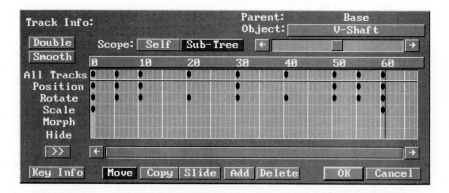

Figure 14.15   The Track Info dialog box showing the keyframe settings for the robot arm motion. Black dots are shown at frames for which positions and rotations have been set. In this example, the settings from frame 0 have been copied to the last frame, number 60 (courtesy of Autodesk, Inc.).

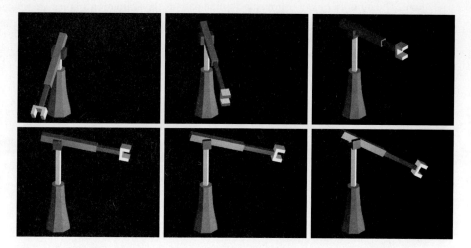

Figure 14.16   Some representative frames from the robot arm animation.

The Keyframer calculates the robot positions in the intermediate frames for playback of the wireframe representation; see some example frames in figure 14.16. A flic preview mode permits shaded low-resolution animations to be run quickly from within 3D Studio. Also, a fully rendered animation can be played on the computer screen, or the frames can be set up for transfer to video.

An Architectural Walkthrough

For this animation, the camera follows a path up to a building and under its overhang. A 3-D spline curve is used to set up the camera target path; see figure 14.17. In 3D Studio, the camera and its target are attached to a dummy object by means of the Hierarchy/Link menu

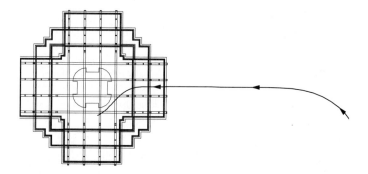

Figure 14.17   Plan view of a building with a spline curve representing the path of the camera target. The building is represented by a surface model of the UCSD Library drawn by Christopher Casey (see figure 12.38e).

item. The dummy object follows the spline path as the animation frames are rendered. The camera, which follows its target and dummy object, automatically rotates to provide a smooth animation sequence.

Figure 14.18 shows some frames from the 3D Studio animation along the path shown in figure 14.17.

Figure 14.18   Some representative frames from the building walkthrough animation created on 3D Studio. The building is a surface model of the UCSD Library drawn by Christopher Casey.

EXERCISES

14.1 Implement the C program subroutine given in section 14.1 for diffuse reflection from a surface of revolution.

14.2 For the special case in which the light direction **L** is a unit vector along the z-axis, show that the components of the reflection vector **R** are expressed in terms of the components of the normal vector **n** by the following relations: $R_x = 2n_z n_x$, $R_y = 2n_z n_y$, and $R_z = 2n_z^2 - 1$. Also, show that when the view vector **V** is along the z-axis (corresponding to lighting from directly behind the observer), the specular reflection term is given by the following expression: $\cos\alpha = R_z = 2n_z^2 - 1$.

14.3 Incorporate a specular reflection component into the program written as exercise 14.1.

14.4 Implement the Gouraud shading subroutine of section 14.1 for a surface of revolution.

14.5 Write a program for a surface of revolution with Phong shading.

14.5 Use your rendering software to reproduce the shading examples shown in figure 14.2.

14.6 With 3D Studio or comparable rendering software, use an opacity map to represent windows and doors as illustrated in the following figure.

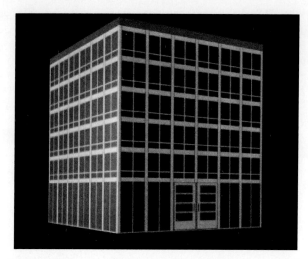

14.7 Write a program to construct a script file for a slide presentation in AutoCAD. Name the slides with a word followed by a number; for example, SLIDE1, SLIDE2, SLIDE3, etc. Place the AutoCAD VSLIDE and DELAY commands in a *for* loop (for all slides after the first one). To write the slide names in the *for* loop, you can write the loop index number *i* next to the string SLIDE to form the slide names SLIDE2, SLIDE3, SLIDE4, etc.

14.8 Use 3D Studio to create an animation sequence for a robot arm.

14.9 Write a 2-D graphics program that incorporates the kinematics of a four-bar linkage. Assume a crank and rocker configuration like that shown on the left below. The length l_1 corresponds to the distance between pins fixed to the ground. The input (driver) of length l_2 rotates continuously through $360°$ while the output (follower) link of length l_4 rocks back and forth. For the animation illustrated on the right below, the lengths satisfy the following relation: $l_2 + l_4 < l_1 + l_3$. Linkages are discussed in mechanical design texts; see for example, Erdman, A. G., and G. N. Sandor, *Mechanism Design: Analysis and Synthesis*, Volume I, 2nd edition, Englewood Cliffs, N. J.: Prentice Hall, 1991

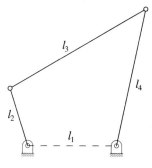

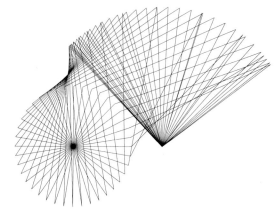

14.10 With 3D Studio or other animation software, create an architectural walkthrough.

14.11 3D Studio and other rendering software provide options for producing stereoscopic views for 3-D viewing. On your CAD system (or by programming), form two perspective views of an object from slightly different (azimuthal) angles to represent the viewpoints of the left and right eyes. The crossed images shown below can be viewed in 3-D by some people without special glasses (the viewing technique involves crossing one's eyes so that three images are seen, with the middle image appearing in 3-D because it is formed by two overlapping images).

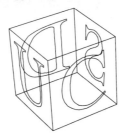 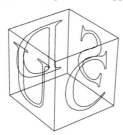

BIBLIOGRAPHY

AutoCAD Release 12: Customization Manual. Sausalito, Calif.: Autodesk, Inc., 1992.

AutoCAD Release 12: Render Reference Manual. Sausalito, Calif.: Autodesk, Inc., 1992.

Autodesk 3D Studio Release 3 Reference Manual. Sausalito, Calif.: Autodesk, Inc., 1993.

Autodesk 3D Studio Release 3 Tutorials. Sausalito, Calif.: Autodesk, Inc., 1993.

AutoShade Version 2: Tutorial. Sausalito, Calif.: Autodesk, Inc., 1990.

AutoShade Version 2: User Guide. Sausalito, Calif.: Autodesk, Inc., 1990.

AutoVision User's Guide and Reference. Sausalito, Calif.: Autodesk, Inc., 1993.

BADLER, N. I., B. A. BARSKY, and D. ZELTZER, eds., *Making Them Move: Mechanics, Control, and Animation of Articulated Figures.* San Mateo, Calif.: Morgan Kaufman Publishers, Inc., 1991.

BARZEL, R., *Physically-Based Modeling for Computer Graphics: A Structured Approach.* Academic Press, Inc., 1992.

FOLEY, J. D., A. VAN DAM, S. K. FEINER, and J. F. HUGHES, *Computer Graphics: Principles and Practice,* 2nd ed. Reading, Mass.: Addison-Wesley Publishing Co., 1990.

GLASSNER, A. S., ed., *An Introduction to Ray Tracing.* San Diego, Calif.: Academic Press (Harcourt Brace Jovanovich Publishers), 1989.

HALL, R., *Illumination and Color in Computer Generated Imagery.* New York: Springer-Verlag, 1989.

ROGERS, D. F., *Procedural Elements for Computer Graphics.* New York: McGraw-Hill Publishing Co., 1985.

UPSTILL, S., *The RenderMan Companion: A Programmer's Guide to Realistic Computer Graphics.* Reading, Mass.: Addison-Wesley Publishing Co., 1990.

WATT, A., *Fundamentals of Three-Dimensional Computer Graphics.* Reading, Mass.: Addison-Wesley Publishing Co., 1989.

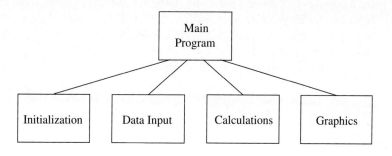

Main Program
Initialization	Data Input	Calculations	Graphics

Appendix A: The Structure of C Programs

The above diagram illustrates the structure of simple programs in the C language. The diagram could have included a box for the program termination, but does not because in this appendix the termination will be just one function call: _setvideomode(_DEFAULT-MODE), which resets the video display to its default mode at the end of the program.

The initialization of a graphics program depends on the system. The program examples given here and in chapter 9 are written in Microsoft C for IBM PC compatible computers. With Microsoft C, initializing the screen for the VGA graphics mode requires just a single statement, _setvideomode(_VRES16COLOR). Functions specific to Microsoft C are described in the tutorial book *Microsoft C Programming for the PC*; many other books also offer instruction in Microsoft C. Procedures in Microsoft C are very similar to Turbo C and other C-language implementations on the IBM PC.

Initializing graphics is more complex on the Macintosh computer, where both the Macintosh Toolbox and the graphics window must be initialized. Macintosh graphics programming with THINKC is described in books by Mark and Reed (1989) and Mark (1990). In addition to the full Microsoft C programs that are presented in this appendix and in chapter

9, program subroutines appear in the other chapters. These subroutines include graphics functions that are similar to the Macintosh functions; for example, MoveTo() rather than the Microsoft C function _moveto(). Table 1.1 in chapter 1 lists some of the key graphics functions for different implementations of C. For most subroutines presented in this book, it is a simple matter to substitute the few functions that are specific to the particular C language you are using.

With the C programming language, comments are enclosed between the /* and */ symbols; the programs below include a one-line comment on the first line to describe the program. The first part of a program comprises a list of header files preceded by #include. The header files define library functions; for example, the functions in the first program listed below require three header files. Note that C is case sensitive, so lowercase and uppercase letters must be used correctly.

Current programming standards recommend that function prototypes be listed for all user-defined functions. For the two function prototypes listed below, the functions do not return values, nor do they have arguments; therefore, their data types and arguments are listed as void. Starting with the function prototypes, each program statement ends with a semicolon.

Data types for global variables are listed before the function main(). That is, if a variable data type is listed before main(), the variable is a global variable, which is defined in subroutines (user-defined functions) as well as in the main function. In the program below, global variables are declared as the type int, which stands for integer.

The main() function must be present in every program. The program execution begins and ends with main(). Program readability is enhanced when main() is short, usually consisting only of calls to functions that carry out major tasks such as initialization, data input, calculations, and graphical output. The function calls within main() in the first program are almost self-explanatory by their names. The functions that start with an underline are Microsoft C graphics functions. These functions are written in lowercase letters, and their arguments are uppercase; for example, _clearscreen(_CLEARSCREEN).

Drawing a Line from Keyboard Input

In the first program, the user-defined function dataPoints() prompts for the coordinates of two points, and the function drawLine() draws a line between the points. In the subroutine dataPoints(), the printf() function prints instructions to the screen, and scanf() reads the values entered on the keyboard. Note that printf() and scanf() are C functions defined in a standard library (UNIX-compatible standard I/O library, identified by the header file stdio.h). In the scanf() function the %d is a conversion character for integers, and the & symbol before the variables signifies "address of." (It is common for beginning C programmers to forget the & symbol in the scanf() function.)

The line drawn on the screen would disappear immediately if the getch() function were not used for a pause (this "get character" function waits for any keyboard input) at the end of the program. The getch() function is defined in the library identified by the header file conio.h (console I/O, which is specific to the PC).

```
/* Program to draw a single line using keyboard input */

#include <stdio.h>      /* needed for printf() and scanf()        */
#include <conio.h>      /* needed for getch()                     */
#include <graph.h>      /* for graphics functions                 */

void dataPoints(void);  /* function prototypes                    */
void drawLine(void);

int xstart,ystart,xend,yend;  /* define global data types         */

void main(void)
{
    _clearscreen(_GCLEARSCREEN);
    dataPoints();               /* call data entry subroutine      */
    _setvideomode(_VRES16COLOR);    /* set VGA mode                */
    drawLine();                 /* line drawing subroutine         */
    getch();                    /* wait for any key to be hit      */
    _setvideomode(_DEFAULTMODE);  /* return to original video mode */
}

void dataPoints(void)
{
    printf("Input the line coordinates:\n");
    printf("xstart ystart xend yend — separated by spaces.\n");
    printf("0 < xstart,xend < 639; 0 < ystart,yend <479\n");

    /* get keyboard input */
    scanf("%d %d %d %d",&xstart,&ystart,&xend,&yend);
}

void drawLine(void)
{
    _moveto(xstart,ystart);
    _lineto(xend,yend);
}
```

The program above draws a line from keyboard input. If the coordinates of the line endpoints are known when the program is written, then it is easier to simply place the values into the program.

Drawing a Polyline from a Data Array

The program below draws a polyline (connected straight-line segments) between six points. The coordinate data are entered into the program with the data type statement for the arrays *xPt*[] and *yPt*[]. In C programs arrays are identified by square brackets. Because a C program statement terminates with a semicolon rather than with a carriage return, the data type statement for an array can contain a large amount of data by occupying many lines enclosed within a single pair of braces { }.

To call the function polyline() from within main(), the square brackets are not included with the array variable names *xPt* and *yPt*. Unlike ordinary variables such as *nPts,* arrays are passed to subroutines by address, rather than by value.

In the subroutine polyline(), the number of points *nPts* in main() is passed to the variable *num* in polyline, and the arrays *yPt*[] and *xPt*[] are passed to *x*[] and *y*[].

The *for* loop in the function polyline() contains the notation $i++$, which stands for $i = i + 1$. The increment operator $i++$ not only provides a shorter notation, but often executes somewhat faster than the full mathematical operation of adding 1 to *i*. Note that there is no semicolon after the closing parenthesis identifying the range of the variable *i;* the semicolons appear only after the individual statements within the braces of the *for* loop. In this subroutine the polyline is plotted between the *num* points by moving to the first point and then drawing line segments sequentially to the remaining points. The *num* points are identified by the array index numbers 0 through $num - 1$.

```
/* Program to draw a polyline using coordinate arrays */

#include <conio.h>                    /* needed for getch()      */
#include <graph.h>                    /* for graphics functions  */

void polyline(int n,int xc[],int yc[]);   /* function prototype  */

void main(void)
{
    int nPts = 6;
            /* values given with data types */
    int xPt[] = {110,40,180,200,135,110};
    int yPt[] = {75,200,200,110,150,75};

    _setvideomode(_VRES16COLOR); /* set VGA mode                */
    polyline(nPts,xPt,yPt);      /* line drawing subroutine     */
    getch();                     /* wait for any key to be hit  */
    _setvideomode(_DEFAULTMODE); /* restore original video mode */
}

void polyline(int num,int x[],int y[])
{
    int i;

    _moveto(x[0],y[0]);
    for (i=1; i<num; i++)
    {
        _lineto(x[i],y[i]);
    }
}
```

Programming for Mouse Input of Data Points

A mouse can be used to enter data quickly. The following program uses the MS-DOS interrupt function int86() to access registers that provide the mouse position and status of the mouse buttons. The name int86() refers to the Intel family of microprocessors for the PC, which started with the 8086 chip. The mouse position is shown on the screen by a cross drawn with the function _putimage(). The drawing mode _GXOR is used with the _putimage() function so that the cross can be erased by drawing over the original cross image. Furthermore, other images under the cross will not be erased when the cross passes over them.

The program also makes it possible to display the cursor position coordinates in a manner similar to AutoCAD. As with AutoCAD, points are entered with the left mouse button, and the sequence is terminated by pressing the return key. The polyline() function of the preceding program is also included in order to draw line segments connecting all of the points entered.

For clarity in reading the program, the #define directive is used to replace numerical values for function arguments with words descriptive of the arguments. Arguments given by the #define directive can be easily recognized if they are written in all capital letters. WHITE is defined as the color index number 15, which is bright white, the default color for drawing lines with the function _lineto().

The structure of C encourages modular programming, so that you can use functions such as mouseInit() and mouseRead() in your own programs even if you do not fully understand all of the program lines within these subroutines. The comments in the listings and the following discussion should help you to understand the key features in these subroutines.

In main(), the mouse is initialized by calling the function mouseInit(). This function call is part of an *if* statement that returns 0 if no mouse is found. If no mouse is detected, the program terminates. Note that the *if* statement requires the relational "equal to" operator == rather than the assignment operator =. Other useful relational operators in C are the following: != for "not equal to," < for "less than," <= for "less than or equal to," > for "greater than," and >= for "greater than or equal to." In *if* statements it is often useful to group comparisons together with the following logical operators: && for AND, || for OR, and ! for negation.

As discussed by Rimmer (1992) and by Ammeraal (1989), the mouse is accessed through int86(), which is a function of three parameters. The first parameter is the interrupt number, which for the mouse is 51; note that in the program below a #define directive has identified the label MOUSE with the number 51. The second parameter represents the registers before the call; the third parameter represents the registers after the call.

The registers AX, BX, CX, and DX are accessed in the subroutine mouseInit(). First, the variable reg.x.ax for the AX resister is set equal to 0 in order to detect a mouse. The variable representing the returned code number, retcode, equals -1 if a mouse is detected and equals 0 if no mouse is detected. If no mouse is detected then the value 0 is returned as the value of mouseInit(). If you have a mouse on your system, but no mouse is detected with this program, then perhaps your mouse driver has not been installed (the mouse driver file

MOUSE.COM is installed by entering MOUSE from the keyboard, or by adding the line DEVICE = MOUSE.SYS to your CONFIG.SYS file).

As shown in the function mouseInit(), the horizontal boundaries for the mouse are prescribed by first setting the AX register variable reg.x.ax equal to 7 and then equating the CX and DX register variables to the desired lower and upper bounds. The horizontal boundaries are given by the global variables $xmin = 10$ and $xmax = 630$. The vertical boundaries are set in the same manner, starting with reg.x.as = 8.

The function cursorInit() sets up the mouse cursor as a small green cross; see figure A.1a. First, the drawing color is set to bright green (identified as the color index number 10 in a #define directive). Then horizontal and vertical line segments 11 pixels long are drawn. Sufficient memory for the cursor image is allocated with C function malloc(), named for m*emory* allocation. In the global data-type declarations, consider the following line: char far *imageCursor. Here the asterisk (*) indicates that the variable *imageCursor* will be used as a pointer, and will point to data having type far char (4-byte character). With C pointers, memory can be manipulated directly. The function _getimage() puts the drawn cursor image into memory.

The expression (char far *) that occurs just before malloc() is an example of type-casting, in which a variable (with its current value) is changed from one data type to another. In the subroutines presented in this book, computations are performed with double-precision floating-point variables that are often changed to integer quantities by type-casting with (int); for example, for using variables with graphics functions that require integers as arguments. In this book the double-precision, floating-point data type *double* is used rather than single-precision data type *float* because it increases precision, and on most

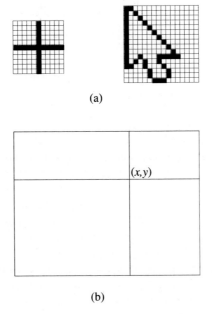

(a)

(b)

Figure A.1 Mouse cursors: (a) pixel representations of the small cross cursor and the arrow cursor; (b) illustration of the large cross cursor, which consists of lines that cross at (x,y) and extend to the edges of the drawing viewport, represented by the bounding rectangle.

systems is no slower (and may be faster) because C compilers are usually designed for double-precision computations.

In the subroutine getData(), the cursor is frequently drawn and erased with the _putimage(). Image placement is referenced to the upper-left corner of the image; therefore, the coordinates $(x - 5, y - 5)$ are used with _putimage() to place the center of the cross at (x, y). The cross center is 5 pixels to the right and 5 pixels down from the upper-left corner of the image shown in figure A.1a.

The reason that _putimage() can both draw and erase is that it is used with the _GXOR drawing mode. In this mode, the cursor image (new image) is combined with the old image (whatever is currently on the screen) using a logical EXCLUSIVE OR. This operation has the effect of changing the cursor color to make it visible against any background color and erasing the cursor (and restoring the background) when the cursor is placed at the same location twice. Although not used in this program, other drawing modes are available with _putimage(): _GAND, which combines the new and old images using a logical AND; _GOR, which combines the images using a logical OR; _GPSET, which just overwrites the old image with the new one in its original color; and _GPRESET, which overwrites the old image with the new one displayed in inverted color.

The main action in the program below occurs in the *do while* loop in the getData() subroutine. This loop repeats execution of the statements in braces only while the criterion at the end (*mouseData* not equal to RETURN) is valid. Unlike the standard *while* loop, which tests the criterion at the top of the loop, the *do while* loop tests the criterion at the bottom of the loop so that it executes the statements at least once, even if the criterion is false.

In the getData() subroutine, the mouse position and button status is read by calling the function mouseRead(). Then the coordinates obtained from mouseRead() are checked to see if they extend beyond the viewport range; if so, they are changed to coordinate values at the edge of the viewport. Next, the function _putimage() is used to erase the cursor at the old position (*xold,yold*) and draw it at the new position (*x,y*). Also, the cursor coordinates are displayed on the screen.

An *if* statement in the getData() subroutine checks to see if the left button of the mouse has been pressed. If so, then the cursor position is stored as a new point in the data array. Also, a small filled red circle is placed on the screen at the point. To avoid interference with the drawn circle, _putimage() is used to erase the cursor before the circle is drawn and to replace the cursor afterward.

In the subroutine mouseRead(), the *do while* loop repeats until the mouse position or button status changes, or until a key is pressed. This latter situation is checked by the *if* statement in which kbhit() is true (nonzero number) if the keyboard is hit, and getch() gets the number for the key hit and returns it as the value of mouseRead(). When the *do while* loop is exited, the values for cursor position and mouse button status are stored in the global reference variables *xref*, *yref*, and *buttonref*. Then the next time mouseRead() is called, the *do while* loop continues until values are changed from the reference values, or until a key is hit. If values were passed back to getData() without waiting for a change, then the constant stream of identical numbers returned would result in a flashing cursor, as it is turned off and on at identical points (*xold,yold*) and (*x,y*). In this program the values *xref* and *yref* are equal to *xold* and *yold,* respectively; however, in the program developed in section 9.1 these values differ when a snap-mode option is introduced.

```
/* Program to enter data points with a mouse */

#include <conio.h>        /* header files needed for functions    */
#include <stdlib.h>
#include <graph.h>
#include <dos.h>
     /* use the #define directive to clarify the program */
#define RETURN        13 /* ASCII number for the return key       */
#define MOUSE         51 /* DOS interrupt number for the mouse     */
#define LEFT_BUTTON   1 /* number for the left mouse button       */
#define RED           4 /* color numbers to use with _setcolor() */
#define GREEN         10 /* bright green for the cursor           */
#define WHITE         15 /* bright white for lines                 */

void    getData(void),cursorInit(void);
int     mouseInit(void),mouseRead(void);
void    polyLine(int n,int xc[],int yc[]);

int     nPts,xPt[200],yPt[200]; /* global variables */
int     x,y,button,xold=5,yold=5,xref=-1,yref=-1,buttonref=-1;
int     xmin=10,xmax=630,ymin=20,ymax=470; /* drawing limits */
char far  *imageCursor;     /* pointer to image memory location */
union REGS  reg;                /* data type needed by int86() */

void main(void)
{
    if (mouseInit() == 0)              /* value 0 means no mouse */
    {
        printf ("Error, mouse isn't working\n");
        exit(1);   /* terminates program if mouse isn't working */
    }
    _setvideomode ( _VRES16COLOR );
    cursorInit();

    getData();
    polyLine(nPts,xPt,yPt);

    getch();
    _setvideomode ( _DEFAULTMODE);
}

void getData(void)
{
    int i,mouseData;
```

```
    i = 0;           /* counter for number of data points entered */

    do               /* loop until RETURN key is pressed           */
    {
        mouseData = mouseRead();
            /* keep cursor in drawing area */
        if (x < xmin) x = xmin; if (x > xmax) x = xmax;
        if (y < ymin) y = ymin; if (y > ymax) y = ymax;

        _putimage(xold-5,yold-5,imageCursor,_GXOR);/* erase cursor */
        _putimage(x-5,y-5,imageCursor,_GXOR);        /* draw cursor  */
            /* display cursor position */
        _settextposition(0,40); printf(" x=%3i y=%3i",x,y);

        if (button == LEFT_BUTTON)    /* button pressed— new point */
        {
            xPt[i] = x; yPt[i] = y; /* store the point in an array */
            i++;                     /* increment the number of points */
            _setcolor(RED);         /* red for filled circle at point */
            _putimage(x-5,y-5,imageCursor,_GXOR);  /* erase cursor */
            _ellipse(_GFILLINTERIOR,x-2,y-2,x+2,y+2);     /* circle */
            _putimage(x-5,y-5,imageCursor,_GXOR);    /* draw cursor */
        }
        xold = x; yold = y;
    } while(mouseData != RETURN);  /* loop until RETURN is pressed */
    nPts = i;                      /* total number of data points  */
    _setcolor(WHITE);              /* reset drawing color to white */
}


void cursorInit(void)
{
    _setcolor(GREEN);     /* cursor image is a green cross */
    _moveto(0,5); _lineto(10,5);
    _moveto(5,0); _lineto(5,10);
        /* allocate memory to store the cursor image */
    imageCursor = (char far *)
                    malloc((unsigned)_imagesize(0,0,10,10));
    _getimage(0,0,10,10,imageCursor); /* put image into memory */
}


int mouseInit(void)
{
    int retcode;

    reg.x.ax = 0;                  /* value 0 checks mouse status    */
    int86(MOUSE, &reg, &reg);   /* function for MS-DOS interrupts  */
    retcode = reg.x.ax;
    if (retcode == 0) return 0; /* code of 0 means no mouse         */
```

```
    reg.x.ax = 7;      /* value 7 sets screen horizontal boundaries */
    reg.x.cx = xmin; reg.x.dx = xmax;
    int86(MOUSE, &reg, &reg);
    reg.x.ax = 8;      /* value 8 sets screen vertical boundaries */
    reg.x.cx = ymin; reg.x.dx = ymax;
    int86(MOUSE, &reg, &reg);
    return retcode;
}


int mouseRead(void)
{
    do
    {
        if (kbhit()) return getch();  /* return number for key hit */
        reg.x.ax = 3;      /* 3 for cursor position & button status */
        int86(MOUSE, &reg, &reg);
        x = reg.x.cx;          /* read cursor x-position    */
        y = reg.x.dx;          /* read cursor y-position    */
        button = reg.x.bx;     /* read mouse button status */
    } while (x == xref && y == yref && button == buttonref);
    xref = x; yref = y; buttonref = button;/* set reference values */
}


void polyLine(int num,int x[],int y[])
{
    int i;

    _moveto(x[0],y[0]);
    for (i=1; i<num; i++)
    {
        _lineto(x[i],y[i]);
    }
}
```

Creating Different Cursors for the Mouse

The mouse cursor in the program listed above is a cross enclosed in an 11×11-pixel square. In AutoCAD the cursor consists of crossed lines that extend to the edges of the drawing viewport; see figure A.1b. This cursor is simulated by the cursorInit() subroutine listed below. In this subroutine two cursor images are stored: one a horizontal line extending between the drawing limits *xmin* and *xmax,* and the other a vertical line extending from *ymin* to *ymax.* The complete cursor is drawn by placing the horizontal line at the current y-position of the cursor, and the vertical line at the x-position. That is, in the above program, _putimage() is replaced in each instance by the following two functions: _putimage(0,*y*, *imageCursor*1,_GXOR); _putimage(*x*,0,*imageCursor*2,_GXOR). Because the starting point for _getimage() is (0,0), placement of the horizontal line at (0,*y*) produces a horizontal line extending from *xmin* to *xmax* at the position *y*. Similarly, the vertical line is placed at *x,* so that the lines cross at (*x,y*). Of course, when the _putimage() functions are used for erasure, they are placed at the old cursor coordinates *xold* and *yold.*

```
void cursorInit(void)
{
    _setcolor(GREEN);
    _moveto(xmin,0); _lineto(xmax,0); /* horizontal line */
    imageCursor1 = (char far *)
                        malloc((unsigned)_imagesize(0,0,639,0));
    _getimage(0,0,639,0,imageCursor1);
    _moveto(0,ymin); _lineto(0,ymax); /* vertical line */
    imageCursor2 = (char far *)
                        malloc((unsigned)_imagesize(0,0,0,479));
    _getimage(0,0,0,479,imageCursor2);
}
```

For some applications an arrow pointer rather than a cross is more appropriate. A standard arrow cursor is contained in the function int86() and can be turned on and off by the functions cursorOn() and cursorOff() listed below. The arrow cursor is based on a 16 × 16-pixel array, as illustrated in figure A.1a. On the PC, the interior of the arrow is white, with a black edge, so that it is visible against any background. On the Macintosh computer, the arrow has the same shape, but with reversed color, since the standard Macintosh background is white, rather than black as for the PC.

Rimmer (1992) describes how the 16 × 16-pixel bitmapped picture of the arrow may be customized in a manner similar to the treatment of bitmapped fonts in chapter 5. The cursor detection point, called the hot spot, remains in the upper-left corner of the array, so that the cross (and box cursor of chapter 9) are best drawn with _putimage().

```
void cursorOn(void)
{
    union REGS reg;

    reg.x.ax = 1;
    int86(MOUSE,&reg,&reg);
}

void cursorOff(void)
{
    union REGS reg;

    reg.x.ax = 2;
    int86(MOUSE,&reg,&reg);
}
```

The arrow cursor accessed by the above functions follows the mouse position; that is, you do not need to place it at the new position (*x,y*) and erase it at the old position (*xold,yold*), as was required with cursors drawn using _putimage(). However, in similar manner to cursors that use _putimage(), the arrow cursor must be turned off when entities are drawn over it, and then turned back on. For example, in the above subroutine, getData(), when circles are drawn at the cursor position with the function _ellipse(), the function cursorOff() must be called right before _ellipse(), and cursorOn() must be called afterwards.

Chapter 9 covers additional interactive features in computer graphics.

BIBLIOGRAPHY

AMMERAAL, L., *Graphics Programming in Turbo C.* New York: Wiley, 1989.

MARK, D., *Macintosh C Programming Primer, Volume II: Mastering the Toolbox Using THINKC.* Reading, Mass.: Addison-Wesley, 1990.

MARK, D., and C. REED, *Macintosh Programming Primer: Inside the Toolbox Using THINK's Light-speedC.* Reading, Mass.: Addison-Wesley, 1989.

RIMMER, S., *Graphical User Interface Programming.* Windcrest/McGraw-Hill, 1992.

THE WAITE GROUP, *Microsoft C Programming for the PC,* 2nd ed. Indianapolis: Howard Sams, 1990.

Appendix B: Program Listings

This appendix contains program subroutines that were too long to conveniently include in the chapters. The listings are labeled by the chapter number, with an extension giving order of the listing in this appendix. Thus listing 7.2 is the second subroutine from chapter 7. Brief discussions of the listings are included with many of the subroutines.

LISTING 3.1: wideLine()

This subroutine draws a wide line, simulating AutoCAD's PLINE command. The subroutine is described in section 3.2, using equations 3.16 and 3.17, and the geometry shown in figure 3.12.

```
void wideLine(double xstart,double ystart,double xend,
              double yend, double hw)
{
    double xtemp,ytemp;
```

```
    if (yend < ystart)
    {
        xtemp = xstart;
        ytemp = ystart;
        xstart = xend;
        ystart = yend;
        xend = xtemp;
        yend = ytemp;
    }
    if (xstart == xend)
    {
        vertLine(xstart,ystart,xend,yend,hw);
    }
    else
    {
        if(ystart == yend)
        {
            horizLine(xstart,ystart,xend,yend,hw);
        }
        else
        {
            diagLine(xstart,ystart,xend,yend,hw);
        }
    }
}

void vertLine(double xstart,double ystart,double xend,double
yend, double hw)
{
    double xstart1,xstart2,x;

    xstart1 = xstart - hw;
    xstart2 = xstart + hw;
    for (x=xstart1; x<=xstart2; x=x+1.)
    {
        MoveTo((int) x,(int) ystart);
        LineTo((int) x,(int) yend);
    }
}

void horizLine(double xstart,double ystart,double xend,double
yend, double hw)
{
    double ystart1,ystart2,y;

    ystart1 = ystart - hw;
    ystart2 = ystart + hw;
    for (y=ystart1; y<=ystart2; y=y+1.)
```

Listing 3.1   wideLine()   **477**

```
        {
            MoveTo((int) xstart,(int) y);
            LineTo((int) xend,(int) y);
        }
    }

void diagLine(double xstart,double ystart,double xend,double
yend, double hw)
{
    double m,m2,dx,dy,xstart1,ystart1,xend1,yend1;
    double xstart2,ystart2,xend2,yend2,y;

    m = (yend - ystart)/(xend - xstart);
    m2 = m*m;
    dx = (m/fabs(m))*hw/sqrt(1+1/m2);
    dy = hw/sqrt(1+m2);
    xstart1 = xstart + dx;
    ystart1 = ystart - dy;
    xend1- dy;
    xstart2 = xstart - dx;
    ystart2- dy;
    xstart2 = xstart - dx;
    ystart2 = ystart + dy;
    xend2 = xend - dx;
    yend2 = yend +dy;

    if (yend1 > ystart2)
    {
        for (y=ystart1+.5; y<ystart2+.5; y=y+1.)
        {
            MoveTo((int) (xstart1-m*(y-ystart1)),(int) y);
            LineTo((int) (xstart1+(y-ystart1)/m),(int) y);
        }
        for (y=ystart2+.5; y<yend1+.5; y=y+1.)
        {
            MoveTo((int) (xstart2+(y-ystart2)/m),(int) y);
            LineTo((int) (xstart1+(y-ystart1)/m),(int) y);
        }
        for (y=yend1+.5; y<yend2+.5; y=y+1.)
        {
            MoveTo((int) (xstart2+(y-ystart2)/m),(int) y);
            LineTo((int) (xend1-m*(y-yend1)),(int) y);
        }
    }
    else
    {
        for (y=ystart1+.5; y<yend1+.5; y=y+1.)
        {
```

```
                MoveTo((int) (xstart1-m*(y-ystart1)),(int) y);
                LineTo((int) (xstart1+(y-ystart1)/m),(int) y);
            }
        for (y=yend1+.5; y<ystart2+.5; y=y+1.)
            {
                MoveTo((int) (xstart1-m*(y-ystart1)),(int) y);
                LineTo((int) (xend1-m*(y-yend1)),(int) y);
            }
        for (y=ystart2+.5; y<yend2+.5; y=y+1.)
            {
                MoveTo((int) (xstart2+(y-ystart2)/m),(int) y);
                LineTo((int) (xend1-m*(y-yend1)),(int) y);
            }
        }
    }
```

LISTING 3.2: fillQuadrilateral()

This subroutine fills a quadrilateral with horizontal lines, as described in section 3.2 and illustrated in figure 3.16.

```
void fillQuadrilateral(double xv[],double yv[])
{
    int     i,imin,j,v0,v1,v2,v3,vd;
    double  xstart,xend,y,ymax,m1,m2;

    imin = 0;
    for (i=0; i<=3; i++)
    {
        if (yv[i] < yv[imin]) imin = i;
    }
    v0 = imin; v1 = (imin+1) % 4;
    v2 = (imin+2) % 4; v3 = (imin+3) % 4;
    if (yv[v3] < yv[v1]) /* exchange v1 & v3 */
    {
        vd = v1; v1 = v3; v3 = vd;
    }
    if (yv[v0] < yv[v1]) /* bottom triangle */
    {
        m1 = (xv[v1]-xv[v0])/(yv[v1]-yv[v0]);
        m2 = (xv[v3]-xv[v0])/(yv[v3]-yv[v0]);
        for (y=yv[v0]+1.; y<yv[v1]; y=y+1.)
        {
            xstart = xv[v0] + m1*(y-yv[v0]);
```

Listing 3.2   fillQuadrilateral()   **479**

```
            MoveTo((int) xstart,(int) y);
            xend = xv[v0] + m2*(y-yv[v0]);
            LineTo((int) xend,(int) y);
        }
    }
    if (yv[v1] < yv[v2]) && yv[v1]<yv[v3]) /* middle quadrilateral */
    {
        if (yv[v3] < yv[v2])
            ymax = vy[v3];
        else
            ymax = yv[v2];
        m1 = (xv[v2]-xv[v1])/(yv[v2]-yv[v1]);
        m2 = (xv[v3]-xv[v0])/(yv[v3]-yv[v0]);
        for (y=yv[v1]; y<ymax; y=y+1.)
        {
            xstart = xv[v1] + m1*(y-yv[v1]);
            MoveTo((int) xstart,(int) y);
            xend = xv[v0] + m2*(y-yv[v0]);
            LineTo((int) xend,(int) y);
        }
    }
    if (yv[v3] < yv[v2]) /* top triangle */
    {
        m1 = (xv[v2]-xv[v1])/(yv[v2]-yv[v1]);
        m2 = (xv[v2]-xv[v3])/(yv[v2]-yv[v3]);
        for (y=yv[v3]; y<yv[v2]; y=y+1.)
        {
            xstart = xv[v2] + m1*(y-yv[v2]);
            MoveTo((int) xstart,(int) y);
            xend = xv[v2] + m2*(y-yv[v2]);
            LineTo((int) xend,(int) y);
        }
    }
    if (yv[v3] > yv[v2]) /* top triangle */
    {
        m1 = (xv[v3]-xv[v0])/(yv[v3]-yv[v0]);
        m2 = (xv[v3]-xv[v2])/(yv[v3]-yv[v2]);
        for (y=yv[v2]; y<yv[v3]; y=y+1.)
        {
            xstart = xv[v3] + m1*(y-yv[v3]);
            MoveTo((int) xstart,(int) y);
            xend = xv[v3] + m2*(y-yv[v3]);
            LineTo((int) xend,(int) y);
        }
    }
}
```

LISTING 7.1: arcFit()

The subroutine arcFit() listed below draws a circular-arc (biarc) interpolation curve that passes through n vertex points prescribed by the coordinate arrays $x[]$ and $y[]$. The equations for this circular-arc fit are given in section 7.2. Also, this subroutine uses the function arc() developed in section 3.1. This subroutine is long because it considers a number of cases, but it is broken up into relatively short parts that are easy to understand.

The first *for* loop in the subroutine calculates the angles σ_i that the polyline segments make with the horizontal, and stores them in the array *sigma[i]*. The second *for* loop involves the calculation of the angle ϕ_i that the tangent vector $\mathbf{t}_i$ makes with the horizontal, which is stored in the array *phi[i]*. That is, equations 7.2–7.5 are used to calculate the horizontal and vertical components (dummy variables f_1 and f_2 in the program) of $\mathbf{t}_i$, from which ϕ_i is obtained using the arctangent function $atan2(f_1, f_2)$. The angle ϕ_0 at the beginning of the curve is then calculated from equation 7.6, with the angle ϕ_{n-1} at the curve end being calculated by a similar formula. Next the angles α_i and β_i are calculated.

The main part of the subroutine is the fourth *for* loop, which extends over the polyline segments $i = 0$ through $n - 2$. First, if α_i is sufficiently small, the arc is drawn as a straight line because if drawn, the actual arc would be indistinguishable from a straight line (the limiting value used corresponds to the radius of curvature being greater than about a million segment lengths). This procedure avoids difficulties that would be associated with trying to draw an arc having a radius value approaching infinity.

Next, the quantity $\sin(\sigma_i - \phi_i)$ is calculated, which determines the variable *ccw* showing whether the segment curve starts to turn in the clockwise or counterclockwise direction. Then the ratio $\sin(\sigma_i - \phi_{i+1})/\sin(\sigma_i - \phi_i)$ is calculated to determine whether the tangent vectors $\mathbf{t}_i$ and $\mathbf{t}_{i+1}$ point to the same side of the segment or to opposite sides. Note that the denominator in this ratio will not be zero because the cases of very small $|\alpha_i| = |\sigma_i - \phi_i|/2$ have already been separated out.

If the tangent vectors point to opposite sides of the segment, the geometry will be that shown in figure 7.7a, and equations 7.7–7.10 will be used to calculate the arc radii and centers. However, if the tangent vectors point to the same side of the segment, then equations 7.11–7.14 will be used.

In each case, the first arc is drawn, then a pixel must be set at the inserted vertex, and then the second arc is drawn. The pixel at the inserted vertex is set because it lies between the two arcs and may be omitted because of round-off errors when the two arcs are drawn. Also, before the arcs are drawn, the program checks the θ_{start} and θ_{end} values to see if an extra 2π factor has appeared because of the specific angle range to which the $atan2()$ function is restricted ($-\pi$ to $+\pi$). If an extra 2π factor has appeared, then θ_{end} is appropriately adjusted by $\pm 2\pi$.

```
void arcFit(int n,double x[],double y[])
{
    double a,b,s,w0,w1,w2,f1,f2;
    double lx[100],ly[100],l[100];
    double sigma[100],phi[100],alpha[100],beta[100];
```

Listing 7.1   arcFit()   **481**

```
double ccw,s1,s2,c1,c2,xint,yint,xm,ym;
double d,d1,d2,r1,r2,xc1,yc1,xc2,yc2;
double startTheta,endTheta;
int i;

s = -1.;
for (i=0; i<=n-2; i++)
{
    lx[i] = x[i+1]-x[i];
    ly[i] = y[i+1]-y[i];
    sigma[i] = atan2(ly[i],lx[i]);
    l[i] = sqrt(pow(lx[i],2)+pow(ly[i],2));
}

for (i=1; i<=n-2; i++)
{
    if (i == 1 || i == n-2)
    {
        a = 1.;
        b = 1.;
    }
    else
    {
        f1 = pow(lx[i+1]/l[i+1]-lx[i]/l[i],2);
        f2 = pow(ly[i+1]/l[i+1]-ly[i]/l[i],2);
        a = sqrt(f1+f2);
        f1 = pow(lx[i-1]/l[i-1]-lx[i-2]/l[i-2],2);
        f2 = pow(ly[i-1]/l[i-1]-ly[i">1f2);
        b = sqrt(f1+f2);
    }
    w0 = .5*((1.+s)*l[i-1]+(1.-s)*l[i]);
    w1 = .5*((1.+s)*l[i]+(1.-s)*l[i-1]);
    f1 = a*w0*l[i]*ly[i-1]+b*w1*l[i-1]*ly[i];
    f2 = a*w0*l[i]*lx[i-1]+b*w1*l[i-1]*lx[i];
    phi[i] = atan2(f1,f2);
}

w0 = .5*((1.+s)*l[0]+(1.-s)*l[1]);
w1 = .5*((1.+s)*l[1]+(1.-s)*l[0]);
w2 = w0 + 2.*w1*cos(sigma[1]-sigma[0]);
f1 = w2*l[1]*ly[0]-w1*l[0]*ly[1];
f2 = w2*l[1]*lx[0]-w1*l[0]*lx[1];
phi[0] = atan2(f1,f2);

w0 = .5*((1.+s)*l[n-3]+(1.-s)*l[n-2]);
w1 = .5*((1.+s)*l[n-2]+(1.-s)*l[n-3]);
w2 = w1 + 2.*w0*cos(sigma[n-3]-sigma[n-2]);
f1 = w2*l[n-3]*ly[n-2]-w0*l[n-2]*ly[n-3];
```

```
f2 = w2*l[n-3]*lx[n-2]-w0*l[n-2]*lx[n-3];
phi[n-1] = atan2(f1,f2);

for (i=0; i<=n-2; i++)
{
    alpha[i] = .5*(sigma[i]-phi[i]);
    beta[i] = .5*(phi[i+1]-sigma[i]);
}

for (i=0; i<=n-2; i++)
{
    if (fabs(alpha[i]) < .000001)
    {
        MoveTo((int) x[i],(int) y[i]);
        LineTo((int) x[i+1],(int) y[i+1]);
    }
    else
    {
        if (sin(sigma[i]-phi[i]) > 0.)
            ccw = 1.0;
        else
            ccw = -1.0;

        if ((sin(sigma[i]-phi[i+1])/sin(sigma[i]-phi[i])) < 0.)
        {
            s1 = sin(.5*(phi[i]+sigma[i]));
            c1 = cos(.5*(phi[i]+sigma[i]));
            s2 = sin(.5*(phi[i+1]+sigma[i]));
            c2 = cos(.5*(phi[i+1]+sigma[i]));
            f1 = (c2*(y[i+1]-y[i])-s2*(x[i+1]-x[i]))/(s1*c2-s2*c1);
            xint = x[i] + c1*f1;
            yint = y[i] + s1*f1;

            d1 = sqrt(pow(xint-x[i],2) + pow(yint-y[i],2));
            d2 = sqrt(pow(xint-x[i+1],2) + pow(yint-y[i+1],2));
            r1 = .5*d1/fabs(sin(alpha[i]));
            r2 = .5*d2/fabs(sin(beta[i]));
            xc1 = x[i] - ccw*r1*sin(phi[i]);
            yc1 = y[i] + ccw*r1*cos(phi[i]);
            xc2 = x[i+1] - ccw*r2*sin(phi[i+1]);
            yc2 = y[i+1] + ccw*r2*cos(phi[i+1]);

            startTheta = -ccw*.5*PI + phi[i];
            endTheta = startTheta + 2.*alpha[i];
            if (endTheta > startTheta+PI) endTheta = endTheta-2.*PI;
            if (endTheta < startTheta-PI) endTheta = endTheta+2.*PI;
            arc(xc1,yc1,r1,startTheta,endTheta);
```

Listing 7.1   arcFit()   **483**

```
            SetPixel((int) xint,(int) yint);

            startTheta = endTheta;
            endTheta = startTheta + 2.*beta[i];
            if (endTheta > startTheta+PI) endTheta = endTheta-2.*PI;
            if (endTheta < startTheta-PI) endTheta = endTheta+2.*PI;
            arc(xc2,yc2,r2,startTheta,endTheta);
        }
        else
        {
            s1 = sin(phi[i]);
            c1 = cos(phi[i]);
            s2 = sin(phi[i+1]);
            c2 = cos(phi[i+1]);

            if (fabs(s1-s2) < .000001)
            {
                xm = .5*(x[i] + x[i+1]);
                ym = .5*(y[i] + y[i+1]);
            }
            else
            {
                f1 = (c2*(y[i+1]-y[i])-s2*(x[i+1]-x[i]))/(s1*c2-s2*c1);
                xint = x[i] + c1*f1;
                yint = y[i] + s1*f1;

                d1 = sqrt(pow(x[i]-xint,2) + pow(y[i]-yint,2));
                d2 = sqrt(pow(x[i+1]-xint,2) + pow(y[i+1]-yint,2));
                d = sqrt(d1*d2);
                f1 = atan2(y[i]-yint,x[i]-xint);
                f2 = atan2(y[i+1]-yint,x[i+1]-xint);
                xm = xint + d*cos(.5*(f1+f2));
                ym = yint + d*sin(.5*(f1+f2));
            }
            f1 = pow(xm-x[i],2) + pow(ym-y[i],2);
            f2 = 2.*(s2*(xm-x[i+1]) - c2*(ym-y[i+1]));
            r1 = fabs(f1/f2);
            xc1 = x[i] - ccw*r1*s1;
            yc1 = y[i] + ccw*r1*c1;
            f1 = pow(xm-x[i+1],2) + pow(ym-y[i+1],2);
            f2 = 2.*(s2*(xm-x[i+1]) - c2*(ym-y[i+1]));
            r2 = fabs(f1/f2);
            xc2 = x[i+1] + ccw*r2*s2;
            yc2 = y[i+1] - ccw*r2*c2;

            startTheta = atan2(y[i]-yc1,x[i]-xc1);
            endTheta = atan2(ym-yc1,xm-xc1);
```

```
                    if (endTheta > startTheta+PI) endTheta = endTheta-2.*PI;
                    if (endTheta < startTheta-PI) endTheta = endTheta+2.*PI;
                    arc(xc1,yc1,r1,startTheta,endTheta);


                    SetPixel((int) xm,(int) ym);


                    startTheta = atan2(y[i+1]-yc2,x[i+1]-xc2);
                    endTheta = atan2(ym-yc2,xm-xc2);
                    if (endTheta > startTheta+PI) endTheta = endTheta-2.*PI;
                    if (endTheta < startTheta-PI) endTheta = endTheta+2.*PI;
                    arc(xc2,yc2,r2,startTheta,endTheta);

                }
            }
        }
    }
```

The above subroutine seems relatively robust and handles most cases without difficulty. However, this subroutine is restricted to open curves with $n \geq 5$. Cases with four or fewer data points must be considered as special cases. The case of $n = 2$ reduces simply to a straight line between the two points. The case $n = 3$ corresponds to a single circular arc being fitted between the three points. This case can be incorporated into the above calculation by setting $A = 1$ and $B = 1$ when $n = 3$. The $n = 4$ case can be incorporated into the arc-fitting procedure by setting $B = 1$ and calculating A according to equation 7.5.

The above subroutine can be changed to the case of a *closed* curve by adding four additional points $i = n, n + 1, n + 2$, and $n + 3$, having coordinates identical to the points $i = 0, 1, 2$, and 3, respectively (that is, for $i = 0$ to 3 set $x[i+n] = x[i]$ and $y[i+n] = y[i]$). The fitted curve can now be plotted starting with segment $i = 2$ and continuing through $i = n + 1$, by means of the general formulas for interior points, equations 7.2–7.5. That is, with the added data points repeating the initial four points, any tangent vector $\mathbf{t}_i$ can be computed from the five surrounding vectors along segments $i - 2, i - 1, i, i + 1$, and $i + 2$. Closed curves are shown in figures 7.3 and 7.4.

LISTING 7.2: natCubicSpline()

The program listing below plots a natural cubic spline interpolated between n data points having coordinates given by the arrays $x[]$ and $y[]$. The equations for the natural cubic spline are given in section 7.5. In that section, an equation involving a tridiagonal matrix was solved to provide equations 7.44–7.46, which are used in the subroutine natCubicSpline() below.

The first *for* loop in the subroutine natCubicSpline() calculates the γ values. The next three *for* loops calculate δ and D values, which are used to compute the arrays $ax[]$, $bx[]$, $cx[]$, and $dx[]$ representing the a_i, b_i, c_i, and d_i coefficients for the $x(t)$ coordinate. The next three loops in the listing carry out the same procedure for the $y(t)$ coordinate. The curve is plotted on the screen in the last *for* loop.

Listing 7.2   natCubicSpline()   **485**

```
void natCubicSpline(int n, double x[],double y[])
{
    int i,j,nsegs,m,xp,yp;
    double ax[50],bx[50],cx[50],dx[50];
    double ay[50],by[50],cy[50],dy[50];
    double der[50],gam[50],del[50];
    double t,dt;

    m = n-1;
    gam[0] = .5;
    for (i=1; i<m; i++)
    {
        gam[i] = 1./(4.-gam[i-1]);
    }
    gam[m] = 1./(2.-gam[m-1]);
    del[0] = 3.*(x[1]-x[0])*gam[0];
    for (i=1; i<m; i++)
    {
        del[i] = (3.*(x[i+1]-x[i-1])-del[i-1])*gam[i];

    }
    del[m] = (3.*(x[m]-x[m-1])-del[m-1])*gam[m];
    der[m] = del[m];
    for (i=m-1; i>=0; i=i-1)
    {
        der[i] = del[i]-gam[i]*der[i+1];
    }
    for (i=0; i<m; i++)
    {
        ax[i] = x[i];
        bx[i] = der[i];
        cx[i] = 3.*(x[i+1]-x[i])-2.*der[i]-der[i+1];
        dx[i] = 2.*(x[i]-x[i+1])+der[i]+der[i+1];
    }
    del[0] = 3.*(y[1]-y[0])*gam[0];
    for (i=1; i<m; i++)
    {
        del[i] = (3.*(y[i+1]-y[i-1])-del[i-1])*gam[i];

    }
    del[m] = (3.*(y[m]-y[m-1])-del[m-1])*gam[m];
    der[m] = del[m];
    for (i=m-1; i<=0; i=i-1)
    {
        der[i] = del[i]-gam[i]*der[i+1];
    }
    for (i=0; i<m; i++)
    {
```

```
        ay[i]  = y[i];
        by[i]  = der[i];
        cy[i]  = 3.*(y[i+1]-y[i])-2.*der[i]-der[i+1];
        dy[i]  = 2.*(y[i]-y[i+1])+der[i]+der[i+1];
    }

    nsegs = 20; dt = 1./(double) nsegs;
    MoveTo((int) x[0],(int) y[0]);
    for (i=0; i<m; i++)
    {
        for (j=1,t=dt;j<=nsegs;j++,t+=dt)
        {
            xp = (int) (ax[i]+bx[i]*t+cx[i]*t*t+dx[i]*t*t*t);
            yp = (int) (ay[i]+by[i]*t+cy[i]*t*t+dy[i]*t*t*t);
            LineTo(xp,yp);
        }
    }
}
```

LISTING 8.1: CONSTRUCTING A GEODESIC DOME
FROM AN ICOSAHEDRON

The program lines listed below can be used to generate a DXF file for the faces of a geodesic dome. The lines starting with the *for* loop replace the *for* loops in the icosahedron program given in section 8.2, and the additional data-type declarations shown below are added to those of the icosahedron program. As discussed in section 8.2, the integer *n* determines the level of division of the icosahedron faces, and the value of 3 given below can be changed to any desired value.

Comments are included in the program lines to clarify the procedures. As illustrated in figure 8.6 of section 8.2, the icosahedron is subdivided into triangles that have vertex coordinates identified by a two-dimensional array; for example, $x[i][j]$, where i and j range from 0 to n. To construct the geodesic dome, the vertices of the original triangle (icosahedron face) are renumbered in the two-dimensional array as (0,0), (0,n), and (n,0). Next the left and right sides of the original triangle are divided into n equal parts by inserting vertices (0,1) through (0,$n - 1$) along the left side and (1,$n - 1$) through ($n - 1$,1) along the right side, as shown in figure 8.6. With these inserted vertices, the interior vertices are readily calculated by the double *for* loop given below.

The new vertex points are then moved out radially to the circumsphere by changing the coordinate values by the value *lenRatio,* which is the ratio of the following lengths: the circumsphere radius 0.9512 and the distance from the center to the vertex point in the plane of the original triangle. Finally, face data are written to the file for all of the small triangles, with separate double *for* loops for upward- and downward-facing triangles.

```
int     j,k,n;
double  iRatio,lenRatio;
```

Listing 8.1   Constructing a Geodesic Dome from an Icosahedron   **487**

```
double xc[3],yc[3],zc[3],xv[4],yv[4],zv[4];
double x[10][10],y[10][10],z[10][10];

n = 3;

for (faceNum=0; faceNum<20; faceNum++)
{
    for (i=0; i<3; i++)
    {
        vnum = vn[faceNum][i];
        xp[i] = vert[vnum][0];
        yp[i] = vert[vnum][1];
        zp[i] = vert[vnum][2];
    } /*    Renumber the three original vertices in a 2-D array.*/
    x[0][0] = xp[0]; y[0][0] = yp[0]; z[0][0] = zp[0];
    x[0][n] = xp[1]; y[0][n] = yp[1]; z[0][n] = zp[1];
    x[n][0] = xp[2]; y[n][0] = yp[2]; z[n][0] = zp[2];

    for (i=1; i<n; i++) /* Insert points along the left and */
    {                   /* right sides of original triangle.*/
        iRatio = ((double) i)/((double) n);
        x[0][i] = (1.- iRatio)*x[0][0] + iRatio*x[0][n];
        y[0][i] = (1.- iRatio)*y[0][0] + iRatio*y[0][n];
        z[0][i] = (1.- iRatio)*z[0][0] + iRatio*z[0][n];
        x[i][n-i] = (1.- iRatio)*x[0][n] + iRatio*x[n][0];
        y[i][n-i] = (1.- iRatio)*y[0][n] + iRatio*y[n][0];
        z[i][n-i] = (1.- iRatio)*z[0][n] + iRatio*z[n][0];
    }
    for (j=0; j<n-1; j++) /* Insert points in the interior */
    {                     /* of the original triangle.     */
        for (i=1; i<n-j; i++)
        {
            iRatio = ((double) i)/((double) (n-j));
            x[i][j] = (1.- iRatio)*x[0][j] + iRatio*x[n-j][j];
            y[i][j] = (1.- iRatio)*y[0][j] + iRatio*y[n-j][j];
            z[i][j] = (1.- iRatio)*z[0][j] + iRatio*z[n-j][j];
        }
    }
    for (j=0; j<n; j++) /* Translate the new points radially */
    {                   /* outward to the circumsphere.      */
        for (i=0; i<n-j+1; i++)
        {
            lenRatio = .9512/sqrt(x[i][j]*x[i][j]
                        +y[i][j]*y[i][j]+z[i][j]*z[i][j]);
            x[i][j] = lenRatio*x[i][j];
            y[i][j] = lenRatio*y[i][j];
            z[i][j] = lenRatio*z[i][j];
        }
```

```
    }
for (j=0; j<n; j++) /* Loop over all upward-pointing */
{                          /* triangles and write the        */
    for (i=0; i<n-j; i++) /* 3DFACE data to the file. */
    {
        xv[0] = xv[3] = x[i][j];
        yv[0] = yv[3] = y[i][j];
        zv[0] = zv[3] = z[i][j];
        xv[1] = x[i][j+1]; yv[1] = y[i][j+1]; zv[1] = z[i][j+1];
        xv[2] = x[i+1][j]; yv[2] = y[i+1][j]; zv[2] = z[i+1][j];
        writeFace(xv,yv,zv);
    }
}
for (j=0; j<n-1; j++)       /* Loop over all downward-pointing */
{                           /* triangles and write             */
    for (i=1; i<n-j; i++) /*3DFACE data to the file.           */
    {
        xv[0] = xv[3] = x[i][j];
        yv[0] = yv[3] = y[i][j];
        zv[0] = zv[3] = z[i][j];
        xv[1] = x[i-1][j+1];yv[1] = y[i-1][j+1];zv[1] = z[i-1][j+1];
        xv[2] = x[i][j+1]; yv[2] = y[i][j+1];zv[2] = z[i][j+1];
        writeFace(xv,yv,zv);
    }
}
}
```

LISTING 9.1: findPline()

The function findPline() is constructed in the same manner as deleteLine() in section 9.2. Here adjacent vertices are identified with the coordinates $(xd0, yd0)$ and $(xd1, yd1)$, because these vertices represent the endpoints of the polyline segments.

```
void findPline(void)
{
    int      j,k,plineFound;
    double   xd,yd,xd0,yd0,xd1,yd1,dx,dy;
    double   t,dbox2,d2,f1,f2;

    imageCursor = imageBox;
    _putimage(xold-5,yold-5,imageCursor,_GXOR);
    plineFound = 0;
    _settextposition(30,1);
    _printf ("             Select polyline.                          ");
    do
    {
        mouseData = mouseRead();
```

Listing 9.2   pedit()   489

```
                    if (x < xmin) x = xmin; if (x > xmax) x = xmax;
                    if (y < ymin) y = ymin; if (y > ymax) y = ymax;
                    _putimage(xold-5,yold-5,imageCursor,_GXOR);
                    _putimage(x-5,y-5,imageCursor,_GXOR);

                    if (button == LEFT_BUTTON)
                    {
                        for (j=1; j<=nPlines; j++)
                        {
                            for (k=0; k<nVertices[j]-1; k++)
                            {
                                xd0 = (double) plines[j][2*k];
                                yd0 = (double) plines[j][2*k+1];
                                xd1 = (double) plines[j][2*k+2];
                                yd1 = (double) plines[j][2*k+3];
                                xd = (double) x; yd =(double) y;
                                dx = xd1 - xd0; dy = yd1 - yd0;
                                t = ((xd-xd0)*dx + (yd-yd0)*dy)/(dx*dx+dy*dy);

                                if ((t >= 0.) && (t <= 1.))
                                {
                                    f1 = fabs(dx)+fabs(dy);
                                    f2 = dx*dx+dy*dy;
                                    dbox2 = 25.0*f1*f1/f2;
                                    f1 = xd0-xd+t*dx;
                                    f2 = yd0-yd+t*dy;
                                    d2 = f1*f1 + f2*f2;
                                    if (d2 < dbox2)
                                    {
                                        plineNum = j;
                                        plineFound = 1;
                                    }
                                }
                            }
                        }
                    }
                    xold = x; yold = y;
                } while((plineFound == 0) && (mouseData != RETURN));
                _putimage(x-5,y-5,imageCursor,_GXOR);
        }
```

LISTING 9.2: pedit()

```
    void pedit(void)
    {
        int i,j,k,xvert,yvert,moveFlag,numVert;
        double xspline[30],yspline[30];
```

```
j = plineNum; numVert = nVertices[j];
k=0;
imageCursor = imageX;
moveFlag =0;
xvert = plines[j][0]; yvert = plines[j][1];
_putimage(xvert-5,yvert-5,imageCursor,_GXOR);
_settextposition(30,5);
printf("Next Previous Move Spline finish edit <RETURN> ");
do
{
    mouseData = mouseRead();
    if (x < xmin) x = xmin; if (x > xmax) x = xmax;
    if (y < ymin) y = ymin; if (y > ymax) y = ymax;

    if (moveFlag == 1)
    {
        _putimage(xold-5,yold-5,imageCursor,_GXOR);
        _setcolor(BLACK);
        _moveto(xvert,yvert); _lineto(xold,yold);
        _setcolor(WHITE);
        _moveto(xvert,yvert); _lineto(x,y);

        _putimage(x-5,y-5,imageCursor,_GXOR);
        redraw(nLines,nPlines);
    }
    if ((mouseData == 'n') || (mouseData == 'N'))
    {
        if (k < numVert-1) k++;
        _putimage(xvert-5,yvert-5,imageCursor,_GXOR);
        xvert = plines[j][2*k];
        yvert = plines[j][2*k+1];
        _putimage(xvert-5,yvert-5,imageCursor,_GXOR);
    }
    if ((mouseData == 'p') || (mouseData == 'P'))
    {
        if (k > 0) k--;
        _putimage(xvert-5,yvert-5,imageCursor,_GXOR);
        xvert = plines[j][2*k];
        yvert = plines[j][2*k+1];
        _putimage(xvert-5,yvert-5,imageCursor,_GXOR);
    }
    if ((mouseData == 'm') || (mouseData == 'M'))
    {
        moveFlag = 1;
        x = xvert; y=yvert;
    }
```

Listing 9.2   pedit()   491

```
          if ((mouseData == 's') || (mouseData == 'S'))
          {
               for (i=0; i[numVert; i++)
               {
                    xspline[i] = (double) plines[j][2*i];
                    yspline[i] = (double) plines[j][2*i+1];
               }
               cubicBSpline(numVert,xspline,yspline);
          }
          _settextposition (1,40);
          printf (" x=%3i y=%3i",x,y);

          if ((button == LEFT_BUTTON) && (moveFlag == 1))
          {
               if ((x != xvert) || (y != yvert))
               {
                    _setcolor(BLACK);
                    if (k == 0)
                         _moveto(plines[j][0],plines[j][1]);
                    else
                         _moveto(plines[j][2*(k-1)],plines[j][2*(k-1)+1]);
                    _lineto(plines[j][2*k],plines[j][2*k+1]);
                    _lineto(plines[j][2*(k+1)],plines[j][2*(k+1)+1]);
                    _moveto(xvert,yvert);
                    _lineto(x,y);

                    _setcolor(WHITE);
                    xvert = plines[j][2*k] = x;
                    yvert = plines[j][2*k+1] = y;
                    moveFlag = 0;
                    redraw(nLines,nPlines);
               }
          }
          xold = x; yold = y;
     } while(mouseData != RETURN);
     _putimage(xvert-5,yvert-5,imageCursor,_GXOR);
}
```

The × cursor used by pedit() is formed by adding the following lines to the subroutine cursorInit().

```
_moveto(0,0);_lineto(10,10);
_moveto(0,10);_lineto(10,0);
imageX = (char far *) malloc((unsigned) _imagesize(0,0,10,10));
_getimage(0,0,10,10,imageX);
_putimage(0,0,imageX,_GXOR);
```

LISTING 9.3: peditDrag()

In the subroutine peditDrag(), the arrays *xsplineOld*[] and *ysplineOld*[] are introduced so that the B-spline curve at the old position can be erased by overdrawing with a black line. The spline and frame motion stop when the RETURN key is pressed, at which time further editing can be done.

```
void peditDrag(void)
{
    int      i,j,k,xvert,yvert,moveFlag,numVert;
    double   xspline[30],yspline[30];
    double   xsplineOld[30],ysplineOld[30];

    j = plineNum; numVert = nVertices[j];
    k=0;
    imageCursor = imageX;
    moveFlag = 0;
    xvert = plines[j][0]; yvert = plines[j][1];
    _putimage(xvert-5,yvert-5,imageCursor,_GXOR);
    _settextposition(30,1);
    printf (" Next     Previous    Move      finish edit <RETURN> ");
    do
    {
        mouseData = mouseRead();
        if (x < xmin) x = xmin; if (x > xmax) x = xmax;
        if (y < ymin) y = ymin; if (y > ymax) y = ymax;

        _settextposition (1,40);
        printf ("   x=%3i y=%3i",x,y);

        if ((mouseData == 'n') || (mouseData == 'N'))
        {
            if (k < numVert-1) k++;
            _putimage(xvert-5,yvert-5,imageCursor,_GXOR);
            xvert = plines[j][2*k];
            yvert = plines[j][2*k+1];
            _putimage(xvert-5,yvert-5,imageCursor,_GXOR);
        }
        if ((mouseData == 'p') || (mouseData == 'P'))
        {
            if (k > 0) k--;
            _putimage(xvert-5,yvert-5,imageCursor,_GXOR);
            xvert = plines[j][2*k];
            yvert = plines[j][2*k+1];
            _putimage(xvert-5,yvert-5,imageCursor,_GXOR);
        }
        if ((mouseData == 'm') || (mouseData == 'M'))
```

Listing 9.4   horDimLine()   **493**

```
                          {
                              moveFlag = 1;
                              _putimage(xvert-5,yvert-5,imageCursor,_GXOR);
                              for (i=0; i<numVert; i++)
                              {
                                  ysplineOld[i] = (double) plines[j][2*i+1];
                                  xsplineOld[i] = (double) plines[j][2*i];
                              }
                          }
                          if (moveFlag == 1)
                          {
                              _setcolor(BLACK);
                              if (k == 0)
                                  _moveto(plines[j][0],plines[j][1]);
                              else
                                  _moveto(plines[j][2*(k-1)],plines[j][2*(k-1)+1]);
                              _lineto(plines[j][2*k],plines[j][2*k+1]);
                              _lineto(plines[j][2*(k+1)],plines[j][2*(k+1)+1]);
                              _moveto(xvert,yvert);
                              _lineto(x,y);
                              cubicBSpline(numVert,xsplineOld,ysplineOld);

                              _setcolor(WHITE);
                              xvert = plines[j][2*k] = x;
                              yvert = plines[j][2*k+1] = y;
                              redraw(nLines,nPlines);

                              for (i=0; i<numVert; i++)
                              {
                                  xsplineOld[i] = xspline[i] = (double) plines[j][2*i];

                                  ysplineOld[i] = yspline[i] = (double) plines[j][2*i+1];
                              }
                              cubicBSpline(numVert,xspline,yspline);
                          }
                      xold = x; yold = y;
                  } while(mouseData != RETURN);
                  _putimage(xvert-5,yvert-5,imageCursor,_GXOR);
          }
```

LISTING 9.4: horDimLine()

In the subroutine horDimLine(), the color of the dimension lines is set to green, and the arrow size parameter *asz* is set equal to the value 2. The counter *dimCount* is set equal to the value 1 before the origin of the first extension line is selected, the value 2 just before the second extension-line origin is selected, the value 3 just before the location of the dimension line is selected, and afterward it is increased to the value 4, resulting in an exit from the *do while* loop.

When the first point is selected with the mouse button, the values (*x,y*) are set equal to the origin of the left extension line (*xl,yl*). When the second point is selected, it is set equal to the right extension line origin (*xr,yr*), unless *x* is less than *xl,* in which case the second point is set equal to (*xl,yl*) and the first point to (*xr,yr*). In this example, the extension lines are drawn starting at a distance *dy* = 3 pixels from the extension line origin, and extending 2*dy* = 6 pixels beyond the extension line position *yc*. In AutoCAD these distances can be adjusted by changing dimension system variables.

At the end of the subroutine the extension lines, dimension line, arrowheads, and text are placed in the drawing. The text (label) is obtained from the dimension line length (*xr* − *xl*). To provide space for this text, its length *dx* in pixels is computed by the function _getgtextextent(). The arrowheads are constructed by drawing a triangle and filling it by using the function _floodfill().

```
void horDimLine(void)
{
    char label[10];
    int  n,dimCount,dx,dy,asz;
    int  xa,ya,xb,yb,xl,yl,xr,yr,xc,yc;

    _setcolor(GREEN);
    asz = 2; imageCursor = imageCross;
    _settextposition(30,1);
    printf("         First extension line origin:                    ");
    dimCount = 1;
    _putimage(xold-5,yold-5,imageCursor,_GXOR);
    do
    {
        mouseData = mouseRead();
        if (x < xmin) x = xmin; if (x > xmax) x = xmax;
        if (y < ymin) y = ymin; if (y > ymax) y = ymax;

        if (snapFlag == 1)
        {
            x = snap*(x/snap); y = snap*(y/snap);
        }
        _putimage(xold-5,yold-5,imageCursor,_GXOR);
        _putimage(x-5,y-5,imageCursor,_GXOR);
        if ((mouseData == 'g') || (mouseData == 'G'))
        {
            gridFlag = 1 - gridFlag;
            gridPlot();
        }
        if ((mouseData == 's') || (mouseData == 'S'))
            snapFlag = 1 - snapFlag;
```

Listing 9.4   horDimLine()   **495**

```
_settextposition (1,40);
printf (" x=%3i y=%3i",x,y);

if (button == LEFT_BUTTON)
{
    switch(dimCount)
    {
    case 1:
        xl = x; yl = y;
        _settextposition(30,1);
        printf("      Second extension line origin:    ");
        break;
    case 2:
        if (x < xl)
        {
            xr = xl; yr = yl;
            xl = x; yl = y;
        }
        else
        {
            xr = x; yr = y;
        }
        _settextposition(30,1);
        printf(" Dimension line location: ");
        break;
    case 3:
        xc = x; yc = y;
    }
    dimCount = dimCount + 1;
}
    xold = x; yold = y;
} while(dimCount < 4);
_putimage(xold-5,yold-5,imageCursor,_GXOR);
sprintf(label,"%d",(xr-xl));
dx = _getgtextextent(label);
if (yc > yl)
    dy = 3;
else
    dy = -3;
_moveto(xl,yl+dy); _lineto(xl,yc+2*dy);
_moveto(xr,yr+dy); _lineto(xr,yc+2*dy);
_moveto(xl+1,yc); _lineto(xl+6*asz,yc-asz);
_lineto(xl+6*asz,yc+asz); _lineto(xl+1,yc);
_floodfill(xl+10,yc,GREEN);
_moveto(xl+12,yc); _lineto((xl+xr-dx-10)/2,yc);
_moveto(xr-1,yc);_lineto(xr-6*asz,yc-asz);
_lineto(xr-6*asz,yc+asz); _lineto(xr-1,yc);
_floodfill(xr-10,yc,GREEN);
```

```
        _moveto(xr-12,yc); _lineto((xl+xr+dx+9)/2,yc);
        _moveto((xl+xr-dx)/2,yc-8);
        _outgtext(label);
        _setcolor(WHITE);
    }
```

LISTING 9.5: SLIDER BAR PROGRAM

In the subroutine slider() contained in the program below, the rectangles and up/down arrows for the slider are drawn first, then a filled rectangle is drawn at the initial position of the scroll box. The last part of slider() contains a *do while* loop that carries out changes to *yval* and to the scroll box position. A switch() function keeps track of the different operations in each of the five regions. When *yval* is changed, the filled box is erased at its old position with the color black, and drawn at its new position in white.

You can easily incorporate this slider program into applications you create.

```
#include <stdio.h>
#include <graph.h>
#include <dos.h>
#define ESC        27
#define MOUSE      51
#define LEFT_BUTTON 1
#define BLACK       0
#define WHITE      15

void     cursorOn(void),cursorOff(void),slider(void);
int      mouseInit(void),mouseRead(void);

union REGS   reg;
int          option,choice,mouseData,sliderFlag;
int          x,y,button,xref,yref,buttonref;
int          xmin=0,xmax=625,ymin=0,ymax=465;

void main(void)
{
    _setvideomode (_VRES16COLOR );
    if (mouseInit() == 0)
    {
        printf ("Error, mouse isn't working\n");
        exit(1);
    }
    cursorOn();
    slider();

    _setvideomode (_DEFAULTMODE);
}
```

Listing 9.5   Slider BarProgram   **497**

```
void slider(void)
{
    int i,region,xsmin,xsmax;
    int yumin,yumax,ylmin,ylmax,yval,yvalold,ybox,yboxold;
    int xarw[] ={1,7,13,10,10,4,4,1};
    int yarw[] = {7,13,7,7,2,2,7,7};

    xsmin = 401; xsmax = xsmin + 14;
    yumin = 224; yumax = yumin + 16;
    ylmin = yumin + 132; ylmax = ylmin + 16;
    yval = yvalold = 50;
    _settextposition(13,47); printf("yval = %d    ",yval);
    _moveto(xsmin-1,ylmin); _lineto(xsmin-1,yumax);
    _moveto(xsmax+1,ylmin); _lineto(xsmax+1,yumax);
    _rectangle(_GBORDER,xsmin-1,yumin,xsmax+1,yumax);
    _rectangle(_GBORDER,xsmin-1,ylmin,xsmax+1,ylmax);
    for (i=0; i<8; i++)
    {
        if (i == 0)
            _moveto(xsmin+xarw[i],yumin+16-yarw[i]);
        else
            _lineto(xsmin+xarw[i],yumin+16-yarw[i]);
    }
    for (i=0; i<8; i++)
    {
        if (i == 0)
            _moveto(xsmin+xarw[i],ylmin+yarw[i]);
        else
            _lineto(xsmin+xarw[i],ylmin+yarw[i]);
    }
    ybox = yboxold = ylmin-yval-1;
    _rectangle(_GFILLINTERIOR,xsmin,ybox-14,xsmax,ybox);

    do
    {
        mouseData = mouseRead();
        if (x < xmin) x = xmin; if (x > xmax-15) x = xmax-15;
        if (y < ymin) y = ymin; if (y > ymax-15) y = ymax-15;

        sliderFlag = 0;

        if ((button == LEFT_BUTTON) && (x > xsmin) && (x < xsmax))
        {
            region = 0;
            if ((y > yumin) && (y < yumax)) region = 1;
            if ((y >= yumax) && (y < (yboxold-14))) region = 2;
            if ((y >= (yboxold-14)) && (y <= yboxold)) region = 3;
            if ((y > yboxold) && (y <= ylmin)) region = 4;
```

```
        if ((y > ylmin) && (y < ylmax)) region = 5;
        switch(region)
        {
            case 1:
                yval = yval + 1;
                if (yval > 100) yval = 100;
                break;
            case 2:
                yval = yval + 10;
                if (yval > 100) yval = 100;
                sliderFlag = 1;
                break;
            case 3:
                yval = ylmin-8-y;
                if (yval > 100) yval = 100;
                if (yval < 0) yval = 0;
                break;
            case 4:
                yval = yval - 10;
                if (yval < 0) yval = 0;
                sliderFlag = 1;
                break;
            case 5:
                yval = yval - 1;
                if (yval < 0) yval = 0;
        }
        if (yval != yvalold)
        {
            _settextposition(13,47); printf("yval = %d    ",yval);
            cursorOff();
            _setcolor(BLACK);
            ybox = ylmin-yval-1;
            _rectangle(_GFILLINTERIOR,xsmin,
            yboxold-14,xsmax,yboxold);
            _setcolor(WHITE);
            _rectangle(_GFILLINTERIOR,xsmin,ybox-14,xsmax,ybox);
            cursorOn();
        }
        yvalold = yval; yboxold = ybox;
    }
} while(mouseData != ESC);
}


int mouseRead(void)
{
    do
    {
        if (kbhit()) return getch();
```

Listing 10.1   Rotary Engine Program   **499**

```
        reg.x.ax = 3;
        int86(MOUSE, &reg, &reg);
        x = reg.x.cx;
        y = reg.x.dx;
        button = reg.x.bx;
    } while (x == xref && y == yref && button == buttonref);
    xref = x; yref = y;
    if (sliderFlag == 0)
        buttonref = -1;
    else
        buttonref = button;
}
```

LISTING 10.1: ROTARY ENGINE PROGRAM

In the rotary engine program below, the variables *e, s, v,* and *w* represent the following Greek variables from the equations in section 10.5: ε, σ, ν, and ω other Greek symbols are written out: *alpha, phi,* and *theta* in the program represent α, ϕ, and θ. All other variables are essentially the same as in the formulas: for example, *rb* and *rg* are the base circle radius (fixed gear radius) and the generating circle radius (interior gear radius). In the program, the formulas include the scale factor *sf* to give the variables appropriate magnitudes for display on the computer screen. Also, plus and minus signs have been reversed in equations for y-variables to account for the reversed directions of screen and world y-values.

In the subroutine wankel(), required quantities are first calculated with equations 10.31–10.34 and 10.39. Next, a *while* loop is continued until any key is pressed. In this loop, the coordinates *xp,yp* of the rotor center path are computed from the angle *w,* which is incremented on each pass through the loop by the program line $w = w - 0.1*PI$. The factor -0.1 is negative so that the rotor will turn clockwise; changing the factor -0.1 to a larger magnitude will speed up the rotor, and a smaller magnitude will slow it down. The rotor and chamber are drawn in white on the black background with the first call of the subroutines rotor() and chamber(). The rotor is drawn before the chamber so that it remains visible while the chamber is being drawn; this reduces the image flicker. The rotor is erased with black when rotor() is called a second time.

The subroutine chamber() draws the epitrochoidal chamber wall described by equations 10.26. The function _ellipse() draws the base circle representing the fixed gear, which is centered on the point (*xcen,ycen*).

The subroutine rotor() first draws the interior gear represented by the generating circle, which has a center moving along the path described by the coordinates *xp,yp*. The first *for* loop cycles through three values of *theta* for the three rotor sides. The geometry relating ϕ_1 and ϕ_2 to θ and α is shown in figure 10.16d. The *for* loop over *phi* draws the arc representing a rotor face, with *phi1* and *phi2* (ϕ_1 and ϕ_2) being the arc boundary angles and *rc* the radius of curvature. The coordinates *xc,yc* for the center of curvature are computed from the rotor's center path point (*xp,yp*), *theta,* and *ro* (R_0 in figure 10.16d).

```c
#include <math.h>
#include <graph.h>

#define PI 3.141593
#define BLACK 0
#define WHITE 15

void     wankel(void),chamber(void),rotor(void);

int      xp,yp,xc,yc,rg,rb;
int      xcen=250,ycen=180;
double   sf=48.0,e=0.45;
double   s,w,v,x,y,rc,r0,h1,w1,alpha,theta,phi,phi1,phi2;

void main(void)
{
    _setvideomode(_VRES16COLOR);
    wankel();
    _setvideomode(_DEFAULTMODE);
}

void wankel(void)
{
    rb = (int) (sf*2*e); rg = (int) (sf*3*e);
    rc = sf*(9- 6*e + 4*e*e)/(3- 4*e);
    r0 = rc - sf*(3- 2*e);
    h1 = sf*1.5*sqrt(3); w1 = sf*(1.5 - 2*e);
    alpha = atan(h1/(rc-w1));
    w = 0.0;

    while (!kbhit())
      {
          xp = xcen - (int) (sf*e*cos(w));
          yp = ycen + (int) (sf*e*sin(w));
          v = w/3;
          _setcolor(WHITE);
          rotor();
          chamber();
          _setcolor(BLACK);
          rotor();
          w=w-0.1*PI;
      }
}

void chamber(void)
{
    for (s=0; s<2.01*PI; s=s+.05*PI)
      {
```

Listing 11.1   Program Subroutines for Walking Through a Scene   **501**

```
        x = sf*(3*cos(s) - e*cos(3*s));
        y = sf*(3*sin(s) - e*sin(3*s));
        if (s == 0) _moveto(xcen + (int) x,ycen - (int) y);
        _lineto(xcen + (int) x,ycen - (int) y);
    }
    _ellipse(_GBORDER,xcen-rb,ycen-rb,xcen+rb,ycen+rb);
}


void rotor(void)
{
    _ellipse(_GBORDER,xp-rg,yp-rg,xp+rg,yp+rg);

    for (theta=v; theta<(v+1.34*PI); theta=theta+2.*PI/3.)
    {
        xc = xp + (int) (r0*cos(theta));
        yc = yp - (int) (r0*sin(theta));
        phi1 = theta + PI - alpha;
        phi2 = theta + PI + alpha;
        _moveto(xc+(int) (rc*cos(phi1)),yc-(int) (rc*sin(phi1)));
        for (phi=phi1; phi<(phi2+.001); phi=phi+.1*(phi2-phi1))
        {
            _lineto(xc+(int) (rc*cos(phi)),yc-(int) (rc*sin(phi)));
        }
    }
}
```

LISTING 11.1: PROGRAM SUBROUTINES FOR WALKING THROUGH A SCENE

The subroutines walkThrough(), drawScene(), and loadLines() given below are incorporated into the interactive viewing program of section 11.4 to provide a walkthrough of the wireframe house shown in figure 11.22. The subroutine walkThrough() replaces moveViewpoint() in the program presented in section 11.4, drawScene() replaces drawCube(), and loadLines() replaces the data for the line arrays given in the earlier program.

In the subroutine walkThrough(), the *if* statement handles two cases determined by whether or not the mouse button is depressed. While the mouse button is depressed, the angle θ changes with the mouse x-coordinate in the same manner as in the subroutine moveViewpoint(), and the viewpoint coordinates (xv,yv) move forward and backward in the view direction with changes with the mouse y-coordinate. Because a unit vector in the view direction from (xv,yv) to (xt,yt) has the components $(cost,sint)$, the relations $xv = xv + 0.2*cost*dy$ and $yv = yv + 0.2*sint*dy$ produce viewpoint motion in the forward and backward directions in response to the mouse motion dy. The 0.2 factor may be changed up or down for faster or slower motion (similarly, the factor 0.01 in the *theta* relation may be changed for faster or slower changes in angle). The position of the target point is updated so that it remains a fixed distance r ahead of the viewpoint in the direction of view. Because here rotation occurs about the viewpoint, rather than about the target point as in the previous subroutines, the value of *r* does not affect the results; this value is set by the initial target and viewpoint positions.

When the mouse button is not depressed, changes in the mouse y-coordinate produce forward and backward motion in the scene, and changes in the mouse x-coordinate result in left and right motion. This result is obtained by the relations for updating *xv* and *yv* in terms of *dx* and *dy* mouse motions given under the *if* statement in the walkThrough() subroutine.

```c
void walkThrough(void)
{
    xold = 600; yold = 0;
    xt = -80; yt = 400; zt = 0;
    xv = xt; yv = yt + 10;
    theta = atan2(yv-yt,xv-xt);
    cost = cos(theta); sint = sin(theta);
    r = sqrt((xv-xt)*(xv-xt)+(yv-yt)*(yv-yt));
    do
    {
        mouseData = mouseRead();

        dx = x-xold; dy = y - yold;
        if (button == LEFT_BUTTON)
        {
            xv = xv + 0.2*cost*dy;
            yv = yv + 0.2*sint*dy;
            theta = theta + 0.01*dx;
            cost = cos(theta); sint = sin(theta);
        }
        else
        {
            xv = xv + 0.2*(- sint*dx + cost*dy);
            yv = yv + 0.2*(cost*dx + sint*dy);
        }
        xt = xv - r*cost; yt = yv - r*sint;
        _clearscreen(_GCLEARSCREEN);
        drawScene();

        xold = x; yold = y;
    } while(mouseData != ESC);

}

void drawScene(void)
{
    int k;
    double xc1,yc1,zc1,xc2,yc2,zc2,xper,yper;
    double zpp=500,zclip=20;
```

Listing 11.1   Program Subroutines for Walking Through a Scene   **503**

```
for (k=0; k<nLines; k++)
{
    xc1 = -sint*(lines[k][0]-xt) + cost*(lines[k][1]-yt);
    yc1 = lines[k][2]-zt;
    zc1 = -cost*(lines[k][0]-xt) - sint*(lines[k][1]-yt) + r;
    xc2 = -sint*(lines[k][3]-xt) + cost*(lines[k][4]-yt);
    yc2 = lines[k][5]-zt;
    zc2 = -cost*(lines[k][3]-xt) - sint*(lines[k][4]-yt) + r;
    if (zc1 > zclip || zc2 > zclip)
    {
        if (zc1 < zclip)
        {
            xc1 = xc2 - (xc2-xc1)*(zc2-zclip)/(zc2-zc1);
            yc1 = yc2 - (yc2-yc1)*(zc2-zclip)/(zc2-zc1);
            zc1 = zclip;
        }
        if (zc2 < zclip)
        {
            xc2 = xc1 - (xc1-xc2)*(zc1-zclip)/(zc1-zc2);
            yc2 = yc1 - (yc1-yc2)*(zc1-zclip)/(zc1-zc2);
            zc2 = zclip;
        }
        xper = xc1*zpp/zc1; yper = yc1*zpp/zc1;
        _moveto(320 + (int) xper,240 - (int) yper);
        xper = xc2*zpp/zc2; yper = yc2*zpp/zc2;
        _lineto(320 + (int) xper,240 - (int) yper);
    }
}
}
```

The subroutine loadLines() is called in main() just before walkThrough(). New global variables are listed below, with the one-dimensional arrays containing data for eight rectangular blocks or boxes. These arrays provide the x and y starting point for a block, and also its width, depth, starting height position, and ending height position. The blocks, each composed of 12 line segments, are used to construct the gallery walls, openings in the walls, hallways to the rooms, and the two rooms. Additional lines are required for roofs, and for floor tiles in the gallery. The viewpoint is set at zero height, so that two-point perspective is achieved by setting $zt = 0$.

```
double lines[230][6];
double x1=4,x2=16,x3=28,h2=20,h3=32;            /* gallery data */
double xstart[] = {0,28,28,32,48,0,-20,-84};    /* block data   */
double ystart[] = {0,0,46,46,20,200,200,176};
double width[] = {4,4,4,16,64,4,20,64};
double depth[] = {260,260,16,16,64,16,16,64};
double height0[] = {-10,-10,-10,-10,-10,-10,-10,-10};
double height1[] = {20,20,10,10,10,10,10,25};
```

```c
void loadLines(void)
{
    int i,j;
    double xs,ys,w,d,h0,h1;
                            /* 8 blocks of 12 lines each for     */
    for (j=0; j<8; j++)     /* gallery walls, openings in walls, */
    {                       /* hallways to rooms, and rooms.      */
        xs = xstart[j]; ys = ystart[j];
        w = width[j]; d = depth[j];
        h0 = height0[j]; h1 = height1[j];
        i = 12*j;

        lines[i][0]=lines[i+2][3]=lines[i+3][0]=lines[i+3][3]=xs;
        lines[i+4][0]=lines[i+4][3]=lines[i+7][0]=lines[i+7][3]=xs;
        lines[i+8][0]=lines[i+10][3]=lines[i+11][0]=lines[i+11][3]=xs;

        lines[i][3]=lines[i+1][0]=lines[i+1][3]=lines[i+2][0]=xs+w;
        lines[i+5][0]=lines[i+5][3]=lines[i+6][0]=lines[i+6][3]=xs+w;
        lines[i+8][3]=lines[i+9][0]=lines[i+9][3]=lines[i+10][0]=xs+w;

        lines[i][1]=lines[i][4]=lines[i+1][1]=lines[i+3][4]=ys;
        lines[i+4][1]=lines[i+4][4]=lines[i+5][1]=lines[i+5][4]=ys;
        lines[i+8][1]=lines[i+8][4]=lines[i+9][1]=lines[i+11][4]=ys;

        lines[i+1][4]=lines[i+2][1]=lines[i+2][4]=lines[i+3][1]=ys+d;
        lines[i+6][1]=lines[i+6][4]=lines[i+7][1]=lines[i+7][4]=ys+d;
        lines[i+9][4]=lines[i+10][1]=lines[i+10][4]=lines[i+11][1]=ys+d;

        lines[i][2]=lines[i][5]=lines[i+1][2]=lines[i+1][5]=h0;
        lines[i+2][2]=lines[i+2][5]=lines[i+3][2]=lines[i+3][5]=h0;
        lines[i+4][2]=lines[i+5][2]=lines[i+6][2]=lines[i+7][2]=h0;

        lines[i+4][5]=lines[i+5][5]=lines[i+6][5]=lines[i+7][5]=h1;
        lines[i+8][2]=lines[i+8][5]=lines[i+10][5]=lines[i+11][2]=h1;
        lines[i+11][5]=lines[i+10][2]=lines[i+9][2]=lines[i+9][5]=h1;
    }
    lines[96][0]=lines[96][3]=x2; lines[96][1]=0; lines[96][4]=260;
    lines[96][2]=lines[96][5]=h3; /* roof beam for gallery */
    for (i=97; i<=150; i=i+2) /* 54 lines for gallery roof */
    {
        lines[i][0]=x1; lines[i+1][0]=x3;
        lines[i][3]=lines[i+1][3]=x2;
        lines[i][1]=lines[i+1][1]=lines[i][4]=lines[i+1][4]=5*(i-97);
        lines[i][2]=lines[i+1][2]=h2;
        lines[i][5]=lines[i+1][5]=h3;
    }
    for (i=151; i<=155; i++) /* long lines for gallery floor tiles */
    {
```

Listing 12.1   Program for a Fractal Mountain   **505**

```
        lines[i][0]=lines[i][3]=8+4*(i-151);
        lines[i][1]=0; lines[i][4]=260;
        lines[i][2]=lines[i][5]=h0;
    }
    for (i=156; i<=221; i++) /* short lines for gallery floor tiles */
    {
        lines[i][0]=x1; lines[i][3]=x3;
        lines[i][1]=lines[i][4]=4*(i-156);
        lines[i][2]=lines[i][5]=h0;
    }
    for (i=0; i<=4; i=i+4)    /* roofs for the two rooms */
    {
        if (i==0) j=4; else j=7;
        lines[222+i][0]=lines[223+i][0]=xstart[j];
        lines[224+i][0]=lines[225+i][0]=xstart[j]+width[j];
        lines[222+i][1]=lines[224+i][1]=ystart[j];
        lines[223+i][1]=lines[225+i][1]=ystart[j]+depth[j];
        lines[222+i][2]=lines[223+i][2]=lines[224+i][2]
                                =lines[225+i][2]=height1[j];
        lines[222+i][3]=lines[223+i][3]=lines[224+i][3]
                        =lines[225+i][3]=xstart[j]+.5*width[j];
        lines[222+i][4]=lines[223+i][4]=lines[224+i][4]
                        =lines[225+i][4]=ystart[j]+.5*depth[j];
        lines[222+i][5]=lines[223+i][5]=lines[224+i][5]
                                =lines[225+i][5]=height1[j]+20;
    }
}
```

LISTING 12.1: PROGRAM FOR A FRACTAL MOUNTAIN

The Microsoft C program listed below builds a fractal mountain by using two subroutines: calcVert() and plotSurface(). Following the procedures described in chapter 8, the subroutine calcVert() uses the matrix $vert[k][j]$ to store vertex coordinates, and the matrix $vn[m][i]$ to store vertex numbers. Recall that the matrix $vert[k][j]$ provides coordinate values for vertex number k, with j = 0, 1, and 2 corresponding to the x, y, and z values. For the triangular faces considered here, $vn[m][i]$ gives the vertex numbers that constitute face m, with the index i taking on the values 0, 1, 2, and 3 for the three vertex points defining the face. With the index i, the first vertex is listed twice, with index 0 for moving to it, and with index 3 for drawing to it at the completion of the face; see the subroutine plotSurface() below.

    The program produces a mountain having an isosceles triangle for its base. On this base triangle, the parameter *side* is the length of the top (unequal) side, and the parameter *height* is the height of the base triangle (distance in the y-direction from the bottom vertex to the top side). For the examples shown in this section, the particular ratio *height/side* = 0.6 was used, although the program can accept any ratio to produce a desired isosceles triangle. The angle α subtended at the bottom vertex is related to the ratio by the following formula: $\alpha = 2 \cot^{-1}(2ratio)$, where $ratio \equiv height/side$. Some special cases of interest are $ratio = \sqrt{3}/2$, which gives an equilateral triangle ($\alpha = 60°$), and $ratio = 1/\sqrt{2}$, which gives a right triangle ($\alpha = 90°$).

The number of horizontal rows of triangular elements in the base is defined as nr in the program, with the total number of triangular elements (faces) being $numFaces = nr \cdot nr$. The total number of vertices equals $(nr + 1) \cdot (nr + 2)/2$. Thus for a mountain of level 5 ($numLevel = 5$), there are 1024 faces and 561 vertices, so the matrices are dimensioned as follows: $vn[1024][4]$ and $vert[561][3]$.

The first set of nested *for* loops (with indices i and j) in the subroutine calcVert() prescribes the vertex coordinates x and y to the values determined by the specified quantities *side, height,* and *numLevel.* These quantities determine the base triangles, which do not change during the program calculations. Also, initial vertical displacements (vertex z values) are set equal to zero.

Vertex numbers start with 0 at the bottom of the base triangle. In the nested i and j *for* loops the index i increases from 0 to nr along the left edge of the base triangle, and j increases from 0 to i along a horizontal line of vertices. A vertex number is given by the relation $k = i(i + 1)/2 + j$, where the first term represents the number of vertices in the triangular region below row i.

In subsequent *for* loops, the vertices are given random displacements in the vertical direction. Integer random numbers from 0 to 32,767 are provided by the function rand(). A fixed set of random numbers is given for each value of a seed number, specified as the argument in the function srand(). That is, different seed numbers give different sets of random numbers, but a particular set of random numbers can be generated whenever its particular seed number is used in srand().

The random integer generated by rand() is changed to a floating-point (double) number, and divided by 32,767 to produce the random number *rnd* that lies between 0 and 1. In the program, the function rand() is called each time a vertex is displaced proportional to *rnd;* thus vertices are displaced by different random numbers to produce a "rough" surface.

The sequence of vertex displacements is illustrated in figures 12.6a–d. Figure 12.6a corresponds to $n = 0$ in the second set of nested *for* loops in the subroutine calcVert(), for a surface of 64 triangular faces ($numLevel = 3$). At this zeroth level, the three corner vertices are displaced from the xy-plane, as illustrated by the arrows. After these corner vertices have been displaced, then all of the other vertices must be moved to positions in the plane formed by the corner vertices. The next set of *for* loops uses linear interpolation to raise the left and right edges of the base triangle to the plane of the corner vertices. After this is done, a set of *for* loops uses these edge vertex positions to raise the interior vertices.

Figure 12.6b illustrates displacements at the first level, corresponding to $n = 1$ in the second set of *for* loops in calcVert(). At this level, the base triangle is divided into four triangles, each with 16 triangular elements (faces). The variable *dRows* denotes the number of rows of triangular elements in a displaced triangular region. For the case $numLevel = 3$ considered in figures 12.6a–d, *dRows* takes on the values 8, 4, 2, and 1 when n equals 0, 1, 2, and 3, respectively.

Listing 12.1   Program for a Fractal Mountain   **507**

Figures 12.6c and d illustrate displacements at levels $n = 2$ and 3. If *numLevel* is set equal to 5, then the 1024 faces result in the surface displacements shown in figure 12.6e. It is evident from figures 12.6 that carrying the fractal subdivision to higher levels corresponds to carrying the random displacements to smaller scales.

In the program, the vertical displacements are given in an *if* loop in the second set of nested *for* loops. These displacements are proportional to the random number *rnd* multiplied by the variables *side* and by *dRows*. The *side* factor is included in order to scale the displacements to the size of the base triangle. The *dRows* factor is included so that the displacements will be larger for the larger triangular regions than for the smaller ones (recall that *dRows* is proportional to the size of the triangular region being displaced). The additional factor of 0.8 shown in the program displacement relation is arbitrary and can be increased or decreased to change the displacement magnitudes.

The *if* statement sets the displacements equal to zero at the edges of the base triangle, as shown in figure 12.6f. Figures 12.6a–e have free edges, computed by replacing the *if* statement with just its last line. Besides the procedure of forcing zero displacements at the base triangle edges, another method of ensuring that the mountain edges reach a common level is to intersect the mountain with a horizontal plane (3Dface) to hide the portion of the mountain below the plane.

```
#include <stdlib.h>
#include <math.h>
#include <graph.h>

#define PI 3.141593

void    calcVertices(void),plotSurface(void);

int     numFaces,vn[1024][4];
double  vert[561][3];

main()
{
    _setvideomode ( _VRES16COLOR );
    calcVertices();
    getch();
    _setvideomode ( _DEFAULTMODE);
}

void calcVertices(void)
{
    int     i,j,k,m,n,i2,j2,k0,k1,k2;
    int     nr,dRows,denom,numLevel = 5;
    double  side,height,exponent,rnd;

    exponent = (double) numLevel;
    nr = (int) (pow(2.,exponent)+.5);
```

```c
    side = 360/nr;              /* length of a triangle side     */
    height = side/sqrt(3);      /* triangle height in y direction */
    numFaces = nr*nr;
    srand(5195);

    for (i=0; i<=nr; i++)
    {
        for (j=0; j<=i; j++)
        {
            k = i*(i+1)/2+j
            vert[k][0] = (j-.5*i)*side;
            vert[k][1] = i*height;
            vert[k][2] = 0; /* start with a flat surface */
        }
    }
    for (n=0; n<=numLevel; n++)
    {
        exponent = (double) n;
        denom = (int) (pow(2.,exponent)+.5);
        dRows = nr/denom;
        for (i=0; i<=nr; i=i+dRows)
        {
            for (j=0; j<=i; j=j+dRows)
            {
                rnd = ((double) rand())/32767;
                k = i*(i+1)/2+j;
                if ((i==nr) || (i==j) || (j==0))
                    vert[k][2] = 0;
                else
                    vert[k][2] = vert[k][2] + 0.8*rnd*side*dRows;
            }
        }
        for (i=0; i<nr; i=i+dRows)
        {
            for <j=0; j<=i; j=j+dRows)
            {
                k0 = i*(i+1)/2+j;
                k2 = (i+dRows)*(i+dRows+1)/2+j;
                for (i2=i+1; i2<i+dRows; i2++)
                { /* left edge of triangle*/
                    k1 = i2*(i2+1)/2+j;
                    vert[k1][2] = vert[k0][2] + (vert[k2][2]-
                                        vert[k0][2])*(i2-i)/dRows;
                }
                k2 = (i+dRows)*(i+dRows+1)/2+j+dRows;
                for (i2=i+1; i2<i+dRows; i2++)
                { /* right edge of triangle */
                    k1 = i2*(i2+1)/2+j+i2-i;
```

Listing 12.1   Program for a Fractal Mountain   **509**

```
                    vert[k1][2] = vert[k0][2] + (vert[k2][2]-
                                      vert[k0][2])*(i2-i)/dRows;
            }
        }
    }
    for (i=0; i<nr; i=i+dRows)
    {
        for (j=0; j<=i; j=j+dRows; i2++)
        {
            for (i2=i+2; i2<=i+dRows; i2++)
            {                  /* downward-pointing triangles */
                k0 = i2*(i2+1)/2+j;
                k2 = i2*(i2+1)/2+j+i2-i;
                for (j2=j+1; j2<=j+i2-i; j2++)
                {
                    k1 = i2*(i2+1)/2+j2;
                    vert[k1][2] = vert[k0][2] + vert[k2][2]-
                                    vert[k0][2])*(j2-j)/(i2-i);
                }
            }
            if (j<i)
            {
                for (i2=i; i2<i+dRows-1; i2++)
                {                  /*upward-pointing triangles */
                    k0 = i2*(i2+1)/2+j+i2-i;
                    k2 = i2*(i2+1)/2+j+dRows;
                    for (j2=j+i2-i+1; j2-j+dRows; j2++)
                    {
                        k1 = i2*(i2+1)/2+j2;
                        vert[k1][2] = vert[k0][2] +
                (vert[k2][2]-vert[k0][2])*(j2-j+i+i-i2)/(dRows+i-i2);
                    }
                }
            }
        }
    }
}
for (i=0; i<nr; i++)
{
    for (j=0; j<=2*i; j=j+2)
    {
        m = i*i+j;                      /* m is the face number */
        k = (i*(i+3)+j+4)/2;
        vn[m][0] = vn[m][3] = k;
        vn[m][1] = k-1;
        vn[m][2] = k-i-2;
        if (j < 2*i)
        {
```

```
                    vn[m+1][0] = vn[m+1][3] = k-i-2;
                    vn[m+1][1] = k-i-1;
                    vn[m+1][2] = k;
                }
            }
        }
    plotSurface();
}

void plotSurface(void)
{
    int      m,k,vnum,xplot,yplot,xcen=320,yb=360;
    double   phi,sinp,cosp,xw,yw,zw,sf = 1.5;

    phi = 70*PI/180; sinp = sin(phi); cosp = cos(phi);

    for (m=0; m<numFaces; m++)
    {
        for (k=0; k<=3; k++)
        {
            vnum = vn[m][k];
            xw = vert[vnum][0]; yw = vert[vnum][1];
            zw = vert[vnum][2];
            xplot = xcen + (int) (sf*xw);
            yplot = yb - (int) (sf*(yw*cosp+zw*sinp));
            if (k==0)
                _moveto(xplot,yplot);
            else
                _lineto(xplot,yplot);
        }
    }
}
```

In the above program listing, the random vertical displacements are proportional to the variable *dRow* to produce displacements that decrease in proportion to the size of the triangular region being displaced. The displacement formula can be generalized so that the displacement is proportional to $(dRow)^s$, where s is a power to be chosen. When $s > 1$, then the displacements of small regions are reduced, whereas for $s < 1$, the displacements of small regions are increased. To keep the average of all displacements approximately the same for different s values, the coefficient is changed from the value 0.8 given in the listing.

Figures 12.7a–c show the effect of decreasing the power s from 1.5 to 1 to 0.5. Figures 12.7a–c were computed with a random seed number equal to 5195, the same as used for figures 12.6. Changing the random seed number provides different random displacements: figures 12.7d–e were calculated with $s = 0.5$, and seed numbers of 14242 and 24929, respectively.

Listing 12.1   Program for a Fractal Mountain   **511**

Another way of changing the shape of the mountain is to add a mean shape to the calculated random displacements. Figure 12.7f has the same seed number (24929) and s value (0.5) as 12.7e, but the random displacements were reduced in magnitude by 1/3 (coefficient of 1.2 rather than 1.8), and the following expression was added to the vertical displacements: $0.05j(i − j)(nr − i)$. This expression represents a smooth mound having zero height at the edges of the base triangle. (The three edges are given by the formulas $j = 0$, $i = j$, and $i = nr$, where the indices i and j are defined as described previously in the discussion of vertex numbers).

Another variation of the mountain program consists of using base triangles with different *height/side* ratios, which can change the steepness on the front sides relative to the back. Also, triangular mountains can be placed in positions where they partially overlap, and they can be intersected with a ground plane placed at any vertical position. These procedures can be used to produce a more complex mountain base when observed with hidden lines removed.

Rendering will make the mountain images more realistic. Even a plan view, which appears as a triangular mesh in line drawings, will look like a top view of a mountain when illumination and shadows are added to the scene.

The plotSurface() subroutine plots the faces on the display screen from a front view ($\theta = -90°$ in equation 11.23), with ϕ being a variable (chosen in the above listing as $\phi = 70°$, corresponding to an angle of 20° above the xy-plane). The painter's hidden-line algorithm discussed in section 12.8 could be added to this plot subroutine. Alternately, the program can write a DXF file to port 3Dfaces to AutoCAD (or other CAD program), which can incorporate hidden-line options along with the other standard display features.

To adapt the above program to writing a DXF file, <graph.h> is replaced by <stdio.h> in the list of include files, and the global variable FILE *dxf is declared. The main() routine is changed to include calls to the following three subroutines: writeStart(), calcVertices(), and writeEnd().

The writeStart() and writeEnd() subroutine are listed in section 8.2. The subroutine calcVertices() is the same as that above, except that lines in plotSurface() are replaced by the following statements.

```
for (m=0; m<numFaces; m++)
{
    for (i=0; i<=3; i++)
    {
        vnum = vn[m][i];
        xw[i] = vert[vnum][0];
        yw[i] = vert[vnum][1];
        zw[i] = vert[vnum][2];
    }
    writeFace(xw,yw,zw);
}
```

The subroutine writeFace(xw,yw,zw) is the same as that given in section 8.2.

LISTING 12.2: PROGRAM FOR A RULED SURFACE

This ruled surface is formed by placing faces between two 3-D B-splines, as illustrated in figure 12.20. In the subroutine ruleSurf() listed below, the two B-splines are identified by the variable *splNum,* which has the value 0 for the first curve and the value 1 for the second curve. The first curve is prescribed by the following arrays of the control points (*xspl*0[], *yspl*0[], and *zspl*0[]. Similarly, the second curve is determined by *xspl*1[], *yspl*1[], and *zspl*1[]. These arrays are dimensioned to handle four additional control points beyond those given in the data because the first and last points are expanded to triple points in the subroutine ruleBSpline().

The B-splines are calculated by extending the subroutine cubicBSpline() of section 7.6 to include z-coordinates and to calculate curve lengths for dividing the curve into *ne* equal lengths. (Here the number of elements *ne* equals the number of faces *numFaces* and corresponds to the AutoCAD system variable SURFTAB1.)

To rule off equal lengths along the spline curves, the subroutine ruleBSpline() is called twice from ruleSurf(), first with the data for the first curve, then with the data for the second curve. At the beginning of the function ruleBSpline(), the first two control points and the last two control points are extrapolated in order to force the cubic B-spline curve to reach the original starting and ending control points. (This procedure requires that the spline have at least five control points; see equations 7.65 and the discussion in section 7.6.)

In ruleBSpline(), after setting the initial distance variable *s* equal to zero, nested *for* loops in *i* and *j* calculate the overall length of the spline curve and store the value in the variable called *length.* The next *for* loop divides the length into *ne* equal parts and stores the values into the array *len*[].

In the remainder of the subroutine ruleBSpline(), the coordinates of the surface vertex points are calculated. Along each B-spline curve, the initial vertex point (xp, yp, zp) is identified by the number *splNum,* which equals 0 and 1 for the two curves. The remaining vertex numbers are determined by stepping an index by 2 along each spline curve; see figure 12.20. The coordinate values for the vertex points along the curve are calculated in the final set of nested *for* loops. These coordinate values are stored in the array *vert*[][].

After the subroutine ruleBSpline() is called in ruleSurf(), a *for* loop calculates the vertex numbers for each face and stores the values in the array *vn*[][]. The formulas for the vertex numbers can readily be checked by referring to figure 12.20.

At the end of the ruleSurf() function, plotSurface() is called to plot the surface. The subroutine plotSurface() is not listed here because it is the same as that given for the mountain program in listing 12.1 above, except that here the faces are quadrilaterals rather than triangles (thus the vertex number loops over five values rather than four values). Also, in plotSurface() a scale factor *sf* of the order of 100 should be used for the particular polylines given below.

```
#include <math.h>
#include <graph.h>

#define PI 3.141593
```

Listing 12.2   Program for a Ruled Surface   **513**

```
void    ruleBSpline(int splNum,int n,double x[],double y[],double z[]);
void    ruleSurf(void),plotSurface(void);

int     vn[12][5],numFaces = 12, ne = 12;
double  vert[26][3];

void    main(void)
{
    _setvideomode ( _VRES16COLOR );
    ruleSurf();
    getch();
    _setvideomode ( _DEFAULTMODE);
}


void ruleSurf(void)
{
    int     i,n1 = 6,n2 = 5;
    double  xspl0[6] = {1,2.5,2.5,2,2.5,3};
    double  yspl0[6] = {1,1,2,2.5,3,3}, zspl0[6] = {0,0,.5,.5,1,1};
    double  xspl1[5] = {3,3,4,5,5};
    double  yspl1[5] = {0,0,1,1.5,2.5}, zspl1[5] = {0,0,1,1,2};

    ruleBSpline(0,n1,xspl0,yspl0,zspl0);
    ruleBSpline(1,n2,xspl1,yspl1,zspl1);

    for (i=0; i<numFaces; i++)
    {
        vn[i][0] = vn[i][4] = 2*i; vn[i][1] = 2*i+1;
        vn[i][2] = 2*i+3; vn[i][3] = 2*i+2;
    }
    plotSurface();
}

void ruleBSpline(int splNum,int n,double x[],double y[],double z[])
{
    int     i,j,k,nisegs,ntsegs;
    double  t,dt,b0,b1,b2,b3,xp,yp,zp;
    double  xstart,ystart,zstart,xend,yend,zend;
    double  s,length,dx,dy,dz,ds,len[12];

    xstart = x[0]; ystart = y[0]; zstart = z[0];
    xend = x[n-1]; yend = y[n-1]; zend = z[n-1];

    x[0] = x[2]+6.*(x[0]-x[1]); x[1] = 1.5*x[1]-.5*x[2];
    y[0] = y[2]+6.*(y[0]-y[1]); y[1] = 1.5*y[1]-.5*y[2];
    z[0] = z[2]+6.*(z[0]-z[1]); z[1] = 1.5*z[1]-.5*z[2];
    x[n-1] = x[n-3]+6.*(x[n-1]-x[n-2]); x[n-2] = 1.5*x[n-2]-.5*x[n-3];
    y[n-1] = y[n-3]+6.*(y[n-1]-y[n-2]); y[n-2] = 1.5*y[n-2]-.5*y[n-3];
```

```
z[n-1] = z[n-3]+6.*(z[n-1]-z[n-2]); z[n-2] = 1.5*z[n-2]-.5*z[n-3];


nisegs = n - 3;
ntsegs = 20; dt = 1./(double) ntsegs;

xp = xstart; yp = ystart; zp = zstart;
s = 0; /* start measuring length with s = 0 at first point */
for (i=3; i<=nisegs+2; i++)
{
    for (j=0,t=0.;j<=ntsegs;j++,t+=dt)
    {
        b0 = t*t*t/6.;
        b1 = (1.+3.*t+3.*t*t-3.*t*t*t)/6.;
        b2 = (4.-6.*t*t+3.*t*t*t)/6.;
        b3 = (1.-3.*t+3.*t*t-t*t*t)/6.;
        dx = b3*x[i-3]+b2*x[i-2]+b1*x[i-1]+b0*x[i] - xp;
        dy = b3*y[i-3]+b2*y[i-2]+b1*y[i-1]+b0*y[i] - yp;
        dz = b3*z[i-3]+b2*z[i-2]+b1*z[i-1]+b0*z[i] - zp;
        ds = sqrt(dx*dx + dy*dy + dz*dz);
        s = s + ds;
        xp = xp + dx; yp = yp + dy; zp = zp + dz;}
    }
}
length = s;
for (k=1; k<ne; k++) /* divide length into ne equal parts */
{
    len[k] = (k*length)/(double) ne;
}
xp = vert[splNum][0] = xstart; yp = vert[splNum][1] = ystart;
zp = vert[splNum][2] = zstart;

s = 0;
for (i=3; i<=nisegs+2; i++) /* calculate vertex coordinates */
{
    for (j=0,t=0.;j<=ntsegs;j++,t+=dt)
    {
        b0 = t*t*t/6.;
        b1 = (1.+3.*t+3.*t*t-3.*t*t*t)/6.;
        b2 = (4.-6.*t*t+3.*t*t*t)/6.;
        b3 = (1.-3.*t+3.*t*t-t*t*t)/6.;
        dx = b3*x[i-3]+b2*x[i-2]+b1*x[i-1]+b0*x[i] - xp;
        dy = b3*y[i-3]+b2*y[i-2]+b1*y[i-1]+b0*y[i] - yp;
        dz = b3*z[i-3]+b2*z[i-2]+b1*z[i-1]+b0*z[i] - zp;
        ds = sqrt(dx*dx + dy*dy + dz*dz);

        for (k=1; k<ne; k++)
        {
            if ((s<len[k]) && ((s+ds)>=len[k]))
```

Listing 12.3   Program for a Bicubic Coons Patch   **515**

```
                    {
                        vert[2*k+splNum][0] = xp + len[k]-s)*dx/ds;
                        vert[2*k+splNum][1] = yp + (len[k]-s)*dy/ds;
                        vert[2*k+splNum][2] = zp + (len[k]-s)*dz/ds;
                    }
                }
                s = s + ds; xp = xp + dx; yp = yp + dy; zp = zp + dz;
            }
        }
        vert[2*ne+splNum][0] = xend; vert[2*ne+splNum][1] = yend;
        vert[2*ne+splNum][2] = zend;
    }
```

LISTING 12.3: PROGRAM FOR A BICUBIC COONS PATCH

The program for the bicubic Coons patch is similar to that given above for a ruled surface, except that the function edgeSurf() listed below is called from the main() function, rather than ruleSurf(). For this example program, the Coons patch is bounded by four cubic B-spline curves. Accordingly, function edgeSurf() includes four function calls to rule BSpline(), which as shown below, differs only slightly from the function of the same name given in the preceding listing.

The global variables, listed on the first two lines below, include different values for *tab*1 and *tab*2, which represent the AutoCAD variables SURFTAB1 and SURFTAB2. Thus the number of elements *ne* along a spline curve equals *tab*1 for splines 0 and 2, and equals *tab*2 for splines 1 and 3; see the *if* statement in the middle of ruleBSpline().

In the subroutine edgeSurf(), the spline control points and patch corners are assigned values, and the subroutine ruleBSpline() is called four times to rule off the spline curves at the appropriate intervals. Then the surface vertex coordinates are calculated with equation 12.5 in a set of nested *for* loops over *i* and *j*. The final set of nested *for* loops draws the surface by calling the function plotSurface().

```
int      vn[120][5],ne,tab1 = 12,tab2 =10,numFaces = 120;
double   vert[143][3];

void edgeSurf(void)
{
    int     i,j,k,m,n0 = 6,n1 = 5,n2 = 5,n3 = 6;
    double  u,v,f1u,f1v,f2u,f2v,rtab1 = 1./12.,rtab2 = 1./10;
    double  xspl0[10] = {1,2.5,2.5,2,2.5,3};
    double  yspl0[10] = {1,1,2,2.5,3,3}, zspl0[10] = {0,0,.5,.5,1,1};
    double  xspl1[9] = {1,1.5,2,2.5,3};
    double  yspl1[9] = {1,.5,.4,.5,0}, zspl1[9] = {0,0,0,0,0};
    double  xspl2[9] = {3,3,4,5,5};
    double  yspl2[9] = {0,0,1,1.5,2.5}, zspl2[9] = {0,0,1,1,2};
    double  xspl3[10] = {3,3.3,3.8,4.2,4.6,5};
```

```
double yspl3[10] = {3,2.6,2.4,2.3,2.4,2.5};
double zspl3[10] = {1,1.2,1.5,1.7,2,2};

vert[0][0] = 1; vert[0][1] = 1; vert[0][2] = 0;
vert[tab2][0] = 3; vert[tab2][1] = 0; vert[tab2][2] = 0;
vert[tab1*(tab2+1)][0] = 3; vert[tab1*(tab2+1)][1] = 3;
vert[tab1*(tab2+1)][2] = 1;
vert[(tab1+1)*(tab2+1)-1][0] = 5;
vert[(tab1+1)*(tab2+1)-1][1] = 2.5;
vert[(tab1+1)*(tab2+1)-1][2] = 2;

ruleBSpline(0,n0,xspl0,yspl0,zspl0);
ruleBSpline(1,n1,xspl1,yspl1,zspl1);
ruleBSpline(2,n2,xspl2,yspl2,zspl2);
ruleBSpline(3,n3,xspl3,yspl3,zspl3);

for (i=1; i<tab1; i++)
{
   for (j=1; j<tab2; j++)
   {
      v = i*rtab1; u = j*rtab2;
      f1u = (2.*u-3.)*u*u+1.; f1v = (2.*v-3.)*v*v+1.;
      f2u = (-2.*u+3.)*u*u; f2v = (-2.*v+3.)*v*v;
      m = i*(tab2+1) + j;
      for (k=0; k<3; k++)
      {
         vert[m][k] = f1v*vert[j][k]
                    + f2v*vert[tab1*(tab2+1)+j][k]
                    + f1u*vert[i*(tab2+1)][k]
                    + f2u*vert[i*(tab2+1)+tab2][k]
                    - (f2v*vert[tab1*(tab2+1)][0]
                    + f1v*vert[0][0])*f1u
                    - (f2v*vert[(tab1+1)*(tab2+1)-1][k]
                    + f1v*vert[tab2][k])*f2u;
      }
   }
}

for (i=0; i<tab1; i++)
{
   for (j=0; j<tab2; j++)
   {
      m = i*tab2 + j;
      vn[m][0] = vn[m][4] = m+i; vn[m][1] = m+i+1;
      vn[m][2] = m+i+tab2+2; vn[m][3] = m+i+tab2+1;
   }
}
```

Listing 12.3   Program for a Bicubic Coons Patch   **517**

```
      plotSurface();
  }

  void ruleBSpline(int splNum,int n,double x[],double y[],double z[])
  {
      int     i,j,k,m,nisegs,ntsegs;
      double  t,dt,b0,b1,b2,b3,xp,yp,zp;
      double  xstart,ystart,zstart,xend,yend,zend;
      double  s,length,dx,dy,dz,ds,len[12];

      xstart = x[0]; ystart = y[0]; zstart = z[0];
      xend = x[n-1]; yend = y[n-1]; zend = z[n-1];

      x[0] = x[2]+6.*(x[0]-x[1]); x[1] = 1.5*x[1]-.5*x[2];
      y[0] = y[2]+6.*(y[0]-y[1]); y[1] = 1.5*y[1]-.5*y[2];
      z[0] = z[2]+6.*(z[0]-z[1]); z[1] = 1.5*z[1]-.5*z[2];
      x[n-1] = x[n-3]+6.*(x[-1]-x[n-2]); x[n-2] = 1.5*x[n-2]-.5*x[n-3];
      y[n-1] = y[n-3]+6.*(y[n-1]-y[n-2]); y[n-2] = 1.5*y[n-2]-.5*y[n-3];
      z[n-1] = z[n-3]+6.*(z[n-1]-z[n-2]); z[n-2] = 1.5*z[n-2]-.5*z[n-3];

      nisegs = n - 3;
      ntsegs = 20; dt = 1./(double) ntsegs;

      xp = xstart; yp = ystart; zp = zstart;
      s = 0; /* start measuring length with s = 0 at first point */
      for (i=3; i<=nisegs+2; i++)
      {
          for (j=0,t=0.;j<=ntsegs;j++,t+=dt)
          {
              b0 = t*t*t/6.;
              b1 = (1.+3.*t+3.*t*t-3.*t*t*t)/6.;
              b2 = (4.-6.*t*t+3.*t*t*t)/6.;
              b3 = (1.-3.*t+3.*t*t-t*t*t)/6.;
              dx = b3*x[i-3]+b2*x[i-2]+b1*x[i-1]+b0*x[i] - xp;
              dy = b3*y[i-3]+b2*y[i-2]+b1*y[i-1]+b0*y[i] - yp;
              dz = b3*z[i-3]+b2*z[i-2]+b1*z[i-1]+b0*z[i] - zp;
              ds = sqrt(dx*dx + dy*dy + dz*dz);
              s = s + ds;
              xp = xp + dx; yp = yp + dy; zp = zp + dz;
          }
      }
      length = s;
      if ((splNum == 0) || (splNum == 2))
          ne = tab1;
      else
          ne = tab2;
      for (k=1; k<ne; k++) /* divide length into ne equal parts */
      {
```

```
        len[k] = (k*length)/(double) ne;
    }
    xp = xstart; yp = ystart; zp = zstart;
    s = 0;
    for (i=3; i<=nisegs+2; i++) /* calculate vertex coordinates */
    {
        for (j=0,t=0.;j<=ntsegs;j++,t+=dt)
        {
            b0 = t*t*t/6.;
            b1 = (1.+3.*t+3.*t*t-3.*t*t*t)/6.;
            b2 = (4.-6.*t*t+3.*t*t*t)/6.;
            b3 = (1.-3.*t+3.*t*t-t*t*t)/6.;
            dx = b3*x[i-3]+b2*x[i-2]+b1*x[i-1]+b0*x[i] - xp;
            dy = b3*y[i-3]+b2*y[i-2]+b1*y[i-1]+b0*y[i] - yp;
            dz = b3*z[i-3]+b2*z[i-2]+b1*z[i-1]+b0*z[i] - zp;
            ds = sqrt(dx*dx + dy*dy + dz*dz);

            for (k=1; k<ne; k++)
            {
                if ((s<len[k]) && ((s+ds)>=len[k]))
                {
                    if (splNum == 0) m = k*(tab2+1);
                    if (splNum == 1) m = k;
                    if (splNum == 2) m = (k+1)*tab2+k;
                    if (splNum == 3) m = tab1*(tab2+1)+k;
                    vert[m][0] = xp + (len[k]-s)*dx/ds;
                    vert[m][1] = yp + (len[k]-s)*dy/ds;
                    vert[m][2] = zp + (len[k]-s)*dz/ds;
                }
            }
            s = s + ds; xp = xp + dx; yp = yp + dy; zp = zp + dz;
        }
    }
}
```

LISTING 12.4: quadBSplSurf()

The subroutine quadBSplSurf() produces a uniform quadratic B–spline surface from a rectangular mesh of control vertices. The boundary control vertices are first extrapolated to stretch the surface to the original corner vertices. Then vertex coordinates for the faces on the smoothed surface are calculated with equation 12.6 from section 12.7. The number of faces drawn on the surface is determined by the parameters *surfu* and *surfv* in the u- and v-directions.

The program lines listed below start with data-type declarations for the global variables *numFaces, vn*[][], and *vert*[][], which are used for plotting faces on the smoothed sur-

Listing 12.4   quadBSplSpurf()   **519**

face with a subroutine like plotSurface(), given at the end of program listing 12.1. The parameter values given in these data declarations and in the subroutine quadBSplSurf() are those for the surfaces shown in figures 12.30–31. The subroutine produces the surface shown in figure 12.31; when the extrapolation of the boundary control points is omitted from the subroutine, the surface in figure 12.30 results. By changing the parameter values, this subroutine can be used with any rectangular mesh that has an array of 3 × 3 or more control vertices. Also, the density of lines plotted on the smoothed surface can be changed by changing the *surfu* and *surfv* values.

The vertices in the control mesh are numbered from 0 through *tab*1 in the u-direction, and from 0 through *tab*2 in the v-direction. The corner vertices are extrapolated after the other boundary vertices are extrapolated in the first two *for* loops of the subroutine quadB-SplSurf().

After the boundary mesh vertices are extrapolated, the increments *du* and *dv* between lines on the smoothed surface are calculated. Then the vertex coordinates (*vert*[k][0], *vert*[k][1], and *vert*[k][2]) are calculated in nested loops with increments of *du* and *dv*. The surface patch that contains a point (*u*, *v*) is identified by the indices *i* and *j* of the spline segments in the u-and v-directions. Thus *u* is increased by increments of *du* in a *while* loop that lies inside a *for* loop over the index *i*. Similarly, *v* is increased by increments of *dv* in a *while* loop lying inside a *for* loop over *j*.

```
int      numFaces = 144,vn[144][5];
double   vert[169][3];

void quadBSplSurf(void)
{
    int     i,j,k,m,n;
    int     tab1 = 3,tab2 = 3,surfu = 12,surfv = 12;
    double  u,v,du,dv,b0u,b1u,b2u,b0v,b1v,b2v;
    double  x[4][4]  = {{0,0,0,0},{1,1,1,1},{2,2,2,2},{3,3,3,3}};
    double  y[4][4]  = {{0,1,2,3},{0,1,2,3},{0,1,2,3},{0,1,2,3}};
    double  z[4][4]  = {{0,0,0,0},{0,3,3,0},{0,3,3,0},{0,0,0,0}};

    for (i=1; i<tab1; i++)
    {
        x[i][0] = 2*x[i][0]-x[i][1];
        y[i][0] = 2*y[i][0]-y[i][1];
        z[i][0] = 2*z[i][0]-z[i][1];
        x[i][tab2] = 2*x[i][tab2]-x[i][tab2-1];
        y[i][tab2] = 2*y[i][tab2]-y[i][tab2-1];
        z[i][tab2] = 2*z[i][tab2]-z[i][tab2-1];
    }
    for (j=1; j<tab2; j++)
    {
        x[0][j] = 2*x[0][j]-x[1][j];
        y[0][j] = 2*y[0][j]-y[1][j];
```

```
        z[0][j] = 2*z[0][j]-z[1][j];
        x[tab1][j] = 2*x[tab1][j]-x[tab1-1][j];
        y[tab1][j] = 2*y[tab1][j]-y[tab1-1][j];
        z[tab1][j] = 2*z[tab1][j]-z[tab1-1][j];
    }


    x[0][0] = 4*x[0][0]-x[1][0]-x[0][1]-x[1][1];
    y[0][0] = 4*y[0][0]-y[1][0]-y[0][1]-y[1][1];
    z[0][0] = 4*z[0][0]-z[1][0]-z[0][1]-z[1][1];
    x[0][tab2] = 4*x[0][tab2]-x[1][tab2]-x[0][tab2-1]-x[1][tab2-1];
    y[0][tab2] = 4*y[0][tab2]-y[1][tab2]-y[0][tab2-1]-y[1][tab2-1];
    z[0][tab2] = 4*z[0][tab2]-z[1][tab2]-z[0][tab2-1]-z[1][tab2-1];
    x[tab1][0] = 4*x[tab1][0]-x[tab1-1][0]-x[tab1][1]-x[tab1-1][1];
    y[tab1][0] = 4*y[tab1][0]-y[tab1-1][0]-y[tab1][1]-y[tab1-1][1];
    z[tab1][0] = 4*z[tab1][0]-z[tab1-1][0]-z[tab1][1]-z[tab1-1][1];
    x[tab1][tab2] = 4*x[tab1][tab2]-x[tab1-1][tab2]-x[tab1][tab2-1]
                    -x[tab1-1][tab2-1];
    y[tab1][tab2] = 4*y[tab1][tab2]-y[tab1-1][tab2]-y[tab1][tab2-1]
                    -y[tab1-1][tab2-1];
    z[tab1][tab2] = 4*z[tab1][tab2]-z[tab1-1][tab2]-z[tab1][tab2-1]
                    -z[tab1-1][tab2-1];

    du = (double) (tab1-1)/(double) surfu;
    dv = (double) (tab2-1)/(double) surfv;
    n = 0;

    for (j=2; j<=tab2; j++)
    {
        if (j==2)
            v = 0.;
        else
            v = v - 1.0;
        while ( v < (1.+.001*dv) )
        {
            b0v = .5*v*v; b1v = .5*(1.+2.*v-2.*v*v);
            b2v = .5*(1.-v)*(1.-v);
            m = 0;
            for (i=2; i<=tab1; i++)
            {
                if (i==2)
                    u = 0.;
                else
                    u = u - 1.0;
                while ( u < (1.+.001*du) )
                {
                    k = m + n*(surfu+1);
                    b0u = .5*u*u; b1u = .5*(1.+2.*u-2.*u*u);
                    b2u = .5*(1.-u)*(1.-u);
```

Listing 12.5   cubicBSplSurf()   **521**

```
                        vert[k][0] = x[i-2][j-2]*b2u*b2v
                            + x[i-2][j-1]*b2u*b1v + x[i-2][j]*b2u*b0v
                            + x[i-1][j-2]*b1u*b2v + x[i-1][j-1]*b1u*b1v
                            + x[i-1][j]*b1u*b0v + x[i][j-2]*b0u*b2v
                            + x[i][j-1]*b0u*b1v + x[i][j]*b0u*b0v;
                        vert[k][1] = y[i-2][j-2]*b2u*b2v
                            + y[i-2][j-1]*b2u*b1v + y[i-2][j]*b2u*b0v
                            + y[i-1][j-2]*b1u*b2v + y[i-1][j-1]*b1u*b1v
                            + y[i-1][j]*b1u*b0v + y[i][j-2]*b0u*b2v
                            + y[i][j-1]*b0u*b1v + y[i][j]*b0u*b0v;
                        vert[k][2] = z[i-2][j-2]*b2u*b2v
                            + z[i-2][j-1]*b2u*b1v + z[i-2][j]*b2u*b0v
                            + z[i-1][j-2]*b1u*b2v + z[i-1][j-1]*b1u*b1v
                            + z[i-1][j]*b1u*b0v + z[i][j-2]*b0u*b2v
                            + z[i][j-1]*b0u*b1v + z[i][j]*b0u*b0v;
                    u = u + du; m++;
                }
            }
            v = v +dv; n++;
        }
    }

    for (n=0; n<surfv; n++)
    {
        for (m=0; m<surfu; m++)
        {
            k = m + n*surfu;
            vn[k][0] = vn[k][4] = k+n; vn[k][1] = k+n+1;
            vn[k][2] = k+n+surfu+2; vn[k][3] = k+n+surfu+1;
        }
    }
    plotSurface();
}
```

LISTING 12.5: cubicBSplSurf()

The subroutine cubicBSplSurf() is similar to quadBSplSurf() in listing 12.4 above, except that the surface is constructed from cubic B-splines rather than quadratic B-splines. The global variables *numFaces, vn[][],* and *vert[][]* have the same parameter values as given in listing 12.4.

For this cubic B-spline case, the extrapolation of mesh vertices involves both the boundary points and the first vertices inside the boundary (recall that the extrapolation procedure for a cubic B-spline given in section 7.6 involved endpoints and the points next to the ends). The cubicBSplSurf() produces the surface shown in figure 12.33. If the extrapolation procedure is omitted, then cubicBSplSurf() draws the surface shown in figure 12.32.

```
void cubicBSplSurf(void)
{
    int      i,j,k,m,n;
    int      tab1 = 4,tab2 = 4,surfu = 12,surfv = 12;
    double   u,v,du,dv,b0u,b1u,b2u,b3u,b0v,b1v,b2v,b3v;
    double   x[5][5] = {{0,0,0,0,0},{1,1,1,1,1},{2,2,2,2,2},
                            {3,3,3,3,3},{4,4,4,4,4}};
    double   y[5][5] = {{0,1,2,3,4},{0,1,2,3,4},{0,1,2,3,4},
                            {0,1,2,3,4},{0,1,2,3,4}};
    double   z[5][5] = {{0,0,0,0,0},{0,3,3,3,0},{0,3,3,3,0},
                            {0,3,3,3,0},{0,0,0,0,0}};

    for (i=1; i<tab1; i++)
    {
        x[i][0] = x[i][2]+6*(x[i][0]-x[i][1]);
        y[i][0] = y[i][2]+6*(y[i][0]-y[i][1]);
        z[i][0] = z[i][2]+6*(z[i][0]-z[i][1]);
        x[i][tab2] = x[i][tab2-2]+6*(x[i][tab2]-x[i][tab2-1]);
        y[i][tab2] = y[i][tab2-2]+6*(y[i][tab2]-y[i][tab2-1]);
        z[i][tab2] = z[i][tab2-2]+6*(z[i][tab2]-z[i][tab2-1]);
    }
    for (j=1; j<tab2; j++)
    {
        x[0][j] = x[2][j]+6*(x[0][j]-x[1][j]);
        y[0][j] = y[2][j]+6*(y[0][j]-y[1][j]);
        z[0][j] = z[2][j]+6*(z[0][j]-z[1][j]);
        x[tab1][j] = x[tab1-2][j]+6*(x[tab1][j]-x[tab1-1][j]);
        y[tab1][j] = y[tab1-2][j]+6*(y[tab1][j]-y[tab1-1][j]);
        z[tab1][j] = z[tab1-2][j]+6*(z[tab1][j]-z[tab1-1][j]);
    }
    for (i=0; i<=tab1; i++)
    {
        x[i][1] = 0.5*(3*x[i][1]-x[i][2]);
        y[i][1] = 0.5*(3*y[i][1]-y[i][2]);
        z[i][1] = 0.5*(3*z[i][1]-z[i][2]);
        x[i][tab2-1] = 0.5*(3*x[i][tab2-1]-x[i][tab2-2]);
        y[i][tab2-1] = 0.5*(3*y[i][tab2-1]-y[i][tab2-2]);
        z[i][tab2-1] = 0.5*(3*z[i][tab2-1]-z[i][tab2-2]);
    }
    for (j=0; j<=tab2; j++)
    {
        x[1][j] = 0.5*(3*x[1][j]-x[2][j]);
        y[1][j] = 0.5*(3*y[1][j]-y[2][j]);
        z[1][j] = 0.5*(3*z[1][j]-z[2][j]);
        x[tab1-1][j] = 0.5*(3*x[tab1-1][j]-x[tab1-2][j]);
        y[tab1-1][j] = 0.5*(3*y[tab1-1][j]-y[tab1-2][j]);
        z[tab1-1][j] = 0.5*(3*z[tab1-1][j]-z[tab1-2][j]);
    }
```

Listing 12.5   cubicBSplSurf()   **523**

```
x[0][0]  = 36*x[0][0]-4*x[0][1]-4*x[1][0]-16*x[1][1]-x[0][2]
           -x[2][0]-4*x[1][2]-4*x[2][1]-x[2][2];
y[0][0]  = 36*y[0][0]-4*y[0][1]-4*y[1][0]-16*y[1][1]-y[0][2]
           -y[2][0]-4*y[1][2]-4*y[2][1]-y[2][2];
z[0][0]  = 36*z[0][0]-4*z[0][1]-4*z[1][0]-16*z[1][1]-z[0][2]
           -z[2][0]-4*z[1][2]-4*z[2][1]-z[2][2];

x[tab1][0]  = 36*x[tab1][0]-4*x[tab1][1]-4*x[tab1-1][0]
              -16*x[tab1-1][1]-x[tab1][2]-x[tab1-2][0]
              -4*x[tab1-1][2]-4*x[tab1-2][1]-x[tab1-2][2];
y[tab1][0]  = 36*y[tab1][0]-4*y[tab1][1]-4*y[tab1-1][0]
              -16*y[tab1-1][1]-y[tab1][2]-y[tab1-2][0]
              -4*y[tab1-1][2]-4*y[tab1-2][1]-y[tab1-2][2];
z[tab1][0]  = 36*z[tab1][0]-4*z[tab1][1]-4*z[tab1-1][0]
              -16*z[tab1-1][1]-z[tab1][2]-z[tab1-2][0]
              -4*z[tab1-1][2]-4*z[tab1-2][1]-z[tab1-2][2];

x[0][tab2]  = 36*x[0][tab2]-4*x[0][tab2-1]-4*x[1][tab2]
              -16*x[1][tab2-1]-x[0][tab2-2]-x[2][tab2]
              -4*x[1][tab2-2]-4*x[2][tab2-1]-x[2][tab2-2];
y[0][tab2]  = 36*y[0][tab2]-4*y[0][tab2-1]-4*y[1][tab2]
              -16*y[1][tab2-1]-y[0][tab2-2]-y[2][tab2]
              -4*y[1][tab2-2]-4*y[2][tab2-1]-y[2][tab2-2];
z[0][tab2]  = 36*z[0][tab2]-4*z[0][tab2-1]-4*z[1][tab2]
              -16*z[1][tab2-1]-z[0][tab2-2]-z[2][tab2]
              -4*z[1][tab2-2]-4*z[2][tab2-1]-z[2][tab2-2];

x[tab1][tab2]  = 36*x[tab1][tab2]-4*x[tab1][tab2-1]
                 -4*x[tab1-1][tab2]-16*x[tab1-1][tab2-1]
                 -x[tab1][tab2-2]-x[tab1-2][tab2]
                 -4*x[tab1-1][tab2-2]-4*x[tab1-2][tab2-1]
                 -x[tab1-2][tab2-2];
y[tab1][tab2]  = 36*y[tab1][tab2]-4*y[tab1][tab2-1]
                 -4*y[tab1-1][tab2]-16*y[tab1-1][tab2-1]
                 -y[tab1][tab2-2]-y[tab1-2][tab2]
                 -4*y[tab1-1][tab2-2]-4*y[tab1-2][tab2-1]
                 -y[tab1-2][tab2-2];
z[tab1][tab2]  = 36*z[tab1][tab2]-4*z[tab1][tab2-1]
                 -4*z[tab1-1][tab2]-16*z[tab1-1][tab2-1]
                 -z[tab1][tab2-2]-z[tab1-2][tab2]
                 -4*z[tab1-1][tab2-2]-4*z[tab1-2][tab2-1]
                 -z[tab1-2][tab2-2];

du = (double) (tab1-2)/(double) surfu;
dv = (double) (tab2-2)/(double) surfv;
n = 0;

for (j=3; j<=tab2; j++)
{
```

```
if (j==3)
    v = 0.;
else
    v = v - 1.0;
while ( v<(1.+.001*dv) )
{
    b0v = v*v*v/6.;
    b1v = (1.+3.*v+3.*v*v-3.*v*v*v)/6.;
    b2v = (4.-6.*v*v+3.*v*v*v)/6.;
    b3v = (1.-3.*v+3.*v*v-v*v*v)/6.;
    m = 0;
    for (i=3; i<=tab1; i++)
    {
        if (i==3)
            u = 0.;
        else
            u = u - 1.0;
        while ( u<(1.+.001*du) )
        {
            k = m + n*(surfu+1);
            b0u = u*u*u/6.;
            b1u = (1.+3.*u+3.*u*u-3.*u*u*u)/6.;
            b2u = (4.-6.*u*u+3.*u*u*u)/6.;
            b3u = (1.-3.*u+3.*u*u-u*u*u)/6.;

            vert[k][0] = x[i-3][j-3]*b3u*b3v
                + x[i-3][j-2]*b3u*b2v + x[i-3][j-1]*b3u*b1v
                + x[i-3][j]*b3u*b0v + x[i-2][j-3]*b2u*b3v
                + x[i-2][j-2]*b2u*b2v + x[i-2][j-1]*b2u*b1v
                + x[i-2][j]*b2u*b0v + x[i-1][j-3]*b1u*b3v
                + x[i-1][j-2]*b1u*b2v + x[i-1][j-1]*b1u*b1v
                + x[i-1][j]*b1u*b0v + x[i][j-3]*b0u*b3v
                + x[i][j-2]*b0u*b2v + x[i][j-1]*b0u*b1v
                + x[i][j]*b0u*b0v;
            vert[k][1] = y[i-3][j-3]*b3u*b3v
                + y[i-3][j-2]*b3u*b2v + y[i-3][j-1]*b3u*b1v
                + y[i-3][j]*b3u*b0v + y[i-2][j-3]*b2u*b3v
                + y[i-2][j-2]*b2u*b2v + y[i-2][j-1]*b2u*b1v
                + y[i-2][j]*b2u*b0v + y[i-1][j-3]*b1u*b3v
                + y[i-1][j-2]*b1u*b2v + y[i-1][j-1]*b1u*b1v
                + y[i-1][j]*b1u*b0v + y[i][j-3]*b0u*b3v
                + y[i][j-2]*b0u*b2v + y[i][j-1]*b0u*b1v
                + y[i][j]*b0u*b0v;
            vert[k][2] = z[i-3][j-3]*b3u*b3v
                + z[i-3][j-2]*b3u*b2v + z[i-3][j-1]*b3u*b1v
                + z[i-3][j]*b3u*b0v + z[i-2][j-3]*b2u*b3v
                + z[i-2][j-2]*b2u*b2v + z[i-2][j-1]*b2u*b1v
                + z[i-2][j]*b2u*b0v + z[i-1][j-3]*b1u*b3v
```

Listing 12.6   quadNURBSurf()   **525**

```
                              + z[i-1][j-2]*b1u*b2v + z[i-1][j-1]*b1u*b1v
                              + z[i-1][j]*b1u*b0v + z[i][j-3]*b0u*b3v
                              + z[i][j-2]*b0u*b2v + z[i][j-1]*b0u*b1v
                              + z[i][j]*b0u*b0v;
                  u = u + du; m++;
              }
          }
          v = v + dv; n++;
      }
  }


  for (n=0; n<surfv; n++)
  {
      for (m=0; m<surfu; m++)
      {
          k = m + n*surfu;
          vn[k][0] = vn[k][4] = k+n;
          vn[k][1] = k+n+1;
          vn[k][2] = k+n+surfu+2;
          vn[k][3] = k+n+surfu+1;
      }
  }
  plotSurface();
}
```

LISTING 12.6: quadNURBSurf()

The subroutine quadNURBSurf() starts with the same control mesh as the subroutines in listings 12.4 and 12.5. Thus the parameters for the global variables *numFaces, vn[][]*, and *vert[][]* are the same.

Unlike the uniform B-spline cases, this nonuniform rational B-spline surface requires that knot vectors and a weight vector be specified. The knot vectors in the u- and v-directions given in the data-type declarations below specify uniform knot placement in both directions. For the knot vectors given below, both u and v vary from 0 to 2 to span the surface.

The weight vector w[4][4] below assigns weights to the four interior vertices that are five times larger than the other weights. For these values, the surface given by the middle illustrations in figure 12.34 is produced. The surfaces on the left in figure 12.34 correspond to the case for which all weights are equal (this case duplicates the surface given by the subroutine in listing 12.4).

The calculations in quadNURBSurf() are similar to those in the two previous listings, except that no special boundary conditions (such as vertex extrapolation) are required to ensure that the smoothed surface extends to the corners of the control mesh. Also, the basis functions are calculated from the NURBS relations given in equation 7.72. The weights are included in the calculation according to equations 12.8–9.

This subroutine can be used with any rectangular mesh having at least three vertices in each direction. For example, the subroutine was used with a particular 3 × 5 mesh and special knot and weight vectors to construct the sections of a spherical surface shown in figure 12.35; see the discussion in section 12.8.

```c
void quadNURBSurf(void)
{
    int     i,j,k,m,n;
    int     tab1 = 3,tab2 = 3,surfu = 12,surfv = 12;
    double  u,v,du,dv,b0u,b1u,b2u,b0v,b1v,b2v;
    double  un1,u0,u1,u2,vn1,v0,v1,v2,bsum;

    double  x[4][4] = {{0,0,0,0},{1,1,1,1},{2,2,2,2},{3,3,3,3}};
    double  y[4][4] = {{0,1,2,3},{0,1,2,3},{0,1,2,3},{0,1,2,3}};
    double  z[4][4] = {{0,0,0,0},{0,3,3,0},{0,3,3,0},{0,0,0,0}};
    double  w[4][4] = {{1,1,1,1},{1,5,5,1},{1,5,5,1},{1,1,1,1}};

    double  uknot[] = {0,0,0,1,2,2,2};
    double  vknot[] = {0,0,0,1,2,2,2};

    du = (uknot[tab1+3]-uknot[0])/(double) surfu;
    dv = (vknot[tab2+3]-vknot[0])/(double) surfv;
    v = 0.; n = 0;

    for (j=2; j<=tab2; j++)
    {
        vn1 = vknot[j-1]; v0 = vknot[j];
        v1 = vknot[j+1]; v2 = vknot[j+2];
        while ( v < (v1+.001*dv) )
        {
            b0v = (v-v0)*(v-v0)/((v2-v0)*(v1-v0));
            b1v = (v1-v)*(v-vn1)/((v1-v0)*(v1-vn1))
                + (v2-v)*(v-v0)/((v2-v0)*(v1-v0));
            b2v = (v1-v)*(v1-v)/((v1-vn1)*(v1-v0));

            u = 0.; m = 0;
            for (i=2; i<=tab1; i++)
            {
                un1 = uknot[i-1]; u0 = uknot[i];
                u1 = uknot[i+1]; u2 = uknot[i+2];
                while ( u < (u1+.001*du) )
                {
                    b0u = (u-u0)*(u-u0)/((u2-u0)*(u1-u0));
                    b1u = (u1-u)*(u-un1)/((u1-u0)*(u1-un1))
                        + (u2-u)*(u-u0)/((u2-u0)*(u1-u0));
                    b2u = (u1-u)*(u1-u)/((u1-un1)*(u1-u0));
                    k = m + n*(surfu+1);
```

Listing 12.6   quadNURBSurf()   527

```
              bsum = w[i-2][j-2]*b2u*b2v + w[i-2][j-1]*b2u*b1v
                   + w[i-2][j]*b2u*b0v + w[i-1][j-2]*b1u*b2v
                   + w[i-1][j-1]*b1u*b1v + w[i-1][j]*b1u*b0v
                   + w[i][j-2]*b0u*b2v + w[i][j-1]*b0u*b1v
                   + w[i][j]*b0u*b0v;

          vert[k][0] = (w[i-2][j-2]*x[i-2][j-2]*b2u*b2v
                     + w[i-2][j-1]*x[i-2][j-1]*b2u*b1v
                     + w[i-2][j]*x[i-2][j]*b2u*b0v
                     + w[i-1][j-2]*x[i-1][j-2]*b1u*b2v
                     + w[i-1][j-1]*x[i-1][j-1]*b1u*b1v
                     + w[i-1][j]*x[i-1][j]*b1u*b0v
                     + w[i][j-2]*x[i][j-2]*b0u*b2v
                     + w[i][j-1]*x[i][j-1]*b0u*b1v
                     + w[i][j]*x[i][j]*b0u*b0v)/bsum;
          vert[k][1] = (w[i-2][j-2]*y[i-2][j-2]*b2u*b2v
                     + w[i-2][j-1]*y[i-2][j-1]*b2u*b1v
                     + w[i-2][j]*y[i-2][j]*b2u*b0v
                     + w[i-1][j-2]*y[i-1][j-2]*b1u*b2v
                     + w[i-1][j-1]*y[i-1][j-1]*b1u*b1v
                     + w[i-1][j]*y[i-1][j]*b1u*b0v
                     + w[i][j-2]*y[i][j-2]*b0u*b2v
                     + w[i][j-1]*y[i][j-1]*b0u*b1v
                     + w[i][j]*y[i][j]*b0u*b0v)/bsum;
          vert[k][2] = (w[i-2][j-2]*z[i-2][j-2]*b2u*b2v
                     + w[i-2][j-1]*z[i-2][j-1]*b2u*b1v
                     + w[i-2][j]*z[i-2][j]*b2u*b0v
                     + w[i-1][j-2]*z[i-1][j-2]*b1u*b2v
                     + w[i-1][j-1]*z[i-1][j-1]*b1u*b1v
                     + w[i-1][j]*z[i-1][j]*b1u*b0v
                     + w[i][j-2]*z[i][j-2]*b0u*b2v
                     + w[i][j-1]*z[i][j-1]*b0u*b1v
                     + w[i][j]*z[i][j]*b0u*b0v)/bsum;
              u = u + du; m++;
          }
      }
      v = v + dv; n++;
  }
}

for (n=0; n<surfv; n++)
{
    for (m=0; m<surfu; m++)
    {
        k = m + n*surfu;
        vn[k][0] = vn[k][4] = k+n;
        vn[k][1] = k+n+1;
        vn[k][2] = k+n+surfu+2;
```

```
                vn[k][3] = k+n+surfu+1;
        }
    }
    plotSurface();
}
```

LISTING 13.1: unionBoundary()

The subroutine unionBoundary() calculates the boundary for the union of the rectangles A and B shown in figure 13.21. This boundary is represented by a closed polyline consisting of *nPts* vertex points with coordinates specified by the arrays *xBrep[i]* and *yBrep[i]*. Thus, to implement the subroutine unionBoundary() given below, the user must specify two corners for each rectangle, after which the rectangles are drawn in one color, then the boundary polyline is plotted in another color. All boundary polylines except those for case 2 are drawn by moving to the starting coordinate $(xBrep[0], yBrep[0]) = (x_{a1}, y_{a1})$, and then drawing line segments from vertex to vertex, ending on the starting point. As shown in figure 13.21, case 2 must be drawn as two separate polylines—the parameter *flag* is included as an argument in the function call polyline() to handle this special case.

The Brep polyline has 4 vertices for case 1, 12 vertices for case 6, and 8 vertices for each of the other cases. The parameter *flag* is set equal to 1 at the start of the subroutine unionBoundary(), and *if* statements then separate out the different cases, with *flag* identifying the case number. Only the first case is not separated out by the *if* statements; thus *flag* = 1 identifies the first case.

Each vertex on the boundary polynomial has an x-coordinate given by one of the four values x_{a1}, x_{a2}, x_{b1}, or x_{b2}, and a y-coordinate given by one of the values y_{a1}, y_{a2}, y_{b1}, or y_{b2}. The vertex coordinates given in the switch() function were determined from the case geometries given in figure 13.21. All cases except cases 2 and 6 have the same coordinates (x_{a1}, y_{a2}) for vertex 7, so these values were set before the switch() function, with a change of the values required only for cases 2 and 6. Also, as mentioned previously, case 2 requires special consideration during plotting; here the arrays have been set up so that plotting proceeds along the following two vertex loops: 0-1-2-3-0 for rectangle A and 4-5-6-7-4 for rectangle B.

```
void unionBoundary(double xa1,double ya1,double xa2,double ya2,
                   double xb1,double yb1,double xb2,double yb2)
{
    int    flag,nPts,i;
    double xBrep[12],yBrep[12];

    flag = 1;
    if ((xb1 < xa2) && (yb1 < ya1))
    {
        if ((xb2 > xa2) && (yb2 > ya1) && (yb2 < ya2)) flag = 3;
        if ((xb2 > xa2) && (yb2 > ya2)) flag = 4;
```

Listing 13.1   unionBoundary()   **529**

```
}
if ((xb1 < xa2) && (xb2 < xa2) && (yb1 < ya1))
{
   if ((yb2 > ya1) && (yb2 < ya2)) flag = 5;
   if ((yb2 > ya1) && (yb2 > ya2)) flag = 6;
}
if ((xb1 < xa2) && (xb2 > xa2) && (yb1 > ya1))
{
   if (yb2 < ya2) flag = 7;
   if ((yb1 < ya2) && (yb2 > ya2)) flag = 8;
}
if ((xb2 < xa2) && (yb1 > ya1) && (yb1 < ya2) && (yb2 > ya2))
                                              flag = 9;
if ((flag == 1) && ((xb1>xa2)||(yb2<ya1)||(yb1>ya2))) flag = 2;

xBrep[0] = xa1; yBrep[0] = ya1; xBrep[7] = xa1; yBrep[7] = ya2;
switch(flag)
{
   case 1: nPts = 4;
       xBrep[1] = xa2; yBrep[1] = ya1; xBrep[2] = xa2; yBrep[2] = ya2;
       xBrep[3] = xa1; yBrep[3] = ya2;
       break;
   case 2: nPts = 8;
       xBrep[1] = xa2; yBrep[1] = ya1; xBrep[2] = xa2; yBrep[2] = ya2;
       xBrep[3] = xa1; yBrep[3] = ya2; xBrep[4] = xb1; yBrep[4] = yb1;
       xBrep[5] = xb2; yBrep[5] = yb1; xBrep[6] = xb2; yBrep[6] = yb2;
       xBrep[7] = xb1; yBrep[7] = yb2;
       break;
   case 3: nPts = 8;
       xBrep[1] = xb1; yBrep[1] = ya1; xBrep[2] = xb1; yBrep[2] = yb1;
       xBrep[3] = xb2; yBrep[3] = yb1; xBrep[4] = xb2; yBrep[4] = yb2;
       xBrep[5] = xa2; yBrep[5] = yb2; xBrep[6] = xa2; yBrep[6] = ya2;
       break;
   case 4: nPts = 8;
       xBrep[1] = xb1; yBrep[1] = ya1; xBrep[2] = xb1; yBrep[2] = yb1;
       xBrep[3] = xb2; yBrep[3] = yb1; xBrep[4] = xb2; yBrep[4] = yb2;
       xBrep[5] = xb1; yBrep[5] = yb2; xBrep[6] = xb1; yBrep[6] = ya2;
       break;
   case 5: nPts = 8;
       xBrep[1] = xb1; yBrep[1] = ya1; xBrep[2] = xb1; yBrep[2] = yb1;
       xBrep[3] = xb2; yBrep[3] = yb1; xBrep[4] = xb2; yBrep[4] = ya1;
       xBrep[5] = xa2; yBrep[5] = ya1; xBrep[6] = xa2; yBrep[6] = ya2;
       break;
   case 6: nPts = 12;
       xBrep[1] = xb1; yBrep[1] = ya1; xBrep[2] = xb1; yBrep[2] = yb1;
       xBrep[3] = xb2; yBrep[3] = yb1; xBrep[4] = xb2; yBrep[4] = ya1;
       xBrep[5] = xa2; yBrep[5] = ya1; xBrep[6] = xa2; yBrep[6] = ya2;
       xBrep[7] = xb2; yBrep[7] = ya2; xBrep[8] = xb2; yBrep[8] = yb2;
```

```
         xBrep[9] = xb1; yBrep[9] = yb2; xBrep[10]= xb1; yBrep[10]= ya2;
         xBrep[11]= xa1; yBrep[11]= ya2;
         break;
   case 7: nPts = 8;
         xBrep[1] = xa2; yBrep[1] = ya1; xBrep[2] = xa2; yBrep[2] = yb1;
         xBrep[3] = xb2; yBrep[3] = yb1; xBrep[4] = xb2; yBrep[4] = yb2;
         xBrep[5] = xa2; yBrep[5] = yb2; xBrep[6] = xa2; yBrep[6] = ya2;
         break;
   case 8: nPts = 8;
         xBrep[1] = xa2; yBrep[1] = ya1; xBrep[2] = xa2; yBrep[2] = yb1;
         xBrep[3] = xb2; yBrep[3] = yb1; xBrep[4] = xb2; yBrep[4] = yb2;
         xBrep[5] = xb1; yBrep[5] = yb2; xBrep[6] = xb1; yBrep[6] = ya2;
         break;
   case 9: nPts = 8;
         xBrep[1] = xa2; yBrep[1] = ya1; xBrep[2] = xa2; yBrep[2] = ya2;
         xBrep[3] = xb2; yBrep[3] = ya2; xBrep[4] = xb2; yBrep[4] = yb2;
         xBrep[5] = xb1; yBrep[5] = yb2; xBrep[6] = xb1; yBrep[6] = ya2;
         break;
   }
   polyline(flag,nPts,xBrep,yBrep);
}
```

Appendix C: Matrix Operations

A summary of basic matrix operations is given in this appendix. Matrices are used for the following graphics calculations: transformations between color spaces in chapter 6, calculation of the natural cubic spline curve in chapter 7, and transformations in 2-D and 3-D physical spaces in chapters 10 and 11.

C.1 MATRIX ADDITION, SUBTRACTION, AND MULTIPLICATION

Matrix Representations

In this book, column vectors are represented as 3×1 and 4×1 matrices (matrices having 3 or 4 rows and 1 column); row vectors are represented as 1×2, 1×3, and 1×4 matrices (matrices having 1 row and 2–4 columns); and transformations are represented as square matrices (2×2, 3×3, and 4×4).

The transformation from the RGB color system to the CMY system is given by equation 6.1 as the following subtraction of column vectors:

$$\begin{bmatrix} C \\ M \\ Y \end{bmatrix} = \begin{bmatrix} 1 \\ 1 \\ 1 \end{bmatrix} - \begin{bmatrix} R \\ G \\ B \end{bmatrix} \qquad (C.1)$$

Transformation from the RGB colors to the CIE XYZ color space is given in equation 6.14 by the following matrix product of a 3×3 matrix with a 3×1 column matrix:

$$\begin{bmatrix} X \\ Y \\ Z \end{bmatrix} = \begin{bmatrix} X_r & X_g & X_b \\ Y_r & Y_g & Y_b \\ Z_r & Z_g & Z_b \end{bmatrix} \begin{bmatrix} R \\ G \\ B \end{bmatrix} \qquad (C.2)$$

In chapter 10, the 2-D transformations for translation, scale, rotation, reflection, and shear are represented by the product of a 1×3 row vector and a 3×3 matrix. Two-dimensional translations by an amount Δx in the horizontal direction and Δy in the vertical direction move a point $\mathbf{P}$ to $\mathbf{P'}$, as given by equation 10.2, which is reproduced below. (The points $\mathbf{P}$ and $\mathbf{P'}$ are represented by the row vectors $[x \quad y \quad 1]$ and $[x' \quad y' \quad 1]$; see section 10.1.)

$$[x' \quad y' \quad 1] = [x \quad y \quad 1] \begin{bmatrix} 1 & 0 & 0 \\ 0 & 1 & 0 \\ \Delta x & \Delta y & 1 \end{bmatrix} \qquad (C.3)$$

Matrix Addition and Subtraction

Only matrices with the same number of rows and columns may be added or subtracted. If [A] and [B] are $m \times n$ matrices, then their sum [C] is represented by the following matrix equation:

$$[A] + [B] = [C] \qquad (C.4)$$

Matrices [A] and [B] have elements represented as a_{ij} and b_{ij}, where the values of i and j denote the row and column location of the element (i ranges from 1 to m and j ranges from 1 to n for the $m \times n$ matrices). For example, a_{23} is the element of [A] that is located in row 2 and column 3. The sum of [A] and [B] yields a matrix [C] with elements that are simply the sum of the elements of [A] and [B]. Thus the elements of [C] in equation C.4 are given by the following equation:

$$c_{ij} = a_{ij} + b_{ij} \qquad (C.5)$$

A similar relation holds for subtraction:

$$[A] - [B] = [C] \text{ with } c_{ij} = a_{ij} - b_{ij} \qquad (C.6)$$

Using this result, the matrix subtraction given in equation C.1 yields the following:

$$\begin{bmatrix} C \\ M \\ Y \end{bmatrix} = \begin{bmatrix} 1-R \\ 1-G \\ 1-B \end{bmatrix} \qquad (C.7)$$

The matrix equation C.7 is equivalent to the following three scalar equations:

$$C = 1 - R, \qquad M = 1 - G, \quad \text{and} \quad Y = 1 - B \tag{C.8}$$

Matrix Multiplication

The multiplication of two matrices is carried out by multiplying the elements in the rows of the first matrix with the elements in the columns of the second matrix (thus, the number of columns in the first matrix must equal the number of rows of the second matrix). Consider the multiplication of a 1×3 row vector [V] and a 3×3 matrix [A].

$$[v_1 \quad v_2 \quad v_3] \begin{bmatrix} a_{11} & a_{12} & a_{13} \\ a_{21} & a_{22} & a_{23} \\ a_{31} & a_{32} & a_{33} \end{bmatrix} =$$

$$[(v_1a_{11} + v_2a_{21} + v_3a_{31}) \quad (v_1a_{12} + v_2a_{22} + v_3a_{32}) \quad (v_1a_{13} + v_2a_{23} + v_3a_{33})] \tag{C.9}$$

Use of equation C.9 to evaluate the product in equation C.3 yields the following results for the translated coordinates x' and y':

$$[x' \quad y' \quad 1] = [x + \Delta x \quad y + \Delta y \quad 1] \tag{C.10}$$

In a similar manner, the matrix product in equation C.2 is evaluated by multiplying the rows of the 3×3 matrix with the column vector:

$$\begin{bmatrix} X \\ Y \\ Z \end{bmatrix} = \begin{bmatrix} X_rR + X_gG + X_bB \\ Y_rR + Y_gG + Y_bB \\ Z_rR + Z_gG + Z_bB \end{bmatrix} \tag{C.11}$$

If the first matrix in equation C.9 were a 3×3 matrix, then the resultant matrix would have three rows: the second formed from the product of the second row of the first matrix and the columns of the second matrix; and the third formed from the product of the third row of first matrix and the columns of the second matrix. The following relation gives the elements c_{ij} of matrix [C] that results from the product [A][B], where [A] has n columns and [B] has n rows.

$$c_{ij} = \sum_{k=1}^{n} a_{ik}b_{kj} \tag{C.12}$$

In equation C.12, the index i ranges from 1 to the number of rows in matrix [A], and j ranges from 1 to the number of columns in matrix [B].

The equations for the natural cubic spline given in section 7.5 are written in terms of a large square matrix that is sparse; that is, it has only a few nonzero elements in each row. This matrix, given in equation 7.42, is called a tridiagonal matrix because there are at most three nonzero elements located in each row on the diagonal or adjacent to it. This matrix is reduced to the matrix in equation 7.43, which has two nonzero elements per row, except for the last row, which has only one nonzero element. The product of this last row and the column vector in equation 7.43 yields the result $D_m = \delta_m$; the product of the second to last row and the column vector yields $D_{m-1} + \gamma_{m-1}D_m = \delta_{m-1}$, with similar results for the other rows; see equation 7.46.

C.2 THE TRANSPOSE, DETERMINANT, AND INVERSE OF A SQUARE MATRIX

The Transpose of a Matrix

The transpose $[A]^T$ of a square matrix $[A]$ is obtained by interchanging rows and columns; that is, by interchanging the elements a_{ij} and a_{ji}. The transpose arises in a number of situations. For example, if coordinates are represented by column vectors rather than by the row vectors given in equation C.3, then the appropriate 3×3 transformation matrix is the transpose of $[A]$. That is, equation C.10 is equally represented by

$$[x' \quad y' \quad 1] = [x \quad y \quad 1][A] \quad \text{and} \quad \begin{bmatrix} x' \\ y' \\ 1 \end{bmatrix} = [A]^T \begin{bmatrix} x \\ y \\ 1 \end{bmatrix}$$

where   (C.13)

$$[A] = \begin{bmatrix} 1 & 0 & 0 \\ 0 & 1 & 0 \\ \Delta x & \Delta y & 1 \end{bmatrix} \quad \text{and} \quad [A]^T = \begin{bmatrix} 1 & 0 & \Delta x \\ 0 & 1 & \Delta y \\ 0 & 0 & 1 \end{bmatrix}$$

The transpose of a matrix also arises when the inverse of a matrix is calculated, as described in the last subsection below.

The Determinant of a Matrix

The determinant of a matrix must be evaluated in a number of situations, including matrix inversion (considered in the next subsection).

The determinant for a 2×2 matrix is evaluated by the following formula:

$$\begin{vmatrix} a_{11} & a_{12} \\ a_{21} & a_{22} \end{vmatrix} = a_{11}a_{22} - a_{12}a_{21}$$ (C.14)

The right side of equation C.14 is composed of product $a_{11}a_{22}$ of the diagonal terms minus the product $a_{12}a_{21}$ of the off-diagonal terms.

The determinant for a 3×3 matrix is evaluated by first expressing it in terms of 2×2 matrices:

$$\begin{vmatrix} a_{11} & a_{12} & a_{13} \\ a_{21} & a_{22} & a_{23} \\ a_{31} & a_{32} & a_{33} \end{vmatrix} = a_{11}\begin{vmatrix} a_{22} & a_{23} \\ a_{32} & a_{33} \end{vmatrix} - a_{12}\begin{vmatrix} a_{21} & a_{23} \\ a_{31} & a_{33} \end{vmatrix} + a_{13}\begin{vmatrix} a_{21} & a_{22} \\ a_{31} & a_{32} \end{vmatrix}$$ (C.15)

$$= a_{11}(a_{22}a_{33} - a_{23}a_{32}) - a_{12}(a_{21}a_{33} - a_{23}a_{31}) + a_{13}(a_{21}a_{32} - a_{22}a_{31})$$

In equation C.15, the determinant is evaluated by an expansion in terms of cofactors. In this procedure, the 3×3 determinant is expanded as products of the elements of its first row and the 2×2 determinants that result when the row and column of the element are omitted. That is, the first element a_{11} multiplies the 2×2 determinant formed by eliminating the first row and first column from the 3×3 determinant. In this expansion, the signs alternate so that for the second term $-a_{12}$ multiplies the 2×2 determinant formed by eliminating the first row and second column from the 3×3 determinant.

The procedure described above can be generalized by defining the cofactor (or signed minor) c_{ij} of matrix element a_{ij} by the following equation:

$$c_{ij} = (-1)^{i+j} |M_{ij}| \tag{C.16}$$

where the minor $|M_{ij}|$ is the determinant of the submatrix $[M_{ij}]$ defined by eliminating row i and column j from the original matrix.

The 3×3 determinant in equation C.15 is expressed in terms of its cofactors by $|A| = a_{11}c_{11} + a_{12}c_{12} + a_{13}c_{13}$. In the same manner, an $n \times n$ determinant can be evaluated as the sum of n products of matrix elements and their cofactors, with the cofactors calculated from determinants of size $(n-1) \times (n-1)$. Cofactors are also required for the matrix inversion procedure described below.

The Inverse of a Matrix

Sometimes it is useful to invert a matrix equation. For example, equation C.2 for XYZ as functions of RGB is presented with specific values in equation 6.16 and then inverted in equation 6.17 to find relations for RGB as functions of XYZ. Let $[A]$ be the 3×3 matrix in equation 6.16, $[XYZ]$ the column vector for the XYZ color variables, and $[RGB]$ the column vector for the colors RGB. Then equation C.2 may be written as $[XYZ] = [A][RGB]$. Inversion of this equation is obtained by multiplying from the left by $[A]^{-1}$, which is the inverse of $[A]$.

The product of $[A]$ with its inverse $[A]^{-1}$ is the identity matrix $[I]$. The matrix $[I]$ has all its diagonal elements equal to 1, and all off-diagonal elements equal to 0. (The $[I]$ matrix should not be confused with the unit matrix $[U_n]$ used in section 6.5 for ordered dithering; $[U_n]$ is an $n \times n$ matrix with *every* element equal to 1.) Thus the following relations hold:

$$[A]^{-1}[A] = [A][A]^{-1} = [I] \tag{C.17}$$

The identity matrix is so named because multiplication of $[I]$ with any matrix returns the original matrix. Thus multiplying the equation $[XYZ] = [A][RGB]$ by $[A]^{-1}$ from the left gives

$$[A]^{-1}[XYZ] = [A]^{-1}[A][RGB] = [I][RGB] = [RGB]$$

or $\tag{C.18}$

$$[RGB] = [A]^{-1}[XYZ]$$

The inverse can be calculated from the relation

$$[A]^{-1} = \frac{[C]^T}{|A|} \tag{C.19}$$

where |A| is the determinant of [A], and $[C]^T$ is the transpose of the matrix [C] formed from [A] by replacing the elements a_{ij} by their cofactors c_{ij}.

As an example of matrix inversion, consider equation 6.16, which corresponds to a particular case of equation C.2; that is, [XYZ] = [A][RGB] with specific values for the elements of [A].

$$\begin{bmatrix} X \\ Y \\ Z \end{bmatrix} = [A] \begin{bmatrix} R \\ G \\ B \end{bmatrix} \quad \text{with } [A] = \begin{bmatrix} 0.478 & 0.299 & 0.175 \\ 0.263 & 0.655 & 0.081 \\ 0.020 & 0.160 & 0.908 \end{bmatrix} \tag{C.20}$$

Replacing the elements of [A] by their cofactors yields the following expressions for [C] and its transpose $[C]^T$:

$$[C] = \begin{bmatrix} 0.581 & -0.237 & 0.029 \\ -0.243 & 0.431 & -0.071 \\ -0.090 & 0.007 & 0.234 \end{bmatrix} \quad \text{and } [C]^T = \begin{bmatrix} 0.582 & -0.243 & -0.090 \\ -0.237 & 0.431 & 0.007 \\ 0.029 & -0.071 & 0.234 \end{bmatrix} \tag{C.21}$$

The determinant of [A] is

$$|A| = 0.478(0.655 \times 0.908 - 0.081 \times 0.160) - 0.299(0.263 \times 0.908 - 0.081 \times 0.020)$$
$$+ 0.175(0.263 \times 0.160 - 0.655 \times 0.020) = 0.212 \tag{C.22}$$

From equation C.19, $[A]^{-1} = [C]^T/|A| = [C]^T/0.212 = 4.71[C]^T$. The product of a scalar with a matrix is evaluated by multiplying each element of the matrix by the scalar. Multiplying the elements of the matrix shown in equation C.21 by 4.71 yields the following equation:

$$\begin{bmatrix} R \\ G \\ B \end{bmatrix} = [A]^{-1} \begin{bmatrix} X \\ Y \\ Z \end{bmatrix} \text{with } [A]^{-1} = \begin{bmatrix} 2.741 & -1.145 & -0.424 \\ -1.116 & 2.030 & 0.033 \\ 0.137 & -0.334 & 1.102 \end{bmatrix} \tag{C.23}$$

The values of the matrix elements in equation C.23 agree with the values given in equation 6.17 to within small round-off errors (as expected from the fact that the initial numbers in equation C.20 are given to only three places).

Index